Western Civilization

Western Civilization

A Brief History

Paul R. Waibel

WILEY Blackwell

This edition first published 2020
© 2020 John Wiley & Sons, Inc.

Registered Office
John Wiley & Sons, Inc., 111 River Street, Hoboken, NJ 07030, USA

Editorial Office
111 River Street, Hoboken, NJ 07030, USA

For details of our global editorial offices, customer services, and more information about Wiley products visit us at www.wiley.com.

Wiley also publishes its books in a variety of electronic formats and by print-on-demand. Some content that appears in standard print versions of this book may not be available in other formats.

Library of Congress Cataloging-in-Publication Data

Name: Waibel, Paul R., author.
Title: Western civilization : a brief history / Paul R. Waibel.
Description: First edition. | Hoboken : John Wiley & Sons, Inc. 2020. |
   Includes index.
Identifiers: LCCN 2019046600 (print) | LCCN 2019046601 (ebook) | ISBN
   9781119160717 (paperback) | ISBN 9781119160779 (adobe pdf) | ISBN
   9781119160786 (epub)
Subjects: LCSH: Civilization, Western–Textbooks.
Classification: LCC CB245 .W255 2020 (print) | LCC CB245 (ebook) | DDC
   909/.09821–dc23
LC record available at https://lccn.loc.gov/2019046600
LC ebook record available at https://lccn.loc.gov/2019046601

Cover Design: Wiley
Cover Image: © R.Tsubin/Getty Images

Set in 9.5/12.5pt STIXTwoText by SPi Global, Pondicherry, India

Printed in the United States of America

V10017365_020520

Contents

Preface

I began teaching survey courses in the history of Western Civilization in 1975 as a graduate teaching assistant at West Virginia University. From then until my retirement from teaching in 2016, I taught survey courses in Western Civilization and World Civilization, as well as upper level courses in everything from ancient history to the history of the twentieth century. During my 40 years of teaching at four colleges and universities, I watched higher education in the United States undergo radical change. Today's students represent a wide range of academic preparation.

The growth of what is commonly referred to as "non-traditional" education has required a rethinking of how core courses are taught and what can be required from the students enrolled in them. Such courses are often marketed as a means for working adults to complete a degree once started, but interrupted. Frequently, adult students need to take a semester or two of history survey to meet a core requirement. Hence, courses in Western Civilization or World History are offered. Students may be required to attend evening classes that meet once a week for six to eight weeks, during which an entire semester's work is completed. At one point in my career, I was assigned to teach a one-semester course in Western Civilization in a weeks as part of a non-traditional adult program. Increasingly, non-traditional courses are taught online, either live or prerecorded. Adult students taking these condensed courses, while at the same time trying to juggle work, family, and other of life's daily demands usually have very little time to spend reading the traditional survey history textbook.

Taking all of the above into consideration, I set for myself the task of writing a Western Civilization text that could be used in the traditional on-campus course, or the non-traditional classes. I wanted the text to be written in an interesting and engaging style, that is to say, I wanted it to be more than a chronological list of dates and names of dead people. What Theodore Roosevelt said of writing in general, I think is especially important in writing a history text for today's student population: "Writings are useless, unless they are read, and they cannot be read unless they are readable." A history text should not be a dry academic piling up of facts. Historian Barbara W. Tuchman described herself "as a storyteller, a narrator, who deals in true stories, not fiction." She also noted that writing readable history is not easy: "One has to sit down on that chair and think and transform thought into readable, conservative, interesting sentences that both make sense and make the reader turn the page."

When writing this and earlier books, I tried, however imperfectly to follow Ms. Tuchman's advice and example. With that in mind, I chose to emphasize topics that students I taught over the many past years found interesting and likely to stimulate class discussion. I am well aware that there is no such thing as true objectivity in teaching or writing history. Merely selecting what historical events and personalities to include in a brief history destroys any such pretense. E.H. Carr called attention to this handicap of every historian in his classic *What is History?* "The belief in a hard core of historical facts existing independently of the historian," wrote Carr, "is a preposterous fallacy, but one that is very hard to eradicate."

Being aware that my own understanding and interpretation of historical events will invariably find its way into my writing to some degree, I nevertheless tried to be faithful to the facts. However, I do have a theme, or organizing idea, around which my story of the rise of Western Civilization is constructed, and it is a rather traditional one.

The roots of Western Civilization are found in the Ancient Near East and the Greco-Roman world. From the former came the Judeo-Christian religious tradition. From the latter came classical humanism. These two different ways of understanding the universe – how it works, whether it has meaning, humankind's place in it, etc. – was synthesized with certain Germanic traditions during the period of the Middle Ages in Europe. By AD 1000, there was in Europe, a new civilization that was different from all others, and armed with a worldview that facilitated both a Scientific Revolution and an Industrial Revolution. With a virtual monopoly on useful (that is, scientific) knowledge, Western Civilization was able to dominate the world by the end of the nineteenth century.

The spread of Western Civilization to the non-Western world enabled those previously more advanced civilizations to "modernize," and liberate themselves from Western imperialism. By the beginning of the twenty-first century, a modernized China, for example, was able to challenge the West for world leadership. Still, the world we live in is a Westernized world.

Acknowledgments

A number of individuals contributed to this project. Students of mine and parents who home schooled their children often asked why I did not write my own history textbook. Well, once I was able to retire, I finally had time to entertain such a challenge. Andrew J. Davidson helped me prepare the proposal for the project. Haze Humbert and Jennifer Manias served as Executive Editors, Janani Govindankutty, Niranjana Vallavan, and Ajith Kumar served as conscientious project managers, Kelley Baylis, Sakthivel Kandaswamy, and many others at Wiley-Blackwell whose names are unknown to me, have played a role in bringing this project to fruition.

My wife Darlene and daughter Elizabeth Waibel edited the individual chapters as I wrote them, correcting grammar and making helpful stylistic suggestions. Former colleagues, friends, and family members contributed images, thus helping to keep the price of the book reasonable. Finally, I wish to thank four professors who imbued in me the love of history and the desire to teach and write history – Benjamin W. Wright, Jr., Clifton W. Potter, Jr., Sheldon Vanauken, and Robert P. Grathwol. A special debt of gratitude is owed to Sheldon Vanauken, who encouraged me to "live under the mercy," and to whose memory I dedicate this book.

Part I

Ancient and Classical Civilization: An Overview

The story of Western Civilization begins around 3500 BC in the area referred to by historians as the Fertile Crescent, a quarter-moon shaped area that stretches from the Nile River valley, along the eastern coast of the Mediterranean Sea, and the river valleys of the Tigris and Euphrates rivers to the Persian Gulf. It was in that area of fertile soil that people learned to farm and irrigate their fields with water from the rivers. Settled farming required organization, which gave birth to the first cities. It was also there that people first learned to write. Organized agriculture and urban life gave rise to a class structure, in which most of the people performed certain tasks, producing the means of livelihood, while a few had the time to contemplate the meaning and purpose of life. Writing made it possible to record not only the mundane affairs of day-to-day life, but also what may be described as philosophical and religious speculation.

If one thinks of an axis around which civilization develops and radiates outward, that axis moved from the Fertile Crescent north-westward to the area of the Aegean Sea, as civilizations appeared along the rim of the Aegean Sea on the island of Crete, the coast of Asia Minor, and the Greek mainland. The Minoan Civilization on Crete and the Mycenaean Civilization on the Greek mainland contributed to the development of classical Greek civilization after 800 BC. With the conquest of the Middle East by Alexander the Great (d. 323 BC) and his successors, the Greek language and humanistic civilization of classical Greece spread throughout the Middle East and Egypt.

The Romans imposed political and, to a degree, cultural unity on the whole Mediterranean world by the end of the second century AD. But, though the Romans conquered the Hellenistic world, they were in turn conquered culturally by the Greeks, thus spreading the Greek language and culture to the western Mediterranean. The axis of civilization shifted westward to the Italian peninsula. It was during the centuries-long rule of Rome, that the religious thought of the ancient Hebrews and early Christians blended with the classical humanism of Greek civilization.

Western Civilization: A Brief History, First Edition. Paul R. Waibel.
© 2020 John Wiley & Sons, Inc. Published 2020 by John Wiley & Sons, Inc.

1

The Cradle of Civilization

Chronology

c. 8000–5000 BC	Neolithic Age
c. 3500 BC	First Cities Appear in Sumer
c. 3300–3100 BC	First Writing Appears in Sumer
c. 3100 BC	Civilization Appears in Nile River Valley
c. 2500 BC	Civilization Appears in Indus River Valley
c. 2150 BC	*Epic of Gilgamesh* is Written Down
c. 2100–2050 BC	Code of Ur-Nammu, Oldest Known Law Code
c. 1900 BC	Abram (Abraham) Leads Hebrews From Ur to Canaan
c. 1754 BC	Law Code of Hammurabi
c. 1500 BC	Civilization Appears in Yellow River Valley
c. 1446 BC	One Possible Date for Hebrew Exodus from Egypt
c. 1393 BC	Birth of Moses
c. 1270 BC	One Possible Date for Hebrew Exodus from Egypt
c. 1024–930 BC	United Kingdom of Israel
722 BC	Assyria Conquers northern Kingdom of Israel
587 BC	Babylonians Capture Jerusalem, Fall of Kingdom of Judah

The story of Western Civilization began during the Neolithic Age (c. 8000 BC–5000 BC), before the appearance of civilization. Humans ceased being hunters and gatherers and began to domesticate animals and cultivate crops. Agriculture enabled human beings to take control of their environment rather than be controlled by it. A technological revolution followed. New tools to cultivate the land and clear forests appeared, along with methods of collecting, storing, and using water from the nearby rivers to irrigate fields. Agricultural centers, or villages, appeared consisting of a group of individuals living together, mutually dependent on one another. As agriculture spread, trade in surplus crops and necessary tools and resources followed.

Discoveries of certain of the Neolithic communities by archeologists are very revealing. Jericho, located in the Jordan valley, was first settled sometime between 10 000 and 9 000 BC.

Western Civilization: A Brief History, First Edition. Paul R. Waibel.
© 2020 John Wiley & Sons, Inc. Published 2020 by John Wiley & Sons, Inc.

By around 9400 BC Jericho occupied about 10 acres (4 ha). There were more than 70 circular dwellings made of sun-dried brick measuring about 15 ft. (4.6 m) across. Estimates of the size of the population vary anywhere from 200 to 300 upward to 2000 or 3000. The village was surrounded by a stone wall more than 12 ft. (3.7 m) high and nearly 6 ft. (1.8 m) wide at the base. Inside the wall stood a stone tower more than 12 ft. (3.7 m) tall with an internal stone staircase. Outside the stone wall was a moat approximately 10 ft. (3.8 m) deep.

The wall served as a defense against potential enemies. The purpose of the tower remains shrouded in mystery. Two archeologists from Tel Aviv University, Roy Liran and Ran Barkai, after studying how the setting sun on the summer solstice interacted with the tower and the surrounding landscape suggest that "the tower was built not just as a marker or a time-keeping device, but as a guardian against the dangers present in the darkness cast by a dying sun's last rays of light" (Sutherland 2018). The dead were buried within the village, often under the floor of the dwelling in which the deceased is assumed to have lived. The skulls were covered in plaster, painted, and placed in the walls. The practice may be evidence of some sort of ancestor worship, but like so much else, that explanation is speculation.

Even more interesting is the Neolithic settlement located in southern Anatolia (modern Turkey) called Çatalhöyük (sometimes spelled Çatal Höyük or Çatal Hüyük), which existed from approximately 7500 to 5700 BC. The site was discovered in the late 1950s and first excavated between 1961 and 1965. Excavations and research by an international team of archeologists began in 1993 and are ongoing.

With a population that ranged between 3000 and 8000, Çatalhöyük was much larger than Jericho. It consisted of about 32 acres (approximately 13 ha) of mud-brick dwellings closely packed together without streets or alleyways. Access to the individual dwellings was through holes in the roofs. The life of the community took place largely on the roofs of what must have resembled a large beehive-like structure. Each dwelling had an oven and furniture that consisted of mud-brick platforms under which deceased family members were buried. The floors were covered in reeds. The walls were covered in bright white plaster, often decorated with colorful frescos. Paintings of bulls on the walls, plastered skulls of oxen embedded in the walls, and the presence of bull horns suggest some sort of religion centered on the worship of bulls, like the religion that appeared later in Minoan Crete (see Chapter 2). One scene painted on a wall depicts a village with a mountain, perhaps Mount Hasan, an inactive volcano. Some art historians regard the painting as the first painted landscape in history.

Most importantly, the people of the Neolithic villages like Jericho and Çatalhöyük did not possess the ability to read and write. Hence, there is no evidence of religious or philosophical thought, no recorded attempts to wrestle with those perennial questions of meaning and purpose. Writing is the defining characteristic of civilization, and so, as impressive as their technologic achievements were, most scholars regard these Neolithic villages as proto-civilizations. To locate the birthplace of civilization, and at the same time, provide some explanation of the difference between a Neolithic village and a civilization, we must look to the fertile land that lies between the Tigris and Euphrates Rivers, an area known as Mesopotamia, or the "land between the rivers."

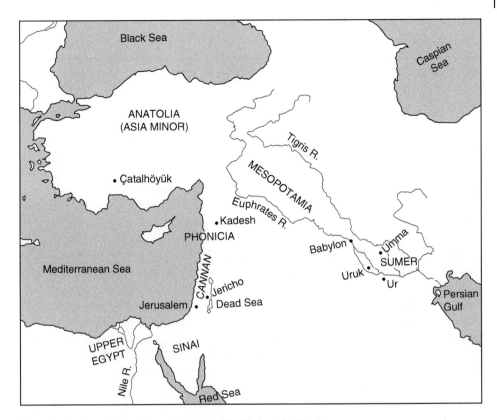

Figure 1.1 Map of the ancient Near East: The Birth of Civilization.

Birth of Civilization

The cradle of civilization lay in the southern most area of Mesopotamia known as Sumer where the Tigris and Euphrates rivers empty into the Persian Gulf. The Sumerians called themselves "the black-headed people" and their home "the land of the black-headed people," or simply "the land." It was in Sumer around 3500 BC that the first cities appeared, and most important, it was in Sumer sometime between 3300 BC and 3100 BC that people first learned to write.[1]

Writing was a byproduct of urbanization. Trade between the cities of Sumer required the ability to communicate. Using a reed with the end cut off, scribes made wedge-shaped marks in small clay tablets that were then allowed to dry in the sun. At first, they made

---

1 Approximately four centuries later, around 3100 BC, civilization appeared in the Nile River Valley of Egypt. It then appeared in the Indus River Valley of India around 2500 BC, and in the Huang Ho (or Yellow) River Valley of China about 1500 BC. The spread of civilization in ancient history, and contacts between ancient civilizations is an interesting topic, but beyond the scope of this survey. Dates of events in ancient history are always approximate and vary widely from one source to another.

marks that represented objects (pictographs), and then marks that represented sounds (phonograms). This style of writing is known as "cuneiform," meaning "wedge-shaped."

Scribes were trained in schools that taught not only the art of writing and reading, but law, medicine, and astrology. Literature appeared as scribes began to write down stories about the gods and heroic figures. The *Epic of Gilgamesh*, considered by many to be the first great work of literature in history, was written down sometime around 2150 BC. It tells the story of Gilgamesh ("Bilgamesh" in Sumerian), king of Uruk, and his companion Enkidu.

In the first half of the epic tale, Gilgamesh and Enkidu go on a series of adventures including a journey to the Cedar Forest, the dwelling place of the gods. There, they defeat the giant monster Humbaba ("Huwawa" in Sumerian), guardian of the Cedar Forest. Gilgamesh spurns the advances of Ishtar, goddess of fertility, love, war, and sex. Ishtar punishes Gilgamesh for his impudence by convincing the gods to kill Enkidu.

The death of Enkidu leads to Gilgamesh's quest to find the meaning of life and death. It is this second half of the epic that is of greatest importance, for in the attempt to answer the perennial questions of meaning and purpose, the *Epic of Gilgamesh* becomes more than an epic tale; it becomes a work of philosophy, another characteristic of a civilization.

Some of the stories related in the *Epic of Gilgamesh* have counterparts in the Old Testament book of Genesis. The flood account in Genesis bears a striking resemblance to the flood story in the *Epic of Gilgamesh*. The two stories have at least 20 points of similarity leading to the obvious conclusion that there must be some connection, but there are significant points in the two accounts that differ. Some who subscribe to the school of thought known as "Panbabylonism," which asserts that the Hebrew Bible and Judaism are derived from Mesopotamian (Babylonian) mythology, consider the Genesis flood story to be modeled after that in the *Epic of Gilgamesh*. Others consider both to be myths with spiritual significance, or accounts of an actual flood that occurred at some time in the past.

Religious beliefs are at the heart of any given civilization's identity. Ultimately, a people's worldview, or understanding of what is real, determines every aspect of life. Since worldview and religious belief are entwined, how a society is governed and organized, as well as its literary and artistic expressions, are rooted in its religious beliefs. Not surprisingly, temples with gods and priests who interceded on behalf of the people were the center of life in Sumerian cities.

For the people of Sumer and Mesopotamia in general, both life and the afterlife were gloomy at best. People were only the pawns of capricious gods who controlled the universe and all that is part of it, and who might bestow blessings or suffering at will. Everywhere there were hostile gods and demons that the people feared. Natural disasters or human actions such as wars were caused by the gods. The people used various means of divination to try and determine what fate the gods might have in store for them as individuals or for the city. Sacrifices, prayers, and magic were employed to appease the gods and ward off the demons. The belief that the will of the gods was revealed in the position of the planets and stars led the Mesopotamians to the study of astronomy and astrology.

People could not look forward to death for relief from uncertainty, anxiety, and fear. The netherworld was understood to be a dark existence governed by a hierarchy of gods. It was not some sort of heaven or hell, a place to which the dead went according to how they lived their lives. Life after death offered only a gloomy existence, a fate that could not be avoided.

Despite their gloomy view of life, the Mesopotamians greatly influenced the history of civilization and continue to influence life today. The number 60, sacred to the sky god An (or Anu), became the basic unit of mathematical calculation and lives on in our division of time into the 60-second minute, the 60-minute hour, and the degrees of a circle. When we add urbanization, the wheel, chariots, and four-wheeled wagons, writing and the first literature, mathematics, and the science of astronomy, and agriculture and animal husbandry to the list, we must acknowledge civilization's debt to the people of ancient Mesopotamia.

Mesopotamia sat at the crossroads of trade, migration, and invasions of conquering armies, all of which spread its culture. Kingdoms and empires rose and fell as power shifted between rival city-states[2] and conquering armies. The appearance of a new technology such as smelting bronze or iron, or the appearance of a new weapon like the first metal arrowheads, the composite bow, body armor, or the war chariot enabled the possessor of the new technology to enjoy its historical moment until the next conqueror appeared armed with some new military technology.

The era of warring city-states ended when Lugalzaggisi, king of Umma, united all of Sumer during his reign, c. 2375–2350 BC. He ruled for only 25 years. In c. 2334 BC, Lugalzaggisi's army was defeated in battle by Sargon (reigned 2334–2279 BC), leader of the Akkadians, a Semitic-speaking people in Mesopotamia north of Sumer. Sargon founded the first multi-national empire. It stretched from the Persian Gulf to the eastern coast of the Mediterranean Sea.

Sargon appointed his daughter, Enheduanna, High Priestess in the temple of the moon god Nanna in the Sumerian city-state of Ur. Enheduanna is the first author and poet known by name in history. She left behind a collection of literary works that include poetry, devotionals, and hymns to Nanna. A collection of her temple hymns known as the "Sumerian Temple Hymns" is considered by some scholars to be the first attempt at a systematic theology.

Sargon's empire ended about 2100 BC. Of the empires that followed, two require mention. First is the Third Dynasty of Ur (Ur III) that lasted from c. 2112 BC to c. 2004 BC. The significance of this brief empire lies in the appearance of one of the oldest known law codes, the Code of Ur-Nammu, king of Ur during the mid-twenty-first century BC. It is not the first written law code. That honor may belong to Urukagina (sometimes spelled Uruinimgina or Irikagina), who ruled the city-state of Lagash in the first half of the twenty-fourth century BC. Though no copy of his law code has been found, its content can be deduced from references to it in other sources from the period.

The Code of Ur-Nammu (r. 2047–2030 BC) consists of 57 laws inscribed on clay tablets. The laws are stated in a simple form: If this is the crime, then this is the punishment. It differs from the later Code of Hammurabi in that it prescribes monetary compensation for crimes that cause physical harm, except in cases of murder, robbery, adultery, and rape, which were capital offenses.

The first two fragments of the Code of Ur-Nammu were found at Nippur in Sumer and translated in 1952. They contained the prologue and five of the laws. Additional tablets were found at Ur and translated in 1965. Something of a social class structure in society at the time can be deduced from the code. All of the people below the king were divided into two classes, free and slave.

---

2 A city and the surrounding territory controlled by it are commonly referred to as a city-state, kingdom, or city-state kingdom.

Figure 1.2 The Ishtar Gate, entrance to the inner city of ancient Babylon, was constructed by King Nebuchadnezzar II c. 575 BC. *Source:* Library of Congress, Prints and Photographs Collections.

Better known is the Code of Hammurabi issued in 1754 BC, during the Old Babylonian Empire. The Code of Hammurabi was found at Susa in 1901 by Jean-Vincent Scheil (1858–1940), a French Dominican scholar. Scheil translated and published the code in 1902. The code consists of 282 laws found on 12 tablets. Unlike the Code of Ur-Nammu, Hammurabi's law code follows the principle of "an eye for an eye and a tooth for a tooth," the law of retaliation, or *Lex Talionis*. Punishment varied according to whether the injured party was a nobleman or a commoner.

If a man has destroyed the eye of a man of the 'gentleman' class, they shall destroy his eye. If he has broken a gentleman's bone, they shall break his bone. If he has destroyed the eye of a commoner or broken a bone of a commoner, he shall pay one mina of silver. If he has destroyed the eye of a gentleman's slave, he shall pay half the slave's price. (From The Code of Hammurabi, 2019)

Around 1600 BC, the Babylonian Empire collapsed when invaded from the north by the Hittites and from the east by the Kassites. The Hittites plundered and then left, but the Kassites remained and ruled Mesopotamia for the next five centuries.

The Hittites were a powerful empire in Anatolia between c. 1700 BC and c. 1200 BC. They spoke an Indo-European[3] language and entered Anatolia as part of a widespread migration of Indo-European people. The Hittites were the first to work iron, although they did not use it for weapons. The fall of the Hittite Empire was a part of the general, catastrophic collapse of the Bronze Age civilizations at the end of the thirteenth century BC. The collapse was brought about by invasions (or migrations) of Indo-Europeans from the north, and repeated attacks from the sea by a mysterious people known as the "Sea People."

Egypt

About the time that cities and writing were appearing in Mesopotamia, civilization was emerging at the southern end of the Fertile Crescent along the Nile River. Ancient Egypt occupied 450 miles (724 km) of the Nile River valley from the first cataract[4] to the Mediterranean Sea. The regular flooding of the Nile created a narrow band of cultivatable land that varied from 5 to 25 miles wide. It was possible to produce two crops per year. It was there, in that narrow band of fertile soil, the "Black Land," that civilization developed. Beyond it on both sides were the vast barren oceans of desert sand, the "Red Land."

Not only did the Nile make agriculture – and with it, civilized life – possible, it was easily navigated, thus providing a measure of unity between Upper (southern) and Lower (northern) Egypt. Relative isolation benefitted ancient Egypt. Invading armies had to either go down the Nile River, where they would be easy targets for defending forces, or cross the Sinai Peninsula, a wide desert. From the beginning of Egypt's history in c. 3100 BC, until it became a part of the Roman Empire in 30 BC, the sight of invading armies was rare. Thus, the Egyptians experienced a sense of regularity, permanence, and security unknown to the people of Mesopotamia.

---

3 The term "Indo-European" refers to a group of languages that originated in the Eurasian Steppes about 6000 years ago.
4 The cataracts are shallow sections of the Nile River where rocks, small islands, and whitewater rapids make navigation difficult or impossible. There are six cataracts.

Neolithic Period	c. 4500 – 3000 BC
Early Dynastic Period	c. 3000 – 2650 BC
Old Kingdom	c. 2650 – 2150 BC
First Intermediate Period	c. 2150 – 2040 BC
Middle Kingdom	c. 2040 – 1640 BC
Second Intermediate Period	c. 1640 – 1550 BC
New Kingdom	c. 1550 – 1070 BC
Third Intermediate Period	c. 1070 – 712 BC
Late Period	c. 712 – 332 BC
Graeco-Roman Period	c. 332 BC – AD 642

Figure 1.3 Chronology of ancient Egypt.

Around 3100 BC, Upper and Lower Egypt were unified by Narmer, who became the founder of the first dynasty and thus the first king, or pharaoh, of Egypt.[5] The history of ancient Egypt is divided into 31 dynasties beginning in c. 3100 BC and concluding in 30 BC, and further divided into the Early Dynastic Period, Old Kingdom, First Intermediate Period, Middle Kingdom, Second Intermediate Period, New Kingdom (or Empire), and Post-Empire.

The pharaohs of the Old Kingdom (c. 2700–c. 2200 BC) ruled from Memphis in Upper Egypt. Unlike the kings in Mesopotamia, who were servants of the gods, the pharaoh was a living god, often associated with the falcon-headed god Horus. Upon death, the pharaoh became Osiris, god of the dead. In life, it was his duty to maintain Ma'at – harmony, continuity, unchanging order, justice, and truth. In so doing, the pharaoh guaranteed the safety and prosperity of the people. If he failed to rule wisely, chaos would return in the form of famine or some other disaster. As the possessor of Ma'at, the pharaoh was the source of law and justice. Hence, the Egyptians never developed a law code. There was no need for one.

During the Old Kingdom only the pharaoh, and those he chose to be with him, enjoyed an afterlife. It was important to preserve the pharaoh's body and to provide him with the things he would need in his afterlife. Pyramids of great size, and later tombs, were constructed and filled with the objects, or models of them, that the pharaoh would need. Scenes depicting hunting or other events that the pharaoh enjoyed in life were carved or painted on the walls. They would become reality in the afterlife.

The Egyptians developed a system of writing that combined pictographs and symbols representing sounds in a script referred to as hieroglyphs ("sacred carvings"), meaning "god's words." By inventing the 24 signs for the sounds of consonants, the Egyptians invented the alphabet, or at least the principle of the alphabet. Because of the abundance of Cyperus papyrus, an aquatic plant that grew along the Nile especially in the Delta, the

---

5 The name of the unifier of Egypt is disputed. Some credit Menes, or Scorpion II, rather than Narmer. The consensus appears to be that Menes and Narmer were the same person, and Scorpion II was a king during the pre-dynastic period. The title "pharaoh" was not used for the Egyptian kings until the reign of Thutmose III (c. 1479–1425 BC) during the period of the New Kingdom, or Empire.

Egyptians were able to make a form of paper known simply as papyrus. Instead of having to make wedge-shaped marks in clay tablets as in Sumerian cuneiform, the Egyptians could use pen and ink to write hieroglyphs on papyrus, as well as carve them or paint them on stone.

The construction of the pyramids during the Old Kingdom testifies to the absolute power of the pharaohs, as well as the engineering skills of the Egyptians. Contrary to the impression one may get from Hollywood, the pyramids were not built by slaves. During the three months each year when the flood waters of the Nile covered the arable land and farming ceased, thousands of peasants were put to work constructing the pyramids. By ensuring the preservation of the pharaoh's body, they were ensuring the continuity of the rhythm of life, especially the regularity of the Nile's flooding upon which life depended.

The pyramids are among the most impressive man-made wonders in history. The first pyramid was built for Djoser (r. c. 2686–c. 2613 BC) at Saqqara, on the west bank of the Nile River opposite Memphis. It has six stepped layers of stone that reached a height of 204 ft. (62 m). The pyramid was surrounded by a 40-acre (16-ha) complex of temples and other buildings enclosed by a 30 ft. (9.1 m) high wall. The Step pyramid, as it is called, was designed by history's first known architect, Imhotep (c. 3000–c. 2950 BC).

Most impressive of the pyramids built during the Old Kingdom is the Great Pyramid, built one century later for Khufu (or Cheops, r. c. 2589–2566 BC). It was the first and largest of the pyramids built at Giza on the west bank of the Nile River close to modern-day Cairo, and is the only one of the Seven Wonders of the Ancient World still standing.

Figure 1.4 The Great Pyramid of Khufu, or Cheops, completed c. 2560 BC. *Source:* Library of Congress, Prints and Photographs Collections.

To build the Great Pyramid, workers cut approximately 2.3 million limestone blocks at quarries 500 miles (804.7 km) away and brought them to Giza. Each block weighed an average of 2.5 tons (2.3 MT), though some were as heavy as 16 tons (14.5 MT). The base is 755 ft. (230.4 m) long on each side (570 000 sq. ft., or 52 954.7 sq. m). The stones are so accurately placed that there is no more than an 8-in. (20.3 cm) difference between the lengths of the sides. The original height was 481 ft. (147 m), making the Great Pyramid the tallest man-made structure well into the nineteenth century AD. The pyramid was encased in smooth limestone. The outer stones fit together so well that a hair cannot be wedged between them. It is estimated that in order to finish the pyramid in 30 years, it would have been necessary to set in place one block every two and a half minutes. The ancient Greek historian Herodotus wrote in *The Histories* (c. 430 BC) that the Egyptians told him it took 100 000 men 20 years to build the Great Pyramid.

A series of weak pharaohs toward the end of the Old Kingdom allowed much of the central government's power to slip into the hands of powerful regional nobles. The result was roughly one century of weak central government and general turmoil between c. 2150 and c. 2050 BC. Mentuhotep II (r. c. 2046–c. 1995 BC), who ruled from Thebes in Upper Egypt, reunited Egypt sometime around the 39th year of his 51-year reign. He was the first pharaoh of the Middle Kingdom, a period of stability and prosperity that lasted from c. 2050 to c. 1652 BC.

The pharaoh's role changed somewhat during the Middle Kingdom. His power over the whole of Egypt was restored, but he was no longer the absolute ruler that he was during the Old Kingdom. The age of the great pyramids was over. The pharaohs of the 11th and 12th dynasties undertook great building projects that benefitted the people by providing employment, but nothing on the scale of the Great Pyramid. It was the pharaoh's role as shepherd of his people that was emphasized. The conquest of Lower Nubia on the southern border of Upper Egypt and military expeditions north along the eastern coast of the Mediterranean Sea enhanced the power of the pharaohs of the Middle Kingdom.

During the latter part of the eighteenth-century BC, Lower Egypt (the Delta region) was invaded by a people whom the Egyptians called the Hyksos (meaning "rulers of foreign lands"). The Hyksos spoke a Semitic language and migrated away from the Middle East after Indo-Europeans migrated into it in the second millennium. The Hyksos kings, or pharaohs, ruled Lower Egypt during the Second Intermediate Period from their capital at Avaris in the eastern Delta.

The Hyksos invaders enjoyed the advantage of advanced military organization and technology. The Egyptian army was outdated both in its weaponry and its emphasis on infantry. They relied on their infantry organized into sections of spearmen, bowmen, and archers. Their main weapons were the mace, a solid shaft with a heavy round head used to bludgeon the enemy, and a simple bow. One can only imagine the fear that must have possessed the Egyptians when confronted with a mobile army of warriors with lightweight, horse-drawn chariots. The Egyptians had never seen horses before. Furthermore, the Hyksos warriors had a new composite bow that could fire an arrow at least 200 yards further than the simple bows used by the Egyptians. They wore helmets and body armor and carried penetrating axes, swords, and quivers of arrows. Weapons made of bronze gave the Hyksos a decisive advantage on the battlefield, and subsequently brought Egypt into the Bronze Age.

The Hyksos controlled Lower Egypt, while Upper Egypt remained under a native Egyptian line that ruled from Thebes. Pharaoh Ahmose I (1570–1546 BC) eventually drove the Hyksos out of Egypt and pursued them north into Palestine as far as the Euphrates River. Ahmose I also led a campaign south into Nubia. Ahmose I's reign marks the beginning of the New Kingdom, or the Egyptian Empire (1550–1069 BC). His conquered lands were consolidated and expanded by his successors, Amenhotep I (1546–1526 BC), Thutmose I (1525–1512 BC), Thutmose II (1512–1504 BC), and Thutmose III (1504–1450). Babylon, Assyria, and the Hittite Empire were compelled to send tribute annually to Egypt.

One of the most interesting rulers of Egypt during the New Kingdom was Queen Hatshepsut (c. 1508–1458 BC). She was the daughter of Thutmose I and the half-sister of her husband, Thutmose II, whom she married when she was only 12 years old. When Thutmose II died in 1479 BC, the heir was an infant son by one of his concubines. Hatshepsut assumed the role of regent for her stepson, Thutmose III. At some point, she assumed the role of pharaoh and co-ruler with Thutmose III.

Hatshepsut's reign was a period of prosperity and peace for Egypt. She succeeded in restoring Egyptian culture and religion, which had been interrupted by the Hyksos, to their former glory. Her extensive efforts to expand Egypt's trade included an expedition she sent to the Land of Punt. The location of Punt is not known for sure, but is usually assumed to be the area of modern Somalia and Sudan. The expedition returned with live myrrh trees, frankincense, and other treasures. Trade between Egypt and Punt continued throughout the New Kingdom.

Upon the death of his stepmother in 1458 BC, Thutmose III became pharaoh in his own right. A gifted military commander, he led his armies north as far as Niya in northern Syria and south into Nubia as far as the fourth cataract. In all, Thutmose III led 17 campaigns during 20 years of his 46-year reign. The Egyptian Empire reached its greatest extent under Thutmose III, who is referred to by some as "the Napoleon of Egypt." He died at 90, a remarkable achievement even in the twenty-first century AD.

If Hatshepsut has a rival for "most interesting of the pharaohs," it is Amenhotep IV, also known as Akhenaten (r. c. 1353–c. 1336 BC). Amenhotep IV attempted to replace the various gods of Egypt with one god, Aten, represented as the sun disk. He changed his name from Amenhotep, which means "Amun is satisfied," to Akhenaten, meaning "Effective Spirit of Aten." Beginning in the first year of his reign, Amenhotep IV built several structures at Karnak dedicated to Aten, including a temple. During the fifth or sixth year he constructed a new capital, Akhetaten ("Horizon of Aten") on the east bank of the Nile, 194 miles (312 km) south of modern Cairo.

Akhenaten's religious revolution gave birth to a new style in art, one more realistic than the stiff, formal style normally associated with ancient Egypt. Traditional artistic styles emphasized the eternal, unchanging nature of the universe that was central to the Egyptian worldview as far back as the Old Kingdom. Akhenaten's new religion and new capital, well away from Thebes and the old gods, ushered in a new artistic style called the Amarna Renaissance that was more realistic. Art from the period includes scenes of Akhenaten, his queen Nefertiti, and their children in everyday settings, playing together beneath "the Aten." Nature in all its beauty likewise became the subject of art. One need only compare the famous bust of Nefertiti[6] with any traditional bust or statue made before or after Akhenaten to see how radically new were the artistic styles.

Literature embraced the artistry of the Amarna period. Akhenaten himself is believed to have written a number of hymn-poems to Aten. The "Great Hymn to Aten," found on the west wall of the tomb of Ay, Akhenaten's chief minister and pharaoh after the death of Tutankhamun (Tutankhaten), is the primary source for the new religion.

> O sole god without equal!
> You are alone, shining in your form of the living Aten.
> Risen, radiant, distant, and near.
>
> (Great Hymn, 47 & 73–74)

The noted Egyptologist Toby A.H. Wilkinson (b. 1969) says that "it has been called 'one of the most significant and splendid pieces of poetry to survive from the pre-Homeric world'" (Darnell and Manassa 2007, p. 41).

Akhenaten's religious reforms may represent a power struggle between the pharaoh and the powerful priesthood of Amun (Amen, Amen Re) at Thebes. Ahmose I emphasized the worship of Amun when he drove the Hyksos out of Egypt, perhaps as an attempt to unify the Egyptian people after roughly one century of foreign rule in Lower Egypt. By the beginning of the reign of Akhenaten, the power of the priests of Amun in Thebes rivaled that of the pharaoh. The fact that Akhenaten changed his name, built a new capital and center for the worship of Aten, and attempted to erase the worship of Amun and the other traditional gods, supports the theory that his religious reforms were a part of an effort to restore the pharaoh's historic position as the sole ruler of Egypt. Also, it is worth noting that the new religion was not in fact true monotheism. Only Akhenaten and his family worshiped Aten. All others worshiped the pharaoh, Akhenaten. The pharaoh was the only access to Aten.

Akhenaten's attempt to establish the worship of Aten did not survive him. His obsession with his new religion meant he neglected his responsibility to rule and defend Egypt. The resulting chaos or appearance of chaos no doubt contributed to the abandonment of Atenism and the restoration of Amun and his powerful priesthood. Akhenaten's son, Tutankhaten (c. 1341–c. 1323), ascended the throne at age nine or ten. The worship of Aten was abandoned along with Akhetaten, which was left to eventually disappear beneath the sand. The temples to Aten were abandoned as well and became the source of building materials for new construction. In the third year of his reign, Tutankhaten changed his name to Tutankhamun, meaning "Living Image of Amun."

Tutankhamun was a minor pharaoh who likely would have been forgotten if the British archeologist Howard Carter (1874–1939) had not discovered his tomb in 1922. The discovery of the only intact tomb of a pharaoh was one of the greatest discoveries in the history of Egyptology. When one considers what was found in King Tut's tomb, one can only wonder what might have been found in the tomb of, say, Ramses II.

Ramses II, also known as Ramses the Great (c. 1303–1213 BC), became pharaoh at 30 and reigned for 67 years. It is not just his longevity that makes him the most celebrated of Egypt's pharaohs. He reasserted Egyptian control over territories lost due to Akhenaten's

---

6 The authenticity of the famous Nefertiti bust was called into question in 2009 in a somewhat sensationalized news release by the Swiss art historian Henri Stierlin (Fake claims 2009). Stierlin has since been proven to be mistaken (Dell'Amore 2009).

neglect. He led successful campaigns north to Syria and south to Nubia. At the Battle of Kadesh (1258 BC) in Syria, Ramses II's forces engaged the Hittites led by King Muwatalli II (c. 1295–1272 BC). Ramses II hailed it as a great victory. He had his account of the battle carved on the walls of the great temple of Abu Simbel. Most scholars today believe the battle was indecisive. The Battle of Kadesh is significant because it resulted in the Treaty of Kadesh, the first known peace treaty in history.

Ramses II is considered by many the greatest pharaoh of the Egyptian Empire. When his mummy was sent to Paris in 1974 to be treated for a fungus, he was issued an Egyptian passport that listed his occupation as "King (deceased)." Upon arrival at Le Bourget Airport near Paris, his mummy was greeted with full military honors and a red carpet.[7] After Ramses II's death, the Egyptian Empire began a steady, prolonged decline. Ramses III (1217–1155 BC) was the last great pharaoh of the New Kingdom. He reigned 1186–1155 BC, during a period of economic decline and foreign invasions.

The whole of the Middle East, indeed the whole of the Mediterranean world, was experiencing a tidal wave of migration and invasion between 1250 and 900 BC. Indo-European-speaking people swept down from the north destroying everything in their path. On the Greek mainland, the Mycenaean civilization, the Greece of Homer's *Iliad* and *Odyssey*, was destroyed by the invaders. The powerful Hittite Empire also succumbed. The Egyptians were driven back into Africa, but were able to beat back repeated assaults by invaders referred to as the "Sea People," some of whom may have been refugees from Greece.

Of those civilizations that were present in 1200 BC, only weakened Egypt survived the cataclysm. In the Middle East, there was a power vacuum. Between c. 1250 and 750 BC, no one power exerted hegemony over the area. This period before the rise of the empires of the Assyrians, Chaldeans (Neo-Babylonian), and Persians is referred to as the "era of the small kingdoms." The Phoenician (or Canaanite) city-states flourished along the eastern coast of the Mediterranean Sea, and the Hebrew Kingdom of Israel rose and fell.

The brief life of the Kingdom of Israel merits attention, for the ancient Hebrews provide one of the three streams of civilization that blend together to produce what we call Western, or European, Civilization. The other two are the Greco-Roman, or Classical, and Germanic traditions. It is primarily to the Hebrews and the Greeks, not the Egyptians or other civilizations of the ancient Near East, that we look to for the spiritual roots of Western Civilization. The Hebrews broke radically with the other peoples of the ancient Near East in how they answered the perennial questions of the meaning and purpose of existence.

Hebrews

Much of what is known about the early history of the Hebrews comes from the Hebrew Scriptures. They are a sacred history, the story of a special, covenant relationship between the one God (Yahweh) and his chosen people, the Hebrews.[8] According to the biblical story, Yahweh is the eternally existing, personal, sovereign creator of all that exists, the one who

---

7 Ramses II is remembered for his remarkable family. He may have had as many as 200 wives and fathered as many as 100 sons and 60 daughters, two of which were included among his wives.
8 Most scholars consider the Hebrew Scriptures to contain passages of reliable history and an indispensable primary source for studying Ancient Near Eastern history.

chose to identify Himself to Moses[9] (Exodus 3) as "I AM." The Hebrew people were a semi-nomadic group of sheep herders who Yahweh chose to be his people. They were not chosen because of who they were, but to become the means by which Yahweh would make himself known to his creation, and through whom he would bless all his creation.

The Hebrew Scriptures relate the story of a group of Hebrews who left the city of Ur in southern Mesopotamia sometime around 1900 BC on a journey westward to the land of Canaan. They were led by Abram, later known as Abraham ("father of a multitude"). Abraham's great-grandson, Joseph, was taken to Egypt, where he was a slave who became a high official of the pharaoh. That was likely during the time when the Hyksos ruled Lower Egypt. Being foreigners themselves, they would not have any reservations about appointing a foreigner to a position of importance in the government.

When a severe famine struck Canaan, Joseph's father, Jacob, went to Egypt with his family. The Hebrews prospered and grew in number until, according to Exodus 1:8, "there arose a new king over Egypt, who did not know Joseph" (ESV). The new pharaoh, perhaps alarmed by the fact that the foreigners were living on the frontier of Egypt through which the Hyksos had invaded Egypt and through which any future invasion would likely come, decided to make forced laborers, or slaves, out of them.

The Hebrews were in bondage in Egypt perhaps 400 (Genesis 15:13) or 430 years (Exodus 12:41). When the period of bondage in Egypt, foretold in Genesis 15:13, was fulfilled, the Hebrew people were led out of Egypt by Moses, a leader raised up by Yahweh for that purpose. Moses led them into the Sinai Peninsula, where they wandered for 40 years. Yahweh renewed his covenant with the Hebrews and gave them a code of laws, both legal and moral. During that period, known as the Exodus, the Hebrews became a nation.

There is much debate over when the Exodus occurred. It took place in the year 2448, according to the Jewish calendar. Some scholars, called biblical minimalists (or the Copenhagen School), do not believe that there ever was such a historical event. They begin with the presupposition that the Bible does not contain reliable evidence for historical events in the history of ancient Israel.

The debate centers around two possible dates for the Exodus. One, that favored by most historians, is c. 1270 BC, during the reign of Rameses II (r. 1279–1213 BC). The second, favored by some biblical scholars, is c. 1446 BC, during the reign of Amenhotep II (r. c. 1450–1425 BC). There are good arguments for and against each one. Given the importance of the event in the history of both Judaism and Christianity the debate is unlikely to ever be resolved.

After a period of 40 years wandering in the wilderness, the Hebrews entered Canaan under the leadership of Joshua, Moses' assistant and successor. The conquest and settlement of Canaan took generations. It was a three-way struggle between the Hebrews, the Canaanites, and the Philistines. The Philistines were an element of the Sea People who were conquering and settling along the coast of the Mediterranean Sea. Following Joshua's

---

9 Dates for Moses are largely speculative and bound up with the problem of dating the Hebrew exodus from Egypt. According to the Jewish calendar, Moses was born on the seventh of Adar of the year 2368 from creation or c. 1393 BC. The same difficulty arises when trying to determine the dates for Abraham, Joseph, Jacob, and Joshua.

death, the Hebrews were organized into a loose confederation of 12 tribes. During crises, they united under charismatic leaders known as judges.

Around 1024 BC, the 12 tribes united as a kingdom. Saul (d. 1010 BC) of the tribe of Benjamin in Israel was chosen king and anointed by Samuel (fl. c. 1000 BC), who, according to rabbinical literature, was the last judge and the earliest of the Major Prophets. Saul was succeeded by his son-in-law, David (c. 1040–c. 970 BC), who completed the conquest of the Canaanites and the Philistines. David established a united kingdom of Israel with its capital at Jerusalem. Israel reached its greatest geographic extent under one of David's younger sons, Solomon (c. 970–931 BC).

Solomon's reign was the "golden age" of Israel. Great prosperity allowed Solomon to engage in a number of impressive building projects, including a very elaborate temple and temple complex in Jerusalem. Jerusalem under Solomon was a very cosmopolitan capital city. Foreigners journeyed to Jerusalem to witness the splendor of Solomon's court. The Old Testament records an account of the queen of Sheba (kingdom of Saba in present day Yemen) who "came to Jerusalem with a very great retinue, with camels bearing spices and very much gold and precious stones" (1 Kings 10:2, ESV). Solomon's wealth was not measured in just gold and silver, but in the size of his harem. According to 1 Kings 11:1-3, Solomon had 700 wives and 300 concubines. Following Solomon's death in 931 BC, Israel was divided into two kingdoms, the northern kingdom of Israel with its capital at Samaria and the kingdom of Judah with Jerusalem as its capital.

The Hebrew people understood themselves to be in a covenant relationship with Yahweh. They were to remain separate from the other nations. They were not to worship other gods, intermarry with foreigners, or mix other cultures with their own. They were, in a word, to remain holy. They failed.

Solomon's building projects brought many skilled laborers to Israel. Israel became the center for much of the trade in the Middle East. The wealth gained from trade brought with it foreign cultural influences. Solomon concluded marriage alliances with foreign states, including Egypt. Not only did he intermarry with women from among the Moabites, Ammonites, Edomites, Sidonians, and Hittites, all of which were forbidden under the covenant with Yahweh, but he committed idolatry by constructing for them places where they could worship their gods. Solomon, himself, joined in worshiping the foreign gods.

Hebrew Contribution to Western Civilization

The roots of Western Civilization, that is, those core values or principles that distinguishes it from other civilizations, are found in its Judeo-Christian and Greek heritage. These include the emphasis on reason, the unique value of the individual, and the conviction that there is meaning and purpose for both history and the individual.

In contrast to the other religions of the ancient Near East that believed in many gods who were in some fashion or other born or created, Yahweh is sovereign and transcendent, eternal and omnipotent, the creator of all that exists. Nature is not an extension of the divine, nor is it the dwelling place of gods, spirits, and demons, but the handiwork of God, created from nothing (*creatio ex nihilo*). Nature is meant to show forth God's glory and inspire worship.

God the Creator alone is to be worshiped, not nature. This demythicizing of nature made possible both the Scientific Revolution and the Industrial Revolution in the West.

Central to Judeo-Christianity is the belief that God created human beings in his own image, distinct from the rest of creation. Since God created an orderly universe, not a universe of random chance, and created human beings in his image, they are able to use reason to understand how the universe works, or as the English philosopher Francis Bacon (1561–1626) said, "capable of thinking God's thoughts after him." But the Hebrews did not create scientific thought, that is, the scientific method. That awaited the Greek philosophers who sought to understand reality beginning with reason alone. The Hebrews were concerned with knowing God and his will for them, not philosophical speculation.

The Hebrews believed that although God was sovereign over all of his creation, he endowed human beings with a free will. Each individual was not only empowered with the ability to choose between right and wrong, good and evil, but obligated to do so: "I call heaven and earth to witness against you today, that I have set before you life and death, blessing and curse. Therefore, choose life ..." (Deuteronomy 30:19, ESV). God alone was the source of what was right or wrong, good or evil. Choosing to obey God's will resulted in blessings; choosing to disobey resulted in death:

> If you obey the commandments of the Lord your God that I command you today, by loving the Lord your God, by walking in his ways, and by keeping his commandments and his statutes and his rules, then you shall live and multiply, and the Lord your God will bless you ... But if your heart turns away, and you will not hear, but are drawn away to worship other gods and serve them, I declare to you today, that you shall surely perish. (Deuteronomy 30: 16-18, ESV)

The Hebrews had an explanation for the existence of evil. It was not the result of the capricious or whimsical will of finite gods who were themselves subject to fate. Rather, evil resulted from the willful choice of the individual to reject God's moral law and act as if autonomous.

Just as the nation of Israel was God's chosen people bound to him by a covenant, so too was the individual. According to the covenant between God and Abraham, the Hebrew people were to make God's moral law known to all the nations of the world by their obedience. There is both parochialism and universalism implied in the covenant. On the one hand, it is a covenant between God and his Chosen People. On the other hand, it is a covenant between God and all humanity. The prophet Isaiah gives a vision of a time when all the nations (i.e. all people groups) of the earth will come to the mountain of the Lord (Isaiah 2:2).

The Hebrew prophets reminded the people that because they were chosen to know God's Law, they had a responsibility to be on the side of justice. They reminded the people that tolerating injustice violated God's Law and would bring upon them God's righteous wrath. Injustice violated the dignity of the individual (both male and female) who bore the image of God, and injustice was therefore an affront to God himself. By reminding the people that their freedom of will impacted the present and the future, the prophets held out the vision of a messianic age free of poverty and injustice. The belief that human beings were able to construct a better world order became one of the core values of Western Civilization.

The worldview of the ancient Hebrews differed dramatically from that of all the other civilizations of the ancient world. It is a "mechanistic" view of a universe that operates by discoverable natural laws, not random chance. Time is understood to be linear with both a beginning and an end not an endless repetition of cycles. There is meaning and purpose for both history and the individual. All this is known by human beings through reason. Because there are moral absolutes implicit in the universe, and because human beings possess a free will, individual choices and actions influence the flow of history. When blended with the worldview of the ancient Greeks (see Chapter 2) and later certain Germanic traditions (see Chapter 4) the result is what is called Western Civilization.

Later Empires

The first of the later empires to arise as the invasions from the north subsided was Assyria. By c. 750 BC, the Assyrians had conquered the whole of Mesopotamia. The northern Kingdom of Israel fell to the Assyrians in 722 BC. The Assyrians scattered many of the Hebrews throughout their empire. Thus, the ten northern Hebrew tribes that made up the northern kingdom of Israel after the division of Solomon's kingdom disappeared as they blended in with the inhabitants of the areas in which they settled. The Assyrian Empire expanded until it eventually included Syria, Phoenicia, and Egypt. It contributed nothing of value to civilization, and its people are remembered primarily for their extreme cruelty.

The Assyrian capital of Nineveh was captured and burned by the Chaldeans in 612 BC. The Chaldean, or Neo-Babylonian, Empire succeeded the Assyrian Empire in Mesopotamia. The empire reached the height of its power under King Nebuchadnezzar II (634–562 BC). Nebuchadnezzar II was a great builder. He transformed the city of Babylon into one of the most splendid cities of the ancient Near East. "In addition to its size," Herodotus wrote, "Babylon surpasses in splendor any city in the known world."

Nebuchadnezzar II invaded and conquered the southern kingdom of Judah in 597 BC. After taking Jerusalem, he deposed Jehoiakim (c. 635–598) and placed on the throne, a new king of his own choosing, Zedekiah (b. 618). When Zedekiah revolted and made an alliance with Egypt, Nebuchadnezzar II invaded and laid siege to Jerusalem. After an 18-month siege, Jerusalem fell. The city and Solomon's Temple were razed to the ground. Zedekiah and several thousand prominent citizens were taken captive to Babylon. Zedekiah died in prison, but those who were taken captive with him endured 70 years of exile in Babylon. The period of the "Babylonian Captivity" became a defining moment in Jewish history.

The Chaldean Empire, impressive as it was, lasted less than a century. In 539 BC, a force of Medes and Persians led by a brilliant military strategist, Cyrus the Great (r. 559–530 BC), brought the curtain down on the Chaldean Empire with the capture of Babylon. Cyrus issued a decree allowing the Hebrew exiles to return to Judah. Many made "the return to Zion" over the next 110 years, where they enjoyed a measure of autonomy under Persian rule. When Cyrus' son Cambyses died in 522 BC, having added Egypt to the empire founded by his father, all of western Asia was under Persian rule. Darius the Great (550–486 BC) abandoned any further conquest, concentrating instead upon transforming the vast conquests into what many call the world's first modern empire.

Persia under Darius was the first empire to be administered by a royal bureaucracy. Darius divided his empire into provinces under the rule of royal officials known as "satraps." Commerce was encouraged by a state-issued coinage, an idea borrowed from the Lydians. Lydia was a wealthy kingdom in west-central Anatolia (modern Turkey). Many believe that the Lydians were the first to mint coins. Cyrus the Great conquered Lydia in 546 BC. Along with the standardized coinage went a common system of weights and measures. A system of roads, including the Royal Post Road, which stretched from Ephesus on the Aegean Sea to Susa near the Persian Gulf, encouraged commerce and unified the empire. A canal linking the Red Sea with the Nile River, originally dug by the Egyptians but since allowed to fill with sand, was reopened. Aramaic became the official language throughout the empire. Zoroastrianism, a dualistic religion that stressed ethics while rejecting blood sacrifices, polytheism, and temple worship, became a universal faith, transcending both the state and the people that gave it birth, thus further unifying the Persian Empire.

The expansion of the Persian Empire through Asia Minor to the Aegean coast brought the Persians into contact with the Greeks. The so-called Persian Wars between 499 and 479 BC, and the subsequent conquest of the Persian Empire by the youthful Alexander the Great of Greece, spread Greek culture throughout the ancient world from Egypt and Greece in the west to the Indus River in the east. It remained for the Romans to complete the mission by unifying the whole of the Mediterranean world, and then pass both the Judeo-Christian and Greco-Roman traditions on to Europe after the fall of the Roman Empire in the West in AD 476.

References

Dell'Amore, C. (2009). Nefertiti's Real, Wrinkled Face Found in Famous Bust? Science News. http://esciencenews.com/sources/national.geographic/2009/03/31/nefertitis.real.wrinkled.face.found.famous.bust (accessed 18 October 2019).

'Fake' claims over Nefertiti bust (2009). BBC News. http://news.bbc.co.uk/2/hi/entertainment/arts_and_culture/8038097.stm (accessed 18 October 2019).

Hammurabi's Code (2019). Hammurabi's Code: An Eye for an Eye. http://www.ushistory.org/civ/4c.asp (accessed 18 October 2019).

Hawass, Z. (2019). Chronology of Ancient Egypt. http://www.guardians.net/hawass/chronology.htm (accessed 18 October 2019).

Sutherland, A. (2018). Mysterious 11,000 – Year-Old Tower Of Jericho: Was World's First Skyscraper A Symbol Of Power Or An Ancient Time-Keeping Device? Ancient Pages. http://www.ancientpages.com/2018/08/31/mysterious-11000-year-old-tower-of-jericho-was-worlds-first-skycraper-a-symbol-of-power-or-an-ancient-time-keeping-device (accessed 18 October 2019).

2

The Ancient Greeks and Their World

Chronology

c. 2500–c. 1100 BC	Minoan-Mycenaean Period
c. 1700–c. 1450 BC	Height of Minoan Civilization
c. 1600–c. 1450 BC	Mycenaean Period
c. 1500 BC	Eruption of Thera (Santorini)
c. 1100–c. 800 BC	Greek Dark Ages
c. 1184 BC	Fall of Troy
c. 800–700 BC	*Iliad* and *Odyssey* written down
c. 800–c. 480 BC	Archaic Period
776 BC	First Olympic Games
c. 510–c. 323 BC	Classical Period
499–449 BC	Persian Wars
454–404 BC	Athenian Empire
431–404 BC	Peloponnesian War
428/427–348/347 BC	Plato
384–322 BC	Aristotle
323 BC	Death of Alexander the Great
c. 323–c. 31 BC	Hellenistic Period

Ancient Greek civilization can be conveniently divided into five historical periods. The first is the Aegean, or Minoan-Mycenaean, civilization (c. 2500–1100 BC), when Greek civilization was centered on the island of Crete and around the city of Mycenae on the Greek peninsula. The period after the collapse of the Minoan-Mycenaean civilization is called the Greek Dark Ages (c. 1100–800 BC), a period during which writing, and with it many aspects of what might be called "civilization," disappeared. The Dark Ages was followed by the Archaic period (c. 800–500 BC), a period during which the *polis*, or city-state, appeared and became the basic political, social, economic, and cultural unit of Greek civilization. The Classical period (c. 500–338 BC) includes the golden age of Greek civilization and culture and the rapid decline and end of the independent city-state. The fifth and final period is known as the Hellenistic. It is the period from the death of Alexander the Great in 323 BC to 30 BC, when Ptolemaic Egypt, the last of the Hellenistic

Western Civilization: A Brief History, First Edition. Paul R. Waibel.
© 2020 John Wiley & Sons, Inc. Published 2020 by John Wiley & Sons, Inc.

kingdoms, was incorporated into the Roman Empire. It was during the Hellenistic period, that Greek culture spread throughout the ancient Mediterranean world.

Minoan Civilization

The Bronze Age civilization centered on the island of Crete, that reached its height between approximately 1700 and 1450 BC, is known as "Minoan." The designation is attributed to the English archeologist, Sir Arthur Evans (1851–1941), who began excavations on the site of Knossos in 1900. During the following three years, Evans unearthed the ruins of what appeared to have been a palace complex he described as "labyrinthine." Like most well-educated English gentlemen at the turn of the twentieth century, Evans was familiar with Greek mythology. The complex layout of the unearthed ruins, together with discoveries such as a double-axe symbol found engraved on columns and depictions of individuals leaping over the backs of bulls, led Evans to associate the palace with the legend of King Minos of Crete, who kept a monster, part bull and part human, in a labyrinth.

Minoan Crete was the center of a vast trading empire that extended well beyond the Aegean Sea and the Greek mainland. They established trading posts in Syria and Egypt and other locations in the Near East and as far west as Sicily and Spain. The need for tin in the production of bronze connected Minoan Crete with such distant locations as Britain and Afghanistan, if only indirectly. Much like the tramp steamers of the nineteenth century that connected Europe with the world beyond its shores, the Minoans played a key role in the diffusion of the more advanced civilizations of Egypt and Southwest Asia to the emerging civilizations along the Mediterranean coast of Europe.

Much of what is known about Minoan life and culture has been deduced from the archeological evidence, rather than the written record. The Minoans were not Greeks, nor was their language Greek. What language they spoke remains unknown and unclassified. The earliest Minoan script is called "Cretan hieroglyphs" and has not been deciphered. A later script referred to as Linear A was in use between c. 1850 and c. 1400 BC. Like Cretan hieroglyphs, it has not been deciphered. A third script, Linear B, was first used in Knossos between c. 1450 and c. 1350 BC after the Mycenaean conquest of Crete. Its use spread from Crete to the Greek mainland. In 1953, Michael Ventris (1922–1956), an English architect and gifted linguist, broke the code. Ventris recognized that Linear B was the written script for an archaic form of Mycenaean Greek dialect.

Minoan settlements were scattered throughout the island of Crete. Whether or not there existed some sort of central authority, as some suggest, cannot be determined from the available archeological evidence. There were four major palace complexes, Knossos being the largest, which apparently exerted some sort of regional authority. The absence of any fortifications indicates that the Minoan civilization was a peaceful one. That assumption is reinforced by frescoes on the walls and in the floors of the palaces that depict tranquil scenes of daily life and nature. Women are portrayed in apparel with their breasts bare.

A small statuette approximately 13½ in. (342.9 mm) tall of a bare-breasted woman holding a snake in each hand is thought to be evidence that Minoan religion revolved around worship of a mother goddess, perhaps the ancestor of the Greek goddess Artemis. A small ivory figurine called "the bull-leaper," a bronze sculpture of an individual leaping over the back of a bull, and wall frescoes of the same subject matter, all found at Knossos, are thought to depict the dangerous sport of bull leaping. Was it only a sport or a ritual involved in bull worship? Evidence of bull worship is found throughout the world.

Though the term Knossos is used today to refer to the Bronze Age archeological ruins, it was more than a palace complex. It is recognized as the oldest city in Europe. At its peak around in 1700 BC, as many as 100 000 people resided at Knossos. The palace covered six acres (2 ha) and included 1300 rooms connected by corridors. Some areas of the palace reached a height of five stories. Fresh water flowed to the palace and surrounding city in aqueducts. The water flowed through the palace in terracotta pipes. A separate closed system drained waste water and sewage to an outside sewer. What is thought to have been the queen's quarters included a water-flushing system toilet and a bathtub.[1]

The Minoan civilization came to an end in the middle of the fifteenth century BC. The cause of its demise remains disputed. The mystery is heightened by attempts to associate Minoan Civilization with the legend of Atlantis. The intermingling of history with legends and mythology increases interest in ancient history, but also increases the difficulty in separating fact from fiction. Current consensus among scholars is that the eruption of a massive volcano 61 miles (100 km) north of Crete on the island of Santorini (Thera) sometime between 1627 BC and 1600 BC may have prepared the way for a subsequent conquest by the Mycenaean Greeks.

Mycenaean Civilization

Mycenaean is the name given to the Bronze Age civilization centered on the Greek mainland from c. 1600 BC to c. 1100 BC. It is named after the fortified city of Mycenae that dominated the Peloponnesian peninsula (southern Greece). As with Sir Arthur Evans and the Minoan civilization, Heinrich Schliemann (1822–1890) ignited interest in Mycenaean civilization, when he began excavations on the site of ancient Mycenae in 1874. Schliemann had already conducted excavations on the site of ancient Troy in 1871.

Schliemann was a wealthy German businessman who retired at age 36 and began a second career as an amateur archeologist. Schliemann's interest in Mycenaean Greece began in early childhood. His father told him tales from the *Iliad* and *Odyssey* and gave him an illustrated world history when he was seven. Schliemann later recalled his fascination with a picture of Troy in flames, and claimed that he decided when he was eight, that he would one day dig up the ancient city of Troy. He realized his dream in 1871–1873, when he excavated Hisarlik ("Place of Fortresses") on the Aegean cost of modern Turkey, 4 miles (6.5 km) from the Dardanelles.

In 1876, Schliemann turned his attention to Mycenae. He believed in the historicity of Homer's *Iliad*. Using the *Iliad* as a guide, along with *Description of Greece*, by Pausanias (d. 180 AD), a second-century AD geographer, Schliemann searched for the grave of King Agamemnon of Mycenae who commanded the Greek forces in the siege of Troy. Schliemann excavated several shaft graves that he believed dated from the time of the Trojan Wars. The graves contained eight men, nine women and two children, together with some of the most impressive archeological treasures ever found.

---

1 The first flush toilets in Washington DC's White House were installed during the presidency of Rutherford B. Hayes (1877–1891).

The bodies were accompanied by precious metals and jewels. The faces of five of the bodies were covered with funeral masks made of gold, one of which Schliemann identified as the mask of Agamemnon. He felt that he had accomplished his lifelong dream of proving that the Trojan Wars were an actual historical event, not just myth. What Schliemann unearthed was not, as he thought, from the period of the Trojan Wars, but from a much earlier period. Nevertheless, his discoveries captured the imagination of Europe like nothing else until the discovery of King Tut's tomb by Howard Carter in 1922.

Unlike the Minoan Civilization centered on Crete, Mycenaean Greece was a warrior culture. There was no unified state, or kingdom. Instead, there were a number of "power centers," including Mycenae, Pylos, Tiryns, Thebes, Athens, Sparta, and other fortress cities in southern and central Greece. There were other differences between the two that make it difficult to differentiate the cultural diffusion between them.

Mycenaean Civilization peaked between c. 1300 BC and 1200 BC. Though a warrior society, the Mycenaeans enjoyed many of the comforts found among the Minoans. Excavations at Pylos on the Mediterranean coast of the Peloponnesus revealed a royal palace with many of the distinctive features of the palace at Knossos. The "Palace of Nestor," named after King Nestor in Homer's *Odyssey*, included wall paintings, storerooms, light wells, a sewage system, and a royal bathroom with bathtub and plumbing.

Sometime around the middle of the fifteenth century BC, the Mycenaeans conquered Crete and, as a result, came under the influence of Minoan culture. Perhaps most

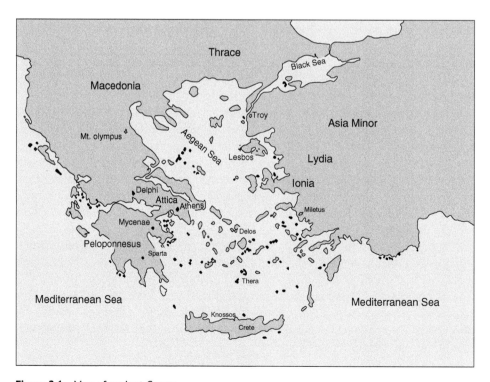

Figure 2.1 Map of ancient Greece.

important for modern archeologists was the appearance of a new writing system referred to by scholars as Linear B Script. It uses the Minoan Linear A Script to write Mycenaean Greek, the earliest form of the Greek language. Linear B was used almost exclusively in the palaces for administrative purposes. It ceased to be used after the collapse of the Bronze Age civilizations between c. 1200 BC and 1150 BC.

The Dark Ages (c. 1100–800 BC)

The collapse of the Bronze Age during the thirteenth century BC was sudden and devastating. Archeological evidence exists throughout the Eastern Mediterranean region in Greece, Turkey, Israel, Syria, Lebanon, and Egypt. "Within a period of forty to fifty years at the end of the thirteenth and the beginning of the twelfth century," writes classical studies scholar Robert Drews, "almost every significant city in the eastern Mediterranean world was destroyed, many of them never to be occupied again" (Drews 1993, p. 4).

What caused the collapse remains a mystery. Many explanations have been offered, but recent scholarship suggests that a "perfect storm" of disastrous events including "climate change; drought and famine; earthquakes; invaders; and internal rebellions" led to a kind of "systems collapse" and ushered in a period referred to as the "Dark Ages" throughout the Eastern Mediterranean regain (Weiner 2015). The Dark Ages lasted from c. 1100 BC to 900 BC in the Near East and until c. 800 BC in Greece. Some scholars prefer 776 BC, the date given by Hippias of Elis (c. 460–400 BC) for the first Olympics.

The art of writing disappeared, cities were abandoned, and the population declined. It is estimated that the population fell to about one-tenth of what it had been in c. 1200 BC. The number of occupied sites in Greece went from about 320 in the thirteenth century to about 40 in the tenth century. What settlements there were during the Dark Ages were small and scattered. Mycenaean culture all but disappeared. The Greeks' self-identity and cultural values, especially the pursuit of excellence, survived in oral transmission to provide the foundation for the classical period.

The Archaic Age (c. 800–480 BC)

Slowly, the turmoil decreased. Agricultural production increased, and with it, the population. The small agricultural villages of the Dark Ages grew into cities and then into city-states (poleis). Typically, a raised area or hill became a fortified area known as the acropolis. Temples to the gods, especially the patron god of the city-state – e.g. the goddess Athena in Athens – were constructed on the acropolis, as well as other official buildings. When the city came under attack, the people would retreat to the acropolis.

At the base of the acropolis was an open area called the agora where merchants and craftsmen conducted their business. It was also the area where free-born citizens would gather to hear public announcements, muster for military campaigns, and attend meetings of the Popular Assembly to discuss and decide matters of importance to the city-state. The philosopher Socrates (see below) frequented the agora in Athens. He would wander about in all sorts of weather barefoot and wearing the same old cloak. He must have been an amusing, if also irritating, figure going about tapping people on the shoulder and asking such questions as "Can you tell me where I can find an honest man?"

Increased population, together with geography and the historical influence of both Minoan and Mycenaean civilizations, led the Greek city-states to look to the sea. During the sixth and fifth centuries BC, Greek colonies existed throughout the Mediterranean world from Asia Minor to Spain. Greek trading posts and settlements existed on the Mediterranean coasts of Spain, France, southern Italy, North Africa, and on the Island of Sicily. They were not colonies in the modern sense. Each was from its founding an independent city-state. Commercial and sentimental ties existed between the sponsoring city-state and the colony, but like the city-states in Greece, and elsewhere, they remained independent.

The overseas colonies provided a market for Greek goods such as wine, olive oil, pottery, and a source of luxury goods and raw materials that found a ready market in Greece. The Greeks, like the Minoans, Myceneans, and the Phoenicians, acted as middle men for the movement of goods throughout the Mediterranean. The Greek colonies acted as important disseminators of Greek culture. They were also a means of relieving political tensions arising in the Greek city-states from over population and/or class conflict. Problems could, in a sense, be exported by founding a colony.

The Greeks never created a unified state. This was due in part to geography, but also the fact that the individual identified first with the city-state. Still, they were conscious of being Greeks. Language was one common denominator. All those who did not speak Greek were regarded as barbarians (*barbaroi*), regardless of their level of civilization, as for example, the Persians. During the eighth century BC, the Greeks reinvented writing by adopting the Phoenician writing system. By adding signs to represent vowels, they created the Greek alphabet. Oral transmission of history and myth could be replaced with written accounts, for example, Homer's *Iliad* and *Odyssey*. Common language and knowledge of a common history and culture was an important source of a common identity. The Olympic Games held on Mount Olympia every four years, beginning in 776 BC, mirrored the independence of the city-states and, at the same time, strengthened their common identity as Greeks.

Mount Olympia is located on the western side of the Peloponnesus where the sanctuary of Altis was located. A temple to Zeus, king of the Greek gods, and a temple to Zeus' wife Hera were located within the sanctuary. The games were held in honor of Zeus. The best athletes from throughout Greece competed as individuals for a garland of wild olive leaves. Participation in the games, in which the athletes competed in the nude, was restricted to men. Married women were not allowed to attend, but unmarried women were permitted as spectators. A separate festival for women in honor of Hera was held at a different time. There, young female athletes competed in what was known as the Heraean Games.

The temple to Apollo, located on the southern slopes of Mount Parnassus was the religious center of ancient Greek religion, as well as a symbol of the unity of all Greeks. It was believed to be the center, or navel, of the world. The oracle of Delphi was located there. It was through the oracle that Apollo made known his will to the Greeks. Individuals would make a sacrifice to Apollo before presenting a question to a male priest. The priest would then present the question to the Pythia, or priestess. The priestess sat on a bronze tripod in the inner chamber of the temple. According to some accounts, the priestess went into a trance induced by fumes arising from a crack in the earth below where she sat, or from chewing laurel leaves. While in the trance, the priestess revealed Apollo's answer, or prophesies. The prophesies were then interpreted by the male priest.

Sparta and Athens

Each city-state was unique, and so it is impossible to describe a "typical" Greek city-state. Instead, Sparta and Athens are often seen in contrast, with Sparta the most atypical and Athens the most typical. Sparta was founded by the Dorians who migrated from northern and northwestern Greece and settled in the Peloponnesus around 950 BC. The city of Sparta dominated the plain of Laconia. The local inhabitants were conquered by the Spartans and became state slaves called "helots." Though there were two kings, a Popular Assembly, and a Council of Elders, Sparta was actually governed by a committee of five Ephors, elected annually by the Popular Assembly. Their role was to guard the rights of the citizens, supervise the kings, conduct foreign affairs, and guard against a revolt of the helots.

Sparta remained an armed camp, on guard against a revolt by the enslaved helots. Much like in a twentieth-century totalitarian state, the individual ceased to exist and became an organic part of the state. Spartans were raised to become but one thing, a soldier ready to die for the city-state. What perplexes the modern mind is the pride with which the Spartan citizen forwent any luxury, any material comfort, and even the desire to think freely for the perceived welfare of Sparta.

The Spartans contributed nothing to philosophy or cultural life. When Sparta's time came to an end, it left behind only the memory of a great warrior tradition, nothing else, not even any impressive ruins. Athens, on the other hand, left behind some of the most impressive ruins of ancient history (e.g. the Parthenon). So rich is the cultural legacy of classical Athens, that it would be difficult, if even impossible, to think of Western Civilization minus Athens.

Athens is located in Attica on the eastern edge of central Greece. It was ruled by kings until 683 BC, when the king was replaced by a board of Archons who served one-year terms. This aristocratic government was corrupt, leading to the oppression of the poor peasants. To avert civil war, Solon (c. 630–c. 560 BC), a moderate Archon, was given authority to institute reforms in the spirit of *noblesse oblige*. Rather than seek answers from the gods, Solon applied reason to the city-state's problems. The ills of society, he reasoned, were due to human behavior, not the will of the gods. Solon sought practical solutions that would restore harmony between man-made laws and the natural laws of the universe.

Solon's reforms included an end to debt slavery, and opening up of opportunities for the commoners to participate, though in a limited way, in the governing process. His economic reforms included the introduction of new industries, including the production of wine and olive oil for export, and the granting of citizenship to foreign craftsmen willing to settle in Athens. Solon stopped short of introducing land reform or democracy. He remained committed to aristocratic government. The lot of the poor did improve, but he meant for the aristocracy to retain the guiding role in government.

Solon's reforms went too far for the aristocrats, but not far enough to satisfy the poor. There followed a period of factional strife. By 560 BC, the citizens were divided into three factions: the landed aristocrats, the new commercial middle class, and the poor small farmers. The stage was set for the appearance of the first tyrant.

Pisistratus (608–527 BC), a nobleman by birth, rose to power on the discontent of the masses. He ruled as tyrant from 546 BC to 528 BC. He gave Athens stability and prosperity. Peisistratus instituted a land reform program through which land, some of it confiscated from aristocrats, and loans were offered to small farmers. An ambitious public works program which beautified the city and provided jobs for the poor was implemented. Olive oil production and trade were encouraged. Peisistratus used public funds to patronize the fine arts and sponsor public festivals. In 566 BC, he founded the Panathenaic Games that included music, poetry, and drama, as well as sporting events. Some believe that Peisistratus' reforms laid the basis for Athens' subsequent cultural leadership. Pisistratus' two sons, Hipparchus and Hippias, tried to continue the tyranny. Hipparchus was assassinated in 514 BC during the Panathenaic Games. The Spartans intervened in 510 BC to restore aristocratic rule. The result was the rise of yet another tyrant, or should one say, reformer.

Reforms instituted by Cleisthenes (c. 570–c. 508 BC) centered on what he called *demokratia*, the rule of the people, that is, the entire body of citizens. Only free, adult males, about 20% of the population of Athens, were citizens. The citizens were divided into 10 tribes, each of which chose by lot 50 of their own who would sit in the new Council of 500. The Council of 500 set the agenda for the Popular Assembly of all of the citizens who

Figure 2.2   The Pnyx was a hill in Athens where the citizens of Athens gathered as the Popular Assembly. *Source:* Photo courtesy of Brent Kooi, private collection.

passed the laws. Cleisthenes also introduced the practice of ostracism, whereby, once a year, the citizens could vote to expel any prominent citizen from the city-state for a period of 10 years. Athenian government as reformed by Cleisthenes served Athens for two and one-half centuries.

Some have chosen to see the political history of Athens as a cycle of government from monarchy, to oligarchy, to tyranny, and finally democracy. But the so-called democracy had little, if anything, in common with modern representative democracy. The latter evolved out of medieval feudalism rather than the *demmokratia* of classical Athens. Classical Greek political theory always subordinated the individual to the city-state. There was no concept of individual rights. Peter Stearns (b. 1936) puts it well when he observes that, "If there was a Geek political heritage, among the chaos of city-states, it was on the whole absolutist, even totalitarian" (Stearns 1977, p. 30).

Cleisthenes passed from the scene around 508 BC, less than one decade before Athens and the rest of the Greek city-states entered upon their most momentous century. It was during the fifth century BC that classical Greek civilization experienced both its golden age and rapid decline. Its moment of greatness was inspired in part by the Persian Wars (499–479 BC). The defeat of Persia was seen by the Greeks as the victory of a free people over a slave empire, and thus inspired greatness in the Greeks, especially the Athenians.

Persian Wars (492–449 BC)

The Greek city-states along the coast of Asia Minor (Ionia) fell under Persian control in 546 BC, when Cyrus the Great (d. 530 BC) conquered the Kingdom of Lydia. In 499 BC, the Ionian Greeks rebelled, led by the city of Miletus. Athens and Eretria sent aid. After a long struggle, the Ionian Greeks were defeated in 494 BC and, once again, were under Persian rule. Darius I, the Great (550–486 BC) decided on a punitive expedition to punish Athens and Eretria.

A Persian expeditionary force crossed the Aegean Sea in 490 BC. Eretria fell after a six-day siege. Shortly after, on the plain of Marathon northeast of Athens, an Athenian army, with some support from Plataea under the command of Miltiades (550–489 BC), met and defeated a Persian force estimated to have been twice as large. The Greek victory brought only a temporary reprieve. Darius I's son, Xerxes I, the Great[2] (519–466 BC) determined to conquer Greece.

Xerxes began his campaign in 480 BC. A Persian army believed to have been between 100 000 and 150 000, crossed the Hellespont and proceeded through Thrace and Macedonia to Greece. At the narrow mountain pass of Thermopylae, a small band of 300 Spartans and 5000 other Greek soldiers died slowing the Persian advance. The decisive battle, however, was fought at sea.

After the Persian defeat in 490 BC, the Athenians heeded the advice of Themistocles (c. 524–459 BC) and built a fleet of 200 triremes, a type of warship with three banks of oars.

---

2 Xerxes I is thought by some scholars to be the Persian King Achashveros in the Old Testament book of Esther.

Themistocles was a veteran of the Battle of Marathon and a populist politician elected archon in 493 BC. The Athenians consulted the Delphic Oracle and were told to "trust in wooden walls." Themistocles argued before the Popular Assembly that "trust in wooden walls" meant build a navy.

In 480 BC after the Battle of Thermopylae, Themistocles once again was able to persuade the Popular Assembly to follow his advice. The Athenians evacuated their beloved city and took refuge on the island of Salamis. The Persians burned Athens. Again, heeding the advice of Themistocles, the Greeks lured the much larger Persian fleet into the narrow Straits of Salamis. An allied fleet led by Athens, attacked the Persian fleet. The Persian ships were large and difficult to maneuver in the narrow straits. The smaller Greek triremes destroyed the Persian fleet, while Xerxes observed the battle from the slopes of Mount Aegaleo.

The final battle took place in the summer of 479 BC near Plataea in southeastern Boeotia. The Persian army was decisively defeated by a Greek army made up of Spartans and soldiers from other Greek city-states. On the same afternoon as the Greek victory in the Battle of Plataea, what was left of the Persian fleet was captured in the Battle of Mycale on the Ionian coast of Asia Minor, opposite the island of Samos. The Greek victories in the two battles ended the Persian threat. The Greeks then went on the offensive.

The Classical Age (c. 480–338 BC)

There were two major results of the Greek victory in the wars with Persia. First, it infused the Greeks with a victorious spirit. The Greeks saw their victory as one of a free people over an empire of slaves. Nothing seemed impossible for them. The result was the golden age of classical civilization, a cultural flowering seldom matched in history (see below). The second outcome was the emergence of Athens as a great power among the Greek city-states. Athenian imperialism would lead to a Greek civil war between Athens and Sparta that would end the golden age and put Greece on a downward slide from which it would never recover.

Athens was rebuilt along with its port, Piraeus, following the Persian defeat. The triumphant Athenian fleet was enlarged. Athens became leader of the Delian League of Greek city-states intended to guard against any revived Persian threat. Once the Persian threat no longer existed, the other members of the Delian League wanted to disband the league. Athens refused. Those city-states who attempted to leave the league were destroyed by Athens. The transformation of the Delian League into an Athenian Empire was complete in 454 BC, when the league's treasury was moved to Athens. Athenian imperialism threatened the traditional Greek lifestyle centered on the independent city-state.

Imperialism brought with it war rather than peace. Athens' attempt to gain hegemony over the Greek city-states led the Athenians into the sin of hubris, that exaggerated pride the Greeks believed led to retribution. Athens' dominance was brief. The end came through the Peloponnesian War (433–404 BC).

Thucydides (460–395 BC), who recorded the Peloponnesian War in his *History of the Peloponnesian War*, said that what caused the war was fear of Athenian imperialism and its threat to the independence of the Greek city-states. Sparta assumed leadership of the Peloponnesian League formed to oppose Athens and defend the liberty of the city-states threatened by Athens' imperialistic goals. The war broke out in 431 BC, when Thebes, an ally of Sparta, attacked Plataea, an ally of Athens.

The war eventually became a contest between Sparta and Athens, while city-states allied with either side would be captured and, at times, their populations massacred. Sparta and Athens, the two most powerful city-states at the time, were not equally matched. Sparta was a land power and Athens was a sea power. Each invaded and lay waste to the opponent's territory on an annual basis, but neither was strong enough to actually capture the enemy city. The Athenians, for example, could retreat behind the city walls to wait out the Spartans. Access to Piraeus, Athens' harbor, was protected by two Long Walls. Their fleet was able to supply Athens. Without a navy, Sparta was not able to blockade Piraeus.

Athens suffered a fatal blow in 429 BC, when the city was struck with a devastating plague. Thucydides recorded the plague in his *History*. From one third to as many as two thirds of the city's population died. The Spartans broke off their siege fearing the plague more than combat. It was the death of Pericles (495–429 BC), architect of the Athenian Empire, that sealed the city's fate. With the loss of Pericles' able leadership, Athenian policy fell victim to the whim of the mob as expressed through the Popular Assembly.

In 415 BC, the Athenians heeded the advice of the youthful and reckless Alcibiades (451/450–404 BC) to launch a campaign against Syracuse on the island of Sicily. The largest force ever assembled by a Greek city-state set sail for Syracuse. The result was a disastrous defeat for Athens in the harbor of Syracuse in 413 BC. With most of its navy gone, Athenian political life deteriorated. No one leader could control the Popular Assembly long enough to implement a strategy. Sparta sought and received financial assistance from Persia to build a fleet.

The Spartans caught the Athenian fleet off guard at Aegospotami in the Hellespont. They captured 160 of the Athenian ships. The Spartans then laid siege to Athens by both land and sea. Without its navy, the proud Athenians were forced to surrender in 404 BC. The Peloponnesian War, sometimes seen as a contest between an elephant and a whale, was won by the elephant.

Sparta's allies demanded that Athens, in defeat, be dealt with as Athens dealt with those whom it defeated, that is, the city destroyed, the men massacred, and the women and children sold into slavery. Sparta refused. Instead, the Delian League was dissolved and Athens was required to surrender what was left of its fleet and dismantle its defensive walls. Aristocratic rule under a government of Thirty Tyrants was imposed on Athens, with Spartan support.

The Greek spirit was broken. The pursuit of selfish interests replaced the old devotion to the city-state. Civil war among the city-states became the order of the day during the fourth century BC, while to the north in Macedonia, the stage was being set for the next phase of Greek history.

After the Peloponnesian War, no individual city-state was able to dominate the rest or impose unity on Greece. Sparta, Thebes, and Athens each, in turn, held brief sway. Finally, in 387 BC, Persia imposed the "King's Peace" on Greece, with Sparta as its agent in supervising the peace. The Ionian city-states remained under Persian control, and all power blocks within Greece were forbidden. Greece remained splintered into numerous independent city-states. Remaining divided, the Greeks were unprepared for the threat presented by Philip II (359–336 BC) and the Kingdom of Macedon in the north.

Philip II studied the battle tactics of the Greeks, especially the heavily armored hoplites, while living in Thebes during his youth. To meet the challenge presented by the hoplites, Philip developed a new formation, the phalanx of 10 ranks of infantry armed with long pikes and small swords. By 357 BC, Philip united Macedonia and gained access to the sea. In 340 BC, he defeated the hastily formed Hellenic League of Greek city-states at the battle of Chaeronea. The independence of the Greek city-states was finally ended, as they were united under Philip's leadership in the League of Corinth. Philip II was the master of Greece.

In 337 BC, the League of Corinth declared war on Persia to avenge the destruction of Greek temples by Xerxes. Philip sent an advance army across the Hellespont in the spring of 336 BC. Philip was assassinated by one of his own bodyguards before he could join his army. Whether the assassin acted alone, or was part of a conspiracy, remains unknown. His son, Alexander, was among those who were rumored to be the instigators of the plot.

Alexander (356–323 BC) succeeded his father at the age of 20. He inherited the war with Persia along with the throne. Thebes rebelled, believing a rumor that Alexander was dead. After destroying Thebes for its treason, Alexander crossed the Hellespont in May, 334 at the exact spot where Xerxes began his invasion of Greece in 480 BC.

Alexander the Great's career has become romanticized and clouded with mystery over the centuries since his death in Babylon in 323 BC at the age of 33. He was, no doubt, a military genius. Even if we grant that the Persian Empire of the time was only a weakened shadow of what it had once been, still Alexander's conquest of it in less than 10 years was a feat seldom, if ever, matched. What his real intentions were for the future can only be guessed. Did he really intend to promote a fusion of cultures and, thus, some sort of new world order as some suggests, or was he merely trying to build a power base from which to launch a conquest of the western Mediterranean? Perhaps in the final analysis, Alexander the Great was only a madman who set out to conquer the world. Whatever his real motives, he changed the world.

The Hellenistic Age (323 – 31 BC)

Shortly after his death Alexander's empire was divided among his leading generals. Alexander's mother Olympia was murdered in 316 BC. His wife Roxana, daughter of a Bactrian chief, and their son were both killed in 310 BC. Roxana had previously killed two of Alexander's other wives fearing they were a threat to her and her son. After dividing the administration of the empire among them, the generals fought one another until 281 BC, when three successor kingdoms were recognized. The Antigonids ruled Macedonia; the Seleucids ruled Asia Minor and Mesopotamia; the Ptolemies ruled Egypt.

During the Hellenistic Age, following the death of Alexander the Great, the independent city-state that characterized the Hellenic Age was replaced by a cosmopolitan world of kingdoms and empires, all of which were permeated by Greek culture. *Koine*, a form of Greek, became the lingua franca throughout most of the Mediterranean world. Alexandria in Egypt, founded by Alexander the Great, became the economic and cultural center of the Mediterranean world. There, Hebrew scholars translated the Old Testament into Greek and began studying Greek philosophy. Historians began to write universal or world histories. The spread of Greek culture from the eastern Mediterranean to the Indus River was one of the great legacies of Hellenization. But this Hellenization remained only a thin veneer limited largely to the urban centers. Outside the cities, in the countryside, there was not even a veneer. There, the old ways remained dominate and the "world" did not extend beyond the immediate experience.

Greek Society

For the sake of brevity, and because we know more about Athens than the other city-states, we will consider Greek society during the classical period as it existed in Athens. The population of Athens and other city-states, except Sparta, consisted of three classes: citizens, resident foreigners (metics), and slaves. Only free adult men were citizens allowed to participate in governing the city-state. Beginning in 451 BC, only male children of parents who were both Athenians were granted citizenship. Resident foreigners, who were often traders and craftsmen, were not citizens. Freed slaves were included in the metics.

Women in Greek Society

Women were Athenians, but little else. Athens was a men's only club. Girls in their mid-teens normally married men in their early thirties. The marriage was arranged by the girl's male guardian. Often the bride did not meet her chosen husband until the wedding day. Once married, her life was largely restricted to the women's quarters. She did not go out in public unless accompanied by a male. Men did the shopping, not women. Wives did not dine with their husbands. They could not act in plays, and if they attended a play, they were required to sit in the rear, away from the men. Married women were not allowed to attend the Olympic Games, where the athletes competed in the nude. The penalty for violating this regulation was death. Unmarried women were allowed to attend the games.

Women were not given any formal education, unless one considers training in household chores an education. A wife's proper station in life was to keep her husband's house and raise his children. Aristotle believed that women were incomplete males. They were necessary for a successful and happy community, but "the male is by nature superior, and the female inferior; and the one rules, and the other is ruled" (Perry et al. 2003, p. 57). The character Procne (sister of Philomela and wife of king Tereus) in Sophocles play, *Tereus*, points to a woman's fate in classical Athens:

> And now I am nothing on my own. But often have I seen women's nature to be like this, since we are nothing. Young girls in their father's house live, I think, the happiest life of all humanity. For folly always brings up children delightfully. But when we have reached the prime of life and are prudent, we are pushed out and sold, away from our ancestral gods and our parents, some of us to foreign husbands, some to barbarians, some to joyless homes, and some to abusive ones. And, when a single night has yoked us, this is what we must approve of and think of as a good life (Sophocles n.d.).

Slaves in Greek Society

Slavery was a part of life throughout the ancient world. A census of Attica taken between 317 BC and 307 BC showed that there were 21 000 citizens, 10 000 metics, and 40 000 slaves. Slaves were the lowest class. Most were purchased from slave traders, though many were obtained as the spoils of war. Most Athenian citizens owned at least one slave. In fact, not being able to afford at least one slave was a sign of poverty.

Domestic slaves were often treated well and considered part of the family. Some served as tutors or domestic servants. Some could even purchase their freedom. Many, perhaps the majority, labored on farms. Some were owned by the city-state. They functioned much like civil servants. It was a slave who attested to the genuineness of the city-state's coinage. They served as policemen and aided in the arrest of criminals. The official executioner was a state-owned slave.

However "good" the life of a slave appeared to be, the fact remained that slaves were legally classified as chattel property. A slave could be sold, punished, or even killed by the master, though killing one's slave was frowned upon in Athens during the classical period. Athenian law required that a female slave be tortured before she could give evidence in court. Aristotle said that slaves were a "sort of living possession." He defended slavery as being "natural," since some human beings lacked the capacity to reason. Such a position, of course, was hard to defend if the slave was another Greek obtained in war.

The lowest of all slaves were those who worked in the Laurium silver mines located less than 40 miles (64 km) southeast of Athens. Much of the wealth that made Athens an imperial power and the glory of the classical period came from the Laurium mines. The mines were owned by the city-state and leased to individuals. Private individuals leased slaves to the miners to labor in the mines or the surrounding facilities that converted the silver ore into coins. About 350 mines employed approximately 20 000 slaves, according to Thucydides, and produced 1000 talents (26 kg or 57 lb.) of silver annually.

Slaves working in the mines were considered disposable slaves. Their life was short and brutal. Naked, the miners descended down a vertical shaft by ladder, and then entered a narrow horizontal shaft. Bent over, they worked with pick and iron hammer to extract the ore. They were poorly fed, savagely beaten, and seldom saw daylight. Because the silver ore contained large amounts of lead, the miners usually died in one to two years from lead poisoning.

Sex in Greek Society

Homosexuality was a characteristic part of society in classical Athens, as elsewhere. In Plato's *Symposium* homosexuality is lauded as "a pure form of Celestial Love." What Plato called the only true love, the love between two males, was really between an adult male and a young boy. It was the norm for an adult male to take a young boy as his lover until the boy was old enough to grow a beard. The relationship between the adult and his lover was considered an educational one. The adult guided his young lover on his way to adulthood.

Intercourse between male and female, husband and wife, was necessary for procreation. "Women for children; boys for pleasure" is an apt description of sexual activity in classical

Figure 2.3 The Erchtheion was a temple dedicated to the goddess Athena on the north side of the Acropolis in Athens, 421–406 BC. *Source:* Photo courtesy of Brent Kooi, private collection.

Athens. It is evident from images on vases and art objects, that love was public as well as private. There are vases with pictures portraying intercourse between two individuals while others look on.

Both Plato and Xenophon, another of Socrates' students, speak of Socrates' well-known fascination with young boys. Both speak of measures taken by Socrates to avoid relationships with the boys from becoming physical, though Plato admits that Socrates did occasionally give in to temptation. Both agreed with their master that the relationship between the adult and the boy could be aimed at both sexual love and "also at obtaining moral wisdom and strength" (Van Dolen 2018).

Greek Philosophy

The greatness of Greek civilization is not found in its political history, but like the ancient Hebrews, in how they tried to answer the perennial questions of the meaning and purpose of existence. The Greeks, like the Hebrews, demythicized nature. But the Greeks were the first to attempt to understand the world, and human beings, relying only on reason. For the Hebrews, there was a natural order to the universe because it was created by a reasonable God. Because the individual was created in God's image, the individual could understand and discover the order of the universe. The Greeks also believed that there was a natural order inherent in the universe. Because the individual possessed the capacity to reason, the individual could discover and understand the natural order of the universe. For the Hebrews the individual's value came from being the image bearer of God. For the Greeks the individual's value came from the capacity to reason. The emphasis by both on the value of the individual and the individual's ability to reason are two fundamental values that distinguish Western Civilization from non-Western civilizations throughout history down to the present.

The Greek philosophers of the Hellenic period may be conveniently divided into cosmologists, or natural philosophers, and the humanistic philosophers. The first philosophers were from Ionia, the Greek colonies along the coast of Asia Minor. They were seeking reasonable explanations for natural phenomena, rather than attributing them to the arbitrary will of the gods or simply random chance. Thales (624–546 BC), Anaximander (610–546 BC), and Anaximenes (585–528 BC) were all from Miletus.

Thales, often called the first philosopher, believed that everything originated in water, the most basic element, and came about by a natural process. Anaximander began with matter, which he called the "boundless" or "unlimited." Life, he reasoned, began in a warm slime. Fish moved onto land and eventually evolved into human beings. It is said that Anaximander supported his theory with a collection of fossils. Anaximenes believed that air was the basic element and all that existed was the result of the thickening and thinning of air.

Matter was the ultimate reality for the philosophers of Miletus. Elsewhere, other Greek thinkers took different approaches. Heraclitus of Ephesus (435–475 BC) postulated change, or flux, as the basic reality. He taught that fire was the basic element. All other elements, and thus all that exist, has its origin in fire. "All things," said Heraclitus, "are an interchange for fire, and fire for all things, just like goods for gold and gold for goods." In contrast, Parmenides of Elea (fl. early fifth century BC) in southern Italy held that reality is one, eternal, and unchanging. In his didactic poem, "Nature," he contrasts "Being" (mass) with "Not Being" (void). Being, that is matter, said Parmenides, is the only object of knowledge, and knowledge can be arrived at through abstract thought. Parmenides is sometimes called the father of formal logic.

Empedocles (495–430 BC) of Agrigentum (a.k.a. Akragas or Agrigento) in Sicily tried to reconcile Heraclitus (change, flux) and Parmenides (eternal, unchanging) with the concept of the four basic elements: earth, air, fire, and water. The four elements were combined or separated by the forces of love and hate. Pythagoras (c. 570–c. 495 BC) of Samos, also in southern Italy, pointed to the importance of mathematics by suggesting that there is an inherent mathematical order to the universe. The visible world and the world of ideas merely reflects the mathematical relationships in the universe. Democritus (460–370 BC), a pupil of Leusippus (c. 460–370 BC), postulated an infinite number of atoms falling through a void. Everything that existed was formed by different combinations of atoms which were governed by natural law. By seeing the universe as a kind of machine operating according to natural laws, whose order was mathematical and subject to logical proof, the natural philosophers discovered the basis of scientific reasoning.

The "scientists" of the Hellenistic period built upon the discoveries of the Hellenic natural philosophers. Euclid (fl. fourth century BC), a mathematician living in Alexandria, wrote a textbook on plane geometry, *Elements of Geometry*, which remained valid into the twentieth century AD. Archimedes (287–212 BC) of Syracuse calculated the value of *pi*, and wrote the first scientific works on statics and hydrostatics. Heraclides Ponticus (387–312 BC) discovered that the earth rotated on its axis. Whether he postulated a heliocentric model of the universe is not known for certain, but Aristarchus (310–230 BC) of Samos did do so. Hipparchus (190–120 BC) of Nicaea, on the other hand, put forth a geocentric model of the universe. It was Hipparchus' model, adopted by the second century AD geographer and mathematician Claudius Ptolemy (90–168 AD), that survived the fall of the Roman Empire in the West and remained dominate until Copernicus revived the heliocentric model in the sixteenth century AD.

The naturalistic philosophers pioneered theoretical reason as the means for understanding nature. Beginning with Socrates (c. 470–c. 399 BC) the humanistic (or metaphysical) philosophers applied reason to the study of the individual and society, which they considered more important than the study of nature.

The ancient Hebrews believed that the individual was endowed by his creator with moral autonomy to choose between obedience to, or disobedience of, God's moral precepts. The individual was not free to create his or her own moral precepts or standard of right and wrong. To disobey God's laws would result in bondage, suffering, and death. The individual existed in a community. For example, the Hebrews were God's chosen people and so, the community likewise, was obligated to conform to God's moral laws. The result would be a just society. This sense of social conscience has been an important part of Western Civilization.

In contrast to the Hebrew writers, Socrates did not believe that moral values originated with an all-sovereign, transcendent God. Rather, moral values were discovered through reason. By a process referred as *dialectics*, that is logical reasoning or logical discussion, individuals in society could acquire knowledge, develop character (virtue), and enjoy the good life. By discovering truth through reason, Socrates did not mean that truth was relative, as did the Sophists of his day.

The Sophists were traveling teachers who offered instruction in useful knowledge for a price. Since rhetoric was definitely a useful skill in democratic Athens, they offered to teach the effective use of language in public speaking. They claimed to teach *arête* (moral virtue or excellence). Socrates loathed the Sophists[3] not only because they made education a business, but also because they were moral relativists. Socrates believed that the pursuit of knowledge had its own rewards. He also taught that truth did exist and could be discovered through dialectical reasoning.

Socrates' most famous pupil was Plato (c. 427–347 BC).[4] Plato is perhaps best known for designing one of the first utopias, or ideal states. In *The Republic*, he tried to define justice by seeing it in the ideal state. Plato's visionary republic, though, turned out to be a totalitarian state. Not even freedom of thought was permitted its subjects. It is in Plato's discussion of where reality lies, that is, his theory of ideas, that his real significance for Western Civilization is found.

---

3 The best known of the Sophists were Protagoras, Gorgias, Antiphon, Hippias, Prodicus, and Thrasymachus.

4 Alfred North Whitehead said of Plato's influence, "The safest general characterization of the European philosophical tradition is that it consists of a series of footnotes to Plato" (Whitehead and Griffin 1978, p. 39).

Plato believed the world we experience from day to day is but a reflection of the real world of ideal forms that exists in the realm of ideas. A chair that we sit on is recognized as a chair because it resembles the one true chair, or chair-form, that exists in the ideal world beyond space and time. The same holds true for such concepts as justice, beauty, etc. The world mankind inhabits is unstable, always in flux. But the realm of ideal forms is eternal and unchanging. This emphasis on universal principles was challenged by Plato's most important student, Aristotle.

Aristotle (385–322 BC) wrote on every subject. He was an organizer, a systematizer. He wrote on botany, zoology, metaphysics, logic, rhetoric, poetry, ethics, and political theory, to name just a few of the areas he examined. Like Plato, who founded the Academy, Aristotle also founded a school, the Lyceum. Like Plato he wrote a book, *Politics*, in which he tried to describe the best form of government. But unlike Plato, Aristotle did not describe a utopia. Instead, he defended the city-state of Hellenic Greece. For Aristotle, law, not a philosopher-king, would rule the affairs of the city-state's citizens.

Aristotle also departed from his former teacher with respect to where he found reality. For Aristotle, reality is in the object itself, not in a perfect realm of ideas. Whereas Plato stressed the universals, Aristotle stressed the particulars. This tension over what is real, or where reality is located, in the universals or the particulars, has troubled Western thought ever since. It became even more of an issue with the enthronement of Aristotle as the philosopher of the Middle Ages by Thomas Aquinas (1225–1274) and other scholastic philosopher-theologians (see Chapter 6).

Simply stated, the problem is, that if you begin with the particulars (e.g. the individual), how do you find ultimate and adequate meaning for the particulars? With Plato, the meaning of the particulars is found in the universals (absolutes) that exist in the realm of ideas. Clearly, Plato and Aristotle are two of the most important thinkers in the history of Western thought and examples of the importance of the classical period for the history of Western Civilization. It would be the task of the Romans to pass on this rich heritage, along with that of the ancient Hebrews, to Europe.

The Greek Legacy

The influence of ancient Greece on Western Civilization is evident everywhere. Walk down just about any street and see the Greek influence in architecture, especially in government buildings. Participate in an election, or witness a trial, where attorneys appeal to the laws of the land before judges and juries sworn to consider the evidence in light of reasoned laws passed by the citizens for the good of the community as a whole. Consider the advances in modern science, whether space exploration or the latest advances in medicine, all possible, because the Greeks established the supremacy of human reason over mysticism, religion, custom, and accepted authority.

The elevation of the individual as a reasoning being who could understand nature and human society, and thereby improve both society and the individual is perhaps the greatest achievement of the Greeks. People could create an organized society in which the people governed themselves. It was possible, they believed, to improve both society and the individual through education, the disciplined pursuit of excellence (*arête*, virtue). They did not see the individual as innately good in the sense that there was no dark side to human nature. Rather, by the creation of laws and public institutions, accepted moral norms, and the building of character, the flaws in human nature could be held in check.

The Greek contribution to Western Civilization can be summed up thus: "Whatever we experience in our day, whatever we set out to find, we see that the Greeks have been there before us, and we meet them on their way back" (Cahill 2003, p. 264).

References

Cahill, T. (2003). *Sailing the Wine-Dark Sea: Why the Greeks Matter*. New York: Nan A. Talese/ Doubleday.

Drews, R. (1993). *The End of the Bronze Age: Changes in Warfare and the Catastrophe Ca. 1200 B.C.* Princeton, NJ: Princeton University Press.

North Whitehead, A. and Griffin, D.R. (1978). *Process and Reality: An Essay in Cosmology*. Corrected ed. New York: Free Press.

Perry, M., Baker, J.W., and Pfeiffer Hollinger, P. (2003). *The Humanities in the Western Tradition: Ideas and Aesthetics. Vol. I: Ancient to Medieval*. Boston: Houghton Mifflin.

Sophocles (2019). Sophocles, Tereus, fr.583 (Radt). Aleator classicus. https://aleatorclassicus. wordpress.com/2012/04/21/sophocles-tereus-fr-583 (accessed 18 October 2019).

Stearns, P.N. (1977). *The Face of Europe*. St. Louis: Forum Press.

Van Dolen, H. (2018). Greek Homosexuality. Livius. https://www.livius.org/articles/concept/ greek-homosexuality (accessed 18 October 2019).

Weiner, J. (2015). What Caused The Mysterious Bronze Age Collapse? Ancient History Et Cetera. http://etc.ancient.eu/2015/05/20/what-caused-the-bronze-age-collapse (accessed 18 October 2019).

3

The Roman World

Chronology

753 BC	Traditional Date of Founding of Rome
509 BC	Rome Becomes a Republic
450 BC	Law of the Twelve Tables
390 BC	Gauls Sack Rome
264–241 BC	First Punic War
218–202 BC	Second Punic War
149–146 BC	Third Punic War and Destruction of Carthage
134–122 BC	Gracchi Brothers' Land Reform
60 BC	First Triumvirate (J. Caesar, Pompey, Crassus)
44 BC	Julius Caesar Assassinated
43 BC	Second Triumvirate (Octavian, Mark Antony, Lepidus)
27 BC	Roman Empire Begins
27 BC–AD 180	*Pax Romana*
19 BC	Virgil's *Aeneid*
c. 4 BC–c. AD 30/33	Jesus of Nazareth
AD 235–285	"Barracks Emperors"
AD 293	Diocletian Founded Tetrarchy
AD 311	Constantine's Edict of Milan
AD 381	Theodosius I Declares Christianity Only Legal Religion
AD 378	Battle of Adrianople
AD 410	Goths Sack Rome
AD 426	St. Augustine's *City of God*
AD 476	End of Roman Empire in the West

According to legend, the city of Rome was founded in 753 BC on a site occupied by an Indo-European people known as the Latins. At about the same time that Rome was being founded, the prophets Amos and Hosea were warning the Kingdom of Judah of God's impending judgment represented by the threat from the Assyrians; Sparta was coming under the rule of Five Ephors; and in Egypt, Piankhi, an Ethiopian, was founding the 25th Dynasty. Farther afield in India, the *Upanishads*, the Hindu scriptures, were being written

Western Civilization: A Brief History, First Edition. Paul R. Waibel.
© 2020 John Wiley & Sons, Inc. Published 2020 by John Wiley & Sons, Inc.

down for the first time, and in China, the original Chou Dynasty was ending, as China slipped into a 500-year-long era of warring barons.

Roman history extends chronologically from the middle of the eighth century BC to the fall of the Roman Empire in the West, traditionally dated in AD 476, and beyond, to the fall of Constantinople, the capital of the Eastern Roman (or Byzantine) Empire to the Ottoman Turks in 1453. Roman civilization is the direct ancestor of Western Civilization. It transmitted to Europe Classical humanism and the Judeo-Christian religious tradition, two primary ingredients of Western Civilization. Its collapse at the end of the fifth century introduced the third major ingredient, the Germanic influence.

Much of what is regarded as typically "Western" originated with or was influenced by the Romans. Many European languages are descended from the Latin spoken by the Romans. Roman law forms the basis of not only the cannon law of the Roman Catholic Church, but of many of the world's legal systems. Roman concepts of government have periodically influenced the development of European governmental institutions. And not least in importance, is the lingering memory of the *Pax Romana* (Roman Peace), roughly 200 years of peace under a "universal" government.

The essence of Roman civilization is often summed up by the saying that it consisted of an army, an arch, and a law. The Roman army was the best the world had yet seen. With weapons no different than most of their opponents, the Roman legions conquered the Mediterranean world. They were also great builders. From Scotland in the north, to North Africa in the south, and from Spain in the west to Mesopotamia in the east, soldiers and merchants traveled in peace on paved roads from city to city. Mighty stone aqueducts carried water from mountain streams to the cities. Amphitheaters, coliseums, temples, and domed structures built of brick and/or stone shaped the skyline of Roman cities. For centuries following the collapse of the Roman Empire, these great structures served as stone quarries for the conquerors, and still today, the surviving ruins testify to the engineering skills of the Romans and the glory that was Rome.

The Roman discovery of a "common law of nature" enabled them to create a system of laws that was suitable for governing a world empire of diverse cultures. They believed that what is right and what is wrong, what is just and what is unjust, is knowable by reason. Natural law refers to a kind of universal conscience that is shared by all humankind. It provides the basis for law that does not merely reflect the will of the stronger or the whim of the masses. It makes a civilized society possible by giving "both privileges or rights, and responsibilities or duties to the truly wise." Natural law has profoundly influenced Western legal systems down to the present.[1]

Early Republic

The early Romans were influenced by both the Greeks who settled independent city-states in the southern "boot" of the Italian peninsula and on the island of Sicily, and the Etruscans, who occupied the area north of Rome between the Arno and the Tiber rivers,

---

1 "Thomas Jefferson explicitly names Cicero as one of a handful of major figures who contributed to a tradition 'of public right' that informed his draft of the Declaration of Independence" (Nicgorski 2017).

known as Etruria. Of the two, the Etruscan influence was the most important. The Etruscans dominated Rome to the end of the monarchy and the founding of the Republic in 509 BC.

The Etruscans remain a mysterious people whose origins are not known with certainty. Recent scholarship supports the Greek historian Dionysius of Halicarnassus whose history of Rome, written around 7 BC, claims that the Etruscans were native to western Italy. Others find merit in Herodotus' belief that the Etruscans originated in Asia Minor and migrated to Italy around 800 BC. Whatever their origin, by the sixth century BC, the Etruscans had established a loose confederation of 12 cities that ruled over most of Italy, except for the Greek city-states in the south.

The Romans inherited the alphabet from the Etruscans, the use of the arch and vault in construction, portrait sculpture, and the practice of divining the future by examining the entrails of animals or observing the flight of birds. The distinctive practice of reclining on low coaches while eating and the distinctive Roman dress, the toga, were also borrowed from the Etruscans. The names of certain Roman gods are Etruscan in origin. The concept of *imperium* – that is, sovereignty or authority to rule in political, military, and religious affairs – originated with the Etruscans. On a darker note, the Romans derived the cruel entertainment of gladiatorial contests from an Etruscan religious ceremony in honor of the dead.

Roman government was initially a monarchy. The king was appointed by the Etruscans who dominated Rome. When the last Etruscan king was driven out in 509 BC by the Romans, Rome became a republic. The *imperium* was transferred to two consuls elected by the *Comitia Centuriata* (a popular assembly) for terms of one year. This transfer of the *imperium* marks the beginning of the Republic. The two consuls shared the *imperium*, each possessing the right of veto. In a time of dire emergency, the consuls, with the approval of the Senate, could appoint a dictator for a limited period of time up to six months. During the designated period, the authority of the consuls was subordinate to that possessed by the dictator.

The Senate was the only continuously-existing deliberative body in government throughout Roman history. The Senate consisted of 300, later 600, members drawn mostly from the landed aristocracy. They were normally ex-magistrates (elected officials) who served for life. The Senate was not a legislative body, but rather an advisory body that gave advice (considered binding) to the consuls and other magistrates. The Senate exercised effective control over the government during the Republican period. It controlled finances, government administration, and foreign affairs.

The population of the Republic was divided by birth into two classes, patricians and plebeians. The patricians were the landowning aristocracy who monopolized the elected offices, and who alone could interpret the unwritten laws of the Republic. The plebeians were mostly peasant farmers and shepherds, but some were merchants, tradesmen, and artisans. They were the backbone of the Roman army, but were excluded from holding public office or serving in the Senate. Kept for the most part in poverty, they were subject to being sold into slavery outside Rome by their creditors for non-payment of debts.

Around 494 BC, the plebeians withdrew from the city to one of the nearby hills, where they set up their own assembly. The patricians were forced to recognize the plebeians' right to elect two, then later ten, magistrates called tribunes, with the power to protect plebeians by vetoing arbitrary acts by the magistrates. The tribune's person was declared sacrosanct. Any person who harmed a tribune could be put to death without trial. Eventually, the tribunes could veto any act of any magistrate (including other tribunes) or any measure passed by the Senate or other assemblies.

The struggle by the plebeians for political, legal, and social equality with the patricians continued for roughly two centuries. In 450 BC, the laws of Rome were codified and published on wooden tablets (or tables) known as the Law of the Twelve Tables. Five years later, plebeians won the right to marry patricians. By 409 BC, elected offices were open to plebeians. Beginning in 342 BC, one of the two consuls was a plebeian. The "Struggle of the Orders," as this early civil rights struggle is often called, culminated in 287 BC with the passage of a law that made decisions of the Plebeian Assembly (*concilium plebis*) binding on all Romans.

Having achieved legal equality with the patricians, the plebeians did not go on to establish a democracy. Instead, they allowed the Senate to continue to rule Rome. A new class struggle appeared, one of rich patricians and plebeians versus poor patricians and plebeians, while the government remained in the hands of a wealthy aristocracy. Evidence of this is found in the fact that between 233 and 133 BC, 26 families provided 80% of the consuls. The same families that monopolized the consulships also controlled the Senate.

Early Conquest Under the Republic

The early Roman army was conscripted for each campaign. The backbone of the army was the infantry, drawn from the small farmers. The wealthy citizens provided the cavalry, while the poor served as light armed infantry troops. The "citizen soldiers" soon proved themselves to be the best army the world had yet seen. In c. 396 BC, the Romans crossed the Tiber River and destroyed the Etruscan stronghold of Veii. Victorious over the Etruscans, the Romans soon suffered a major defeat at the hands of the invading Gauls (Celts) from the north. The Gauls captured and sacked the city of Rome in 390 BC. No enemy army penetrated the walls of Rome for the next 800 years.

During the fourth and early third centuries BC, Roman armies defeated the Etruscans, the Gauls, and another neighboring tribe, the Samites. By 265 BC, Rome controlled all of Italy south of the Po River. Even the Greek city-states in Sicily acknowledged Roman authority. Roman presence in Sicily set the stage for the decisive showdown between Rome and Carthage on the northern coast of Africa. Carthage originated as a Phoenician colony on the Mediterranean coast of Africa. By the beginning of the third century BC, it dominated the western Mediterranean Sea, including the western side of Sicily. At first the Carthaginians, whose navy controlled the seas, appeared to be the more formidable foe. But after a series of three wars known as the Punic Wars, between 264 and 146 BC, Carthage was utterly destroyed and Rome was master of the western Mediterranean world.

Rome entered the First Punic War (264–241 BC) against Carthage, a naval power, without a navy. The Romans built a navy and in 241 BC won a decisive victory in a naval battle off the coast of Sicily. In addition to paying a huge indemnity in silver, Carthage surrendered the island of Sicily. Rome added the islands of Corsica and Sardinia to its emerging empire in 238 BC. With the annexation of Sicily, Corsica, and Sardinia, Rome became a major power in the western Mediterranean Sea.

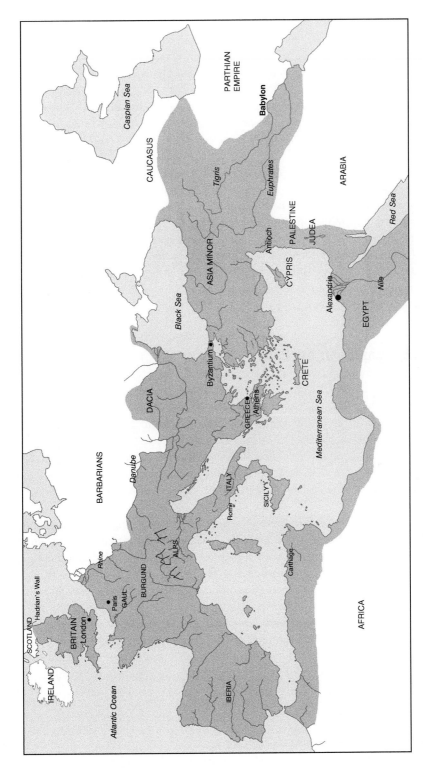

Figure 3.1 Map of the Roman Empire, AD 117.

The Second Punic War (218–202 BC) broke out when Carthage attacked the city of Saguntum, a Roman ally in Spain. The Carthaginian general, Hannibal (247–183 BC), invaded Italy by taking a largely mercenary army across the Alps into the Po valley. Though he won a number of impressive victories against the Romans in Italy, he was never strong enough to attack Rome itself. The Romans took the war to North Africa in 204 BC with an army under the command of Publius Cornelius Scipio (236–183 BC), later know as Scipio Africanus. Hannibal returned home to defend Carthage, only to suffer defeat by Scipio at the battle of Zama in 202 BC. Carthage was defeated and forced to surrender Spain, pay a huge indemnity, and disarm.

The Third Punic War (149–146 BC) was more a massacre than a war. Roman hatred of Carthage was fueled by Carthage's growing commercial prosperity. In 150 BC, the Romans seized upon a minor incident to demand that the Carthaginians abandon Carthage and move 10 miles inland. When they refused, the Romans declared war and laid siege to the city. Carthage finally fell in 146 BC after a three-year siege. The Romans sacked and burned the city. Those citizens who survived were sold into slavery. Scipio ordered the city totally destroyed, leaving not one stone on top of another, and decreed that no city should ever exist, or crop ever grow again on the site of Carthage.[2] Rome was now the foremost military power in the western Mediterranean. Soon its attention turned to the Hellenistic east.

Roman Expansion in the East

Roman victory in the Punic Wars did not make Rome an empire. Some historians suggest that the Roman Republic reluctantly became an empire. There was no plan of conquest. The Romans tried to avoid involvement beyond the Italian peninsula. But Rome soon discovered that peace in the Mediterranean world was vital for Rome's survival and future prosperity. That realization compelled Rome to intervene again and again in disputes between various powers at the eastern end of the Mediterranean Sea. During the last two centuries BC, the Roman Republic became an empire ruling over the whole of the Mediterranean world.

Rome was drawn into the wars between the three successor kingdoms of Alexander the Great's empire – the Kingdom of Macedon, the Seleucid Empire, and the Ptolemaic Kingdom of Egypt. As Rome expanded, it became increasingly dependent upon Egypt for grain. Instability in the East threatened Rome's prosperity. In a series of so-called Macedonian Wars, fought between 214 and 148 BC, Rome became master of Greece.

When the Corinthian-led Achaean League revolted in 146 BC, Rome crushed the revolt and brought Greece under Roman rule. Though Athens, Sparta, and Delphi remained nominally independent as Roman allies, Corinth was utterly destroyed,[3] and the remainder of Greece was placed under the authority of the Roman governor of Macedon. Attalus III (c. 170–133 BC), the last king of Pergamum, willed his kingdom to Rome in 133 BC.

---

2 The popular story that the Romans sowed the soil with salt so that nothing could grow there in the future is only a modern myth. It was said that Scipio Africanus wept while the city burned and wondered if the same fate would one day befall Rome.
3 The Romans destroyed Corinth in 146 BC, the same year they destroyed Carthage.

It became the Roman province of Asia in 129 BC. Only Egypt and the Seleucid kingdom remained independent, albeit at the mercy of Rome.

Rome, the small city-state on the banks of the Tiber River in Italy, was now the master of a vast empire that dominated the Mediterranean world. The impact of such success brought a whole host of economic and social changes that fundamentally altered the character of Roman civilization and called into question the ability of republican institutions to govern such a vast empire.

Decline of the Republic

The growth of a vast overseas empire brought both prosperity and increasing stress on the old republican institutions. Three issues in particular became critical during the last century of the Roman Republic. The first problem was how a city-state could successfully govern such a vast empire. A city-state was geographically small with a small population and culturally homogeneous. Republican institutions that might work in a very small world were not suited to empires, especially lacking modern communication. A second issue was the question of how Rome could adjust to the economic and social changes caused by the influx of great wealth and the growth of a slave-based economy. Finally, Rome faced the problem of finding a focus of unity for the empire, as the empire grew and became increasingly more pluralistic and multicultural. Efforts to solve these issues eventually destroyed the Republic.

The growth of empire meant a steady stream of wealth and cheap labor in the form of slaves. Together, they transformed the social and economic life of the Republic. The senatorial class and the equestrians (*equites*) benefitted from the expansion. The equestrians were large landowners, bankers, merchants, and public contractors (e.g. tax farmers) who supplied the needs of the new empire. The lower classes, especially the small farmers, did not benefit. They suffered.

The appearance of large estates, or plantations called *latifundia*, and the passing of the small independent farmers was a particularly destructive trend. Wealthy landowners acquired public lands, which they turned into large plantations producing cash crops for a commercial market, for example cattle and sheep in southern Italy, or olives and wine in central Italy. These plantations were worked by large gangs of slaves, who were often sold as disposable slaves in the mines when they became old or feeble. It is estimated that approximately one-third of the population of Italy in the first century BC was slaves.

The small farmers could not compete with the large estates worked by slave labor. They were often forced, by circumstances, to sell out to the large landowners. They then drifted into Rome, where, together with returning veterans, they formed a troublesome and potentially powerful voting bloc. Two brothers, Tiberius and Gaius Gracchus, recognized this potential.

The Gracchi brothers were grandsons of Scipio Africanus, the hero of the Second Punic War. They were reformers in the tradition of the two Greeks, Solon and Cleisthenes. They believed it was necessary to restore the class of independent farmers in order to restore the old Roman virtues. Though of the nobility, they used the office of tribune to become champions of the lower classes.

Tiberius Gracchus (c. 163–133 BC) was elected tribune in 134 BC. His goal was to restore the class of small farmers through a program of land reform. He proposed that public lands acquired illegally by the large landowners should be returned to the state. The state would then give them out in small allotments to the poor. The program would be paid for out of the treasury of Pergamum, willed to Rome in 133 BC by Attalus III.

In pursuit of his goal, Tiberius violated custom by ignoring the Senate and attempting to implement his land reform program through the Plebeian Assembly. Also, his plan to use funds from the treasury of Pergamum violated the tradition of the Senate's control of foreign affairs. Tiberius committed a further offense by standing for reelection as tribune. Tribunes were elected for only one year. Such disregard for accepted traditions alienated the senatorial class. Resorting to violence rather than reason and compromise, a mob, urged on by members of the Senate. killed Tiberius and 300 of his supporters in the summer of 133 BC.

Tiberius' younger brother Gaius (153–121 BC) was elected tribune in 124 BC. He was a more astute politician than his brother. In addition to continuing the land reform policies of Tiberius, Gaius sought other means of helping the lower classes. He founded new colonies on public lands in Italy. Perhaps, most significant, was his plan to stabilize the price of grain in Rome, a matter of critical importance for the poor. The government began buying grain in bulk and then reselling it at fixed prices to the poor. Once begun, no Roman leader to the end of the Empire dared stop subsidizing the price of grain.

Gaius also tried to ally himself with the equestrian class of government bureaucrats and contractors. He initiated road-building projects and allowed equestrians to participate in the courts that tried officials for corruption. In effect, those who benefitted from corruption became their own judges. A law passed since his brother's death that allowed tribunes to be reelected enabled Gaius to be reelected tribune in 123 BC. Then his fortunes began to change.

Gaius Gracchus' downfall came when he proposed granting citizenship to all of Rome's Italian allies. That was a policy rejected by all of the classes of Roman citizens – senators, equestrians, and lower classes alike. His proposal to found a colony on the site of ancient Carthage was also unpopular. When he stood for reelection to a third term as tribune, he was rejected. Once again, the opposition resorted to violence. Urged on by a consul who offered to pay its weight in gold for Gaius' head, a mob murdered Gaius and 3000 of his followers in 121 BC.

With the passing of the Gracchi brothers, the Republic was plunged into a series of civil wars between popular generals that lasted until 27 BC. The first conflict was between Gaius Marius (157–86 BC), a general of equestrian rank who obtained fame in the Jugurthine War (111–105 BC) in North Africa, and Lucius Cornelius Sulla (138–78 BC) who gained fame in the Social War (91–88 BC) between Rome and its Italian allies. Sulla was a champion of the Senate. When the Senate refused to grant Roman citizenship to allied cities, Italy was plunged into an unnecessary civil war.

The conflict between Marius and Sulla broke out over who would command the Roman legions sent to the Middle East to put down a revolt led by Mithridates (134–63 BC), king of Pontus. Sulla, elected one of the consuls in 88 BC, was given command of the legions by the Senate. The Popular Assembly, ignoring the Senate's choice, elected Marius to command the legions against Mithridates. Sulla marched his legions into Rome, forcing Marius to seek refuge in North Africa. Sulla then left for the Middle East. Marius took advantage of Sulla's absence to capture Rome and put Sulla's supporters to the sword.

After suppressing Mithridates with a systematic brutality that would become his trademark, Sulla returned to Italy in 83 BC to renew the civil war with Marius' followers; Marius having died in 86 BC. A list of between 2000 and 9000 of Marius' followers was published. They could be freely killed and their property seized and distributed to Sulla's supporters. Sulla declared himself dictator for an indefinite term and began instituting reforms aimed at restoring the Senate to power, before retiring to private life on his country estate in Campania.

Perhaps the most fatal consequence of the struggle between Marius and Sulla was a fundamental change in the Roman army, introduced by Marius. Historically, the Roman legions were conscripted for short-term duty from among the property-owning citizens. Marius changed that practice when he began recruiting soldiers from among the property-less poor for long-term enlistments. Professional armies recruited by the generals replaced the citizen soldiers of the early Republic. This resulted in a basic shift in the loyalty of the legions from the Republic to the general who recruited them, and to whom they looked for their pay, a share in the booty from successful campaigns, and a grant of land to retire on when their enlistment was over. Such "professional" armies could be, and were, used by ambitious generals against the Republic.

The career of Julius Caesar (100–44 BC) is an apt example. Julius Caesar was an ambitious aristocrat who in 59 BC was able to form what is referred to as the First Triumvirate with two other equally ambitious and talented figures, Gnaeus Pompey (106–48 BC) and Marcus Licinius Crassus (112–53 BC).

Pompey was a very popular general. He had fought as an ally of Sulla against Marius, defeated Mithridates of Pontus, rid the Mediterranean Sea of pirates, suppressed the slave revolt led by Spartacus (111–71 BC), and was elected consul in 70 BC along with Crassus. Pompey was also married to Julius Caesar's daughter Julia.

Unlike Pompey and Caesar, Crassus lacked military talent, but made up for the deficiency by being rich. Indeed, he was called *Dives*, "the rich!" Following Caesar's election as consul in 59 BC, the three co-conspirators, although still rivals, joined together in an informal, illegal conspiracy to dominate the Roman Republic. Each member of the First Triumvirate sought to further his career. Crassus hoped to gain a reputation as a successful general by attacking the Kingdom of Parthia in the East. The disastrous campaign resulted in one of the most humiliating defeats for the Roman legions and the death of Crassus at the hands of the Parthians.

Pompey, being the senior partner in the Triumvirate, remained in Rome, while Julius Caesar became a proconsul over Gaul (modern France). In a series of brilliant military campaigns, Caesar conquered Gaul, twice invaded Britain, and crossed the Rhine River in an expedition against the Germans. Caesar kept his admiring public informed of his exploits in regular dispatches, written in the third person. Caesar's *Commentaries on the Gallic War* remain one of the classics of Latin literature.

Caesar's growing popularity led to a rupture in his relationship with Pompey, especially after the death of Julia, who worked hard at keeping the peace between the two rivals. In 52 BC, Pompey was elected sole consul and given dictatorial powers. When the Senate called upon Caesar to give up his military command, he sensed a conspiracy to bring about his downfall, and perhaps his death. In 49 BC, Caesar led his loyal legions against Rome. Pompey fled to Greece, where he was decisively defeated by Caesar at the battle of Pharsalus in 48 BC.

Pompey sought refuge in Egypt following his defeat, where he was murdered as he disembarked at Alexandria. Caesar spent the years between 48 and 45 BC subduing Pompey's supporters in North Africa, Spain, and the Middle East. While in Egypt, Caesar was entertained by Queen Cleopatra (c. 70–30 BC). Cleopatra gave birth to a son by Julius Caesar in 47 BC. She named him Caesarion, "little Caesar" (47–30 BC).

When Caesar returned to Rome, his enemies vanquished, he quickly gathered together in his hands all of the power of the principle offices of the Republic. Apparently, Caesar recognized that the republican government was unsuited for governing so vast an empire and felt that only a dictatorship could restore peace and stability, and provide efficient government. He used his powers to institute far-reaching reforms, including codification of the laws, colonies, and land reform for the poor, an end to tax farming, a new calendar, and a reorganization of local government in Italy.

Not everyone was pleased with Caesar's reforms. A conspiracy formed within the Senate among those who feared Caesar might reestablish a monarchy. On the Ides of March (March 15) 44 BC the conspirators led by Gaius Cassius Longinus (c. 85–42 BC) and Marcus Junius Brutus (85–42 BC) assassinated Caesar in the Senate chambers.

If the conspirators felt that by murdering Julius Caesar, they could save the Republic, they were mistaken. A Second Triumvirate soon took form, as two of Caesar's lieutenants, Mark Antony (Marcus Antonius, c. 82–30 BC) and Marcus Aemilius Lepidus (c. 89/88–13/12 BC) joined forces with Julius Caesar's nephew and heir, Octavian (Gaius Julius Octavianus, 63 BC–AD 14). The Senatorial armies, led by Brutus and Cassius, were defeated at Philippi in Greece in 42 BC by Mark Antony and Octavian. Brutus and Cassius chose suicide, rather than being taken captive. Lepidus was forced to retire to North Africa in 36 BC. Mark Antony and Octavian divided the empire between them, with Mark Antony taking the peaceful and more prosperous East, and Octavian taking the West along with Rome, itself.

Once in the East, Mark Antony fell fully under the spell of Queen Cleopatra of Egypt, with whom he took up residence in Alexandria. In 37 BC, Mark Antony divorced his pregnant wife, Olivia, Octavian's sister, and married Cleopatra. Mark Antony's lifestyle took on the appearance of an oriental potentate. In a grand ceremony staged in 34 BC, Mark Antony proclaimed Caesarion to be Julius Caesar's rightful heir. He also gave Roman provinces in the East to Cleopatra and her three sons.

Octavian was quick to publicize Mark Antony's outrageous act and portray him and Cleopatra as a threat to Rome. The Senate outlawed Mark Antony and declared war on Cleopatra in 31 BC. The decisive battle of Actium took place the next year off the coast of Greece. Cleopatra and Mark Antony fled back to Egypt. Mark Antony committed suicide, followed by Cleopatra, when she discovered that Octavian would not become her next conquest.

Pax Romana

When Octavian returned to Rome following the defeat of Antony and Cleopatra, he was the undisputed master of the Roman Republic. In the years that followed, he proved himself to be a gifted politician and one of history's truly great rulers. Presenting himself as savior of the Republic and the one who restored peace, he completed the transformation of the Republic begun by Julius Caesar. Realizing that he had to avoid alienating the Senate and thereby avoid suffering the same fate as Julius Caesar, Octavian created an imperial system of government and civil service that concentrated power in the emperor's hands, while giving the illusion of republican rule for those who chose to believe it so. For example, Octavian allowed the Senate to govern the provinces that were at peace, while reserving to the emperor all of the frontier provinces where the legions were stationed under command of the emperor. Ultimately, Octavian's power rested on his command of the army, as did that of all subsequent emperors.

Octavian ruled constitutionally by monopolizing the key offices of the Republic. While this practice maintained the fiction of a Republic, it created a fatal problem that was never successfully resolved, the question of succession. How does the transition from one emperor to the next take place peacefully? This problem was solved only once, during the period of the so-called "Five Good Emperors," between AD 96 and 180.

The form of imperial government established by Octavian is referred to as the *Principate*, taken from the title he preferred, *Princeps*, or "First Citizen." Octavian was granted a variety of titles, among them Imperator Caesar Augustus, or simply Augustus (the Revered), conferred on him by the Senate in 27 BC, and by which he is known after that date. As the emperor Augustus, he promoted the restoration of the old Roman virtues, became a great patron of the arts, and tried to stabilize the borders of the Empire.

Augustus' reign inaugurated a period in history known as the *Pax Romana*, or Roman Peace, roughly a 200-year period from the beginning of Augustus' reign to the end of the reign of Marcus Aurelius (121–180), the last of the Five Good Emperors in 180. It was a period of peace and prosperity unparalleled in history until perhaps the so-called *Pax Britania* during the nineteenth century. Under the *Pax Romana*, the Roman Empire became a unified community of over 70 million people, stretching from Britain and Spain to Mesopotamia and the Arabian Desert, and from the Rhine and Danube Rivers to the Sahara Desert. It was an urban, cultured world held together by paved roads and an efficient administration, and defended by the best army known to history at that time.

The first four successors of Augustus were related to him or his third wife Livia. The first was his stepson, Tiberius (42 BC–AD 37). He was, on the whole, a good administrator, at least during the early years of his reign. During the last 10 years of his reign, he lived on the island of Capri, where he became increasingly more paranoid. Many suffered torture and death as a result. Nevertheless, he left behind an empire that was strong, well administered, and with a full treasury.

Tiberius chose as his successor, his grandnephew, Caligula (12–41). Caligula reigned for only four years. Though he launched a number of building programs, including a lighthouse at Boulogne and a new amphitheater in Pompeii, he showed signs of insanity. He delighted in inflicting cruelty, and demonstrated his contempt for the Senate by reportedly awarding his horse, Incitatus, a consulship. He was assassinated in January 41, by the Pretorian Guard, an elite military unit charged with protection of the emperor and his family.

The Pretorian Guard declared Caligula's uncle, Claudius (10 BC–AD 54), emperor. Claudius was the first emperor appointed by the Pretorian Guard, a precedent that augured badly for the future. His reign proved to be a good one. Claudius was well educated and wrote extensively, especially histories. Unfortunately, none of his writings survive.

He undertook a number of public works programs and gave generous support to public games, especially gladiatorial contests, and even staged naval battles. He added new provinces to the empire, including Britannia, with its capital at Camulodunum (modern Colchester in Essex). Claudius died from poisoned mushrooms fed to him by his third wife, Agrippina, in a successful plot to make her son, Nero, emperor.

Nero (37–68) was only 16 when he became emperor. The charge that he fiddled while a portion of Rome burned in 64 is not true. In fact, Nero did much at his expense to relieve the suffering caused by the fire. It is possible that the rumor has its origin in the fact that Nero prided himself on being a great actor and musician, and insisted on performing publicly. The Roman citizens were more offended by his pretensions to talent in the creative arts than by his debauched lifestyle, his brutal persecution of Christians in Rome following the fire, or his execution of those he felt offended or threatened by, including his mother. Nero ended his own life in June 68. His last words: "What an artist dies in me!"

Nero's death was followed by civil war, as the generals battled one another for the throne. Four emperors reigned in one year. Two were executed. One committed suicide. The last of the four, Vespasian (9–79) emerged the victor in the civil war. He was declared emperor by the Senate in December 69.

Vespasian founded the Flavian dynasty that included him and his two sons. Titus (39–81) was the first. He is best remembered for his capture and destruction of Jerusalem in 70, including the Second Temple. Domitian (51–96), the younger son, ruled for 14 years.

Figure 3.2 The Pantheon in Rome was completed c. 125 during the reign of Hadrian and served as temple. *Source:* Photo courtesy of Bruce Erik Bezaire, private collection.

Though he did much to restore stability, his authoritarian rule led to his assassination in September 96. He was the last of the three Flavian emperors.

Domitian was followed by the period of "The Five Good Emperors" – Nerva (30–98), Trajan (53–117), Hadrian (76–138), Antoninus Pius (86–161), and Marcus Aurelius (121–180). It was a period of relative prosperity and peace, at least until the later years of Marcus Aurelius' reign. The Roman Empire reached its greatest extent geographically during Trajan's reign between 98 and 117. From the reign of his successor, Hadrian, the question was how to hold onto what was already a part of the Empire in the face of increasing pressures from without and growing signs of decline within.

Roman Cultural Life

While considering the period of the *Pax Romana*, it is fitting to pause and look briefly at the cultural achievements of the Romans. Their achievements in Latin literature may be divided chronologically into three periods, the Age of Cicero, the Augustan Age, and the Silver Age. The first was during the Republic and was dominated by Marcus Tullius Cicero (106–43 BC). Cicero was not only the greatest orator of his day, but also a poet, author, and philosopher. He left behind many speeches, political treatises, letters, and books, including his unfinished *Republic*, considered one of the earliest treatises on the concept of natural law.

Cicero's Latin prose is regarded as the finest ever written. It remained the standard for Latin through the Renaissance (mid-fourteenth century to early seventeenth century), and some would say even to our own day. Second to Cicero was Julius Caesar. Though his speeches are lost, his *Commentaries on the Gallic War* is still read and studied by students of the classics. Two other names from the Age of Cicero worthy of note in this brief summary are Titus Lucretius Carsus (c. 99–c. 55 BC) and Gaius Valerius Catullus (84–54 BC).

Lucretius was an Epicurean philosopher and poet best remembered for his long didactic poem, *On the Nature of the Universe*. Its significance lies in the fact that it presents the atomic theory, along with the essence of Epicurean philosophy. Catullus, on the other hand, is remembered for his love poems about one Lesbia. In real life, Lesbia was a notorious woman named Clodia, with whom Catullus had an affair until she abandoned him for a friend of Cicero.

The period in Roman cultural life that parallels the reign of Augustus is referred to as the Augustan Age. Latin scholars are prone to call it the Golden Age. Augustus monopolized the patronage of all of the artists of the period with two goals in mind. He wanted to glorify his own reign, and he wanted to promote his campaign of restoring the virtues and morality of the old Roman Republic. Among the "greats" whom Augustus patronized, four names stand out as particularly noteworthy, Virgil (70–19 BC), Horace (65–8 BC), Livy (59 BC–AD 17), and Ovid (43 BC–AD 17).

Virgil's *Aeneid* is considered the greatest piece of Roman poetry by Rome's greatest poet. It relates the exploits of Aeneas, son of Anchises and hero of the Trojan War after the fall of Troy. In so doing, it tells the story of the founding of Rome. The *Aeneid* became a national epic, and, like Homer's *Iliad* and *Odyssey*, served as an inspiration and model for many subsequent epics in Western literature, including those of Dante and John Milton.

Horace was Virgil's successor. His *Odes* is a collection of lyric poems on love, pleasure, the brevity of life, and nature. Some of the poems eulogize Augustus, while others exalt the Greek philosophical notion of the "golden mean," finding tranquility in life by avoiding extremes. He influenced later writers, among them William Wordsworth, Ben Jonson, W.H. Auden, Robert Frost, and many more.

Livy was a historian whose *History* recorded the history of Rome from its foundation to Livy's own day. Only 35 of its 142 books have survived. The main theme in Livy's portrayal of Rome's history is the moral decline and corruption of the Roman citizens following the end of the Punic Wars. The pursuit of personal peace and luxury replaced the old virtues of civic duty.

Ovid was a prolific poet and one of the leading figures in Roman society until his *Art of Love*, a sort of poetic handbook on how to seduce a lover, earned him the wrath of Augustus. His works were banished, and he was exiled to a remote corner of the Empire on the Black Sea.

The Augustan Age was followed by the Silver Age, referring to a group of writers who wrote during the period between the death of Augustus and c. 130. Their works are considered "great," but not of the caliber of the Augustan Age. Noteworthy in this group are the stoic philosopher, Senecca (4 BC–AD 65); Petronius (27–66), author of *Satykricon*; the historian Tacitus (56–117), who recorded the period 14–96, and tells us much of what we know about the Germanic tribes in his *Histories*, *Annals*, and *Germania*; Juvenal (c. 55–127 AD) who satirized the immoral lifestyle of the Roman aristocracy in *Satires*; Suetonius (70–130), whose sensational *Lives of the Caesars* portrays in tabloid fashion, the decadent lives of the Caesars from Julius to Domitian; and finally Plutarch (45–120), who provides parallel biographical sketches of famous Greeks and Romans in *Parallel Lives*.

In other areas of cultural expression, the Romans tended to copy the Greeks. Roman sculptures are mostly copies of Greek originals. Portrait sculpture was one area in which the Romans broke with the past. They turned away from the idealized portraiture of the Greeks and portrayed the subject as he or she really was, with all the warts, scars, wrinkles, and other defects faithfully presented. Mosaics found wherever Romans settled was another area in which the Romans excelled. Few examples of Roman painting have survived, mostly in the ruins of Pompeii and Herculaneum, buried in 79 by the eruption of Mt. Vesuvius. Of Roman music, nothing remains. Those who have studied the references to it in Roman literature have concluded that we are not poorer for its loss.

The Rise of Christianity

The nearly two centuries of world peace known as the Pax Romana, or Peace of Rome, was one of Rome's greatest achievements. Though it was a period of unparalleled peace and prosperity, looking back from the present, we can see there were signs of trouble ahead. One that played an increasingly important role in Rome's long decline was what was happening to the "soul" of the Roman Empire.

The Roman Empire was a multicultural, pluralistic, inclusive society. The benefits of Roman civilization – a unified world empire, paved roads that connected prosperous urban centers, a military force that assured peaceful movement of people and goods throughout the empire, a system of law and jurisprudence that was not limited by cultural prejudices, a common language through the adoption of *Koiné* Greek, and much more – eventually caused doubt about what it meant to be "Roman." Strange and exotic foods and other products were not all that became common place in Rome, however.

The Mediterranean world was experiencing a spiritual crisis during the *Pax Romana*. The official state cults rooted in Greek mythology no longer provided answers to the perennial questions of meaning and purpose. Neither did Greek philosophy with its emphasis on reason. Stoicism, the most popular pseudo-religion of the sophisticated classes, was fatalistic. Like the state cults, it did not provide any emotional satisfaction or hope for the individual. There was a widespread, unsatisfied spiritual longing among the masses who felt that their age was increasingly bankrupt, both morally and spiritually.

Many people turned to the mystery religions that provided mysticism, emotional experience, and contact with the divine. The mystery religions originated in the East. Included among them were the cults of Cybele (Asia Minor), Isis (Egypt), Mithras (Persia), and the Unconquered Sun (Syria). The mystery religions were secret societies with elaborate initiatory rites. Most featured a god who had died and was resurrected. Initiates into the cult of Cybele, for example, were baptized in a shower of blood as a bull was slaughtered above them. The mystery religions had certain things in common with Christianity, but there were profound differences.

A major difference between the mystery religions and Christianity was that Jesus of Nazareth (c. 4 BC–c. AD 30/33), the founder of Christianity, was an actual, historic figure, not a myth. Jesus was born in Bethlehem, an obscure corner of the empire, during the reign of Augustus and died during the reign of Tiberius. Virtually nothing is known of his youth, and what is known of his adult life and teaching is found in the Bible's New Testament.

When Jesus was about 30 years old, he began to proclaim the coming of the Kingdom of God, a messianic message derived from the Jewish scriptures, the Old Testament of the Christian Bible. He taught a revolutionary interpretation of the Mosaic Law that emphasized ethics rather than a slavish legalism. Justice and mercy were more important than fulfilling the letter of the Law. Asked what the greatest commandment was in the Law, he answered: "You shall love the Lord your God with all your heart and with all your soul and with all your mind. This is the great and first commandment. And a second is like it: You shall love your neighbor as yourself. On these two commandments depend all the Law and the Prophets."[4]

Jesus gathered a following over a period of three years during which he traveled throughout Judea, Samaria, and Galilee, accompanied by 12 followers whom he chose to be his disciples. His teachings were a clear threat to the Jewish establishment, whose teaching was based on a strict adherence to tradition. On the eve of the Jewish Passover, probably in the year 33 or 34, Jesus was executed by order of Pontius Pilate, Roman procurator (actually prefect, or governor) of Judea.

The death of Jesus did not halt the spread of his teaching. Within days, rumors spread that Jesus had risen from the dead and was seen by his followers. The belief that Jesus was in fact the savior-God who became human, lived, suffered, died, and rose from the dead on the third day after his death by crucifixion became the central doctrine of the new religion.

---

4 Matthew 22:37-40. ESV

The belief that the risen Jesus appeared before his followers and commanded them to take the news of what they saw and heard while he was with them to people everywhere became the central motivation for the spread of Christianity.

Christianity had an appeal like no other religion, cult, or philosophy of the time. It offered meaning and hope to all, of whatever class, ethnic identity, or level of education, through a personal relationship with God, and membership in a family in which all were equal and bound together by love for one another. "By this all people will know that you are my disciples," Jesus told his followers, "if you have love for one another."[5] God was no respecter of persons. Rich and poor, free and slave, male and female, all were equal in his sight. It was a message of compassion for those who suffered. It bestowed a sense of dignity on the common person who was considered of little or no value in the ancient world.

Christianity may well have remained a minor sect within Judaism except for the conversion of Saul (c. 5–c. 67), a highly educated and devout Jew. Saul was a Roman citizen by virtue of being born a citizen of the city of Tarsus on the south-central coast of Asia Minor (modern Turkey). Initially a persecutor of the followers of Jesus, he was himself converted and spent the rest of his life teaching that Jesus was the promised Messiah of the Jewish Scriptures.

Saul of Tarsus became Paul the Apostle. His knowledge of the Jewish Scriptures and his extensive education enabled him to transform a sect within Judaism, a national religion, into a religion for all humanity. Paul's significance in the history of Christianity is evident in the fact that 14 of the 27 books of the New Testament are attributed to him.

Decline of the Empire

Dio Cassius (155–235), a Roman historian of the second to third centuries, said that after Marcus Aurelius, the last of the Five Good Emperors, the Roman Empire declined from "a kingdom of gold to one of iron and rust." The stresses that contributed to the decline and eventual fall of the Roman Empire in the West were already evident before the death of Marcus Aurelius and the reign of his insane son, Commodus (161–192).

The wealth and prosperity of the *Pax Romana* began to decline during the first half of the second century after the Empire ceased to expand. Though the wealth and prosperity of the Empire declined, the cost of government escalated. The imperial budget increased by at least 25% during the third century. Rising costs for the army, bread, and circus for the masses in Rome, a growing government bureaucracy, and expensive wars all contributed to the rising costs. Commodus increased the soldiers' pay, which was then doubled by Septimius Severus (142–211). During Marcus Aurelius' reign a daily distribution of pork, oil, and bread was given to the urban poor. As apathy became more and more prevalent, government expenditures on public spectacles such as gladiatorial contests became a significant part of the imperial budget.

There was a decline in the population beginning in the second century. Though its exact cause is uncertain, no doubt the devastating impact of the plague which ravaged the Empire during the latter part of the second century, and again in the middle of the third century,

---

5 John 13:35. ESV

contributed to it. The first outbreak may have killed a quarter of the population by 180. During the second outbreak, between 252 and 267, about two-thirds of the population of Alexandria perished. Alexandria was the economic heart of the Empire. Such a blow to the city had a negative impact throughout the Empire. At its height, 5000 people a day are believed to have died in Rome. The Empire never fully recovered from the economic and psychological effects of the plague.

Inflation and depreciation of the currency both contributed to, and were in turn caused by, the economic decline. A *denarius*, the equivalent of a day's wages, lost 80% of its value by the reign of Augustus, and 98% by the reign of Diocletian (244–311). The economic woes were made all the more significant by the growing pressures along the frontiers from the Germans in the north and the Persians in the east.

Marcus Aurelius was forced to spend much of his reign along the Danube River frontier holding back the Germans. Defending the frontiers became a major preoccupation of his successors, many of whom were generals who "militarized" the administration of the Empire. After the murder of Commodus in 192, chaos reigned in Rome until Septimius Severus restored order in 196.

Severus was basically a military man. He was born in North Africa and had little regard for Rome or its residents. He introduced reforms that had the effect of transforming the Principate into a thinly veiled military dictatorship. Much of the work of governing the Empire at all levels was taken over by the army. But as more and more soldiers were used for non-military functions, fewer were available to defend the frontiers.

Severus' eldest son and successor, Caracalla (188–217), resorted to buying off the barbarians for peace, while granting a 50% increase in wages to the Roman soldiers. He unsuccessfully tried to solve the financial crisis by reforming the currency. He granted citizenship to all free men in the Empire in 212 in an attempt to shore up popular support for the Empire and increase tax revenue.

Another practice with fateful consequences for the future of the Empire, was that of inviting German tribes along the frontiers to settle just inside the borders, become "Roman," and join in the defense of the Empire. With time, this practice led to a "barbarization" of the army. During the fifth century, when the Germans came pouring into the Empire, they were no longer met by the traditional disciplined Roman legions of the late Republic and early Empire, but by Roman legions made up of Germans who fought like Germans. The military advantage was lost, and with it, the Empire in the West.

Caracalla's immediate successors, Elagabalus (203–222) and Severus Alexander (208–235) were mere teenagers when they donned the imperial purple. Both were murdered. Maximinus (173–238) was the first Roman Emperor not born a Roman citizen. He could barely speak Latin and was the first of 26 emperors known as the "Barracks Emperors" who reigned between 235 and 285. All were soldiers. Only one died a natural death.

No one thing can be pointed to as "the cause" of the fall of the Roman Empire in the West. But the inability of the central government to provide peace and law and order at the local level was certainly one of the most important causes of the decline. During the era of the Barracks Emperors, several provinces tried to separate from the Empire and govern themselves. Trade was hampered. The Empire was an urban empire, a collection of cities tied together by trade. When the trade was interrupted, the cities began to die, and with them the Empire.

A major overhaul of the imperial government was undertaken at the end of the third century by Diocletian (244–311) in a bold attempt to halt the downward spiral. He sought to solve the problem of succession by setting up a new form of administration known as the Tetrarchy. The administration of the Empire was divided between four men with power divided on a territorial basis. The Empire was divided in half with Italy in the West. Each half was divided into two administrative districts. There were two co-emperors, one in the West and one in the East, with the title "Augustus." Each Augustus had a junior emperor with the title "Caesar." None of the four chose Rome as his capital. The plan was for each Caesar to move up and become the Augustus upon the death of his senior partner. Thus, was a smooth succession to replace the civil wars that followed the death of an emperor. It did not work.

Diocletian and his co-emperor, Maximilian (c. 250–310), retired in 305. Instead of a smooth succession, civil war broke out once again. By 310, there were five rival Augusti. The victor in 324 was Constantine (272–337) son of Constantius (250–306), who served as Caesar in the West between 293 and 305 and as Augustus, 305–306. Constantine ruled alone from 324 until his death in 337. In 330, he moved the capital to "New Rome," later renamed Constantinople (today's Istanbul) in his honor, located on the site of the ancient Greek city of Byzantium on the Bosporus Strait.

Figure 3.3   The Arch of Constantine in Rome commemorates Constantine's victory Battle of Milvian Bridge in 312. *Source:* Photo courtesy of Bruce Erik Bezaire, private collection.

In addition to the Tetrarchy, Diocletian instituted other reforms. He attempted to establish a uniform and stable currency. He issued the Edict of Maximum Prices in 301 in an attempt to deal with inflation. A maximum price was set for each kind of labor and article. Also, individuals were frozen in their occupations and place of residence. None of these reforms really worked, despite the threat of death for violating them.

Constantine's reign resulted in the most fundamental and lasting change in the Roman Empire since its founding by Augustus. Whereas Diocletian and his predecessors saw Christianity as a threat to the Empire, Constantine saw it as the potential cement that could hold the Empire together and even strengthen it. Constantine issued the Edict of Milan in 311, named after the city from which he was governing at the time. It read in part, "Our purpose is to grant both to the Christians and to all others full authority to follow whatever worship each person has desired, whereby whatsoever Divinity dwells in heaven may be benevolent and propitious to us, and to all who are placed under our authority." Theodosius I (347–395) made Christianity the state religion in 381. The Roman Empire became a "Christian" empire with far-reaching consequences for both church and state.

Despite the decline of central government in the West, the Roman armies, barbarized though they were, were able to defend the frontiers until the last quarter of the fourth century. During the 370s, the German tribes came under pressure from a nomadic Mongolian people known as the Huns. In 376, the eastern emperor Valens (328–378) permitted the Visigoths (West Goths) to peacefully cross the Danube River and seek refuge inside the Empire. When imperial bureaucrats abused the Goths, they rose in revolt. At the battle of Adrianople in 378, one of history's decisive battles, the Romans were defeated and Valens taken captive. Unable to lay siege to Constantinople, the Goths went on the rampage.

The Goths laid siege to the city of Rome in 409. Twice, the citizens paid a ransom, but twice the Goths returned. Many barbarian slaves escaped from Rome and joined the Goths. Then, in August of 410, the gates of Rome were opened by a slave, and the Goths poured into the city. Only the churches of St. Peter and St. Paul were spared, for the Visigoths were Arian Christians. All else was subjected to the wrath of the barbarians. Rome, the eternal city, capital of the greatest empire in history, was captured for the first time since 390 BC.

The winter of 406-407 was unusually cold in Europe. The Rhine River froze over. Many of the Roman soldiers along the Rhine had been recalled to defend Rome threatened by the Gothic king Alaric (c. 370–410). A mixed group of Germans including Vandals, Suevi, and Alans crossed the Rhine near Mainz. A flood of Germans, followed by the Huns in the middle of the fifth century, began plundering and carving out petty kingdoms in the western half of the Empire. Rome was sacked again in 455 by the Vandals. Roman emperors remained on the throne in the West at the pleasure of German warrior-kings until 476.

Julius Nepos (430–480) was appointed emperor in the West in 474 by Leo I (401–474), emperor in the East. Nepos was deposed by the commander of his army, Orestes (d. 476), who named his teenage son Romulus-Augustulus (b. 460) emperor.[6] His reign was brief, only 10 months. He was deposed on September 4, 476, by Odoacer (433–493), an army commander who led a revolt against Orestes. Odoacer was proclaimed king by his army. The young Romulus-Augustulus was granted an annual pension and retired under a kind of house arrest in Campania. The Roman Senate, still in existence, accepted Odoacer as king.

---

6 Since Julius Nepos was appointed by Leo I, Nepos was the *de jure* emperor in the West.

The Senate sent a delegation to Constantinople to inform Emperor Zeno (c. 425–491) that an emperor was no longer necessary in the West. Thus, the year 476 is regarded as the "official" end of the Roman Empire, at least in the West.

By the end of the fifth century, the Roman Empire in the West existed as a patchwork of Germanic kingdoms – The Vandals in North Africa, the Visigoths in Spain, the Ostrogoths (East Goths) in Italy, the Franks in Gaul and the Rhineland, and the Angles and Saxons in Britain. In each case, the Germanic kings pretended to govern under the authority of the emperor in Constantinople, but in practice ruled alone. The Roman Empire in the East lived on as the Eastern Roman, or Byzantine, Empire until 1453. In the West, the memory of a universal state survived in the Christian Church, the medieval concept of Christendom, and after 961, in the Holy Roman Empire.

References

Nicgorski, W. (2017). Cicero and the Natural Law. Natural Law, Natural Rights, and American Constitutionalism. http://www.nlnrac.org/classical/cicero (accessed 18 October 2019).
Wright, D.F. (2015). 313 The Edict of Milan. Christianity Today. http://www.christianitytoday.com/ch/1990/issue28/2809.html (accessed 18 October 2019).

Part II

Europe in the Middle Ages: An Overview

When the last Roman Emperor in the West was deposed in 476, any semblance of central government vanished with him. A plurality of Germanic kingdoms replaced what was the Roman Empire in the West. By the beginning of the ninth century, a strong Frankish kingdom appeared to be assuming the role of the former Roman imperial authority. Charlemagne was crowned Emperor of the Romans by Pope Leo III on Christmas Day, 800. Charlemagne unified much of what today comprises France, the Low Countries, Germany, and Italy down to Rome.

Charlemagne established a palace school at his court in Aachen (Aix la Chapelle) that is credited with stimulating a revival of learning known as the Carolingian Renaissance. The Frankish Kingdom fragmented following Charlemagne's death in 814. The successor kingdoms were unable to provide protection from the Viking raids during the ninth century. The need to provide for law and order and livelihood at the local level in the absence of any central government gave rise to feudalism. A feudal pyramid with the king at its peak and levels of warrior nobility owing personal loyalty to one another in exchange for land emerged throughout Europe.

The legacy, or myth, of a universal Christian empire was kept alive by the emergence of a Western Christian faith unified theologically and with a governmental administration centered in Rome. Where there was once an emperor, there was now a pope, and where there was once a Roman civil administration, there were archbishops, bishops, priests, and monastic abbots, all answerable to the bishop of Rome, the successor of St. Peter and vicar of Christ on earth. The people looked to the church for guidance more than to any secular feudal lord.

During the High Middle Ages, the eleventh through thirteenth centuries, central political authority began to reappear in the form of feudal monarchies in England, France, and the Holy Roman Empire, where the imperial title was revived after 961. A thirteenth-century Renaissance created a synthesis of the Judeo-Christian religious tradition with Classical Humanism and the Germanic traditions resulting in what became known as Western Civilization.

Western Civilization: A Brief History, First Edition. Paul R. Waibel.
© 2020 John Wiley & Sons, Inc. Published 2020 by John Wiley & Sons, Inc.

4

The Birth of Europe

Chronology

c. 500	Ambrosius Aurelianus Wins Battle of Mons Badonicus in Britain
506	Clovis I Converted to Christianity
527–565	Byzantine Emperor Justinian Codifies Roman Law
532–537	Church of Holy Wisdom (Hagia Sophia) constructed in Constantinople
c. 610	Muhammad Begins Preaching New Muslim Religion
732	Charles Martel Defeats Arab-Muslim Army in Battle of Tours
714–768	Pepin III, First Carolingian King of Franks
753	Pope Stephen II Grants Pepin III Title, Patrician of the Romans
781	Alcuin of York Becomes Head of Court School in Aachen
793	Monastery of Lindisfarne Destroyed by Vikings
800	Charlemagne Crowned Emperor of the Romans by Pope Leo III
843	Treaty of Verdun Divides Charlemagne's empire
865	Twelve-year Viking Invasion of Britain Begins
878	Treaty of Wedmore between Alfred the Great and Danes
1016–1028	Cnut the Great Unites England, Denmark, and Norway
1042	Edward the Confessor Becomes King of England
1066	Battle of Hastings
1066	Duke William of Normandy Crowned King of England

The collapse of the Roman Empire in the West marked the end of the classical, or Greco-Roman, period of history. The last emperor in the West, Roumulus-Augustulus, was deposed in 476, but the myth lingered on. A patchwork of Germanic kingdoms emerged, ruled by tribal chiefs, or kings, who pretended to rule in the name of the successors of the Caesars now resident in Constantinople. The Italian peninsula was ruled by Ostrogoths (East Goths). The Visigoths (West Goths) established a kingdom in Spain, having driven the Vandals into North Africa. The Angels and Saxons crossed from northern Germany to Britain, where they established several small kingdoms. The Celts were pushed west into Wales, Cornwall, and Cumberland. The Franks settled in what is today the Low Countries, northeastern France, and western Germany. Other Germanic tribes – Sueves, Jutes, Burgundians, Danes – occupied their own little pieces of the former Roman Empire.

Western Civilization: A Brief History, First Edition. Paul R. Waibel.
© 2020 John Wiley & Sons, Inc. Published 2020 by John Wiley & Sons, Inc.

When centralized government vanished, when goods could no longer move across Europe safely on the roads built by the Romans, when commerce and coinage vanished, and the cities died, a new way of life, feudalism, evolved to provide for law and order and livelihood at the grassroots level. The Early Middle Ages was in many ways a "Dark Age," a period of uncertainty and fear of both the present and the future. But, as the twelfth century approached, and the new invasions of the Vikings, Magyars, and Muslims came to an end, a new civilization began to appear, a synthesis of Classical Civilization, Judeo-Christianity, and Germanic traditions. Western, or European, Civilization was born.

Early Germanic Kingdoms

Goths

After he deposed the last Roman emperor in the West, Romulus-Augustulus, in 476, Odoacer ruled as King of Italy over a kingdom that included the Italian peninsula, Sicily (477), and the eastern coast of the Adriatic Sea (480). Odoacer tried to preserve what was left of Roman civilization in his kingdom. He enjoyed the support of the Roman Senate, which continued in existence until c. 580. The fact that he remained at peace with the Roman Catholic Church, even though he was himself an Arian, testifies to his wisdom as a ruler. The Eastern Roman emperor, Zeno (425–491), granted Odoacer the title, "patrician." The title was honorary. It was a means by which both the barbarian rulers and the Eastern Roman emperors could keep alive the myth of a united Roman Empire.

Encouraged by Zeno, Theodoric (454–526), King of the Ostrogoths, invaded Italy in 488. Odoacer's army was repeatedly defeated. When he took refuge in Ravenna in 489, Theodoric besieged the city. In February, 493, the bishop of Ravenna negotiated an agreement whereby Odoacer and Theodoric would rule jointly. Theodoric murdered Odoacer at a banquet to celebrate the agreement, and then proceeded to purge all of Odoacer's family and supporters.

Like Odoacer, Theodoric tried to preserve Roman civilization. Part of his plan was to establish justice for all of his subjects, which meant maintaining peace between the Roman population and the Goths (both Ostrogoths and Visigoths), and between the Trinitarian Christians (Roman Catholic) and the followers (mostly Goths) of the Arian heresy, while at the same time protecting his Jewish subjects. He reformed the laws so as to make them more equitable and repaired the old Roman aqueducts and buildings. Though he could neither read nor write, he encouraged learning.

It appears that Theodoric's aim was to civilize his own people within a Roman environment while maintaining peace among Italy's diverse population. In the end, he failed. The Italians (the native Roman population) were never reconciled to rule by the Ostrogoths, whom they saw as foreigners and worse, heretics. Between 535 and 554, the Byzantine emperor Justinian I (482–565) reconquered Italy in a vain attempt to reconstitute the Roman Empire in the West. The Goths were driven out across the Alps, while what was left of Roman civilization in Italy was destroyed. All Odoacer's and Theodoric's efforts to save Roman civilization in Italy came to naught in the end.

Franks

It was the Kingdom of the Franks that proved to be the most important for the future emergence of a new European civilization. Unlike the other major Germanic kingdoms, only the Franks retained contact with their homeland along the eastern bank of the Rhine River. Thus, the Franks were able to receive continued growth from further Frankish immigrants. The other Germanic kingdoms were cut off from their places of origin. More important, most of the Germanic tribes that were converted to Christianity were converted to Arian Christianity. Only the Franks were orthodox Christians.

The Franks were united by Clovis I (c. 466–511) after his succession to the throne in 481. In 493, he married a Burgundian princess who was an orthodox Christian. Clovis converted to orthodox Christianity in 506. Their king's conversion meant the conversion of the Franks, also. By becoming Roman Catholic Christians, the Franks gained the support of the native population and the Roman Catholic Church with its organized bureaucracy throughout Western Europe. Clovis could, and did, lead his Frankish armies into battle against the other German tribes as the defender of the true Christian faith.

Gregory of Tours (c. 538–594), bishop and author of *History of the Franks*, recorded how Clovis' wars with the Arian Germans were seen as crusades to liberate Christians suffering under the rule of Arian heretics. Not only did the Christian population view Clovis as God's warrior, so too did the Byzantine emperor Anastasius I (c. 431–518). Anastasius granted Clovis the title Counsel following Clovis' defeat of the Arian Visigoths in 501. The relationship between the Franks and the Roman Catholic Church was mutually advantageous. The Franks gained the support of the Christian population, while the Roman Catholic Church gained a military defender.

The Merovingian dynasty continued to rule the Kingdom of the Franks until 751, when Clovis' kingdom was divided into three parts: Neustria, Gaul, and Austrasia. During the sixth and seventh centuries the Merovingian kings grew weak. Real power passed into the hands of those who held the office of Mayor of the Palace, manager of the king's household.

Pepin of Herstal (635–714) became Mayor of the Palace in Austrasia in 680. He united all of the Franks through a military victory in 687. Pepin did not become king. He remained Mayor of the Palace in all three of the Frankish kingdoms, plus Burgundy. He was succeeded as Mayor of the Palace by his illegitimate son, Charles Martel (c. 688–741).

In early October 732, Charles Martel stopped an invasion of Western Europe by an Arab-Muslim army that crossed the Pyrenees Mountains from Spain into France. Today, historians dispute the military significance of the Battle of Tours, but what is certain is that throughout the Middle Ages and beyond, Charles Martel and the Franks were credited with saving Christendom from conquest by Islam. The perception that the Franks had saved Christianity further cemented the alliance between the Franks and the Catholic Church.

Charles Martel was succeeded by his son, Pepin III (714–768), also known as Pepin the Short, who deposed the last Merovingian king and became the first Carolingian king of the Franks. Pope Zachary (r. 741–752), who was dependent upon the Franks to protect the Church from the Arian Lombards who were threatening Rome, gave his blessing to the transition of power.

Pope Zachary's successor, Stephen II (r. 752–757) crossed the Alps in 753 to seek Pepin's aid. He anointed and crowned Pepin King of the Franks and conferred upon him and his sons the title "Patrician of the Romans." Pepin invaded Italy in 756, defeated the Lombards, and gave Stephen the territories in central Italy formerly belonging to the Byzantine Empire.

The grant of territory to the papacy, known as the Donation of Pepin, later became the Papal States. It was a mixed blessing for the papacy. The papacy was henceforth free of secular control, at least in theory, but the pope was required to wear two hats, one spiritual and one political. He was both the head of the Christian church and ruler of the Papal States. The need to defend the independence of the Papal States and, with it, the independence of the Roman Catholic Church, became a major issue during the Middle Ages and beyond to the twentieth century.

Pepin's son and successor, Charlemagne (742–814) was the most significant figure during the early Middle Ages. During his long reign of 46 years, he created an empire that stretched from the Pyrenees in the west to the Ebro River in the east, and from the North Sea to central Italy. Though it did not long survive him, no other European leader would impose such unity in Europe until Napoleon Bonaparte at the beginning of the nineteenth century and Adolf Hitler in the middle of the twentieth century.

Charlemagne was in Rome during the Christmas season in 800. His journey was due, in part, to the alliance between the Franks and the papacy established by his grandfather and father. Pope Leo III (r. 795–816) was facing a rebellion in Rome by a political faction that was opposed to his reign. Leo called upon Charlemagne for aid. Upon his arrival in Rome, Charlemagne heard the charges brought against Leo III by his enemies. Leo swore that he was innocent. Charlemagne declared Leo innocent and banished his enemies.

On Christmas Day, Charlemagne attended mass in St. Peter's Basilica. As he knelt before the tomb of the apostle to pray, Leo placed a crown upon his head. Then those present in the church shouted three times in unison: "To Charles Augustus, crowned by God, great and peace-giving emperor, life and victory." For the first time since 476, there was once again a Roman Emperor in the West. Charlemagne's new title, Emperor of the Romans, was not recognized by the Byzantine emperor until 812.

Charlemagne's empire had a semblance of centralized government and administration. There were 350 counties, each under an administrator with the title of Count, who was charged with administering justice, keeping the peace, providing soldiers for Charlemagne's campaigns, collecting taxes, and seeing that crops were planted and harvested. Royal inspectors, called *missi dominici*, visited the counties to ensure that the counts were carrying out their duties honestly and to report back to Charlemagne on the state of the kingdom. Charlemagne issued laws that were a blend of German customs and Christian principles.

Charlemagne's interest in educational reform led him to found a palace school at his capital in Aachen, also known as Aix-la-Chapelle. He sent to York in Northumbria, the cultural center of Western Christendom at the time, for the Anglo-Saxon scholar, Alcuin (735–804) to oversee his school. Under Alcuin's tutelage, the palace school became the nucleus of an intellectual and cultural revival known as the Carolingian Renaissance. Monks were put to work copying (and thus preserving) the Latin classics. Nearly all of the earliest known manuscripts of classical literature are copies made by the medieval monks, many of them Carolingian copies. Monks were sent out from the palace school to revive the monastic and cathedral schools.

Charlemagne's empire was not a true rebirth of the old Roman Empire in the West. There were no urban centers, and no rebirth of trade, commerce, or banking. The old Roman cities continued to decay into ruins. The old Roman aqueducts and roads were used as stone quarries to build castles. At the beginning of the ninth century, there were less than 20 000 people living in Rome, a city that during the second century had a population of over one million.

Charlemagne's empire was a Germanic kingdom supersized, a vast area temporarily held together by the force of Charlemagne's personality. Those within the empire gave personal loyalty to Charlemagne. There was no revival of the Roman concept of a state, as summed up in the motto, "The Senate and People of Rome." Such concepts were totally foreign to the German mind in the ninth century. Hence, the empire did not survive his death, but it did serve an important function. It kept alive the idea of a universal Christian empire.

Anglo-Saxons

According to tradition, the Rhine River froze over in December 406, an unusual occurrence. Large numbers of Germans fleeing before the advancing Huns poured across the river into Gaul. The Visigoth invasion of northern Italy was halted, but only temporarily. Desperate for soldiers loyal to Rome, Honorius (384–423), emperor in the West, recalled the legions from Britain. With the legions gone, the Anglo-Saxon invaders met little resistance from the defenseless inhabitants of Britain. In 410, the year that the Visigoths sacked Rome, Honorius informed the people of Britain that they must see to their own defense. The legions were not going to return.

The inhabitants of Britain resisted the invaders, but by the middle of the fifth century much of what is modern England was overrun. There is very little in the historical record of this period in Britain's history. As the Romanized population vanished or migrated westward into Wales, Cornwall, and Cumberland, literacy vanished with them. Something of the resistance to the Anglo-Saxons can be gleaned from "On the Ruin and Conquest of Britain" by St. Gildas (c. 500–570), a sixth-century monk.

In the first part of "On the Ruin and Conquest of Britain," Gildas relates the history of Britain from the Roman conquest to his own time. Of particular interest is Gildas's account of a Christian Romanized Britain, Ambrosius Aurelianus, who rallied the Britons to resist the Anglo-Saxon invaders. He won 12 battles, most famously, the Battle of Mons Badonicus, or Battle of Badon, in c. 500. Ambrosius Aurelianus is a shadowy figure. From the ninth century on, his identity became absorbed into the legend of King Arthur of Camelot and the Knights of the Round Table.

By 650, the Anglo-Saxon invaders settled down in seven separate kingdoms referred to historically as the Heptarchy: East Anglia, Essex, Kent, Mercia, Northumbria, Sussex and Wessex. War among the seven kingdoms was constant. From time to time, the kingdoms recognized one king as the Bretwalda, or "High King" of Britain. By the middle of the ninth century, the seven kingdoms were consolidated into three: Northumbria, Mercia, and Wessex.

Viking raids (mostly Danes) were common during the ninth century. In 865, a large Viking army originating in Denmark began a 12-year campaign in Britain. The "Great Heathen Army," as the invaders were called by the Britons, came to conquer and settle, not merely raid and plunder. Only the Kingdom of Wessex, where Alfred the Great (849–899) was king, remained unconquered. A decisive battle (Battle of Edington) was fought in 878, from which Alfred emerged victorious over the Danish king Guthrum (d. 890).

With the Treaty of Wedmore (878) that followed Alfred's victory, the Vikings agreed to settle in an area that comprised northern and eastern England, where the laws of the Danes ruled. It became known as the Danelaw. Guthrum accepted baptism, took the Christian name Athelstan, and became Alfred's godson. In 937, Alfred's grandson, Athelstan, King of the Anglo-Saxons (924–927) and King of the English (927–939), defeated an invasion by a combined force of Irish, Norse, Scots, and Northumbrians, thus preserving the independence of both the Danelaw and the Kingdom of Wessex.

England was once again invaded in 1003 by Sweyn Forkbeard (960–1014) of Denmark. He was proclaimed king on Christmas Day, 1013, but died less than six weeks later on February 3, 1014, uncrowned. Sweyn's son, Cnut (995–1035), also known as Canute (Cnut the Great) the Dane, in 1016 became the first ruler of all England since the Roman era. He was crowned King of Denmark in 1018 and King of Norway in 1028. Together, the kingdoms are referred to as the North Sea Empire or the Anglo-Scandinavian Empire.

The period of Cnut's reign was a pleasant respite from the turmoil that preceded and followed him. He brought more than two decades of peace and prosperity to England. He reformed the laws, promoted trade, and strengthened the coinage. Cnut was a generous patron of the Church. He rebuilt the churches and monasteries that were looted by the Vikings and built new ones. He gave gifts of money and relics to the English Church and promoted monastic reforms. In 1027, he made a pilgrimage to Rome to attend the coronation of the Holy Roman Emperor Conrad II and obtain favors for English Christians directly from the pope.

Cnut's Anglo-Scandinavian Empire did not survive him. Like Charlemagne's empire, Cnut's empire fragmented as his heirs intrigued and battled for the pieces. The English crown returned to the House of Wessex with Edward the Confessor (1003–1066) in 1042. Edward proved a saintly, but ineffective ruler, who left the affairs of state largely to Godwin, Earl of Wessex, and his son Harold. When Edward died childless, the Witan (royal council of nobles and church leaders) elected Harold Godwinson King of England.

Harold, known as Harold II, was immediately faced with two challenges to his rule – the first from his brother Tostig (c. 1026–1066), supported by King Harald III Hardrada of Norway, who invaded England, and the second from Duke William II of Normandy (1028–1087), a cousin of Edward the Confessor. Harold surprised Tostig and Hardrada at Stamford Bridge in Yorkshire on September 25, 1066. Both Tostig and Hardrada were killed in the battle, and their army virtually annihilated.

Immediately following the Battle of Stamford Bridge, Harold force-marched his army to the south coast of England to confront an invading army led by Duke William of Normandy. The battle that ensued on October 14, known as the Battle of Hastings, proved historically significant for several reasons. Harold's Anglo-Saxon army fought on foot with the battle ax as their preferred weapon. William's army was made up of armed, mounted knights, supported by infantry armed with bows. The battle lasted the entire day. At its end, Harold lay dead, shot through the eye with an arrow, and his army destroyed.

Figure 4.1 Duke William of Normandy's victory over King Harold of England at the Battle of Hastings in 1066 marked the end of Anglo-Saxon England. *Source:* The Miriam and Ira D. Wallach Division of Art, Prints, and Photographs: Print Collection, The New York Public Library.

The period of Anglo-Saxon England ended with the death of its last king. The Norman Conquest of England followed. William was crowned King of England on Christmas Day, 1066. Though William retained those aspects of Saxon customs and laws that strengthened the king's position, he introduced a highly centralized form of feudalism in England. Saxon nobles were displaced and their lands given to those, largely Norman, who participated in the conquest. French, the language of the Normans, became the language of government and administration. Henceforth, the dominant cultural influence in England came from across the channel.

Disintegration of the Carolingian Empire

On September 11, 813, Charlemagne crowned his eldest son, Louis, emperor. Louis ruled as co-emperor with his father until the latter's death in January, 814. Charlemagne recognized that when Pope Leo III crowned him emperor on Christmas Day, 800, it appeared that the title was the pope's to bestow on whomever he chose. Was the emperor subject to the pope? Charlemagne's crowning of his son, without consulting the pope, was one way of clarifying the relationship between secular and papal authority. Louis, however, allowed himself to be crowned a second time by Pope Sylvester IV (816–817) in October 816, as if to say that he was not truly emperor until given the pope's blessing.

Louis proved to be an ineffective ruler. Lacking his father's ability to inspire awe, his reign was marked by war between his four sons and among the Frankish nobility. Upon his death in 840, his three surviving legitimate sons fought over the division of the empire. The two younger sons, Charles the Bald (823–827) and Louis the German (c. 804–876), joined forces against their older brother, Lothair I (795–855), who inherited the imperial title and attempted to hold the empire together.

Charles the Bald and Louis the German met together with their armies at Strasbourg in February 842. The two brothers swore an oath of unity against their older brother. The oath was taken in the vernacular languages of their followers: "*romana lingua*," the precursor of modern French, and "*teudisca lingua*," the precursor of modern German. It was already evident by the middle of the ninth century that there were two distinct languages and cultures emerging that would evolve into modern France and Germany.

The Treaty of Verdun was concluded between the three brothers in August 843. It divided the administration and territory of the Carolingian Empire between the three. Charles the Bald was given the French speaking western Frankish lands, roughly medieval France. Louis the German was given the German speaking eastern Frankish lands. Lothair retained the imperial title and control of the so-called "Middle Kingdom," a strip of territory stretching from the North Sea to northern Italy. When Lothair died in 855, his lands were divided, according to Frankish custom, between his three sons. From its creation to middle of the twentieth century, the territory given to Lothair was fought over by the heirs of Charles and Louis.

New Invasions

The fragmentation of the Carolingian Empire and the resulting civil strife of the ninth century exposed Europe to a new wave of invasions during the ninth and tenth centuries. The new invaders were the Muslims, the Magyars, and the Vikings. Of the three, the Vikings were the most devastating and had the greatest historical impact.

The Muslims were defeated by the Franks in 732 at the Battle of Tours, thus preventing their advance into Western Europe beyond the Pyrenees Mountains. During the ninth century, they raided the southern coast of Europe, especially Italy, from bases in Muslim-controlled North Africa. By the middle of the ninth century they occupied Sicily, Corsica, Sardinia, the Balearic Islands, and southern Italy. They sacked Rome in 846 and again in 876, and burned Monte Cassino in 883.

The Magyars were a Turkic people related to the Huns who migrated from the Russian Steppes to the Carpathian Basin, where they founded the principality of Hungary at the end of the ninth century. From their base in Hungary, they were able to conduct swift raids throughout Central Europe. Their armies consisted mostly of light cavalry armed with a reflexive bow. Their raids were so destructive and terrifying, that contemporary Christian authors likened them to the biblical Gog and Magog who will wage war against God at the end of the world. The Magyars were decisively defeated at the Battle of Lechfield in 955. They settled down and became the founders of modern Hungary.

The invaders who had the greatest impact on the future were the Vikings. They came from the area referred to as Scandinavia – Norway, Sweden, and Denmark. Their significance is evident in that the period from the late eighth to the end of the eleventh century is sometimes referred to as the "Viking Age." Why they began migrating is open to many interpretations. Overpopulation was one reason. Given the agricultural technology at that time, it was easy for the growth in population to outstrip the food supply. The gradual appearance of strong central monarchies in the Scandinavian kingdoms was another.

As pagan warriors, adventure and booty were also motivations. The absence of any strong central authority capable of mounting a rapid response to the swift Viking raiders left the towns and monasteries along the coasts and rivers of Europe and the British Isles easy prey. As pagans, the Vikings did not have any scruples about burning a monastery and nailing the monks to the church door, as they sometimes did. The monastery of Lindisfarne on the coast of Northumbria was looted and burned in 793. Lindisfarne was a center of art and learning, a bright light in a dark age. The Anglo-Saxon Chronicle records the tragic event:

> This year came dreadful fore-warnings over the land of the Northumbrians, terrifying the people most woefully: these were immense sheets of light rushing through the air, and whirlwinds, and fiery, dragons flying across the firmament. These tremendous tokens were soon followed by a great famine: and not long after, on the sixth day before the ides of January in the same year, the harrowing inroads of heathen men made lamentable havoc in the church of God in Holy-island [of Lindisfarne], by rapine and slaughter. (The Anglo-Saxon Chronicle 2019)

"God, save us from the wrath of the Norsemen" was a prayer offered up from the churches and monasteries during the Viking Age.

The Viking migration followed three main routes. The Norse followed a northern or eastern route to Scotland, Ireland, Iceland, Greenland, and eventually the island of Newfoundland off the eastern coast of Canada. They colonized the Faeroes, Shetland, Orkney, and Hebrides Islands, Ireland, and the Isle of Man by 800. They settled Iceland in 874 and Greenland in 986. The Norse established two settlements in Greenland, one on the western coast (Western Settlement) and one on the southern tip (Eastern Settlement). Together, they accommodated several hundred farms and more than 3000 settlers at their peak. The Western Settlement was abandoned around 1400, and the Eastern Settlement within the next 50 years.

The Norse Vikings established a presence along the Canadian coast, an area they called Vinland. The exact location of Vinland has been disputed. Popular myth has placed it as far inland as Minnesota. Excavations undertaken at L'Anse aux Meadows on the northern tip of Newfoundland beginning in 1960 uncovered the remains of a Norse settlement. The style and structure of the buildings found at the site are identical to those found in Greenland and Iceland from the same period. Recent excavations during 2016 at Point Rosee on the southern tip of Newfoundland reveal a second Norse settlement on the island. No archeological evidence has been found of Norse settlements or trading posts on the North American mainland, but New Brunswick is a likely location for future discoveries.

The Vikings out of Sweden, called Rus or Varangians, took an eastern route down the rivers of Eastern Europe, especially the Don and Dnieper. They engaged in a profitable trade between the Baltic and Black Seas. Byzantine merchants and Arab traders along the Volga River and on the shores of the Sea of Azov engaged in trade with the Vikings. The Vikings traded amber, furs, honey, slaves, wax, and weapons for silks, silver, and other luxuries. There was a major trading center on the future site of Novgorod as early as the middle of the ninth century. According to the Russian Chronicles, Prince Oleg of Novgorod (r. 879–912) founded the state of Kievan Rus' in 907 with Kiev as its capital. Prince Oleg negotiated a trade treaty with the Byzantine Empire in 911.

The Vikings (mostly Danes) raided down the rivers of continental Europe as the Carolingian Empire fragmented. Their longboats were long, narrow, and had a shallow draft that made them ideally suited for swift raids on monasteries and settlements along the rivers. A longboat could carry 40–60 warriors. The raiders could appear suddenly and be gone before word of their arrival ever reached the one who was expected to raise an army for defense. The Annals of St. Bertin, records the Danish raid on Dorestad, a trading center, in 834:

> Meanwhile a fleet of Danes came to Frisia and laid waste a part of it. From there, they came by way of Utrecht to the emporium called Dorestad and destroyed everything. They slaughtered some people, took others away captive, and burned the surrounding region. (Nelson 1991, p. 30).

By the middle of the ninth century, the Viking raiders came in fleets of as many as 350 ships and several thousand warriors. They began to winter over in the lower Seine Valley in 851. From there, they were able to harry the largely defenseless former Carolingian empire.

In 911, Charles the Simple (879–929) signed the Treaty of Saint-Clair-sur-Epte with the Viking leader, Rollo (b. c. 846), in which Charles ceded to Rollo the territory later known as Normandy, "land of the Northmen." Rollo became a Christian and agreed to serve Charles and protect the Seine estuaries from further Viking incursions. It was Rollo's great-great-great-grandson, William, Duke of Normandy, who invaded and conquered England in 1066. The Battle of Stamford Bridge (1066), where Harold Godwinson defeated King Harald III Hardrada of Norway, and the Battle of Hastings, where Duke William defeated Harold Godwinson, mark the end of the Viking Age.

Feudalism

After the collapse of Charlemagne's empire, there was no longer a central government and no great warrior like Charlemagne to defend Christendom from the new invaders. As one chronicler put it, "Once we had a king, now we have kinglets" (Dowley 2018, p. 140).

Or as another said in 909, "every man does what seems good in his own eyes, despising laws human and divine and the commands of the Church. The strong oppress the weak; the world is full of violence against the poor and of the plunder of ecclesiastical goods" (Bokenkotter 2005, p. 112). In the midst of the chaos, a system known generally as feudalism evolved to provide for law and order and economic livelihood at the grassroots level.

In attempting to describe feudalism, one is forced to describe it in theory, since it evolved over several centuries and differed from place to place and from time to time. It is doubtful that feudalism in practice ever fully reflected feudalism in theory. The highly centralized version introduced in England following the Norman Conquest in 1066 is probably the closest practice ever came to approximating theory.

The political, economic, and social order of medieval Europe is referred to by the generic term "feudalism." A distinction is made between the governmental side of feudalism and the economic side of feudalism. The governmental side is referred to as the feudal system, and the economic side is referred to as the manorial system.

Medieval society divided people into two classes – nobles and commoners. The emergence during the late Middle Ages of a third class, the middle class (bourgeoisie), which could not be fitted into feudalism, was a leading cause of its slow decline. The feudal system involved only the members of the nobility, and had to do with the relationship between lord and vassal. The manorial system involved both the nobility and the commoner, and had to do with the relationship between the lord of the manor and the commoners (serfs, peasants, villeins, yeomen) who lived on the manor and worked the land.

Feudal System

The primary function of the feudal system was to exchange land for military service. Land was the one valuable commodity in the agricultural world of medieval Europe. In theory, the land belonged to the king, or in the case of the Holy Roman Empire, the emperor. Without money to hire soldiers, the king used the one thing he possessed, that is, the land. The king would give use, not ownership, of a piece of land to a nobleman in exchange for military service. Depending on the size of the land that the nobleman received, he was required to provide a certain number of armed mounted knights to serve in the king's army for a certain number of days each year.

The one granting the land became the lord, and the one receiving the land became the lord's vassal. The grant of land, itself, was called a fief. A fief contained one or more manors, that is, self-sufficient agricultural units roughly similar to a plantation. Serfs or peasants came with the land. Their role was to work the land and perform other various duties for the one who possessed the land, and who was their lord, the lord of the manor. The lord of the manor used the income from the land to provide the necessary armament, weapons, and warhorse for himself and, if necessary, the other knights he agreed to furnish.

The exchange of land for services took the form of an investiture ceremony. The vassal knelt before his lord, placed his hands between the lord's hands and swore to be the lord's man and perform the duties agreed to, some of which were traditional and others were specific. The lord would then hand a clump of dirt, or other object symbolizing the land grant, to the vassal. Thus, the vassal was invested with his fief.

There was both a property element and a personal element in the feudal system. The land (fief) granted to the vassal was the property element. The oath of loyalty that established a personal bond between lord and vassal was the personal element. It was not a one-sided arrangement. The vassal was obligated to serve the traditional 30 or 40 days of military service, provide lodging for the lord and his retinue when they visited the vassal's manor, and all other duties agreed to in the investiture ceremony. The lord was obligated to defend his vassal in the event of war and provide justice for his vassal in the lord's court.

The important thing to understand is that these relationships were between individuals, not between an individual and the state, kingdom, or other political unit. If the vassal did not fulfill his obligations, the lord could recover the fief, a process known as forfeiture. Upon the death of either the lord or vassal, a new feudal contract was agreed to between the survivor and the heir of the deceased. Upon the death of a vassal whose heir was either a minor or a daughter, the lord exercised wardship and enjoyed the income from the fief until the heir reached majority or he found a husband for his ward, the deceased's daughter.

In the feudal system, every man was a vassal, having sworn fealty to a lord. Often an individual was a vassal of more than one lord, and himself a lord with vassals. The feudal system was, theoretically at least, a feudal pyramid with the king, or emperor, at the peak of the pyramid with a string of vassals under him. Each of the king's vassals might have a string of vassals under him, and so forth as the pyramid fanned out in a process referred to as subinfeudation. A king could be a vassal of another king. William I of England was both King of England and Duke of Normandy. As the Duke of Normandy, William was a vassal of the king of France. In 1213, King John surrendered England to the pope and then received it back as a vassal.

Manorial System

The manorial system was the economic side of feudalism. Its function was to provide for the livelihood of those living on the manor and support the feudal system by providing the wealth with which the lord of the manor fulfilled his feudal obligations to his lord. As in the feudal system, the serf or peasant swore an oath of fealty to the lord of the manor in a ceremony similar to the one in which the lord received his fief from his lord. This was the personal element. In exchange for his service, the serf, or peasant, received a portion of the manor's arable land to farm, the property element. In addition, he owed a portion of the produce from the land he farmed to the lord of the manor.

A manor was meant to be a self-sufficient unit. It consisted of both arable and non-arable land. The arable land was that which could be farmed. It was usually divided into three large fields, which were then divided into strips of about one half-acre (2023.4 sq. m.) each. The strips were allotted to the peasant families in rotation, so that each received a portion of the good and the bad land. The practice had the added benefit of requiring the peasants to work the land according to a common plan. Scattered throughout the fields in the same manner as those of the peasants was the lord's portion, called the lord's demesne. The peasants were required to work approximately three days each week on the lord's demesne.

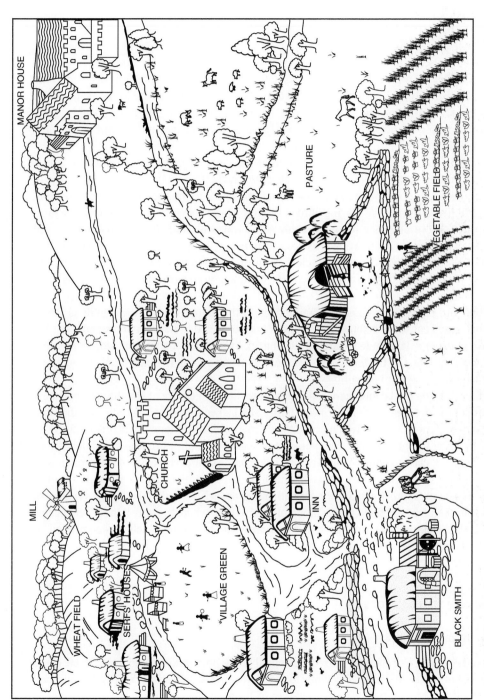

Figure 4.2 A Medieval Manor was an economically self-sufficient world of its own.

The introduction of the three-field system greatly increased production. Two fields were cultivated each year, one devoted to winter crops and one devoted to summer crops. The third lay fallow so as to replenish its nutrients. An acre (4046.9 sq. m.) would produce about seven bushels (approx. 0.035 cubic meter) of wheat in an average year. Two bushels would be retained for seed for the next year. After the lord's portion and a 10% church tax were deducted, little was left for the serf. Also, a portion was paid to the lord for use of his mill to grind the wheat into flour and for use of the lord's oven to bake the bread. Grain (mostly wheat, but also barley and rye) in the form of bread or gruel was the staple in the serf's diet. Cabbage, onions, peas, beans, and turnips were also a part of the serf's diet.

In addition to the arable land, a portion of the manor consisted of non-arable land – forest, common pasture, orchard, and meadow. The serfs lived in the manorial village in windowless, one-room huts with a dirt floor and a hole in the roof to let out smoke from a small fire in the center. During winter, the serf's family shared the space with the farm animals whose presence helped provide some warmth. Since bathing was considered unhealthy, and little attention was paid to personal hygiene by even members of the nobility, it is unlikely that the stench of the animals bothered the residents. The manorial village included a church for the serfs, complete with a priest chosen by the lord of the manor.

The lord of the manor and his family lived in the manor house. It was built as a residence, not a castle for defense. The manor house reflected the wealth and standing of the lord. In general, it included a Great Hall, chapel, living quarters, kitchen, storerooms, and servants' quarters. If the lord possessed more than one manor, the individual manors were managed by a steward or bailiff.

Together, the feudal and manorial systems provided a measure of stability during an era that lacked any meaningful central authority and lacked a money economy. Whether lord or serf, each held a recognized place in the divinely ordained hierarchical order referred to as the Great Chain of Being. Each person enjoyed all the rights, privileges, and obligations of the social class to which the individual belonged. As hard as the life of a serf often was, the serf possessed customary rights that the lord of the manor could not ignore. Of course, reality seldom approximated theory. Whether lord or serf, life in the Middle Ages was harsh and short and always filled with a monotonous routine, where the only hope of relief came with death and an eternity spent in God's presence, access to which was controlled by the church.

Europe's Neighbors

The Byzantine Empire

In the year 330, Constantine moved the capital of the Roman Empire to the East. He chose the site of Byzantium, a Greek colony founded in c. 667 BC. It was a strategically important location on the European side of the Strait of Bosporus that connects the Mediterranean Sea with the Black Sea. The city overlooked the Sea of Marmora and the Bosporus. On the northern side was the Golden Horn, an excellent harbor.

Rome ceased to be the capital of the empire when Diocletian created the Tetrarchy in 293. The Tetrarchy provided for four administrative centers, or capitals, but the economic and political center of the empire was increasingly in the East. The eastern provinces of the empire – Asia Minor, Syria, and Egypt – were the wealthiest part of the empire. There, were found the most prosperous cities with a vibrant urban culture. There was also an abundant labor supply, and productive agriculture, especially in Asia Minor.

Constantine named his new capital simply "New Rome." After his death in 337, the city was known as Constantinople in his honor, and remained so until 1923. Greek was the popular language and Latin the official language. It was not until the middle of the eighth century, when the Byzantine Empire was reduced to Greek-speaking Asia Minor, the Balkans, and a portion of southern Italy, that the empire became culturally Greek. Justinian (c. 482–565) was the last emperor to use the title "Caesar." By 750, the emperor's official title was "king" (*basileus*) and Greek was the official language.

Justinian was the greatest of the Byzantine emperors, the one most responsible for the image we have today of the Byzantine Empire. He became emperor after the death of his uncle, Justin I (450–527), an illiterate peasant and swineherd who rose to become Commander of the Palace Guard. Justin became emperor when Anastasius I died in 518. In April, 527, just four months before his death, Justin named Justinian, who was already co-emperor, his successor. This soldier of humble origins became one of the most historically important figures of late antiquity and the early Middle Ages.

Justinian tried to reunite the old Roman Empire. With his armies under the command of Belisarius (500–565), a brilliant military commander who ranks along with Julius Caesar, Alexander the Great, and Napoleon Bonaparte, Justinian won back most of Italy, eastern Spain, and the coastline of North Africa, but at a great price. What remained of Roman civilization in Italy after the fall of the empire in the West was destroyed in the struggle between the Goths and Belisarius' army. The necessary taxes to finance the conquest in the West and the wars with Persia in the East placed stress on the empire's resources and caused unrest among the populace. Almost all of the reconquered territories were lost after Justinian's death. Only in southern Italy did the Byzantine Empire remain in control into the eleventh century. It was from southern Italy and Sicily that the Byzantine culture exerted a lasting influence on the development of European civilization.

Justinian's greatest achievement was the *Corpus Iuris Civilis* ("Body of Civil Law"), the first comprehensive compilation and codification of Roman law. The task began in 527, when Justinian ascended the throne, and was not complete until 565, the year of Justinian's death. Its impact was felt well beyond the Byzantine Empire. The revived interest in Roman law at the new European universities during the tenth century, especially the University of Bologna in Italy, led to it becoming the basis of the Roman Catholic Church's canon law. It eventually became a major influence in most of the world's legal systems.

Justinian took a deep interest in Christianity, which he saw as a major support for the state. Unlike the Roman Catholic Church in the West that fought for the independence of the church from secular control, the Patriarch of the Orthodox Church was subordinate to the emperor. Religious conformity was enforced. Heretics were prosecuted. "It is right that those who do not worship God correctly," said Justinian, "should be deprived of worldly advantage too" (Galli and Olsen 2000, p. 313). Justinian closed the Academy in Athens in 529; he regarded it as a center of pagan learning.

Next to the *Corpus Iuris Civilis*, Justinian's greatest achievement was the construction of the Hagia Sophia, Church of Holy Wisdom, in Constantinople. Justinian was a great builder who constructed churches throughout the empire during his 38-year reign. Construction began in February, 532, and the cathedral was inaugurated by the emperor and the patriarch on December 27, 537. Until the construction of St. Peter's Basilica in Rome between 1506 and 1626, it was the largest and most spectacular church in the world. In Europe, it was often referred to simply as "the Church." A Roman Catholic cleric who visited the Hagia Sophia said that when he entered the church, it was as if he entered heaven.

It was in the Byzantine East that classical, Christian, and oriental cultures synthesized. The Byzantine Empire was a continuation of the urban based civilization of the Hellenistic and Roman eras. To these, was added the increasingly important cultural influences of the revived Persian (Sassanian) Empire. While Europe was going through its "Dark Ages" during the fifth through ninth centuries, the resources of the ancient world, especially Greek literature and Roman law, were preserved in the Byzantine Empire until they could be reintroduced to Europe during the High Middle Ages and the Renaissance. Also, until the fall of Constantinople in 1453 to the Ottoman Turks, the Byzantine Empire guarded the eastern frontier of Europe from the conquering armies of Islam.

Rise of Islam

At the beginning of the seventh century, the Arabian Peninsula was a vast desert with a few cities here and there along its coasts. The cities were trading centers for luxury goods from the Indian Ocean regions that were carried by caravans across the desert to the urban centers along the coast of the Mediterranean Sea. The desert regions were occupied by Bedouins, nomadic Arab tribes that herded sheep and goats, and raided the caravans and coastal cities to supplement their pastoral lifestyle. Religiously, the Arabs were influenced by Christianity, Judaism, and Zoroastrianism (from Persia). The Bedouins remained largely pagan, worshipping a variety of tribal gods.

The city of Mecca, located 43 miles (70 km) inland on the eastern coast of the Red Sea, was a place of worship of the various pagan gods, and therefore "sacred" to the Bedouins and city dwellers alike. By the beginning of the seventh century, Mecca was a trading center, especially for the lucrative spice trade. A cube-shaped granite structure called the Kaaba is located in Mecca. It was a worship center for the various pagan deities. Inside the Kaaba was the Black Stone, that all of the tribes believed was sent to earth by Allah, the most powerful of the gods.

Muhammad was born in Mecca, probably in 570, and died in Medina in 632. When he was 40 years old, he claimed that the angel Gabriel visited him and delivered to him the first of an unknown number of revelations from Allah. They were later, years after Muhammad's death, collected and became the Islamic holy book, the Quran (or Koran).

Muhammad began preaching a radical form of monotheism to the residents of Mecca in about the year 610. The Meccans did not welcome his message. In 622, he was forced to leave the city. He went to Medina, where his preaching began to enjoy some success. The flight to Medina and the time spent there is referred to as the Hegira.

From the beginning in 622, Muhammad spread his new religion of Islam by military conquest. After each victory, the men were executed and the women and children were either taken as booty or sold into slavery. By the end of 630, Mecca and all of the Arabian Peninsula was ruled by Muhammad. The first encounters between Christian (Byzantine) and Muslim armies occurred during the 630's. Both Antioch and Jerusalem were conquered in 637. Muslim armies spread Islam rapidly west and east of the Arab Peninsula. By 732, they conquered North Africa, crossed into Spain, and continued across the Pyrenees Mountains until halted by the Franks at the Battle of Tours (732). By 750, they expanded eastward to India and as far as the Talas River Valley in Central Asia. A major battle was fought in July, 751, in the Talas River Valley between an Arab-Persian army and a Chinese army of the Tang dynasty. The battle is significant because the Muslim victory halted the westward expansion of the Chinese.

Islamic culture impacted European culture in a variety of ways, most often through Spain, Sicily, and southern Italy where there was close contact over a long period of time. Understandably, there was an unconscious assimilation in such areas as food, vocabulary, the fine arts, and architecture. Much more important was the importation of the vast quantity of classical literature. Most important were the works of Aristotle and the commentaries on his works by Middle Eastern scholars. Aristotle became "the philosopher" of the Middle Ages, and the subsequent challenge to his influence helped to spark the Scientific Revolution in the last half of the sixteenth century. We shall return to this part of the story in the next three chapters.

References

The Anglo-Saxon Chronicle (2019). The Online Medieval and Classical Library. http://mcllibrary.org/Anglo/part2.html (accessed 21 October 2019).

Bokenkotter, T. (2005). *A Concise History of the Catholic Church*, rev. ed. New York: Doubleday.

Dowley, T. (2018). *A Short Introduction to the History of Christianity*. Minneapolis, MN: Fortress Press.

Galli, M. and Olsen, T. (2000). *131 Christians Everyone Should Know*. Nashville, TN: Broadman & Holman.

Nelson, J.L. (1991). *The Annals of St-Bertin. Manchester*. UK: Manchester University Press.

5

Dawn of the Age of Faith

Chronology

405	St. Jerome Completed the Latin Vulgate Translation of the Bible
529	Benedict of Nursia Founded a Monastery at Monte Casino
c. 590	Pope Gregory I's *Pastoral Care*
664	Synod of Whitby Unites Celtic Church with Roman Catholic Church
910	Duke William of Aquitaine Grants Charter for Cluny Abbey
962	Otto I Becomes First Holy Roman Emperor
1054	Great Schism Between Roman Catholic and Orthodox Churches
1078–1122	Investiture Controversy
1086	*Domesday Book*, or Great Survey of England and Parts of Wales
1095	Pope Urban II Calls for Crusade to Liberate Holy Land from Muslims
1122	Concordat of Worms Ends Investiture Controversy
c. 1150	Gratian's *Decretum*, Textbook on Cannon Law
1154	Henry II Crowned King of England
1215	Fourth Lateran Council Convened by Pope Innocent III
1215	King John of England Agrees to the *Magna Carta*, or Great Charter

There are good reasons why past historians liked to refer to the Middle Ages as the "Age of Faith." When the Roman Empire in the West collapsed during the fifth century, and with it, classical civilization, the sense of permanence, security, faith in the future, optimism, and hope that comes from an awareness of the continuity between past, present, and future vanished. The light of civilization went out and, in its place, there was despair, fear of the present and the future, violence, and an all-pervasive sense of being immersed in a dark sea of moral chaos. There was no meaning or purpose for history or the individual. The psychological impact of the collapse of classical civilization was greater than its material impact.

It was Christianity that kept alive the glowing embers of civilization during the Early Middle Ages. Many historians believe that civilization survived the long night from the end of the fifth to the eleventh centuries largely due to the efforts of the Christian church. The church was able to provide an explanation for the present uncertainty and offer hope for the future. By the end of the fourth century, the cannon of the New Testament was agreed upon and formally accepted at the Synod of Rome (382) and the Synod of Carthage (397).

Western Civilization: A Brief History, First Edition. Paul R. Waibel.
© 2020 John Wiley & Sons, Inc. Published 2020 by John Wiley & Sons, Inc.

By the time of Pope Leo I (d. 461), the bishop of Rome was generally recognized in the West as the supreme head of the church. Monasticism spread from the East to the West during the second half of the fourth century. Through these three means – canon, pope, and monks – the Christian church tamed and converted the barbarians, synthesized classical civilization and Germanic traditions with Christianity, and provided a new worldview that became the foundation of a new medieval civilization referred to as "Christendom."

Rise of the Papacy

The church in the East during the early centuries of the Byzantine Empire enjoyed a prosperous and settled environment. It was in the East that the early heresies arose and were combated. By defending the faith in controversies that often arose from the influence of Greek philosophy, the Church Fathers formulated creeds, defined doctrine, and developed a Christian theology. Church polity was not an issue in the East, where the emperor was both head of state and church. In the West, where central civil authority was rapidly vanishing under pressure from barbarian invasions, church polity was the most urgent need. Western Christians unified the church by developing a monarchical form of church government centered in Rome.

The rise of the papal monarchy during the Middle Ages was the result of several historic developments. There was what might be called historical accident, if indeed there is such a thing. Rome was the only apostolic city in the West. An apostolic city (apostolic see) is one in which the church in that city was founded by one of Jesus's 12 apostles. With contact between Christians in the West and the East interrupted, it was only natural for the faithful in the West to look to the bishop in Rome as the leader of the church. The belief that the apostles possessed authority which they passed on to their successors led to the logical conclusion that Peter's authority as the first bishop of Rome was perpetuated in the bishops of Rome. The bishop of Rome's leadership of the church was supported by the Petrine Theory.

The Petrine Theory is based on an incident recorded in Matthew 16:13–19, when Jesus asked his disciples who the people thought he was. After they gave various answers, Jesus then asked them, "But who do you say that I am?" It was Peter who answered: "You are the Christ, the Son of the living God." Jesus then told Peter that the truth he had just spoken was not the result of logical reasoning, but divine revelation. Jesus then went on to say, "And I tell you, you are Peter, and on this rock I will build my church, and the gates of hell shall not prevail against it. I will give you the keys of the kingdom of heaven, and whatever you bind on earth shall be bound in heaven, and whatever you loose on earth shall be loosed in heaven" (ESV).

The crucial word in these verses is, of course, the "rock" upon which Jesus said he would build his church. Christians in the West increasingly understood the "rock" to refer to Peter, the man, not the divinely revealed truth that Jesus was the "Christ, the Son of the living God." The authority given by Jesus to Peter was the "power of the keys," or the authority to act as Christ's vicar on earth.

Peter is identified as the first bishop of Rome in the earliest known list of Roman bishops. Christians in the West concluded that the authority given by Jesus to Peter was passed on to his successors, the bishops of Rome. His early successors were referred to as the Vicar of

Peter, but by 495 the title became Vicar of Christ. The title "pope," from the Latin *papa* and Greek *pappas* meaning father, was first used by Siricius (r. 384–399).

The first bishop of Rome to claim the authority of Peter as outlined in the Petrine Theory was Damasus I, who served as pope from 366 to 384. Damasus I was also the first to refer to Rome as the Apostolic See ("seat of the apostle"). He further enhanced the position of the bishop of Rome by commissioning Jerome (c. 347–419/420), perhaps the most learned of the early Church Fathers, to prepare a new Latin translation of the Bible. Jerome's translation, the Vulgate, became the authoritative Bible for the Roman Catholic Church.

Jerome, Augustine (354–430), Ambrose (c. 347–420), and Gregory I, "the Great" (r. 590–604) were the four great Latin Church Fathers. Gregory I's administrative skills made the Roman bishopric wealthy. He used the income to finance the government of Rome, care for the

Figure 5.1 "St. Jerome's Latin translation of the Bible (390–405), known as the Vulgate, was affirmed by the Council of Trent (1545–1563) as the official Latin Bible of the Roman Catholic Church." *Source:* The Miriam and Ira D. Wallach Division of Art, Prints, and Photographs: Print Collection, The New York Public Library.

city's poor, and buy off the Lombards who threatened Rome. His *Pastoral Care* was one of the most widely read religious book of the Middle Ages. In 596, Gregory sent Augustine (d. c. 604), prior of the Benedictine monastery of St. Andrew in Rome, to the Kingdom of Kent in England to evangelize the Anglo-Saxons. In 597, Gregory appointed Augustine the first archbishop of England. It was in Britain that the two orthodox versions of Christianity in the West came into direct contact.

Celtic Christianity developed in Ireland, when many Christian Britons fled Britain following the end of Roman rule and the invasion of Britain by the pagan Anglo-Saxons. During the sixth and seventh centuries Irish monks founded monasteries in Scotland, England, Belgium, Germany, France, and even northern Italy. Celtic and Roman Christianity differed in some areas of practice – how to ordain bishops, how to shave the head of monks, and most important, how to calculate the date of Easter. Though the differences seem minor by modern standards, they were serious matters in the seventh century.

King Oswiu (c. 612–670) of Northumbria called for a meeting of monks representing the two churches to decide which practice, Celtic or Roman, was correct. The meeting took place at Whitby Abbey in 664. When the Celtic monks acknowledged that Peter, the founder of the church in Rome, was the successor of Jesus Christ, Oswiu ruled in favor of Roman Christianity. Following the Synod of Whitby, Celtic Christianity came under the authority of the Pope. A unified Christianity in the West greatly enhanced the papal claim to supreme authority in Christendom.

The authority of the papacy was enhanced further by the increasing distinction between the laity and the clergy. Only the clergy who were in the line of apostolic succession could minister to the laity the sacraments through which God's grace was dispensed to the faithful. According to the Petrine Theory, the authority to minister the sacraments emanated from the pope through the clergy. The church was an essential intermediary between the individual and God.

Rise of Monasticism

Christian monasticism first developed in Egypt and Syria during the late third and early fourth centuries. The first monks were individuals who lived as hermits, a form of monasticism known as anchoritic. It spread to the West during the latter part of the fourth century. The environment in Western Europe was not conducive to the harsh asceticism of the hermit monks. Hence, it was a communal form of monasticism known as cenobitic, that became the rule.

Monasticism was not invented by the early medieval Christians, but there were a variety of reasons for its attraction. One was the view, originating in part in Greek philosophy, that there was an inherent conflict between the flesh and spirit. The spirit was good; the material was evil. Some believed that by mortifying the flesh, one could become more spiritual.

Some Christians felt the need to separate themselves from a society and church that was becoming corrupted by material excess. After Theodosius I made Christianity the only legal religion in the Roman Empire (381), the number of those who professed to be Christians rose to about 90%. This influx of nominal converts led to a lessening of religious zeal. The end of persecution meant the end of martyrdom. For some, asceticism substituted for martyrdom. Anyone could become a martyr by renouncing the world and becoming a monk, either as a hermit in the desert or a monk in a monastery.

The first-century Christians met in homes or in the synagogues. During the second half of the third century, they began to construct buildings for worship. Corporate worship was further encouraged by the emergence of the monarchical bishop and the sacramental system. Becoming a monk was one way that an individual could return to an individualistic mode of worship.

The identity of the first Christian monk is lost to history. The founder of anchoritic monasticism was a wealthy Coptic peasant from Egypt. Anthony of Egypt (c.251–356) took to heart Jesus' advice to the rich young man: "If you would be perfect, go, sell what you possess and give to the poor and you will have treasure in heaven; and come, follow me" (Matthew 19:21 ESV). When Anthony was about 20, he sold all of his possessions, gave the proceeds to the poor, and became a hermit. He spent 20 years alone in the Egyptian desert. He fasted, gave up bathing, put on a hair shirt, and devoted himself to a life of prayer, Bible study, meditation, and battling real or imagined demons.

The founder of what became the definitive form of Western monasticism was Benedict of Nursia (c. 480–543), the son of a Roman nobleman. After a brief experiment as a hermit living in a cave for three years, he founded a monastery at Monte Cassino, not far from Naples in 529. Monte Cassino was founded to be a completely self-contained, self-supporting, self-governing world of its own. Life in the monastery was characterized by a communal life of absolute regularity, strict discipline, and unvarying routine.

Benedict devised a daily routine that prescribed 4 hours of communal liturgical prayer and worship, 4 hours of private meditation, prayer, and reading, 6 hours of physical labor, and 10 hours reserved for eating and sleeping. The mortification of the flesh practiced by the anchoritic monks was prohibited. Instead, each monk was responsible for making sure that his brother monks ate regular meals, and that special care was given to the elderly, the sick, and the young. Silence was not required, but idle talk was discouraged, and bathing was discouraged as an unnecessary luxury. As the Order of Benedict spread throughout the West, regulations changed. The Benedictine monks in England were allowed take three or four baths per year.

By the end of the ninth century, the Rule of Benedict became the basic rule for all Western monasteries, except those in Ireland. With time, however, they became more than a refuge from the world for those seeking a more spiritual lifestyle. They became educational centers that supplied bishops, popes, and scholars to serve as royal chancellors and advisers. It was in the monasteries that literacy and literature survived the dark period of the Early Middle Ages. Ninety percent of the literate population between 600 and 1100 were educated in monastic schools.

Feudalism and the Church

In the absence of any strong central government following the fragmentation of the Carolingian empire, the church was caught up in the emerging feudalism. Priests, bishops, archbishops, abbots of monasteries, even the pope, became feudal appointees of secular lords. Having lost its independence, the church entered upon a period of rapid and dramatic moral decline that lasted until the middle of the tenth century. Church offices were awarded by secular lords to individuals with little, if any, interest in spiritual matters. Those who did were plagued by divided allegiances.

Church offices were sought for the wealth and power that came with them. Seventeen popes sat on the Holy See between 897 and 955, one of which was poisoned and crushed to death by his enemies. Pope Stephen VI (r. May 896-August 897) followed the brief two-week reign of Pope Boniface VI (April 896), who either died of gout or was murdered. Stephen VI had the decaying body of Pope Formosus (r. 891–896), Boniface's predecessor, exhumed, dressed in his papal vestments and seated on the papal throne, then tried before the so-called "Cadaver Synod." The trial was held in the Basilica of St. John Lateran in Rome in January 897 with Stephen VI presiding. After being convicted of perjury and usurping the office of bishop, Formosus' corpse was stripped of its vestments, the three fingers of the right hand used to pronounce blessings were cut off, the body dragged through the streets, and finally, after a brief burial, disinterred, and dumped in the Tiber River. After Formosus' body washed up on the banks of the river and was alleged to perform miracles, Stephen VI was deposed, imprisoned, and strangled.

Two rivals occupied the papal throne in 903. Both ended their brief careers in prison. From 904 until the reforms imposed by the Holy Roman Emperor Otto I (912–973), the papacy was controlled by an Italian family whose debauchery equaled that of the worst Roman emperors. Actual control of the papacy lay in the hands of three powerful women who passed the papal throne between their paramours and illegitimate children. The low point of the papacy came with the reign of John XII (r. 955–964). John became pope at only 18 years of age. So absolute was his moral corruption, that his reign is known in church history as the "papal pornocracy."

Church Renewal

The scandal of the medieval church, corrupted by its entanglement in the feudal system, led to the emergence of a reform movement that began in the monasteries. It began as a movement to revitalize Benedictine monasticism, that many felt was corrupted by involvement with the world outside the walls of the monasteries.

The reform movement originated at the monastery of Cluny in eastern France. It is known as both the Cluniac and Gregorian Reform movement. The charter granted by Duke William I of Aquitaine in 910 for the establishment of Cluny Abbey stipulated that the monastery was to be free of all lay and ecclesiastical control. It was to be under direct control of the papacy, which, given the state of affairs in Rome at the time, meant that the monastery was able to chart its own course. Monasteries that adopted the Cluniac reforms were headed by a prior who was under the abbot of Cluny. Discipline and commitment to the reform ideals was maintained, since each monk in the order was a monk of Cluny.

The Cluniac reformers were committed to ending the corruption and immorality that came to characterize the life of the church. They focused on three primary abuses, the trafficking in church offices (simony), the appointment of relatives to church offices (nepotism), and violation of the vow of clerical celibacy. In addition, cultivation of spiritual life and an emphasis on worship were required of all the monks.

The spirit of reform took hold in Rome with the election of Pope Leo IX (r. 1049–1054). Leo IX surrounded himself with reformers, most importantly, Hildebrand of Sovana. When Hildebrand was elected Pope Gregory VII (r. 1073–1085), the stage was set for one of the most dramatic events in the struggle to reform the church – the showdown between Gregory VII and Holy Roman Emperor Henry IV. Gregory's passion was to restore the moral character of the papacy and the power of the pope. For Gregory that meant an end to the practice of lay investiture, the practice of a secular lord investing a bishop, abbot, or other churchman with the insignia of his spiritual office (see the Investiture Controversy below).

The pope's authority over the church and his power and influence within Christendom was furthered by the development of a centralized and very efficient papal curia and the compilation and application of canon law during the twelfth century. Urban II (r. 1088–1099) is credited with developing the papal curia consisting of a chancery, papal chapel, treasury, and the whole administrative system for the day-to-day governing of the church.

The compilation of canon law was inspired by the study of Roman law at the University of Bologna in Italy. Gratian (fl. early twelfth century), a Benedictine monk in a monastery near Bologna, prepared a systematic digest of some 3800 texts from a broad spectrum of sources including the Bible, the Church Fathers, conciliar canons, and papal decrees. Gratian's *Decretum* (*Harmony of Discordant Canons*) became the basic "textbook" for the study of canon law for centuries. Canon law provided a foundation for papal authority and a kind of guidebook for the administrative machinery of the church.

The emphasis on papal authority that reached fruition in the reign of Innocent III (r. 1198–1216) brought the differences between the Roman Catholic Church in the West and the Greek Orthodox Church in the East to a crisis resulting in a formal split between the two. There were many differences between the two churches, just as there was between the Celtic Church and the Roman Catholic Church that were resolved by the Synod of Whitby in 664. Unlike the Celtic Christians, the Orthodox Christians never accepted the claims of papal supremacy. The Eastern bishops were willing to acknowledge the bishop of Rome as the first among equals, but not as the supreme head of Christendom.

In 1054, the contested issue was the use of unleavened bread in the Eucharist by the church in the West. When Patriarch Cerularius (r. 1043–1059) condemned the practice, Leo IX sent his closest advisor, the fiery defender of papal supremacy, Hildebrand, to Constantinople to resolve the issue. When Cerularius ignored the papal delegation, Hildebrand marched into the Church of Saint Sophia on July 16, 1054, and placed a bull of excommunication on the high alter. Cerularius responded by convening a Synod and excommunicated Hildebrand and his supporters. The mutual excommunications finalized the split between the two churches.[1]

---

1 In January, 1964, Pope Paul VI (r. 1963–1978) and Ecumenical Patriarch Athenagoras (r. 1948–1972) met in Jerusalem and lifted the dual excommunications.

Crusades

At the end of the eleventh century, Europe was ready to launch its first expansion beyond the borders of Europe proper. Between 1095 and the end of the thirteenth century, European armies embarked on a series of crusades to liberate the Holy Land from Muslim control. Though largely French in origin, participants from across Europe took part in nine crusades that were both a sign of progress in Europe and an expression of widespread popular religious piety.

In 1071, the Seljuk Turks, a tribe of Tartars from Central Asia, defeated a Byzantine army at the Battle of Manzikert north of Lake Van in eastern Turkey. The Turks gained control of much of the Anatolia Peninsula. In 1095, Emperor Alexius I Comnenus (1056–1118) sent an urgent appeal to Pope Urban II for military aide against the Turks.

Urban II made a dramatic speech at the Council of Clermont in south-central France in November 1095, calling upon the Christian nobility of Europe to go to the Holy Land and liberate Jerusalem and the other holy places from the infidel Turks. He promised that all who answered the call would "obtain the remission of your sins and be sure of the incorruptible glory of the kingdom of heaven" (Thatcher 1905, p. 520). When he finished his speech, the crowd shouted out repeatedly, "God wills it."

Those who heeded the call shared a variety of motives. Some Crusaders went for economic gain or simply adventure. For most, however, the Crusades were a pilgrimage. The eleventh and twelfth century chroniclers never speak of "crusades." Instead, they speak of the "Jerusalem journey," the "journey to the Holy Sepulcher," or the "pilgrimage to Jerusalem." Participation on a crusade served as penance for a sinful life corrupted by a wicked world. For many of them in the Age of Faith, there was a longing to see the birthplace of God's Son, and perhaps to die there.

There were nine crusades and at least two well-known unofficial crusades. The First Crusade (1096–1099), composed mostly of French knights, set out for the Holy Land in August 1096 and arrived before the walls of Jerusalem in June 1099. The city fell to the Crusaders after the second assault. After entering the city, the Crusaders spent seven days slaughtering the population, both Muslims and Jews. Many of the Crusaders returned home. Those who remained established four so-called "Crusader States": Jerusalem, Edessa, Antioch, and Tripoli. They were feudal states subject, at least in theory, to the Pope.

In 1146, Edessa was retaken by Muslim forces, who slaughtered most of the population and sold the rest into slavery. The fall of Edessa led to the Second Crusade (1147–1149) led by King Louis VII (1120–1180) of France and Conrad III, King of Germany. Louis and Conrad assembled an army of 50 000 and attacked Damascus in Syria. After a brief siege of the city, the Crusaders were forced to retreat. The Second Crusade, unlike the First Crusade, ended in a humiliating failure.

Sultan Saladin (c. 1137–1193) began a campaign against the Crusader Kingdom of Jerusalem in 1187. Saladin's capture of the city in October 1187 led to the Third Crusade, often called the King's Crusade (1189–1192), because it was led by Holy Roman Emperor Frederick I Barbarossa (1122–1190), King Philip II Augustus of France (1165–1223), and King Richard I the Lionheart (1157–1199) of England. Frederick died on route and most of

Figure 5.2 Woodcut from c. 1486 depicting Pope Urban II at the Council of Claremont (1095) urging kings and nobles to go on a crusade to liberate the Holy Land from Muslim control. *Source:* Library of Congress, Prints, and Photographs Collections.

his army returned to Germany. Philip II and Richard I captured the port city of Acre in July 1191. The two quarreled over how to proceed, resulting in Philip returning to France, leaving Richard to carry on alone. Richard defeated Saladin's army at the Battle of Arsuf near Jerusalem in September. A year later Richard and Saladin signed a treaty that left Jerusalem in Muslim hands, but granted Christians access to Jerusalem and the holy places.

The extent to which the original motive for the Crusades gave way to conquest and plunder was evident in the Fourth Crusade (1202–1204) called by Pope Innocent III (r. 1198–1216). The original goal of the crusade was to recapture Jerusalem by first invading Egypt. Instead, the Crusaders agreed with the Venetians to attack the Christian city of Zara on the eastern coast of the Adriatic Sea. Zara was a commercial rival of the Republic of Venice. After the fall of Zara, again agreeing to entreaties from the Venetians, the Crusaders attacked Constantinople. The lure of plunder and power was greater than their commitment to fight the Muslims and liberate Jerusalem.

The capture of Constantinople by the Crusaders was followed by a frenzy of looting, burning, and slaughter. The Crusaders did not spare the churches or the monasteries. The destruction and looting of the artistic treasures of Constantinople is considered one of history's great cultural disasters, comparable to the Muslim capture of Alexandria in 641 and the bombing of Dresden in February 1945. Pope Innocent III excommunicated both the Crusaders and the Venetians, and condemned the Fourth Crusade. The victors established the Latin Empire of Constantinople out of the remnants of the old empire. It lasted until 1261, when it was dissolved and a weakened Byzantine Empire was restored.

Innocent III called for a fifth crusade in 1213. Preparations for the crusade continued after his death in 1216, under his successor Pope Honorius III (r. 1216–1227). The crusade meant to follow the original plan for the Fourth Crusade by attacking Egypt. It ended in the surrender of the Crusaders to Sultan Al-Kamil (c. 1177–1238), a nephew of Saladin.[2] It was the last official crusade under papal patronage.

Holy Roman Emperor Frederick II (1194–1250) organized and led the Sixth Crusade (1228–1229) even while under a sentence of excommunication by Pope Gregory IX (r. 1227–1241). Frederick was able to achieve by diplomacy what the previous crusades failed to achieve through war. Sultan Al-Kamil agreed to a treaty with Frederick in which he ceded Jerusalem (not including the Mosque of Omar), Nazareth, and Bethlehem to Frederick and agreed to a 10-year truce. Frederick and Gregory IX were reconciled in 1230. Gregory lifted the bull of excommunication, but still threatened by Frederick's power in Italy, excommunicated him again in 1239.

The Seventh Crusade (1248–1254) was led by King Louis IX (1214–1270). Louis proved to be a poor military strategist. He was defeated, taken captive, and after a ransom was paid, he returned to France. Louis planned another crusade, commonly referred to as the Eighth Crusade (1270). Shortly after landing his army in Tunis, dysentery swept through the camp killing many of the crusaders. Louis, himself died on August 25, without having conquered any territory.

A final feeble attempt at a crusade occurred in 1271. It was led by Prince Edward of England (1239–1307). After arriving in Acre, Edward found little support for another crusade and returned to England. In 1291, Acre, the last Crusader outpost in the Holy Land, fell to a Muslim army after a brief siege. Those who were unable to escape were slaughtered. Jerusalem and the Holy Land remained in Muslim hands until the end of the First World War in 1919.

---

2 An interesting sidelight of the Fifth Crusade is a meeting between Sultan Al-Kamil and St. Francis of Assisi (c. 1181–1226) during an interlude in the siege of Damietta in the Nile River Delta.

There were two "crusades" that deserve mention because of what they show about the Middle Ages as an Age of Faith. They were in a sense spontaneous and without any real organization or leadership. The first, commonly called the "People's Crusade," occurred in 1096, while the First Crusade was preparing to depart for the Holy Land. The second, the so-called "Children's Crusade," took place in 1212, after the Fourth Crusade ended in the sacking of Constantinople. Both were disastrous.

The leader of the People's Crusade, was a barefoot, bare-headed monk called Peter the Hermit (1050–1115). Peter traveled through Italy, France, and Germany speaking in churches or wherever he could gather a crowd. He called upon any and all to go to the Holy Land and liberate Jerusalem and the holy sites from the hands of the infidels.

The disorganized band of mostly common people – peasants, men, women, children, and some landless knights – passed overland along the Danube River and through the Balkans like a dark cloud of locusts. Citizens of towns along the route fled when they learned of the approaching horde. Once they arrived at Constantinople, the emperor quickly transported them across the Bosporus Strait to Asia Minor (Turkey). Without adequate food or water, and lacking any military leadership or strategy, they were quickly massacred or captured and sold into slavery by the Turkish armies. Peter, however, survived and eventually returned to Flanders, where he founded a monastery.

Reliable facts about the Children's Crusade of 1212 are difficult to come by. There were two movements, or crusades. One was led by Nicholas of Cologne, a young shepherd boy, and the other led by Stephan of Cloyes in France, also a young shepherd boy of about 12 years.

Both boys believed that they were called by God to lead a children's crusade that would succeed where the adults had failed. The innocent children would not win by fighting, but by the direct intervention of God. They believed that once they reached the Mediterranean coast, the sea would miraculously part, and the Children would walk across on dry land to the Holy Land, where the Muslim armies would simply melt before them. It did not happen that way.

Stephen led a band of perhaps 30 000 youth, mostly boys, through France to Marseilles on the Mediterranean coast. Only about half actually made it to Marseilles. The others either became discouraged and abandoned the crusade or perished from hunger and hardship. Those who remained found that the sea did not open for them. Two merchants convinced them to board seven ships for the journey. Once out to sea, and after two ships sank, the remaining five were met by a squadron of Saracen slave traders who purchased the children and sold them in the slave markets of Egypt, Algeria, and Baghdad.

Nicholas' band headed for Genoa. Many perished while crossing the Alps. Once in Genoa, they also found that the Mediterranean Sea did not part for them as they expected. Some boarded two ships headed for Palestine and were never heard from again. Some chose to accept an invitation from the city leaders to remain in Genoa. The remainder eventually arrived in Rome, where they met with Pope Innocent III. He told them to return to their homes and wait until they grew up to fulfill their vows to go on a crusade. Very few ever returned to their homes.

The Crusades had both positive and negative influences. The Italian port cities, especially Genoa and Pisa, and the Republic of Venice, prospered from the increased trade with the Crusader States. The Republic of Venice benefitted greatly from the Fourth Crusade's capture of Constantinople, Venice's main commercial rival. The stimulation of trade, and the growth of towns along the trade routes from northern Italy to the markets in the coastal area of northwestern Europe hastened the emergence of a commercial class and the emergence of what would later be called a capitalist economy. That in turn enabled the monarchs to forge an informal alliance with the new middle class to weaken the power of the nobility, thereby strengthening central government and hastening the decline of feudalism.

European culture was enriched by increased contact with the Muslim world, where much of classical civilization was preserved. Classical manuscripts of the Greek philosophers and dramatists, as well as treatises on them by Muslim scholars, became increasingly available to Westerners, especially those associated with the emerging universities. However, it is generally assumed that the cultural influence came mainly through Spain, Sicily, and southern Italy rather than as a direct result of the Crusades.

Unfortunately, the Crusades apparently initiated the first widespread outburst of anti-Semitism in Europe. During the First Crusade, Jewish communities in the Rhineland cities of Speyer, Worms, and Mainz were destroyed by mobs of mostly peasants aroused by charismatic preachers. The Crusaders, themselves, extorted funds from the more prosperous Jews to help finance the crusades. Pogroms became more commonplace throughout Europe afterwards during difficult times of economic distress.

The Fourth Lateran Council convened by Pope Innocent III in 1215 institutionalized religious anti-Semitism. Jews were required to live in ghettos, restricted areas of cities that were often gated. They were required to be inside the ghetto at nightfall, when the gates were closed. Jews were required not to appear in public during Holy Week, and required to wear distinctive clothing and/or what came to be called the "Jewish badge." The design of the badge varied from country to country and from time to time. During Edward I of England's reign, for example, "[a] piece of yellow taffeta, six fingers long and three broad, was to be worn above the heart by every Jew over the age of seven years" (Jewish Identification 2008).

Feudal Monarchies

During the eleventh and twelfth centuries, the kings of England and France were able to transform the role of the king from the peak of a feudal pyramid to the focal point of a strong centralized government. Stiff resistance from both the feudal nobility and the church prevented the same from occurring in the Holy Roman Empire. The church itself was experiencing a reform movement that strengthened the pope's position as the divinely appointed absolute monarch of a highly centralized and efficient bureaucracy.

The kings enjoyed certain advantages in their efforts to bring their "over mighty" vassals into submission. The king's position was divinely sanctioned. The crowning of a monarch by a bishop, or sometimes the pope, was a sign that the person being crowned was God's chosen, just as in ancient Israel when Samuel anointed Saul king of Israel. To oppose the king was tantamount to being in opposition to God.

Feudal kings were able to enhance their power through successful wars and dynastic marriages. Duke William of Normandy (c. 1028–1087) became King of England by conquest. His grandson, Henry II (1133–1189), acquired Aquitaine, Poitou, and Gascony by marriage to Eleanor of Aquitaine (1122–1204). Together with Normandy, Anjou, Maine, and Touraine acquired by inheritance, Henry II controlled 10 times as much of France as the French king who was Henry II's feudal lord.

The development of a government administration that enabled the crown to touch the lives of all of its subjects, both noble and commoner, was another means of strengthening the king's position vis-à-vis his vassals. Once again, Henry II of England is a good example. His efforts to make royal justice the common law of England, and his creation of the Exchequer (treasury) strengthened his authority as king.

The revival of trade and the rebirth of cities led to the birth of a money economy and a new class of merchants and bankers. The kings found, in the emergence of a commercial class, the opportunity to acquire the funds with which to force their vassals into submission. The things that a commercial class required – money, standardized weights and measures, commercial as opposed to feudal laws, protection from the arbitrary rule of local lords – required central government. The kings could grant such needs in exchange for fees and taxes. Thus, a partnership was forged between the crown and the commercial class. The ability of the kings to hire soldiers, however, undercut the original motive behind the feudal system, which was exchanging land for military service.

England

Following his victory at the Battle of Hastings in 1066, William the Conqueror proceeded to impose a centralized form of feudalism modeled after that in practice in Normandy. In theory, all of England belonged to the crown. One-sixth to one-fifth was retained as the royal demesne. The great Anglo-Saxon estates were confiscated and parceled out as fiefs to William's Norman followers. The lands held by the church, approximately one-fourth of the total land in England, remained in church hands. After all, Pope Alexander II (r. 1061–1073) blessed William's invasion and conquest.

Those who held a fief directly from William (tenants-in-chief) were allowed to grant portions of their lands to individuals who became their vassals (subinfeudation). In 1086, William required all vassals throughout England to take an oath of primary vassalage, or allegiance, to the crown. Thus, all land holders were made vassals of the crown, even if they held their fief from a lesser lord.

The Anglo-Saxon system of governmental administration consisting of shires, hundreds (groups of villages), and sheriffs (shire reeves), and the Anglo-Saxon system of taxation were retained and improved upon. The Witan was replaced by the Great Council (*Magnum Concilium*), an assembly of royal officials, great barons, and church leaders. It met when called by the king to discuss matters presented to it and give advice. A smaller group referred to as the Small Council, or King's Court (*Curia Regis*), met more frequently for the same purpose.

In 1086, William I sent royal commissioners throughout his new realm to take a census, not only of people, but of every acre of land, every plow, every animal, indeed, every item of value. People were put under oath and questioned as to what they knew about who owned a piece of land in the past, how much it produced in a normal year, etc. This census, known as the *Domesday Book*, was the first ever undertaken in Europe. Today, it provides a look at England frozen in time, from which scholars are able to construct a picture of life in England during the eleventh century.

Based on the statistics in the *Domesday Book*, historians are able to estimate the population of England at approximately 2 million, of which between 9 and 20% (depending on the area) were slaves; 85% were serfs; 3.5% were burghers and other residents of towns, 0.5% were members of the clergy (priests, monks and nuns), and 1% were nobles.

Henry I (1068–1135), William I's third son became king in 1138. He expanded and refined the royal administrative and justice systems, while restoring a measure of prosperity to the kingdom. After the death of his son and heir, Henry named his daughter Matilda (c. 1103–1147) as his successor. Matilda married Geoffrey Plantagenet (1113–1151), Count of Anjou in 1112. When Henry I died in 1135, Stephen of Blois (d. 1154), the son of Henry I's sister, Adela, seized the throne and was crowned king. England was engulfed by civil war between those who supported Stephen and those who supported Matilda's claim to the throne. In 1153, Stephen recognized Matilda's son, Henry (1133–1189), as his successor. When Stephen died in the summer of 1154, Henry was crowned Henry II, the first of the Plantagenet dynasty.

Henry II was a natural born leader, whose very appearance – handsome, athletic, cultured – inspired confidence among those loyal to the crown. Walter Map (1140–1210), a courtier, wrote that Henry II possessed a countenance "upon which a man might gaze a thousand times, yet still feel drawn to" (Cahill 2006, p. 137). Henry not only restored peace and prosperity to England, he strengthened the royal government. By inheritance, marriage, and conquest he created the "Angevin Empire" that included England, half of France, and parts of Ireland and Wales.

Henry II sent royal justices throughout the kingdom to hear cases that previously were heard only in the local lord's court. The Assizes of Clarendon (1166) established what later became known as the grand jury. Henry's judicial reforms extended royal authority, increased revenues, and perhaps most important for the future, laid the foundation of English common law.

Henry II was succeeded by his son Richard I the Lionheart, who spent less than 6 months of his 10-year reign in England. His role in the Third Crusade, and his appearance in the Robin Hood stories, made him a romantic figure in English history. Perhaps the best assessment of Richard I's reign was given by historian Steven Runciman: "[H]e was a bad son, a bad husband, and a bad king, but a gallant and splendid soldier" (Runciman 1952, p. 75). Richard I died on April 6, 1199 from an arrow wound he received while attacking the castle of Châlus-Chabrol in France. Richard's younger brother John (1166–1216), the favorite son of Henry II, was immediately crowned king. Neither popular legend nor historians have been kind to John's memory.

Unlike his brother, John was not "a gallant and splendid soldier." In fact, he was called "John Softsword," among other things. He had the misfortune to confront two of the most powerful monarchs of the High Middle Ages, Pope Innocent III and Philip Augustus of France. A dispute between John and Hugh of Lusignan (1183–1249), both of whom were vassals of Philip, led to Hugh appealing to their lord, Philip, for justice. When John refused to appear in Philip's court, Philip declared his French lands forfeited. In the war with Philip that followed, John lost all of his French lands north of the Loire River. France became the dominant power in Europe.

A depleted treasury and inflation alienated John's barons. His position was further weakened when he found himself in conflict with Innocent III over the pope's choice of Stephen Langton (c. 1150–1228) as Archbishop of Canterbury in 1207. Innocent III excommunicated John and placed England under an interdict in 1208. When that failed to force John's submission, Innocent declared John deposed and called upon Philip Augustus to execute his decree. Faced with an invasion and lacking support from his English barons, John was forced to submit. He did homage to Innocent III for England and Ireland, which he received back as a fief, and agreed to pay an annual tribute.

John's misfortunes reached a climax in mid-June 1215, in a meadow along the River Thames called Runnymede. It was there that King John was forced to yield to the demands of his barons that he adhere to the feudal contracts he had with them. The document known as the *Magna Carta*, or Great Charter, was a feudal document clarifying the mutual obligations between the king and his vassals, and between the king and the church. Embedded in it, however, were principles like the supremacy of law, judicial review, and representative government that with time transformed the Great Charter into a founding document of English Constitutional history.

The reign of John's son, Henry III (1207–1272), was a turbulent period. His inability to control the barons, his expensive failures in foreign affairs, and the increasing power of the church during his reign all contributed to a split among the barons into one party willing to use force to bring about reform and another supportive of the king. The former was led by Simon de Montfort (c. 1208–1265), Henry III's brother-in-law. Simon de Montfort's forces defeated Henry III at the Battle of Lewes in 1264. Henry was taken captive, briefly giving de Montfort control of England.

De Montfort ruled England in the king's name from May 1264 until August 1265. In January 1265, de Montfort summoned a meeting of the king's council, called Parliament since the 1240's. He included not only the barons, leaders of the church, and knights from the shires, but two burgesses from each borough. It was the first time that representatives of the major towns were included in a Parliament. The practice was continued by Edward I (1236–1307), when he became king in 1272, after defeating de Montfort's army at the Battle of Evesham.

Edward I proved to be a wise and able ruler. He is sometimes referred to as the first English king, and at other times, as the English Justinian, because of his legislative reforms. Among his judicial reforms was the establishment of three royal common law courts. The Court of the King's Bench handled civil criminal cases; the Court of Exchequer handled cases dealing with royal finances; and the Court of Common Pleas handled civil cases between subjects of the crown.

Edward I's writ calling for a meeting of Parliament in 1295 included the phrase, "let that which toucheth all be approved by all." Opinions differ as to whether it was Simon de Montfort's Parliament in 1265 or Edward I's Parliament in 1295 that was the "first" English Parliament. By the end of Edward's reign, William I's Great Council, an assembly of royal officials, great barons, and church leaders called by the king to discuss matters presented to it and give advice, had evolved into a Parliament representing what jurists of the time were beginning to call the "community of the realm."

France

Louis V (c. 966/67–987) was the last of the Carolingian dynasty to rule West Francia (France). Because he died childless, the assembly of French barons elected Hugh Capet (938–996) as their king. Hugh Capet was the first of the Capetian dynasty that ruled France until 1792.

Hugh was a feudal lord with a royal title that meant very little other than that he and his title were sanctified by the church. His own feudal domain was limited to an ill-defined area known as the *Ill-de-France* surrounding Paris. Even there, his vassals were able to exercise considerable independence. As for Hugh's vassals who held royal fiefs, they recognized him as their lord, but since they were often more powerful than he, their loyalty was limited by their own interests. The task set before Hugh Capet and his successors was slowly, but steadily, to expand the *Ill-de-France* into the Kingdom of France.

Philip II Augustus (1165–1223) took advantage of feudal law to deny the English kings their lands in France, which they held as vassals of the French king. He not only enlarged the kingdom, he also created a royal bureaucracy to administer the kingdom, collect revenues, and expand royal justice. He granted charters to towns, winning him the support of the growing commercial class and increasing royal revenue. Revenues acquired from the towns enabled him to finance the royal bureaucracy and hire a professional army, both of which strengthened the central government and checked the independence of the barons.

Philip II's grandson Louis IX (1214–1270) ascended the throne 1226, when he was only 12 years old. His mother, Blanche of Castile, was a devout Christian, who raised her son to be a model Christian ruler. She served as regent until Louis began his personal reign around 1234, and continued as his trusted advisor until her death in 1252.

Louis IX saw that royal justice was extended to all of his subjects equally. He transformed the King's Court (*Curia Regis*) into what became known as the Parlement of Paris, the supreme court of France. As with Henry II in England, Louis IX allowed local cases to be transferred to royal courts. He was even known to sit beside a tree and invite local people to bring their cases before him for judgment.

Louis IX is remembered most for his piety. No other ruler of the Middle Ages came closer to embodying the feudal ideal of the king or emperor as a vassal of God, charged with ruling justly. His reputation was such that he was called upon to arbitrate international disputes, as for example between Henry III of England and his barons. So popular was Louis IX that the people considered him a saint, even before he was canonized in 1297 by Pope Boniface VIII (r. 1294–1303).

Holy Roman Empire

The Carolingian Kingdom of East Francia (Germany) suffered most from the invasions of the ninth and tenth centuries. The royal successors of Louis the German, Charlemagne's grandson, were unable to defend the kingdom from the Vikings, Magyars, and Slavs. It fell upon the powerful dukes of the so-called "stem (i.e. tribe) duchies" to defend their own territories. When the last Carolingian king, Louis the Child (893–911) died, the German magnates elected Conrad, Duke of Franconia as the new king of East Francia. Franconia was one of the five stem duchies.

Conrad I (c. 881–918) was unable to establish his authority over the remaining stem duchies, and thus failed to establish his family as a new dynasty. Before his death, Conrad urged the dukes to elect his chief rival, Henry Fowler, Duke of Saxony, as his successor. Henry I (c. 876–936) was the first of the Ottonian Dynasty, sometimes referred to as the Saxon Dynasty. All efforts by Henry I and his successors to construct a strong centralized monarchy failed. Ultimately, it was their conflict with the papacy, and their inability to check the independence of their vassals, that defeated all their efforts. Henry I was succeeded by his eldest son, Otto.

Otto I the Great (912–973) led his armies into Italy in 962 to defend Pope John XII (955–964) from his rivals in the Papal States. In return for his aid, the pope crowned Otto I Emperor of the Romans. Historians recognize Otto I's coronation as the founding of the Holy Roman Empire that lasted until it was dissolved by Napoleon I in 1806.[3] Otto I deposed John XII in 963 and oversaw the election of Leo VIII as the new pope. When Leo VIII died in 965, Otto returned to Rome to see his candidate elected. He once again asserted his will over the selection of a new pope in 972. For Otto and his successors, control of the church was vital to their rule over the Holy Roman Empire.

During the history of the Holy Roman Empire, the title of Emperor was a major reason why Germany, unlike England and France, never developed into a unified nation until after the Holy Roman Empire ended. The title clearly implied a revival of the Roman Empire in the West, that is, the Christian Roman Empire of the fourth and fifth centuries. In reality it was, as the eighteenth-century French philosophe, Voltaire, quipped: "neither holy, nor Roman, nor an empire."

The pretense of being a revival of the Roman Empire meant that the emperors expended most of their energies and treasure in futile attempts to extend their rule over Italy down to, and including, Rome. That effort, one is tempted to say "addiction," brought them into a life or death struggle with the papacy. The papacy saw itself and the church as above all human institutions, a vital link between the secular realm and God. Therefore, the popes were destined to defend the independence of the church and of the Papal States. It also meant that the Holy Roman Empire must remain, like Germania, a geographic reference, a patchwork quilt of territories presided over by an emperor whose actual authority was limited to whatever the princes were willing to grant at any one point in time.

The emperors granted fiefs to churchmen in Germany. Since they had no "legitimate" heirs, when they died, the fiefs reverted back to the emperor. Thus, the emperors could use the clergy as a kind of royal administration, while also having access to the church's wealth. However, when they expected the popes to show the same subservience as their appointed bishops in Germany, they found themselves faced with a resistance that was insurmountable. The Middle Ages was an age of faith. Most people still lived in awe of God, his church, and his vicar on earth, the pope.

---

3 Charlemagne was crowned Emperor of the Romans on Christmas Day 800, but the title was not used after 924 until revived with the crowning of Otto I. Some historians prefer to mark the founding of the Holy Roman Empire with Charlemagne, but 962 is the traditional date.

The fatal flaw in the emperors' dependence upon control of the church was never more evident than in what was known as the "Investiture Controversy." When the emperor appointed a bishop, the newly appointed bishop appeared before the emperor to swear fealty to his lord, the emperor, and receive from the emperor the bishop's ring and crozier (staff), the symbols of his spiritual office. A secular lord was investing a churchman with an ecclesiastical office. This practice, called lay investiture, was a clear example of how the feudal system had impressed itself on the church, effectively making the church a captive of the secular lords.

The Gregorian reform movement that began during the middle of the eleventh century made ending the practice of lay investiture a major goal in freeing the church from secular control. If successful, the Holy Roman Emperors would be left without a power base from which to combat the nobles's efforts to prevent the emergence of a strong central monarchy. Neither emperor nor pope was able, or willing, to yield. The showdown came in a confrontation between Pope Gregory VII (r., 1073–1085) and Emperor Henry IV (1050–1106).

Gregory VII threw down the gauntlet in 1075, when he issued a decree forbidding a clergyman from being invested with a spiritual office (bishopric, abbey, or church) by a secular lord: "we decree that no one of the clergy shall receive the investiture with a bishopric or abbey or church from the hand of an emperor or king or of any lay person, male or female" (Tierney 1983, p. 143). If Henry IV respected Gregory VII's decree, he would lose his most important allies in his struggle with the nobles, and the military and financial support they provided. To Henry IV, Gregory VII was a religious fanatic meddling in the internal affairs of the Empire, not Christ's appointed vicar defending the independence and spiritual authority of the church. With the support of his appointed German bishops, Henry rejected the papal decree.

Gregory VII had at his disposal two powerful weapons he could use to bring a recalcitrant individual into submission. One was excommunication, and the other was the interdict. Excommunication denied the disobedient individual access to the sacraments, not including the sacrament of penance. If fear of damnation did not force a non-cooperative ruler such as Henry IV to submit, then an interdict could be placed on the ruler's territory. An interdict forbade certain of the sacraments and Christian burial to all believers in a given geographic area. It was meant to motivate the people to put pressure on the ruler to submit.

Pope Gregory VII excommunicated Henry, declared him deposed, and his vassals released from all oaths of allegiance to Henry. It was an open invitation to the German nobles to revolt, which they did. They called for a meeting chaired by Gregory to resolve the conflict by election of a new emperor.

While passing through northern Italy en route to Germany in January, 1077, Gregory stopped over at Canossa Castle in northern Italy. Henry went to Canossa, where he knelt in the snow asking the pope for forgiveness. After three days, Gregory forgave Henry and welcomed him back into the church. It appeared that Henry lost, since he was forced to humble himself before his arch enemy. But it was not necessarily so.

Henry knew that the pope was a priest, and as a priest, he could not refuse to forgive a penitent sinner. Once Gregory absolved Henry of his sins, which he was bound to do, the oaths of allegiance of his vassals were once more binding. The rebellious nobles felt betrayed by Gregory. Their revolt collapsed.

Three years later, in 1080, Gregory once again excommunicated Henry and tried to depose him. In response, a synod of prelates from Germany and northern Italy deposed Gregory and elected Guibert of Ravenna as Pope Clement III (r. 1080–1100).[4] Henry then invaded Italy and besieged Rome. Robert Guiscard (1015–1085), the Norman conqueror of southern Italy and Sicily and the pope's ally, drove Henry out of Rome. When Henry's army sacked Rome, Gregory was forced to flee. He died in exile in 1085.

A compromise in the Investiture Controversy was reached in 1122 between Henry V (1086–1125) and Pope Calixtus II (r. 1119–1124) known as the Concordat of Worms. According to the terms of the concordat,[5] the free election of German bishops was guaranteed, though the emperor had the right to be present at the election. The emperor invested the bishop with the symbols of his secular authority, while the pope, or his representative, invested the bishop with the symbols of his spiritual authority.

The Concordat of Worms did not end the struggle between pope and emperor. During the final phase of the struggle, Frederick I Barbarossa (1122–1190) and his grandson Frederick II (1194–1250) clashed head on with Pope Innocent III, during whose reign the papacy reached the height of its power and influence during the Middle Ages. Pope Innocent III boldly defended the supremacy of papal authority in all affairs, both ecclesiastical and secular.

Frederick I sought to restore the imperial image and make the Holy Roman Empire a strong, centralized feudal monarchy. Unfortunately, he felt it necessary to assert imperial rule over northern Italy. The northern Italian cities were wealthy, but also independent. Frederick's aims were, once again, a threat to the independence of the Papal States. The papacy joined in an alliance with the northern Italian cities called the Lombard League in 1167. When the imperial armies crossed the Alps in 1176, they suffered a devastating defeat in the Battle of Legnano. Frederick I's defeat did not end the conflict. The duel between emperor and pope continued under Frederick II, nicknamed "the Wonder of the World" (*Stupor mundi*).

Frederick II is one of the most interesting personalities in medieval history. He was an educated, and in many ways, an enlightened ruler, who spoke several languages, wrote books, composed music, and promoted the arts. At a time when most rulers were illiterate, Frederick II was said to be able to speak nine languages and read seven. His book on falconry, *The Art of Hunting with Birds*, has earned him the title "first scientific ornithologist." He is credited with contributing to the lyric quality of the Italian language by providing a refuge for individuals fleeing the Albigensian Crusade in Southern France (1209–1229) called for by Pope Innocent III.

After the death of his father in 1197 and his mother in 1198, Frederick became a ward of Innocent III. He was crowned Holy Roman Emperor in St. Peter's Church in Rome in 1220 by Pope Honorius III (r. 112–1130), who was his tutor when Innocent III was his guardian. In 1228, he led a crusade that resulted in a treaty with al-Kamil, the sultan of Egypt, without fighting a single battle (see above).

---

4 Clement III was never recognized as a legitimate pope and is, therefore, remembered as one of the antipopes.

5 A concordat is a treaty or agreement between the Roman Catholic Church and a secular government.

Frederick created a secular state based in Italy and Sicily that was incompatible with the independence of the Papal States, which were squeezed between the two as if in a vice. It was his secular outlook, that quality which tempts us to call him the first modern ruler, as much as anything, that led Pope Gregory IX to label Frederick the Antichrist.[6] Frederick was a religious skeptic, who allegedly referred to Moses, Jesus, and Muhammad as the three great frauds in history. His interest in science and education, combined with his religious skepticism, led him to found the first secular university in Europe, the University of Naples.

Frederick II's greatest failure, like that of the emperors who preceded him, was to neglect Germany while trying to build a strong centralized monarchy in Italy and Sicily. Frederick bought the support of the German nobility by granting them ever more political autonomy. Preventing the growth of strong central government became a given for both the German princes within the empire and the emerging nation states of Europe for centuries. By threatening the independence of the papacy and by fomenting conflict within the Papal States, Frederick compelled the papacy to seek alliances with France, which in turn, set in motion the long decline of papal power culminating in the Protestant Reformation two-and-a-half centuries later.

Frederick II was succeeded as Holy Roman Emperor in 1250 by his son, Conrad IV (1228–1254), who reigned for only four years. He was the last of the Hohenstaufen dynasty. Anarchy followed Conrad's death as no one was able to establish rule over Germany. In 1273, Rudolph of Hapsburg was elected emperor. He was the first of the Hapsburg dynasty that would play a key role in European history until the early twentieth century.

References

Cahill, T. (2006). *Mysteries of the Middle Ages: The Rise of Feminism, Science, and Art from the Cults of Catholic Europe*. New York: Doubleday.

Jewish Identification (2008). Jewish Badge. http://www.jewishvirtuallibrary.org/jewish-badge (accessed 21 October 2019).

Runciman, S. (1952). *A History of the Crusades. Volume III, the Kingdom of Acre and the Later Crusades*, 75. Cambridge: Cambridge University Press.

Thatcher, O.J. (1905). *A Source Book for Medieval History: Selected Documents Illustrating the History of Europe in the Middle Ages*. New York: Charles Scribner's Sons.

Tierney, B. (ed.) (1983). *The Middle Ages, Vol. I: Sources of Medieval History*, 4e. New York: Alfred A Knopf.

---

6 Medieval popes commonly referred to heretics as the Antichrist. Later, the Protestant Reformers applied the term to the popes.

6

The High Middle Ages, 1000–1300

Chronology

426	Augustine's *City of God*
524	Boethius' *Consolation of Philosophy*
874	Viking Settlements on Iceland
c. 1000	Vikings Settlements on Greenland
1077–1078	Anselm's Ontological Argument for the Existence of God
1090–1153	Bernard of Clairvaux, Defender of Orthodoxy Against Abelard
1115–1117	Abelard's Sic *et non* (*Yes and No*)
1265–1274	Thomas Aquinas' *Summa Theologiae* (*Systematic Theology*)
c. 1308–1320	Dante Alighieri Writes *The Divine Comedy*
1337–1453	Hundred Years' War Between England and France
1346	Battle of Crécy
1347–1351	Plague Ravages Europe
1353	Giovanni Boccaccio's *The Decameron*
1355	Battle of Poitiers
1358	French *Jacquerie*
1400	Geoffrey Chaucer's *The Canterbury Tales*
1415	Battle of Agincourt
1431	Martyrdom of Joan of Arc

Historians no longer refer to the Middle Ages as the Dark Ages, but the term does have merit when applied to the period between 500 and 1100. The collapse of classical civilization in the West brought with it the end of trade and commerce, the end of urban life, and the decline and near disappearance of intellectual life. The accumulated knowledge and achievements of past civilizations all but vanished. The flame grew dim, but it did not die out. Here and there, in monasteries scattered throughout Western Europe, monks labored diligently copying and preserving what manuscripts survived the barbarian conquest. Literacy did not die out entirely. Books did not disappear entirely. As the centuries passed, and political and economic order slowly reemerged, Western Europe provided the incubator for the birth of a new civilization that made possible the advances in science, economics, political theory, and philosophy that, in turn, produced modern civilization. Civilized

Western Civilization: A Brief History, First Edition. Paul R. Waibel.
© 2020 John Wiley & Sons, Inc. Published 2020 by John Wiley & Sons, Inc.

life continued in the East where both Byzantine and Islamic civilizations made advances that later filtered into and enriched the West, but it was in Europe that Western civilization emerged.

During the period of the early Middle Ages, the remnants of classical civilization and Christianity, both a part of the heritage of the Roman Empire, intermingled with Germanic influences. Classical civilization was exhausted by the end of the Roman Empire. It was not able alone to be the basis for the revival of civilization in the West. Christianity, though still in its infancy, was a new and vibrant cultural and intellectual force. The disappearance of any meaningful political unity meant that the Christian Church, with its administrative structure that extended throughout the former empire, was able to keep alive the memory of a unified civilization, and provide the integrating force for the birth of a new, Western, European civilization.

Faith and Reason

During the period of intellectual and cultural poverty, those few who were literate, primarily engaged in salvaging what they could of the classical heritage. They were committed to their Christian faith, but held a deep appreciation of the Greco-Roman classics that were available to them. Whether consciously or unconsciously, they synthesized the two traditions – Christian and classical – thereby creating a new Christian culture. In effect, they "Christianized" the classical inheritance. However, it was not without a struggle. From the time of the early Church Fathers, there was a latent hostility between knowledge obtained through human reason and knowledge from revealed truth. Tertullian (c. 155-c. 240) acknowledged the problem in his admonition:

> What indeed has Athens to do with Jerusalem? What concord is there between the Academy and the Church? what between heretics and Christians? Our instruction comes from "the porch of Solomon," who had himself taught that "the Lord should be sought in simplicity of heart." Away with all attempts to produce a mottled Christianity of Stoic, Platonic, and dialectic composition! We want no curious disputation after possessing Christ Jesus, no inquisition after enjoying the gospel! With our faith, we desire no further belief. (Tertullian 2017, p. 476)

Following the sacking of Rome by the Visigoths in 410, Saint Augustine, Bishop of Hippo (354–430) in North Africa, tried to make sense of the event in his *City of God* (*De civitate Dei*, c. 413–426), the first Christian philosophy of history. Augustine made a distinction between the earthly city of Rome (the City of Man) and the heavenly Jerusalem (the City of God). The two cities were in perpetual conflict, but the City of God was eternal. The City of Man was destined for destruction. The Christian's focus must be on the City of God, not the City of Man in which the Christian was only a temporary resident. Augustine's doctrine of the two cities implies a rejection of the defining characteristic of classical civilization, that is, that reason alone can create a just society, or put another way, education can create a virtuous person. For Augustine, faith trumps human reason, just as God's grace trumps human effort.

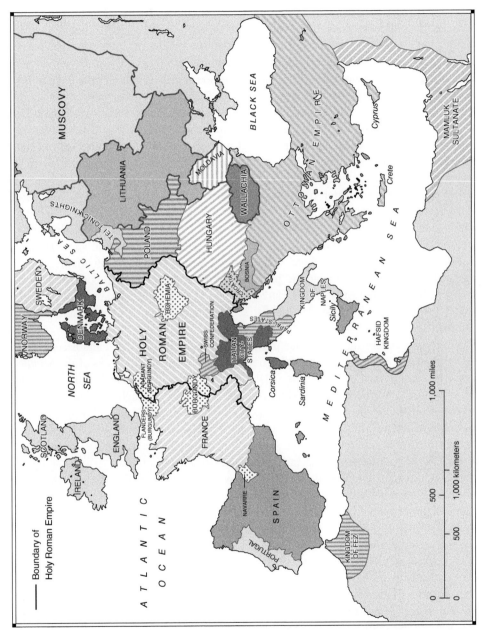

Figure 6.1 Map of Europe during the Middle Ages.

Augustine lived with the struggle between faith and reason. His father was a pagan. His mother was a devout Christian. He received an education in the classics. His reading of Cicero led to a love of Greek philosophy, especially the Neoplatonic philosophy of Plotinus (204–270). His search for an understanding of the problem of evil led to his efforts to synthesize Neoplatonism with Christianity. He remained faithful to the primacy of biblical teaching, but realized the necessity of a classical education, if Christianity was to be given a hearing within the intellectual climate of his day.

Augustine addressed the task of communicating God's truth as found in the Bible in his *On Christian Teaching* (*De doctrina christiana*). The first three volumes were published in 397, and the fourth in 426. The classical authors, said Augustine, were useful for interpreting the Bible. Therefore, one who wished to communicate biblical truth to the educated populace must be versed in the liberal arts. Knowledge of languages, history, and the sciences, combined with skill in the use of logic and eloquent speech (rhetoric) were necessary tools in the Christian apologist's toolbox.

A key figure in the transition from the late Roman to the medieval period was Anicius Manlis Severinus Boethius (c. 480–524). Boethius was born into an aristocratic, Christian family. Given a classical education, he became chief official in the court of Theodoric, the Ostrogoth king of Italy. He was the last Latin-speaking scholar in the West who mastered both the Greek language and Greek philosophy. He wrote treatises on mathematics, translated works by the Neoplatonic philosopher, Porphyry (c. 234–c. 305), and most important, he translated Aristotle's works on logic into Latin. Until the thirteenth century, virtually the only works of Aristotle known to scholars in the West were those translated by Boethius.

Boethius was caught up in a palace intrigue and imprisoned in 1523 and executed in 1524. While awaiting execution, he wrote one of the most important books of the Middle Ages. *The Consolation of Philosophy* is a dialog between Boethius and Lady Philosophy on how to reconcile human free will with an omnipotent God. Though Boethius does not mention Christianity directly, he effectively Christianizes classical philosophy. Lady Philosophy reassures him that the individual human being is not a victim of impersonal fate or living in a meaningless universe. Rather, humanity inhabits a universe imbued with meaning by the all-knowing, all-seeing presence of God.

In *The Consolation of Philosophy* and his other writings, Boethius demonstrated that reason and faith were not in conflict. Knowledge obtained from secular literature could aid in understanding the Bible. Knowledge of the holy was not beyond human reason. "As far as you are able," wrote Boethius, "join faith to reason." The troubled relationship between faith and reason continued until the twelfth and thirteenth centuries, when the scholastic scholars, most notably Thomas Aquinas (1225–1274), demonstrated that there is no ultimate conflict between faith and reason. All truth is God's truth.

The rebirth of cities contributed to a revival of knowledge. The monastic schools preserved manuscripts and kept literacy alive, but the demands of urban life led to the appearance of cathedral schools and the first universities. The cathedral schools flourished or waned depending on who occupied the bishop's chair. With the appearance of the first universities at the end of the tenth century, higher education received the freedom necessary to produce what is commonly referred to as the Twelfth Century Renaissance.

The first universities began as guilds of either students or faculty. A guild was an association of merchants or craftsmen in a given urban center. Its purpose was to assure employment, control the quality of goods or services, and guarantee profits for its members by restricting trade. The first university, the University of Bologna, was founded in 1088 by students who banded together in order to bargain collectively with both faculty and town leaders. In 1158, the Holy Roman Emperor Frederick I Barbarossa granted the university a charter considered the first recognition of the principle of academic freedom. The University of Bologna served as a model for subsequent universities, which were originally communities of students and scholars, not collections of buildings.

The different universities were known for different disciplines. For example, the University of Bologna was noted for the study of civil and canon law, Salerno for medicine, and Paris for Theology, "the queen of the sciences." The University of Paris was founded about 1150, as a corporation of students and faculty. It was chartered by Philip II Augustus in 1200, and recognized by Pope Innocent III (r. 1198–1216) in 1215. Students were studying at Oxford, England as early as 1096. A migration of professors from Oxford led to the founding of the University of Cambridge in 1209.

The core curriculum was the seven liberal arts: grammar, rhetoric, and logic (the trivium) and geometry, arithmetic, music, and astronomy (the quadrivium). Professors gave lectures, or read aloud from a Latin text, together with their comments, while the students took notes. Since books were handwritten and therefore beyond the reach of most students, it was necessary to write down as much as possible. Disputations, formal debates conducted according to strict rules, were also a part of the curriculum.

By the third quarter of the thirteenth century, virtually all of Aristotle's works were available along with commentaries by Jewish and Arab scholars. As Aristotle became more and more the dominate influence in medieval education, the breadth and scope of his writings posed serious problems for Christian scholars. Aristotle's understanding of reality came from the application of human reason, not divine revelation. The attempt to understand reality beginning with reason alone and making no appeal to supernatural or mythical explanation was, after all, the great achievement of classical Greek civilization (See Chapter 2). Did human beings inhabit a universe that was eternal and mechanistic as Aristotle taught, or a universe that was finite, created by an infinite, personal God who was sovereign over history? The apparent conflict between faith and reason demanded resolution.

The important role played by Aristotle in the faith versus reason debate is evident in the case of Berengar of Tours (c. 999–1088). Berengar was a gifted scholar and master of the Cathedral School of St. Martin at Tours in France. Berengar denied the doctrine of transubstantiation, that the bread and wine become the actual flesh and blood of Jesus Christ in the Eucharist. The "Real Presence of Christ" in the communion bread and wine was accepted by both the Roman Catholic and Orthodox churches. Berengar's view that Christ's presence in the Eucharist is spiritual, not physical, was declared heretical in 1050 by the Council of Vercelli, and again at church councils held in 1075, 1076, and 1078.

Lanfranc (1005–1089), archbishop of Canterbury and a personal friend of Berengar took up the task of refuting Berengar. Lanfranc's rebuttal is found in *On the Body and Blood of the Lord* (*De corpore et sanguine Domini*) written sometime between 1060 and 1063.

What is significant about Lanfranc's defense of orthodoxy is his extensive use of Aristotelian logic, in particular Aristotle's distinction between substance and accident. Substance is that which exists in itself. Accident is that which requires a substance within which to exist. In the statement, "Paul is a man," "Paul" is the substance and "man" is the accident.

The question of the Real Presence of Jesus Christ in the Eucharist was one aspect of the chief philosophical debate of the Middle Ages, the debate over universals. The question of universals simply put is the question of what is real. It is Plato's distinction between the real world of ideal forms that exists in the realm of ideas (reality) and the world we experience from day to day that is only a reflection of the ideal world beyond space and time, versus Aristotle's assertion that reality is in the object itself, not in a realm of ideas (See Chapter 2). To our modern mind, this problem of universals may appear to be "much ado about nothing," but it was the cornerstone of the medieval worldview.

For the medieval theologians, God was the final reference point, the universal that gave identity and meaning to all of creation. Knowledge of God came by way of revelation, that is, the Bible. But, creation could be understood by logic and reason. Was it possible then, for reason to affirm what was known from revelation? Was there a reasonable argument for the existence of God? It was the task of the scholastic theologians of the eleventh through thirteenth centuries to demonstrate through rigorous logical argument that what was known from revelation agreed with what could be discovered through reason. Their solution is called the Medieval Synthesis. The three most important scholastic theologians were Anselm of Canterbury, Peter Abelard and, most importantly, Thomas Aquinas.

Anselm (c. 1033–1109) held that reason played an important role in aiding the individual's understanding of what was already known by faith. Faith and reason are compatible, but faith is a prerequisite for understanding. Faith establishes boundaries within which reason may operate freely. Thus, reason is not autonomous, and must not be allowed to undermine faith in that which is known to be true.

Anselm's so-called "ontological argument for the existence of God" is a good illustration of both the scholastic method and scholasticism's synthesis of faith and reason. Anselm's argument can be summarized thus: "We can conceive of no being greater than God. But if God were to exist only in thought and not in actuality, his greatness would be limited; he would be less than perfect. Hence, he exists" (Perry et al. 2003, p. 245). Anslem does not begin, "If God can be proven to exist." Rather he assumes the existence of God as fact, because it is found in Holy Scripture, God's revelation. This is deductive reasoning. His goal is to demonstrate that God is knowable through both faith and reason.

Whereas Anslem said that he must believe in order to understand, Peter Abelard (1079–1142) said that he must understand in order to believe. Abelard was troubled by the fact that there were divergent opinions on fundamental Christian doctrines, and that certain biblical verses appeared to contradict other verses. In his book, *Sic et Non* (*Yes and No*) Abelard compiled a list of 158 philosophical and theological questions without comment. Then, for each question, he presented passages from the Bible, the Church Fathers, and other authorities to demonstrate that they disagreed on basic Christian dogma.

Abelard did not attempt to refute church doctrine, which he, like Anselm, accepted. "All knowledge," he said, "derives from God." He advocated using deductive reasoning to defend doctrine. However, since he demonstrated the contradictions without resolving them, he left himself open to the charge of using dialectical argument to attack and undermine faith. That was the charge brought against him by Bernard of Clairvaux (1090–1153), the eloquent defender of orthodoxy. Bernard denounced what he called the scholastics's "scandalous curiosity" that the divine mysteries could be reduced to the level of human reason. Bernard rejected Abelard's claim that all Christian dogma could be rationally explained. Abelard said that, "By doubting we are led to question, by questioning we arrive at the truth" (Shelley 1995, p. 197). Bernard countered by declaring that doubt leads to heresy.

The differences between Anselm and Abelard reflected the different positions they took on the problem of universals. The scholastic theologians divided into two schools on the question of universals, a division that originated in the different philosophies of Plato and Aristotle. The "realists" held that the individual objects are only reflections of the universal ideas in the mind of God, embedded by God in human reason. Anselm was a realist. The opposite position, originating with Aristotle, was called "nominalism." The nominalists argued that the individual objects alone are real. Ideas, or concepts, are only names. Abelard did not deny the reality of universals, but did insist that the universal idea could not be separated from the particular object.

The modern student may wonder why the medieval theologians were so passionate about the question of universals or the related question of faith and reason. A brief look at how realism and nominalism affected the dogma of the Real Presence of Jesus Christ in the Eucharist will shed some light. Realism supported the belief that the bread and wine became in reality the flesh and blood of Jesus Christ while remaining bread and wine. Nominalism, on the other hand, did not. According to the nominalist, the reality is in the object itself. Thus, the words flesh and blood are only words. The bread and wine remain bread and wine. They are symbols of Jesus Christ's flesh and blood, but only symbols.

The greatest and most prolific of the scholastic theologians was the Dominican friar, Thomas Aquinas (1225–1274). Aquinas taught at the University of Paris between 1252 and 1274. It was during that period that he wrote his two greatest works, *Summa Contra Gentiles* and *Summa Theologia*, together totaling 10 000 double-column folio pages. A *summa* is a concise summation of knowledge on a particular subject.

Aquinas addresses knowledge that can be known by application of reason in *Summa Contra Gentile*.[1] It explains the Christian faith with truths (including theological truths) that anyone can know by reason. The *Summa Theologia* (*Systematic Theology*) is an encyclopedic exposition of truths of the Christian faith that can be known, though not always understood, only through faith in God's revelation. His method is dialectic reasoning. He poses a question, suggests answers, confronts the answers with objections, refutes the objections, and draws conclusions.

Aquinas distinguished between natural truth, that which can be known by reason, and revealed truth, that which can be known only by faith. Since all truth comes from God, there can be no conflict between the two. Revealed truth may not be understood, but it remains true. Natural truth, if it contradicts revealed truth, is in error. For example,

---

1 The English translation of the titles varies. *Of God and His Creatures* and *On the Truth of the Catholic Faith* are two examples.

Aristotle argued that the world was eternal, a belief that contradicts the Biblical teaching that the world, being created, is finite. Only God is eternal. Therefore Aristotle erred, but Aristotle did not have the benefit of revelation. That was the problem the scholastics were trying to resolve. The solution to the relationship between faith and reason was to subordinate reason to faith. The role of revelation was to establish limits within which reason can operate. Reason can be used to understand faith, but it exceeds its competency when it is used to validate revelation.

Not everyone accepted Aquinas' teaching. Twenty of his propositions were included in a condemnation of 219 propositions that were said to violate the omnipotence of God issued by the Bishop of Paris in 1277. By the time of the Council of Trent (1545–1563), Aquinas' teachings were widely accepted. The *Summa Theologia* was placed on the high altar next to the Bible and the papal decrees. His theology guided the Council as it sought to define Roman Catholic dogma under attack by the Protestant Reformation. In 1879, Pope Leo XIII (1878–1903) declared Thomas Aquinas' theology the clearest exposition of true Catholic doctrine. He further directed that: "teachers ... do their best to instill the doctrine of Thomas Aquinas into the minds of their hearers; and let them clearly point out its solidity and excellence above all other teaching" (Summa 2018).

Medieval Synthesis

Setting aside the question of material comfort, there was no better time in which to live than the Middle Ages. Those things that disturb modern individuals most – finding meaning and purpose in everyday life – were non-existent for most people living during the Middle Ages. Everyone knew, or could know, the meaning and purpose of life in the here and now, and one's ultimate destiny once life here on earth came to an end. Thanks to Thomas Aquinas and the scholastic theologians who removed the apparent contradictions between revealed truth and classical philosophy, the medieval world was blessed with a systematic worldview that answered life's most pressing questions and was easy to understand.

The medieval worldview was based on the acceptance of authority, that is to say, it was based on known truths that came from two sources, the Bible and classical philosophy. If one wished to know whether the solar system was geocentric or heliocentric, one need only consult either Aristotle or the Bible. Any confusion was easily resolved by referring the question to the church. In the Age of Faith, "Christianity was the matrix of medieval life."

> [E]ven cooking instructions called for boiling an egg "during the length of time wherein you say a Miserere" [One of the Penitential Psalms, e.g., Psalm 51]. It governed birth, marriage, and death, sex, and eating, made the rules for law and medicine, gave philosophy and scholarship their subject matter. Membership in the Church was not a matter of choice; it was compulsory and without an alternative, which gave it a hold not easy to dislodge. (Tuchman 1978, p. 32)

Because Christianity was at the core of the medieval worldview, all created things, including time (history) itself, were pregnant with meaning and purpose. The belief that one lived in an orderly universe was everywhere evident. It did not violate common sense and was emotionally pleasing. One could also say that the medieval view of the universe was scientific, given the fact that reason and observation were really the only instruments available to the individual.

According to medieval Christian teaching, God's creation was orderly and hierarchical. The cosmos was made up of two realms, or regions, that were different in composition and governed by different laws. This distinction originated with Aristotle. The dividing line was the moon. The region below the moon was the terrestrial (material) realm composed of the four basic elements (see below). It was a realm in which things changed. Living things, for example, were born, grew old or became sickly, and died. Above the moon was the celestial realm of unchanging perfection. Once Aristotle was brought into conformity with church dogma, the two realms became an earthly realm and a realm of grace, or a higher region of perfection and a lower region of imperfection.

The medieval model of the solar system was based on that of Claudius Ptolemy (100–168), a Greek mathematician and astronomer who lived in Alexandria, Egypt during the second century. Ptolemy included the geocentric (earth-centered) model in a mathematical treatise written around 150. It was translated into Arabic in about 827, when it was given the title *Almagest*. It was translated into Latin and found its way into Europe during the last half of the twelfth century. How the Ptolemaic model became the model of the solar system during the Middle Ages is a good example of how much of the classical inheritance came to Europe by way of the Muslim world.

Medieval Model of the Universe

According to Ptolemy's geocentric model of the solar system, the earth sits motionless at the center. It is surrounded by seven concentric crystal spheres, each of which has embedded in it one of the seven planets. The first is the moon, then Mercury, Venus, the Sun, Mars, Jupiter, and Saturn. The spheres are transparent, solid, and move at uniform speeds around the earth. The seven spheres are enclosed by an eighth sphere in which the fixed stars are embedded.

The medieval version of Ptolemy's model added three additional heavenly spheres. The first is the Crystalline Heaven. The second is called the Prime Mover. It is the sphere through which God transmits motion to the seven planetary spheres. The third is the Empyrean Heaven, the abode of God and the angels. It was commonly referred to as Paradise, where the redeemed dwelled in God's presence.

The order of the solar system bore evidence that all of creation was organized in a hierarchy from the lowest to the highest. The earth, being the abode of fallen humanity, was at the center of the solar system as far removed from God's presence as possible. Hell, the abode of the devil and place of eternal punishment for those who rejected God's grace, was located in the center of the earth.

There was a distinction made between the earthly realm, a lower world of imperfection, and the realm of grace, a higher world of perfection. Different sets of laws governed the earth and the heavens. Gravity, for example, operated in the earthly realm but not in the heavenly realm. Once again, the two realms mirrored Aristotle's distinction between that which existed below the moon and that which existed above the moon.

God created rocks that occupied space, plants that occupied space and were alive. Animals came next with existence, life, and motion. Human beings were created in God's image. They were capable of reasoning and grasping some part of God's universal truth. After human beings came the angels. At the top of this great chain of being was God, eternal, personal, and creator of all that existed. Knowledge of God and his revelation passed down through the great chain of being from God to the prophets and the apostles and then to the masses.

God created Adam and Eve, the first two human beings from whom all humanity is descended. They were created perfect and given free will to either obey or disobey God. When they disobeyed, they suffered a fall from grace. As a result, human nature became flawed, no longer perfectly good. Humans could, by God's grace, overcome the effects of the Fall, as the event is commonly called. God, himself, entered into history as Jesus Christ, who suffered and died to reverse the effects of the Fall. This revelation, known as the gospel, was entrusted to the Church, through which God's redeeming grace passed to the individual. Apart from God's grace, human beings were helpless.

Medieval people understood the existence of evil to be a moral problem, not an environmental problem. All of humanity since Adam and Eve is in rebellion against God. Altering the environment, as the eighteenth-century Enlightenment would later propose, would not solve the problem. Education cannot produce a morally good person.

Figure 6.2 Dante Alighieri, author of the Divine Comedy, perhaps the greatest literary work of the Middle Ages. *Source:* From the New York Public Library.

From the Greeks, by way of Aristotle, came the belief that everything on earth was composed of four basic elements – earth, air, fire, and water. There were four corresponding qualities. Earth was cold and dry; air was hot and wet; fire was hot and dry; and water was cold and wet. The practice of medicine consisted of balancing the four elements. A fever, for example, meant too much fire. Diarrhea was indicative of too much water. There were also four "humors" – blood, yellow bile, black bile, and phlegm. Corresponding to the four humors were the four temperaments – sanguine, choleric, melancholic, and phlegmatic. Whichever of the four humors was dominant determined the individual's personality.

This medieval worldview that we call the Medieval Synthesis (or premodernity) provided those living in the Age of Faith with answers to the perennial questions of meaning and purpose for both history and the individual. This vision of reality as a spiritual hierarchy can be seen in Dante Alighieri's poetic masterpiece, *The Divine Comedy*, in the architecture of the gothic cathedral, and in Thomas Aquinas' *Summa Theologia*.

Medieval Art and Literature

The creative works of the thirteenth and fourteenth centuries were in no way inferior to those of the classical period. The architecture of the gothic cathedrals with their beautiful stained glass windows, pointed arches, and flying buttresses are just as impressive as the Parthenon in Athens or the Coliseum in Rome. Dante's *Divine Comedy* is as great a piece of literature as either Homer's *Iliad* and *Odyssey* or Virgil's *Aeneid*.

Much of medieval sculpture and painting was in the service of religion. It was after all the Age of Faith. The gothic cathedrals were adorned with statues. There are more than 2000 statues in the porches of Chartres Cathedral in France. Though the influence of ancient Greek sculpture is clearly evident, for example, in the drapery of the figures, it is not a slavish imitation. The figures are not all of saints, Bible characters, angels, and demons, or even religious in subject. There are realistic figures of people and animals, both real and mythical. And one must not neglect to take note of those fanciful, frightening, and even terrifying gargoyles that are both functional and artistic.

Medieval paintings often had a didactic function. In the absence of printed books, paintings were used to educate the illiterate masses in basic biblical stories and church doctrines, much like the stained glass windows in the cathedrals. Most medieval artists painted directly on the stone or wood walls, rather than on canvas. For that reason, much has been lost to forces of climate and fire.

Music was one area in which medieval Europe surpassed the classical world. Musicians in Western Europe during the eleventh century developed the system of musical notation still in use. No longer was it necessary to memorize a piece of music. Musical notation made it possible to produce rich polyphonic music. Secular music was free from the constraints imposed by church tradition and thus able to pursue its own direction. The troubadours (*trouvères* in northern France; *minnesingers* in Germany) developed melodies that would seem modern by those who enjoy the modern folk music of the latter twentieth century.

Latin was the *lingua franca* of the Middle Ages just as Koiné Greek was for the Hellenistic world. It was the official language of the church. It was used in diplomacy, education, literature, poetry, and the humorously vulgar and satirical ballads sung by the goliards[2] in courts and taverns. Medieval Latin was not the same as the Latin of Cicero, Virgil, or Julius Caesar. It was richer in vocabulary and more informal than classical Latin. It would take the slavish imitation of Cicero by the Renaissance to render Medieval Latin a "dead" language.

The increase in the literate population outside the monasteries and churches created a demand for vernacular literature that drew from European legends and myths rather than traditional classical or Christian themes. Epic poems like the *Song of Roland* and the German *Niebelung* stories were written in the vernacular for a male aristocratic audience. These *chansons de geste*, as they were called, emphasized chivalric ideals. Romantic tales of King Arthur and the Knights of the Round Table, Tristan and Isolde, and the Quest for the Holy Grail appealed to both men and women.

Late Middle Ages, 1300–1500

Europe experienced economic prosperity and steady population growth between 1100 and 1300. Estimates of Europe's population in 1300 vary widely from as few as 70 million to as many as 100 million. The actual figure no doubt lies somewhere in between. Most sources put the total population somewhere around 80 million. What can be said with confidence is that Europe was over populated in 1300, when a series of crises struck causing the population to plummet to about 50 million. The three major crises were famine, plague, and war.

Famine

With roughly 743 million people in Europe today, it is hard to imagine how the continent could be over populated with only 80 or so million. The lack of technology, coupled with a scarcity of land for cultivation, meant that only a limited amount of food could be produced. Competition for available farm land intensified. Parents divided farms among surviving children. As the size of farms decreased, landlords increased rents.

A change in climate beginning in the early fourteenth century brought to an end what is referred to as the Medieval Warm Period (900–1300). Temperatures in Europe were the mildest in over 8000 years during the Medieval Warm Period. New, often marginal lands were brought under cultivation. The food supply increased, and with it the population.

The Vikings took advantage of the warmer weather to establish colonies in Iceland (874) and Greenland (c. 1000). The Greenland settlers were farmers who raised cattle, sheep, and goats. A lively trade existed between the Greenland settlements and Europe by way of Iceland and Norway until the climate changed with the onset of what is called the Little Ice Age (c. 1300–c. 2000).

There was a precarious balance between the food supply and the population at the beginning of the fourteenth century. The climate began to change just when any shortfall in crop production would have a devastating impact. Summers were cooler, wetter, and shorter.

---

2 Young clergy who wrote satirical Latin poetry.

Early frosts were followed by colder and longer winters. Hunger became common, especially among the laboring classes in the countryside.

Heavy and persistent rains, together with unusually cool temperatures during the spring and summer of 1315, and again in 1316, set the stage for the Great Famine of 1315 to 1322. Wet, muddy fields were near impossible to plow. Seeds rotted before they germinated. What crops were harvested were much smaller than earlier. Grain reserves vanished. There was not enough fodder to feed the livestock. After eating the seed grain and slaughtering the draft animals for food, people began to scavenge in the woods for anything edible. In some areas, there were reports of infants and small children being abandoned and starving people resorting to cannibalism. The Great Famine left a population weakened and susceptible to disease and vulnerable to the effects the pandemic of plague and the Hundred Years' War that lay just over a decade in the future.

Plague

The population of Europe was weakened and still traumatized by the effects of the famine when the plague struck in the summer of 1347. Like ripples in the water after a stone has been tossed into a pond, the plague spread across Europe over the next three years. It followed the complex maze of trade routes until all of Europe was infected. Some isolated pockets off the trade routes were bypassed. Towns and cities, with their crowded and unsanitary conditions, were the hardest hit. By the time the plague ran its course in 1351, anywhere from 30% to 60% of Europe's population perished.

The traditional account of the plague identifies it as bubonic plague, or Black Death, caused by the bacterium *Yersinia pestis*. It was thought that the plague originated in Mongolia. The traditional trade routes through Central Asia known as the Silk Road were cut off by the Mongolian conquest known as the Golden Horde (mid-thirteenth century to the end of the fourteenth century). For that reason, the plague did not move eastward across Russia into Europe.

In the autumn of 1346, the Mongols attacked the Crimean port of Caffa (modern Feodosia) on the Black Sea. The plague broke out among the Mongols and spread to the city. Italian merchant ships carried it from there to Constantinople, Alexandria, and the Mediterranean Sea ports. In October, 1347, Genoese ships docked in the port of Messenia on the island of Sicily. Among the goods aboard ship were rats infected with the plague. The rats aboard ship were black rats, also known as "house rats" or "ship rats," who liked to live close to people, not the gray rats who prefer living in sewers. The rats went ashore, taking with them a host of fleas.

Personal hygiene in the fourteenth century was such that people carried on their person a variety of vermin such as lice and fleas. It was considered bad manners for a gentleman to crush vermin that crawled out from his sleeve while in the presence of a lady. People were accustomed to being bitten by vermin. What was another bite, unless it was the bite of an infected flea? The plague passed from person to person. Not only were rats and people infected, but also sheep, cows, goats, pigs, and chickens.

Recent research has raised many questions concerning the traditional account. If the plague was spread by fleas on black rats, there should be skeletal evidence of large numbers of dead rats, as there are of humans, but there are not. DNA studies done in France in 2010 and 2011 indicate that pathogens responsible for the *Yersinia pestis* caused other forms of plague in addition to the bubonic plague. Other avenues of research have suggested that there were a variety of infectious diseases active at the same time, including smallpox, typhus, various respiratory infections, and even a hemorrhagic epidemic like Ebola.

The plague returned in 1361–1363, 1374–1375, 1390, and 1400. The first outbreak was the most devastating. It is not surprising that the loss of so many people in such a short period had a profound impact in every area of life. Without any knowledge of how disease spreads, all sorts of theories were put forth. Some attributed it to divine punishment. From the University of Paris came the suggestion that a conjunction of Jupiter, Mars, and Saturn caused dense clouds of infected air to form. This so-called miasmatic theory taught that diseases were caused by foul-smelling air containing small particles of decaying organic matter. Avoiding sex, exercise, and baths were believed to help prevent bad air from entering the body through the pores.

The reaction of the people to the suffering caused by famine and plague varied. Some fled to the countryside in hopes of escaping. An example is found in the *Decameron*, written in the vernacular by Giovanni Boccaccio (1313–1375). It tells the story of seven individuals who fled from Florence to a country villa to escape the plague in 1348. In order to while away the time, they tell each other stories of various sorts. Others resorted to a riotous lifestyle in a sort of "live and make merry for tomorrow we die" attitude. Some chose to mock death by publicly performing what was called the "Dance of Death" (*Danse Macabre*). Still others joined bands of flagellants who went from place to place flogging themselves and each other. They thought that through mortifying their flesh they could atone for the sins of the world and thereby obtain God's mercy.

Some accused the Jews of poisoning the water supplies, leading to the massacre of Jews in various areas. Efforts by the church to protect the Jews failed. Pope Clement VI (r. 1342–1352) pointed out that the Jews were dying from the plague as well as the Christians. Would the Jews poison themselves? Also, the plague was killing many Englishmen, though there weren't any Jews in England since Edward I expelled them in 1290.

The sudden drop in population caused a shortage of labor in both the countryside and in the towns and cities. In an era when nine-tenths of the population earned their living in agriculture, the rural economy was hardest hit. The shortage of labor meant that the peasants were able to demand higher wages. Those bound to the land were able to become renters. The lords's income from such traditional monopolies as mills and ovens that serfs were required to use decreased substantially. Inflation was added to the mix of economic woes caused by an increase in the per-capita supply of gold and silver.

Taken together, the economic impact not only threatened the lifestyle of the nobility, but what they believed to be part of a divinely ordained social hierarchy. A part of their response came in the form of laws passed in England, Spain, Portugal, and parts of Germany aimed at forcing the peasants to work for fixed wages. In England, for example, Parliament passed the Ordinance of Laborers in 1349 and the Statute of Laborers in 1351 aimed at forcing a return to wage rates prevailing in 1346.

At various times and in various places, the peasants rose up in defense of their traditional rights. They defended their actions by arguing that if all people are the children of Adam and Eve, then all were equal and entitled to justice. To the landlords, the peasants who revolted were simply sinners. Their response was swift and brutal. Suppression of the peasant revolt known as the *Jacquerie* in northern France during the summer of 1358, resulted in the death of an estimated 20 000 peasants. Evidence that the peasant revolts were seen by the nobility as a threat to the established order of society can be seen in the fact that the French and English nobility engaged in the Hundred Years' War at the time suspended their fighting in order to join forces to put down the *Jacquerie*.

A similar course of events played out in the urban centers. Towns and cities were unhealthy even in the best of times. The death rate was always higher than the birth rate. The only way cities grew was by adding new residents from outside. The crowded conditions made them even more vulnerable to outbreaks of the plague. Available records provide some idea of the deaths from the plague.

> In Avignon, 400 people died daily over a period of three months (36 000 out of a population of 50 000). A single graveyard received more than 11 000 corpses in six weeks. In a three month period in 1349, 800 people died daily in Paris, 500 daily in Pisa, and 600 daily in Vienna. In Frankfurt 2000 people died over a period of ten weeks in 1349 and in that same period 12 000 lost their lives in Erfurt. (Kreis 2004)

Workers tried to benefit from the demand for labor, while merchants and craftsmen tried to protect their privileged positions. The guilds became more restrictive, making it very difficult for a journeyman to become a master craftsman and open his own shop.

Unrest occurred in some urban centers where the ruling oligarchies, often the guilds, tried to prevent the workers from benefitting from the labor shortage. One of the better known was the revolt of the *ciompi* (wool carders) in Florence in 1378. It was a revolt of artisans, laborers, and craftsmen who were not members of the guilds. Other urban revolts took place in Ghent, Paris, and elsewhere. Like the peasant revolts, the urban revolts were brutally crushed. What gains were made were short lived as the old social and economic order was restored.

Hundred Years' War, 1337–1453

Suffering caused by the plague was made all the worse by the Hundred Years' War between England and France. The Hundred Years' War was actually a series of wars between England and France fought over a period of 116 years, a period that witnessed the transition from the Middle Ages to the early modern period. It was the era during which the new nation-states began to displace the old feudal monarchies. A sense of national identity arose among the French and English, which in a little over two centuries, during the French Revolution (1789–1799), would emerge as modern nationalism. These changes, and more, resulted in part from new weapons and ways of conducting warfare.

All wars are preceded by a series of events collectively referred to as the causes of the war. And then there is that one event labeled the immediate cause, which serves as the excuse for war. In the case of the Hundred Years' War, there were several long-term causes. First, there was the fact that England ruled over a significant portion of France ever since William, Duke of Normandy, invaded and conquered England in 1066. The French kings slowly whittled away at England's holdings until, on the eve of the war, only two provinces, Gascony and Guienne (Guyenne), remained. A second cause was the lucrative English wool trade with Flanders, a part of France. The wool trade was a vital part of England's economy, but the significance of the wool trade as a cause of the war is more the product of historical hindsight than contemporary reality.

A third cause of the war was Edward III's claim to the French crown. When Charles IV (1294–1328), last of the Capetian dynasty, died without a male heir, Edward III appeared to be the next in line for the French crown. Edward's claim was based on his mother being the daughter of Philip IV. French Salic law did not allow for a woman to inherit property. Thus, she could not serve as the conduit through which Edward could claim the throne of France. The crown passed to Philip of Valois, the nearest male relative of Charles IV. Philip was crowned Philip VI (1293–1350), the first of the Valois dynasty.

Tensions between Edward III and Philip VI reached a climax in May 1337, when Philip declared Edward in breach of his feudal contract. Philip declared Aquitaine forfeit and

Figure 6.3 Statue of Joan of Arc by Emmanual Fremiet in Paris. *Source:* Library of Congress Prints and Photographs Division.

began an invasion of Guienne. Edward responded by laying claim to the French crown and sending an expeditionary force to France. What awareness most people today have of the Hundred Years' War is largely limited to the heroic stories surrounding the role of Joan of Arc (*Jeanne d'Arc*), "The Maid of Orléans." Joan was a mere teenage girl, the illiterate daughter of a tenant farmer, when she appeared before *Dauphin* Charles (Charles VII, 1403–1461) claiming that God had spoken to her and told her that she was to lead the French armies to victory over the English.

The French armies were in desperate straits when Joan appeared from out of nowhere. They had suffered repeated defeats. The soldiers, the court, and the people of France were demoralized. Charles, perhaps feeling there was nothing to lose, allowed her to accompany the army in an attempt to relieve the city of Orléans, then under siege. Joan of Arc did not command the army. But the mere presence of this young maiden wearing a borrowed suit of armor, sitting on a borrowed horse, with a borrowed sword, and a borrowed banner, inspired the French army and turned almost certain defeat into victory.

The victory before Orlèans in 1429 was followed by others. To the French, Joan of Arc was a sign that God was on the side of France. To the English, she was bewitched, a servant of the devil. On May 23, 1430, Joan was captured by Burgundian allies of the English. The Burgundians turned her over to the English for a significant sum. She was subsequently tried and convicted of witchcraft and heresy. The charge that doomed her was of cross-dressing. She was burned at the stake in Rouen on May 30, 1430. Her ashes were gathered and thrown into the Seine River. Pope Callixtus III (r. 1455–1458) authorized a retrial in 1455. The following year, the appellate court ruled that Joan of Arc was innocent and died a martyr. She was officially recognized as a saint by the Roman Catholic Church in 1920, concluding a canonization process begun in 1869.

Three battles during the Hundred Years' War changed the art of warfare. The introduction of a new battle tactic or a new weapon could quickly alter the course of history. The use of the longbow by the English at the battles of Crécy (1346), Poitiers (1355), and Agincourt (1415) proved that the armored mounted knight and the foot soldier equipped with a crossbow were henceforth obsolete. Clouds of arrows, fired off by English archers armed with longbows, darkened the sky over the heads of the charging French cavalry. The shower of arrows decimated the ranks of French knights before they could reach the English soldiers. The longbow had a range of up to 250 yards and could penetrate two layers of chain-mail armor. The long bowman could shoot at least five arrows to every one shot by a soldier armed with the cumbersome crossbow.

At Crécy, the much larger French cavalry and infantry charged the English force of 8000 men, including archers. Fifteen times they charged and each time they were cut down by the hail of arrows fired by the English long bowmen. The French losses were enormous, including 1500 knights. The French knights chose to fight on foot at Poitiers. Encased in armor they advanced slowly, only to be slaughtered by the English archers. About 2000 French prisoners were taken, including the king of France. The French blunder was repeated at Agincourt. Dismounted French knights in plate armor walked across a muddy field to engage a small English army of mostly archers. When the battle ended, the French lost 5000 and had another 1000 taken prisoner. The English suffered only 500 casualties.

Edward III used cannons when he captured the port city of Calais following the battle of Crécy. The cannons were of limited value, however. They fired only small stones or metal objects. As a siege weapon used against castles or city walls, they proved very effective as they were improved over time. The early cannons were not useful in defending castles and towns, since the cannon's recoil shook the stone walls, causing them to collapse. Hand guns made an appearance during the Hundred Years' War, but did not have a major influence until the sixteenth century. What can be seen with the benefit of hindsight is that by the middle of the fifteenth century, individual valor and the role of armored mounted knights were becoming obsolete.

The end of feudal warfare had a profound impact. As infantry grew in importance and cavalry declined, professional armies, often private companies of mercenaries available for hire, became common. Charles VII created the first standing army in Western Europe since the Roman Empire. It was funded by a permanent tax called the *taille*, granted by the Estates General. The role of the nobility declined and the role of the middle and lower classes increased. Just as in classical Greece following the Persian Wars, when the role of the navy powered by oarsmen from the lower classes lessened the role of the hoplite warriors from the upper classes, the rise in importance of the infantry lessened the role of the knight on horseback, and with him, the aristocratic class from which he came. That, together with the cannons to knock down the castle walls of recalcitrant nobles, aided the emergence of strong central governments. When the growing sense of national identity was added to the mix, the result was the rise of the nation-state.

References

Encyclical by Leo XIII (2018). Codex Hammurabi (King Translation) - Wikisource, the Free Online Library. https://en.wikisource.org/wiki/Summa_Theologiae/Encyclical_of_Leo_XIII (accessed 21 October 2019).

Kreis, S. (2004). Satan Triumphant: The Black Death. The History Guide. http://www.historyguide.org/ancient/lecture29b.html (accessed 21 October 2019).

Perry, M., Baker, J.W., and Hollinger, P.P. (2003). *The Humanities in the Western Tradition: Ideas and Aesthetics, Vol. I: Ancient to Medieval*. Boston, NY: Houghton Mifflin Company.

Shelley, B.L. (1995). *Church History in Plain Language*. Nashville, TN: Thomas Nelson Publishers.

Tertullian, Q.S.F. (2017). *The Writings of Tertullian - Volume II*. Ontario: Devoted Publishing.

Tuchman, B.W. (1978). *A distant mirror*. London: Macmillan.

Part III

Birth of Modern Europe: An Overview

The fourteenth through the eighteenth centuries was the period during which Western Civilization established its distinctive identity among the world's civilizations. The Renaissance that began in the fourteenth century, and lasted until the end of the sixteenth century, shifted the focus of understanding from God and his revelation to the individual human being's ability to discover how God's universe worked. The Scientific Revolution of the mid-sixteenth century through the end of the eighteenth century, though still acknowledging God as the creator and sustainer of the universe, discovered that the universe was a kind of cosmic machine that operated according to cause and effect natural laws.

The religious unity of the Middle Ages was shattered by the Protestant Reformation that began in 1517 and lasted until the last half of the seventeenth century. Like the Scientific Revolution, the Reformation shifted, for some, the authority from the church's interpretation of God's revelation in Scripture to the individual's understanding of God's revelation in Scripture, the final authority in all matters of faith and practice.

The Protestant Reformation and what is often called the Catholic Counter Reformation encouraged an outburst of creativity in intellectual and cultural life in the West. The paintings and sculptures of the Northern Renaissance reflected the new Protestant influence, just as the artworks of the Southern Renaissance reflected its humanistic emphasis, and the Baroque style of the seventeenth century reflected the grandeur of the renewed Roman Catholic Church.

The eighteenth-century intellectuals were impressed with the new natural law model of the universe and the new scientific method of inquiry that revealed it. They believed that similar natural laws governing human relations could be discovered. With that knowledge, human institutions could be altered so as to liberate the natural goodness of humankind as originally created by God. Evil existed as an environmental problem, not a moral problem as Christians believed. Utopia on earth was within reach of human beings empowered by reason. The Enlightenment began the secularization of Western thought and society that continued through the nineteenth century.

Western Civilization: A Brief History, First Edition. Paul R. Waibel.
© 2020 John Wiley & Sons, Inc. Published 2020 by John Wiley & Sons, Inc.

7

The Renaissance and Reformation

Chronology

1371	Brethren of the Common Life Founded by Geert Groote
1378–1417	Great Schism of the Western Church
1415	Council of Constance Declares John Wycliffe a Heretic
1415	Martyrdom of Jan Hus by Council of Constance
1427–1444	Leonardo Bruni Translates Works of Plato
c. 1440	Lorenzo Valla's *The false Donation of Constantine*
1462	Marsilio Ficino Becomes Head of Platonic Academy in Florence
1496	Pico della Mirandola's *Oration on the Dignity of Man*
1501–1504	Michelangelo's *David*
1513	Niccolò Machiavelli's *The Prince*
1513	Giovanni dé Medici Elected Pope Leo X
1516	Erasmus' New Greek Translation of the New Testament
1516	Thomas More's *Utopia*
1517	Leonardo da Vinci's *Mona Lisa*
1517	Martin's Luther's *Ninety-Five Theses*
1528	Baldassare Castiglione's *The Book of the Courtier*
1534	English Parliament Passes Act of Supremacy
1534	Society of Jesus (Jesuits) Founded by Ignatius Loyola
1536	John Calvin's *Institutes of the Christian Religion*
1545–1563	Council of Trent
1549	Thomas Cranmer's *Book of Common Prayer*
1559	Pope Paul IV Issues *Index of Prohibited Books*
1563	English Parliament Passes Thirty-nine Articles

Renaissance Italy

During the fourteenth and fifteenth centuries the struggle between the papacy and the Holy Roman emperors continued, even as the power of both declined. Europe north of the Alps was preoccupied with the Hundred Years' War between France and England and

Western Civilization: A Brief History, First Edition. Paul R. Waibel.
© 2020 John Wiley & Sons, Inc. Published 2020 by John Wiley & Sons, Inc.

the struggle within the Holy Roman Empire over the imperial crown. Northern and central Italy was nominally a part of the Empire. However, in the absence of actual imperial control over the area, the Italian peninsula became a world of its own, a kind of miniature Europe. The prosperous, trade-rich Italian cities developed into powerful independent city-states.

The political map of Italy during the Renaissance, roughly 1350 to 1600, resembled that of ancient Greece. The northern Italian city-states began as urban communes with republican constitutions. Conflicts between the two centers of power, the nobles whose wealth was based in land and the merchants whose wealth was based in commerce, encouraged the rise of despots. The inability of the republican governments to deal with the stresses caused by the spread of the plague in the middle of the fourteenth century, and the increasing dependence of the city-states on mercenary soldiers (*condottieri*) for defense were contributing factors in the shift to despotism.

By the mid-fifteenth century, there were five major powers within Italy: Venice, Florence, Milan, the Papal States, and the Kingdom of Naples. Both Venice and Florence were republics, though Florence was a republic in name only. Less than 4000 out of an estimated population of 100 000 were able to vote. Beginning in the 1430s, Florence was controlled from behind the scenes by the powerful Medici banking family. Cosimo dé Medici (1389–1464) ruled Florence much like a modern political boss. Pope Pius II (1458–1464) described Cosimo's role: "Political questions are settled in [Cosimo's] house. The man he chooses holds office ... He it is who decides peace and war ... He is king in all but name" (Byfield 2010, p. 217). Cosimo's grandson, Lorenzo the Magnificent (1449–1492), ruled Florence more openly from 1480 until his death in 1492.

The Republic of Venice was the only one to remain a republic throughout the Renaissance. Venice was an aristocratic republic in which participation in decision making was limited to a few thousand of the wealthiest males. It was one of the best governed states in Europe during the fifteenth century. At the peak of its power, it was the greatest naval and trading power in the Mediterranean. In 1410, Venice had a naval force of 3300 ships, manned by an estimated 36 000 men, mostly disposable galley slaves. Its trading vessels sailed as far as Iceland.

Venice's foreign policy was determined by its need to control trade through the Mediterranean Sea and its dependence upon imports of food and raw materials. It diverted the Fourth Crusade (1204) from its original mission to capturing Constantinople, its chief trade rival. In 1380, Venice defeated the Republic of Genoa in the War of Chioggia, eliminating Genoa as a trading rival in the Adriatic Sea. The war, basically a naval war, saw the first use of seaborne cannons.

Milan was strategically located to control the trade routes between the Italian peninsula and Europe north of the Alps. Milan became a duchy in 1395, when Gian Galeazzo Visconti (1351–1402) purchased the title of hereditary duke from the Holy Roman Emperor Wenceslas (1361–1419). The Visconti family ruled the Duchy of Milan until 1447. Following the death of Filippo Maria in 1447, the last of the Visconti dukes, the Milanese attempted to reestablish a republic that lasted for only three years.

In February, 1450, Francesco Sforza (1401–1466), a *condottieri* (mercenary soldier) employed by Filippo Maria, who was also Francesco's father-in-law, was chosen by the city senate to be the Duke of Milan. Under his son, Ludovico Maria Sforza (1452–1508), called "Il Moro" because of his dark complexion, Milan flourished as a center of Italian

Figure 7.1 The Doge's Palace, established in 1340, was the residence of the Doge, or Duke, the chief magistrate and leader of the Republic of Venice. *Source:* Courtesy of Bruce Erik Bezaire.

Renaissance art and culture. He lavished patronage on artists, poets, and musicians, including the architect Donato Bramante (1444–1514) and Leonardo da Vinci (1452–1519), the foremost polymath of the Renaissance.

The Papal States were in turmoil during most of the Renaissance period. Between 1305 and 1378, the papacy was located at Avignon, a papal enclave in south-eastern France, in effect, a captive of the French monarchy. None of the Avignon popes are remembered for their piety. Rather, they are remembered for their innovative ways of raising money to support their lavish lifestyle. When what was known as the Babylonian Captivity ended in 1378, the return of the papacy to Rome resulted in the Great Schism of the Western Church, 1378–1417, when there was one pope in Rome and another in Avignon.

The scandal of two popes, at one point three, together with the worldliness of the Renaissance popes, greatly undermined the spiritual power of the church. The scandal of two popes created a serious spiritual problem for the laity. The individual Christian was taught to believe that the church dispensed salvation through the sacraments. But what if the parish priest, from whom the individual received the sacraments, was ordained by a false pope? The link going back to St. Peter was broken. The individual's soul was in danger of eternal damnation, and there was nothing he or she could do about it.

The schism divided Europe along political lines. France and her allies sided with the popes in Avignon. England, at war with France, naturally recognized the popes in Rome. Italy, the Holy Roman Empire, Scandinavia, and Hungary joined with England. The schism

Figure 7.2 Map of Renaissance Italy.

finally ended with the Council of Constance (1414–1418). Because it was a church council that ended the schism, a new issue arose. Did a general council of the church have a greater authority than the pope? Was the Roman Catholic Church in danger of becoming a constitutional monarchy? The answer came in the form of a papal bull, *Execrabilis*, issued by Pope Pius II (r. 1458–1464), in which he condemned any future appeals to a general council. The papal bull brought to an end the so-called Conciliar Movement. Henceforth, any reform of the church had to be initiated by the pope.

The Kingdom of Naples was the only monarchy among the Italian city-states. It was a feudal kingdom occupied by mostly poverty-stricken peasants, ruled over by feudal barons with very little interest in culture. When King Ferdinand I (1423–1494) died in 1494, Charles VIII (1470–1498) of France invaded Italy with an army of about 30 000 soldiers and 70 large bronze cannons. His excuse was a rather tenuous claim to the throne of Naples through his paternal grandmother, Marie of Anjou (1404–1464).

The small mercenary armies employed by the Italian city-states were no match for Charles VIII's professional army. His army advanced down the Italian peninsula as if on parade. Charles's rapid conquest provoked Spain's intervention. What followed was the so-called Italian Wars that lasted until 1559. The invasion of Italy and the continuous warfare that followed destroyed the Renaissance spirit in Italy.

Renaissance Humanism

The term "Renaissance" is a French word meaning "rebirth," first used by the French historian Jules Michelet (1798–1874) in 1858, to define the cultural awakening that occurred in Europe during the fourteenth through sixteenth centuries. In 1860, the Swiss art historian Jacob Burckhardt (1818–1897) published his study of Italy during the Renaissance titled *The Civilization of the Renaissance in Italy*, one of the most influential books in modern historiography. Burkhardt did not focus on just one area – e.g. art and culture. He included the political and social institutions as well. Burkhardt was one of the romantic historians of the latter half of the nineteenth century who believed that each nation had a spirit (*Geist*), and that the history of a nation should be understood and presented as a biography of the nation. His study led him to conclude that it was in Italy during the Renaissance that the modern world was born.

Not every historian agreed with Burkhardt. The Dutch historian Johan Huizinga (1872–1945) undertook a similar comprehensive study of the period. Huizinga's study focused on France and the Netherlands during the same period. In his book, *The Waning of the Middle Ages* (1919), Huizinga saw the period as one of pessimism and cultural despair, during which the medieval world was dying. Hence, it is appropriate to refer to the period as the Late Middle Ages when looking at Europe north of the Alps (See Chapter 6) and the Renaissance when looking at Italy, or the spread of the Renaissance north of the Alps in the sixteenth century.

Many historians today see the Renaissance as the continuation of a cultural revival already underway in the twelfth and thirteenth centuries. The environment of the Italian city-states during the fourteenth and fifteenth centuries was conducive to the renewed interest in classical civilization. Italy was more densely populated than the rest of Europe. It was the funnel through which both trade and ideas flowed into Europe. Its prosperous trade and industry created a vibrant capitalism that required and encouraged individualism. Commerce required large numbers of individuals literate in both the use of words and numbers. Life expectancy was short, so young men were driven to seek material success early. The model of the self-made, rags-to-riches man resulted in a social structure where men with wealth, rather than inherited titles, were the leaders. Wealth encouraged patronage of the arts as a sign of success. And the art the wealthy patronized was not only religious, but increasingly secular – portraits, landscapes, and themes drawn from classical civilization.

It is important to understand the terms "humanism" and "humanist" as they apply to the Renaissance. Simply put, a humanist was anyone engaged in the study of the "*studia humanitatis*," or humanities. The *studia humanitatis* was a revision of the *Trivium*, which together with the *Quadrivium*, was the heart of scholastic education at the medieval universities. It consisted of grammar, poetry, rhetoric, history, and moral philosophy. "The *studia humanitatis* excluded logic, but they added to the traditional grammar and rhetoric not only history, Greek, and moral philosophy, but also made poetry, once a sequel of grammar and rhetoric, the most important member of the whole group" (Kristeller 1990, p. 178).

The Italian humanists were living in a world that was very different from that of the Middle Ages. It was an urban, secular environment largely dominated by the bourgeoisie. The Italian humanists looked to the classics, especially the Greek classics, because they found there, a world like their own. It was a world in which the dignity of human beings was found in their ability to reason, to understand the world in which they lived, and to shape it according to their will. The focus and energy of the Italian Renaissance was summed up in the ancient Greek philosopher Protagoras' axiom, "Man is the measure of all things." William Shakespeare (1564–1616), sometimes called the last Renaissance man and the first modern man, expressed it thus: "What a piece of work is a man! how noble in reason! how infinite in faculty! in form and moving how express and admirable! in action how like an angel! in apprehension how like a god" (Shakespeare, *Hamlet*, Act 2, scene 2).

The humanists resurrected the classical Greek concept of *aretē*. Though there is no English word that accurately conveys the meaning of *aretē*, it can be understood as the belief that the individual human being is capable of achieving excellence in every area of life. Put another way, the individual becomes truly human when the individual strives, as he or she must, to become all that he or she can be. Unlike their predecessors in the Middle Ages, who believed that the individual was hopeless apart from God's grace, the Renaissance believed that education could produce a good person. Giovanni Pico della Mirandola (1463–1494) in his *Oration on the Dignity of Man* (1496) has God say to the individual created in his image:

> We have given you, O Adam, no visage proper to yourself, nor endowment properly your own, in order that whatever place, whatever form, whatever gifts you may, with premeditation, select, these same you may have and possess through your own judgement and decision. The nature of all other creatures is defined and restricted within laws which We have laid down; you, by contrast, impeded by no such restrictions, may, by your own free will, to whose custody We have assigned you, trace for yourself the lineaments of your own nature. I have placed you at the very center of the world, so that from that vantage point you may with greater ease glance round about you on all that the world contains. We have made you a creature neither of heaven nor of earth, neither mortal nor immortal, in order that you may, as the free and proud shaper of your own being, fashion yourself in the form you may prefer. It will be in your power to descend to the lower, brutish forms of life; you will be able, through your own decision, to rise again to the superior orders whose life is divine. (Pico della Mirandola 2014)

To fully understand how different the Renaissance humanist view of humanity was from that of the Middle Ages, we need only compare della Mirandola's *Oration* to a few verses from Psalm 8:

> When I look at your heavens, the work of your fingers,
> the moon and the stars, which you have set in place,
> what is man that you are mindful of him,
> and the son of man that you care for him?
>
> (3-4, ESV)

The shift to a more secular worldview is also evident in how the humanists viewed historical time. They were conscious of living in a time very different from the recent past. The medievalists divided history into two periods, a period of darkness from the Fall to the coming of Jesus Christ, and a period of light from the birth of Jesus Christ until his return at the end of history. The Renaissance humanists, beginning in the middle of the fourteenth century, divided history into three periods, a period of light that ended with the fall of the Roman Empire, followed by an age of darkness, followed by the rebirth of civilization in their own day. This Renaissance division of history into three periods survives today in the traditional ancient, medieval, and modern paradigm.

Leading Italian Humanists

Francesco Petrarca, better known as Petrarch (1304–1374), is considered the father of humanism. He traveled extensively, recovering Latin manuscripts long lost in monastic libraries. He regarded Medieval Latin barbarous, and encouraged others to emulate Cicero's style of prose. Petrarch also held up Cicero as a model for the humanist's active participation in the life of the city, what is called civic humanism. The Renaissance humanist, he believed, must be a person of action as well as learning.

Giovanni Boccaccio (1313–1375), author of the *Decameron*, was a friend of Petrarch and fellow Florentine. He wrote both prose and poetry. His emphasis on realism and use of the vernacular contributed to the development of Italian humanism. The characters in the *Decameron* "must wrestle with fate," but also learn that to achieve happiness in life, the individual must pursue "realistic goals, and not chase after dreams that are not humanly possible" ("*Boccaccio*" 2016). Like Petrarch, Boccaccio served Florence on diplomatic missions to the papacy, Romagna, Milan, Naples, and Venice. He learned Greek, urged to do so by Petrarch who was never able to, and encouraged the translation of works by Homer into Latin.

Leonardo Bruni (1370–1444) exemplified civic humanism. He wrote a biography of Cicero, in which he presented Cicero as an example of what it meant to be a citizen. Just as Cicero placed all of his talents in service to the Roman Republic, the citizen of Florence must be an active citizen, making use of all his talent and resources. Bruni served as a chancellor of Florence from 1427 until 1444. He translated works by Plato, Aristotle, and Plutarch into Latin. His history of Florence is considered by some to be the first modern history.

The critical approach to primary sources is one of the important contributions by Renaissance humanists to modern scholarship. Lorenzo Valla (1407–1457) mastered both Latin and Greek. His study of Latin led him to idealize the style of the late Roman Republic and early Empire. By doing so, he contributed to the secular flavor of Italian humanism. By limiting classical Latin to these periods, Valla effectively confined Italian humanism to pagan authors. The Christian humanists of the Northern Renaissance, mid-fifteenth through the sixteenth centuries, placed less emphasis on the pagan authors and gave more attention to the Hebrew and Greek texts of the Bible and writings of the early Christians.

Valla is best remembered for his use of textual criticism to expose the Donation of Constantine as an eighth century forgery. The Donation of Constantine was allegedly an imperial decree in which the Emperor Constantine gave authority over the western half of the Roman Empire to the pope. In another publication, *Adnotationes*, he revealed errors in the Latin Vulgate translation of the Bible by Jerome. For these and other embarrassments he caused the church, Valla was investigated by the Inquisition and found guilty of heresy. Alfonso I, king of Naples (1396–1458), whom Valla served as royal secretary and historian, was able to protect Valla from martyrdom. Because Valla's works were used later by the Protestant Reformers, both *Adnotationes* and *Declamation Concerning the False Donation of Constantine* were placed on the *Index of Forbidden Books* in the mid-sixteenth century.

Cosimo dé Medici chose Marsilio Ficino (1433–1499) as head of the Florentine Academy that he founded in 1462 for the study of Greek and the Greek classics, especially the works of Plato and Plotinus (204–270), the founder of Neo-Platonism. What became known as the Platonic Academy was an intellectual oasis for inquiring minds from Northern Europe as well as Italy.

Figure 7.3 The "Hospital of the Innocents" in Florence, Italy was designed by Filippo Brunelleschi, 1419–1427.

Ficino synthesized Platonism and Christianity in such a way as to stress the dignity and creative abilities of the individual human being. He did not make a distinction between *revealed* truth and inspired truth. Truth was found in the writings of the ancient philosophers as well as in the Bible and the early Christian thinkers. Human beings were spiritually linked to God because they possessed a soul. They were linked to the material world through their bodies. Humans are unique among all creatures, in that they are able to transcend their place in the Great Chain of Being and achieve spiritual union with God, the purest spirit.

Niccolò Machiavelli (1469–1527) was arguably the Renaissance humanist who had the greatest influence on modern history. His two treatises on politics, *The Discourses on the First Ten Books of Livy* and especially the thin volume titled *The Prince*, earned him the title of the father of modern political science. The classical philosophers, such as Plato and Aristotle, assumed that the state was part of the natural order of the universe, whose purpose was to create an environment in which its citizens could live a virtuous life. Christian thinkers understood the state to be divinely ordained, a necessity in a fallen world. The goal was to create an earthly city, according to divine mandates revealed in the Bible, as interpreted by the church. Machiavelli, in contrast to both, viewed the state as a purely human creation.

Machiavelli chose to study politics objectively, using reason to understand how politics are practiced in the real world. He began with the assumption that the goal of politics is to serve the interests of the state. Whatever ensures the existence and well-being of the state is good. Whatever threatens or harms the state is bad. Politics must be amoral, if it is to perform its true function. Because people are by nature evil, "no attention should be paid either to justice or injustice, to kindness or cruelty, or to its being praiseworthy or ignominious. On the contrary, every other consideration being set aside, that alternative should be wholeheartedly adopted which will save the life and preserve the freedom of one's country" (Donnelly 2000, p. 174).

Machiavelli did not suggest that a prince should be wicked or cruel for no reason. Nor was he implying that the prince could not be a moral person. Rather he said that private morality must not be allowed to impede his public duty. If necessary, for the good of the state, the prince must be willing to act in a way that normally would be considered morally wrong. The wise prince should give the appearance of being virtuous and religious, since that enables him to rule efficiently, but must act in accordance with what is best for the state. All things will be forgiven except that which harms the state.

Machiavelli's view of history and his amoral approach to politics was well ahead of his time. Historically, rulers have acted much in line with Machiavelli's advice given in *The Prince*, but none would want to admit to being "Machiavellian." Machiavellian has become a pejorative term to describe someone who is unscrupulous, crafty, cunning, deceitful, the list goes on. We recognize these characteristics in politics as being distinctively modern, but it was not until the late-seventeenth century with the political philosophies of Thomas Hobbes and John Locke (See Chapter 9) that political theory became unapologetically secular.

If Machiavelli's *The Prince* was a handbook for the successful Renaissance prince, then *The Book of the Courtier* by Baldassare Castiglione (1478–1529) did the same for the Renaissance courtier. The successful courtier is one who is well-rounded, that is, educated in the humanities, athletic, practices refined manners, and able to display knowledge of, and competence with, the sword as well as a musical instrument. Above all, the courtier must be able to demonstrate his many qualities without pretense or exaggerated display, and "to practice in everything a certain nonchalance [*sprezzatura*] that shall conceal design and show that what is done and said is done without effort and almost without thought" ("Excerpts" 2000).

The spirit of the Italian Renaissance focused on this world and on individuals and what they could achieve. Leon Battista Alberti (1404–1472) summed it up well when he said, "Men can do all things if they will." From the work of artists and sculptors, who portrayed biblical characters as real people in a real world rather than symbols of spiritual truths, to architects who built buildings scaled down to human proportions rather than soaring gothic cathedrals, the new world of the Italian Renaissance was one in which people found meaning in their own achievements. The emphasis shifted away from the God-centered universe of the medieval synthesis, where God was the reference point that gave meaning to all of his creation.

Northern Renaissance

The period of the Renaissance is normally divided into the Italian Renaissance and the Northern Renaissance. There was only one Renaissance that began in Italy in the mid-fourteenth century and lasted until the end of the sixteenth century. The Renaissance spread north of the Alps in the latter part of the fifteenth century, especially after the French invasion of Italy in 1494. Europe north of the Alps was very different from Italy, as noted earlier. The Renaissance was slow to spread to the North, and as it did, it developed differently as it adjusted to the new environment.

Whereas Italy was a world of mostly city-states in which wealth from industry and commerce was concentrated in urban centers, in the North the economy was still largely agricultural. There were fewer and less populated cities scattered over a much greater geographic area. The landed aristocracy possessed greater prestige, and unlike in Italy, where they often lived in the cities, those in the North did not mix with the urban elite. Nation-states were developing in the North, as well as a sense of national identity. Northerners did not pass their daily lives among the ruins of classical civilization. Hence, they did not have the same reverence for the past. For the Italian humanists, a reverence for classical civilization was a source of national identity and sentiment. The Roman Catholic Church in the North, though declining in political power, remained the main source of intellectual life. The nobility was the major source of patronage for the arts and humanist scholars, whereas in Italy it was the princes, wealthy merchant families, and the church.

Though the Italian Renaissance was clearly secular in spirit the Northern Renaissance was more religious. The secular humanists in Italy were primarily interested in the classical authors and languages of ancient Greece and Rome. The humanists in the North, often referred to as Christian humanists, turned their attention to the writings of the early church. They hoped to find there a purer form of Christianity that could bring reform to the church of their day.

Leading Christian Humanists

The greatest humanist of the Northern Renaissance, some would say of the whole Renaissance, was Desiderius Erasmus (1466–1536). Erasmus was born the illegitimate son of a cleric and the daughter of a physician. He was educated in the Deventer School of the Brethren of the Common Life, founded by Geert Groote (1340–1384), a successful educator. The Brethren of the Common Life was a lay movement that emphasized a personal life of piety and service. The members sought to reform the Roman Catholic Church by following the example of Jesus Christ and living a simple life style. They placed great emphasis on education, which led them to found a number of schools for boys. Both Erasmus and the Protestant Reformer, Martin Luther, studied in schools founded by the Brethren of the Common Life.

His early association with the Brethren of the Common Life influenced Erasmus' understanding of Christianity as "the philosophy of Christ." Erasmus' philosophy of Christ meant returning to the simplicity of the early church. Inner piety and a lifestyle modeled after the teachings of Jesus Christ, not rituals, sacraments, and veneration of relics, would bring about renewal. Christian humanism, of which Erasmus was the foremost example, shared in common with the secular humanists and the ancient Greek philosophers the belief that education could produce a moral person. The philosophy of Christ was the Christian humanists's answer to the corruption of the institutional church. They believed the church doctrine was sound. What was needed was to remove the corrupt individuals and replace them with morally upright men.

On a visit to England in 1499–1500, Erasmus was introduced to John Colet (1467–1519), Dean of St. Paul's Church, by his host, Thomas More (1478–1535). It was Colet who encouraged Erasmus to study Greek. Using the earliest manuscripts then available, Erasmus produced a new Greek translation of the New Testament, and along with it, a new Latin translation in 1516. The Greek New Testament, together with his *Handbook of the Christian Knight* (1503) and *The Praise of Folly* (1511), contributed to the Protestant Reformation. Some of Erasmus's enemies in the Roman Catholic Church accused him of being Luther's inspiration. Luther, they said, hatched the egg Erasmus laid.

Erasmus's devoted friend, Thomas More, was England's leading humanist and a good example of civic humanism. Unlike Erasmus, More chose a career in politics. He served as a lawyer, civil servant, Member of Parliament, and eventually Lord Chancellor of England. Like Erasmus, More acknowledged the corruption in the church and desired its reform. Also, like Erasmus, he believed that the doctrine of the Roman Catholic Church was sound, and that reform would come from within by removing the abuses of doctrine and replacing corrupt churchmen with well-educated, morally upright, and spiritual men.

Thomas More's best known work is his satirical book, *Utopia* (1516). More shared the humanist's faith in the innate goodness of human nature, and the ability of human beings to construct a just society. This "utopian" vision is clear in More's fictional narrative of an imaginary society on an island in the Atlantic, where the citizens of Utopia were willing to give up their individual rights, including private property, for the common good.

More was a friend of Henry VIII (1491–1547). When Henry dismissed Cardinal Thomas Wolseley (1473–1530) as Lord Chancellor in 1529, he chose Thomas More as his successor. Wolseley was dismissed for his failure to secure from the pope an annulment of Henry

VIII's marriage to Catherine of Aragon. Because of his religious faith, More was unable to accept Henry's divorce of Catherine as legitimate. Nor was he willing to acknowledge Henry as the supreme head of the church in England. More resigned his post as Lord Chancellor, was subsequently charged and convicted of treason, and was executed on July 6, 1535.

Renaissance Art and Culture[1]

The Renaissance artists continued to use religious themes, but with a new twist. The secular humanism of the Italian Renaissance is evident in its art and architecture. Both Donatello (c. 1386–1466) and Michelangelo (1475–1564) created free-standing, nude statues of the biblical figure David. Donatello used bronze, whereas Michelangelo used marble. Both are equal to the best statuary produced during the classical period. However, if they were not titled, "*David*," no one viewing either one would recognize either as a statue of the biblical David. Donatello's *David* (c. 1428–1432) is graceful, but effeminate. He used a bust of the Emperor Hadrian's lover, the youthful Antinous, as the model for the head of his *David*. Michelangelo's *David* (1501–1504) is more like a Greek god than any living man. It exudes a spirit of confidence, determination, and heroism. Neither *David* is circumcised, yet another indication of the secular, humanist spirit of the Italian Renaissance.

The lesser-known Florentine, Andrea del Verrocchio (c. 1435–1488) made a bronze statue of David sometime between 1473 and 1475. His *David* is clothed in classical attire, holds a sword in his right hand, and has the severed head of Goliath at his feet. Take away Goliath's head, and again one would not know it was the biblical David. Compare all three with the marble statue of *David* (1623) by Gian Lorenzo Bernini (1598–1680), done during the Baroque artistic period that was inspired by the Catholic Reformation. The observer instantly recognizes Bernini's David as the heroic Old Testament giant killer.

It was in painting that the Renaissance excelled. There were no classical paintings to inspire or to copy. Both religious and pagan themes were used. Sandro Botticelli (1445–1510) painted the *Allegory of Spring* (c. 1482) and *Birth of Venus* (c. 1485) inspired by classical mythology. He also painted *Adoration of the Magi* (c. 1475–1476), clearly inspired by the New Testament gospels. The latter serves as a good example of Renaissance artists injecting realism in religiously themed paintings. Botticelli incorporated portraits of Cosimo dé Medici, his sons Piero and Giovanni and his grandsons Lorenzo and Giuliano in the painting. Similarly, Jean Fouquet (c. 1420-1477/81) used Agnès Sorel, the mistress of the French king Charles VII, as the model for the Virgin Mary in his painting titled *Virgin and Child Surrounded by Angels* (a.k.a., *The Red Virgin*). Some argue that this sort of realism changed the meaning of the scene, that is, inhibited the viewer's ability to see the religious meaning of the scene.

Renaissance artists were true Renaissance men. Michelangelo not only carved *David* and the beautiful *Pietà* (1499), he also painted the ceiling of the Sistine Chapel in Rome. Raphael

---

1 It is not possible to do justice to the history of art in a survey history text such as this. The reader is encouraged to consult the many studies of the arts through history available on DVD.

(1483–1520) is perhaps best known for his painting, *School of Athens* (1509–1511) in the Vatican Palace, but he was also one of the most popular architects in Rome during Julius II's reign. Leonardo da Vinci painted two of the most famous paintings in history, the *Mona Lisa* (1517) and the *Last Supper* (1494). But he was much more than just a painter. His sketch books (more than 5000 pages) contain drawings of all sorts of machines and gadgets, as well as detailed anatomical sketches of the human skeleton, muscles, nerves, and blood vessels.

Protestant Reformation

On October 31, 1517, Martin Luther (1483–1546), a monk of the Augustinian Order and professor at the University of Wittenberg, made the 15-minute walk from the Augustinian Cloister to the Castle Church in Wittenberg. It was October 31, the eve of All Saints. Wittenberg was filled with pilgrims waiting for the church doors to open so that they could walk through its halls viewing and venerating the vast collection of holy relics assembled by Elector Frederick the Wise (1463–1525). In one hand, Luther carried a rolled-up document. In the other, he carried a hammer. When he arrived at the church's north entrance, where the large wooden door served as the university bulletin board, he unrolled the document and nailed it to the door.

The document known ever since as the *Ninety-Five Theses* was written in Latin and bore the title, *Disputation on the Power and Efficacy of Indulgences*. By nailing the *Disputation* to the church door, Luther was inviting his colleagues in the academic community to debate what he believed was the abuse of the doctrine of indulgences. An indulgence was the forgiveness of all or part of the temporal punishment for sins already confessed and forgiven. The authority to forgive sins and the punishment due for them was believed to reside with the church, ultimately with the pope. It became standard practice from the eleventh century on, however, for indulgences to be given on condition of contributions to a church or monastery. By posting the *Ninety-Five Theses*, Luther hoped to call attention to the abuse of the indulgence system. It was meant only as an invitation to his colleagues at the university to debate the issue, but instead triggered the Protestant Reformation.

Background

Late Medieval Christendom did not fracture over the issue of indulgences. The underlying cause was much more complex. Ultimately, it was a question of authority: What is truth? For Luther, personally, it was how to be certain that God had forgiven him for his sins. The church taught that forgiveness of sins and restoration of fellowship with God (salvation) was a gift of God's grace as a result of the life, death, and resurrection of Jesus Christ. God's grace, however, was dispensed by the church through the sacraments, most importantly the Eucharist, or Mass. This was the issue that troubled many Christians throughout the Middle Ages. Was the institutional church a necessary intermediary between the individual and God, or did the individual have direct access to God based only on faith in Jesus Christ?

Among those commonly referred to as the "forerunners" of the Protestant Reformation, those who advocated one or more of the cardinal doctrines of the Reformation, were Peter Waldo, John Wycliffe, and Jan Hus. Peter Waldo (c. 1140–1205) was a prosperous merchant from Lyons, France. Sometime during the 1160s, he chose to live a life of poverty and began preaching and teaching. His followers were known as the Poor Men of Lyons, or Waldensians. The Waldensians preached without ecclesiastical permission, questioned the existence of purgatory, and embraced a symbolical interpretation of the Eucharist. Peter Waldo was excommunicated in 1184 for preaching without permission. The teachings of his followers were pronounced heretical by the Fourth Lateran Council in 1215.

John Wycliffe (c. 1330–1384) was a distinguished professor at Oxford University and rector of St. Mary Church in Lutterworth, England. Many of his teachings were at odds with the official doctrine of the Roman Catholic Church. He taught that only those predestined to be saved were members of the true church; the sacraments were invalid if administered by a sinful priest; and that the rulers should determine how much property church officials could own. Most important was his denial of transubstantiation and his belief that the Bible was the final authority in matters of faith and practice and should be made available to all to read in their own language.

Wycliffe was instrumental in producing the first English translation of the Bible. His followers, known as Lollards, were an unauthorized movement of lay preachers who used the new English translation of the Bible and pamphlets written by Wycliffe. When Henry IV (1367–1413) became king in 1399, the Lollards came under persecution. Parliament approved the burning of heretics in 1401, resulting in the martyrdom of many of the Lollards. In 1415, the Council of Constance declared Wycliffe a heretic and his teachings heresy.

During Wycliffe's tenure as a professor at Oxford University, some students from Bohemia, among them Jerome of Prague (1379–1416), took copies of Wycliffe's writings back to Bohemia. They influenced the popular preacher of Bethlehem Chapel in Prague and rector of the University of Prague, Jan Hus (1369–1415). Soon Hus was preaching against indulgences and appealing to the authority of Scripture.

Hus went to the Council of Constance under a guarantee of safe conduct which was withdrawn upon his arrival. He was subsequently convicted of heresy and burned at the stake in July 1415. Jerome of Prague, who journeyed to Constance to join Hus, was imprisoned, convicted of heresy, and burned at the stake in May 1416.

A link exists between Wycliffe, Hus, and Luther, in that all three, to one extent or another, advocated what became the three basic doctrines of the Protestant Reformation: the authority of the Bible (*sola scriptura*) and salvation by grace (*sola gratia*) through faith (*sola fide*) in Jesus Christ, alone. Two questions that beg to be answered, however, are why did the Reformation occur at the beginning of the sixteenth century and not earlier with Wycliffe or Hus? And why was Martin Luther not silenced or martyred?

Europe at the beginning of the sixteenth century was very different than a hundred years earlier. The Avignon Papacy, followed by the scandal of two popes and the church's failure to minister to the spiritual needs of the people traumatized by plague and war, contributed to the decline of papal power and seriously weakened the church's spiritual influence. The spiritual influence of the church in the lives of the people was further shaken by the Renaissance popes, who displayed the characteristics, both good and bad, of the Italian Renaissance. Many were great patrons of the arts. Most were astute princes of the Papal States.

The papal election of Innocent VIII (r. 1484–1492) was a fraud. It was common practice at the time for the candidates to simply purchase votes, and Innocent outbid his rivals. The general of the Augustinian order was thrown into prison for saying of Innocent, "In darkness Innocent was elected, in darkness he lives, and in darkness he will die" (Schaff 1910, p. 437). Rome became a refuge for criminals during Innocent's reign. When Innocent's vice-chancellor, Rodrigo Borgia was asked why the laws were not enforced, he supposedly answered: "God desires not the death of a sinner, but rather that he pay and live" (Schaff 1910, Volume V, p. 437.). One Italian poet commented that Innocent deserved to be called father, since he had 16 illegitimate children, all by married women. The lifestyle of many of the cardinals mirrored that of Innocent VIII.

Only five of the cardinals who voted in the election of Rodrigo Borgia (1431–1503) as Alexander VI (r. 1492–1503) did not sell their votes. As pope, Alexander VI devoted his reign to furthering the careers of his illegitimate children. Among his children, were two memorable personalities of the Italian Renaissance, Cesare Borgia (1475–1507) and his sister Lucrezia Borgia (1480–1519). Cesare Borgia served as the model for Machiavelli's ideal ruler in *The Prince*. Lucrezia Borgia was known for her beauty, intelligence, and administrative talent.

Julian Ravere, was elected Julius II (r. 1503–1513) following the brief, month-long pontificate of Pius III (r. 1503). He is remembered as the "Warrior Pope," because of his practice of leading his armies of Swiss mercenaries into battle against the French. But he is best remembered for his patronage of the arts, and his employment of such famous Renaissance artists as Michelangelo, Raphael (1483–1520), and Bramante (1444–1514). His primary goal as pope was to strengthen the political authority of the papacy.

Lorenzo dé Medici's second son, Giovanni, was elected Pope Leo X (r. 1513–1521), the last Renaissance pope. His life, in many ways, exemplified the corruption plaguing the church on the eve of the Protestant Reformation. He benefitted from the three major violations of church law that characterized the church hierarchy during the Renaissance, nepotism, pluralism, and absenteeism. He took holy orders at age seven and was given the abbey of Fonte Dolce. At eight years of age, he was nominated for an archbishopric. Innocent VIII appointed him a cardinal, the youngest ever. In all, he held nearly 30 church offices while still a teenager. On a positive note, Leo X made Rome a center for the arts. Ironically, shortly before his death, Lorenzo wrote to his son warning him that Rome was a sink of all iniquities and exhorted him to live a virtuous life.

Other developments during the fifteenth century that contributed to the Reformation included a widespread movement of popular piety on the eve of the Reformation. Pilgrimages to the tombs of saints and venerating saints' relics were popular. Geoffrey Chaucer 's *Canterbury Tales*, written between 1387 and 1400, is a fictional account of a group of 30 pilgrims on a journey to the shrine of St. Thomas Becket at Canterbury. The emergence of a sense of national identity, and the emergence of a commercial class that benefitted from the growth of the nation-states and was, therefore, willing to support the new monarchs when they sought to gain control of the church in their territories, also prepared the way for reform and revolt in the church. Finally, the appearance of the printing press in the latter half of the century made possible the rapid dissemination of the ideas of the reformers. Some historians have characterized the Reformation as war of pamphlets and books.

Mainline and Radical Reformation

The Reformation did not result in a single Protestant alternative to the Roman Catholic Church. From the beginning, the Protestant movement fragmented into those often referred to as the Mainline, or Magisterial, Reformation and those referred to as the Radical Reformation. All subscribed to the authority of the Bible and defended their distinctive doctrines with appeals to the Bible.

The Mainline Reformation consisted of those churches that followed the teachings of Martin Luther, John Calvin, and Huldrich Zwingli. They continued the practice of a territorial church, which meant that everyone within a given territory had to be of one faith. The territorial church fit well with the emerging nation-states, since a national church fostered a sense of national identity and could be controlled by the state. The principle *cius regio eius religio*, meaning that the prince determined the religion of his subjects, was the desired norm.

Those churches that made the most radical break with the beliefs and practices of the Roman Catholic Church made up the Radical Reformation. They consisted of a diverse group of minor sects that held certain beliefs and practices in common, especially the "gathered out," or "believer's church," and believer's baptism. Only those who made a confession of faith and were subsequently baptized were to be admitted to membership in the church. Logically, this led to the separation of church and state, and for some, but not all, the sharing of material goods, pacifism, and a refusal to take oaths or serve the state. Because the mainline Reformers envisioned a close cooperation between church and state, the radicals were perceived as social, economic, political, and religious rebels. Therefore, they suffered persecution in both Roman Catholic and Protestant states.

Martin Luther

Martin Luther's posting of the *Ninety-Five Theses* on October 31, 1517, marks the beginning of the Protestant Reformation. The *Ninety-Five Theses* circulated among Luther's friends at first, but by the end of November or early December 1517, they were appearing in print in both Latin and German throughout Germany and even in Switzerland. When a copy reached Pope Leo X, he dismissed it, saying "it's only a drunken German, who will feel differently when he sobers up" (Simon 1968, p. 142).

Leo was unable to immediately silence Luther, once he realized the threat represented by Luther's challenge. The election of a new Holy Roman Emperor was pending, and Luther's prince and protector, Frederick the Wise, was one of the seven princes who would elect the next emperor. Leo hoped that by not angering Frederick, he could influence Frederick's vote in favor of his candidate. A debate in Leipzig between Luther and a leading Roman Catholic scholar, Johann Eck (1486–1543) was arranged for July 1519. During the course of the famous Leipzig Debate, Eck was able to get Luther to admit that some of his views, especially as to the question of authority, were identical to those of Jan Hus, condemned as a heretic by the Council of Constance. Luther, in effect, admitted that he, too, was a heretic, as defined by the church. Leo X excommunicated Luther in January 1521.

The newly elected emperor, Charles V (1500–1558), a devout Roman Catholic, yielded to the persuasion of his uncle, Frederick the Wise, and granted Luther a hearing before the

Imperial Diet of the Empire meeting in April 1521 in the city of Worms on the Rhine River. He also granted Luther a safe conduct to Worms and his return to Wittenberg after the meeting. Luther was not allowed to defend his views as he expected. Instead, he was given an opportunity to recant or be condemned. When he refused to recant, the Imperial Diet declared him to be an outlaw, and placed him under the ban of the Empire. His works were banned, and he was to be hunted down, arrested, and put to death.

Frederick the Wise arranged for Luther to be spirited away to his fortress castle at Wartburg, where he remained in hiding for 11 months. Luther spent much of his time on a German translation of the New Testament. He made use of Erasmus's Greek New Testament and published grammars and glossaries by Johannes Reuchlin (1455–1522), a noted German humanist. Luther's German New Testament appeared in print in September 1522. He spent the next 12 years translating the Old Testament into German using the Latin Vulgate as his basic source text, but also consulting Hebrew translations of the Psalms and a Hebrew Old Testament. Luther's first complete German translation of the Bible including the Apocrypha appeared in print in September 1534.

Thanks to the printing press, Luther's writings, unlike those of Wycliffe and Hus, spread rapidly throughout Europe. Luther's goal was to reform the Roman Catholic Church, not to found a new church. Repeated attempts were undertaken to repair the widening rift between Luther and the Roman Catholic Church. The term "Protestant" was first used at the Diet of Speyer in 1529, to describe Luther's followers. Luther's friend and colleague, Philip Melanchthon (1497–1560), drew up a confession of faith with Luther's approval, which was presented to the Diet of Augsburg in 1530 by the Lutheran princes. Rejected by the Diet, the Augsburg Confession later became the authoritative doctrinal statement of the Lutheran churches.

Huldrich Zwingli

Huldrich Zwingli (1484–1531) led the Reformation in Switzerland. He was a Swiss patriot as well as a religious reformer who desired a reform of society and the church. Zwingli worked closely with the governmental authorities. The thirteen Swiss cantons had representative governments and Zwingli believed that the Reformation should be instituted by those representative governments. His method was to engage in a public debate with representatives of the Roman Catholic Church, after which, the governmental authorities would introduce the Reformation. Zwingli was killed in 1531 at the Battle of Kappel between Protestant and Catholic cantons. In 1531, Zwingli's followers merged with the Calvinists through the Consensus of Zurich.

John Calvin

John Calvin (1509–1564) was a French scholar who studied law and theology at the universities of Orléans, Paris, and Bourges. He was exposed to Luther's writings as a student. In his only recorded reference to his conversion, Calvin said only that "by an unexpected conversion [God] tamed to teachableness a mind too stubborn for its years" (Estep 1986, p. 225).

His great contribution to the Protestant Reformation was *Institutes of the Christian Religion*, first published in 1536, when Calvin was only twenty-seven years old. Within the framework of St. Augustine's theology, the *Institutes* presented a clear, reasoned summation of Reformation theology. The influences of Luther, Zwingli, and Erasmus's Christian humanism are present. Calvin's theology is often summarized and perhaps oversimplified, by the acronym TULIP: **T**otal depravity, **U**nconditional election, **L**imited atonement, **I**rresistible grace, and **P**erseverance of the saints.

Calvin moved to Geneva, Switzerland in 1536. Under his influence, Geneva became a kind of Calvinist theocracy. The private and social lives of Geneva's citizens were regulated through church courts. Church and state were separate, but the state government followed Calvin's guidance on moral and economic issues. Religious refugees from all over Europe went to Geneva to study under Calvin at the university he founded. Though many who disagreed with Calvin's influence left Geneva, many more came. Many left Geneva to spread Calvin's teachings to France, England, Scotland, and the Netherlands. Calvinism supplanted Lutheranism as the missionary wing of the Protestant Reformation.

Reformation in England

It was passion of a different sort that led Henry VIII (1491–1547) to separate the church in England from Rome. Henry did not have a legitimate male heir, and feared that if he died, with his daughter Mary by his wife Catherine of Aragon (1485–1536) as his only legitimate heir, civil war would break out in England. Henry sought an annulment of his marriage to Catherine. When negotiations with Pope Clement VII (1478–1534) broke down, Henry decided to act through Parliament. In 1531, the English clergy were coerced into accepting Henry as the head of the church in England, "as far as the law of Christ allows." In the following year, he appointed Thomas Cranmer (1489–1556) Archbishop of Canterbury. As Archbishop, Cranmer convened a church court in 1533 that promptly granted Henry a divorce. The Act of Supremacy passed by Parliament in 1534 declared Henry to be the "only supreme head" of the Church of England. The English church became a national church, but not a Protestant church.

Henry VIII never abandoned his belief in the correctness of Roman Catholic doctrine. Pope Leo X granted Henry the title "Defender of the Faith" in 1521, which has remained one of the titles of the English monarch into the twenty-first century. In accordance with Henry's wishes, Parliament passed the Six Acts in 1539, affirming Roman Catholic doctrine in the English church. The pope was no longer head of the church in England, but it remained Roman Catholic in doctrine so long as Henry VIII was alive.

The Protestant Reformation came to England during the reign of Henry VIII's son Edward VI (1537–1553). Edward VI was only nine years old, when he came to the throne. The introduction of the Protestant Reformation was largely the work of Archbishop Thomas Cranmer, who wrote the *Book of Common Prayer* in 1549 to provide a Protestant liturgy for the Church of England.

Upon Edward VI's death in 1553, Parliament restored Henry VIII's marriage to Catherine of Aragon and declared their daughter Mary to be legitimate heir and Queen of England. Mary, like her mother, was a devout Roman Catholic believer. She initially hoped that her subjects would return to what she believed to be the true church. When they failed to do so, she began using force, including the burning of heretics beginning in 1555. It was not her persecution of Protestants, which earned her the epithet "Bloody Mary,"[2] that alienated her subjects, but her marriage to King Philip II (1527–1598) of Spain. She died in 1558.

Mary's half-sister and successor, Elizabeth I (1533–1603), cared little about religion except as it affected the well-being of her realm. She took the title "supreme governor of the Church of England," rather than "supreme head." A modified *Book of Common Prayer* was adopted. It, together with the Thirty-nine Articles passed by Parliament in 1563, defined the doctrine and practice for Church of England. The service of Holy Communion was made vague enough that those who wished to do so could believe that it affirmed transubstantiation. Roman Catholic believers could celebrate Mass in private without fear, unless treason was suspected. Thus, in various ways, life was made comfortable in England for moderate Catholics.

Catholic Reformation

The Catholic Reformation was more than a response to the Protestant Reformation. It was part of a spiritual revival underway in the late-fifteenth century that embraced reform along the lines suggested by the Christian humanists. Members of the Oratory of Divine Love founded in Florence in 1497, believed that reform might come through the practice of love and moral improvement. Among its members was Gasparo Contarini (1483–1542), a well-educated scholar and diplomat.

Contarini wanted to see reconciliation between the Protest Reformers, some of whose opinions he shared, and the Roman Catholic Church. He served as Pope Paul III's representative at the Colloquy of Regensburg (1541), where moderate Catholic theologians met with moderate Protestant theologians, most notably Martin Luther's successor as leader of the Lutheran movement, Philip Melanchthon. A young John Calvin was also present at the Colloquy. The participants were able to reach agreement on such key issues as free will, original sin, and most importantly, on justification by "faith and grace, dependent on the merits of Christ," with the justifying grace being made "lively and efficacious through works of charity." They could not agree on the issue of the Lord's Supper, or Eucharist. Contarini, peacemaker though he was, refused to compromise on the doctrine of transubstantiation.

The Colloquy failed to achieve its goal of reconciliation. Those who attended, both Protestant and Roman Catholic, were severely criticized back home for having compromised as much as they had. Recognizing the reconciliation was not going to happen, the Roman Catholic Church went on the offensive. The instruments employed were essentially medieval, including the founding of new religious orders, the Council of Trent, the Inquisition, the Index, and direct use of military force by Catholic monarchs.

---

2 Interestingly, Mary's half-sister, Elizabeth I, martyred many more people than Mary, yet she is remembered as "Good Queen Bess." Sadly, history is not always fair.

Most important of the new religious orders was the Society of Jesus, popularly known as the Jesuits, founded by Ignatius Loyola (1491–1556), a former Spanish soldier. The Jesuits concentrated on three goals: education, winning back those areas lost to Protestantism, and foreign missions. Having taken an oath of absolute obedience to the pope, the Jesuits became the shock troops of the Catholic Church's counteroffensive against Protestantism. They played a major role in halting the spread of Protestantism and winning back large areas to the Roman Catholic Church. Their greatest and most heroic efforts were expended overseas evangelizing America, Africa, and Asia. Wherever Spanish and Portuguese explorers went, Jesuit missionaries went with them.

Of the 270 bishops who attended the Council of Trent called by Pope Paul III (r. 1534–1549), 187 were Italians, two were German, and the remainder were from France and Spain. The council met in three sessions between 1545 and 1563. No attempt was made at reconciliation with the Protestants. It reaffirmed and clarified Roman Catholic doctrine as it existed before the Protestant Reformation. Many of the more blatant abuses, such as the selling of indulgences, were dealt with. Bishops were instructed to reside within their dioceses. Seminaries were established for the training of clergy. A catechism was developed so that Catholics could distinguish truth from error. Thomas Aquinas was established as the dominant theological influence in the revitalized Roman Catholic Church. For the next 400 years, until the Vatican II Council (1961–1965), the Roman Catholic Church remained as defined at the Council of Trent.

Reestablishment of the Inquisition was authorized in 1542 by Pope Paul II in the papal bull, *Licet ab Initio*. It operated differently and, with varying success, depending on the secular authority in a given area. France, though a Catholic country, refused to allow it to operate in France. Its most infamous reputation was earned in Spain, where it was used primarily as a political weapon. In Italy, where Cardinal Caraffa, the future Pope Paul IV (r. 1555–1559), served as one of the Inquisitors-General, the Inquisition applied terror and torture to snuff out all stirrings of Protestant or liberal Catholic thought.

One of Pope Paul IV's final acts was to issue the first *Index of Prohibited Books* in 1559. It "included all works written by heretics, all books without identifiable authors or printers, and all books printed by heretic printers regardless of the nature of the book" (Rye 1981, p. 69). Also included were all books on divination, magic (including necromancy), astrology, and all Talmudic books. The Council of Trent issued an expanded *Index* in 1564, that included all the works of Erasmus and vernacular translations of the Bible. The *Index* was updated periodically until it was abolished in 1966.

Conflicts among the Protestant Reformers

When Martin Luther nailed his Ninety-Five Theses on the church door in Wittenberg in 1517, he did not intend to create a new church, much less be responsible for a never-ending fragmentation of the Protestant movement that continues to our own day. Nevertheless, he did. Luther believed that the medieval church's teaching that God's grace was dispensed to the believer through the sacraments that could only be ministered by a priest in apostolic succession was not only unbiblical, but also a means by which the church hierarchy held the laity in bondage. The individual did not have direct access to God's grace. The institutional church was an indispensable intermediary.

When Luther stood before the Diet of Worms in 1521, he defended himself by an appeal to the Bible as the supreme authority: "Unless I am convinced by the testimony of the Scriptures or by clear reason ... I am bound by the Scriptures I have quoted, and my conscience is captive to the Word of God" (Jones 1985, p. 44). During that same year, Luther published two pamphlets in which he attacked the sacramental system and set forth the doctrine of the priesthood of all believers. No longer was there a teaching authority to which the individual could appeal for clarification of a biblical passage.

The authority of Scripture was the doctrinal assumption on which the Protestant Reformation rested. All of the Reformers, mainline and radical alike, agreed on that fundamental point. But agreement on the authority of the Bible is not the same as agreeing on what the Bible says. The doctrine of the priesthood of believers guaranteed that fragmentation would characterize the history of Protestantism. The Reformers agreed on the Bible alone, grace alone, and faith alone, but often disagreed passionately on the meaning of Communion, the meaning and manner of baptism, church polity, forms of worship, and many other issues. The very same differences that divided all Protestants from the Roman Catholic Church, also divided the various Protestant sects.

Assessment

Perhaps what makes the Protestant Reformation and the Catholic Reformation that followed so interesting and relevant for today is the insight it gives into the perennial search for truth and meaning. From time to time throughout history, great men and women – philosophers, mystics, religious thinkers, and artists – have asked if there is in fact an ultimate truth, and if so, how that truth can be known, if in fact it can be known.

Individuals of the Christian faith hold to the belief that the ultimate reality is a personal infinite God, who exists independent of, and is the creator of, the material universe. For them, truth, that is ultimate truth, does exist and originates in the creator – God. Christians during the sixteenth century, whether Roman Catholic, Greek Orthodox, or followers of the Protestant Reformation, believed that God had made himself known in the Old and New Testaments (i.e. the Bible). The Roman Catholics believed that the church, ultimately the pope, was entrusted with the authority to interpret the Scriptures. Therefore, there were two pillars of authority, the Scriptures and church tradition (decisions of church councils, papal decrees, etc.).

For the Protestant Reformers, the Bible alone was the sole authority in all matters of religious faith and practice. That is what Luther asserted in his defiant stand at the Diet of Worms. The Reformation was not a struggle between various truths, or ideas, but really a struggle over who correctly understood and taught "the Truth." Since the eternal destiny of human beings depended on knowing the truth, individuals on both sides were willing to die, even kill, to defend the truth as they understood it. Tragically, the history of the Protestant Reformation and the Catholic Reformation is written in the blood of the martyrs (Waibel 2005, pp. 106–107).

References

Boccaccio (2016). New World Encyclopedia. http://www.newworldencyclopedia.org/entry/
Boccaccio (accessed 21 October 2019).

Byfield, T. (2010). *The Christians: Their First Two Thousand Years*, vol. 8. Edmonton: Christian
History Project.

Donnelly, J. (2000). *Realism and International Relations*. Cambridge: Cambridge University
Press.

Estep, W.R. (1986). *Renaissance and Reformation*. Grand Rapids, MI: W.B. Eerdmans Pub. Co.

Castiglione, B. (2000). Excerpts from The Book of the Courtier by Baldesar Castiglione. https://
www.oneonta.edu/faculty/farberas/arth/arth200/artist/castiglione_courtier.htm (accessed
21 October 2019).

Jones, R.T. (1985). *The Great Protestant Reformation*, 44. Downers Grove, IL: Intervarsity Press.

Kristeller, P.O. (1990). *Renaissance Thought and the Arts: Collected Essays*. Princeton, NJ:
Princeton Univ. Press.

Pico della Mirandola, G. (2014). Oration on the Dignity of Man. https://ebooks.adelaide.edu.
au/p/pico_della_mirandola/giovanni/dignity (accessed 21 October 2019).

Rye, M. (1981). Index Librorum Prohibitorum. *Journal of Rutgers University Libraries* 43 (2)
http://jrul.libraries.rutgers.edu/index.php/jrul/article/viewFile/1611/3051 (accessed
February 10, 2019.

Schaff, P. (1910). *History of the Christian Church*. In: *The Middle Ages*, vol. 5, pt. 2,
(ed. P. Schaff). New York: Charles Scribner's Sons.

Shakespeare, W. (1603). *Hamlet*. Act 2, Scene 2.

Simon, E. (1968). *Luther Alive: Martin Luther and the Making of the Reformation*. London:
Hoddar and Stroughton.

Waibel, P.R. (2005). *Martin Luther: A Brief Introduction to his Life and Works*. Wheeling, IL:
Harlan Davidson, Inc.

8

New Horizons

Chronology

1488	Bartolomeu Dias Sails Round the Cape of Good Hope
1497	Vasco de Gama Reaches India
1497	John Cabot Sailed to the Canadian Maritime Islands
1492	Christopher Columbus Reached the Bahamas
1496–1550	René Descartes, "I think therefore I am" (*Cogito ergo sum*)
1519–1522	The Spanish Sail Around the World
1543	Nicolaus Copernicus' *On the Revolution of the Celestial Spheres*
1555	Peace of Augsburg (Who's Realm, His Religion)
1571	Battle of Lepanto
1588	Spanish Armada
1598	Edict of Nantes
1609–1619	Kepler's Three Laws of Planetary Motion
1618–1648	Thirty-Years' War
1620	Francis Bacon's *Novum Organum* (*New Method*)
1623	Galileo Galilei's *The Assayer*
1649	Execution of Charles I by the "Rump Parliament"
1649–1660	English Interregnum
1653	Oliver Cromwell Becomes Lord Protector of England
1657–1701	Scientific Societies Founded in France, England, and Germany
1667–1714	Wars of Louis VIV
1682	Palace of Versailles Becomes Royal Residence (France)
1687	Isaac Newton's *Mathematical Principles of Natural Philosophy*
1688–1689	Glorious Revolution

The fifteenth through the seventeenth centuries was a period of transition from the medieval world to the modern world. The Renaissance and the Reformation were only two aspects of that transition. Contemporary with them was the appearance of the modern nation-state, as opposed to the old feudal monarchies, that made possible the Age of Exploration and Discovery beginning in the middle of the fifteenth century and the Scientific Revolution beginning in the middle of the sixteenth century. They were all part

Western Civilization: A Brief History, First Edition. Paul R. Waibel.
© 2020 John Wiley & Sons, Inc. Published 2020 by John Wiley & Sons, Inc.

of a whole that replaced the Great Chain of Being with a new understanding of the universe and humankind's place in it.

Rise of the Nation-States

Nation-state building required monarchs to subdue, or at least neutralize, the two chief centers of opposition, the church and the nobility. At the same time, they had to promote a sense of national identity on the part of their subjects. These goals were achieved during the sixteenth through the seventeenth centuries in Spain, France, and England, but not in the Holy Roman Empire or Italy. Out of the process of nation-state building emerged the modern European state system.

The new sovereign monarchs benefitted from the Reformation. The churches that emerged from the Reformation were national, or state, churches. Some monarchs, or princes in the case of individual states within the Holy Roman Empire, supported the Protestant Reformation, because by doing so, they gained control of the church within their territory. In countries where the Roman Catholic Church remained, it became a state church controlled by the monarch. This was true especially in Spain and France. National identity and religious identity became one and the same, especially in Spain. To be truly English, for example, meant membership in the Established Church of England. Likewise, to be truly Spanish meant being Roman Catholic.

Taxation provided the funds with which to build standing armies, which were used both to combat resistance to strong centralized government and to promote national identity. Taxation, and to a lesser extent conscription, touched the lives of people at the local level. As a particular territory and language became a part of a nation-state's identity, the medieval idea of Christendom imaged in the Roman Catholic Church and the Holy Roman Empire faded into history. Throughout, the new monarchs were supported by the rising bourgeoisie, the business-wise townspeople.

Spain

The marriage of Queen Isabella I (1451–1504) of Castile and King Ferdinand II (1452–1516) of Aragon in 1469 is generally considered the beginning of the Kingdom of Spain. Their defeat of Granada, the last Muslim kingdom in Spain, in 1492, brought to an end the long struggle to drive the Muslims out of the Iberian Peninsula. The Roman Catholic Church in Spain was brought under royal control. Under "The Catholic Monarchs," as Ferdinand and Isabella were known, Spanish identity was based on religious conformity and ancestry. An individual was considered a Spaniard only if no Jewish or non-Spanish ancestry existed. The Jews were expelled in 1492, and the Muslims, known as Moors, between 1609 and 1614. A reign of terror under the Inquisition, introduced in Spain in 1478, was used to root out all opposition to the monarchy and enforce religious conformity.

Spain became the greatest power in Europe during the reign of Charles I (1500–1558), grandson of Ferdinand and Isabella. In 1519, he was elected Holy Roman Emperor as Charles V. He expelled the French from Italy. The Peace of Augsburg (1555) established the principle of *Cuius regio, eius religio* ("Whose realm, his religion") as the basis for peace between the Protestant and Catholic princes in the Holy Roman Empire. He halted the advance of the Ottoman Turks into Eastern Europe in 1529, before the walls of Vienna. Charles V retired to the Monastery of Yuste in 1556, leaving Spain, Italy, the Netherlands, and the overseas empire to his son, Philip II (1527–1598), and the Holy Roman Empire to his brother, Ferdinand I (1503–1564).

Charles V left his son an efficient civil service and the best army in Europe. Great wealth flowed into Spain from its colonies. In his offensive, against the Protestants, Philip II benefitted from the fact that France was distracted by civil war between Protestant and Catholic factions. The Treaty of Cateau-Cambresis (1554) between Philip II and Henry II of France gave Spain control of Italy. A combined Spanish and Venetian fleet dealt the Ottoman Turks a decisive defeat in the Battle of Lepanto (1571) in Gulf of Corinth. In 1578, Philip united Portugal with Spain, adding Portugal's vast overseas empire to that of Spain. The dynastic union, known as the Iberian Union, lasted until 1640.

With the benefit of historical hindsight, one can see that the decline of Spanish power was already underway during Philip II's reign. The oppressive atmosphere caused by the Inquisition stifled individual initiative. Spanish students were not allowed to study outside of Spain, thus cutting Spain off from the progressive forces that produced the Scientific Revolution and Enlightenment. Corruption at all levels became the rule in the bureaucracies of both Church and State. Spain never developed a middle class. A rigid class structure kept Spain a nation of wealthy land owners and exploited peasants.

Philip II assembled an Armada of 130 ships in 1588 for an invasion of England. The Armada was to transport some 30 000 soldiers from the Spanish Netherlands to England. A total of 55 000 soldiers were mustered for the invasion. Bad weather and English seamanship defeated the Armada. Protestants throughout Europe saw it as a sign that God was on their side. Had not the pope blessed the Armada, allowed Philip to collect a crusade tax to finance it, and granted the Spanish soldiers and sailors an indulgence?

In retrospect, the Armada debacle, together with the loss of the Netherlands in 1609, marks Spain's decline to a second-rate power. The verdict was confirmed in 1643, when a French army defeated the once unbeatable Spanish army at the Battle of Rocroi on the border of modern Belgium. Spain never recovered.

France

France was unfortunate to suffer a series of internal wars known as the French Wars of Religion (1562–1598) between Huguenots (French Calvinists) and Catholics. It was both a religious and a dynastic struggle. When Henry II (1519–1599) died, he was succeeded by three sons wholly unsuited to rule. The Queen Mother, Catherine de Médici (1519–1589), ruled France as regent. Since it was generally assumed that none of Henry II's sons would produce an heir, the struggle was over who would succeed to the throne upon the death of Henry III (1551–1589). The two rivals were King Henry III of Navarre (1553–1610) and Henry I, Duke of Guise (1550–1588). Henry of Navarre was Head of the House of Bourbon, and Duke Henry was founder of the Catholic League formed to block the former's more legitimate claim. Henry of Navarre was a descendant of Louis IX, married to Henry III's sister.

The end of the dynastic struggle came with the War of the Three Henrys (1584–1589). Henry III arranged for the murder of Duke Henry of Guise. He was subsequently assassinated by an Ultra-Catholic monk, leaving only Henry of Navarre, who converted to Catholicism and succeeded to the throne as Henry IV. "Paris," he is alleged to have said, "is worth a Mass." Upon ascending the throne, Henry IV issued the Edict of Nantes (1598), which granted limited religious tolerance to Protestants and brought a measure of religious peace and stability to the realm.

Henry IV was assassinated in 1610, leaving behind his nine-year old son to succeed him as Louis XIII (1601–1643). Once again, the Queen Mother, Marie de Médici (1575–1642), became regent. Under Cardinal Richelieu (1585–1642), her chief minister, and Cardinal Jules Mazarin (1602–1661), Richelieu's chosen successor, France supplanted Spain as the dominant power in Europe. Richelieu, who is considered one of the greatest statesmen in European history, had as his objective, to enhance the power of the crown in France and to restore France's great power status in Europe.

Richelieu used a carrot and stick approach with the nobility. They enjoyed appointments in the army and in government and the diplomatic service as well as tax exemption. In exchange for such privileges, they were forced to dismantle their fortified strongholds. Garrisoned towns guaranteed the Huguenots by the Edict of Nantes were seized, and the Huguenots disarmed. However, they continued to enjoy freedom of worship.

The nobles, assisted by some wealthy bourgeoisie of Paris, revolted between 1648 and 1653. The revolt known as the *Frondes*, occurred when the new king, Louis XIV (1638–1715), was a child and France was governed by a regency council. In reality, Cardinal Mazarin was the actual ruler during Louis XIV's youth. When Mazarin died in 1661, Louis XIV assumed personal direction of France's internal and foreign affairs.

Louis XIV's experience as a child during the *Frondes* left him determined to rule as an absolute monarch and to make France not just the most powerful nation in Europe but the most splendid as well. He worked diligently and conscientiously as few monarchs in history have before or since. He developed an efficient government by choosing men of proven ability from the middle-class as his chief ministers. Jean Baptiste Colbert (1619–1683), the son of a merchant, served as his finance minister. Colbert approached his office with the same sense of duty as his sovereign. By reducing fraud, increasing efficiency, and promoting industry, Colbert increased state revenue.

The aristocracy was reduced to a life of meaningless frivolity. By requiring them to be in residence at his palace of Versailles, and by decreeing that any nobleman who entered a trade would automatically forfeit his title, Louis XIV was able to keep them absent from their geographic bases of power and, at the same time, burdened them with the expenses of an extravagant lifestyle. The Parlement of Paris and the provincial parlements, traditional strongholds of the aristocracy, were reduced to impotency. Louis XIV never called a meeting of the Estates General. In fact, the Estates General did not meet between 1614 and 1789, a total of 165 years.

Louis XIV was deeply religious and a devout Roman Catholic. He believed that a unified nation-state required religious uniformity. That belief and his desire to combat heresy led him to revoke the Edict of Nantes in 1685. Huguenots were forced to convert to Catholicism or flee France to refuge in neighboring Protestant states or abroad in North America, South Africa, or the West Indies. Those who remained were subjected to torture, imprisonment, and servitude in the French galleys. A meeting of the French Catholic clergy in 1682 approved the four Gallican Articles, which effectively limited the pope's authority over the Catholic Church in France to spiritual matters, and affirmed the independence of the king in all temporal matters.

Under Louis XIV, France became not only the greatest power in Europe, but also the grandest. French replaced Latin as the language of diplomacy and the common tongue of the educated elite. The manners and dress of Louis XIV's court at Versailles were copied by the courts of kings and princes throughout Europe. It is not possible to accurately estimate the cost of construction of the palace of Versailles, but attempts to do so put the price, in today's currency, at several billion U. S. dollars. The silver balustrade in the ceremonial chamber of Louis XIV's Grand Apartment contained more than one ton (907.2 kg) of silver. The palace, more than one third of a mile (0.54 km) across and able to accommodate 10 000 residents, was surrounded by acres of formal gardens decorated with splendid fountains and 300 different trees. Versailles was a suitable residence for Louis XIV, known in his lifetime as the "Sun King" and the "Grand Monarch." The cost for operating such a monument to power and vanity consumed 5% of the annual state budget.

Louis XIV's attempt to extend the borders of France to what he believed were France's "natural borders" – the Rhine, the Alps, and the Pyrenees –threatened to establish French hegemony in Europe. The result was four major wars between 1667 and 1714, known collectively as the Wars of Louis XIV. England joined with various states on the continent to defend the "Liberty of Europe," which meant maintaining a balance of power in Europe. When the wars ended with the Peace of Utrecht in 1714, France was nearly bankrupt. When Louis XIV died in 1715, he left France with a financial crisis that led eventually to revolution in 1789.

England

Elizabeth I was the last of the Tudor monarchs. Upon her death, James VI of Scotland became James I of England, the first of the Stuart dynasty. James I (1566–1625) was the son of Mary I, Queen of Scotland (1542–1587) and Lord Darnley (Henry Stuart). Because Elizabeth I never married, and therefore did not have any children, Mary Queen of Scots, as she was known, was next in line as England's sovereign. Because she was Roman Catholic, many plots to remove Elizabeth and place Mary on the throne revolved around her. In 1586, she was implicated in a plot to assassinate Elizabeth that included the invasion of England by Spain and the Catholic League of France. Tried and convicted of treason, Elizabeth gave her consent for Mary's execution.

After Mary's death, her son was next in line to succeed Elizabeth. James Stuart was separated from his mother as an infant and raised as a member of the Presbyterian Church of Scotland, founded by the firebrand Calvinist Reformer, John Knox (1505–1572). James I remained a committed Protestant,[1] but one who believed in the episcopal form of church

---

1 James I sponsored an English translation of the Bible between 1604 and 1611, later known as the *Authorized King James Version* (KJV) in his honor.

government in the Established Church of England, not the congregationalism of the Scottish Kirk. Episcopal government complimented his belief in divine right monarchy. "No bishop, no king" summed up James I's view of the relationship between church and state.

A struggle emerged between James I, who believed in divine right monarchy, and Parliament, which claimed that the English sovereign was a constitutional monarch subject to Parliament. Both parties were, in fact, trying to change how England was governed. Under the Tudors, king and Parliament worked as a partnership, but one in which the monarch was clearly the senior partner. Divine right monarchy and constitutional monarchy both represented a new departure.

The Tudor monarchs were careful to obtain the approval of Parliament as evident in Henry VIII's separating the English church from Rome, his seizure and sale of monastic lands, and Elizabeth I's Act of Uniformity. Ever since the reign of Edward I (1272–1307), the English monarchs understood that it was easier to rule with the support of the realm as represented in Parliament, so long as Parliament's function was to advise and approve. However, it became established practice for Parliament to approve grants of revenue for the crown. It was Parliament's control of the purse that led to open war between the Stuarts and the Parliamentarians.

Charles I (1600–1649), James I's successor, lacked the skills necessary to reach a peaceful settlement with Parliament. In his third year as king, Parliament passed the Petition of Right (1628) demanding that the king not levy taxes without Parliament's approval nor imprison an individual without a trial. Charles I dissolved Parliament, and did not call another for the next 11 years.

William Laud (1573–1645) served as Archbishop of Canterbury during the period that Charles I ruled without Parliament. Laud was an authoritarian church leader. He desired to restore the Church of England to the prominence it enjoyed before the Reformation. The Puritans (English Calvinists) feared that such high church practices as an emphasis on ritual, priestly authority, and sacraments would be forced upon them, also. Puritans, lawyers, and influential country gentlemen joined forces in opposition to Laud and his church reforms. They also shared as a common cause, resistance to divine right monarchy.

When Archbishop Laud tried to force the Prayer Book of 1637 on the Scottish Presbyterian Church, the Scots revolted. Charles I was forced to call a meeting of Parliament in April 1640, to request funds to suppress the Scottish revolt. When Parliament refused to act unless Charles first addressed their grievances, he dissolved Parliament in May. Desperate for funds, Charles I called Parliament to meet in November 1640. Known as the "Long Parliament," it lasted until 1660.

Civil War broke out in 1642 between the royalists (Cavaliers) and the Parliamentarians (Roundheads). The Royalists were concentrated in northern and west-central England. They tended to be from the gentry, Anglican clergy, and the peasantry. The Roundheads were concentrated in East Anglia, London, and southern England. The middle classes, great merchants, and many nobles tended to support the Parliamentarian cause. The Puritans, of course, were among the Parliamentarians.

Oliver Cromwell (1599–1658) created the New Model Army, a disciplined force trained in the military tactics of the new continental armies. Cromwell was a Puritan zealot, who believed that he was an instrument of God's will. His army won a decisive victory over the

Royalists at the Battle of Naseby in June 1645. A division occurred among the Parliamentarians between a majority who favored a monarchy with an established Presbyterian church and those who opposed such a settlement. Cromwell and the army sided with the minority.

In December 1648, the army purged Parliament of those members who favored a settlement with Charles I. The event is known as Pride's Purge, named after the officer in command of the soldiers who carried out the purge. Those who remained, approximately 80 members of the House of Commons, declared themselves "the supreme power in this nation" on January 4, 1649. This "Rump Parliament," as it is known, established a High Court of Justice that tried and convicted Charles I of high treason. Charles I's death on January 30, 1649, may be viewed as either regicide or a lawful execution. His two sons, Charles and James, went into exile in France. Charles (1630–1685) became Charles II, *de jure* King of England upon the death of his father.

The Rump Parliament established a republican form of government called the Commonwealth of England. A written constitution, known as the Instrument of Government, the only written constitution in England's history, was drafted in 1649. Cromwell led the government, but found that he was no more suited to work with Parliament, even his Rump Parliament, than Charles I. He dispersed Parliament by force in April 1653 and ruled England for the next five years as a military dictator with the title of Lord Protector of England. By the time Cromwell died in 1658 and was succeeded by his son, Richard, England was tired of Puritan rule. A Convention Parliament of 556 members met in April 1660, and proclaimed Charles II king. Charles II returned to London on May 29 to the sound of cheering crowds.

Arguments over religion and the relationship between Parliament and the king continued during the reigns of Charles II and his brother James II (1633–1701). Charles II was at least sympathetic to Catholicism. Parliament passed the Test Act in 1673, which required all civil and military officials to take an oath denouncing Roman Catholicism and take communion in the Church of England. When James refused, his earlier conversion to Roman Catholicism became public knowledge. In 1673, James married Mary of Modena, a Roman Catholic believer. A controversy arose over whether or not James, now a Roman Catholic, could succeed his brother as king, since Charles II would die without a legitimate heir. Parliament was divided between those who were willing to accept James as king (Tories) and those who wanted to exclude James (Whigs) in favor of his Protestant daughter, Mary, from his first marriage.

James became king as James II in 1685. He began to appoint Roman Catholics to high positions in the military and government. Parliament was forced into action, when much to everyone's shock, his wife gave birth to a son. Faced with a Catholic succession, Parliament invited James II's daughter Mary and her husband William of Orange, stadtholder of the United Provinces of the Netherlands, to become joint monarchs as Mary II and William III. James II fled to France together with his wife and son.

In January 1689, the Convention Parliament declared the throne of England vacant and offered it to William and Mary. They accepted and agreed to rule as constitutional monarchs under the terms of the Declaration of Rights, enacted into law by Parliament on December 16, 1690, as the Bill of Rights. Taken together, the events of 1688 and 1689 became known as the Glorious Revolution.

Holy Roman Empire

While Spain, France, and England were developing into strong nation-states, the Holy Roman Empire was undergoing internal religious and dynastic struggles that would leave it a loose confederation of sovereign states until its dissolution in 1806. As noted earlier, the abdication of Charles V in 1556, divided the vast Habsburg Empire into two. His son, Philip II, received Spain, Italy, the Netherlands, and the overseas empire in the New World. His brother, Ferdinand I, received Austria, the Habsburg territories in Eastern Europe, and the imperial title of Holy Roman Emperor. The new arrangement resulted in two conflicts that influenced the future of Europe.

France remained, as during Charles V's reign, surrounded by Habsburgs. What was different at the beginning of the seventeenth century was the decline of Spanish power and the emergence of France as the dominant power in Europe. France was committed to confronting Habsburg interests whenever and wherever possible. The Austrian Habsburgs were committed to consolidating their hold over the Holy Roman Empire by asserting authority over the hundreds of individual political entities within the Empire and reestablishing religious unity under Roman Catholicism. These conflicting interests provided the backdrop to the Thirty Years' War (1618–1648).

At the dawn of the seventeenth century, the Holy Roman Empire was divided into two hostile camps, Protestant and Catholic. King Ferdinand I of Bohemia and Holy Roman Emperor after 1619 (Ferdinand II [1578–1637]), began the war in 1618, when he canceled privileges granted to Protestants by his predecessor and embarked upon a policy of forcing Roman Catholic conformity on Bohemia and Austria. The Protestants sought help from the Protestant Union, a military league of Protestant states within the Empire led by Frederick V (1596–1632), Elector Palatine and for one year the King of Bohemia (1619–1620). Ferdinand II received aid from the Catholic League led by Maximilian I (1573–1651) of Bavaria. The Protestant forces were decisively defeated at the Battle of White Mountain in November 1620.

Ferdinand II proceeded to eradicate Protestantism in the Habsburg territories. He then sent his armies under the command of Albrecht von Wallenstein (1583–1634) against the Protestant princes in the Empire. The Protestants formed an alliance with Denmark. By 1629, Wallenstein's army had conquered much of the Protestant territories and invaded Denmark. The defeat of the Protestants and the rising power of the Habsburgs alarmed not only the Protestant states in Europe, but Catholic France as well. In 1630, subsidized by France, Gustavus Adolphus (Gustav II Adolf [1594–1632]) of Sweden joined the Protestant cause. His victorious army reversed the course of the war. Tragically, he was killed while leading a cavalry charge at the Battle of Lützen (1632).

Protestant successes were checked in 1634, when a Spanish army defeated the Swedish-led Protestants at the Battle of Nördlingen. The Swedish army retreated to Northern Germany, while the Protestants signed the Treaty of Prague (1635) with Ferdinand II. The civil war, that at least on the surface appeared to be a war between Catholics and Protestants, came to an end. France, however, was threatened all along its borders by the victorious Habsburgs.

The final phase of the Thirty Years' War was clearly a decisive struggle for supremacy between the Bourbon rulers of France and the Spanish and Imperial Habsburgs. Cardinal Richelieu, Chief Minister for Louis XIII, decided the situation called for more than financial support of the war against the Habsburgs. France declared war on Spain in May 1635 and sent a French army into the Spanish Netherlands. The French defeated the Spanish in the Battle of Rocroi in 1645. The Swedish army went on the offensive against the Habsburgs, defeating them at the battles of Wittstock (1636), Breitenfeld (1642), and Jankau (1645). A combined Swedish and French army defeated the Habsburg army in the Battle of Zusmarshausen in1648, one of the last battles of the war.

The Thirty Years' War ended with the Peace of Westphalia in 1648, one of the most significant peace settlements in history. Peace negotiations were underway since 1644 in the cities of Osnabrück and Münster. The most important outcome of the Peace of Westphalia was recognition of the sovereignty of the individual German states within the Holy Roman Empire. Individual states within the Empire – e.g. Austria, Brandenburg, Bavaria – developed into nation-states while remaining a part of the Holy Roman Empire, henceforth, a loose confederation with an emperor and an Imperial Diet. It remained in the interest of the European great powers for the next two centuries to maintain the Peace of Westphalia, and by so doing, prevent the emergence of a unified Germany in the heart of Europe.

The economic and social consequences of the Thirty Years' War were far reaching for Central Europe. For 30 years, the mercenary armies lived off the land causing widespread disruption of the agricultural and commercial life of Germany, and with it, famine and starvation. An outbreak of plague between 1634 and 1639 contributed to the population decline. Estimates of the decline vary from 15% to 30%. Some areas suffered more than others. The city of Magdeburg, for example, had a population of 25 000 in 1618, but only 2464 in 1644 (History Learning 2015). The population of Germany did not recover until the first quarter of the eighteenth century.

Exploration and Discovery

Europeans began to search in earnest for new seaborne routes to India and Asia in the middle of the fifteenth century. The Mongols controlled Russia. The Ottoman Turks captured Constantinople in 1453, and advanced into Southeast Europe and North Africa. The traditional routes over which trade moved between Europe and parts of Asia were cut off. The interruption of trade that had been taking place for centuries came at a time when the new nation-states along the Atlantic coast possessed the necessary resources to launch such ventures and the new technology to guarantee their success.

From the mid-fifteenth century through the sixteenth century, overseas exploration and discovery was dominated by Portugal and Spain. From the beginning, the primary motivation was economic gain. But, along with the desire for profits, went a desire to Christianize the world. Ogier Ghiselin de Busbecq (1522–1592), Austrian ambassador to Constantinople, referred to the confusion of motives when he wrote, "Religion supplies the pretext and gold the motive" (Davidson 1997, p. 277). This dual motivation was also true for the Dutch, English, and French, who began overseas exploration and colonization in the seventeenth century. Differences existed. For example, the Portuguese and Spanish ventures were sponsored by their governments, while those of their competitors were normally underwritten by government-chartered, private companies.

A Portuguese prince known as Prince Henry the Navigator (1394–1460) is credited with launching the Age of Discovery. Though he was not a sailor, himself, he sponsored voyages down the western coast of Africa. Bartolomeu Dias (1450–1500) rounded the Cape of Good Hope and entered the Indian Ocean in 1488. Nine years later, Vasco de Gama (1469–1524) sailed around Africa and reached India.

Ferdinand and Isabella of Spain agreed to sponsor a voyage westward across the Atlantic Ocean by an Italian sailor, Christopher Columbus (1451–1506). Columbus set sail on August 3, 1492, and on October 12 reached what he believed was Asia. In fact, he landed on one of the islands of the Bahamas. In all, Columbus made four voyages to the islands of the Caribbean Sea. He died in 1506, believing that he had reached the islands off the coast of China.

Ferdinand Magellan (1480–1521) set sail from Spain in September 1519 in search of a route to the Spice Islands by sailing around South America and across the Pacific Ocean. Magellan was killed in April, 1521 in a battle in the Philippine Islands. Almost exactly three years after setting sail from Spain, only one (the smallest) of the original ships, and only 18 of the original 237 sailors, returned to Spain, having completed the first circumnavigation of the earth.

John Cabot (c. 1450–c. 1499), like Columbus, believed that the shortest route to Asia was to sail westward, but unlike Columbus, he believed the distance across the Atlantic Ocean was shorter, if one sailed from Northern Europe. With the backing of King Henry VII of England, Cabot sailed from Bristol with one ship and a crew of 18 sailors in early May 1497. He returned to Bristol on August 6, 1497 having reached Canada, possibly one of the Maritime Islands. Like Columbus, Cabot died believing he had found a shorter route to Asia.

Giovanni da Verrazzano (1485–1528) and Jacques Cartier (1491–1557) undertook voyages to the coast of North America sponsored by Francis I (1494–1547) of France. Verrazzano explored the eastern coast of North America on his first voyage in 1524. He made two subsequent voyages in 1527 and 1528. On his final voyage, he anchored off the coast of Guadeloupe, an island in the eastern Caribbean Sea. He, and the small landing party that accompanied him, were taken prisoner by the island's natives, who proved to be cannibals. Verrazzano and his companions were killed and eaten, while his brother and those who remained onboard ship looked on unable to intervene. Jacques Cartier made three voyages to North America between 1534 and 1541, where he explored the St. Lawrence River. The voyages by Verrazzano and Cartier were the basis for French claims to territory in North America. Neither England nor France, however, successfully established colonies until the early seventeenth century. The English tried to establish a colony on the island of Roanoke off the coast of North Carolina in 1587, but the effort failed.

European exploration and colonization of various hitherto unknown lands, and new encounters with other often much older and more advanced civilizations of the world, had a great impact on the course of Western Civilization, both positive and negative. A new world literally opened up to Europeans. New ship technology, nautical maps, and maps of the new territories brought Europe and the world beyond its horizons into intimate contact. The result was what historians call the Colombian Exchange.

The term Colombian Exchange is used primarily in reference to the impact of Europe on the New World of the Western Hemisphere and of the New World on Europe. A similar process of cultural exchange was taking place between the West and Asia for centuries, but intensified as European nations came into more direct contact with the Asian civilizations after the middle of the fifteenth century.

The positive influences of European expansion in the Western Hemisphere included the introduction of horses. Native Americans were, at first, terrified of the horses, which later revolutionized transportation and labor. Cattle, pigs, chickens, sheep, and goats, all of which were passengers on Columbus' second voyage in 1493, provided new food sources and future sources of revenue. Sheep's wool later fueled the nineteenth-century Industrial Revolution. Cats and domesticated dogs were also among the newcomers to the Americas.

The quality of European life was significantly enhanced by the introduction of new plants from the Americas. These included potatoes (including sweet potatoes), maize (American corn), beans, squash, tomatoes, and cacao (chocolate). Of them, potatoes and American corn were perhaps the most important, though it would be hard to imagine the modern diet without tomatoes. Potatoes became a staple in the diet of Europeans, especially for the lower classes.[2]

Not every aspect of the Colombian Exchange was positive for its participants. Not all of the plants and animals were intentionally introduced. Along with the horses, cattle, etc. came various insects and that ever-present stowaway onboard ships, the rat. Among the insects were the Asian cockroach, Japanese beetle, gypsy moth, killer bees, and Dutch elm disease. Rats are believed to have arrived with Columbus' first voyage. Cats kept intentionally aboard ships to help control the rat population followed the rats ashore. Both adapted well to the new environment. By the 1700s, both were found throughout North and South America.

There was an exchange of diseases that caused immense suffering in Europe and the Americas. Europeans brought with them Old World diseases like smallpox, measles, malaria, yellow fever, influenza, and chicken pox. They took back with them such New World diseases as syphilis, polio, hepatitis, and encephalitis. Many of the diseases introduced by the Europeans were spread through the air or by touch. They spread rapidly among the Native Americans whose immune systems were not able to combat the new invaders. Some estimates of the death toll among Native Americans due to the new diseases are as high as 90%.

Mercantilism was the dominant economic theory in Europe. According to mercantilist theory, colonies existed for the good of the mother country. They were expected to produce cheap raw materials and provide markets for home industries. Colonies were meant to remain underdeveloped and dependent upon the mother country. Since agricultural and mineral products were extracted from the colonies, a cheap labor force was necessary. At first, the colonial masters tried to make use of the Native Americans, but when they proved unsuited to forced labor, black Africans were imported.

Europeans did not invent the African slave trade. The slave trade was an established part of life in Africa south of the Sahara for centuries. The emergence of a plantation economy in the New World, especially in the Caribbean Sea and the southern portion of the future

---

2 Frederick the Great of Prussia ate meals of potatoes in public to encourage their consumption. On the other hand, he tried to prevent the drinking of coffee, like tea, an import from the "Old World" of the Middle East and Asia.

United States, dramatically increased the demand for African slaves. The production of sugar, tobacco, rice, and cotton were all labor intensive, requiring large numbers of cheap labor. The Portuguese and Spanish began using African slaves in their American colonies in the early sixteenth century. African leaders along the western coast of Africa acquired the slaves by force from the interior tribes, and then traded them for manufactured goods they desired from the European and American slave traders.

Supplying the New World colonies with African slaves became a very profitable part of the transatlantic trade. The Spanish, Portuguese, Dutch, Danish, French, British, and Americans all profited from the trade in human beings. The first American slave ship, *Desire*, was built in Massachusetts and launched in 1636. Four years later, Massachusetts became the first British colony in North America to legalize slavery. According to some estimates, as many as 9 300 000 Africans were forcibly transported to the Americas as slaves, the majority making the so-called Middle Passage from Africa to the Americas during the eighteenth century.

From the beginning of the sixteenth century to the middle of the seventeenth century, vast quantities of silver and gold flowed through Spain into the rest of Europe causing a price revolution and stimulating the growth of commercial capitalism. The expansion of European influence around the world was concurrent with the Scientific Revolution and the Enlightenment. Europe was gaining a monopoly on useful knowledge that would result in the Industrial Revolution, setting the stage for the Age of Western Imperialism at the end of the nineteenth century through the first half of the twentieth century. The forces loosed during the early modern era resulted in the Westernization of the world in the twentieth century.

Scientific Revolution

The Scientific Revolution that began in the middle of the sixteenth century and extended until near the end of the seventeenth century affected every area of life. By establishing a new understanding of the universe and a new methodology for discovering the true nature of the universe, it altered the basic values of Western Civilization and accelerated its future development. The Scientific Revolution, together with the Enlightenment and the Industrial Revolution that followed directly from it, enabled the West to gain a monopoly on useful (i.e. technological) knowledge that made it possible for Western Civilization to effectively dominate the world at the end of the nineteenth century.

By synthesizing, or uniting, medieval theology with classical philosophy (metaphysics), Thomas Aquinas and those scholastic theologians-philosophers who followed him, framed a systematic worldview that answered life's most pressing questions and was easy to understand. We refer to it as the medieval synthesis, or premodernity. It was based upon the acceptance of authority. Questions about how the universe worked were answered by simply referring to the appropriate authority, whether it was Aristotle, Ptolemy, or the church.

The dependence on accepted authority can be illustrated by an experiment undertaken by Galileo Galilei (1564–1642). Aristotle taught that if two objects, one larger and heavier than the other, were dropped at the same time, the larger and heavier object would hit the earth first. Rather than accept Aristotle's answer as definitive, Galileo chose to test it.

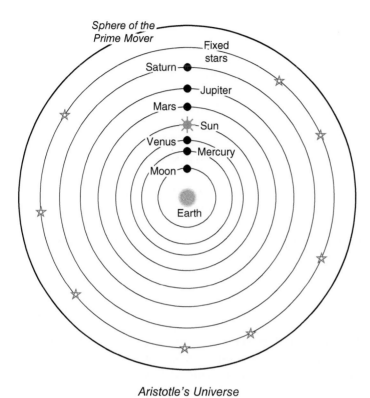

Aristotle's Universe

Figure 8.1 The geocentric model of the universe, also known as the pre-scientific or Aristotelian model, placed the earth at the center.

In about the year 1590, he dropped two balls of different weight from the top of the Leaning Tower of Pisa. They both hit the ground at the same time. During the preceding nineteen centuries no one thought to test Aristotle's assertion. There was no need to. Aristotle's findings were, according to the church, in harmony with the Bible. How could Aristotle be mistaken?

Many previously unknown classical manuscripts were brought to light during the Renaissance. The appearance of the printing press in the middle of the fifteenth century meant that they were more readily available. The availability of new ancient manuscripts resulted in a community of inquisitive minds across Europe willing to question Aristotle. Reverence for the accepted authorities was replaced by a willingness to verify their conclusions. One example was the discovery of Archimedes' reference to the lost work of Aristarchus (d. 230 BC), in which Aristarchus proposed a heliocentric model of the universe. Awareness of Aristarchus' heliocentric model encouraged Nicolaus Copernicus to propose his own heliocentric model of the universe in 1543.

As noted above (See Chapter 6) reason and observation were the only two instruments available during the Middle Ages to the individual who was trying to understand the universe he inhabited. Observation affirmed that the earth was the center of the universe as Aristotle taught and the church believed to be in the Bible. Did not the sun rise in the morning and go down in the evening? Did not an object fall down, rather than up?

The invention of basic scientific instruments during the seventeenth century made closer observation of nature possible, while at the same time, making it possible to discover answers to existing and newly formed questions. Galileo was able to make use of the newly invented telescope and microscope. The barometer, thermometer, air pump, and first pendulum clock all made their appearance during the middle of the seventeenth century. Perhaps the most important instrument for the progress of scientific investigation was the use of mathematics.

A number of advances in mathematics were made during the seventeenth century. The symbols for addition, subtraction, multiplication, and division came into general use along with Arabic numbers during the seventeenth century. The first tables of logarithms were published in 1614 and 1620. William Oughtred (1574–1660), an English mathematician and Anglican minister, invented the first slide rule in 1621. Blaise Pascal (1623–1662), a French mathematician and religious philosopher, invented the first calculator between 1642 and 1644, called the Pascaline or Arithmetic Machine. Isaac Newton (1642–1727) and Gottfried Leibniz (1646–1727), independently and almost simultaneously, discovered differential and integral calculus in the middle of the century. René Descartes (1596–1650) and Pierre de Fermat (1607–1665), both French mathematicians, independently developed analytic geometry in the 1630s. Without these advances in the science of mathematics, the Scientific Revolution could not have occurred when it did. Mathematics is the language of science.

Armed with the new instruments, the natural philosophers of the Scientific Revolution were able to go beyond merely knowing how things worked to discovering, or understanding, why. They began to develop a new method of inquiry, one that turned away from accepted authority, whether the classical philosophers or the medieval theologians, and embraced "systematic observation, measurement, and experiment, and the formulation, testing, and modification of hypotheses" (Oxford Dictionaries 2019).

From Copernicus to Newton

On May 24, 1543, Nicolaus Copernicus (1473–1543), a Polish astronomer and Catholic priest, died in Frauenburg, Poland. As he lay dying, he was handed a copy of his recently printed book, *On the Revolution of the Celestial Spheres*. The appearance of Copernicus' book is commonly considered to mark the beginning of the Scientific Revolution. Copernicus agreed with the commonly held belief of the day that the simpler something was, the more likely it was to be true, and the geocentric model of the universe was very difficult to prove mathematically. He discovered that the order of the planets made much more sense mathematically by simply placing the sun at the center with the earth revolving around it, and the moon revolving around the earth. He kept the crystalline spheres and the 24-hour revolution of the planets. By placing the sun at the center and making the earth just another planet going around the sun, Copernicus destroyed medieval cosmology and the medieval synthesis.

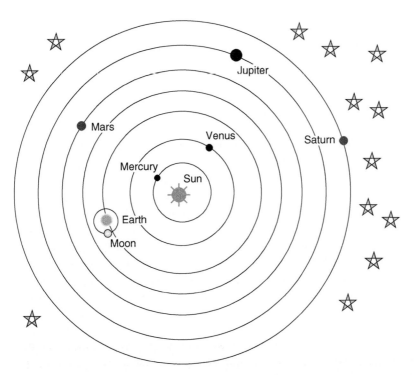

Figure 8.2   The heliocentric model of the universe, also known as the Copernican model, placed the sun at the center.

Copernicus' model was largely ignored at first. Most individuals remained loyal to the Aristotelian-Ptolemaic model that did not contradict either common sense observation or the medieval church's interpretation of the Bible. Was not the earth too heavy to move? If the earth rotated on its axis as required by the Copernican model, why didn't objects on the earth fly off into space? Did not Joshua command the sun to stand still while the Israelites were battling the Amorites? It fell upon Johannes Kepler to discover the laws of planetary motion that confirmed the Copernican model.

Johannes Kepler (1571–1630) was a mathematician, astronomer, and practicing astrologer who cast horoscopes for friends and patrons alike. In 1600, he became an assistant to Tycho Brahe (1546–1601), a Danish astronomer who kept detailed records of astronomical observations he conducted at his observatory, Uraniborg, on an island off the coast of Denmark. When Brahe died in 1601, Kepler inherited his data on the movement of the planets. Using Brahe's data, Kepler was able to define and mathematically prove three laws of planetary motion.

The first states that the orbits of the planets are elliptical, that is, like the outline of an egg shell with the sun at one focus of the ellipse. The second states that the speed of a planet's orbit varies with its distance from the sun. The closer the planet is to the sun, the faster its speed. The third law, simply stated, is that the larger the planet's orbit, the slower is its average speed. Gone were the crystalline spheres with the planets embedded in them moving in a circular motion around the sun. Kepler proved mathematically the heliocentric model.

A mechanistic model of the universe was beginning to take shape. But problems remained. Why, for example, did not the planets fly off into space? What held them in their orbits?

Galileo Galilei built a telescope in 1609, which he used to view the moon, and later, Jupiter. He discovered mountains on the moon and moons around Jupiter. If there were mountains on the moon, then the moon was not a pure orb composed of divine ether. Rather, it was made of a solid substance like the earth. If Jupiter had moons around it, then it was possible for the moon to revolve around the earth, while the earth revolved around the sun. No longer was there one set of laws for the earth and another set of laws for the heavens. One set of natural laws applied to both.

Galileo demonstrated better than anyone before him the important role that mathematics plays in science. He believed that the whole of nature was governed by certain universal truths, or natural laws, that could be verified mathematically. Whereas Aristotle and the medieval scholastic philosophers relied on *a priori* principles and common sense, Galileo advocated direct observation and mathematics as the means for achieving knowledge about nature. Galileo argued that nature in its most minute details, whether an atom or a planet, displayed mathematical regularity. For him, the universe was rational, but it was a rationality of mathematics, not scholastic logic. In his last book titled *The Assayer* (1623), Galileo wrote:

> Philosophy [i.e. physics] is written in this grand book — I mean the universe — which stands continually open to our gaze, but it cannot be understood unless one first learns to comprehend the language and interpret the characters in which it is written. It is written in the language of mathematics, and its characters are triangles, circles, and other geometrical figures, without which it is humanly impossible to understand a single word of it; without these, one is wandering around in a dark labyrinth. ("Works of Galileo" 2004)

What was real was what could be measured.

The discoveries and theories of Copernicus, Kepler, and Galileo were synthesized by Sir Isaac Newton (1642–1727), an eccentric genius and professor of mathematics at Cambridge University in England. Newton worked out the mathematical proofs for the universal law of gravity in 1666, but did not publish his findings until 1687. It was his friend and fellow mathematician, Edmund Halley (1656–1742), who encouraged Newton to make his discovery public. The result was Newton's *Mathematical Principles of Natural Philosophy* (1687), commonly referred to as *Principia*, one of the most influential books ever published.

Kepler was not able to answer the question of what kept the planets in their orbits. Newton discovered that every object, whether atom or planet, everywhere in the universe, is attracted to every other object in the universe by an invisible force he called universal gravity. The result was a new model of the universe as a machine, or clock, that operated by cause and effect natural laws. The universe and all that existed in it, including human beings, were subject to the same unchanging natural laws.

Newton's "clockwork universe" was not a closed system. Newton was a deeply religious man who believed that God created the universe and was "everywhere present" in it. The invisible force he called universal gravity was simply God's will. For Newton and the other scientists of his day, the discoveries they made about the universe proclaimed the glory of its creator. "This most beautiful System of the Sun, Planets and Comets," wrote Newton in

Figure 8.3   Aristotle, Ptolemy, and Copernicus are pictured discussing astronomy. *Source:* Engraving by Stefano Della Bella (1632).

Principia, "could only proceed from the counsel and dominion of an intelligent and powerful being" (Newton 2009). And later in *Optics* (1704), Newton said that the universe of natural laws "can be the effect of nothing else than the Wisdom and Skill of a powerful ever-lasting Agent" (Haycock 2005). The question of whether or not a mechanistic universe required divine intervention arose later during the Enlightenment.

Bacon and Descartes

Francis Bacon (1561–1626) served as Lord Chancellor of England under James I. Though he was not himself a scientist, he was one of the more important figures of the Scientific Revolution. Bacon vigorously campaigned for use of the scientific method in *Novum*

Organum (*New Method*) published in 1620. He advocated the pursuit of knowledge through observation and inductive reasoning. From experience and observation facts are arrived at which "ultimately arrived at the knowledge of the laws which govern the material world" (Lewis 1871, p. 126).

Bacon believed that use of the scientific method would lead to an accurate understanding of nature that, in turn, would lead to the improvement of society. In *New Atlantis*, an unfinished utopian novel published a year after his death, Bacon argued that scientific knowledge would lead to a future society where "generosity and enlightenment, dignity and splendour, piety and public spirit" (Bacon 2018, p. 3) would be realized. It was the practical application of scientific knowledge, rather than pure scientific research that concerned Bacon. Knowledge meant power over nature, and power over nature meant progress. In making the connection between knowledge and progress, Bacon foreshadowed a leading characteristic of the eighteenth-century Enlightenment, faith in progress and optimism about the future.

There was one important flaw in Bacon's methodology. He was not a mathematician, and therefore did not understand the important role that mathematics played in science. That was not the case with the Frenchman, René Descartes (1596–1650), who was at the same time a philosopher, mathematician, and scientist. Descartes invented coordinate geometry, also known as analytic or Cartesian geometry.

Beginning by doubting everything except his own existence, and through a process of rigorous reasoning, Descartes believed one could discover the true nature of the universe and human beings. He was convinced that the one thing he could know for certain was that he was thinking, therefore he existed. He could not doubt his own existence unless he existed. This methodical doubt is referred to as Cartesian doubt, or skepticism, and summed up in the famous saying, "I think therefore I am" (*Cogito ergo sum*).

It was by doubting that Descartes proved the existence of God. He, an imperfect being, could only conceive of a sovereign perfect being – God! – because that being placed the idea in his mind. Descartes further asserted the separation of mind and matter, an idea that existed at least as early as Plato and Aristotle. "Cartesian dualism" is the term applied to Descartes' appropriation of this ancient philosophical concept.

Descartes divided reality into two entities, the extended substance and the thinking substance. The extended substance is matter, everything that occupied space. It was objective and could be understood and explained mathematically with formulas and equations. Mathematics ruled supreme over the extended substance. The thinking substance was all things that exist only in the mind – e.g. consciousness, subjective experience – and are not subject to mathematical analysis.

Descartes' two realities created a problem for modern philosophy, earning for him the title of the first modern philosopher. How can the two realities, both created by God, be connected? What connects the soul to the material body? This dualism of mind and body, spirit and matter, results in what some call an upper and lower story. Since Descartes, humans live in two worlds. Much of life is lived in the lower story, a world that can be explained "scientifically," but is unable to provide emotional satisfaction. To satisfy that which makes a human being "human," one must leap upstairs into the spiritual realm that cannot be explained mathematically.

The problem of dualism introduced by Descartes, keeping in mind that it is at least as ancient as Plato and Aristotle, was not a problem for Descartes or the other natural philosophers of the Scientific Revolution. They understood their quest to discover how the universe worked as thinking God's thoughts after him, or as Kepler put it, "O God, I am thinking Thy thoughts after Thee" (Johann Kepler 2018).

Significance of the Scientific Revolution

The Scientific Revolution was the most significant development in the history of civilization since the Neolithic Revolution. The medieval model of the universe, Dante's cosmology, was overthrown, and replaced by a wholly new model and methodology for investigating and understanding the universe. The impact of this paradigm shift was not immediately apparent. The medieval synthesis was mortally wounded, but not yet deceased. The Scientific Revolution served as a bridge to the eighteenth-century Enlightenment.

Human beings were no longer at the mercy of providence, but henceforth masters of their own fate. By the middle of the seventeenth century, the governing classes supported scientific investigation. Scientific societies and academies appeared to encourage the scientists. They provided funds and equipment, and a community in which the new scientific discoveries were discussed and made public in published journals and books. Florence's Academy of Experiments was founded in 1657, England's Royal Academy of Science in 1662, the French Academy of Science in 1666, and the Berlin Academy in 1701. The scientific societies were a means by which the scientists were able to bypass the universities and especially the Roman Catholic Church, both of which continued to defend the Aristotelian-Ptolemaic model. Newton's discoveries were generally rejected by the faculty of Cambridge University in England as late as 1718.

Strong opposition to the new clockwork universe of the scientists came from the Roman Catholic Church. There was much more at stake for the Catholic Church than for the leaders of the nation-states. If the geocentric model was wrong, if the same natural laws applied everywhere in the universe, what was to become of the Great Chain of Being? If the earth and Jupiter were made of the same material, if they were both "just planets" orbiting the sun, then were peasants and nobles both creatures created by God in his image, neither greater than the other? Everything was upset. The eighteenth-century English poet, Alexander Pope (1688–1744), born in the year Newton's *Principia* was published, summed up the significance of the change presented by Newton's synthesis in his couplet:

> Nature and Nature's Laws lay hid in Night:
> God said, "Let Newton be!" and all was light.
> (Duffy 2018)

The light of scientific discovery contradicted the Roman Catholic Church's interpretation of Scripture, contradicted the medieval synthesis, and challenged the church's authority. It was not only the Protestant Reformers who threatened the pope's authority.

The Catholic Church's reaction to the Scientific Revolution was influenced by its response to the Protestant Reformation. The scientists found the freedom to investigate nature in the Protestant lands. When Galileo was forced to repudiate the Copernican theory and placed under *de facto* house arrest, he was able to continue to write, and his work was published in Protestant Holland. His books, together with those of Copernicus, Kepler, and Descartes were placed on the Index of Forbidden Books.

Giordano Bruno (1548–1600), Italian Dominican Friar and mathematician, was burned at the stake in 1600, and Galileo censored in 1633, for defending the Copernican theory declared heretical by the Roman Catholic Church. At the same time, Roman Catholic scholars made use of the Copernican theory in their reform of the calendar in 1582. In Spain, where the Inquisition was most infamous, the crown offered a generous reward to the inventor of an accurate clock. The same offer was made in England, Portugal, Venice, and France.

Christians, both Roman Catholic and Protestant, were faced with difficult questions that demanded answers. Was God the creator and sustainer of the universe, as Newton and the other scientists of the Scientific Revolution believed, or was he the great architect? If the new Newtonian universe was a cause and effect natural law mechanism, how were the miracles recounted in the Bible to be explained? Some called for a new synthesis of Christianity and science. Pascal was one such person. Christian apologists, since the early days of Christianity, insisted that there is no conflict between Christianity and science. Science seeks to explain how; religious faith seeks to explain why. For many of the intellectuals who followed the Scientific Revolution and were part of the eighteenth-century Enlightenment, the answer to the presumed conflict was found in Descartes' dualism. All things that could not be proven true by the scientific method were assumed to be either false, or irrelevant, that is, simply kicked upstairs as part of the thinking substance.

References

Bacon, S.F. (2018). *The New Atlantis: A Utopian Novel*. CreateSpace Independent Publishing Platform.

Davidson, M.H. (1997). *Columbus Then and Now: A Life Reexamined*. Norman, OK: University of Oklahoma Press.

Duffy, E. (2018). Far from the Tree. The New York Review of Books. https://www.nybooks.com/articles/2018/03/08/isaac-newton-far-from-the-tree (accessed 21 October 2019).

Haycock, D.B. (2005). Chapter 1: 'Standing on the Sholders of Giants.' http://www.newtonproject.ox.ac.uk/view/texts/normalized/OTHE00018 (accessed 21 October 2019).

History Learning (2015). Population and the Thirty Years War. http://historylearning.com/the-thirty-years-war0/social-economic-thirty-years/population-thirty-years-war (accessed 21 October 2019).

History of Science (2004). The Works of Galileo. Two New Sciences. https://hos.ou.edu/exhibits/exhibit.php?exbgrp=1&exbid=15 (accessed 21 October 2019).

Kepler, J. (2018). Leben. https://leben.us/johann-kepler (accessed 21 October 2019).

Lewis, G.H. (1871). *The history of Philosophy from Thales to Comte. Vol. II, Modern Philosophy*. London: Longmans, Green, and Company.

Newton, I. (2009). 'General Scholium' from the Mathematical Principles of Natural Philosophy (1729). http://www.newtonproject.ox.ac.uk/view/texts/normalized/NATP00056 (accessed 21 October 2019).

Oxford Dictionaries (2019). Definition of scientific method in English by Oxford Dictionaries. https://en.oxforddictionaries.com/definition/scientific_method (accessed 21 October 2019).

9

Age of Enlightenment and Revolution

Chronology

1598	James I's *The True Law of Free Monarchies*
1651	Thomas Hobbes' *Leviathan*
1690	John Locke's *Essay Concerning Human Understanding* and *Two Treatises on Government*
1709	Jacques-Benigne Bossuet's *Politics Derived from the Words of Holy Scripture*
1733	Voltaire's *Philosophical Letters on the English*
1740–1748	Seven Years' War
1765–1783	American Revolution
1751–1772	*Encyclopedia* Edited by Denis Diderot
1757	David Hume's *Natural History of Religion*
1762	Jean-Jacques Rousseau's *Social Contract*
1789–1791	Moderate Phase of French Revolution
1790	Civil Constitution of the Clergy
1791	*Declaration of the Rights of Woman and the Female Citizen*
1793–1794	Reign of Terror in French Revolution
1799	*Coup d'état* of 18–19 Brumaire, Napoleon Bonaparte
1800–1810	Codification of French Law under Napoleon, *Code Napoléon*
1801	Concordat of 1801 Between France and Roman Catholic Church
1804	Napoleon Becomes Emperor of First French Empire
1812	Napoleon Invades Russia
1815	Battle of Waterloo; Napoleon Exiled to island of St. Helena

The eighteenth-century Enlightenment flowed out of the Scientific Revolution and led directly to the French Revolution and Napoleon. Newton's *Principia* discredited the universe of the philosophers and theologians and put in its place a clockwork universe of cause and effect natural laws. John Locke's *Essay Concerning Human Understanding* and *Two Treatises on Government* advanced the belief that once the natural laws of society were discovered, it would be possible for rational human beings to construct a just society. When the French people attempted to realize the Enlightenment's promise in the

Western Civilization: A Brief History, First Edition. Paul R. Waibel.
© 2020 John Wiley & Sons, Inc. Published 2020 by John Wiley & Sons, Inc.

revolution of 1789, the Enlightenment's faith in progress and optimism about the future was shattered by the Reign of Terror and the Napoleonic wars.

Enlightenment

The natural philosophers of the Scientific Revolution changed forever how human beings view the universe they inhabit. Their discovery that the universe was a kind of gigantic cosmic machine operating according to cause and effect natural laws raised new questions. What does it mean to be human and how do humans fit into the cosmic machine? It was by using the scientific method – observation, experimentation, mathematical reasoning – as advocated by Francis Bacon, that the true nature of the universe was revealed. The natural philosophers, or scientists, did not believe that by rejecting ancient and church authorities and embracing the scientific method they were contradicting anything taught in the Bible. Indeed, they believed that they were merely discovering the natural laws instituted by God when he created the universe.

The eighteenth-century intellectuals, commonly referred to as philosophes, assumed that the universe was created by God. After all, it was reasonable to assume that if a clock exists, there must be a clockmaker. However, unlike Newton, the philosophes did not believe it necessary for God to be actively involved in his creation. It was possible that the clockmaker, having made the clock, wound it up and let it operate as designed without any further attention from its maker. With few and very rare exceptions, the intellectuals of the Enlightenment were not so daring as to suggest that the universe could exist without a creator. That radical idea had to wait another hundred years or more.

The philosophes were daring enough to take a bold leap of faith and assume that if there were natural laws governing how the universe worked, there must also be natural laws governing human society. The Scientific Revolution was a revolution in physics. The philosophes wanted to apply its discoveries to the study of human society and how human beings influence and shape the world in which they live. They assumed a mechanical view of both the natural world and human nature. It was only reasonable, they thought, to ask if there were natural laws governing human institutions waiting to be discovered.

The philosophes were neither atheists nor even agnostics. They were theists of a variety known as deists. The deists accepted the existence of God as creator of the universe-machine, but not as redeemer. They believed that God, being God, created a universe without flaws. Human beings were created good and remain by nature good. So, asked the deists, why do people who are innately good do bad things? How can injustice exist in a perfect world? The answer seemed logical. What Christians saw as the effects of sin in a fallen world, the Enlightenment intellectuals understood to be the corruption of naturally good people by history, poor education, and faulty institutions. Since humans were by nature good and able to reason, it followed that they could discover the natural laws of society and bring the faulty institutions into line with natural law. To continue the machine imagery, it was possible to tune-up the universe machine.

Knowledge of the natural laws of nature made it possible to construct wonderful gadgets that would improve the quality of life as foreseen by Francis Bacon in his utopian novel, *New Atlantis*. The philosophes believed that knowledge of the natural laws of society would lead to the removal of the injustices in society. Progress was possible. Rational human beings could create a utopia here on earth. Thus, the intellectuals of the Enlightenment had faith in progress and great optimism about the future.

It was the English philosopher, John Locke (1632–1704), who provided the intellectual basis for the Enlightenment's faith in progress and optimism. Locke wrote two of the most influential books of the Enlightenment, *Essay Concerning the Human Understanding* and *Two Treatises on Government*, both published in 1690. In the first, Locke tried to answer the epistemological question of how we know what we know. He rejected the belief held by the Scholastic philosophers and René Descartes that human beings are born with certain innate ideas implanted in the mind by God. He held that the human mind at birth is a blank slate (*tabula rasa*). Data from the environment flows into the mind through the five senses – sight, hearing, taste, smell, and touch. All knowledge comes from experience.

Human beings as individuals are products of their environment. A bad environment and bad education over time produced flawed institutions which, in turn, caused innately good humans to behave badly. A good environment and good education would produce virtuous people and a just society that functioned as originally designed. Locke's environmentalism was foundational to the Enlightenment.

It has been said that the intellectuals of the Enlightenment were propagandists. They wanted to communicate the new model of the universe and the new methodology discovered by the Scientific Revolution to the literate classes, in order to enlist them in the cause of building a better world. The publication of the *Encyclopedia*, published between 1751 and 1772, was a major effort to publicize the new worldview, and, "to change the way people think" (Rae and Thompson 2019). Denis Diderot (1713–1784) and Jean-Baptiste le Rond d'Alembert (1717–1783) began the monumental project as co-editors in 1751. D'Alembert withdrew from the editorship in 1759, leaving Diderot to continue as editor until its completion in 1772. More than 150 individuals, known collectively as the Encyclopedists, contributed articles, many of them multiple articles. Louis de Jaucourt (1704–1779) was the most prolific contributor. Between 1759 and 1765, Jaucourt wrote 17 266 articles, an average of eight per day, or 25% of the entire *Encyclopedia*.

Armed with Locke's empiricism, the philosophes believed that as science-based knowledge displaced superstition and ignorance, the innate goodness of human beings would shine forth assuring material and moral progress. No one better illustrated the Enlightenment's unbounded faith in human progress than Nicolas de Condorcet (1743–1794), a contributor to the *Encyclopedia*:

> The time will therefore come when the sun will shine only on free men who know no other master but their reason; when tyrants and slaves, priests and their stupid or hypocritical instruments will exist only in works of history and on the stage; and when we shall think of them only to pity their victims and their dupes; to maintain ourselves in a state of vigilance by thinking on their excesses; and to learn how to recognize and so to destroy, by force of reason, the first seeds of tyranny and superstition, should they ever dare to reappear amongst us. (Kreis 2006)

Ironically, Condorcet wrote those words shortly before being found dead in his prison cell, waiting a likely appearance before the guillotine in 1794. Diderot was a more realistic observer of the time, when he wrote, "We preach wisdom to the deaf and we are still far indeed from the age of reason" (Gay 1995, p. 20).

In their mission to redeem society by changing the way people think, the philosophes declared war on the Christian-based medieval synthesis. Only knowledge that could be verified by the scientific method was valid. Thus, the Christian belief that the cause of injustice was a moral problem, that is, that the descendants of Adam and Eve were in rebellion against God, was dismissed as myth. Centuries of Christian teaching stood in the way of clear thinking. The new way of thinking had to first discredit Christianity's claim to infallible truth, and the organized church and its priesthood as guardians of that truth.

David Hume (1711–1776), the radical Scottish skeptic and author of *The Natural History of Religion* (1757), referred to religious beliefs as "sick men's dreams," that at times have "been embraced by men of the greatest and most cultivated understanding" (Hume 1817, p. 451). Francois-Marie Arouet (1694–1778), better known as Voltaire, the greatest of the French philosophes, regarded all religions as social phenomena. He called Christianity "the Christ-worshiping superstition" that led to intolerance. As with most of the philosophes, Voltaire believed Christianity and all organized religion would one day be replaced by "natural religion" based on reason alone. The Enlightenment initiated the secularization of Western society that characterized the nineteenth century.

Enlightenment Political Theory

Divine Right Monarchy was the standard form of government, at least in theory, in most of the European nation-states during the eighteenth century. Simply stated, the monarch's authority to rule derives directly from God, not the people. God alone is sovereign over all of his creation, and it is he who grants sovereignty over the nation to his chosen servant, the monarch, who rules by the "grace of God." The argument for the divine right of monarchy was most clearly stated in *The True Law of Free Monarchies* (1598) by James I and *Politics Derived from the Words of Holy Scripture* (1709) by Bishop Jacques-Benigne Bossuet (1627–1704).

James I, in a speech before Parliament on March 21, 1609 and in *The True Law of Free Monarchies,* directly compared the king's role with that of God. "Kings are justly called gods," wrote James I, "for that they exercise a manner of resemblance of divine power upon earth: for if you will consider the attributes of God, you shall see how they agree in the person of a king" (Jokinen 1999). Just as it is blasphemy to question God's actions, "so is it sedition in subjects to dispute what a king may do in the height of his power" (Jokinen 1999). James I also argued that his authority and power was a part of the "ancient rights and possessions" he inherited from his "predecessors."

Bishop Bossuet was court preacher to Louis XIV and tutor to his eldest son, Louis, *Le Grand Dauphin.* In *Politics Derived from the Words of Holy Scripture*, published five years after his death, Bossuet based his defense of the divine right of kings on Scripture. He argued that God placed the king on the throne as "the representative of the divine majesty, sent by His providence for the execution of His designs" (Bossuet 1959). Just as in the Old Testament, he placed Saul and David on the throne of Israel and had them anointed by his prophet, Samuel. Any attempt to limit the king's sovereignty by placing any institution, such as

Parliament in England or the Estates General in France, between the king and God is rebellion against God. Throughout Scripture, argued Bossuet, whenever the people opposed the one whom God chose to rule over them, they were opposing God himself. Only God can judge the king. But as God's servant, the king must rule wisely, and not think that he is free to abuse his authority. The king must exercise his power "with fear and restraint as a thing which has come from God, and for which God will demand an account...." (Bossuet 1959).

Needless to say, the absolutism of a divine right king was in practice far from absolute. There were numerous historical institutions, such the privileges enjoyed by the church, nobility, guilds, knights, and even the peasantry, that could not be totally ignored, as the Stuarts learned from the Glorious Revolution in England and the Bourbon kings of France were to learn in the French Revolution at the end of the eighteenth century. The political theorists of the Enlightenment considered monarchy supported by a state church as archaic and corrupt. They looked to new forms of polity that were grounded in the natural laws of society, rather than appeals to theology. Thomas Hobbes, John Locke, and Jean-Jacques Rousseau formulated social contract theories of government. Others looked to the role of historical institutions, as for example, Montesquieu. Voltaire preferred enlightened despotism, which was a merger of divine right and social contract theories.

Social Contract Theorists

The social contract theorists refer back to the "state of nature," the time before the existence of organized society. There is no way of knowing what such a period was like. Thus, the so-called state of nature is purely hypothetical, and differs with each theorist. There are three social contract theorists, Thomas Hobbes, John Locke, and Jean-Jacques Rousseau. Each began with a different picture of what life was like in the state of nature. Each believed that society and government arose from a social contract between people in the state of nature, and each deduced a different form of government.

Thomas Hobbes

Life in the state of nature according to Thomas Hobbes (1588–1679) was one of constant conflict, "a war of all against all." The problem was that each individual possessed the natural right to determine what was right or wrong (judicial power), and the right to use force (executive power). In order to protect themselves from their own selfishness and establish harmony, the people entered into a social contract by which they created organized society and government. Each individual surrendered his or her judicial and executive powers to a single individual, who retained his own judicial and executive powers along with those of all other members of society. The result was an absolutist government in which the ruler's will was the law. The fear of the people revolting, even though there was no right of revolt against an unjust ruler in the social contract, would compel the absolute ruler to rule justly.

Hobbes presented his theory in *Leviathan* (1651), written during the English Civil War (1642–1651). Some scholars believe that Hobbes was attempting to justify Oliver Cromwell's autocratic rule during the Interregnum (1649–1660). The Enlightenment intellectuals agreed with Hobbes' secularism, but found his pessimistic view of human nature incompatible with the Enlightenment's fundamental assumption that people were created and remained by nature good.

John Locke

Of the three social contract theorists, John Locke is the most important. Locke presented his theory in *Two Treatises on Government* (1690), written, it is believed, to justify the Glorious Revolution in England in 1688 (see Chapter 8). Locke assumed that in the state of nature, human beings lived in harmony with one another as individuals who were by nature rational and good. People were endowed with certain inalienable natural rights, they being life, liberty, and property. The people entered into a social contract to create an organized society and government whose purpose was to protect those rights. They agreed to delegate, not surrender, their executive power to elected individuals, who would govern on their behalf. They retained their judicial power, that is, the right to determine what is right and wrong.

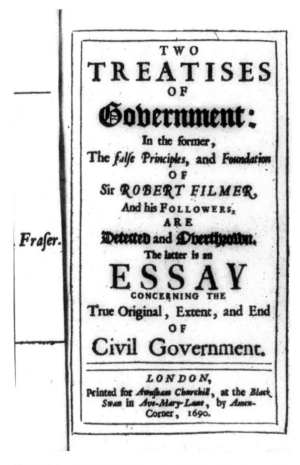

Figure 9.1 The title page from Locke's Two Treatises of Government (1690).

According to Locke's theory, King James II did not use the executive power delegated to him by the people represented in Parliament to protect their natural rights. On the contrary, he violated the terms of the contract by imprisoning individuals without due process of law, taxing the people without their approval, and various other arbitrary actions. Therefore, Parliament, acting on behalf of the people, had the right to take back the executive power from James II and immediately grant it to a new executive, William and Mary. Because James II did not rule by the grace of God, but by the will of the people, Parliament was justified in bypassing James II's son, the infant James, called James III by the Stuarts. The form of government resulting from Locke's theory is what is variously called parliamentarianism, constitutionalism, or simply representative government.

Though Locke was writing about England, the new United States of America that came out of the revolution of 13 of England's North American colonies is the best example of Locke's social contract theory. Following the revolution, elected representatives of the residents of the colonies met in Philadelphia, Pennsylvania in 1787 to form a new federal government. The instrument they drafted begins with the words:

> We the People of the United States, in Order to form a more perfect Union, establish Justice, insure domestic Tranquility, provide for the common defense, promote the general Welfare, and secure the Blessings of Liberty to ourselves and our Posterity, do ordain and establish this Constitution for the United States of America.

It then goes on to define the rights of the people and the role of government. The people are sovereign. The role of government is to guarantee and defend the natural rights of the citizens. It is a secular document. The United States of America is clearly created by and for the people, not by the grace of God. This is not to say that Christian influences were not present. As with the whole of the Enlightenment, the Judeo-Christian influence lies quietly in the background. However, the influence of John Locke is clear.

Jean-Jacques Rousseau

Jean-Jacques Rousseau (1712–1778) believed that people enjoyed absolute freedom in the state of nature. The individual was naturally good, sought only his or her own welfare, and felt compassion for those who suffered. The appearance of social organization caused the individual to become selfish, prideful, and to lose compassion for one's fellow members of society. In short, the individual in civil society lost his or her freedom and became a slave. Since it is not possible to return to the state of nature, the people created the semblance of freedom through a social contract. Rousseau presented his version of the social contract in what may well be his most famous work, *Social Contract* (1762).

According to Rousseau, every individual in society surrenders both executive and judicial authority to every other individual in society. At first it appears that the result is anarchy. Not so for Rousseau. There emerges from the whole a consensus, or General Will (the will of the community as a whole), that is in harmony with the individual's will. The collective whole is sovereign, just as each member is sovereign. Because the General Will is the individual's will, there can be no majority and minority will. The individual's will is fulfilled in the General Will. Thus, the individual is truly free when his or her will is one with the General Will.

If Hobbes' social contract resulted in absolutism and Locke's in constitutionalism, what results from Rousseau's social contract? Traditionally, Rousseau's vision is understood to be that of a popular democracy, such as many believed existed in the ancient Greek city state of Athens. Some find in Rousseau's social contract, not so much a popular democracy, as a theoretical justification for what became known in the twentieth century as totalitarianism.

Montesquieu

All three of the social contract theories are riddled with problems. Since there is no verifiable historical evidence regarding the so-called state of nature, the assumption made by each of the three theorists is purely hypothetical. Yet, upon that first assumption, hangs the outcome of the social contract. Also, one might justly ask of Locke, what is the origin of the inalienable rights that people allegedly possess? Here as elsewhere the intellectuals of the Enlightenment, by limiting the role of God in his creation to that of the clockmaker, forced themselves to rely on abstract principles in structuring a new worldview to replace the medieval synthesis.

Charles-Louis de Secondat, Baron de La Brède et de Montesquieu (1689–1755) was a nobleman from the south of France who, like his fellow philosophes, was a deist, but unlike them was an admirer of the Middle Ages. Montesquieu held a hereditary seat in the Parliament (*Parlement*) of Bordeaux, a medieval institution that functioned as a stronghold of noble privilege. He looked not to abstract principles, but to historical institutions such the *parlements* and the church as safeguards against royal despotism.

Montesquieu's political philosophy is found in *The Spirit of Laws* (1748). There is not one form of government suitable for everyone, everywhere. Despotism, wrote Montesquieu, works best in large empires, and democracy was suited only to small city-states. For France, and other European states, he advocated a separation and balance of powers as found in practice in England. Over centuries, England had successfully developed a system of government that restrained royal power while guaranteeing the people's liberty. The best form of government is one in which the three powers found in every state – legislative, executive, and judiciary – are separated and able to balance and check the power of each other.

The Founding Fathers who drafted the American Constitution were well acquainted with Montesquieu's theory of separation and balance of powers. Over the past two-hundred plus years the document they produced has proven to be an ingenious blend of Locke's social contract and Montesquieu's separation of powers. Perhaps its success may be attributed, at least in part, to the fact that the Founding Fathers built upon centuries of English constitutional history with its defense of liberty rooted in historical institutions rather than abstract principles.

Enlightened Despotism

Not all were as concerned about liberty and inalienable natural rights as Locke, Rousseau, and Montesquieu. Voltaire was, like Locke and Montesquieu, an admirer of England. His two books, *Philosophical Letters on the English* (1733) and *Elements of the Philosophy of*

Newton (1738) did much to publicize Newton's physics, Bacon's inductive philosophy, and Locke's empiricism across Europe and especially in France. What Voltaire admired most about England was its freedom of worship and the press, and the honor accorded to men of letters like himself. He was not really concerned with the issue of political liberty.

Voltaire held Louis XIV in great esteem, something very evident in his *Age of Louis XIV* published in 1751. His staunch defense of religious liberty, however, led him to prefer enlightened despotism, often referred to as enlightened absolutism. He visited Frederick the Great (1712–1786), the French-speaking, flute-playing, absolutist King of Prussia. He held Frederick up as an enlightened ruler, because Frederick promoted the arts and sciences and practiced religious toleration in his realm. Voltaire, who detested the Roman Catholic Church in France, praised Frederick for not recognizing any religious authority.

Divine right monarchy and enlightened despotism differed more in their theoretical bases than their practice. Louis XIV summed up the relationship between divine right kingship and the state in his famous statement, "I am the state" ("L'État, c'est moi"). In contrast to Louis XIV, Frederick the Great, who exemplified enlightened despotism, referred to himself as the "first servant of the state" ("*erster Diener des Staates*").

Enlightened rulers did not claim any divine mandate or special accountability to God. They justified their rule by claiming to use their power to establish enlightened policies that would remove the injustices that were a by-product of the entrenched privileged groups such as the noble landlords, clergy, and corrupt and inefficient bureaucracies. They would promote economic growth by developing the state's infrastructure, rationalize the collection of taxes, and replace mercantilist restrictions with free enterprise. Religious toleration (including Jews) was an important part of enlightened government. The Jesuits were expelled from most Catholic countries during the 1760's, and the order disbanded by Pope Clement XIV (r. 1769–1774) in 1773.[1]

By rationalizing government administration at all levels, and by suppressing the traditional limitations on central authority, enlightened despotism was a more enhanced and efficient form of absolutism than its predecessor, divine right monarchy.

French Revolution and Napoleon

The French Revolution marks the end of the Old Order (*Ancien Régime*) in France. It is sometimes compared with the Russian Revolution of 1917 as a pivotal event that impacted all that followed. It began in 1789 and lasted until 1799, or 1815, if one chooses to include the Napoleonic period, as is often the case.

Background

France was the most advanced and perhaps wealthiest country in Europe on the eve of the Revolution. France was more than twice as populous as Great Britain in 1789. French was spoken by the educated classes of Europe and North America. Paris was the intellectual

---

1 The order was restored by Pope Pius VII in 1814.

and cultural capital of Europe. French styles and tastes were copied everywhere Western Civilization extended. It was no wonder that the Revolution sent shockwaves throughout Europe.

There were long-term causes, such as the influence of the Enlightenment, but none was more important than the ongoing bankruptcy of the French government. The end of the Wars of Louis XIV in 1714, followed by the death of the Sun King himself in 1715, left the French government bankrupt. It was a problem that intensified as the century progressed. France went to war against England in both the War of Austrian Succession (1740–1748) and the Seven Years' War (1756–1763). Defeat in both wars deepened the financial problem. The final blow came with the American Revolution (1765–1783).

France began providing money and materials to the American revolutionists in 1775, and recognized the United States of America in the Treaty of Alliance of February 6, 1778. Britain responded with a declaration of war against France in March. French support for the American Revolution was vital to its success. Finding itself at war with France, which was supported by Spain and the Netherlands, and without allies, Britain chose to make peace. The 13 American colonies gained their independence in the Treaty of Paris (1783). The war between Britain and France ended with rather insignificant territorial adjustments.

The financial cost to France was enormous. The French government exhausted its credit, causing a financial crisis during the 1780's that led directly to the outbreak of revolution in Paris in 1789. The only solution to the crisis appeared to be for the church and the nobility to surrender some of their tax-exempt privileges. But when Louis XVI tried to impose a small tax on the nobility, the Parlement of Paris protested. The king, who usually yielded when faced with opposition, agreed in May 1788 to call for a meeting of the Estates-General in May 1789.

Since the Estates-General had not met since 1614, questions immediately arose about how members would be selected and how they would meet and vote. The French population was divided into three estates, based on class and rank. The first estate consisted of the clergy, the second of the nobility, and the third included everyone who was not a member of the first two estates. The clergy numbered about 130 000 out of a population of approximately 27 million.[2] The church owned roughly 10% of the land, and was tax exempt, but did make a "voluntary" contribution to the state every five years. The higher clergy came from the aristocracy and tended to side with the nobility, while the lower clergy were often from the commoners and sympathized with the third estate.

The second estate included about 350 000 noblemen, who owned between 25 and 30% of the land. They were also tax exempt. Because France did not practice primogeniture, the title and property of a deceased nobleman was passed to all of his sons, rather than to the eldest as in England. As with the clergy, some were very wealthy, and some were very poor. They had been stripped of most of their political power by the early Bourbon monarchs. The second estate was revolutionary in that the nobility looked forward to the meeting of the Estates-General as an opportunity to turn the clock back before the reign of Louis XIV, when king, church, and nobility shared power.

---

2 The statistics for population, land ownership, etc. vary widely from one source to another.

The third estate included about 95% of the population. It included the bourgeoisie, who made up about 8% of the population and owned between 20 and 25% of the land. Wealthy entrepreneurs, small shopkeepers, professionals, industrialists, and bankers were all part of the third estate. Also included, were the peasants, about 80% of the total population. Between 35 and 40% of the land was owned by the peasants, but roughly half of them owned plots too small to support them, or owned no land at all. The peasants still owed seigneurial obligations to the nobles who formally owned the land they occupied, as well as a tithe to the church. The working poor were also included.

The peasantry was particularly hard hit during the 1780's. There was a succession of crop failures. At the same time, the government increased the *taille*, a land tax owed by the peasants and other non-noble land owners, and the salt tax. As conditions in the countryside worsened, the destitute drifted into the towns seeking work that was not available. Rents rose by 140% in Paris for those who were employed. The crop failures caused a rapid rise in the price of bread, which accounted for three-fourths of the average worker's diet and consumed as much as one-half of his or her income.

During the year between Louis XVI's call for a meeting of the Estates-General in May 1788 and its convening in May 1789, the three estates chose delegates. Historically, the three estates would meet separately and have one vote each. Since the dominate portion of both the first and second estates were from the aristocracy, it was natural for them to vote together, thus rendering the third estate's vote a mere formality. Therefore, the third estate demanded that it have the same number of delegates as the first two combined, and that all three estates meet together and each delegate cast a single vote. Since there were some among those representing the first two estates who sympathized with the third estate, the latter would be able to transform the Estates-General into a constitutional convention. Louis XVI agreed to "doubling the Third." The first two estates would have 300 hundred delegates each, while the third estate would have 600.

The American Revolution served a second important role in addition to deepening the financial woes of the French government. Until the successful American Revolution, John Locke's social contract theory was just that, a theory. But once the 13 American colonies became independent and drafted a constitution, there was a historical example of a people who came together through their chosen representatives and drew up, and agreed to, a written social contract that defined the liberties of the citizens and the limits of governmental authority.

Moderate Phase, 1789–1791

The convening of the Estates-General on May 5, 1789, with much pomp and ceremony, was the event that triggered the revolution. After several weeks of fruitless debate, on June 17, the bourgeois-dominated third estate proclaimed itself a National Assembly. It was an illegal act by which they effectively assumed sovereignty. Thus, June 17, 1789 can be considered the start of the French Revolution. On June 20, the delegates from the third estate met in an indoor tennis court, and took an oath known as the Tennis Court Oath to continue meeting until they gave France a constitution. Some members of the first two estates joined with the third. Louis XVI once again yielded. On June 27, he ordered the first and second estates to join what he recognized as the National Assembly.

Amidst the turmoil, the price of bread soared. Rumors circulated that Louis XVI was making preparations to use force against the National Assembly. In response, the working class in Paris, called the *sans-coulottes*, organized a volunteer militia known as the National Guard. On July 14, a mob stormed the Bastille, a fortress prison that served as a symbol of the Old Order, where arms were stored. As royal authority melted away in Paris and throughout the countryside, panic swept through France.

During the evening of August 4, the National Assembly passed reforms that removed the last remnants of the privileged status of the nobility and clergy. The Declaration of the Rights of Man and of the Citizen, a summary of the Enlightenment principles of individual liberty, freedom of speech and religion, and equality before the law, was issued by the National Assembly on August 27. The bourgeois dominance in the National Assembly was evident in its emphasis on the sanctity of private property. Also, women were considered equal to men only in the abstract. Olympe de Gouges (1748–1793), a playwright and crusader for women's rights and abolition of slavery, responded with the *Declaration of the Rights of Woman and the Female Citizen* (1791), a defense of gender equality. She was subsequently executed by guillotine in 1793 during the Reign of Terror.

The National Assembly committed two blunders, which together contributed to the ultimate failure of the Revolution. To deal with the financial crisis that grew deeper by the day, the Assembly issued bonds called *assignats*, which were declared legal tender. The *assignats*, in effect paper money, lost value rapidly as the amount of *assignats* in circulation increased. By the end of 1795, the total face value of *assignats* in circulation was 45 billion livres. Their actual value was only one-quarter of 1% of their face value. They were virtually worthless.

In order to provide backing for the *assignats* when they were first issued, the National Assembly made a second major blunder when it decided to "reform" the Roman Catholic Church. Church lands were seized and, subsequently, sold at auction to redeem the *assignats*. Monastic vows were prohibited. In July 1790, the National Assembly passed the Civil Constitution of the Clergy. The clergy were henceforth to be elected and required to take an oath of allegiance to the nation. Their salaries were paid out of public funds. The clergy soon divided into two factions. Those who took the oath were known as the "juring," or "constitutional clergy." Those who did not were known as the "non-juring," or "refractory clergy."

The National Assembly's war on the Catholic Church turned much of countryside against the Revolution. The peasantry remained faithful to the church and became fertile soil for counterrevolution. Pope Pius VI (1717–1799) issued the encyclical *Charitas* (April 13, 1799) in which he condemned both the Civil Constitution of the Clergy and the Declaration of the Rights of Man and of the Citizen. The hostility between the Revolution and the Roman Catholic Church was not ended until 1801, when Napoleon Bonaparte and Pope Pius VII (1742–1823) signed the Concordat of 1801.

The Constitution of 1791 was adopted on September 3. France was defined as a constitutional monarchy with sovereignty vested in the "Nation." There was a separation of powers, with the executive vested in the king, the legislative vested in the Legislative Assembly, and the judicial vested in the courts. Citizens were divided into active and passive citizens. Active citizens were men at least 25 years old and paying a tax equal to three days labor. Passive citizens enjoyed equality in civil liberties, at least in theory, though women were not guaranteed the right to an education or freedom of speech. Free public education was guaranteed, at least for males. Marriage was defined as a civil contract.

Members to the Legislative Assembly were chosen by electors who were elected by the active citizens. There were property requirements for voting for electors, being an elector, and being a member of the Legislative Assembly. The influence of the wealthy few was also evident in the "inviolability of property" and prohibition against laborers organizing for collective bargaining. Despite all of the "checks and balances" in the political process that ensured the dominance of wealth, many more people were able to vote in France under the Constitution of 1791 than could vote in Great Britain at that time. The decision by members of the National Assembly to exclude themselves from membership in the Legislative Assembly was most unfortunate for the new experiment in constitutional government. The only Frenchmen with any practical experience with representative government were barred from serving in the first elected Legislative Assembly.

Radical Phase, 1792–1794

On April 20, 1792, the Legislative Assembly declared war on Austria, thus beginning a war that would continue on and off until Napoleon's final defeat at Waterloo in 1815. The war went badly at first for France. Prussia allied with Austria. In July, the French armies, commanded in part by Marquis de Lafayette (1757–1834), a hero of the American Revolution, suffered reverses. Possible defeat raised fear of a restoration of the Old Order. Insurrection broke out in Paris. Mob violence forced the Legislative Assembly in August to suspend the monarchy and call for the election by universal male suffrage of a National Convention to draft a new constitution for a republic.

The newly elected National Convention abolished the monarchy, declared France a republic, placed Louis XVI on trial, and executed the king on January 21, 1793. The dauphin, Louis-Charles, was recognized by supporters of the monarchy as Louis XVII. He died in prison at the age of ten, never having been crowned.

The leaders of the Revolution when it began were disciples of John Locke. With the election of the National Convention, leadership passed into the hands of those who were disciples of Jean-Jacques Rousseau. There were three centers of power in the National Convention: the Committee of General Security, the Paris Commune, and the Committee of Public Safety with 9, later 12, members. As the more radical factions competed for power, Maximilien François Marie Isidore de Robespierre (1758–1794), a member of the Committee of Public Safety, who as a former provincial criminal judge had opposed to the death penalty, emerged as the dominant person in the government.

Under the leadership of Robespierre and the Jacobin Club, a Reign of Terror was instituted throughout France. Robespierre was a visionary who wanted to create a utopian Republic of Virtue based on reason and the innate goodness of human beings. He and his supporters believed that the Constitution of 1793, declaring France a Republic, could not be implemented until France was purged of all counterrevolutionaries and enemies of the Republic.

The Reign of Terror lasted for ten months from September 5, 1793, when the government decided to make "Terror" the order of the day, until the fall and execution of Robespierre at the end of July 1794. There is no way of knowing for certain how many people died. The numbers vary widely. Official records indicate that 16 thousand were guillotined over nine months in public executions that served as a kind of macabre entertainment for the crowds that watched. The slaughter was greatest in the Vendée, a province on the Atlantic coast, where one-quarter of the population, including men, women, and children, fell victim to the Terror. Contrary to popular myth, most victims of the Reign of Terror were ordinary citizens randomly selected, not members of the aristocracy.[3]

The Enlightenment philosophes's crusade against Christianity and the Roman Catholic Church, in particular, bore fruit during the Revolution. On September 2, 1792, three bishops and over 200 priests were massacred by mobs in Paris. During the Reign of Terror, a new, de-Christianized calendar beginning with the Year 1 of the Revolution was introduced. There were 12 months of 30 days each, divided into three weeks of ten days each. The months and days were given new names in an attempt to remove all Christian influence. All religious holidays were banned and replaced with holidays to celebrate the Revolution.

The anti-Christian crusade climaxed with an attempt to introduce a new religion, the Cult of the Supreme Being. A previous attempt at establishing a Cult of Reason, essentially atheism, failed to attract a following beyond the intellectuals and some from among the *sans-culottes*. Robespierre believed that the extremes of the anti-Christian crusade alienated the masses. He also believed that a belief in God and religious faith was necessary for instilling moral values in the people, something that he felt was a necessity for a Republic of Virtue. Thus, in June, 1794, Robespierre introduced the "Worship of the Supreme Being." Both the existence of God and belief in the individual soul's immortality were recognized. Freethinkers who admired Voltaire accused Robespierre of being a reactionary. Their resistance contributed to his fall from power on July 27, 1794.

End of the Terror and Return of the Moderates, 1794–1799

It was said that when Robespierre rose in the National Assembly to denounce enemies of the Republic, his hand would move up and down like the blade of the guillotine. As former allies of Robespierre became victims of the Terror, fear led to conspiracies against Robespierre among members of the National Assembly. On July 27, 1794, he was not allowed to speak and expelled from the Convention. He was arrested, and on July 28 (*10 Thermidor*, the month of heat according to the French Republican Calendar), Robespierre was guillotined along with 21 of his associates.

---

3 "According to one estimate, among those condemned by the revolutionary tribunals, about 8 percent were aristocrats, 6 percent clergy, 14 percent middle class, and 70 percent were workers or peasants accused of hoarding, evading the draft, desertion, rebellion, and other purported crimes. Of these social groupings, the clergy of the Roman Catholic Church suffered proportionately the greatest loss" Brian Gardner (2012). "Dechristianization of France During the French Revolution." *Dechristianization of France During the French Revolution: Western Civilization II Guides* (April 30). http://westerncivguides. umwblogs.org/2012/04/30/dechristianization-of-france-during-the-french-revolution (accessed February 12, 2019).

The fall of Robespierre was followed by the Thermidorian Reaction. The Jacobins went into hiding throughout France as the Great Terror was followed by a counterterror. Those perceived to be supporters of Robespierre and the Jacobins were purged from the government and the military. The republican constitution of 1793 was annulled. Back in control, the moderate followers of John Locke drafted a new constitution.

The Constitution of the Year III (1795) established a new form of government known as the Directory. Instead of a single Legislative Assembly, there was a bicameral legislature consisting of a lower house known as the Council of 500 and an upper house called the Council of Elders with 250 members. The Council of 500 proposed legislation, while the Council of Elders either accepted or rejected the proposed legislation. Members of both houses were chosen by electors who were elected by the active citizens defined as all tax-paying males over 21. Property requirements limited the prospective pool of electors to a mere 30 000 out of a population of more than 27 million. The executive branch consisted of five individuals called directors who were selected by the Council of Elders from a list provided by the Council of 500.

The period of the Directory was a troubled period. Graft and corruption were rampant. France was still at war, though the war was going well for France at the time. The economy was such that the rich grew richer and the poor suffered. Food shortages, rebellion in the Vendée supported by the British and the French royalists who hoped for a restoration of the monarchy, and renewed hopes among the Jacobins due to the complete collapse of the value of the *assignats*, made restoration of stability virtually impossible.

François-Noël Babeuf (1760–1797), known as Gracchus Babeuf, emerged as a champion of the poor.[4] Babeuf was a journalist and publisher of *Le tribun du people* ("the tribune of the people"). "What," asked Babeuf, "is the French Revolution? An open war between patricians and plebeians, between rich and poor" (Doyle 1989, p. 324). Among his goals was the abolition of private property and private enterprise. Babeuf's Conspiracy of Equals, as it became known, was supported by the Jacobins. Believing that an armed uprising was likely, the Directory acted to crush the movement. Babeuf was arrested on May 10, 1796, and executed on May 27, 1797. The Directory limped on, increasingly dependent upon the military for its survival until November 9, 1799 (18 *Brumaire*, Year VIII according to the French Republican Calendar), when it was overthrown in a *coup d'état*.

Napoleonic Period, 1799–1815

Napoleon Bonaparte was born August 15, 1769, on the island of Corsica, recently acquired by France from the Republic of Genoa in the Treaty of Versailles (1768). His father was a member of the lesser Italian nobility. He entered military school just months before his tenth birthday and graduated from the *École Militaire* in Paris with the rank of second lieutenant in the artillery at age 16. After a victory over a British supported royalist rebellion at the Battle of Toulon in December 1793, he was promoted

---

4 The nickname "Gracchus" is a reference to Tiberius and Gaius Gaius Gracchus, tribunes during the Roman Republic who championed the cause of the poor. See Chapter 3.

to the rank of brigadier general. As his military successes followed one after the other, Napoleon's military career flourished.

After defeating the Austrians in Italy in 1797, Napoleon returned to Paris a hero. Hoping to force Britain to accept peace by attacking British interests in the Middle East, he took an army to Egypt. His successful campaigns in Egypt and Syria were further evidence of his military genius. When English Admiral Horatio Nelson (1758–1805) destroyed the French fleet in the Battle of the Nile, also called the Battle of Aboukir Bay, in August 1798, the army was marooned in Egypt. Napoleon returned to Paris, leaving his army in Egypt. The last of the French soldiers in Egypt were repatriated back to France in 1801 during a truce in the war between France and Great Britain.

The *Coup d'état* of 18–19 Brumaire (November 9–10, 1799) ended the Directory and paved the way for Napoleon's rule. Many consider it to mark the effective end of the French Revolution, preferring to view the Napoleonic period as something distinct from the Revolution itself. Others see it as the natural conclusion of the Revolution. The Constitution of the Year III was abolished and replaced by a new Constitution of the Year VIII. The Directory was replaced by a three-member Consul with all real power vested in the First Consul, Napoleon. It was approved by 99.9% of those who voted in a referendum held on February 7, 1800. A second referendum held on August 2, 1802, approved the Constitution of the Year X making Napoleon First Consul for life. Two years later in 1804, the Constitution of the Year XII established the First French Empire with Napoleon as Emperor of the French. The imperial title was made hereditary in Napoleon's family.

By 1810, Napoleon dominated all of continental Europe except the Balkan Peninsula. The Grand Empire consisted of an enlarged France, a host of vassal states, some ruled by his relatives, and states that were reluctant allies, including Austria, Prussia, Russia, Sweden, and Denmark. Napoleon believed his victories were responsible for his success. "My power proceeds from my reputation," he said in 1802, "and my reputation from the victories I have won" (Johnston 1910, p. 166). Arthur Wellesley, Duke of Wellington (1769–1852), who together with Prussian Field Marshall Gebhard Leberecht von Blücher (1742–1819) defeated Napoleon at the Battle of Waterloo (1815), said that Napoleon's "presence on the field made a difference of 40,000 men" (Chandler 1966, p. 157). It was his ability to inspire greatness in ordinary people that made Napoleon a great leader. In Napoleon's own words: "You must speak to the soul in order to electrify the man" (Chandler 1966, p. 155).

Enlightened Despot

Napoleon was more than a conqueror. He was the classic example of an enlightened despot. Enlightenment ideals guided his rule of France and were carried throughout Europe wherever his armies went. Some of his reforms were begun during the radical phase of the Revolution and brought to fruition by him. He rationalized and centralized government administration. Tax collection was centralized and made more efficient. Government corruption and waste were curtailed. Careers in government service were opened to men of talent rather than birth. Ability and performance became the criteria for promotion. In two areas, church-state relations and the economy, Napoleon succeeded where all of those before him failed.

As one shaped by the Enlightenment, Napoleon was not a religious person, but neither was he hostile to religion. Unlike the philosophes, he did not foresee a utopia in the future. He believed that society would always be one of inequality. Some would prosper and others would suffer. Therefore, the masses needed religion to comfort them, to enable them to accept the inequalities in this life and have faith in a future justice beyond this life guaranteed by their faith in God. Belief in God was a necessary basis for public and private morals. A person who did not believe that all would one day be fairly judged could not be trusted. "No society," said Napoleon, "can exist without morality; there is no good morality without religion. It is religion alone, therefore, that gives to the state a firm and durable reform" (Markham 1963, p. 93).

Napoleon made peace between the French Revolution and the Roman Catholic Church with the Concordat of 1801, and by doing so, undercut the peasants' support of the royalists. According to the terms of the Concordat, Catholicism was recognized as the religion of the majority of the French people, but not as the state church. The government nominated bishops with papal approval. The bishops appointed the clergy. The state paid the salaries of the clergy. The papacy gave up any claim to church lands that were confiscated and sold during the Revolution. The Organic Articles of 1802 extended religious liberty to Protestants and Jews.

The French economy that Napoleon inherited from the Directory was in shambles. To promote economic development, he improved the infrastructure by building roads and canals that served both economic and military functions. Unnecessary restrictions were removed. Taxes and tax collection were reformed, and government began to work together with industrial and commercial interests for the good of both private and state interests. Most important, perhaps, was the creation of the Bank of France to grant loans and regulate a new currency based on a gold standard system.

Napoleon also applied Enlightenment principles to his reform of education. He established a public educational system that was secular and focused on preparing men for public service and to serve as officers in the military. It was a highly centralized educational system under the supervision of the University of France, a national board of education that determined the curriculum and established standards for the nation as a whole. His enlightened approach did not extend to girls, however.

Napoleon's supreme achievement, even by his own measure, was the *Code Napoléon*. There was a confusion of law codes in France before the Revolution. They included elements from Justinian's codification of Roman law in the sixth century, feudal Frankish and Germanic institutions, Canon Law of the Roman Catholic Church, royal decrees, case law emanating over time from the various *parlements*, and local customs. Voltaire quipped that a traveler in France "changes his law almost as often as he changes his horses" (Voltaire 2016).

Napoleon appointed a committee of lawyers in 1800 to begin work on the code, but also took a personal interest in the overall process. The *Code Civil des Français* was completed and became official in 1804. By 1810, the *Code Napoléon*, as it was then known, was supplemented by criminal, commercial, military, and penal codes. The revolutionary principles of liberty and equality before the law, freedom of religion, and private property rights were enshrined in the Napoleonic Code. These, however, were compromised by reactionary elements such as allowing for judicial torture, giving fathers authority over their children, husbands authority over their wives, and denying labor the right to organize.

Empire

Though Napoleon was, in many ways, an "enlightened" ruler, in the end he failed. The reforms he brought to France and through conquest to the rest of continental Europe mark the end of the Old Order in France and Europe as well. But the glories he brought to France and the French people could only be sustained through conquest. Once the conquests ended, the burdens placed upon the client states and allies to benefit France undermined the enlightened principles he hoped would unite Europe under French leadership. Napoleon was unable to end the war with England, and as long as England would not accept French hegemony over Europe, the war continued until Napoleon was finally defeated. Also, he was never able to get European rulers to accept his imperial title as legitimate. To them Napoleon remained forever the "Corsican Monster."

Figure 9.2 Portrait of Napoleon I by Nicolas-Toussaint Charlet (c. 1821).

With the founding of the First Empire in 1804, the French Revolution came full circle. The empire was, in fact, a revival of the pre-revolution absolute monarchy, only made more efficient by enlightened rationalization of government institutions. Napoleon established a new nobility based on talent rather than birth, and an imperial grandeur more splendid than the Bourbon court. He divorced Joséphine de Beauharnais (1763–1814) in 1809, and in April 1810, married Marie-Louise (1791–1847), the eldest daughter of Francis II (1768–1835), emperor of Austria. He hoped the marriage would result in a male heir and acceptance of the legitimacy of the Bonapartist dynasty in France. A son was born March 24, 1811, Napoleon's only legitimate heir, and given the title "King of Rome."

The Treaty of Amiens between France and Great Britain and her allies was signed in March 1802, as a "Definitive Treaty of Peace." It proved to be only a cease fire. The war was renewed in May 1803. Admiral Horatio Nelson, who previously won the Battle of the Nile in 1789, dealt Napoleon a crushing defeat in the Battle of Trafalgar off the coast of Spain in October 1804. Without losing a single ship, Nelson's fleet sunk 22 out of 33 ships of the line of a combined French and Spanish fleet. Any hope of a French invasion of Britain went down with the warships.

Napoleon's fortunes were much better on the battlefield, where he personally controlled the course of events. He defeated the Austrians and Russians at the Battle of Austerlitz in December 1805, and the Prussians at the Battles of Jena and Auerstadt in October 1806. As a result, the Holy Roman Empire was terminated and replaced with the Confederation of the Rhine, making all of Germany except Austria, Prussia, Brunswick, and Hesse a protectorate of France. The former Holy Roman Emperor was henceforth the Emperor of Austria. Russia was once more defeated at the Battle of Friedland in June 1807, following which Russia and Prussia signed the Treaties of Tilsit, recognizing the Confederation of the Rhine and the creation of the Grand Duchy of Warsaw out of territory ceded by Prussia.

Unable to engage Britain in a decisive battle where his Grand Army would have the advantage, Napoleon resorted to economic warfare to compel Britain to make peace. His goal was to close European ports to trade with Great Britain. What became known as the Continental System resulted from two decrees, the Berlin Decree of 1806 and the Milan Decree of 1807. Britain countered with the Orders in Council (1807), which was a counter blockade of France and all the continental nations allied with Napoleon.

Napoleon overestimated Britain's dependence on trade with the continent. Its control of the seas meant that it had access to necessary supplies from overseas. However, the Continental System proved disastrous for Napoleon's allies, especially the Low Countries, who were dependent on their trade with Britain. Economic suffering encouraged smuggling. In 1810, Tsar Alexander I (1777–1825) withdrew from the Continental System, a move that led to Napoleon's invasion of Russia in 1812.

Napoleon's Grande Army of approximately 600 000 crossed the Niemen River into Russia on June 26, 1812. About one-half were French. The remainder were provided by Napoleon's allies and client states. His goal was to engage the Russian army in a major battle, one he felt confident of winning, and then dictate terms to Tsar Alexander I. The Russian army numbered about 200 000. Because Napoleon expected a quick victory, his army was not prepared for an extended campaign that would include Russia's bitter cold winter. Neither did he plan to supply his vast army for an extended period of time, or a campaign that would extend deep into Russia.

The Russian army retreated, scorching the earth as they did, denying the Grand Army the ability to live off the land. As its supply lines became ever more overextended, and the weather turned wetter and colder, the Grand Army's condition worsened. Still, Napoleon pursued the Russian army deeper into the Russian interior. Two bloody battles were fought. One was at Smolensk (August 17–19), and the second at Borodino on September 7.

When the Grand Army reached Moscow on September 14, Napoleon found the city abandoned and burning. Napoleon waited for Alexander I to sue for peace. With supplies depleted and as snow began to fall, the Grand Amy began its retreat from Moscow on October 19. Freezing, starving, and constantly harassed by Russians and Cossacks, Napoleon's army began to melt away in November. Only a remnant, perhaps around 100 000, returned to France.

As the Russians advanced into Central Europe, Austria, Prussia, and Sweden switched sides. What is referred to by Germans as the War of Liberation occurred during the period between March 1813 and May 1814. The decisive Battle of the Nations was fought just east of Leipzig on October 16–19, 1813. It was the first time Napoleon was defeated on the field of battle. The Grand Army retreated toward Paris. Napoleon was unable to prevent the coalition forces from invading France. Meanwhile, the Duke of Wellington invaded France from Spain. Napoleon was left with no choice but to abdicate on April 4, in favor of his son with Empress Marie-Louise as regent.

Suspecting Napoleon intended to rule through his son and wife, the Allies compelled him to abdicate unconditionally on April 11, 1814. Louis XVI's brother, the Count of Provence, returned to France as Louis XVIII (1755–1824). According to the Treaty of Fontainebleau (1814), Napoleon was exiled to the island of Elba off the coast of Italy. He was allowed to keep the title of Emperor and given an annual allowance from the French treasury. Elba was recognized as a sovereign principality with its own flag and an army of 600 soldiers. During his 300 days as ruler of Elba, Napoleon proved himself once again a son of the Enlightenment. He did much to develop the island's infrastructure and raise the standard of living for the island's roughly 12 000 inhabitants.

But Napoleon's understanding of his own destiny did not allow him to be content as the enlightened ruler of Elba. On March 1, 1815, he appeared on the French coast near Cannes and began the journey back to Paris. Soldiers sent by Louis XVIII to intercept and arrest Napoleon joined him instead. Louis XVIII left Paris for Ghent. Napoleon entered Paris on March 20, welcomed by cheering crowds. When news of Napoleon's return to power reached the Allies, who were gathering in Vienna to restore order to Europe after the disturbances of 1789–1815, they agreed to remain at war with Napoleon until he was finally defeated and removed as a threat to the peace of Europe.

The last battle of the Napoleonic Wars took place near the village of Waterloo just south of Brussels, Belgium. The battle began at noon on June 18, 1815. Initially Napoleon's army of 72 000 engaged an allied army of about 68 000 commanded by the Duke of Wellington. In the late afternoon the battle was going poorly for Wellington, until a Prussian army of 30 000 under the command of Field Marshall Blücher arrived. The arrival of the Prussians changed the course of the battle. Napoleon was defeated. According to some accounts, he left the battlefield in tears.

Napoleon abdicated a second time in favor of his son, considered by some to have reigned for a few days as Napoleon II. Napoleon left Paris on June 25. He departed for America aboard a French frigate on July 6, the same day that Louis XVIII returned to Paris. Napoleon never reached America. His journey was interrupted by a British fleet. He was transported to the remote island of St. Helena in the South Atlantic Ocean, 1200 miles from the nearest landmass, accompanied by a small entourage. He spent his remaining years writing his memoirs. Napoleon died on May 5, 1821, at age 51, most likely from stomach cancer.

References

Bossuet, B.J-B. (1959). The Divine Right of Kings. http://www.iupui.edu/~histwhs/H114.dir/H114.webreader/H114.read.a.Bossuet.html (accessed 21 October 2019).

Chandler, D. (1966). *The Campaigns of Napoleon*. New York: Macmillan.

Doyle, W. (1989). *The Oxford History of the French Revolution*. Oxford: Oxford University Press.

Gay, P. (1995). *The Enlightenment: The Rise of Modern Paganism*. New York: W. W. Norton & Co.

Hume, D. (1817). *Essays and Treatises on Several Subjects: in Two Volumes*, vol. 2. Edinburgh: Bell & Bradfute.

Hume, D. (1956). *The Natural History of Religion*. London: Adam and Charles Black.

Johnston, R.M. (ed.) (1910). *The Corsican: A Diary of Napoleon's Life in his Own Words*. Boston: Houghton Mifflin.

Jokinen, A. (1999). James I's Speech Before Parliament (1609). http://www.luminarium.org/sevenlit/james/1609speech.htm (accessed 4 November 2019).

Kreis, S. (2006). Condorcet, Sketch for a Historical Picture of the Progress of the Human Mind (1795). The History Guide. http://www.historyguide.org/intellect/sketch.html (accessed 21 October 2019).

Markham, F. (1963). *Napoleon*. New York: New American Library.

Pearcy, T. and Dickson, M. (1997). King James I, On Divine Right of Kings. http://www.wwnorton.com/college/history/ralph/workbook/ralprs20.htm (accessed 21 October 2019).

Rae, J. and Thompson, S. (2017). Denis Diderot. http://alphahistory.com/frenchrevolution/denis-diderot (accessed 21 October 2019).

Rae, J. and Thompson, S. (2019). Denis Diderot. French Revolution. Alpha History. https://alphahistory.com/frenchrevolution/denis-diderot (accessed 4 November 2019).

Voltaire (2016). Philosophical Dictionary, by Voltaire. CUSTOMS-USAGES. https://ebooks.adelaide.edu.au/v/voltaire/dictionary/chapter145.html (accessed 21 October 2019).

Part IV

Nineteenth Century: An Overview

With Napoleon defeated, the victors met in Vienna to restore order and peace in Europe. Conservatives who put their trust in historical precedent rather than abstract principles were in command. They were guided by the belief that a balance of power among the Great Powers was the basis for a lasting peace. They also believed that sovereignty rested in the legitimate hereditary rulers, rather than with the people. Their attempt to restore the old order, however, merely put a lid on the forces and ideas released by the Enlightenment and the emerging Industrial Revolution.

Napoleon's conquests spread the social contract theories of Jean-Jacques Rousseau and John Locke. The restored rulers could try repressing them, but they could not eliminate either liberalism or nationalism. Revolutions broke out during the first half of the nineteenth century that were led by the middle class, and had as their goal, the establishment of constitutional governments, free trade, and nation-states based on national identity.

A combination of new scientific knowledge about agriculture and husbandry resulted in an agricultural, or green, revolution during the early eighteenth century, which in turn caused an increase in population. The growth in population provided the necessary labor force for the Industrial Revolution that began in Britain during the last decades of the eighteenth century. With abundant and easily accessible coal supplies, and command of the seas, Britain was ideally situated to become the world's only truly industrialized nation by the middle of the nineteenth century.

The Industrial Revolution spread to the European continent after 1815. At the same time, a second scientific revolution was underway that changed the understanding of reality. Humanity was increasingly understood to be engaged in an evolutionary process, in which those who were higher on the ladder of evolution did by right and necessity dominate and exploit those who were lower. Armed with a monopoly on useful knowledge (meaning scientific knowledge), driven by the laws of *laissez faire* economics, and liberated from any real human conscience, the European nations, joined by the two non-European nations, the United States of America and Japan, embarked on a new age of imperialism. By the end of the nineteenth century, virtually all of the habitable world was dominated and economically exploited by the West. Europe, once the backwater of world civilization, had become the center of the world.

Western Civilization: A Brief History, First Edition. Paul R. Waibel.
© 2020 John Wiley & Sons, Inc. Published 2020 by John Wiley & Sons, Inc.

10

Europe's Great Powers in the Nineteenth Century

Chronology

1814–1815	Vienna Congress
1818–1822	Concert of Europe
1821–1829	Greek War for Independence
1823	Monroe Doctrine
1825	Decembrist Revolt in Russia
1830	July Revolution in France; Louis Philippe King of the French
1834	*Zollverein* (Customs Union) Founded by Prussia
1839	Treaty of London Guarantees Belgium's Neutrality
1848	Revolutions Throughout Europe
1848	Revolution in France; National Workshops; "Bloody Days of June"
1848	Louis-Napoléon Bonaparte Elected President of France
1848–1849	Frankfurt Parliament
1852	Louis- Napoléon Bonaparte Proclaimed Emperor Napoleon III
1853–1856	Crimean War
1861	Kingdom of Italy Proclaimed
1864	German-Danish War
1866	Austro-Prussian War (Seven Weeks' War)
1867	Dual Monarchy (Austria-Hungary)
1870–1871	Franco-Prussian War
1871	Proclamation of German Empire
1871	Paris Commune

After Napoleon Bonaparte's first abdication in April 1814, the Quadruple Alliance exiled Napoleon to the island of Elba off the coast of Italy and recognized the eldest of Louis XVI's surviving brothers as Louis XVIII (1755–1824). Louis XVI's son, Louis-Charles (1785–1795), recognized as Louis XVII but never crowned, died in captivity. Desiring to strengthen a restored Bourbon dynasty, the Allies signed a generous treaty with France, known as the First Treaty of Paris (May 30, 1814).

The First Treaty of Paris restored France's borders of 1792, which included territories not within France's borders before the Revolution in 1789. Britain returned France's former

Western Civilization: A Brief History, First Edition. Paul R. Waibel.
© 2020 John Wiley & Sons, Inc. Published 2020 by John Wiley & Sons, Inc.

colonies, with the exception of Tobago and St. Lucia in the Caribbean, Mauritius in the Indian Ocean, and Malta in the Mediterranean Sea. France was not required to pay any indemnities. The treaty did not, however, address the issue of territorial changes made in Europe under Napoleon. That task was left to the Vienna Congress, hosted by Emperor Francis I of Austria (1768–1835), formerly Francis II, Holy Roman Emperor.

Vienna Congress

Heads of state and representatives from across Europe and beyond attended the Vienna Congress that convened in September 1814, and lasted until June 1815. The whole Congress never met together. Most delegates spent their time enjoying Vienna, one of the most beautiful and culturally alive cities in Europe. All of the negotiations and decisions were made by the members of the Quadruple Alliance, joined by France in January 1815. The five Great Powers – Britain, Austria, Prussia, Russia, and France – remained the five Great Powers of Europe, one could say of the world, until the Great War of 1914–1918.

The Vienna Congress was the third such peace conference at which the powers that had been at war for an extended period of time met and attempted to construct a peace settlement that would assure peace in Europe for the future. The previous two were the Peace of Westphalia (1648) and the Peace of Utrecht (1713). The Vienna Congress proved to be the most successful peace conference in Western history. For one hundred years until 1914, there was not a major war involving the Five Great Powers.

The representatives of the Five Great Powers, while pursuing their own objectives, were guided by three basic principles. The first was their shared belief that a lasting peace depended upon a balance of power among the Great Powers. Therefore, they determined to restore the balance that existed before 1789 and take steps to assure that no one power would again attempt to gain dominance (hegemony or universal monarchy) in Europe.

The second guiding principle was compensation, which meant that in redrawing international borders, territorial adjustments would be made to promote the balance of power. If one of the five gained territory, the others would be granted new territory as necessary to assure a balance of power.

The third guiding principle was legitimacy. Not only had Napoleon altered the national borders throughout much of Europe, he also removed heads of state and, in some cases, replaced them with members of his family. The diplomats agreed that, in such cases, the legitimate ruler of a given state, or his legitimate heir, would be restored. The principle of legitimacy was not followed in every case that arose.

The diplomats were all gifted negotiators. Klemens von Metternich (1773–1859) represented Austria. He was the dominate personality at the Congress. His influence is evident in the fact that some modern historians call the period in European history between 1815 and 1848 the "Age of Metternich." Robert Stewart, commonly referred to as Lord Castlereagh (1769–1822), represented Britain. Prussia was represented by Prince Karl von Hardenberg (1750–1822) and Wilhelm von Humboldt (1767–1835), a noted philosopher and linguist. Prince Charles de Talleyrand (1754–1838), the prime example of a government bureaucrat, represented France. Talleyrand was a survivor. He served the French revolutionary governments, Napoleon, Louis XVIII, and following the Revolution of 1830, Louis Philippe, the July Monarch. Tsar Alexander I (1777–1825) chose to represent himself, assisted by Count Karl Nesselrode (1780–1862).

The members of the Quadruple Alliance agreed in advance of the Congress to retain certain territories and advantages they gained during the Napoleonic Wars. Russia was to retain Finland and refused to discuss issues relating to either Turkey or the Balkans. Britain, with command of the seas and clearly the only "world power," kept certain of the former French colonies (see above) and the Cape of Good Hope and Ceylon, formerly belonging to the Dutch. In addition, Britain refused to discuss freedom of the seas and overseas colonies. The revolt of the Spanish colonies in the Western Hemisphere was allowed to run its course.

To guarantee against a renewed threat from France, the Kingdom of the Netherlands was resurrected with Belgium added. The Kingdom of Sardinia was strengthened with the addition of the former Republic of Genoa. Most of the left bank of the Rhine River was given to Prussia. Prussia was also given Polish and Swedish territories in Eastern Europe, as well as most of the Kingdom of Saxony. The Polish-Saxon question split the Quadruple Alliance and threatened to destroy hope of a lasting peace.

Tsar Alexander I wanted to restore the Kingdom of Poland with himself as constitutional king. Prussia wanted to annex all of the Kingdom of Saxony. Both proposals were viewed by Metternich as direct threats to Austria. Metternich was supported by Castlereagh, who considered Russia a greater threat to future peace in Europe than a revived France. The split in the Allies gave Talleyrand the opportunity to establish France as an equal partner in the negotiations. Talleyrand signed a secret treaty with Britain and Austria, agreeing to join them in a war with Russia and Prussia, if necessary, to block their aims. When the terms of the secret treaty leaked, Alexander proposed a compromise.

The threat of war was defused. The Congress created a new, miniature "Congress Poland" with Alexander I as its king and with a constitution granted by Alexander. Prussia was given two-thirds of Saxony, with the remainder being retained by the King of Saxony. The settlement of the Polish-Saxon question set Prussia on the path of becoming the dominate power on the European continent by the end of the century.

Among other important actions of the Congress was the decision not to resurrect the Holy Roman Empire, dissolved in August 1806 as a result of Napoleon's victory at the Battle of Austerlitz and Francis II's abdication as Holy Roman Emperor. In its place, the Congress created the German Confederation, a loose federation of sovereign German states and free cities, without either an executive or judiciary. A Diet (assembly) of delegates sent by the governments of the member states, presided over by an Austrian delegate, met regularly in Frankfurt.

While the Vienna Congress was in session, Napoleon escaped from Elba and returned to France. On March 20, he entered Paris to cheering crowds, reestablished his rule and began raising a new army. The members of the Quadruple Alliance formed a new alliance, pledging themselves to remain in the field until Napoleon was finally and decisively defeated. On June 18, the two armies met at Waterloo in Belgium. Napoleon was defeated by the joint efforts of the Duke of Wellington and Field Marshal Blücher. Napoleon abdicated a second time on June 22 and was exiled to the island of St Helena in the South Atlantic. The Allied armies entered Paris on July 7 and restored Louis XVIII.

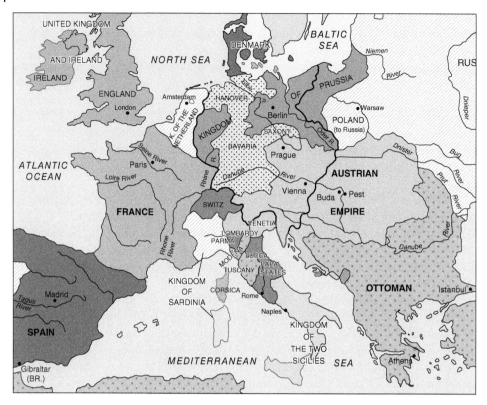

Figure 10.1 Map of Europe at Mid-1800's.

The First Treaty of Paris was voided and replaced by the less generous Second Treaty of Paris on November 20, 1815. France's borders were reduced to those of 1790, essentially the same as 1789. In addition, France was required to pay for the cost of defeating Napoleon for a second time, set at 700 million francs. The Allies were allowed to establish 17 fortresses along France's northern and eastern frontiers at France's expense. The treaty was signed in Paris on September 26, 1815, by Russia, Austria, and Prussia. Subsequently, most of the European states signed.

Tsar Alexander I called upon Europe's rulers to join him in forming a Holy Alliance, an agreement to follow Christian teachings in their relationship with one another and with their subjects. During the period 1815–1848, the Holy Alliance referred to the cooperation between the three conservative East European monarchies – Russia, Prussia, and Austria – intent on suppressing any signs of nationalism or liberalism, the two isms that threatened their very existence. Only Britain, the Pope, and the Sultan of Turkey refused to sign.

Concert System

The General Treaty of the Final Act of the Congress of Vienna was signed on June 9, 1815, just nine days before the Battle of Waterloo. With Napoleon's final defeat and exile, the members of the Quadruple Alliance turned their attention to the question of how to assure the settlement's future security. They met in Paris on November 20, and formally reaffirmed their commitment to prevent a revival of Bonapartism and to maintain the balance of power in Europe. They agreed to meet in conference periodically to discuss any threat to the peace of Europe and, if necessary, take action to guarantee it. There were four meetings of what historians refer to as the Concert of Europe between 1818 and 1822.

The first meeting of the Concert took place in 1818 at the Congress of Aix-la-Chapelle (a.k.a., Aachen). A number of items were discussed, including the international slave trade, the Barbary pirates, granting the title of "King" to the former Electors of the Holy Roman Empire, and a plea from Napoleon's mother that her son be allowed to return to Europe. The really significant decision of the Congress was to withdraw the allied troops from France and allow private banks to assume the indemnity imposed on France by the Second Treaty of Paris. Also, France joined the Quadruple Alliance, making it a Quintuple Alliance. Tsar Alexander I's visionary proposal to form some sort of permanent European union, together with an international military force, got nowhere due in part to the threat such an arrangement would pose to the sovereignty of the member states.

In 1820, liberal-inspired revolutions broke out in Spain and Naples. The corrupt governments of the two restored monarchies collapsed with little resistance. Ferdinand VII (1784–1833) of Spain was forced to restore the constitution of 1812 that established a constitutional monarchy with sovereignty vested in the nation. Ferdinand IV (1751–1825) of Naples agreed, under coercion, to grant a constitution. The revolutions were both inspired by liberalism, with a measure of nationalism mixed in, especially in Naples.

A second meeting of the Concert was held at the Congress of Troppau in Silesia during October 1820. Alexander I and Francis I attended in person, Wilhelm III (1770–1840) of Prussia was represented by the crown prince, while Britain and France sent observers. The Congress was dominated by Metternich, who proposed that they approve a protocol granting the members of the Quintuple Alliance the right to intervene in the internal affairs of any European state where the "legitimate" government was threatened by revolution. Both Britain and France refused to sign the protocol, making it clear that a rift was widening between the two Western powers and the Holy Alliance. Though the Troppau Protocol, embodying the principle of intervention, was signed by the three members of the Holy Alliance on November 19, 1820, no intervention in the revolutions in Spain or Naples was authorized. Instead, the Congress adjourned, agreeing to reconvene in January, 1821, at Laibach in Slovenia.

When the Congress of Laibach convened in January, 1821, the rift between the two constitutional powers of Britain and France and the three autocratic powers of the Holy Alliance was beyond repair. Metternich's desire to transform the Concert into an anti-revolutionary alliance synonymous with the Holy Alliance was largely complete. Once again, Britain was represented by an observer without authority to act on behalf of the British government. France, however, did send a diplomat with authority to represent its government. Against British objections to the general principle of intervention championed by Metternich, the Congress chose to authorize Austria to intervene militarily to crush liberal revolutions in both Naples and Piedmont.

The final meeting of the Concert took place in Verona, Italy, between October 20 and December 14, 1822. The primary reason for the Congress of Verona was Louis XVIII's request that the Concert approve French intervention in Spain. Austria, Russia, and Prussia gave their approval to the French request. In the spring of 1823, a French army of 20 000 crossed the Pyrenees and restored Ferdinand VII to his throne.

Latin America, Britain, and the United States

Two very important issues that were of special interest to Britain were hauntingly present in the background at the Congress of Verona. One was Spain's desire, in accordance with the principle of legitimacy, to regain its colonies in the Americas. The second was the Greek revolt against Turkish rule that broke out in March, 1821.

Spanish power was in decline at least since France's victory over Spain in the Battle of Rocroi in 1643. British commercial penetration of Spain's American colonies had been underway for well over a century. During the Napoleonic Wars, British trade with Latin America increased dramatically. The prospect of restoring Spanish rule there was definitely against British interests. Britain wanted the former Spanish colonies to become independent and able to enter into trade agreements with Britain. Of course, there was no chance of intervention in Latin America, if such intervention was opposed by the British navy.

Britain's efforts to ensure the survival of the newly formed Latin American republics found support from the United States of America, that only eight years earlier signed the Treaty of Ghent, in which Britain acknowledged defeat by the United States in the War of 1812. There was strong moral support among the citizens of the United States for the new republics. The new British Foreign Secretary, George Canning (1770–1827), found in that sentiment support for Britain's position with respect to the former Spanish colonies.

Canning proposed that the United Kingdom and the United States issue a joint declaration against any European power attempting to restore the new republics to their former colonial masters. The United States was basking in a wave of nationalism following its victory in the War of 1812. For President James Monroe (1758–1831), then in his second term as president, to appear to cooperate with Britain would have been very unpopular. Furthermore, Monroe's Secretary of State, John Quincy Adams (1767–1848), hoped to succeed Monroe as president. Adams suggested that the United States take unilateral action. Monroe declared what became known as the Monroe Doctrine in his annual message to Congress on December 2, 1823, declaring that the United States of America would consider as hostile any interference by any European power in the Americas.

There was no way the United States could enforce its newly declared foreign policy, but the European states understood that it was really British policy and would be enforced by the British navy. It was a win-win for both parties. Monroe and Adams avoided appearing to cooperate with Britain, and Britain avoided openly proclaiming a policy that violated the principle of legitimacy. With time, the Monroe Doctrine became the cornerstone of the United States' foreign policy toward its Latin American neighbors.

Greek War for Independence

The Greek War for Independence was a cause on which the European Great Powers were able to find common ground. Greece had been under Ottoman Turkish rule since the mid-fifteenth century. According to the principle of legitimacy, the Sultan of Turkey was the legitimate ruler of Greece. When the Greeks revolted in 1821 and proclaimed their independence in 1822, the initial response from the Great Powers was negative. Metternich correctly understood that the Greek revolt was inspired by both nationalism and liberalism.

A positive response to Greek pleas for aid would mean encouraging the two greatest threats to the tranquility of Europe as established by the Vienna Congress.

Many liberals and nationalists in the West saw in the Greek struggle for independence a replay of the ancient Greeks' struggle against the Persians. Ancient Greece was seen as the birthplace of Western Civilization, especially by liberals. The struggle of the Christian Greeks for freedom and liberty after almost four centuries of occupation by the infidel Turks was destined to capture the hearts of Western intellectuals and inspire poets and painters under the spell of romanticism. The death of the popular romantic poet, Lord Byron (George Gordon, 1788–1824), in Missolonghi, Greece, where he went to join the Greek cause, encouraged widespread support in Britain.

Though ruled by Muslim Turks, the Greeks were allowed to remain Greek Orthodox Christians. Orthodox Christians, however, looked to the Tsar of Russia as the defender of Orthodox Christianity since the fall of Constantinople in 1453. The persecution of Orthodox Christians in Greece, during their struggle for independence provided an excuse for Russia's intervention. Russia's strategic interests in the Balkans and its desire to one day control Constantinople and the Dardanelles was perhaps an even more compelling reason for Russian intervention. Fearful of a Russian presence in the eastern Mediterranean, Britain, and France were drawn into the conflict. Their goal was to shore up Turkey, the "Sick Man of Europe," check the advance of Russian influence, and see Greece become independent.

An independent Greek state was recognized by the Great Powers in 1829. However, it was not until 1832, that Turkey recognized the independence of Greece in the Treaty of Constantinople. Representatives of Britain, France, and Russia met in London in May 1832. Without consulting the Greeks, they agreed that Greece should be a monarchy with the Bavarian prince, Otto von Wittelsbach (1815–1867), as its king.

Decembrist Revolt

Tsar Alexander I died on December 1, 1825. The Tsars were, until the Russian Revolution in 1917, the most autocratic rulers in Europe. Alexander I was somewhat of an exception. His grant of a constitution for Congress Poland, with himself as constitutional monarch, met with only limited success. His early liberalism, like his proposed Holy Alliance and vision of a unified Europe, were influenced by both Enlightenment ideas and religious mysticism.

Alexander I pursued Napoleon to Paris following Napoleon's disastrous invasion of Russia in 1812. Educated officers of the Russian army were thus exposed to the ideas of the Enlightenment. Some hoped that Alexander would grant a constitution for Russia and introduce other liberal reforms. Alexander, himself, turned conservative after the mutiny of the Semyonovsky Lifeguard Regiment, one of the two oldest guard regiments in the Russian imperial army in October 1820, and after coming under the influence of Metternich at the Congress of Troppau.

When Alexander I died unexpectedly in 1825 without a legitimate male heir, he was survived by two brothers, Constantine (1779–1831) and Nicholas (1796–1855), neither of whom wanted to be Tsar. Nicholas swore allegiance to Constantine, despite the fact that Constantine had renounced his right of succession in 1822, in a manifesto signed by

Alexander I. Constantine swore allegiance to Nicholas, making clear that he would not become Tsar. Only then, did Nicholas publish the manifesto of 1822 after which he became Tsar of Russia.

On December 26, 1825, three thousand soldiers stationed in St. Petersburg mutinied in what is known as the Decembrist Revolt. They marched into Senate Square chanting "Constantine and Constitution." Nicholas acted quickly to crush the mutiny. Five of the leaders were hung. Many were sentenced to forced labor in Siberia. Others were stationed at distant outposts in the empire. All hope of liberal reform vanished. Nicholas I proved to be the very personification of a ruthless autocratic ruler. Alexander I left the door open to possible change, but Nicholas I slammed the door shut. He chose to see it as his divinely ordained duty to defend the existing order, especially the absolute authority of the Tsar, and the Orthodox Christian Church.

Revolutions of 1830–1832

One can never turn back the clock of history. The attempt by the Vienna Congress to restore the old order was bound to fail. Once the ideas of the Enlightenment and French Revolution were loosed, no amount of reaction could contain them. The appeal of both liberalism and nationalism was destined to overcome all resistance by the end of the nineteenth century.

When Louis XVIII was restored to his throne for the second time after Napoleon's defeat at Waterloo, he recognized that it was not possible to go back to the old order of pre-1789 France. He granted his subjects a constitution (*Charte Constitutionnelle*) in June 1814. The Charter of 1814, as it was called, created a constitutional monarchy with a king who was, in theory, a divine right monarch. It recognized such basic human rights as equality before the law, freedom of religion, and freedom of thought. A two-chamber legislative assembly with advisory power was provided for. Suffrage was limited to a mere 90 000 very wealthy male citizens. The strongest opposition to the Charter of 1814 came from the *ultras*, a group of aristocrats led by the king's brother, Charles-Philippe, comte d'Artois (1757–1836). The *ultras* were committed to restoration of Old Order.

Charles-Philippe ascended to the throne in 1824 as Charles X. His actions soon alienated virtually all Frenchmen except the *ultras*. The Catholic Church began to retake control of the schools. An indemnity was granted to the aristocrats who lost their property during the Revolution. When opposition appeared in the press, Charles X imposed censorship. He dissolved the Chamber of Deputies and called for new elections after it passed a vote of no-confidence in his government. When the elections only strengthened the opposition, Charles issued the "July Ordinances" on July 26, 1830. The new legislature was dissolved without ever meeting. The suffrage was reduced to mainly the old aristocracy. Freedom of the press was suspended.

Barricades went up in the streets of Paris from July 27 to 29. When most of the army refused to fire on the demonstrators, Charles X abdicated and fled into exile in England. The students, intellectuals, and workers who manned the barricades wanted to establish a republic. The middle class, including bankers, merchants, and industrialists, wanted a constitutional monarchy. The Marquis de Lafayette (1757–1834), hero of both the American and French revolutions, offered Louis Philippe (1773–1850), Duke of Orleans, as a constitutional monarch who would rule under the Charter of 1814.

Orleans was a cadet branch of the House of Bourbon. Louis Philippe's father, known as Philippe Égalité (1747–1793), participated in the French Revolution. He voted for the execution of Louis XVI and was himself guillotined during the Reign of Terror. Like his father, Louis Philippe was a member of the Jacobin Club and served in the National Assembly. He became king on August 9, 1830 with the title King of the French. The new title identified him with the people, rather than the territory of France. During his reign, which lasted until the Revolution of 1848, he was variously known as the "Citizen King" and the "July Monarch," and his reign as the "July Monarchy."

News that the Parisians were in revolt inspired revolutions to break out in Belgium, Poland, and Italy. The revolution in Belgium was largely nationalist in inspiration. A provisional government was formed, which declared Belgium's independence on October 4, 1830. A National Congress was elected on November 3 that drafted and adopted a constitution on February 7, 1831.

The five Great Powers met in London in 1830 and recognized the independence of Belgium. The Netherlands, however, did not accept the loss of Belgium until 1839. Leopold I of Saxe-Coburg (1790–1865) was chosen as Leopold I, King of Belgium. The independence of Belgium was recognized and its neutrality guaranteed in the Treaty of London (1839), signed by the European Great Powers, Belgium, and the Netherlands.[1]

Revolution broke out in Warsaw in November 1830. Nicholas I sent an army of 100 000 into Poland to put down the revolution. Unwilling to grant reforms demanded by the peasants and workers, the revolutionary leaders were unable to muster sufficient support. By September 1831, the dream of Polish independence was ended. Congress Poland came to an end as Poland was absorbed into Russia. Thousands of Poles were sent to Siberia. The repressive rule of Nicholas I replaced the constitutional monarchy.

Lessor revolutions occurred in Italy, in Modena and the Papal States, during 1831, and in Piedmont and Genoa in 1833–1834. They lacked any organization for a common military defense, and soon became divided between those who desired a republican form of government, and the middle-class liberals who feared such radicalism and were willing to find common cause with the absolute rulers of the old order. Austria, fearful of liberal and nationalist ideas spreading to its territories in northern Italy, sent armies into Italy to restore order.

Revolutions of 1848

The year 1848 is known as the "Year of Revolutions." On February 22, 1848, revolution once again broke out in Paris. Soon, all of Europe was engulfed by revolution as students, workers, peasants, and the middle classes rose up demanding that the reactionary governments established by the Vienna Congress grant constitutions, extend suffrage and, in many cases, national unity. The Vienna Settlement, sometimes referred to as the Metternichian System, was designed to eradicate, or at least contain, the forces of liberalism and nationalism. Once again, history would demonstrate that ideas cannot be snuffed out once they find expression.

---

1 The Treaty of London of 1839 played an important role in the outbreak of the Great War in 1914.

France

The students, workers, and lower middle class that manned the barricades in 1830 and forced Charles X to flee into exile, felt betrayed by Louis Philippe's government. Though called "King," he did not surround himself with any of the glitter that characterized the Bourbon kings or other divine-right monarchs. He dressed in a businessman's suit and presided over a government that served the interests of the very wealthy upper middle class and those aristocrats who resigned themselves to the end of the old order.

France, and most of Europe, was suffering during the "hungry forties." Europe was still experiencing the aftershocks of the 1837 depression. The decline in domestic and foreign trade meant lower production which, in turn, meant lower wages and less work. Crop failures, especially in wheat and potatoes, resulted in famine and disease. Rigid commitment to the iron laws of classical economics left no room for government intervention to relieve the suffering of the masses.

With censorship of the press and a prohibition on public meetings, the moderate middle-class liberals turned to hosting banquets at which a speaker would call for expanding the suffrage and restoration of liberty. A large banquet was scheduled for February 22, 1848 in Paris. When the government prohibited the "monster banquet," barricades went up. The National Guard and the army garrison in Paris refused to support the government. On February 24, Louis Philippe abdicated and, like Charles X in 1830, fled to England. On the same day, the Chamber of Deputies formed a provisional government and proclaimed a republic, the Second French Republic.

From the beginning, a split between two factions within the provisional government mirrored a basic division within France that originated in the French Revolution and continues into the twenty-first century. There was a right wing of moderate republicans with mainly moderate liberal objectives. There was also a left wing of more radical republicans who saw a republic as a means to more sweeping political, economic, and social reforms. The right wing was led by Alphonse de Lamartine (1790–1869), a romantic poet and statesman. The left wing was led by Louis Blanc (1811–1882), a historian, socialist, and popular speaker.

The provisional government authorized the formation of "National Workshops," perhaps as a concession to Louis Blanc. They were not what Blanc advocated in his writings, which were meant to lead to socialism. Rather, they were a form of temporary relief for the unemployed of Paris. The unemployed were assigned daily jobs sweeping streets and similar tasks, for which they were paid a small sum at the end of the day. When word of the National Workshops spread throughout the countryside, unemployed workers poured into Paris. The program was soon overwhelmed and short of funds. To the property owners, whether peasant farmers or urban middle class, such schemes were a waste of public funds and worse, they reeked of socialism. It was easy for the bourgeoisie, who feared the working class and branded them as dangerous radicals, to raise the specter of socialism as an effective weapon against their demands.

The election of a National (or Constituent) Assembly took place on April 23. Louis Blanc's left wing won only 80 of the 880 seats. The National Assembly replaced the provisional government with a temporary executive board of five members, all of whom

Figure 10.2 Barricade Scene from the June Days in Paris during the Revolution of 1848 by Adolphe Hervier.

were opposed to Blanc and his followers. On June 21, the National Workshops were closed. Barricades once again appeared across the streets in Paris. The government proclaimed martial law and called upon General Louis-Eugène Cavaignac (1802–1857) to suppress the uprising. Class warfare lasted for three days in Paris, the "Bloody June Days" of June 24–26. The outcome was never in doubt. Approximately 10 000 were killed or wounded. Another roughly 11 000 were taken prisoner and immediately deported to the colonies.

The new republican constitution was completed on November 4, 1848. It provided for a strong president and a single chamber legislature. Both the president and the members of the legislature were elected by universal manhood suffrage. The first presidential election took place on December 10. There were six candidates, including General Cavaignac, Alphonse de Lamartine, and Louis-Napoléon Bonaparte (1808–1873), nephew and heir of Napoleon I. Louis-Napoléon won by a landslide with 74.4% of the vote, compared to 19.65% for Cavaignac, and 0.28 for Lamartine.

Louis-Napoléon's victory was due to more than just name recognition. He was a man with a program. He won the support of the middle classes, the church, the property-owning peasants, and the workers. Unable to run for reelection according to the constitution, Louis-Napoléon dissolved the National Legislative Assembly on December 2, 1851. In a national plebiscite held December 20–21, the French people overwhelmingly approved Louis-Napoléon succeeding himself as president in violation of the constitution. A second plebiscite on January 14–15, 1852, approved reestablishment of the Empire with Louis-Napoléon as Emperor Napoleon III.

Germany

The German Confederation, created by the Vienna Congress to take the place of the old Holy Roman Empire, was intended to accomplish two goals: keep peace between the member states and between the Confederation and the rest of Europe, and guarantee the independence of the member states. For Metternich, that meant the suppression of any signs of liberalism or nationalism. The Diet of the Confederation consisted of representatives chosen and instructed by the governments of the member states. They did not represent the German people. The meetings of the Diet were presided over by the Austrian delegate.

Prussia was the hope of German liberals and nationalists during the period between 1815 and 1848. Prussia instituted liberal reforms, including free trade and abolition of serfdom, following its defeat by Napoleon in 1806. The spirit of German nationalism was born in the resistance to French occupation, especially in the War of Liberation (1813) led by Prussia. It found fertile soil after 1815 among the intellectuals, poets, professors, and students at the universities. It was in response to these smoldering embers of German nationalism and liberalism that Metternich proposed the Carlsbad Decrees, passed by the Diet in 1819. Strict censorship was imposed, nationalist student organizations (*Burschenschaften*) were banned, and the universities were placed under supervision.

Metternich predicted that if the restraints on liberalism and nationalism were removed, revolution would spread throughout Europe. By the end of March 1848, revolutions had broken out in Milan, Vienna, and Berlin. On March 13, Metternich resigned his office and fled to exile in England. In Berlin, Friedrich-Wilhelm IV (1795–1861) announced that he would grant Prussia a constitution and lead the movement for German unification. He ended censorship of the press and withdrew his troops from Berlin.

On May 18, an all-German National Assembly, commonly referred to as the Frankfurt Parliament, began drafting a constitution for a united Germany. The 800 delegates represented the members of the German Confederation, minus Austria. Most were middle-class liberals with university degrees. It was, perhaps, the best educated parliament ever assembled. There was only one delegate who could be classified as working class. He was of Polish nationality and ignored.

The Frankfurt Parliament was soon bogged down in a debate over what constituted a German, and what should be the borders of a united Germany. The first question was easy to answer. During the first half of the century, nationality was largely determined by language. A German was one who spoke German. The second question was much more difficult. Two solutions were proposed, one called the "Greater Germany" (*Großdeutschland*), which referred to a union of all German-speaking peoples. The second was called "Little Germany" (*Kleindeutschland*), which excluded Austria from a unified Germany.

A constitution for a united Germany, according to the Little German solution, was completed on March 27, 1849. The following day, the Frankfurt Parliament elected Friedrich-Wilhelm IV as emperor. A delegation was sent to Berlin to offer the crown to the king of Prussia. Friedrich-Wilhelm refused the crown, saying that he would not accept "a crown up from the gutter." In a letter to his sister, the Tsarina of Russia, he said that "in order to give, you would first of all have to be in possession of something that can be given" (Steinberg, 2011, p. 102). It was a clear rejection of the liberal (Enlightenment) principle that the people are sovereign. For Friedrich-Wilhelm IV, sovereignty was vested by God in the princes. Only the princes of Germany could offer a crown of a united Germany.

By rejecting the crown offered by the Frankfurt Parliament, Friedrich-Wilhelm IV also rejected the constitution. Liberalism in Germany was defeated, but the national aspirations of the German people suffered only a temporary setback. Germany would become united, but from above, not below. The future united Germany would have a constitution, but one given to the German people by their sovereign, not one of their own making.

Austria

The Hapsburg Empire was still a feudal, dynastic, crazy-quilt empire including 11 major ethnic groups (mostly Slavic), six officially recognized Slavonic languages plus German and Italian, and three major religions (Roman Catholic, Orthodox, and Muslim). It had a largely agricultural economy dominated in the east by large, wealthy landowners who ruled over a mass of ignorant and impoverished peasants still suffering under the remnants of medieval feudalism. The only thing that this diverse bundle of humanity had in common was that they were all ruled by the Hapsburg emperor in Vienna.

Demonstrations occurred in Vienna, Prague, and Budapest in March 1848. Middle-class liberals in Vienna called for a constitution. Students and workers manned the barricades. As in Germany, the initial response of the imperial government was shock followed by concessions. A constitutional assembly met in August to draft a liberal constitution.

Hungary, where Magyar nationalism was strong, was granted autonomy within the Austrian empire. Under the leadership of Louis Kossuth (1802–1894), a constitution was drafted and liberal reforms introduced, including freedom of religion and a free press, the end of serfdom, and universal manhood suffrage for Magyars. In April 1849, Hungary declared its independence. An intense program to "Magyarize" the non-Magyar speaking population (more than half) was introduced.

A Slovak National Council that convened in Vienna in September 1848 called for an autonomous Slovakian state within the Kingdom of Hungary. Slovakian nationalism clashed head on with Magyar nationalism and the government's efforts to Magyarize the kingdom's non-Magyar population.

Revolutions broke out in Austria's north-Italian provinces of Lombardy and Venetia. The Venetians proclaimed a republic in March 1848. Charles Albert (1798–1849),

King of Piedmont-Sardinia, declared war on Austria and invaded Lombardy in hopes of annexing both Lombardy and Venetia.

The initial reaction to the outburst of revolution in the Hapsburg lands was like that in the German states. Ferdinand I (1793–1875) ended censorship and in April he granted a liberal constitution by royal decree. In mid-May, Ferdinand and the royal family left Vienna for Innsbruck. Soon the tide turned in favor of a counterblow against the revolution.

The middle-class liberals who led the revolution feared nothing more than the radicalism of the working class and peasants. Once it became time to settle down to constructing a new government, the leaders of the revolution had to confront the demands from the lower classes, students, and some intellectuals for a republic with universal manhood suffrage. The middle-class liberals desired a political revolution resulting in a constitutional monarchy, but the working class wanted to go further with a social revolution as well. Ethnic clashes came to the forefront providing further opportunities for the royal government to divide and conquer.

The Czech revolt was over by June, when General Alfred Windischgrätz (1787–1862) took Prague by force. Martial law was imposed. Field Marshal Joseph Radetzky (1766–1858) crushed an Italian army commanded by Charles Albert at the Battle of Novara (March 23, 1849) not far from Milan. In August, Venice surrendered to Radetzky after a lengthy siege. Austrian rule was restored in northern Italy.

General Joseph Jellachich (1801–1859) began a campaign against the revolution in Hungary in September 1848. Fear that a victory by Jellachich in Hungary would lead to a military assault on Vienna led to a radical uprising in Vienna in October. Windischgrätz, supported by Jellachich, besieged Vienna. The city surrendered after five days. Windischgrätz occupied Budapest on January 5, 1849. When the Austrians were unable to crush the revolution in Hungary, Nicholas I sent a Russian army into Hungary to assist them. The Magyar forces were no match for the combined Austrian and Russian armies. The Hungarian revolution ended in August. Louis Kossuth fled to Turkey, visited the United States and Britain, and died in exile in Turin, Italy in 1894.

Ferdinand I abdicated on December 2, 1848, in favor of his 18-year old nephew, Franz Joseph (1830–1916), who reigned until 1916. Government reforms resulted in a strong centralized government. The Constitution of 1849 was repealed, and all representative bodies at all levels were prohibited. Subject minorities, especially the Hungarians, were suppressed, as the old order was reestablished throughout the Hapsburg empire.

Rome

There were revolutions throughout Italy in 1848. Their goal was to drive Austria out of northern Italy and create a unified nation state. Both Austria and the Papacy were obstacles to any unification of Italy. Pope Pius IX (r. 1846–1878) began his reign as a liberal reformer. When revolution broke out in Italy in 1848, Pius IX tried to avoid conflict with its leaders, but soon discovered that the interests of the Papacy were incompatible with the inherent anticlericalism of classical liberalism. Also, he had to accept the fact that a united Italy would threaten the independence of the Roman Catholic Church, something the popes were committed to defending since the end of the Roman Empire in the West.

Pius IX left Rome in November 1848, taking refuge in the Kingdom of the Two Sicilies. A Roman Republic was proclaimed in February 1849, under leadership of Giuseppe Mazzini (1805–1872), a romantic nationalist who devoted his life trying to unite Italy as a liberal republic. The pope condemned the republic, excommunicated its participants, and called upon France, Austria, Spain, and Naples to intervene.

On April 25, 1849, a French army sent by Louis Napoleon, the newly elected president of France, arrived in Italy. Though Louis Napoleon participated in a revolt against the Pope in 1831, he, like his famous uncle, recognized the importance of securing the support of French Catholics. The French siege of Rome lasted from June 1 to June 29. They entered Rome on July 3 and restored the Pope's temporal rule. Pius IX, himself, did not return to Rome until April 1850. A French garrison remained in Rome until 1870.

Why the Revolutions Failed

When the revolutions first broke out, the conservative governments were taken by surprise. Rather than use military force to quickly crush the revolutions, as Nicholas I did in 1825, they hesitated. Concessions were granted, constitutions promised and, in some cases, the rulers temporarily left their capitals for a secondary residence, where they could wait out the upheaval. Once the inevitable conflict between the various revolutionary leaders surfaced, causing fragmentation among them, the conservative governments counterattacked. The idealism and enthusiasm of the revolutionary forces proved no match for the regular armies.

There were many reasons for the failure of the revolutions, but two stand out. First, was fear of the lower classes of workers and peasants by the propertied middle classes. For the latter, the primary responsibility of government was to protect the inalienable natural rights of the individual – life, liberty, property – all of which were property rights. Participation in the political life of the nation had to be limited to property owners. Granting universal manhood suffrage, as demanded by the lower classes who called for a republic, was understood by the middle classes as a license for the propertyless to attack their property, and hence their liberty. Economic and social justice was never a goal of classical liberalism. Faced with a choice between a republic with universal manhood suffrage or joining forces with the old order to crush the threat of lower-class radicalism, the bourgeois liberals chose the latter.

The second primary reason for the failure of the revolutions was the clash of nationalities. This was particularly true in central Europe. Before the Revolutions of 1848, liberals envisioned a community of nation states based on nationalities living in harmony with one another. The revolutions in the German states and the Hapsburg lands proved such optimism was an illusion. However one drew the borders of a united Germany, a Kingdom of Hungary, or any other of a number of possible nation states within the Hapsburg lands, there would be frustrated national minorities within those nation states. Nationalists were not willing to recognize the rights of national minorities within their borders, as was demonstrated by the zeal with which the Magyars tried to Magyarize Hungary's non-Magyar population.

Some positive gains resulted from the Revolutions of 1848. Frenchmen gained universal manhood suffrage. Serfdom came to an end in the eastern German states and in the

Hapsburg lands. Both proved a mixed blessing for the future. Napoleon III built a constitutional dictatorship on the basis of popular sovereignty. The liberated peasants of Eastern Europe proved immune to bourgeois liberal ideas. They sided with the conservative governments against the liberal revolutionists during the upheaval and supported the conservative counter-revolution.

The Vienna Settlement survived the revolutions of 1848–1849. Liberalism was defeated, especially in central and eastern Europe. The middle classes in Italy and Germany retreated from politics. The unification of both was achieved within the next two decades, but by the conservatives on the battlefields, not by the people in the streets or the bourgeois liberals in constituent assemblies.

Unification of Italy and Germany

There was peace among the European Great Powers during the nineteenth century, except of course for the Crimean War (1853–1856), which was little more than a prolonged siege of Sebastopol by the British and the French. The peace of Europe was interrupted between 1859 and 1871 by the wars of Italian and German unification. The birth of nationalism, a kind of secular faith born in the French Revolution and Wars of Napoleon, suffered a setback in the Revolutions of 1848, but erupted again in 1859, resulting in the unification of Italy and Germany and the end of the Vienna Settlement.

During the first 50 years after the Vienna Congress, there were two major nation states in Europe, Great Britain (or the United Kingdom) and France. In central Europe (Germany), there were smaller states that were fragments of a "nation." As understood by the ideology of nationalism, a nation consists of a people identifiable by a common language, a shared sense of a common history, ancestry, and destiny, and who occupy a definable geographic area. Thus, in German history, it is common to speak of a German nation, all those who speak German, as distinct from the political entities within which the German people live. During the period prior to the unification of Germany in 1871, there was one German nation, but many states within and without the German Confederation in which Germans lived. The same was true of the Italian or Apennine Peninsula prior to the unification of Italy, where the Italian people lived scattered among a number of states.

In addition to the fragments of nation states in Germany and Italy, there were also large, old-fashioned dynastic states, or empires, consisting of different people groups, or "nations," who had in common only that they are were ruled by the same sovereign, or dynasty. The obvious examples during the nineteenth century were Russia, the Hapsburg Monarchy (or Austrian Empire), and the Ottoman Empire. They were, in some sense, holdovers from the old order prior to the French Revolution.

Italy

After the fall of the ill-fated Roman Republic in 1849, the task of achieving the unification of Italy fell to the Kingdom of Piedmont-Sardinia and Count Camillo Benso di Cavour (1810–1861). Cavour was a practitioner of what was called *realpolitik*, a realistic, rather than idealistic or romantic, approach to achieving clearly defined goals, unhampered by ethical considerations. To achieve unification, it was necessary to expel Austria from northern Italy and the Bourbons from the Kingdom of Naples without provoking intervention by Napoleon III. To do so, Cavour began to modernize Piedmont by developing its infrastructure so as to encourage industrialization and trade, overhaul the kingdom's finances, and strengthen Piedmont's image and position in Europe.

During the Crimean War, Cavour allied Piedmont-Sardinia with Britain and France against Russia, even though Piedmont had no issue at stake with Russia. The alliance did secure Cavour a place at the Congress of Paris (1856) and Napoleon III's assistance in forcing Austria out of northern Italy. In July 1858, Cavour and Napoleon III met and agreed that France would aid Piedmont in the event of war between Piedmont and Austria. France was to receive French-speaking Savoy and Nice from Piedmont, and Piedmont would receive Lombardy and Venetia from Austria, and be allowed to annex Modena and Parma and part of the Papal States.

Cavour cleverly maneuvered Austria into declaring war on Piedmont in April 1859. The Austrian army was defeated at the battle of Magenta (June 4) by a combined Piedmontese and French army. A second, indecisive and particularly bloody battle was fought ten days later at Solferino, after which Napoleon III made a separate peace with Austria. Piedmont did receive Lombardy from Austria, but not Venetia. Meanwhile successful revolts occurred in Modena, Parma, Tuscany, and Romagna, after which the new revolutionary governments agreed to annexation by Piedmont-Sardinia.

Meanwhile, Giuseppe Garibaldi (1807–1882), a colorful Italian patriot and soldier of fortune, was uniting southern Italy. On May 11, 1860, he arrived on the island of Sicily with a band of followers known as the Redshirts. In less than a month, Garibaldi was in control of Sicily. On August 22, he crossed the Strait of Messina and arrived in Naples, the capital of the Kingdom of the Two Sicilies. Garibaldi was above all else a patriot, who was happy to see Italy united under Victor Emmanuel II (1820–1878) of Piedmont-Sadinia. After surrendering southern Italy to the Piedmontese, and a private meeting with Victor Emmanuel II, Garibaldi returned to his farm on the island of Caprera.

The Kingdom of Italy was proclaimed on March 17, 1861, with Florence as its capital. In 1866, following its defeat in the Austro-Prussian War, Austria ceded Venetia to France which, in turn, ceded it to Italy. French troops were withdrawn from Rome at the beginning of the Franco-Prussian War in 1870. Rome was then occupied by Italian troops and became the capital of Italy. Pope Pius IX retreated into the Vatican, refusing to recognize Italy's annexation of Rome. The "Roman Question," as the conflict between church and state in Italy after 1870 was called, was not resolved until 1929.

Germany

The Austrian-dominated German Confederation was dissolved during the Revolutions of 1848. In 1850, Prussia tried taking advantage of Austria's preoccupation with troubles caused by the revolutions to propose a reorganization of the German states under Prussian leadership known as the Erfurt Union. Faced with the threat of war with Austria and Bavaria, supported by Russia, Prussia was forced to abandon the Erfurt Union and accept revival of the German Confederation under Austrian leadership. The struggle between Prussia and Austria for leadership and eventual unification of Germany continued.

Prussia did have a distinct advantage in the struggle with Austria as a result of the *Zollverein*, a customs union of 18 German states providing for free trade among its members, founded by Prussia in 1834. Prussia was careful to exclude Austria from the *Zollverein* as it expanded under Prussian leadership. By expanding the *Zollverein*, Prussia was effectively uniting Germany economically. At the same time, the German states looked more and more to Prussia as the leader in Germany.

The unification of Germany was the work of Otto von Bismarck (1815–1898), appointed prime minister and foreign minister of Prussia by Wilhelm I (1797–1888) in 1862. Bismarck was a member of the Prussian nobility, or *Junker* class, and a conservative devoted to his sovereign, Wilhelm I. Above all, he was a master of *realpolitik*. Bismarck achieved German unification through three wars. Whether he carefully planned and orchestrated the wars, or merely took advantage of opportunities as they arose, is much debated by historians. In either case, Bismarck skillfully used the wars to accomplish his singular goal.

The first war was the German-Danish War of 1864, over the two provinces of Schleswig and Holstein on the Jutland Peninsula. Both duchies had large German populations. Both were ruled by the king of Denmark, who was the Danish Duke of Schleswig, and, because Holstein had been a part of the Holy Roman Empire and was a member of the German Confederation, the German Duke of Holstein.

In November 15, 1863, Christian IX (1818–1906), succeeded to the Danish throne. He immediately agreed to a new constitution that united both Schleswig and Holstein with Denmark. It was an open invitation to Bismarck to assert Prussian leadership in a crisis that aroused German national feeling. Claiming that Denmark had seized territory belonging to the German Confederation by annexing Holstein, Prussia and Austria invaded Holstein on behalf of the German Confederation.

Denmark was quickly defeated. In the Treaty of Vienna (1864) between Denmark, Austria, and Prussia, Christian IX ceded Schleswig and Holstein to Prussia and Austria. The Convention of Gastein (1865) between Austria and Prussia declared both Austria and Prussia to be sovereign over both duchies, with Prussia administering Schleswig and Austria administering Holstein. By placing Austria in Holstein with Prussian forces to the north in Schleswig and Prussia on the southern border of Holstein, Bismarck guaranteed conflicts would emerge between the two rivals leading to the outbreak of the Austro-Prussian War, or the Seven Weeks' War, in 1866.

The Prussian railroads and the modernizing of the Prussian army proved decisive. The Prussians simply outmaneuvered the Austrians. The Prussian commander, Helmuth von Moltke (1800–1891), made use of a lesson learned from the American Civil War, that is, the coordination of railroads and telegraph to rapidly deploy a mass army. The fact that the Prussian soldiers were equipped with breech-loading rifles, while the Austrians were still using muzzle-loading rifles, gave the Prussians a definite advantage. The outcome was decided at the Battle of Sadowa (or Königgrätz) on July 3.

The Treaty of Prague (August 23, 1866) gave Prussia full possession of Schleswig and Holstein, and allowed it to annex the Kingdom of Hanover, Electoral Hesse, the Duchy of Nassau, and the Free City of Frankfurt. Austria ceded Venetia to Italy, exited German affairs, and paid an indemnity. The German Confederation came to an end and was replaced by the North German Confederation under Prussian leadership. The constitution of the North German Confederation served as a model for the unified German Empire in 1871.

Austria's defeat forced a reorganization of the Austrian Empire. The Hapsburg monarchy came to terms with its largest minority, the Magyars. In the Compromise (or *Ausgleich*) of 1867, the Austrian Empire became Austria-Hungary, commonly referred to as the Dual Monarchy. Franz Joseph ruled as the Emperor of Austria and the King of Hungary with separate diets, or parliaments, in Vienna and Budapest. The two were autonomous states, though foreign affairs and the military were controlled in Vienna. The arrangement merely put off the inevitable disintegration of the Hapsburg monarchy until 1918.

Bismarck was magnanimous toward both Austria and the South German states of Baden, Wuerttemberg, and Bavaria that allied themselves with Austria. No doubt he was thinking ahead to the climatic struggle with France, in which he would need their neutrality, if not their participation.

The occasion for war with France arose when a revolution in Spain resulted in Queen Isabella II (1833–1904) being deposed. One of the candidates for the vacant throne was Prince Leopold (1835–1905), a relative of Wilhelm I. Napoleon III opposed Leopold's candidacy, since it would place France between two Hohenzollern kingdoms. While visiting a health spa at Bad Ems in Western Germany, Wilhelm I was approached by the French ambassador with a request that Wilhelm affirm his decision to withdraw Prince Leopold's candidacy. Wilhelm sent a telegram to Bismarck detailing his discussion with the French ambassador. Bismarck published the telegram after editing it so as to appear insulting to Napoleon III. Bismarck intended for it to provoke Napoleon to declare war. It worked. France declared war on Prussia on July 19, 1870.

The Franco-Prussian War of 1870–1871, was a repeat of the Austro-Prussian War. Austria declared neutrality. The south German states, regarding France the aggressor, joined Prussia. The German mobilization was efficient, quickly deploying 360 000 troops to the front within 18 days, whereas the French mobilization was confused and delayed. The main French army with Napoleon III present was surrounded and defeated at the Battle of Sedan on August 31. The French surrender and capture of Napoleon III effectively ended the war.

Paris refused to accept defeat. A government of national defense was formed, which declared Napoleon III deposed and proclaimed the Third French Republic. The German army began a siege of Paris on September 19 that lasted until January 28, 1871. Ten days earlier, on January 18, Wilhelm I was acclaimed German Emperor in the Hall of Mirrors at Versailles. Wilhelm, who would not accept the crown of a united Germany offered by the Frankfurt Parliament in 1849, accepted the imperial crown of the German Empire, offered to him on behalf of the German princes by Ludwig II (1845–1886), King of Bavaria. According to the Treaty of Frankfurt, signed on May 10, 1871, Germany annexed the two provinces of Alsace and Lorraine and France agreed to pay a 5 billion francs indemnity. German troops remained in northern France until September 1873, when payments were completed.

Figure 10.3 Napoleon III surrendering to Wilhelm I following the Battle of Sedan, 1870.

Paris Commune

The conflict between the conservative mood in the French provinces and the radicalism that prevailed in Paris, led to armed conflict between the provisional government of the newly proclaimed Third Republic and Paris. Elections were held in February 1871 for a National Assembly. The majority of the new delegates were monarchists, whereas the people of Paris wanted a republic. Fearful that the National Assembly might restore the monarchy, radicals of various convictions, including anarchists and socialists, formed a commune government on March 26.

The response of the government to the Paris Commune mirrored that of 1848. A military assault on the city was launched. The army entered Paris on May 21 and immediately engaged in a street by street, building by building, assault on the Communards. The week of May 21–28 is remembered as the "Bloody Week." The numbers of those killed fighting or executed by hastily organized military tribunals, is much debated. Recent research by historian Robert Tombs puts the number of those killed at between six and seven thousand, rather than the commonly given figure of about 20 000. The French army, at the time, recorded 43 522 prisoners taken during and after the week of May 21–28. What can be said with confidence is that thousands died and thousands more were deported or sentenced to prison.

The French Constitution of 1875 provided for a republic. The Third Republic was, as Adolphe Thiers (1797–1877), its first president characterized it, "the government that divides us least." The royalists who dominated the National Assembly wanted a monarchy, but were unable to decide on which royal house. Bourbon? Orleans? Bonaparte? In July 1871, Henri, Count of Chambord (1820–1883), grandson of Charles X, was offered the crown, but refused to govern under the tricolor flag. He insisted on the white *fleur-de-lis* flag of the Bourbons. Thus, the Third French Republic became a republic by default.

The unification of Italy and Germany destroyed the balance of power among the five traditional Great Powers. In the succeeding decades, Germany emerged as the dominant power on the European continent. By the end of the nineteenth century, Germany was the shining example of the triumph of Western Civilization. Not only did it possess the greatest army in Europe, it also led economically and culturally.

The Third French Republic was plagued by a deep division between conservatives, monarchists, and Christians on the right, and radical republicans, socialists, and secularists on the left. A weak central government was offset by a professional civil service that provided stability. Confusion might reign in Paris, but throughout France, at the local level, government bureaucrats went to work each day, making sure that France remained a modern, progressive nation.

The United Kingdom remained what it was since 1815, the world's only Great Power, the arbiter of world affairs. The nineteenth century was the era of the *Pax Britannia*. That reality was never more evident than during the period of Western Imperialism from about 1875 to 1914. Britain built a worldwide empire on which the sun never set. London remained the financial center of the world.

In Eastern Europe, both Russia and Austria-Hungary remained outdated dynastic empires that remained members of the club of the world's Great Powers only by virtue of their size and history. As a result of the unification of Italy and Germany, the traditional flexibility of borders in Central Europe ended, and the "hot spot" of Europe shifted to the Balkans, where Russia and Austria-Hungary were rivals for the European territories of the shrinking Ottoman Empire.

In the world beyond Europe, two nations were emerging as Great Powers. The United States of America was rapidly developing its vast natural resources. By the end of the century, it was arguably the world's leading economic power, though reluctant to assume its place as a major player on the world stage. Japan, forced open by the United States in 1853, was modernizing at a speed unknown at any time before. By the end of the century, Japan was a modern imperialist power aspiring to become the dominant power in the Pacific.

References

Steinberg, J. (2011). *Bismarck: A Life*. Oxford: Oxford University Press.

Tombs, R. (September 2012). How bloody was la Semaine sanglante of 1871? A revision. *The Historical Journal* 55 (3): 619–704.

11

Industrial Revolution

Chronology

1733	John Jay Invents the Flying Shuttle
1765	James Hargrave Invents the Spinning Jenny
1769	Richard Arkwright Invents the Water-Powered Spinning Frame
1771	Richard Arkwright Opens the First Factory
1776	Adam Smith's *An Inquiry into the Nature and Causes of the Wealth of Nations*
1785	First Use of Steam Power in a Cotton Mill
1798	Eli Whitney's "Uniformity System" of Interchangeable Parts
1798	Thomas Robert Malthus' *An Essay on the Principle of Population*
1799	Samuel Compton Invents the Spinning Mule
1830s	Beginning of Railroad Boom
1830s–1840s	Parliamentary Acts Limit Child Labor
1832	Great Reform Bill Passed by Parliament
1834	New Poor Law (England) Opens Workhouses
1839	People's Charter (England)
1842	Owen Chadwick's *The Sanitary Conditions of the Labouring Population*
1846	British Parliament Repeals Corn Laws
1848	Karl Marx's *Communist Manifesto*
1851	Great Exhibition
1884–1885	First Skyscraper (10 Stories) in Chicago, USA
1911	Winslow Taylor's *The Principles of Scientific Management*

What historians refer to as the Industrial Revolution was the most significant development in human history since the Neolithic Revolution. Every aspect of human life was changed, and continues to change as a result. Not only how humans live, but also what they think, how they understand what it means to be human, and whether history has any meaning at all, were impacted by industrialization. It began in England during the last quarter of the eighteenth century, spread to the European continent after 1815, and by the end of the nineteenth century, made the rise of Western Civilization the central theme in the story of World Civilization.

Western Civilization: A Brief History, First Edition. Paul R. Waibel.
© 2020 John Wiley & Sons, Inc. Published 2020 by John Wiley & Sons, Inc.

Origins

It was a revolution in agriculture that made the Industrial Revolution possible. A population explosion beginning in the mid-eighteenth century did not result in the usual famine and mass migration that previously occurred when the population outstripped the food supply. Instead, the growth in population provided the demand which in turn brought forth the technological advances that gave birth to the Industrial Revolution. The population growth that began in the middle of the eighteenth century, and continued in the West until the latter half of the twentieth century, was due to the increase in life expectancy. More people were living longer and healthier lives than before due to the increase in both the output and variety of the food supply. The agricultural revolution removed the limitations on the production of food that existed since the Neolithic Revolution, thus unleashing the economic laws that in part drive historical progress.

The Glorious Revolution in England in 1688 effectively marked the ascendency to power of the property-owning aristocracy of landlords and wealthy merchants. The political life of Britain was securely in the hands of the landowning aristocracy and "squirearchy." The titled nobility sat in the House of Lords, while the practice of primogeniture assured that their younger sons or male siblings filled the seats in the House of Commons. Along with political power came control of the economic life of the kingdom until the middle of the nineteenth century.

The medieval manor contained, in addition to the open fields farmed in strips by the peasants, certain portions of land that were owned by the lord of the manor. But, the peasants who lived in the manorial village were allowed certain rights of usage of "the commons" under common law. The "common rights" of the villagers could not be changed or abolished except by an act of Parliament.

During the eighteenth century, the landlords desired to take advantage of the new and evolving agricultural technology in order to increase production and, of course, income. Parliament cooperated with the landlords by passing what were known as enclosure acts that allowed the landlords to enclose, or "fence in," the commons and open fields. The villagers lost their historic rights to usage of the commons, as the landlords assumed private ownership and management of the commons. Individual plots of land, or farms, worked by tenant farmers replaced the open fields and commons. Improving landlords were able to work with individual tenants to introduce the new "scientific" methods of farming the land, newly invented farm implements, new crops, and experimental methods of selective breeding of livestock aimed at producing larger sheep that produced more wool and fatter beef cattle and dairy cows that produced more beef and dairy products.

The enclosure movement meant that by the early nineteenth century, land ownership in England was concentrated in relatively fewer hands than anywhere else in western or central Europe. As agriculture became more efficient, one might say more "capitalistic," many individuals found themselves without any, or insufficient, land to support their families. Some were fortunate enough to find work as agricultural wage laborers. Many were left unemployed. They became the labor force necessary for industrialization.

The enclosure movement was contemporary with a period of proto-industrialization characterized by what is called "cottage industry," or the "putting-out system." Individuals, often merchants who accumulated excess wealth (capital) resulting from the commercial revolution, invested in raw materials that could be transformed into finished, marketable merchandise, while bypassing the restrictions on quality and labor imposed by the guild system. The production of wool cloth provides a good example.

An entrepreneur might purchase a quantity of raw wool, and then take it to cottagers in the country who, in turn, would spin it into yarn. The cottager was paid according to the amount of yarn produced. The yarn was either the finished product to be sold, or was taken to other cottagers who wove the yarn into cloth. Again, the cottager was paid for piecework. Thus, the entrepreneur was able to avoid the controls on production imposed by the guilds and engage in what is today referred to as "free enterprise," or laissez-faire economics.

There existed a link between enclosure, cottage industry, and industrialization, though it was not the only path to the Industrial Revolution or the only explanation of why the Industrial Revolution occurred first in England and in textiles. England, during the eighteenth and nineteenth centuries, provided a fertile environment for industrialization. All of the necessary ingredients were present in England as nowhere else.

The Treaty of Paris in 1763, that resulted from England's victory over France in the Seven Years' War left England with a colonial empire and command of the seas. England's command of the seas, a reality that lasted until after the First World War (1918), guaranteed its access to necessary raw materials and markets throughout the world. Increased overseas and domestic commerce produced investment capital, while the agricultural revolution fostered population growth and additional capital for investment. A business-friendly government encouraged and rewarded the entrepreneurial spirit and pursuit of profits that became characteristic of the English aristocracy.

Such was the importance of the wool trade in the history of England that since the reign of Edward III in the middle of the fourteenth-century, the Lord Speaker in the House of Lords sits even today on a cushion stuffed with wool, known as the "Woolsack." The textile trade was an essential part of the English economy well into the nineteenth century. Entrepreneurs saw the promise of steadily increasing profits from investments, if new means of producing woollen cloth could be found. Further incentive was provided by the growing demand for cotton cloth, but the traditional methods of spinning and weaving textiles meant that cotton cloth produced in England could not compete with cotton cloth imported from India or Egypt. The answer was provided by a series of inventions that moved the production of textiles from the cottage to the factory.

John Jay's invention of the flying shuttle (1733) increased the amount of cloth a single weaver could produce, resulting in an increased demand for yarn. The increased supply of yarn was made possible by James Hargraves' spinning jenny (1765). The traditional spinning wheel had only one spindle on which thread was produced. The spinning jenny had eight spindles. In 1769, Richard Arkwright (1732–1792) patented his water-powered spinning frame that was able to spin 128 threads.

Arkwright's water-frame spinning machine was too large to be placed in a cottage or operated by hand. In 1771, Arkwright joined together with two others to found the first textile mill (or factory) in Cromford, Derbyshire. Arkwright built cottages near the factory to house workers recruited from throughout Derbyshire. In addition to his own factories, Arkwright was a shareholder in 110 of 143 factories using the technology he invented. At his death in 1792, Arkwright, a man born into poverty, was worth an estimated at £500 000, or roughly $200 million today.

Samuel Crompton (1753–1827) invented the spinning mule in 1779, which effectively combined Hargrave's spinning jenny and Arkwright's water-frame machine. By 1812, there were an estimated 360 mills using Crompton's invention. Edmond Cartwright (1743–1823) invented the first power loom in 1785. By 1813, there were 2400 power looms in operation in England. By 1850, the number rose to 250 000.

With spinning and weaving fully automated and done in factories, supplying the demand for raw cotton became a serious problem. Between 1783 and 1790, the amount of cotton imported by England rose from 9 million pounds (4 082 331 kg) to 28 million pounds (12 700 586.36 kg) annually. By 1812, that figure rose to 63 million (28 576 319.31 kg) and in 1825 to 228 million pounds (103 419 060.36 kg) (Mirsky and Nevins 1952, p. 91). The answer to the problem of supplying raw cotton to the English factories was found in the invention of the cotton gin in 1793 by the Connecticut Yankee inventor, Eli Whitney (1765–1825). Whitney's cotton gin enabled a single individual to remove the seeds from more cotton in one hour than multiple workers could in one whole day using their hands.

The cotton gin was not Eli Whitney's only contribution to the Industrial Revolution. In 1798, the United States' government granted Whitney a contract to produce 10 000 muskets. To produce the muskets, Whitney developed what he called his "uniformity system," which was the manufacture of interchangeable parts from which individual muskets were assembled. Prior to Whitney's "uniformity system," each musket was constructed as a unique piece by a skilled craftsman. Whitney proved that it was possible to mass produce identical, interchangeable parts at low cost using unskilled labor and specially designed machinery. Whitney may not have invented the idea, but he made a major contribution to the Industrial Revolution by demonstrating the concept's feasibility.

The early factories were located along rivers, since water was required to power the machines. With the appearance of the first practical steam engines developed by James Watt (1736–1819), steam power began to replace water power in the textile mills. The first use of steam power in a cotton mill occurred in 1785. Edmund Cartwright converted his factories over to steam power in 1790, using steam engines developed and manufactured by James Watt and Matthew Boulton (1728–1809). Steam power meant that factories no longer had to be located along rivers. Steam engines required coal, a lot of coal, meaning that factories were located in areas where large quantities of coal were found near the surface. Coal production soared. Ten million metric tons (10 000 000 000 km) of coal were mined in Great Britain in 1800 (Trueman 2019).

Putting a steam engine on wheels and then on rails was both a logical step and a revolution. In 1825, the Stockton and Darlington Railroad began transporting coal from the mines near Darlington in northeastern England to Stockton on the coast, a distance of 8 miles (12.9 km) at 15 miles (24 km) per hour. The Stockton and Darlington Railroad and, five years later, the Liverpool and Manchester Railroad (40 miles [64 km]), carried both passengers and freight. The steam locomotives used on both railroads were built by George

Stephenson (1781–1848). His *Rocket*, introduced in 1829, traveled at an astonishing speed of 36 miles (58 km) per hour.

The early 1830s marked the beginning of the railroad boom. Whereas there were 95 miles (152.89 km) of railroad track in Britain in 1830, there were 20 000 miles (32 186.88 km) in 1890 (Butler 2007). The first railroads in the US and France appeared in 1829 and in Germany in 1835. Railroad expansion connected the interiors of nations with ports and the world beyond. The Transcontinental Railroad across the US constructed between 1863 and 1869, the Orient Express that linked Paris and Istanbul in 1889, and the Trans-Siberian Railway across Russia constructed between 1891 and 1916, are the three classic examples of how the development of railroads stimulated economic development.

At the middle of the nineteenth century, Britain was the world's only truly industrialized nation. Britain's leadership was put on exhibit for the whole world to see at the Great Exhibition, held in London between May and October, 1851. Roughly 100 000 items were on display from a hydraulic press that could lift 1144 pounds (518.10 kg) and "a steam-hammer that could, with equal accuracy, forge the main bearing of a steamship or gently crack an egg," (Picard 2009) to finely crafted surgical instruments and hairpins. The exhibit hall was an immense structure, 1848 ft. (562 m) long and 408 ft. (124 m) wide with a cast-iron skeleton that supported 300 000 plate-glass sheets measuring 4 ft. and 1 in. (1.3 m) long and 10 in. (25.3 cm) wide (Building the Museum 2019).

Despite the growth of industry in Britain, at the time of the Great Exhibition, there were still more people engaged in agricultural-related work than manufacturing. More people were employed "in service" as domestic servants than in factories.

Figure 11.1 Steam powered agricultural equipment on display at the Great Exhibition, or Crystal Palace, in London in 1851. *Source:* Library of Congress Prints and Photographs Division.

Between 1851 and 1871, the number of those employed in domestic service in England rose from 900 000 to 1.4 million (Ashton 1997).

A Second Industrial Revolution

A second industrial revolution was underway beginning in the 1870s, characterized by a marriage of science and technology that resulted in new industries such as petroleum, electricity, and chemicals, and new forms of transportation and communication. The centralization of ownership and management in the hands of a few became the norm in industrial organization. The monopolies, cartels, trusts, and syndicates, as they were known, were formed to control the prices of raw materials and manufactured products. Some sought to dominate entire industries. Some were national, while others were international in their reach. They were headed by individuals popularly referred to as captains of industry, moguls, or robber barons.

The opening of new geographic areas in the American West and overseas colonial possessions, fueled industrial growth by providing an abundant supply of natural resources and markets. The steady increase in population meant that there was an ample supply of labor. The rapid expansion of industry in the United States following the end of the Civil War (1865), was made possible by the steady stream of immigrants from Europe and Asia.

The railroads enabled manufacturing to be concentrated in towns. In some cases, industrial towns appeared where none existed before. Since clocks were rare in the first half of the nineteenth century, and too expensive for most workers to own during the second half of the century, factory workers had to live close enough to the factory or mine to hear the whistle blow. The workers were, in effect, appendages of the machines. Their lives were ordered by the blowing of the factory whistle. Hence, workers were housed in crowded, bleak tenements around the factories.

The percentage of people living in cities and towns across Europe rose from 17% in 1801 to 54% in 1891. The population of London rose from 960 000 in 1800 to 2.4 million in 1851, and 6.5 million in 1900. Berlin's population rose from just under 500 000 in 1850 to roughly 2 million in 1900. Across the Atlantic Ocean, Chicago, where the first skyscraper (10 stories high) was erected in 1884–1885, population increased from 300 000 in 1871 to over 1 million in 1890.

The active role played by the continental governments differed from the more *laisses-faire* approach in England, where early industrial development was largely financed by private capital, that is, individuals reinvesting profits. They took an active part in promoting industrial development by often providing funds to develop railroads, mines, dockyards, and other infrastructure. They encouraged the appearance of joint-stock investment banks that were able to provide the large capital investments necessary. Investors' liability was limited to the amount they invested. Examples of these investment banks included the Crédit Mobilier Bank in France (1852), the Darmstadt Bank in Germany (1853), and the Kreditanstalt Bank in Austria (1855).

Applied science became an integral part of manufacturing by the end of the century, especially in the new industries such as chemicals. The Scientific and Industrial Revolutions united to produce new products. The invention of the internal combustion engine in the 1870s and the diesel engine in the 1890s, together with the development of gasoline and diesel fuels, are obvious examples. Employment of engineers and applied scientists in industry was normal by 1900.

Science was applied to management as well, with what became known as "Taylorism," or scientific management, named after its founder, Frederick Winslow Taylor (1856–1915). The goal was to find the "one best way" of performing a task so as to increase efficiency and thus reduce cost. Workers became, in effect, like machines that performed a specific task repeatedly in such a manner that increased productivity and lowered labor costs per item produced or task performed. The "right" person, Taylor argued, should be carefully selected for the task he or she was assigned to perform:

> ...one of the very first requirements for a man who is fit to handle pig iron as a regular occupation is that he shall be so stupid and so phlegmatic that he more nearly resembles in his mental make-up the ox than any other type. The man who is mentally alert and intelligent is for this very reason entirely unsuited to what would, for him, be the grinding monotony of work of this character. (Taylor 1911, p. 59)

Taylorism, combined with the assembly line developed by Henry Ford (1863–1947), resulted in the mind-numbing labor that characterized manufacturing plants in the twentieth century.

The growth of large industrial conglomerates meant that those who controlled access to investment capital, large banks and other financial institutions, were able to influence business policies. Their representatives were found on the boards of directors of the firms dependent upon them for capital. They often encouraged the formation of cartels and other means of limiting competition in order to boost earnings.

Free Trade

The nineteenth century was the English century, much as the twentieth century has been called the American century. Being the first country to industrialize, and with command of the seas, Britain was the de facto leader of the West until the end of the First World War. London was the financial center of what was becoming a world economy. Britain's leadership was due in part, at least until the latter part of the nineteenth century, to its practice of free trade.

In 1815, following the end of the Napoleonic Wars, Parliament passed the Corn Laws aimed at helping the landed aristocrats by restricting the importation of grain. Peace opened up Britain to cheap wheat from Eastern Europe. The Corn Laws allowed the importation of duty-free wheat only when the average price reached 80 shillings per bushel. Peace also meant that there was a backlog of manufactured goods that could not be absorbed by either the domestic or foreign markets. Unemployment soared as thousands of workers were laid off and an estimated 400 000 soldiers were demobilized, further depressing the price of wheat.

Opposition to the Corn Laws came from both the workers and the middle-class industrialists. The former suffered from the high cost of food at a time when employment was hard to find and wages were low. The industrialists wanted to lower the price of food for the workers, thus enabling them to pay lower wages. Both were at odds with the landowners who held power in Parliament. While serving as Prime Minister between 1828 and 1830, the Duke of Wellington, Arthur Wellesley (1769–1852), was able to get Parliament to pass the Corn Law Act of 1828, that provided a sliding scale for the tariff on imported wheat. Finally, Parliament passed the Importation Act of 1846, which repealed the Corn Laws.

Repeal of the Corn Laws signaled that Britain embraced free trade. Preferential treatment of Britain's colonies was also abandoned. By 1860, the transition to free trade was complete. Backers of free trade saw it as an integral part of a self-regulating economy that would promote growth and benefit everyone. It sent a signal to the landed aristocracy that like other classes, they should not look to the state to protect their interests. Free trade was popular with both the middle and working classes, both of whom wanted to keep government out of the economic life of the nation.

Those who favored free trade believed that if all nations embraced it, prosperity would result and it would be a force for peace. When depression hit in the 1870s, the other nations began to put up tariff walls to protect their infant industries from cheap goods imported from Britain. During the 1880s and 1890s, Britain expanded its colonial empire, thus opening new markets as protectionism spread on the continent and was adopted by the US. Still, Britain remained committed to free trade until the early 1930s.

Having been the world's first industrial nation, Britain's competitive advantage was lost during the Second Industrial Revolution. Germany began rapidly industrializing after unification in 1871. Likewise, the United States experienced a surge in industrial growth in the last quarter of the nineteenth century, fueled in part by a corresponding surge in immigration. Both were able to profit from Britain's example. Germany and the United States were able to enter the new industries, such as chemicals, and open "modern" factories powered by new sources of energy including diesel fuel and electricity. British industry was outdated and slow to adopt the new technology. Germany was quick to catch up with and surpass Britain. By the end of the century, Germany was Europe's leading industrial power, with the United States the world's leader.

Impact of the Industrial Revolution on Society

The textile mill opened by Richard Arkwright in 1771 is considered the first factory. It was the prototype of the factories that appeared during the Industrial Revolution. Shortly after opening, the factory employed 300 workers. By 1789, there were 800 employed. With the exception of a few, who in retrospect might be called engineers, the bulk were unskilled. As such, they had no choice but to submit to the rhythm of the machines and the tyranny of the foremen whose job was to make sure the workers kept pace with the machines.

The early factories were crowded, dirty, poorly ventilated, dark, and dangerous to work in. The author and social critic Charles Dickens (1812–1870) and the poet William Blake (1757–1827) both referred to the factories as "dark Satanic Mills." Whether male or female, child or adult, workers labored up to 16, or as many as 18 hours a day, with only an hour off for lunch or supper. Fines were levied for being tardy to work or for talking, singing, or whistling during work. The workweek was six days. Saturday afternoons off became common toward the end of the century. Injuries, especially among the children and women, were frequent. According to a report commissioned by the House of Commons in 1832, injured workers were often "abandoned from the moment that an accident occurs; their wages are stopped, no medical attendance is provided, and whatever the extent of the injury, no compensation is afforded" (Simkin 2015). A German visiting Manchester, England in 1842, commented that he saw so many people missing a leg or arm, that it was like "living in the midst of the army just returned from a campaign" (Simkin 2015).

Child Labor

Because only unskilled labor was required, the factories relied heavily on women and children. Factory owners "pointed out that children were ideal factory workers because they were obedient, submissive, likely to respond to punishment," and a "cheap source of labor that allowed them to stay competitive" (Child Labor n.d.). And of course, children did not attempt to form labor unions. The life of the child laborer, sometimes as young as five or six, was grim. They worked between 12 and 15 hours a day, 6 days a week, often having to take their meals while working and were subjected to being "strapped" as they grew tired.

The early textile mills relied heavily on "child apprentices." Child apprentices were paupers acquired from orphanages, and after passage of the New Poor Law in 1834, from the workhouses. The children were hired out by the workhouses that housed, clothed, and fed them, but did not pay them any wages for their labor. It was conservatively estimated that approximately one-third of those employed in the textile mills in England in 1784 were child apprentices. The percentage in individual mills reached as high as 80 or 90%. A British Parliamentary Report in 1834, found that of the children employed in the textile mills in 1833, between one-sixth and one-fifth were under the age of 14 (Child Labor n.d.).

Children made up a large portion of workers in the coal and metal mines in Britain. Child labor was especially used underground in the coal mines, where small children were able to move about in the narrow mineshafts better than adults. Some, called "thrusters," pushed wheeled carts filled with coal through the mines. The carts were pulled in front by a "hurrier," a child or woman harnessed to the cart like a draft animal. Tubs without wheels filled with coal were pulled by "drawers," either a child or woman in harness. Along the shafts were trapdoors that had to be opened and closed as the carts or tubs of coal moved through the shafts. The trapdoors were "manned" by small children as young as five or six called "trappers," sitting in the dark with only a candle for light and no one to talk to. A child working in the mines could go down into the mine before the sun came up in the morning and return to the surface after the sun had gone down in the evening.

One-third of the workers in the coal mines in Britain in 1842 were under the age of 18. A mine accident in 1838, in which 26 children (11 girls and 15 boys) between the ages of 7 and 17 died, was brought to the attention of Queen Victoria (1819–1901). The queen ordered an inquiry into the disaster (Huskar Colliery 2019). Lord Anthony Ashley-Cooper, 7th Earl of Shaftesbury (1801–1885), a Tory MP, headed a commission that reported to the

House of Commons on the plight of women and children working in the coal mines. The report, together with engraved illustrations and personal testimonies, was published in May 1842. The public was shocked, but shock was not sufficient to pass the Mines Act of 1842 banning boys and girls under ten years from working underground in the mines. In order to secure its passage, Lord Ashley pointed out that the girls and women worked in the mines dressed in trousers and bare-breasted along with boys and men, which "made girls unsuitable for marriage and unfit to be mothers" (Evans 2017).

The textile mills and factories in England served as a prototype for the spread of industrialization during the nineteenth century. Working conditions and the use of cheap child and women labor were similar whether in Britain, on the continent, or in the United States. The experience with child labor did differ, however. Parliament was much quicker than the American Congress to end the practice. The Factory Act of 1833 prohibited employment of children under 9 years of age, limited those between 9 and 13 to no more than 9 hours per day, and those between 13 and 18 to no more than 12 hours per day. Inspectors were provided to inspect the factories, but with limited success. The Factory Act of 1847, known as the Ten Hours Act, restricted employment of youth between the ages of 13 and 18 to no more than ten hours per day.

Subsequent legislation passed by Parliament, further restricted the age at which children could be employed, the hours and time of day they were permitted to work, and also addressed safety concerns. In 1878, children under 10 were barred from employment anywhere. Those between 10 and 14 could be employed for half days. The minimum age was raised to 11 in 1891 and 12 in 1901. The Factory Acts gave increasing attention to the need to provide a minimum of education for children of the working class. The Elementary Education Act of 1880 made primary education compulsory for children between age 5 and 10. Subsequent Education Acts raised the leaving age to 11 in 1893, and 12 in 1899. The Factory Acts and the Elementary Education Acts together resulted in a steady decline in the employment of children in the United Kingdom.

The employment of children in the United States during the nineteenth-century was not unlike in Britain, except of course, for the practice of slavery in the South until 1865. According to the 1900 census, one out of every six children between 5- and 10-years old were employed in what were termed "gainful occupations." Eighteen percent of America's workforce in 1900 was under the age of 16. Twenty-five percent of the workers in the Southern cotton mills were less than 12 years old. As in Britain, public opinion was aroused, but measures to address the problem were much slower in the United States.

By 1899, 28 of the 43 states had child labor laws. Congress passed the Keating-Owen Child Labor Act in 1916. It prohibited the employment of children under 14 in factories and under 16 in mines by prohibiting the sale in interstate trade of any products by firms that violated its provisions. The Supreme Court declared the Act unconstitutional in 1918. A further attempt by Congress to restrict child labor in 1918 was likewise declared unconstitutional. An attempt to add a child labor amendment to the Constitution in 1924 failed to be ratified by the necessary three-quarters of the states. Opposition was strong in the South, where attempts to restrict child labor were viewed as an "effort of northern agitators to kill the infant industries of the south" (Whittaker 2005, p. 5). The Fair Standards Act of 1938, passed as part of the New Deal legislation, finally placed limits on child labor that effectively ended the employment of children under 16 in factories and mines.

Women

A woman's daily life during the Industrial Revolution was never an easy one. Women, like children, were a cheap source of labor in an environment where labor was but one cost factor in the production of an item, and one without a human face. They worked beside the children in the factories and mines doing the same, or similar, monotonous tasks for 10–15 or more hours, day after day, week after week. Fortunate was the woman who was able to marry and trade working in the factory or mine for the domestic labor of raising children and caring for the home. Not all were able to do so. Many married women with children had to work the long hours in the factory or mine and also care for their families.

Testimonies given before Parliamentary commissions in Britain and Congressional Committees in the United States are replete with accounts of the horrors endured by women workers during the nineteenth century. Jane Goode was a working-class mother who testified before a British Factory Commission in 1833. She gave birth to 12 children, five of whom died before they were three months old. Two daughters and a son started working when they were seven. Jane Goode's example illustrates the high infant death rate, especially among the working class.

Betty Wardle was interviewed in 1842 by a Parliamentary Commission investigating women workers in the mines. She began working in the mine when she was six years old. She had four children; two were born while working in the mine. When asked if she had to work while pregnant, she answered: "Ay, to be sure. I had a child born in the pits, and I brought it up the pitshaft [sic] in my skirt" (Pike 2006, p. 258). When asked if she had to wear a belt and a chain, a harness used to haul coal wagons up to the surface, she answered: "Yes, sure I did" (Pike 2006). The Factory Act of 1847, limited women's work to 10 hours per day. Further limitations came with the Factory Act of 1878, which limited women to 56 hours a week. Finally, in 1891, Parliament passed the Factory Act of 1891, prohibiting women from working until four weeks after giving birth.

The Industrial Revolution brought to the forefront the question of what was the proper role for women in society, especially during the last half of the nineteenth century, the so-called "Victorian Age." Women in Britain had virtually no identity apart from men. They were effectively denied any opportunity for an education that would enable them to be financially independent of men. Women could not vote, sue, or own property, and once married, could not sign a contract, or keep as her own any earned wages. The Victorian ideal of womanhood was a life centered on the family, motherhood, and respectability, or as the German maxim put it: *"Kinder, Küche, Kirche"* ("children, kitchen, church").

The working-class woman was unable to relate to the Victorian Ideal of femininity that emphasized family, motherhood, and respectability. It was the upper and middle-class woman who was expected to live by the code that defined a respectable woman as being beautiful with a measure of elegance, polite, and of course, sexually restrained. Middle-class mothers guarded their daughters' virginity like the family bank account. Young men were expected to "sow their wild oats" before settling down, but no such libertine behavior was to be found in the life of a respectable middle-class daughter in the market for a suitable husband.

Of course, ideal and reality often clashed. The "Cult of True Womanhood" or "Cult of Domesticity," was an idealized set of values that characterized the middle and upper classes. The only alternatives to working in the factory or mine for single working-class women was either prostitution or domestic service, the latter being the preferred alternative. A single woman from the working class who found a position as a domestic servant could contribute to her family's income while preparing herself for marriage.

Urbanization

As noted above, the rapid growth of cities was spawned by the Industrial Revolution. Prior to the Industrial Revolution, cities were primarily centers of government and/or church administration, craft manufacturing, commerce, and banking. Towns and cities were always unhealthy. Until the mid-nineteenth century, the only way they increased population was from immigration, since death rates were always higher than birth rates. The agricultural revolution of the eighteenth century, that made the Industrial Revolution possible by improving nutrition and thus triggering a population boom, did not have a positive impact on life expectancy in the urban centers. On the contrary, the unprecedented growth of the cities caused by industrialization made them, if possible, even more unhealthy.

There exist from government reports and novels by such authors as Charles Dickens, Benjamin Disraeli (1804–1881), Elizabeth Gaskell (1810–1865), and Émile Zola (1840–1902), vivid descriptions of the horrid conditions that existed in the early industrial towns. Charles Dickens's description of the fictional Coketown in his novel, *Hard Times* (1854), enables the reader to understand and feel emotionally how industrialization scarred the once beautiful countryside and the human spirit:

> It was a town of red brick, or of brick that would have been red if the smoke and ashes had allowed it; but as matters stood, it was a town of unnatural red and black like the painted face of a savage. It was a town of machinery and tall chimneys, out of which interminable serpents of smoke trailed themselves for ever and ever, and never got uncoiled. It had a black canal in it, and a river that ran purple with ill-smelling dye, and vast piles of building[s] full of windows where there was a rattling and a trembling all day long, and where the piston of the steam-engine worked monotonously up and down, like the head of an elephant in a state of melancholy madness. It contained several large streets all very like one another, and many small streets still more like one another, inhabited by people equally like one another, who all went in and out at the same hours, with the same sound upon the same pavements, to do the same work, and to whom every day was the same as yesterday and to-morrow, and every year the counterpart of the last and the next. (Dickens 1905)

Coketown was a fictional creation, but not Manchester, the site of large textile mills. The French writer Alexis de Tocqueville (1805–1859) visited Manchester in 1835, and commented on its wretched working-class neighborhoods: "From this foul Drain the greatest stream of human industry flows out to fertilize the whole world. From this filthy sewer pure gold flows. Here humanity attains its most complete development and its most brutish, here civilization works its miracles and civilized man is turned almost into a savage" (Hobsbawm 1962, p. 44). The average life span of workers living in Manchester in the mid-nineteenth century was an alarming 17 years, 15 in Liverpool (The Peel Web 2016).

As the industrial cities developed, they reflected the emerging class structure of the industrial age. The wealthiest residents lived on the outer fringe of the city on lots with a private home, garden, and carriage house. Just inside the city limits, was found the middle class living in comfortable accommodations that were a humble reflection of their wealthier neighbors. Next came the abode of the lower middle class, a mixture of small houses and reasonably comfortable row houses of one- to two-stories with perhaps a small patch of green grass.

In the center of the city, crowded around the factories were three- to four-story, poorly built row houses, back-to-back in blocks of 4–20 houses, each block having a common pump and a common toilet or outhouse. The row houses, often built by the factory owners as cheaply as possible to house their workers, were dark, poorly ventilated, and always overcrowded. The streets were dirt, muddy when it rained, with a ditch that ran down the center into which garbage of all sorts and dead animals were thrown. The "night soil" from the outhouses was collected by "soil men," who hauled the solid waste away to the country where it was sold as fertilizer.

The lack of sanitation and clean water meant that the inner cities were breeding grounds for the many communicable diseases and the outbreak of epidemics, especially cholera. Until the emergence of the germ theory of disease, thanks to the work of the French microbiologist Louis Pasteur (1822–1895) and the German microbiologist Robert Koch (1843–1910), cholera was believed to be caused by "bad air" coming from decaying organic matter. As knowledge of the existence of microorganisms and their role in the spreading of cholera and other diseases became known, the middle and upper classes began calling for public authorities to "sanitize" the germ-infested inner cities as a matter of self-defense.

Even before the germ theory of disease, public officials were making a connection between filth and the spread of cholera and other diseases that made no distinction between classes. In England, Owen Chadwick (1800–1890) was able to demonstrate the relationship between the lack of public sanitation and disease in *The Sanitary Conditions of the Labouring Population* (1842). The appearance of Chadwick's report, followed by a cholera outbreak in 1848 that lasted 2 years and claimed 52 000 lives in England and Wales, prompted Parliament to pass the Public Health Act of 1848. A Central Board of Health was established, signaling a public commitment to improving public sanitation. A much more comprehensive Public Health Act was passed in 1875, that called upon local authorities to provide clean water and removal of waste. It also addressed the need for building codes for future construction. Similar steps were taken in France, Germany, and the United States as they awakened to the need for public authorities to assume responsibility for public health.

Responses to Industrialization

Looking back from the twenty-first century, one must wonder why it took so long for governments to awaken to the suffering caused by rapid industrialization. The squalor in the inner core of industrial cities was evident to anyone with eyes to see or a nose to smell with.

At the end of the eighteenth century, it was said that a traveler approaching London could smell the city before seeing the spires of its churches on the horizon.

Government authorities could not simply look to historical precedent to find solutions to the problems arising from urbanization. There was no precedent for the Industrial Revolution. There were no urban planners or environmental engineers to consult or employ. True, ancient Knossos had flushing toilets and a drainage system that carried away sewage. Roman cities were supplied with fresh water from great distances by skillfully built aqueducts. No Roman city of any size was without at least one public toilet where individuals would gather to relieve themselves and visit. It was not until the late 1850s that Paris installed a water and sewage system in part of the city. Still, as late as 1914, only 68% of the buildings in Paris were connected to the sewer system.

The Industrial Revolution was possible because of the Scientific Revolution, but it was also a product of the Enlightenment. Both the political and economic philosophy that dominated the nineteenth century was what is commonly referred to as classical liberalism. Politically, classical liberalism called for written constitutions that spelled out the rights of citizens and the limits of government authority, and regularly scheduled elections for representatives of the citizens who meet in regularly scheduled meetings of a representative assembly. The classical liberals were not democrats, however. Only those who met certain property requirements were allowed to vote.

John Locke, whose *Two Treatises on Government* (1690) provided the philosophical foundation for political liberalism, held that all rights are property rights. Any attack on a person's property was an attack on that person's liberty, that is, one's inalienable natural rights of life, liberty, and property. As noted earlier, Locke's *Two Treatises on Government* was an attempt to justify the Glorious Revolution (1688), which transformed England from an absolute monarchy into a constitutional monarchy with political power resting safely in the hands of the landed aristocracy.

Adam Smith's *An Inquiry into the Nature and Causes of the Wealth of Nations* (1776) was for classical economic liberalism what Locke's *Two Treatises* was for political liberalism. Like the other intellectuals of the Enlightenment who claimed to discover the natural laws of society, Adam Smith believed that he discovered certain "natural laws" of economics, for example, the law of supply and demand, and the law of diminishing returns.

Adam Smith was one of a group of economic theorists who are sometimes referred to as the "dismal scientists." Thomas R. Malthus (1766–1834) and David Ricardo (1772–1823) were also members. Malthus is best remembered for his *An Essay on the Principle of Population* (1798). Population, said Malthus, will continue to increase until it is greater than what the food supply can support. Then famine, disease, war, infanticide, etc., sets in until the population drops below the food supply, thus allowing the population to increase until once again it outstrips the food supply. Thus, population flows through history like a wave, and any attempt to alleviate the suffering will only cause greater suffering in the future. It is better to allow the law of population to make the necessary adjustments without interference.

David Ricardo is best remembered for his "iron law of wages," so named at mid-century by Ferdinand Lasalle (1825–1864), one of the founders of German Social Democracy. Simply put, the iron law of wages states that in a free economy, real wages, or real income, will always be at the minimum subsistence level. In Ricardo's words, "... Profits depend on high or low wages, wages on the price of necessaries, and the price of necessaries chiefly on the price of food because all other requisites may be increased almost without limit" (Ricardo 1821, p. 119).

What today is referred to as simply "economics" was called "political economy" at the beginning of the nineteenth century. The term "dismal science" is variously attributed to the English historian, Thomas Carlyle (1795–1881) or the German writer, Johann Wolfgang von Goethe (1749–1832). The term is fitting when referring to classical economic liberalism, or even in the twenty-first century when referring to what is commonly called economic imperialism. It was the belief that the natural laws of economics were ironclad laws, that is, that nothing could be done to alter them without courting disaster, that made them "dismal."

Opponents of the classical economists used the term "laissez-faire" (lit. "let do") to describe classical economics. Theoretically, economic relationships occur according to self-governing natural laws, such as the law of supply and demand. If each person in society follows his or her own self-interest, the result will be beneficial to all. The whole process is guided by what Adam Smith called an "invisible hand." He did not mean some sort of divine interference, but simply how the natural laws of economics work. Government should not meddle with the economy, rather keep its hands off, hence the term laissez-faire. The only legitimate role for government is to act as a kind of referee making sure that competition remains free. Workers must accept the iron law of wages and expect no more than the minimum standard of living. Laissez-faire "is the system, the natural system – there is no other" (Palmer and Colton 1965, p. 430).

The classical liberal response to the suffering of the working poor was the New Poor Law of 1834. The New Poor Law replaced the Elizabethan Poor Law of 1601, under which poor relief was administered through the church parishes. The New Poor Law was based on the assumption that relief should go only to those who were truly deserving. In order to receive relief, the poor would have to go into the Workhouse, where conditions were intentionally so bad that only those who were truly destitute would seek relief.

Liberalism changed during the course of the nineteenth century from the Grim Reaper of classical liberalism to liberalism as it is commonly identified in the twenty-first century. As the working class gained a class identity, and the right to vote, political parties had to listen to the workers' demands for justice. As a result, liberalism today believes in universal suffrage, called "radicalism" in the early nineteenth century, and a proactive role for government in securing a more just, or equitable, distribution of wealth. There is, one should note, a constant in the history of liberalism. It is the concern for the individual.

Classical liberalism held that the interest of the individual was best served if government limited itself to the role of referee. Modern liberalism recognizes that the playing field is not level for everyone. The lone worker is at a disadvantage trying to bargain for a higher wage with the factory owner. Hence government has a responsibility to help level the playing field through legislation and other means of regulating the economy.

Early Reform Efforts

The new industrial environment during the nineteenth century created a new class structure. In the old medieval order, each individual enjoyed the rights and privileges of the estate to which he or she belonged. No such security existed in the new laissez-faire society where the only value seemed to be one's economic value, or put another way, one's utility. So prevalent was the commitment to laissez-faire, that the natural instinct of the working class to organize for self-defense against the greed of those who owned the factories, was understood by the factory owners as a threat to the natural order as determined by the natural laws of economics. Everywhere, laws were enacted, such as the Combination Act of 1799 in Britain, that prohibited workers from forming any association aimed at collectively bargaining with employers for wages or improved working conditions.

As noted earlier, the political life of Britain was securely in the hands of the property-owning aristocracy of landlords and wealthy merchants. But with the growth of a wealthy class of industrial entrepreneurs in the new environment, where industrial wealth often trumped landed wealth, pressure mounted for reform of the electoral system. There were demands to lower the property requirements for suffrage and granting, or increasing, representation of the industrial areas in order to provide representation in Parliament for the new industrial middle class. Parliament responded with passage of the Great Reform Bill of 1832.

The Great Reform Bill of 1832, was the first major overhaul of the electoral system in Britain since the reign of Elizabeth I. The need for reform was demonstrated by the electoral borough of Old Sarum, which consisted of an old farmhouse, several fields, and a bunch of sheep. Old Sarum was represented in Parliament by two MPs appointed by 43 men who did not live in the borough. Boroughs like Old Sarum were referred to as "rotten" or "pocket" boroughs. The need to eliminate such boroughs was evident in the fact that the industrial city of Manchester with a population of 400 000 was not represented in Parliament.

The Great Reform Bill passed the House of Lords only with the intervention of King William IV (1765–1837). Fifty-six boroughs were eliminated and 31 were reduced to one member. Sixty-seven new boroughs were created that granted representation to the new industrial areas. Property requirements for voting were reduced, effectively granting suffrage to the middle class (The Reform Act n.d.). The working class, some of the lower middle class, and women were not included. Even so, the electorate was nearly doubled as a result of the reforms.

The balance of power did not immediately change. The Reform Bill in effect recognized the growing power of the wealthy middle class, while the landed aristocracy retained control of Parliament, the bureaucracy, the church, and the military. Perhaps the most significant impact of the Great Reform Bill was that, when considered together with other reform measures passed by Parliament during the 1820s and 1830s – Catholic Relief Act (1829), abolition of slavery in the British Empire (1833), Municipal Corporations Act (1835) – Parliament demonstrated that reform was possible in Britain without revolution. The United Kingdom was spared the revolutions that swept across the continent in 1848.

Left out of the Great Reform Bill of 1832, the working class turned to a movement known as Chartism, a reform movement whose aims were stated in the People's Charter of 1838. The Chartists called for universal manhood suffrage, a secret ballot, annual parliamentary elections, and the end of property requirements, together with paid salaries for Members of Parliament. The last two were meant to make it possible for members of the working and lower middle classes to become Members of Parliament.

There were three charters presented to Parliament, the first in 1839 with 1.2 million signatures, the second in 1842 with over 3 million signatures, and a third in 1848 with perhaps 6 million signatures. All three were rejected. However, by 1918, all of the aims of the Chartists, except annually elected Parliaments, were enacted. With Chartism's failure in 1848, workers turned their attention to labor organization.

At mid-century, Members of Parliament were aware that further electoral reform was necessary, if Britain was to avoid a revolution from below. Benjamin Disraeli (1804–1888), leader of the Conservative Party, secured passage of the Reform Act of 1867 which, in effect, doubled the voting population of England and Wales by enfranchising most of the urban population. In doing so, Disraeli was acknowledging the fact that the urban working class was going to get the vote, and he wanted the Conservative Party to get credit for it.

A further advance toward universal manhood suffrage was made in 1884, when the Liberal Party led by William E. Gladstone (1809–1898) pushed the Reform Act of 1884 through Parliament. The provisions of the Reform Act of 1867 were extended to the counties, effectively enfranchising the rural working class. Property requirements still kept about 40% of the male population from voting. All property requirements for adult males over age 21 were removed by the Representation of the People Act in 1918. The act also granted the vote to women over 30 years of age who met certain minimum property qualifications. Fear of women becoming a majority of the electorate kept Parliament from granting the vote to women on the same grounds as men until 1928.

Marxism and the Working Class

The alternative to a society based on laissez-faire would be one based on cooperation. That is the starting point for those who advocated what is called socialism. The term is often used with the assumption that all parties in the discussion understand what is meant by socialism. Unfortunately, that is seldom the case. Socialism is not the same as Marxism, and Marxism is not the same as Marxism-Leninism, or communism. Utopian Socialism, Social Democracy, Christian Socialism, and Fabian socialism are all different, though they all have some things in common. And of course, there are the other two isms, anarchism and syndicalism, that are often confused with the others.

Prior the mid-nineteenth century, those who offered a vision of a society based on cooperation were referred to as socialists, or Utopian socialists. They essentially believed that if people were placed in an ideal community where all property was held in common and all worked for the common benefit of all, they would live in peaceful harmony with one another. Those most often identified by historians as Utopian socialists include Henri de Saint-Simon (1760–1825), Charles Fourier (1772–1837), Étienne Cabet (1788–1856), and Robert Owen (1771–1858).

Robert Owen, was a successful textile manufacturer from Wales, and leader of the trade union movement as well as a socialist. Among the 130 or so attempts to establish a utopian society in the United States, 16 were founded or inspired by Owen. Charles Fourier advocated small communities of approximately 1600 people called *phalansteries*. He recognized that human beings have a natural desire for rewards, so he allowed that individuals would be rewarded according to their special skills or responsibilities within the community. Efforts to create utopian communities in America inspired by Fourier's ideas included Utopia, Ohio and Brook Farm, Massachusetts.

Étienne Cabet was founder of a utopian movement known as the Icarians. The name was derived from the title of a science fiction novel by Cabet, *The Voyage to Icaria*, published in 1840. Five Icarian communities were founded in America beginning in 1848. The longest lasting was the Corning Icarian Community in southwest Iowa, which lasted from 1852 to 1898. It was the longest lasting utopian socialist community founded in America.

Henri de Saint-Simon differed from the other utopian socialists, and is not always included among them, because he envisioned a scientifically organized society managed by a trained elite of technocrats. Emperor Napoleon III of the Second French Empire (1852–1870) is sometimes referred to as "Saint-Simon on Horseback," because of his economic policies. Napoleon III believed that the government had an important role to play in stimulating economic expansion. The imperial government was able to promote the banking and credit institutions that financed public works programs and development of the nation's infrastructure, all of which benefitted the working class.

The appearance in 1848 of the *Communist Manifesto* by Karl Marx (1818–1883) and Friedrich Engels (1820–1895) changed the definition of socialism and its historical development. It is arguably the most influential political pamphlet in modern Western, even world, history. It contains, in less than 50 pages, the political and economic philosophy of Karl Marx that perhaps more than anything else gave to the working class a class identity. It opens a new way of understanding history: "The history of all hitherto existing society is the history of class struggles" (Marx and Engels 1948, p. 9).

Figure 11.2 Karl Marx, author of The Communist Manifesto (1848), one of the most influential books in modern history. *Source:* Library of Congress Prints and Photographs Division.

Karl Marx borrowed from the German metaphysical philosopher, Georg Wilhelm Friedrich Hegel (1770–1831) his belief that history advanced according to a dialectical process. Hegel believed that history was the unfolding of the Universal Spirit by a process of clashes between the spirit of the age and an opposing spirit, resulting in a new spirit of the age that is a synthesis of all that went before. Theoretically, the Universal Spirit will be fully revealed at some point in the future.

Marx, as a materialist, regarded Hegel's talk of a Universal Spirit as just so much German metaphysical nonsense, but he found Hegel's view of historical progress as a series of clashes between opposing forces helpful. Marx substituted a dialectical conflict between classes defined by their economic interests. In each period of history, there was a clash between those who owned and controlled the means of producing wealth and those who owned nothing but their labor. In the pre-industrial world, the clash was between the landowners and those who worked the land.

The Industrial Revolution produced a society in which the class struggle reached its final stage. The bourgeoisie (capitalists), who own most of the wealth and the means of producing wealth, are opposed by the proletariat, the class of wage workers. Since the transition from one stage to the next was always by violent revolution, the proletariat will rise up and overthrow the bourgeoisie, after which private property will be abolished, and with it, all class conflict. Marx was not very clear as to what follows the final revolution. Apparently, a brief dictatorship of the proletariat would follow as the state slowly withered away.

Marxism's Appeal

Marxism proved appealing for a number of reasons. First, like most of the isms that emerged from the Enlightenment, or in reaction to it, Marxism assumes that human beings are by nature good, only corrupted by history. If that is true, then it is only necessary to adjust the environment in order to end the injustices inherent in an industrial society. Also, Marx assumed that human nature, like the natural physical world, is governed by scientific laws. He believed that he had discovered the natural laws of the historical process. With his discovery of what is commonly called dialectical materialism, he could accurately predict the future outcome of the historical process. The simplicity of it is very attractive to those who desire to be optimistic about the future, and have faith in progress.

Some scholars have pointed out that when rightly understood, Marxism is a total worldview. Understanding Marxism as a Christian heresy, or an ersatz religion, helps one to understand its appeal for those suffering from the injustices of an industrial society that knows no ethic other than laissez-faire, or its appeal for the poor in underdeveloped countries. David Lyon, Professor of Sociology at Erasmus University in Rotterdam, writes:

> Marxism has an appeal similar to that of the Christian gospel. A root problem is isolated, its manifestations described, release is promised, a savior is available and new life will follow. The Creator is now man; creation, work; the fall, division of labour; sin, capitalism; the savior, intelligentsia plus working class; salvation, revolution; the church, the people or the party. (Lyon 1979, p. 14)

Orthodoxy and Revision

Karl Marx's view of history was very deterministic. He was convinced that wealth was being concentrated in fewer hands, and that parallel to that, the suffering of the proletariat was increasing. It was only a matter of time before the great proletarian revolution would occur, as is evident in the closing lines of the *Communist Manifesto*:

> The Communists disdain to conceal their views and aims. They openly declare that their ends can be attained only by the forcible overthrow of all existing social conditions. Let the ruling classes tremble at a Communistic revolution. The proletarians have nothing to lose but their chains. They have a world to win. (Marx and Engels 1948, p. 44)

By the early 1860s, it was obvious to some of Marx's followers that the future need not unfold exactly as Marx insisted it must. Perhaps the way to the future socialist utopia was by evolution, not revolution.

In 1863, Ferdinand Lassalle (1825–1864) founded the General German Workers' Association (ADAV) committed to achieving socialism through the electoral process. In essence, the goal was to first gain suffrage for the working class, then use the legislative process to advance working-class goals until one day a socialist Germany was a reality. In 1869, Wilhelm Liebknecht (1826–1900) and August Bebel (1840–1913) founded the Social Democratic Workers' Party (SDAP) with support from the trade unions. The ADAV and the SDAP both were committed to achieving socialism in Germany by lawful means. The two political parties merged in 1875 to form the Socialist Workers' Party of Germany (SAPD) with a program urging "universal, equal, direct suffrage." The 1890 party conference renamed the party the Social Democratic Party of Germany (SPD).

What became the ideology of the SPD after 1890 was "revisionism" associated with Eduard Bernstein (1850–1932). The revisionists abandoned Marx's revolutionary socialism in favor of a pragmatic approach that substituted private initiative and cooperation for class conflict. Private property and capitalism would not vanish as Marx predicted. Instead, a steady progress of reform legislation and strong labor unions would lead to an ever more just society for all classes.

The revisionists could point to the social legislation passed by the Reichstag during the 1880s that made Germany the most progressive nation in the world. Kaiser Wilhelm I (1797–1888) gave his support to the legislation in a letter to the Reichstag in 1881: "...those who are disabled from work by age and invalidity have a well-grounded claim to care from the state" (Social Security n.d.). The Health Insurance Act of 1883 provided compensation for workers when sick. The Accident Insurance Act of 1884 provided compensation for injured workers. In 1889, old age pensions were added. The Pensions and Disabilities Act of 1889 provided pensions for workers who reached age 70. Chancellor Otto von Bismarck (1815–1898), who sponsored the legislation, hoped that it would reconcile the working class to the state.

Socialism in Britain

Though Karl Marx lived most of his life in England, the working class in Britain never found Marxism attractive. Instead, they embraced a vision of a welfare state, what was commonly called "gas and water socialism." As noted earlier, the Liberal and Conservative parties vied with one another for working class support. Legislation passed by Parliament in 1871 and 1876 protected labor unions, allowing for the growth of a strong labor union movement more interested in humanizing laissez-faire than eliminating private property.

Intellectuals in Britain who were attracted to socialism found a home in the Fabian Society, founded in 1884 to advance the cause of evolutionary socialism. The husband and wife team of Sidney and Beatrice Webb (1859–1947; 1858–1943) were the most influential members. Other well-known members were the philosopher George Bernard Shaw (1856–1950) and the writer H.G. Wells (1866–1946). The Fabians rejected class conflict in favor of a future welfare state brought about gradually through legislation. Fabian socialists, ethical and Christian socialists, and the trade unions joined forces to found the Labour Party in 1900.

Anarchism

The laboring classes in countries with an industrial economy and constitutional government that allowed for their participation, limited though it was, were attracted to socialist ideologies that emphasized equality of reward over equality of opportunity. Where the political system offered the working-class real opportunities to influence governments to address the workers' grievances, the evolution of socialism was in the direction of the modern welfare state. The urban and rural unemployed in the more backward regions of Eastern and Southern Europe were attracted to anarchism.

The anarchists sought the violent overthrow of all existing order and the establishment of a stateless, voluntary order in its place. Marx believed that the proletarian revolution was inevitable. The anarchists believed an act of terrorism, such as the assassination of a head of state, would trigger a revolution that would result in the overthrow of all order, after which, a voluntary society would rise from the ruins.

Mikhail Bakunin (1814–1876), a Russian anarchist and friend of Karl Marx, criticized Marx's theory. He believed that the Marxist revolution would simply result in establishing a new class of exploiters to replace the capitalists. Bakunin's criticism of Marxism proved prophetic during the twentieth century. Both Marxism and anarchism share a fundamental error. They are both based on the Enlightenment's belief that human beings are good, but corrupted by history. Both must end in failure. A society without order would be anarchy, and no society can exist in such a state. The dictatorship of the proletariat must become authoritarian, because people who are neither good nor evil by nature, but capable of both, will not simply chose to behave as Marxism insists that they will. When people do not behave as predicted, coercion must be used to compel them to behave according to the theory. Eventually, the state that was meant to liberate the exploited, must become authoritarian. History since the publication of the *Communist Manifesto* has proven that neither idealistic Marxism nor unrestrained capitalism can produce a just society.

References

Ashton, T.S. (1997). *The Industrial Revolution: 1760–1830*. Oxford: Oxford University Press.

Butler, C. (2007). Railroads and Their Impact (c.1825–1900). The Flow of History. http://www.flowofhistory.com/units/eme/17/FC112 (accessed 13 February 2019).

Dickens, C. (1905). *Hard Times*. New York: Charles Scribner's Sons. https://www.gutenberg.org/files/786/786-h/786-h.htm#page18 (accessed 14 February 2019).

Evans, R.J. (2017). *The Pursuit of Power: Europe, 1815–1914*. London: Penguin Books.

Hobsbawm, E.J. (1962). *The Age of Revolution: 1789–1848*. New York: New American Library.

Lyon, D. (1979). *Karl Marx: A Christian Assessment of His Life & Thought*. Downers Grove, IL: InterVarsity Press.

Marx, K. and Engels, F. (1948). *The Communist Manifesto*. New York: International Publishers Co.

Mirsky, J. and Nevins, A. (1952). *The World of Eli Whitney*. New York: Macmillan Company.

MSIA (2019). Huskar Colliery 1838 – Mining Accident Database. http://www.mineaccidents.com.au/mine-accident/202/huskar-colliery-1838 (accessed 21 October 2019).

Palmer, R.R. and Colton, J. (1965). *A History of the Modern World*. New York: Alfred A Knopf.

Picard, L. (2009). The Great Exhibition. The British Library. https://www.bl.uk/victorian-britain/articles/the-great-exhibition (accessed 21 October 2019).

Pike, E.R. (2006). *Human Documents of the Industrial Revolution in Britain*. London: George Allen & Unwin.

Ricardo, D. (1821). *On the Principles of Political Economy and Taxation*. London: John Murray.

Simkin, J. (2015). Factory Accidents. Spartacus Educational. http://spartacus-educational.com/IRaccidents.htm (accessed 21 October 2019).

Social Security (n.d.). Reports, Facts and Figures. Press Office. Social Security Administration. https://www.ssa.gov/history/ottob.html (accessed 21 October 2019).

Taylor, F.W. (1911). *The Principles of Scientific Management*. New York: Harper & Brothers.

The Peel Web (2016). Public Health: background. http://www.historyhome.co.uk/peel/p-health/pubheal.htm (accessed 21 October 2019).

Tuttle, C. (2001). Child Labor during the British Industrial Revolution. https://eh.net/encyclopedia/child-labor-during-the-british-industrial-revolution (accessed 21 October 2019).

Trueman, C.N. (2019). Coal Mines in the Industrial Revolution. History Learning Site. http://www.historylearningsite.co.uk/britain-1700-to-1900/industrial-revolution/coal-mines-in-the-industrial-revolution (accessed 21 October 2019).

UK Parliament (n.d.). The Reform Act 1932. http://www.parliament.uk/about/living-heritage/evolutionofparliament/houseofcommons/reformacts/overview/reformact1832 (accessed 21 October 2019).

Victoria and Albert Museum (2019). Building the Museum. http://www.vam.ac.uk/content/articles/t/the-crystal-palace (accessed 21 October 2019).

Whittaker, W.G. (2005). Child Labor in America: History, Policy, and Legislative Issue. CRS Report for Congress. http://digitalcommons.ilr.cornell.edu/cgi/viewcontent.cgi?article=1204&context=key_workplace (accessed 21 October 2019).

12

Nineteenth-Century Intellect and Culture

Chronology

1650	Bishop James Usher's *Annals of the Old Testament*
1770s–mid-1800s	Romanticism
1730s–1770s	First Great Awakening (USA and UK)
c. 1790–1840s	Second Great Awakening (USA)
1830–1833	Charles Lyell's *Principles of Geology*
1830–1842	Auguste Comte's *Course of Positive Philosophy* ("law of three stages")
1856	Gustave Flaubert's *Madame Bovary*
1859	Charles Darwin's *On the Origin of Species by Means of Natural Selection*
1860s–1903	Herbert Spencer Advocates Social Darwinism
1865	Gregor Johann Mendel's *"Experiments on Plant Hybrids"*
1871	Charles Darwin's *The Descent of Man, and Selection in Relation to Sex*
1879	Henrik Ibsen's *Doll's House*
1882	Friedrich Nietzsche's *The Gay Science*
1883	Francis Galton Introduces Theory of Eugenics
1899	Sigmund Freud's *Interpretation of Dreams*
1905	Albert Einstein's Theory of Relativity

The intellectual and cultural history of the nineteenth century was characterized by rebellion, rebellion against all accepted standards of "good taste" and "correct thinking," which occurred against a backdrop of political revolution, industrialization, and secularization. At the beginning of the century, the pendulum swung from an emphasis on reason and rationalism to an emphasis on intuition, emotion, and mystery, known as Romanticism. The pendulum swung back in the direction of an emphasis on reason and rationalism in the middle of the century, as a second scientific revolution pushed Romanticism, religion, and metaphysics to the background, in favor of careful observation and scientific scrutiny of the empirical world. During the latter decades of the century to the outbreak of the Great War, the emphasis shifted once again. The blending of romantic myth and Darwinism, in an atmosphere of continued secularization of life and thought, produced a new age of nonreason that would characterize the twentieth century.

Western Civilization: A Brief History, First Edition. Paul R. Waibel.
© 2020 John Wiley & Sons, Inc. Published 2020 by John Wiley & Sons, Inc.

Romanticism

The Romantic Revolt dominated the intellectual and cultural history of the period from the 1770s to the middle of the 1800s. It was primarily in the creative arts and literature, but also greatly influenced the rise of radical nationalism during the latter decades of the nineteenth century. It began in Germany and France as a revolt against the Enlightenment's emphasis on reason and spread throughout Europe and America.

As noted earlier (Chapter 9), the Enlightenment marked the transition from the medieval synthesis (premodernity) to the Enlightenment tradition (modernity). Whereas the medieval synthesis looked to accepted authorities (e.g. Bible, authoritative church teachings, and the classical philosophers) for a true understanding of reality, the Enlightenment tradition looked to the scientific method, or reason. Premodernity found order and meaning in a universe created by a God who maintained it in existence by his continued involvement. Modernity found order in a mechanistic universe of cause and effect natural law created by God, but operating like a clock without divine intervention.

The philosophes's reliance on the scientific method, what they called the application of reason, left no room for humanness, that which separates human beings from animals. They reduced human beings to soulless thinking machines. By focusing on the generic human being, they lost the uniqueness of the individual. They allowed for an autonomous mind capable of reasoning, but did not allow for "personality," that characteristic which makes the individual unique from all other humans. Such things as love, hate, good, bad, and beauty are real but cannot be explained, only experienced. In short, the philosophes reduced human beings to numbers.

Not surprisingly, the human spirit revolted against such an attempt to banish it. During the Enlightenment, the pendulum swung too far in the direction of rationalism. With the romantic revolt, it swung back in the direction of emotion, intuition, instinct, passion, experience, mystery, and individualism. By liberating the human spirit from the restraints imposed on it by the Enlightenment, romanticism unleashed a creative energy in the arts that had not been seen since the Renaissance, and which continues to influence the creative arts into the twenty-first century.

Whereas the philosophes believed that emotions were obstacles in the search for truth, the romantics felt that all rules must be swept aside and the spirit set free to find through intuitive feelings, a higher truth, a more authentic understanding of reality and oneself. "I feel it," said Rousseau, "and it is this feeling which speaks to me more forcibly than the reason which disputes it" (Abbs 2008). To Descartes's "I think, therefore I am," the romantic replied, "I feel, therefore I am."

Creativity could not be learned. One did not become a poet, painter, or composer by studying technique. A creative work could not be appreciated by comparing it to some rubric. Its message, or meaning, had its genesis in the artist's unconscious mind and therefore must be felt, or experienced, to be understood and appreciated.

Central to romanticism were the emotions, or feelings, that occupy the individual's soul and unconscious, and find expression in the music, art, and especially poetry. Because poetry flows directly from the heart, it was the dominate cultural expression of romanticism.

Many expressions of the romantic spirit, whether poetry, art, or music, express what the Germans call *sehnsucht*, a sense of longing for something more, something missing in the individual's life that cannot be identified or defined. Johann Wolfgang von Goethe (1749–1832) expressed it in his poem, *Only those who know the longing* (*Nur wer die Sehnsucht kennt*):

> Only the Yearning, they
> Know what I suffer!
> Alone, and far away
> From all joy severed,
> Seeing the sky always
> On every side.
> Who love me and know me, they
> Distantly hide.
> I'm dizzied: I'm burned, all day
> Inwardly shudder.
> Only the Yearning, they
> Know what I suffer!
>
> (Goethe 2004)

The observer experiences this feeling of *sehnsucht* when viewing Casper David Friedrich's paintings, especially *Wanderer above the Sea of Fog* (1818) or *Man and Woman Contemplating the Moon* (1824).

The romantics were enthralled with nature, not the nature-machine designed by the clockmaker God of deism, but nature alive with a divine spirit, unscarred by the sound and sight of the "dark satanic mills" that polluted the rivers, filled the sky with dark clouds of smoke, and blackened the beauty of virgin nature with a blanket of soot. To experience life fully, one had to go out into the woods, sit in a clearing and listen to the sounds of leaves and branches made alive by the movement of the air, or sit on the seashore and listen to the crash of the waves upon the beach, or sit beside a waterfall. William Wordsworth (1770–1850) said it best in his poem, *The Tables Turned*:

> One impulse from a vernal wood
> May teach you more of man,
> Of moral evil and of good
> Than all the sages can.
>
> (Wordsworth 2018)

The God to whom the romantics were attracted to was neither the clockmaker God of deism nor the God of Judeo-Christianity. Their God was a spiritual force that animated nature and inspired people. The romantics criticized the philosophes for attempting to subject religious faith to the scientific method. They saw the individual as a spiritual being. By choosing to see the individual as a thinking machine, the philosophes alienated the individual from the spiritual side of his or her nature, thus making the individual less than human.

The romantics were attracted to the medieval period of history. They were deeply moved by the liturgy of the medieval Roman Catholic Church that nourished the individual's longing (*sehnsucht*) for communion with the infinite, especially the eucharistic liturgy of the Mass wherein the bread and wine are miraculously transformed into the flesh and blood of Jesus Christ.

Their world of the Middle Ages was "romantic," in that it was an idealized world of knights in shining armor rescuing fair damsels from fiery dragons and dark knights. The romantic believed that the corporate nature of medieval society provided for harmony among the classes. Churchman, noble, merchant, and peasant all found fulfillment in their assigned place in the Great Chain of Being. Of course, their picture of the medieval world was far from reality. Their fascination with the Middle Ages gave birth to a gothic revival in architecture and what became known in literature as the *Gothic Romance*. Emily Brontë's *Wuthering Heights*, Charlotte Brontë's *Jane Eyre*, Mary Shelley's *Frankenstein*, Victor Hugo's *The Hunchback of Notre Dame*, and Goethe's *Faust* are all classic examples of the Gothic genre of romantic literature.

More than anyone else, the German composer Richard Wagner (1813–1888) brought together all of the characteristics of Romanticism in his operas. He took the themes for his operas from the legends and myths of the Germanic people and the Middle Ages. Wagner combined all of the creative arts, in what he called *Gesamtkunstwerk* (an "all-embracing art form" or "total artwork"). *Parsifal*, *Lohengrin*, and *The Ring of the Nibelungs* were perhaps the truest expression of the Romantic movement.

Through the study of religion, history, folk traditions, legends, and linguistics, the romantics felt they could connect with the unique soul of a particular people group. They believed that just as the individual had a soul, so also did a group of people. For example, each German had a soul, but so did what was called the German nation, as distinct from the political entity known as the nation state. This aspect of romanticism later influenced the rise of a radical nationalism during the latter part of the nineteenth century (Chapter 13).

The overemphasis on reason within Christianity, both Roman Catholic and especially the Protestant churches, resulted in a new emphasis on experiencing a personal relationship with Jesus Christ and less on the intellect. It began in Germany as a reaction to the emotionally dead orthodoxy of the Lutheran state churches and spread to England and from there to America. In Germany, it was called Pietism, Evangelicalism in England, and the Great Awakening in America. Among the key figures associated with the movement were John and Charles Wesley and George Whitefield in England, and Jonathan Edwards in America.

John Wesley (1703–1791) became a Christian through his contact with followers of Count Nicholaus von Zinzendorf (1700–1760), founder of the Moravian Brethren and the modern Protestant foreign mission movement. George Whitefield (1714–1770) was the bridge between the Evangelical revival in England and the Great Awakening in America. Wesley and Whitefield often traveled together in both England and America. The revivalists stressed three things: the terror of the law to sinners, the unmerited grace of God, and the new birth in Jesus Christ. They did not ignore the intellectual side of the Christian religion as is evidenced in the preaching and writings of Jonathan Edwards (1703–1758), regarded by many scholars as one of the greatest philosopher-theologians in American history.

Figure 12.1 John Wesley, a leader of the First Great Awakening, is depicted preaching while standing on his father's grave. *Source:* Library of Congress Prints and Photographs Division.

There was a second so-called Great Awakening in America during the first half of the nineteenth century that emphasized the experiential aspect of religion. The camp meetings on the western frontier characterized the Second Great Awakening. When news spread along the frontier that a camp meeting was to take place, families and individuals came from as many as 100 miles away by foot, wagon, or whatever means was available. They brought with them tents and food so that they could camp out for as long as the enthusiasm lasted.

The Second Great Awakening combined religious enthusiasm with a concern for social reform. Charles G. Finney (1792–1875), a lawyer who gave up the practice of law to become an ordained Presbyterian minister, president of Oberlin College, and revivalist preacher, was a major force in linking the Second Great Awakening with social reform – including abolition of slavery and women's rights.

Romantic Revolt and Immanuel Kant's Idealism

Romanticism raised the question of whether reality was in the individual's mind or the environment. It is an epistemological question: How do we know what we know? As noted earlier (Chapter 9), John Locke's empiricism effectively made the mind a prisoner of the environment. He held that the human mind at birth is a blank slate (*tabula rasa*). Data from the environment flows into the mind through the five senses – sight, hearing, taste, smell, and touch. All knowledge comes from experience.

The Scottish empiricist, David Hume (1711–1776), argued that nothing can be known for certain through the senses. His radical skepticism undermined faith in reason that characterized both the Scientific Revolution and the Enlightenment. In response, the German philosopher Immanuel Kant (1724–1804) rejected both Locke's and Hume's empiricism.

Kant said that the mind is not a blank slate at birth. Rather, it is equipped, *a priori*, with certain forms and categories like perception, space, time, and cause and effect. The mind imposes order and meaning on what is experienced through the senses. Because the physical world must conform to the forms and categories implanted in the mind, the universe as defined by Newtonian physics really exists. Without the rational structure that exists *a priori* in the mind, our sensory knowledge of the material universe would be a "hopeless jumble," or as William James put it, "a great blooming buzzing confusion" (Stromberg 1994, p. 26).

Kant saved the modernist understanding of the universe from Hume's radical skepticism. We do live in a cause and effect natural law universe that can be reliably known. The knowledge we have of the universe machine (e.g., the natural laws), however, does not come from the machine itself. Rather, the order of the universe originates in the mind and is imposed on the raw sensory data by the mind.

Before leaving Kant, one must make note of the fact that he made a distinction between the scientific knowledge of something, for example, the natural laws that regulate the universe machine, and knowledge of the universe machine's origin, or ultimate reality. Kant acknowledged that there are questions the answers to which cannot be known through reason. The existence of God, for example, cannot be proven by the scientific method. Nevertheless, we know that he exists. That knowledge is intuitive, or the result of transcendental reason. Humans are condemned to live knowing that their scientific knowledge is exact but only superficial. We can have true knowledge of how the universe works, but never why it exists.

A Second Scientific Revolution

In the middle of the nineteenth century, the pendulum swung back in the direction of reason and objective reality. A second scientific revolution, together with rapid advances in technology captured the public's attention, leading to a renewed faith in the scientific method as the only reliable means of discovering a true understanding of reality. Many people saw in the "benefits of science" the promise of solutions to many of the social problems caused by industrialization. Romanticism, metaphysics, and religion all lost ground to a growing materialist, secular worldview, the belief that matter is the ultimate reality and everything non-material is merely the product of physical forces. The secularization of Western Civilization, begun during the Enlightenment, continued at an accelerated pace during the nineteenth century.

The most important and influential event in the intellectual life of the nineteenth century was the appearance of Charles Darwin's theory of evolution. Darwin was the Newton, the great synthesizer, of the second scientific revolution. By the end of the century, the theory of evolution was widely accepted and became a basic assumption of modern science.

Darwin and Evolution

The origin of life by some process of evolution did not originate with Charles Darwin. The ancient Greek natural philosopher, Anaximander, theorized that life began in the warm water, or slime, on the earth's surface. At first, there were only sea creatures, but when they had evolved to the point where they could survive outside the water, they crawled up on land; thus, accounting for the land animals from which humans eventually evolved. The theory of evolution reappeared again and again during the centuries between Anaximander and Darwin. It is not difficult to understand the persistence of the theory of evolution over time. If one begins with matter as the ultimate reality, then life must have originated in that matter by some sort of random chance evolutionary process.

Until the publication of Darwin's *On the Origin of Species by Means of Natural Selection* in 1859, followed by *The Descent of Man, and Selection in Relation to Sex* in 1871, the theory of evolution was not widely regarded as having much merit. Among its advocates in the eighteenth century were the naturalist and pioneer botanist, Chevalier de Lamarck (1744–1829) and Charles Darwin's grandfather, Erasmus Darwin (1731–1802), a physician and poet.

Lamarck argued for an evolutionary process based on acquired characteristics in response to the environment that were passed on to the organism's offspring. Erasmus Darwin advocated an evolutionary process similar to Lamarck's but added the suggestion that the earth was millions of years old, a belief not widely held at the time. The question of the age of the earth was a major obstacle to the widespread acceptance of theories of evolution prior to Charles Darwin. Most people of all levels of education, historical scholars, as well as the literate public, believed that the earth was only thousands of years old.

One of the most widely read histories of the world, *Universal History, in Perspective*[1] by Emma Willard (1787–1870), a pioneer in progressive education, puts the year of creation at 4004 BC. The chronology employed by Ms. Willard is that of James Usher (or Ussher, 1581–1656), Anglican Archbishop of Armagh and Primate of All Ireland between 1625 and 1656. In 1650, Bishop Usher published his *Annals of the Old Testament, Deduced from the First Origins of the World*, the fruit of 20 years of scholarly labor.

Usher was no lightweight when it came to scholarly research. Stephen Jay Gould (1941–2002), noted paleontologist, evolutionary biologist, and historian of science, paid tribute to Usher in 1991: "Ussher represented the best of scholarship in his time" (Woods 2016). From his research, Usher concluded that: "In the beginning, God created heaven and earth, which beginning of time, according to this chronology, occurred at the beginning of the night which preceded the 23rd of October in the year of the Julian period" (Linder 2019). Usher gave 4004 BC as the date in "Christian" time.

Usher's chronology was supported by the theory known as catastrophism," which was itself supported by Usher's chronology. Catastrophism sought to explain the fossil remains by the occurrence of sudden catastrophic geological events such as the flood referred to in the biblical book of Genesis. Catastrophism was displaced by the geological theory known as "uniformitarianism," associated with the noted geologist, Charles Lyell (1797–1875).

---

1 Emma Willard's *Universal History* was first published in 1835. Classic reprint editions were still being published in 2019 by Forgotten Books (London, UK).

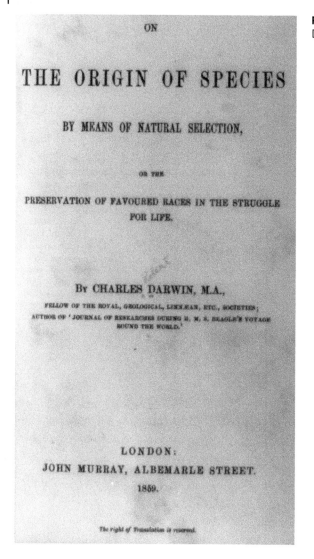

Figure 12.2 The title page from Darwin's *The Origin of Species*.

Lyell recognized that the accepted theories regarding the geological age of the earth were based on the creation account in Genesis. Between May, 1828 and February, 1829, Lyell studied geological formations in France, northern Italy, and on the island of Sicily. The first volume of his monumental study *Principles of Geology* appeared in 1830. The two additional volumes appeared in 1832 and 1833. In *Principles of Geology*, Lyell offered the theory of uniformitarianism as an alternative to catastrophism.

According to uniformitarianism, the geological laws as they operate today have always operated so without any interruption or catastrophe such as the Genesis flood. To determine the earth's age, one must begin with the present and calculate backwards to its origin. "The present is the key to the past" became the catchword. Thus Lyell, in a single blow, provided the one thing requisite to any credible theory of evolution, an earth old enough to include an evolutionary process. Instead of the earth being thousands, or even millions of years old, it could be "billions and billions" of years old – in fact as old as the theory (and Lyell's conjectures) required.

Darwin was able to take the first volume of *Principles of Geology* with him, when he embarked on a five-year voyage to the South Pacific aboard the *HMS Beagle* (1831–1836). He received the second and third volumes while on voyage. Lyell provided the timeframe. It was Thomas Robert Malthus' *"Essay on the Principle of Population"* (1798) that helped Darwin formulate a theory of organic evolution that involved a process of "natural selection" and "survival of the fittest." Darwin described his discovery in one of his notebooks:

> (Ridley n.d.)

> In October 1838, that is, fifteen months after I had begun my systematic enquiry, I happened to read for amusement 'Malthus on Population,' and being well prepared to appreciate the struggle for existence which everywhere goes on from long-continued observation of the habits of animals and plants, it at once struck me that under these circumstances favourable variations would tend to be preserved, and unfavourable ones to be destroyed. The result of this would be the formation of new species. (Darwin 2013a)

Simply put, if an organism is born with attributes that were better suited to the environment, it would survive and pass those attributes on to its progeny. Eventually, a new species would emerge. Those members of the species with attributes less suited to the environment would eventually become extinct.

Charles Darwin was not only a scientist; he was also a master communicator. Darwin did not present his theory encumbered by scientific terms and complicated mathematical formulas as if written for a select audience, such as a scientific society. *Origin of Species* is, as the late Roland N. Stromberg, a noted intellectual historian, put it, "a masterpiece of scientific argumentation... thoroughly comprehensible to almost any literate person, yet scientifically impressive" (Stromberg 1994, pp. 108–109). An individual with an inquisitive mind who read Darwin's book could hardly fail to be convinced that the theory of evolution was at least plausible.

In *Origin of Species*, Darwin limited himself to a discussion of plant and animal species. He did not apply his theory to humans, though it would be unlikely for the reader not to make the connection. It was in his second book, *The Descent of Man*, first published in 1871 and extensively revised in 1874, that Darwin addressed the subject of human evolution. He clearly stated his purpose for *The Descent of Man* in the introduction:

> The sole object of this work is to consider, firstly, whether man, like every other species, is descended from some pre-existing form; secondly, the manner of his development; and thirdly, the value of the differences between the so-called races of man. (Darwin 1871, p. 3)

The Descent of Man was given a lengthy review in *The Annual Register*, an annual review of British and world history begun in 1758. "The point," commented the reviewer, "as we need hardly say, which Mr. Darwin seeks to demonstrate is that man is descended from the great apes" (Respect of Literature 1871). The reviewer also noted the controversy that

Darwin stirred up with *Origin of Species*, and concluded: "Mr. Darwin's work, in short, is one of those rare achievements which effect a transformation throughout the whole range of intellectual effort" (Darwin 1871). Nothing more accurate could be said about the impact of Darwin's theory and the controversy that has surrounded it to the present.

Reaction to Darwin's Theory of Evolution

Darwin's *Origin of Species* sold out on its first day of publication, but the impressive sales figures did not necessarily mean that everyone who purchased a copy was in agreement with its author. Most scientists already accepted the theory of evolution. Nevertheless, Darwin's theory met with strong opposition within the scientific community and among noted intellectuals of the day. The resistance tended to focus on Darwin's assertion that "natural selection" was the mechanism of evolution. Twelve years after the publication of *Origin of Species*, a conference of French anthropologists concluded that there was "no proof or even presumption" of natural selection as the engine of evolution (Stromberg 1994, pp. 109–110).

Karl Ernst von Baer (1792–1876), a pioneer in physical anthropology and father of comparative embryology, refused to accept a theory that reduced human beings to the level of animals originating in matter. Adam Sedgwick (1785–1873), professor of geology at Cambridge University and a friend of Darwin's, wrote Darwin explaining his reaction to *Origin of Species*. In his letter dated November 24, 1859, Sedgwick said that he read the book with mixed feelings of "more pain than pleasure." He commented: "Parts of it I admired greatly; parts I laughed at till my sides were almost sore; other parts I read with absolute sorrow; because I think them utterly false & grievously mischievous" (Darwin Correspondence Project 2018). The Lamarckian theory of evolution continued to command a following until after 1900, in part because it allowed one to affirm evolution without accepting natural selection.

Darwin was handicapped by his lack of knowledge about the role of heredity. Gregor Johann Mendel (1822–1884), an Augustinian Friar and botanist, discovered the basic principles of heredity by conducting experiments on peas in his monastery garden between 1856 and 1863. He presented his findings in 1865 to a meeting of the Natural Science Society in Brno, in present day Czech Republic, and in an essay titled "*Experiments on Plant Hybrids*," in the society's journal. Mendel's discoveries, which earned him the epitaph," father of modern genetics," were ignored until after 1900.

Darwin believed that evolution occurs slowly at a constant rate over millions of years as species adapt to the changing environment until the whole species becomes a new species. "As natural selection acts solely by accumulating slight, successive, favourable variations," Darwin concluded, "it can produce no great or sudden modification; it can act only by very short and slow steps" (Darwin 2013b). The process, known as "phyletic gradualism" may be pictured as a straight, upward leaning line, or reduced to a simple formula of time plus chance equals change. The theory of evolution has itself evolved. Today evolution is understood to occur by a process referred to as "punctuated equilibrium," whereby "new species evolve over relatively short periods of time (a few hundred to a thousand years), followed by longer periods in which little genetic change occurs" (American Heritage 2019).

Christian Response to Darwin

Darwin did not directly attack religious faith or the Bible. He considered himself an agnostic on questions of ultimate reality. He appears to accept theism in the conclusion to *Origin of Species*, but soon gave up whatever religious faith he possessed and concluded that he could find no evidence of divine creation. His loss of belief in a providential God was due in part to Charles Lyell's *Principles of Geology*, his acceptance of natural selection, and the loss of his beloved daughter, Annie.

Since the appearance of *Origin of Species* in 1859, much attention has been given to the obvious conflict between Darwin's theory and a literal interpretation of the Bible. The length of the days of creation, Adam and Eve and the Fall, the Flood, and other such obvious conflicts between the biblical book of Genesis and Darwin's theory of evolution provided ample topics for public debate, pulpit sermons, and the tabloid press of the Victorian period, as they do today. In fact, many Christians, such as the old-fashioned Calvinist clergy, and scientists who identified themselves as Christians, found little difficulty in harmonizing evolution and the Bible. A noted example of the latter was Henry Drummond (1851–1897), biologist, author, and lecturer on natural science, of whom the famous evangelist, Dwight L. Moody (1837–1899) said: "He was the most Christlike man I ever met" (Dorsett 1997, p. 372).

Despite the efforts of Drummond and others to reconcile evolution and the Bible, there remained implications of Darwin's theory that appeared irreconcilable with Christianity, many of which were not different from those of Baer, Sedgwick, and other scientists who were alarmed by the implications of natural selection. Two objections, in particular, were obvious.

First, according to Darwin, humans were not a special creation, created by God in his image, but just a higher form of animal life, albeit thinking animals. Life may have begun as a chance event in some primeval slime, but by Darwin's day, evolution of life progressed to the stage of a reasoning biped (e.g. Darwin).

The need to explain the perceived differences between humans and non-humans, what is referred to as the "evolutionary predicament," became a major point of contention in the debate. How can one make a distinction between humans and non-humans, when the logic of evolutionary theory says that there is none? Still, historical experience insists that human beings are not the same as non-humans. Stated differently, are human beings animals like other animals, that is, merely evolved apes, or something more? If the old belief that humans constitute a distinct moral category is abandoned and a category of non-humans welcomed (for example, apes) to the human community because of shared characteristics, then the whole concept of human rights crumbles to dust.

The famed British philosopher Bertrand Russell could find no logical reason for distinguishing between humans and oysters, in which case, Russell preferred oysters. Darwin himself felt "it would be impossible to fix on any definite point when the term 'man' [i.e., 'human'] ought to be used...." The question itself, he felt, was "a matter of very little importance" (Fernandez-Armesto 2004, p. 127). For Christians and many scientists in the second half of the nineteenth century, the moral and ethical implications of the question alone were staggering.

In addition to reducing human beings to the status of thinking animals, a second major objection was the element of chance, or accident, and the purposeless nature of the evolutionary process, and therefore of history in general, which contradicted the providential nature of history as depicted in the Bible. The idea that the historical process lacked design or purpose was a challenge not just to biblical teaching, but to both the medieval synthesis (premodernity) and the Enlightenment tradition (modernity).

Social Darwinism

Some of those who embraced Darwin's theory of biological evolution applied it to other areas with tragic consequences. One such application was Social Darwinism, associated with Herbert Spencer (1820–1903). Spencer was a largely self-educated Victorian, whose interests ranged from philosophy through biology, anthropology, sociology, to classical liberal political theory. He wanted to create a grand theory of evolution that applied to the whole universe. It was Spencer, rather than Darwin, who coined the phrase "survival of the fittest" to describe the logic of evolution. Though he was more of a Lamarckian evolutionist than a Darwinist, Darwin considered Spencer a far greater intellect than himself.

Spencer believed that the only "facts" that could be accepted were those that could be verified empirically. He assigned to the "unknown" the perennial questions of ultimate reality. He taught that competition, or struggle for survival, unencumbered by ethical questions leads to progress. Spencer's knowledge of classical liberal economic theory influenced his conclusions. Like the Dismal Scientists before him, Spencer believed that attempts to relieve suffering in the present would only result in greater suffering in the future. It is in the best interest of future humanity to allow the weaker to perish.

Social Darwinism was a logical by-product of Darwin's theory of evolution. The only ethic that can be derived from evolution is the law of the jungle. Those who can, adapt and survive; those who cannot, perish. Nature does not distinguish between combatants. Hence, Social Darwinism became a convenient justification for every manner of injustice and inequality. The exploitation of the laboring classes by the barons of industry, racism, war, and imperialism were all justified by an appeal to the unforgiving laws of nature.

Herbert Spencer's writings, like those of Charles Darwin, were widely read. Both men were gifted communicators. Spencer was more forthright in acknowledging the harsh consequences of evolution once understood as more than just a biological theory. During the new age of imperialism, beginning with the last quarter of the nineteenth century, Europeans came into direct contact with various people groups living in societies without the benefits of modern technology. It was easy to justify exploiting them by suggesting that they were not as far "evolved" as Europeans and therefore not able to adapt to the changing environment.

Darwin and Spencer believed that the "primitive" people encountered by Europeans abroad were simply late starters on the road to where Europeans were in the late-nineteenth century. They were bound to suffer in competition with the more advanced European civilization. It was only logical, and right, said Darwin, that "an endless number of lower races will be eliminated by the higher civilized races throughout the world" (Firchow 2015, p. 152). By the end of the century, many scientists and other intellectuals were suggesting that knowledge of the laws of biological evolution could be beneficial, just as was knowledge of the natural laws of physics and economics. This led to the pseudoscience of eugenics.

Darwin's half-cousin, Francis Galton (1822–1911), coined the term "eugenics" in reference to the practice of controlled breeding with the goal of improving the human race. For eugenicists, nature (genes) was far more important than nurture (environment) in determining the future health of the human race. There were two sides to the practice of eugenics. Encouraging the proliferation of the desirable genetic stock was called "positive eugenics." Preventing the proliferation of undesirable genetic stock was called "negative eugenics."

The eugenics movement enjoyed widespread support among biologists and social scientists as well as prominent public figures and government leaders. It was regarded as a serious field of study after 1900, providing scientific support for laws restricting immigration, marriage, and forced sterilization of individuals deemed "undesirable" for a variety of reasons. The constitutionality of eugenics laws in the US was upheld by the Supreme Court in 1927.[2]

Positivism

Just as Immanuel Kant's philosophical idealism harmonized with Romanticism, Auguste Comte's positivism fit well with the renewed emphasis on empiricism and increasing secularism. Like the intellectuals of the Enlightenment, Comte (1798–1857) believed that there were natural laws governing society comparable to the laws governing the physical world. Those natural laws of society could be discovered by a careful scientific study of history and society.

Comte is best remembered for his "law of three stages," according to which, he tried to link intellectual evolution with social evolution. The three stages are the theological, metaphysical, and scientific. During the theological stage, reality is understood by appealing to supernatural forces, as for example, the "will of God." During the metaphysical stage, divinity is replaced by abstract ideas as, for example, when the philosophes spoke of "natural rights," the existence of which cannot be proven empirically. In the final scientific, or positivist, stage all theological explanations or appeals to abstract ideas give way to reliance on an empirical knowledge of the natural laws that govern both the physical world and human society.

Interestingly, though Comte did away with God entirely in his final stage of development, he found it necessary to retain religion for the purpose of providing moral guidance for the individual and unity within society. The object of worship was not a divinity, but rather humanity, "which must be loved, known, and served" (Bourdeau 2008). Comte found little support for his Religion of Humanity, but it does serve to illustrate the ongoing secularization of thought during the nineteenth century.

---

2 Enthusiasm for eugenics waned after World War II, when its role in the Holocaust was revealed, but never disappeared. Individual states began repealing their eugenics laws in the 1970s, but sterilization of certain inmates in prisons and hospitals continue in the twenty-first century (Stern 2016).

Realism and Naturalism

Just as poetry was the dominant cultural expression of Romanticism, the novel was the dominant cultural expression of Realism and Naturalism. The realists turned their attention away from the inner world of the mind, emotions, feelings, and mysticism to focus on the world as it really is, the objective world. In their novels, the realists depicted the everyday life of ordinary people engaged in mundane everyday activities. The naturalists went a step further. They tried to show a relationship between the environment and the character traits of those living in that environment.

Perhaps the best example of the realist novel is Gustave Flaubert's *Madame Bovary* (1856). Flaubert (1821–1880) presents the life of Emma Bovary, trapped in a dull life from which she cannot escape; she seeks fulfillment through adulterous affairs that lead to her financial ruin and suicide. Other noted realist writers include Honoré de Balzac (1799–1850), George Eliot (1819–1880), Leo Tolstoy (1828–1910), Charles Dickens, and Henry James (1843–1916).

The realist playwright, Henrik Ibsen (1828–1906) put the lifestyle of the middle class under the microscope, calling attention to the hypocrisy and pretentiousness of their bourgeois lifestyle that smothered any individual identity. In the concluding scene of his play, *Doll's House* (1879), Nora Helmer attempts to explain to her husband why she must leave him and their children in order to try to discover who she really is as an individual:

> Isn't there one thing that strikes you as strange in our sitting here like this? ... We have been married now eight years. Does it not occur to you that this is the first time we two, you and I, husband and wife, have had a serious conversation? .... In all these eight years – longer than that – from the very beginning of our acquaintance, we have never exchanged a word on any serious subject .... When I was at home with papa, he told me his opinion about everything, and so I had the same opinions; and if I differed from him I concealed the fact, because he would not have liked it. He called me his doll-child, and he played with me just as I used to play with my dolls. And when I came to live with you ... I was simply transferred from papa's hands into yours. You arranged everything according to your own taste, and so I got the same tastes as your [*sic.*] else I pretended to, I am really not quite sure which – I think sometimes the one and sometimes the other. When I look back on it, it seems to me as if I had been living here like a poor woman – just from hand to mouth. I have existed merely to perform tricks for you, Torvald. But you would have it so. You and papa have committed a great sin against me. It is your fault that I have made nothing of my life. (Shmoop Editorial Team 2008)

Naturalism was a more extreme version, or extension, of realism but with a difference. Like the realist writers, they portrayed common people in everyday life, but with a scientific objectivity. The writer is an observer who remains detached from his subject matter, as if recording observations of an experiment in a lab manual. Central to the naturalist novel is the belief that the character and destiny of the individual is determined by the environment.

There is no free will. Examples of naturalist writers include Emile Zola (1840–1902), Edith Wharton (1862–1937), Frank Norris (1870–1902), and Stephen Crane (1871–1900).

Realist painters sought to honestly portray the everyday life of people in all their beauty and ugliness. Whereas the romantic painters, for example, romanticized the peasants in their environment, realist painters like Gustave Courbet (1819–1877) portrayed the harshness of the peasants' life, void of any romantic idealism. Courbet described his own mission, as well as that of other realists' painters, when he wrote in his manifesto (1855), that his principle aim was "to translate the customs, the ideas, the appearances of my epoch" (Witt 2005).

Revolt Against Reason

The Enlightenment intellectuals believed in progress and were optimistic about the future. They believed that human beings were by nature good, though corrupted by a faulty environment. John Locke's environmentalism, as presented in his influential *Essay Concerning Human Understanding* (1689) provided a basis for their faith in progress and their optimism. The application of reason allowed the scientists to discover the natural laws of the universe. Knowledge of the natural laws enabled mankind to improve their material wellbeing. The Enlightenment thinkers went a step further. They assumed that there must be natural laws governing society comparable to the natural laws discovered by the scientists. Again, reason could be used to discover those natural laws of society, and with that knowledge, the flawed environment could be restored to its natural state, thus restoring human beings to their natural goodness. A better future, perhaps a utopia, was within reach.

In order to boldly use reason to alter society, that is, to bring it into line with natural law, it was necessary to change the way people think. That required shaking off the shackles of accepted authority, especially the Christian understanding of reality, or worldview. The Enlightenment promised a future of humanity guided by the light of reason. The individual, designed and created by the Architect, the god of Deism, was a thinking, reasoning creature, and thereby the master of his or her own fate and of history.

Prior to the Enlightenment, the role of reason was to understand revealed truth. Known truths set the limits within which reason might operate. Revelation provided an absolute reference point for reasoning. The Enlightenment secularized reason by adopting Deism. God, as creator, remained the ultimate reference point, but reason was free to discover the natural laws that governed God's creation.

During the last decades of the nineteenth century, and the early years of the twentieth century, the pendulum swung once again in the direction of an emphasis on emotions, intuition, and irrationalism. A new set of intellectuals questioned whether human beings were rational creatures living in an orderly and meaningful universe. They began to see human beings as irrational animals adrift in a random chance universe. The drift into irrationalism led ultimately to the death of reason after the Second World War, announcing the beginning of the era of postmodernity, or the Enlightenment tradition in disarray. No one individual represents the attack on reason more than the German philosopher Friedrich Nietzsche (1844–1900).

Friedrich Nietzsche

Nietzsche was well ahead of this time. He is often considered one of the first existentialist philosophers, though existentialism did not become popular until the last half of the twentieth century. Nietzsche saw clearly that autonomous reason would lead to the death of reason, that is, nihilism. That is what he meant, when he wrote, "God is dead." He was not saying, as some have thought, that God actually died. He could not, because there never was an actual transcendent God as understood in the Judeo-Christian religious tradition. God never existed, only the idea of God, created by human beings in order to give order and meaning to existence. But, the discoveries of modern science and philosophical reasoning had led to the conclusion that the "myth" of God was no longer tenable, therefore "God is dead." By rendering the myth of God untenable, humanity cut itself loose from its essential reference point, leaving humankind adrift in a universe without meaning.

Nietzsche explained the implications of the death of God in the parable of the madman in *The Gay Science* (1882):

> "Have you not heard of that madman who lit a lantern in the bright morning hours, ran to the market place, and cried incessantly: 'I seek God! I seek God!' – As many of those who did not believe in God were standing around just then, he provoked much laughter. Has he got lost? asked one. Did he lose his way like a child? asked another. Or is he hiding? Is he afraid of us? Has he gone on a voyage? emigrated? – Thus, they yelled and laughed.'"

> "The madman jumped into their midst and pierced them with his eyes. 'Whither is God?' he cried; 'I will tell you. *We have killed him* – you and I. All of us are his murderers. But how did we do this? How could we drink up the sea? Who gave us the sponge to wipe away the entire horizon? What were we doing when we unchained this earth from its sun? Whither is it moving now? Whither are we moving? Away from all suns? Are we not plunging continually? Backward, sideward, forward, in all directions? Is there still any up or down? Are we not straying, as through an infinite nothing? Do we not feel the breath of empty space? Has it not become colder? Is not night continually closing in on us? Do we not need to light lanterns in the morning? Do we hear nothing as yet of the noise of the gravediggers who are burying God? Do we smell nothing as yet of the divine decomposition? Gods, too, decompose. God is dead. God remains dead. And we have killed him.'"

> "'How shall we comfort ourselves, the murderers of all murderers? What was holiest and mightiest of all that the world has yet owned has bled to death under our knives: who will wipe this blood off us? What water is there for us to clean ourselves? What festivals of atonement, what sacred games shall we have to invent? Is not the greatness of this deed too great for us? Must we ourselves not become gods simply to appear worthy of it? There has never been a greater deed; and whoever is born after us – for the sake of this deed he will belong to a higher history than all history hitherto.'"

> "Here the madman fell silent and looked again at his listeners; and they, too, were silent and stared at him in astonishment. At last he threw his lantern on the ground, and it broke into pieces and went out. 'I have come too early,' he said

then; 'my time is not yet'. This tremendous event is still on its way, still wandering; it has not yet reached the ears of men". "Lightning and thunder require time; the light of the stars requires time; deeds, though done, still require time to be seen and heard. This deed is still more distant from them than most distant stars – *and yet they have done it themselves.*"

"It has been related further that on the same day the madman forced his way into several churches and there struck up his *requiem aeternam deo.* Led out and called to account, he is said always to have replied nothing but: 'What after all are these churches now if they are not the tombs and sepulchers of God (Kreis 2012)?'"

Nietzsche saw clearly the fallacy in the heart of the Enlightenment tradition. It is not possible to separate God the great architect from God the redeemer, or to put it another way, one cannot reject Christianity and retain Christian ethics.

In the absence of a creator God, there is no right or wrong, no truth, only the individual alone in a godless universe raising his or her fist defiantly in the face of the dark emptiness of space. Facing the reality that there is no God leads to nihilism, the belief that there are no valid religious or moral principles to live by and that ultimately existence is meaningless. But there is, Nietzsche claimed, a way to escape the nihilism.

Liberated from the Christian slave morality, either in its religious or secular forms, the superman (the *Übermensch*, or overman) faces the nihilism defiantly by the force of his will and creates for himself a new myth to replace that of the God myth. The individual's will to power, to dominate, is inherent in human nature. Nietzsche understood that a world in which there is no right and wrong is a brutal and frightening world.

There can be no doubt that Nietzsche was one of the foremost intellects of the nineteenth century. The son of a Lutheran minister who at first studied theology with the goal of becoming a minister, Nietzsche gave up all religious faith when he was 20. When he was only 24 years old, he was awarded an honorary doctorate by the University of Leipzig and offered a professorship of classical philology at the University of Basel in Switzerland, evidence of his genius.

During the period 1879 to 1889, Nietzsche wrote several of the most influential works of nineteenth-century philosophy, including *The Gay Science, Thus Spoke Zarathustra, Beyond Good and Evil,* and *The Antichrist.* He suffered a mental breakdown in January 1889, from which he never recovered, and died in August 1900, in Weimar, the birthplace of Goethe.

Bergson, Sorel, Freud, and Einstein

Henri Bergson (1859–1941) and Georges Sorel (1847–1922) concluded that humans are driven by dark instinctual drives. They are irrational, not rational. Bergson believed that intuition, not science, was the way to truth. Sorel recognized the importance of myth as a motivational force for political action. People needed something to die for as well as something to live for. That myth might be the future utopia envisioned by Karl Marx, the thousand-year Reich of Adolf Hitler's imagination, or Sorel's choice, the general strike. None, however, was more influential in advancing the drift into irrationalism than Sigmund Freud (1856–1939), the founder of psychoanalysis.

According to Freud, the individual's personality, or psyche, consists of an id, ego, and superego. The id exists in the unconscious part of the mind. It is the primitive, instinctual, and impulsive part of the psyche, always demanding instant gratification. The superego operates as a moral conscience. It is a reservoir of moral standards and values learned from one's parents and society. The ego operates as a mediator between the id and superego. It acts as a link between the unconscious mind and reality.

A newborn infant is all id. It demands to be fed and cries until its demands are met. As the infant develops, it soon learns that its demands are not always met as soon as it wishes. As the child grows into an adult, it learns that certain behaviors are unacceptable. The id's amoral demands must at times be suppressed. The result is that every individual suffers anxiety, since every individual must learn to deny his or her true self in order to conform to society's standards or suffer the consequences. As a result, according to Freud, all human beings, whether as individuals or as a collective (society), are neurotic.

Though Freud clung to the Enlightenment's belief that reason and scientific inquiry made civilization possible, his conclusion that humans are motivated by primitive, irrational drives, hidden deep in the subconscious, tended to undermine the Enlightenment's image of humanity. Also, Freud rejected both the Christian belief that evil was essentially a moral problem and the Enlightenment's assumption that it was an environmental problem. Rather, Freud believed that evil was rooted in human nature. For him, there was no utopia in the future. Faith in progress and optimism about the future no longer had a basis. Human beings as the thinking (reasoning) higher animals of Darwin's vision, like human beings created in the image of God, were now obsolete.

The meditations and musings of the philosophers and other intellectuals of the nineteenth century were a threat to the Enlightenment tradition, but what threw it into disarray was the revolution in physics from the 1890's to the 1920's. The Enlightenment tradition rested on the seemingly firm foundation of Newton's synthesis, or as it is commonly referred to as classical physics. Classical physics was challenged, and some would say effectively over-thrown, by the discoveries of Max Planck (1858–1947), Niels Bohr (1885–1962), Werner Heisenberg (1901–1976), and especially Albert Einstein (1885–1962).

Newton's universe was a three-dimensional, objective reality, whose properties could be measured from an absolute reference point. It was a universe of predictable cause and effect natural laws. The individual, an autonomous being, was capable of using reason to understand the universe and his or her role in it. It was a universe of meaning. But with the emergence of the new atomic physics, objective reality vanished. Space and time did not exist independent of the observer. Uncertainty took the place of certainty. Optimism was replaced by pessimism and despair, for the individual was only a random chance "happening" thrown up by an impersonal universe, and his or her ultimate reality was only the molecules of which he or she was composed.

Anxiety characterized the mood of society at the end of the nineteenth century. All scientific and religious certainty was disappearing. Fear of an uncertain future replaced the optimism of mid-century realism. If the individual was governed by irrational forces beneath the conscious mind, then society, a collective of individuals, was also governed by irrational forces. Of the artists who gave visual representation to the new age of anxiety, none did better than Edvard Munch (1863–1944) in his painting *The Scream of Nature* (1893).

The transition to postmodernity (Enlightenment tradition in disarray) that was underway at the end of the nineteenth century would intensify during the period between the two world wars. The trenches of the First World War, the Great Depression, the horrors of the Second World War, including the Holocaust, carpet bombing of cities, and the atomic bombing of Hiroshima and Nagasaki, would make it increasingly more difficult for people at the end of the twentieth century to have faith in progress or be optimistic about the future. Despair seems more appropriate for human beings who believe themselves to be amoral descendants of primates rather than creatures created in the image of a loving God.

References

Abbs, P. (2008). The Full Revelation of the Self: Jean-Jacques Rousseau and the Birth of Deep Autobiography. Philosophy Now: A Magazine of Ideas. https://philosophynow.org/issues/68/The_Full_Revelation_of_the_Self_Jean-Jacques_Rousseau_and_the_Birth_of_Deep_Autobiography (accessed 21 October 2019).

Bourdeau, M. (2008). Auguste Comte. Stanford Encyclopedia of Philosophy. https://plato.stanford.edu/entries/comte/#RelHum (accessed 21 October 2019).

Darwin, C. (1871). *The Descent of Man, and Selection in Relation to Sex*, 1e, vol. 1. 2 vols. New York: D. Appleton and Company.

Darwin, C. (2013a). The Autobiography of Charles Darwin. Project Gutenberg. https://www.gutenberg.org/files/2010/2010-h/2010-h.htm#link2H_4_0002 (accessed 6 November 2019).

Darwin, C. (2013b). On the Origin of Species By Means of Natural Selection. 1st Ed. http://www.gutenberg.org/files/1228/1228-h/1228-h.htm (accessed 21 October 2019).

Dorsett, L.W. (1997). *A Passion for Souls: The Life of D. L. Moody*, 372. Chicago, IL: Moody Press.

Fernandez-Armesto, F. (2004). *Humankind: A Brief History*. Oxford, UK: Oxford University Press.

Firchow, P.E. (2015). *Envisioning Africa: Racism and Imperialism in Conrad's Heart of Darkness*. Lexington, KY: University Press of Kentucky.

Goethe (2004). Poetry in Translation. https://www.poetryintranslation.com/PITBR/German/Goethepoems.php#anchor_Toc74652048 (accessed 21 October 2019).

Kreis, S. (2012). Nietzsche, Freud and the Thrust Toward Modernism. Historyguide.org. http://www.historyguide.org/europe/madman.html (accessed February 15, 2019).

Linder, D.O. (2019). Bishop James Ussher Sets the Date for Creation. Famous Trials. http://www.famous-trials.com/scopesmonkey/2102-ussher (accessed 21 October 2019).

Shmoop Editorial Team (2008). A Doll's House Full Text: Act Three Page 15. https://www.shmoop.com/dolls-house/act-three-full-text-15.html (accessed 21 October 2019).

Stern, A.M. (2016). That Time The United States Sterilized 60,000 Of Its Citizens. Huffpost. https://www.huffingtonpost.com/entry/sterilization-united-states_us_568f35f2e4b0c8beacf68713 (accessed 21 October 2019).

Stromberg, R.N. (1994). *European Intellectual History since 1789*. Englewood Cliffs, NJ: Prentice Hall.

The American Heritage® Science Dictionary (2019). Houghton Mifflin Company. http://www.dictionary.com/browse/punctuated-equilibrium (accessed 21 October 2019).

University of Cambridge (2018). Darwin Correspondence Project. Letter No. 2548. http://www.darwinproject.ac.uk/DCP-LETT-2548 (accessed 21 OCtober 2019).

Witt, M.A.F. (2005). *The Humanities: Cultural Roots and Continuities*. Boston: Houghton Mifflin.

Woods, M. (2016). Why Did Archbishop Ussher Believe the Earth Was Created in 4004 bc? Christian News on Christian Today. Christianity Today. https://www.christiantoday.com/article/why-did-archbishop-ussher-believe-the-earth-was-created-in-4004-bc/82341.htm (accessed 6 November 2019).

Wordsworth, W. (2018). The Tables Turned by William Wordsworth. Poetry Foundation. https://www.poetryfoundation.org/poems/45557/the-tables-turned (accessed 21 October 2019).

13

Nineteenth-Century Imperialism

Chronology

1803–1867	United States Expands Across Continent to Pacific Ocean
1839–1842	Opium War in China
1846–1848	Mexican-American War
1853	US Commodore Matthew Perry Forces Japan Open
1856–1860	Arrow War in China
1857–1858	Revolt in India Against British East India Company's Rule
1858	Treaty of Tientsin
1868	Meiji Restoration in Japan
1876	Leopold II Begins Exploitation of Congo in Central Africa
1884–1885	Berlin Congress Sets "Rule of the Game" for Africa
1887	Annam, Tonkin, Cochinchina, and Cambodia become French Indochina. Laos Added in 1893
1894–1895	Sino-Japanese War
1896	Ethiopians Defeat Italian Army's Invasion in Battle of Adwa
1898	Spanish-American War
1898	Battle of Omdurman in the Sudan
1998	United States Annexes Hawaii
1899–1901	Boxer Rebellion in China
1899–1902	Boar War in South Africa
1902	Anglo-Japanese Alliance
1904	Roosevelt Corollary
1904–1905	Russo-Japanese War
1911–1912	Chinese Revolution and End of Qing Dynasty

If we think of imperialism as the domination of one group of people by another group of people, then imperialism is as old as the history of humanity. The first civilizations of the Fertile Crescent and Asia were all imperialistic. The desire to engage in warfare and dominate other humans seems to be, unfortunately, a part of human nature. Archeologists have discovered human skeletons from the Neolithic period (c. 8000–c. 4000 BC) with arrowheads embedded in them. Sargon (r. 2334–2279 BC), leader of the Akkadians in

Western Civilization: A Brief History, First Edition. Paul R. Waibel.
© 2020 John Wiley & Sons, Inc. Published 2020 by John Wiley & Sons, Inc.

Mesopotamia, is credited with founding the first multi-national empire. The Persian Empire, founded by Cyrus the Great (r. 559–530 BC), is considered the first "modern" empire, in that it was administered by a royal bureaucracy.

Western Civilization that developed in Europe following the collapse of the Roman Empire in the West was no exception. Internecine warfare among the various Germanic tribes continued until the end of the eleventh century, when the feudal monarchies of Europe embarked upon their first expansion beyond the borders of Europe proper. Between 1095 and 1291, European crusader armies conquered portions of the Middle East along the Mediterranean coast, where they established feudal kingdoms modeled after those in Europe.

The various civilizations of the world were never as isolated from one another as is commonly believed. As early as the Neolithic period, trade existed between the different regions that together comprise the gigantic landmass of Eurasia and Africa, sometimes referred to as the "world island." During the ancient and medieval periods, luxury goods, foodstuff, and raw materials moved across Eurasia along trade routes that connected the Mediterranean area and Europe in the West with India and China in the East.

Acre, the last outpost of the Crusader States, fell in 1291. The breakup of the Mongol Empire in 1260, and expansion of the Ottoman Empire during the fourteenth and fifteenth centuries, cut off the traditional trade routes between Europe and Asia. European demand for Asian goods, however, did not slacken. European merchants sought new oversea routes to Asia. The new nation states along the Atlantic coast possessed the necessary resources to launch such ventures and the new technology to guarantee their success.

The primary motivation behind the so-called Age of Exploration and Discovery between c. 1450 and c. 1650 was economic. Portugal and Spain led the way in the sixteenth century, followed by England, France, and the Netherlands during the seventeenth century. They sought luxury goods like silk and spices from Asia, ivory and slaves from Africa, and land that produced cash crops like tobacco and cotton in the Americas. Colonies were established in the Americas, but mostly trading posts along the coasts of Africa and Asia and on the various islands, especially in the East Indies.

The interest in overseas empires waned during the late-eighteenth century and first half of the nineteenth century, due in part to the Napoleonic Wars, the spread of industrialization, and the rise of nationalism. The classical liberal economic theory that fueled the Industrial Revolution emphasized free trade, which did not require control of the areas with which one traded. The struggle for unified nation states based on national identity, tied as it was to liberalism during the first half of the nineteenth century, deflected attention away from overseas territorial acquisitions. The lack of interest, as late as 1871, was evident in Otto von Bismarck's opposition to Germany's pursuit of overseas colonies, at least until 1884. The general feeling among European leaders was that, apart from a few exceptions, colonies cost more than they were worth. Why be burdened by tracts of overseas territory that were expensive to administer and provided little in return?

Everything changed during the 1870s and 1880s. The earlier contacts were, except for the Americas and Africa, with civilizations older and more advanced than Europe. If one considers the world as a whole during the early modern period, it was Asia, not Europe, that was the most advanced part of the world and the residence of the world's most powerful rulers. The Chinese thought of their empire as the Middle Kingdom, occupying the center of the world and ruled by an emperor who enjoyed the mandate of heaven and ruled on behalf of the gods. All those who lived outside China were regarded as barbarians who owed submission and tribute to China's emperor, the "Son of Heaven." When European merchants first appeared, they were treated as barbarians who had nothing to offer but gold and silver in exchange for the tea, porcelain, and silk and other textiles they desired.

The world during the last quarter of the nineteenth century was a very different reality. The West had experienced both the Scientific and Industrial Revolutions. The West had unlocked the secrets of nature and applied that knowledge to suddenly surge ahead of the rest of the world which continued to cling to a prescientific worldview. The most influential people in the West were no longer the philosopher-theologians of the medieval synthesis, but the scientists, entrepreneurs, and statesmen adept in the art of *Realpolitik*. When European and American ships appeared in the harbors of the non-Western empires in the mid-nineteenth century and later, they were no longer viewed as barbarians. It was the non-Westerners who were awestruck by the technological superiority of those who came to impose a global economy dominated by the industrialized West, and with it, Western political domination of the non-Western world.

New Imperialism

Historians variously date the beginning of the period of the new imperialism anywhere between 1870 and 1880. One could, if one so chose, push the date back to 1853, when the United States forced Japan to open its ports to trade with the West. We need not be too pedantic about dates for the beginning or ending of the new imperialism. A cursory look at a map of Africa in 1870 with another in 1910, or similar maps of Asia during the same time period, provides a graphic image of how the new imperialism differed from that of the fifteenth, sixteenth, and seventeenth centuries.

In 1870, the Western presence in Africa was limited to trading posts along the coasts, and the British and Dutch settlements at the southern tip of the continent. The interior remained a "dark continent," unknown to Westerners. A very different reality appears on a map of 1910. All of Sub-Saharan Africa is divided into colonies of the various European powers. The rest is either colonized or under indirect rule. Only two nations in Africa in 1910 remained independent: Liberia on the western coast, established by the United States as a homeland for liberated slaves who wished to return to Africa, and Ethiopia (Abyssinia), one of the oldest countries in world history, located on the Horn of Africa. A similar reality existed in Asia by 1910, where only Siam (Thailand) and Japan remained independent. China, nominally independent, was divided into spheres of influence by the Western powers, including the United States, and Japan, now Westernized and imperialistic. It is no exaggeration to say that on the eve of the First World War, almost every landmass and every island in the world was under direct or indirect Western control.

Motives

Economic reasons were the most important and longest lasting motivation for the new imperialism. The dynamic industrialization of Europe and the United States during the nineteenth century led logically to the creation of an integrated global economy. The factories had an

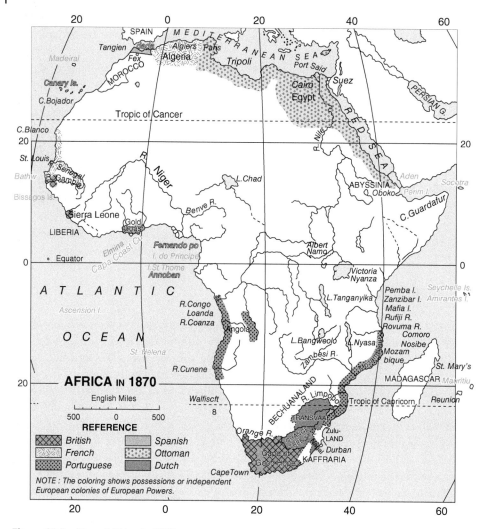

Figure 13.1 Map of Africa in 1870.

insatiable appetite for natural resources and products not available at home. Industrial development led to population growth, which, in turn, increased demand for manufactured products and imports desired by an increasingly more affluent population, such as coffee, tea, cotton, and copra.

Industrialization also created a need for foreign markets for industrial products that exceeded the demand at home. Also, industrial production created investment capital in search of opportunities abroad. European and American investors reaped immense profits not only by extracting the desired natural resources, but also by developing the infrastructure of railroads, harbors, mines, and plantations that the economic exploitation of an area required. Labor was also available and cheap. In some cases, when deemed necessary, forced labor accompanied by extreme brutality was employed.

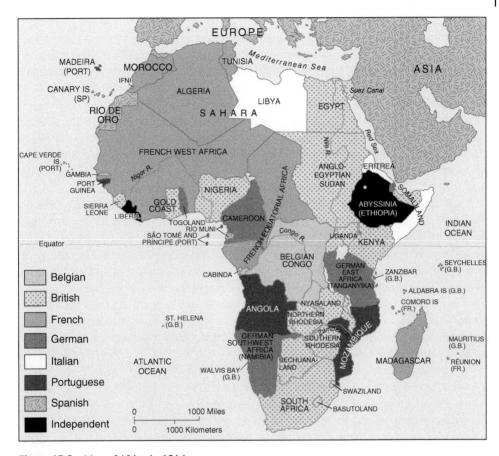

Figure 13.2 Map of Africa in 1914.

Investors were motivated by the lure of easy profits, not by any desire to improve the lives of the native populations. The introduction of Western capitalism and Western legal concepts effectively destroyed the centuries-old lifestyles of the native people of Africa and North America, making them victims of a clash between two totally incompatible economic, legal, political, and social systems. They were plunged into what can only be described as a Social Darwinist struggle for survival, which they could only lose.

Not surprisingly, exploitation resulted in resistance. Investors in turn demanded protection. Their governments met the need in a variety of ways. The removal, or near extinction, of the native population and expropriation of their property (e.g., North America), indirect rule and/or treaties of extraterritoriality (e.g., India and China), or direct acquisition and colonization (e.g., Africa and Asia) were employed. Colonies required navies to protect supply lines and fueling stations (i.e., ports) for naval and merchant ships. By the end of the nineteenth century, colonies and navies were necessary signs of great power status among the Western nations. Since it could be argued that overseas colonies were a vital part of the national economy, their possession and protection were considered a matter of national security, as well as national prestige.

It would be a gross oversimplification, even incorrect, to imply that greed and glory were the only motives behind the new imperialism. There was still unexplored areas and unknown people groups to be discovered. Scientific expeditions were undertaken to further peoples's knowledge of the "unknown" world. Such knowledge not only served to satisfy the scholar's curiosity, but at the same time, opened new areas to economic exploitation. The wealthier members of European and American society were able to satisfy their desire for adventure or the thrill of a big game hunt. Some simply desired to visit the strange places with strange sounding names that they read about in popular periodicals or heard about from those who had been there. Whatever the motive, it was always assumed that wherever they chose to go in the world, for whatever purpose, they were entitled to enjoy the security that any individual from the civilized world enjoyed at home.

If any Westerners went to the colonies with what they considered purely altruistic motives, it was the Christian missionaries. Since the origin of the Christian religion during the first century, Christians have journeyed throughout the world seeking converts to the faith. They often built orphanages, hospitals, schools for both boys and girls, and often tried to defend the native people from their colonial exploiters. Governments of the colonial empires often encouraged missionary activity. The charge that missionaries were in danger from uncivilized natives provided a convenient excuse for intervention and occupation of desirable territory. The missionaries were not always unwilling participants in the deception. Many Protestant Christians of the period believed that the Westernization of the world meant the Christianization of the world.

The humanitarian impulse to take the benefits of modern civilization, such as modern medicine, agricultural technology, and education to their colonies, was often used by the imperialists as an excuse for the domination and exploitation of the non-Western world. Westerners during the new era of imperialism viewed the occupants of the underdeveloped areas of the world through lenses colored by theories of evolution and Social Darwinism. Like the planter aristocracy of the American South, Europeans saw the native people of Africa and much of Asia as child-like creatures in need of "uplifting" from the darkness in which they lived.

The new imperialism was romanticized by such ardent imperialists as the English writer Rudyard Kipling (1865–1936), many of whose works are set in India and relate the interactions between the British colonials and subject Indians. The best known of Kipling's pro-imperialist poems is *The White Man's Burden* (1899), composed to commemorate the United States's victory in the Spanish-American War (1898) and America's annexation of the Philippine Islands. In it, Kipling urged the United States to join Britain in the pursuit of empire and the spread of Western civilization:

> Take up the White Man's burden–
> Send forth the best ye breed–
> Go bind your sons to exile
> To serve your captives' need;
> To wait in heavy harness,
> On fluttered folk and wild–
> Your new-caught, sullen peoples,
> Half-devil and half-child.

* * *

Take up the White Man's burden–
And reap his old reward:
The blame of those ye better,
The hate of those ye guard–
The cry of hosts ye humour
(Ah, slowly!) toward the light:–
"Why brought he us from bondage,
Our loved Egyptian night?"
(Kipling 1899, p. 290)

Not everyone in Europe or America shared Kipling's skewed view of imperialism. There were many responses to his poem, among them *The Brown Man's Burden* by Henry Du Pré Labouchere (1831–1912):

Pile on the brown man's burden
To gratify your greed;
Go, clear away the "niggers"
Who progress would impede;
Be very stern, for truly
'Tis useless to be mild
With new-caught, sullen peoples,
Half devil and half child.
...* ...* ...*
Pile on the brown man's burden,
And if his cry be sore,
That surely need not irk you–
Ye've driven slaves before.
Seize on his ports and pastures,
The fields his people tread;
Go make from them your living,
And mark them with his dead.
(Boulos 2010)

Westerners assumed that they, like all human beings, were the product of the natural laws of evolution, only they believed that they were further evolved than those who occupied the non-Western world. When contrasting life in the developed nations of Europe and America with life in the underdeveloped areas, or even with life in the ancient empires of Asia, it was easy to argue that Westernization offered more than a few benefits.

By almost any standard of measurement, Westerners at the end of the nineteenth century enjoyed a higher standard of living than people anywhere else in the world. Life expectancy was higher, infant mortality rates were lower, and whereas literacy rates in northwestern Europe were nearly 100%, they were barely above zero in the non-Western world. Non-Westerners, even those in the ancient civilized areas of Asia, still lived in fear of unseen forces. They still worshiped nature and demonic forces, whereas Westerners had unlocked the mysteries of the universe machine. Europeans no longer lived in fear of unseen forces. Scientific knowledge had given them mastery over nature, showering upon them a cornucopia of material blessings.

Human rights, both corporate and individual, were regarded in the West as the mark of a civilized people. Women possessed the same human rights as men, even though they did not yet possess the right to vote and did not enjoy equality in employment and education. And where human rights clashed with cultural or religious practice, human rights were deemed superior. Women were not subjected to such barbarous practices as genital mutilation or *suttee*, the burning of a Hindu widow on her husband's funeral pyre. Nor were they condemned to a lifetime of illiteracy and unquestioned submission to the arbitrary will of father or husband. This message of universal and inalienable human rights, the true mark of civilization, went wherever the might of Western imperialism was felt. Unfortunately, the twisted logic of Social Darwinism did not require the imperialists to treat their colonial subjects as equals.

Colonial Empires

The leading imperialist nations at the end of the nineteenth century were Great Britain, France, Germany, the United States, Italy, Belgium, and Russia. Russia created a continental empire by expanding across the Eurasian continent to the Pacific Ocean, annexing, rather than colonizing, vast areas of eastern and central Asia. In a similar manner, the US expanded across the North American continent to the Pacific Ocean, before acquiring overseas colonies, called "territories." Both Italy and Belgium were minor players, whose imperialistic activity was restricted to Africa. Germany, a latecomer to empire building, acquired colonies in Africa and an assortment of islands in the western Pacific Ocean. The French competed with Great Britain for possessions in both Africa and Southeast Asia. The most successful of the imperialists was Great Britain. With command of the seas throughout the nineteenth century until after the First World War, the British built an empire of more than 12 million square miles ($31\,079\,857.324\,km^2$) on which the sun never set.

Scramble for Africa

The new imperialism was triggered by events in the interior of Africa in the late 1870s. Prior to that time, Sub-Saharan Africa was of little interest to Europeans, except as a supplier of slaves. Slavery was an established institution in Africa. European and American slave traders were able to restrict their activity to the coastal areas, where Africans captured by other Africans[1] in the interior were brought and secured until sold to the slave traders. Thus, it was not necessary for the European traders to venture into the interior to capture the slaves. The tropical climate and diseases were deadly for Europeans who were confined to the coastal areas where mortality rates reached between 25 and 50%.

---

1 African chiefs who supplied the slaves received as much as £20–£36 for a single slave, depending on sex, age, and other factors.

The transatlantic slave trade provided huge profits for all of its participants for more than four centuries, despite the fact that as many as half or more of the individuals captured in the interior died during the journey to the coast, and another 10–55% died during the average sixty-day "middle passage" to the markets in the Americas. The Spanish crown awarded, for a suitable fee, a license known as the *asiento*, which granted a monopoly on supplying slaves to the Spanish colonies in the Americas. The Treaty of Utrecht (1713), that ended the War of Spanish Succession, awarded the *asiento* to Great Britain, which held it until 1750, when Britain and Spain agreed to end it in the Treaty of Madrid.

Great Britain abolished slavery in all British territories in 1833. The British navy enforced the ban on the international slave trade by authorizing its warships to seize ships of any nation carrying slaves. With the ending of the legal slave trade, the legitimate trade with Africa dwindled to the point where many of the coastal areas held by European nations were abandoned. Interest in gaining colonies waned, that is, until after 1870, when the advance of industrialism in Europe created renewed interest.

The individual whose actions triggered the Scramble for Africa and launched the new age of imperialism was King Leopold II of Belgium. In 1876, Leopold hosted a Geographical Conference on Central Africa which resulted in the founding of the International Association for the Exploration and Civilization of Central Africa. Leopold advertised the association as an instrument for promoting the end of slavery and the introduction of civilization to Central Africa: "To open to civilization the only part of our globe which it has not yet penetrated, to pierce the darkness which hangs over entire peoples, is, I dare say, a crusade worthy of this century of progress" (Hochschild 1998, p. 49). Many prominent people gave financial and moral support to Leopold's altruistic sounding venture. The reality was very different.

Leopold served as chairman of the International Association that never met after 1876. It served as a front for Leopold's acquisition of the Congo as his personal property. He employed the popular journalist and explorer, Henry Morton Stanley (1841–1904), to secure treaties with tribal chiefs, by which they signed over to Leopold's International Association more than 900 000 square miles (2 330 989.3 km^2) of the Congo.

The merciless brutality employed by Leopold to extract the rich natural resources – gold, ivory, and rubber – of the Congo stands as one of the most shocking examples of imperialism in modern history. The ruthless use of forced labor resulted in the deaths of an estimated one-half of the native population during the 25 years that the Congo remained the personal property of Leopold, who gave it the name, "Congo Free State."

To extract the Congo's natural resources, the territory was divided into districts, and quotas were imposed on what each district and each worker was required to produce. To protect his interests and to pacify the Congo, Leopold established the *Force Publique* ("Public Force"), a military and police force with officers recruited from Europe, the British Empire, and the United States. White mercenaries were employed, and Africans were recruited or drafted into its ranks.

Individual laborers who failed to meet their quotas suffered the amputation of a hand or a foot. If their continued labor was needed, their wives and children endured the amputations. Labor gang bosses delivered baskets of severed limbs, mostly hands, to their superiors as evidence that they were doing their jobs. To ensure that members of the *Force Publique* were not wasting expensive bullets hunting, they were required to turn in a right hand for every bullet fired.

The atrocities committed in the Congo under Leopold II's ownership became known in Europe from graphic accounts and photographs provided, despite Leopold's efforts to prevent such, by missionaries and others who were horrified by what they witnessed. In 1908, ownership of the Congo was transferred to the Kingdom of Belgium. Its name was changed to the Belgian Congo, and cosmetic changes made to improve the image of what was henceforth a Belgian colony until granted independence in 1960.

The riches reaped by Leopold II from the Congo awakened interest in Africa by other European powers. In order to prevent competing claims from leading to war between them, Otto von Bismarck called for a conference of the European nations with an interest in Africa to meet in Berlin and agree to an orderly plan for the colonization of the continent. The Berlin Conference met between November 15, 1884 and February 26, 1885. Twelve European nations, plus Turkey and the United States attended the conference. None of the African people were either consulted or represented.

The Berlin Conference established what were referred to as the "rules of the game" for the further exploitation of the African continent. One of the primary reasons for the conference was to assure all parties enjoyed free access to the Congo Free State by recognizing Leopold's private ownership of the territory. But there was more. The so-called Principle of Effectivity was agreed to. In order to claim an area as a colony, the interested power had to make treaties with the local leaders, establish a police force, administer the area, and, perhaps most important, provide for the economic development of the area.

Within two decades of the Berlin Conference, all of Africa was partitioned among the European powers, except Liberia and Ethiopia. An attempt by the Italians to conquer Ethiopia in 1896 was defeated by a French-trained and armed Ethiopian army in the Battle of Adwa. The British fought a three-year war (1899–1902) in South Africa with the Orange Free State and the Republic of the Transvaal (South African Republic or ZAR), two areas occupied by descendants of Dutch and Huguenot settlers of the seventeenth century referred to as Afrikaners or Boers.

The British sent most of the captured Boer soldiers abroad, while internment camps, later commonly referred to as concentration camps, were established to house mostly women and children. An estimated 26 000 Afrikaner women and children perished in the camps before peace was restored in 1902. Camps were also established for Black Africans, of which more than 14 000 perished, like the Afrikaners, from malnutrition and the unsanitary conditions in the camps. In 1910, the Cape of Good Hope, Natal, and the two former Boer republics were united to form the Union of South Africa.

Germany was a latecomer to the contest for colonies. Bismarck at first opposed ventures outside Europe, but in 1884, yielded to popular clamor. The first German colony was Angra Pequena, later named German South-West Africa. Other possessions followed in Africa and the Pacific. Resistance to German rule was dealt with swiftly and decisively. When the Herero revolted in 1904, the German forces suppressed the revolt and, while doing so, reduced the Herero population from an estimated 80 000 to an estimated 15 000. Similarly, in German South-East Africa, the Maji uprising of 1905–1907 was put down at the cost of between 80 and 100 thousand African lives.

The carving up of Africa occurred rapidly and with little armed conflict. When the European powers found it necessary to employ military force, it was always small armies of one or two thousand, mostly African soldiers, trained and commanded by European officers. Europeans found it easy to employ one tribe against another in a game of divide and conquer. When the imperialists encountered resistance, the African natives were no match for Western military technology. The Battle of Omdurman (1898) in the Sudan serves as an excellent example.

In January 1885, Khartoum, the capital of the Sudan in southern Egypt, fell to a radical Islamic army led by Al-Mahdī (1844–1885), a self-proclaimed prophet. The garrison at Khartoum was commanded by the popular British General Charles George ("Chinese") Gordon (1833–1885). After the fall of Khartoum, the entire garrison and Gordon were massacred. A combined British and Egyptian force of 8000 British regulars and 13000 British-trained and commanded Egyptian soldiers invaded the Sudan in 1898. The decisive battle was fought outside Omdurman, the Mahdist capital. Beginning on the morning of September 2, the Mahdist army of 50000 charged the British forces who were armed with Maxim machine guns that fired 600 rounds per minute. When the battle was over, the British suffered 48 dead and 380 wounded, while the Mahdist suffered 10000 dead and 14000 wounded.

The Battle of Omdurman was between two organized armies. Battles that were fought in Sub-Sahara Africa were fought against undisciplined natives armed with spears. To the traumatized natives, Europeans were an unbeatable force against which resistance was hopeless. The technological advantage enjoyed by the Europeans in Asia was not as great, but no less effective.

India

India in 1900 was the jewel of the British Empire. Never more than about four thousand British, assisted by several hundred thousand British-trained Indian civil servants, governed an area that included three-hundred million people, who together spoke around three hundred languages, shared three major religions, and represented a variety of "races" and cultures. How was it possible for this home of one of the world's most ancient civilizations to become a colony of a small island nation off the coast of Europe?

The once mighty Mughal Empire, that was founded in 1529, was in an advanced state of decline at the beginning of the nineteenth century. Though Muslim and Turkic-Mongol in origin, the Mughal rulers effectively integrated both Muslim and Hindu followers into an economically prosperous state. At its peak, the Mughals ruled most of the Indian subcontinent and portions of Afghanistan. As it declined during the eighteenth century, competing princes replaced the once efficient central government. It was easy for the British to play the princes off against one another, thus replacing the Mughal rulers.

In addition to the British, the Portuguese, Dutch, French, and Danes established trading posts along the Indian coast in past centuries. By the end of the eighteenth century, the Dutch and French holdings were in British hands. The Danes sold their holdings to Britain in 1845. Only the Portuguese continued to hold territory in India through the period of British rule that ended in 1947, and remained until compelled to leave by Indian military action in 1961.

British India was originally administered by the East India Company, a joint-stock trading company. The East India Company developed its own civil service and military forces consisting largely of Indian recruits, trained and commanded by the British. A series of parliamentary acts beginning in 1773, placed the East India Company's administration under close royal supervision.

An assortment of British policies, including the building of railroads and telegraph lines, opening of Western-style schools, aggressive Christian missionary practices, legalization of remarriage for widows, and prohibition of infanticide and *suttee*, led to what is referred to as the Indian Mutiny of 1857. The immediate cause of the mutiny by Indian soldiers serving in the British army, called Sepoys, was the introduction in February 1857, of gunpowder cartridges for the Enfield rifle, rumored to be greased with cow and pig fat. Since it was necessary for the soldiers to bite off the tip of the cartridge with their teeth, both Hindu and Muslim soldiers violated their religious beliefs by doing so.

The rebellion began in May 1857 and lasted until June 1858. Atrocities were committed by both sides during the revolt. Once peace was restored, the East India Company's rule ended, the Mughal Empire was officially dissolved, India became a colony of the British Empire, and Queen Victoria was given the title Empress of India. As an indication of India's importance, governance of the British Raj, as India was referred to between 1858 and 1947, was assigned to the Secretary of State for India, who was a member of the cabinet. The chief British government official in India was the governor-general, or viceroy.

During the nineteenth century, India became a major source for jute, oil seeds, wheat, and cotton. The surplus capital produced by the export of India's natural resources could have financed the industrialization of India. That, however, was not in the best interest of Britain. Under the neo-mercantilist economic policies, India was to remain a source of raw materials and a market for finished goods produced in Britain.

Cotton provides an example. Raw cotton was exported to Britain, where it was transformed into cotton cloth. The machine-made cotton cloth was then exported back to India, where it was profitably sold to the Indian consumer at prices cheaper than cotton cloth produced by hand in India. British policies prevented the development of cotton mills in India. The same neo-mercantilist policies were applied throughout the empire, resulting in what is called "aborted modernization," condemning India and the other colonies to an agricultural economy.

British rule had a profound impact on the intellectual life of India. Thomas Babington Macaulay (1800–1859), a distinguished historian and Whig parliamentarian, was instrumental in persuading the East India Company to introduce English education to India. In his Minute on Education (1835), Macaulay made very clear why it was advisable for the British to introduce a Western educational curriculum along with the English language:

> I feel ... that it is impossible for us, with our limited means, to attempt to educate the body of the people. We must at present do our best to form a class who may be interpreters between us and the millions whom we govern, a class of persons Indian in blood and colour, but English in tastes, in opinions, in morals and in intellect. To that class we may leave it to refine the vernacular dialects of the country, to enrich those dialects with terms of science borrowed from the Western nomenclature, and to render them by degrees fit vehicles for conveying knowledge to the great mass of the population. (Macaulay 1835)

Once introduced, the English curriculum produced a small English-speaking, Hindu upper class. The Hindus embraced the English schools, while the Muslim population initially rejected both Western schools and Western books. The masses remained untouched and illiterate.

British rule in India had both a positive and negative impact that remains even in the twenty-first century. British rule introduced modern civilization to the Indian subcontinent. Political and linguistic unity was imposed for the first time. Railroads, schools, hospitals, and orphanages were built. The most important positive influence was the introduction of the ideas of the Enlightenment, the secularized core values of Western Civilization. They include the unique value of the individual person, the inalienable rights of freedom of thought and expression, and the equality of all individuals regardless of race, religion, social, or economic status, and, in the twenty-first century, sexual orientation.

The introduction of Western education, the creation of an educated upper class with English as a common language, and their exposure to Western literature and political thought, created Indian nationalism. Those who were educated and embraced Western political ideas and human rights found themselves out of place at home, while at the same time, desiring to liberate their homeland from the imperialists. It was particularly true of those who, like Mahatma Gandhi (1869–1948), received a university education at Oxford or Cambridge Universities, or other Western universities. They used Western political theories and Western political practices – newspapers, pamphleteering, mass meetings, petitions, organized political parties – to eventually achieve independence. They argued that John Locke's and Thomas Jefferson's declarations, that all men are created equal and endowed with certain inalienable rights, and that those principles are self-evident, were true for all people, not just those in the West.

China

Over four thousand years, China developed a civilization that viewed itself as the world, the Middle Kingdom (*Zhonggou*), inward looking, with nothing to learn from the "barbarians" who lived beyond its borders. Trade existed between Europe and East Asia for many centuries before direct contact was established. Emissaries from the Roman Empire apparently arrived in China in 166 AD and again in 226 and 284, according to Chinese records. There was continuous contact, mostly trade, between Europe and China during the period of the Middle Ages and Early Modern period of European history. Merchants, explorers, and often Christian missionaries journeyed to and from the Far East.

John of Montecorvino (Giovanni da Montecorvino, 1247–1328), a Franciscan missionary who led the earliest Roman Catholic missions in India and China, was consecrated archbishop of Peking (Beijing) in 1307 by Pope Clement V (r. 1305–1314). Europeans were welcomed in China during the Yuan Dynasty (1279–1368). The Yuan were Mongolian, and therefore a foreign dynasty. A native Chinese dynasty, the Ming Dynasty (1368–1644), followed the Yuan. In 1368, all foreigners were expelled from China, but not all contact with the outside world was ended. Between 1405 and 1433, Cheng Ho (Zheng He, 1371–1433), admiral and diplomat, led seven maritime missions that sailed around Southeast Asia and India to the eastern coast of Africa. The first fleet consisted of 62 ships and 27 800 men.

Impressive as Cheng Ho's voyages were, they ended with his death in 1433, when an imperial order called a halt to any further missions. In 1477, when a new expedition was proposed, the vice president of the Ministry of War argued that the immense cost of such ventures was not justified by the "wonderful precious things" brought back, things that China neither needed nor desired. In 1525, all oceangoing ships were ordered destroyed. The largest navy in history, an estimated 3500 ships, was no more, as China turned inward.

The Ming Dynasty came to an end in 1644, when the Manchus, an ethnic minority from the northeastern region known as Manchuria, conquered China and established the Qing Dynasty. They ruled China until 1912, following the Chinese Revolution of 1911. Under the Qing Dynasty, China remained a closed society with an agricultural economy, administered by a scholar bureaucracy. Contact with the outside world was restricted to a few ports: Chusan (Zhoushan), Amoy (Xiamen), and especially Canton (Guangzhou). Beginning in 1757, foreign trade was limited to Canton and had to be conducted through a group of Chinese merchants known as the *Cohong*. Foreign traders were not allowed to enter China. Their living quarters were restricted to a small area of Canton along the Pearl River.

China was forced open to the West by Great Britain in 1842. It was an industrialized Britain that confronted China in the Opium War of 1839–1842. Historically, Western merchants did not have anything but silver and gold to offer the Chinese in exchange for the silks, tea, and porcelain they desired. As the demand for Chinese products increased, the need to find a product desired by the Chinese increased, also. The answer was found in opium, a product grown in India and exported to China by the East India Company.

By the 1820s, China was paying for an ever-increasing quantity of opium with silver, despite the Chinese government outlawing the production or importation of the drug in 1800, and imposing severe penalties on violators. For the Chinese officials, the opium trade was a moral issue, an evil that was destroying Chinese society. The East India Company, British merchants, and those who smuggled the opium into China argued that China was simply out of touch with the "civilized" nations of the world and unwilling to engage in free trade and normal conduct of international relations with other nations.

In June 1839, Chinese authorities seized 1.2 million kg (2.6 million lbs.) of opium and destroyed it. War broke out between China and Great Britain in November. Chinese military technology was still what it was in the sixteenth century and no match for the British. What was later called the First Opium War ended in 1842 with the Treaty of Nanking (Nanjing). China ceded Hong Kong to Great Britain, agreed to pay a huge indemnity, and opened five additional "treaty ports." In October 1843, the British Supplementary Treaty of the Bogue (Humen) granted "most favored nation" status to Britain and the right of extraterritoriality for British subjects. Most favored nation status meant that whatever concessions China made to any other foreign nation in the future would automatically apply to Britain. The right of extraterritoriality meant that British subjects residing in China were not subject to Chinese law. They remained under British jurisdiction.

War broke out again in October 1856 and lasted until October 1860. Britain was joined by France in the Second Opium War, also known as the Arrow War. China was once again easily defeated and humiliated. According to the 1858 Treaty of Tientsin (Tianjin) between China and Great Britain, France, Russia, and the United States, 11 additional ports were opened to trade; foreign vessels (including war ships) could navigate freely the Yangtze River; foreigners could travel freely and engage in trade or missionary activities throughout

China; the four Western powers opened legations in Peking; and China was required to pay a huge indemnity. Also, China agreed to refrain from referring to British subjects and officials as "barbarians." In the 1860 Convention of Peking (Beijing), China made territorial concessions to both Great Britain and Russia.

The United States engaged in military action against China at the beginning of the Second Opium War. Two American warships landed 150 marines and sailors in Canton to protect American citizens. As the force was being withdrawn on November 15, a Chinese garrison fired on a small American boat. In retaliation, an American warship sailed up the Pearl River and attacked Canton's coastal forts. A landing force of under 300 marines and sailors engaged a Chinese force of 3000 soldiers. When the battle was over, the American force suffered 7 dead and 22 wounded. Chinese casualties were estimated at 250–500 killed and wounded. The United States's victory led to America remaining out of the war until June 1859, when it supported the British and French in the Second Battle of Taku Forts.

Russia took advantage of China's vulnerability during the war to complete expansion across Eurasia to the Pacific Ocean. China ceded both banks of the Amur River to Russia as well as coastal territory from the mouth of the Amur River to the border of Korea. In 1860, Russia founded the city of Vladivostok on the coast near the Korean border.

Most humiliating for the proud Chinese was their defeat in the Sino-Japanese War of 1894–1895. The war broke out over Korea, a long-time client state of China. Japan, with a modern army and navy modeled after those of Germany and Great Britain, quickly defeated the much larger Chinese forces and, after landing forces in Manchuria that threatened the sea approaches to Peking, forced China to sue for peace. In the Treaty of Shimonoseki (1895), China ceded the island of Formosa (Taiwan), the Pescadores (P'eng-hu Islands), and the Liaotung Peninsula (Southeastern Manchuria) to Japan and recognized the independence of Korea. Japan's surprising defeat of China alarmed the European powers. Protests from Russia, Germany, and France compelled the Japanese to return the Liaotung Peninsula to China.

After 1860, China lay prostrate before the imperialists. Because of centuries of rule by the scholar-bureaucrats who were schooled in Confucianism, the Chinese were convinced that China had nothing to learn from the outside world and no need to make any concessions to the modern world that was now imposing itself on the Middle Kingdom. Western gunboats patrolled the rivers. Western civil servants controlled, directly and indirectly, the country's finances. Western missionaries and merchants roamed the countryside, protected by extraterritoriality rights from Chinese laws and customs.

In 1898, China was in danger of being partitioned as happened to Sub-Sahara Africa. Fearful of Japanese and Russian designs on China, the European powers and the United States all extorted further concessions from China. Each took control of a portion of Chinese territory, commonly called "spheres of influence." Fearful for what the partition of China might mean for American commercial interests in China, the United States proposed that all interested parties agree to what was called the "Open Door" policy. It merely meant, that while respecting the territorial integrity of China, the country would remain open to economic exploitation by all without any restrictions.

A final, but futile, attempt to drive out the foreigners and defend traditional Chinese ways from modernism came in the form of what was called the "Boxer Rebellion" in 1899–1901. The Boxers, as they were called by Westerners, were members of a secret society known as the "Righteous and Harmonious Fists" (Yihequan). They were violently opposed to all foreign influence, especially that of the Christian missionaries. With support from the Empress Dowager Tz'u-hsi (Cixi, 1835–1908), the Boxers attacked foreigners, Christian missionaries, and Chinese suspected of being Christian converts across northern China.

For 55 days between June 20 and August 14, 1900, the Boxers besieged the Peking Legation Quarter were approximately 900 European, American, and Japanese soldiers, together with about 2800 Chinese Christians took refuge. An international force of European, Japanese, and American soldiers entered Peking on August 14. The first to enter the Legation Quarter were Sikh and Rajput soldiers from India commanded by British officers. The Empress Dowager and her court fled to Hsi-an (X'ian) in Shaanxi Province. Following the defeat of the Boxers and the imperial army, Peking was subjected to what a British officer called one of the "unwritten laws that a city which does not surrender at the last and is taken by storm is looted" (Bickers and Tiedemann 2008, p. 54).

Many saw the defeat of the Boxers as yet more evidence that Western civilization was superior to any non-Western civilization. Others in Europe and America saw it differently. George Lynch, a journalist for the *British Daily Express* wrote: "there are things that I must not write, and that may not be printed in England, which would seem to show that this Western civilization of ours is merely a veneer over savagery" (Lai-Henderson 2015, p. 61). According to the Treaty of 1901 (Xinchou Treaty), ten high-ranking officials were to be executed, and China was to pay reparations to the victors in the amount of 450 million taels of fine silver (roughly $9.4 billion, or £7 billion in 2018).

Empress Dowager Tz'u-hsi died November 15, 1908, the day after her son, the Hsuan-tung (or Zuantuong) Emperor (1875–1908), died of arsenic poisoning. Puyi (1906–1967), the two-year old son of Prince Chun (or Zaifeng, 1883–1951), chosen by the Empress Dowager, became the last emperor of China. The Qing dynasty ended with the Revolution of 1911.

Japan

Francis Xavier (1506–1552), a Jesuit missionary who followed the Portuguese to India, Ceylon, Malaya, and the East Indies, arrived in Japan in 1549. As part of their emphasis on converting the upper classes and, through them, the lower classes, the Jesuit missionaries adopted the Japanese lifestyle. They dressed like their hosts, ate their food, and even adjusted to the Japanese emphasis on personal cleanliness. The Franciscans arrived in Japan in 1593. Unlike the Jesuits, they focused on the poor. Dutch and English Protestant missionaries began to arrive in the early 1600s.

The missionaries did not encounter any real hostility until the beginning of the seventeenth century. The spread of Christianity, and the intrigues between the various Christian sects, caused alarm among the Japanese leadership. In 1603, Tokugawa Ieyasu (1543–1616) established a centralized feudal state in Japan known historically as the Tokugawa Shogunate that ruled Japan for the next 250 years. Ieyasu and his successors ruled Japan as the supreme military commander, or *shogun*, appointed by the emperor who resided in Kyoto.

In 1606 Christianity was prohibited, and in 1614, Ieyasu published an edict ordering the destruction of Christianity in Japan. Christian converts who refused to belong to a Buddhist temple were martyred, as were the missionaries who did not leave the country. Ieyasu's successors closed Japan to all Western influence. By 1637, only a small group of Dutch merchants remained, who were restricted to Deshima (Dejima) an artificial island of 2.2 acres ($9000\,m^2$) in Nagasaki harbor. After 1715 only two ships annually were allowed to dock at Deshima. To further cut Japan off from the outside world, all Japanese were forbidden to travel outside of Japan.

Japan's isolation came to an abrupt end on July 8, 1853, when United States Naval Commodore Matthew Perry (1794–1858) sailed into Edo Bay with a letter from President Millard Fillmore (1800–1874) requesting Japan begin trade relations with the United States. Perry made it clear that the alternative was war. Perry returned in February 1854, and on March 31 signed the Treaty of Kanagawa that opened the ports of Shimoda and Hakodate to trade and granted other commercial and diplomatic rights to the United States. The Treaty of Amity and Commerce (or Harris Treaty) between the two nations was signed on July 29, 1858. It granted extraterritoriality to the United States, freedom of religion for foreigners, prohibited the opium trade, and opened additional ports to trade. Similar treaties were negotiated between Japan and the European nations.

Figure 13.3 United States Naval Commodore Matthew Perry arriving in Japan in July 1853, forcing Japan open to world trade for the first time in 200 years. *Source:* Library of Congress Prints and Photographs Division.

Japan's response to the imperialist threat was the opposite of China's. Both the Tokugawa *shogun* and the reigning emperor died in 1868. The Tokugawa *shogun* was replaced by a new leadership of young samurai, who accepted the need for Japan to modernize, if it was to avoid the same fate as China. The political, economic, and social transformation of Japan that occurred between 1868 and 1912 is called the Meiji Restoration. "Meiji" was the reign name of Mutsuhito (1852–1912), who reigned as Emperor Meiji from 1867 to 1912. "Restoration" refers to ending the military dictatorship of the Tokugawa Shogunate and the restoration of the emperor's personal rule. To emphasize the change, the emperor's residence was moved from Kyoto to Tokyo.

The goal of the samurai to modernize and westernize Japan was made clear in the emperor's announcement in his Charter Oath of 1868, that "Knowledge shall be sought all over the world, and thereby the foundations of imperial rule shall be strengthened" (Kissinger 2011, p. 79). They wanted Western learning, meaning science and technology, not Western culture. Westernization meant strengthening Japan, not changing its religion or culture. Teachers were brought to Japan, and Japanese students were sent abroad to study and return to teach. The educational system was modernized and centralized to assure uniformity of purpose, meaning literacy, not individualism.

The old feudal levies were replaced with a modern conscript army. German officers were brought to Japan to create an army modeled after the most admired army in Europe at that time. A small modern navy was built with guidance from the British, whose navy dominated the world's oceans.

The economy was modernized in order to support the new military establishment. The government took an active role in founding and providing finances to launch light and heavy industries required for a modern nation. Railroads, mining, steel production, shipbuilding, and other industries were started under government direction, then once established, were sold to private interests at bargain prices.

The legal and judicial systems were completely remade so as to embody such Western concepts as individual rights, due process, and the rule of law. Western values, or Enlightenment values – private property, freedom of religion, freedom of speech, freedom of association – were guaranteed by a constitution adopted in 1889. In drafting the Western style constitution, Germany once again served as the model. It provided the form of a parliamentary system, while leaving real power in the hands of the emperor and the ruling oligarchy. Article One made clear that the emperor, who was "sacred and inviolable" (Article 3), was sovereign: "The Empire of Japan shall be reigned over and governed by a line of Emperors unbroken for ages eternal."

Japan accomplished something that no colonial possession was able to do. A nation that was still living in the Middle Ages when Commodore Perry sailed into Edo Bay in 1853 was transformed into a modern, industrial nation within three decades. In 1894, Great Britain and the United States agreed to give up their extraterritoriality rights within five years. Similar Western nations with those rights concluded similar treaties around the same time. Extraterritoriality came to an end in Japan in 1899. Japan succeeded in modernizing without compromising its culture. It was modern, but it was not Western.

Japan did, however, mimic the Western imperialist nations in one other way. In 1894, it proved that it, too, was an imperialist nation, when it went to war over Korea with China. As a result of the Sino-Japanese War (1894–1895), Japan gained Taiwan (or Formosa), a portion of the Liaodong Peninsula, the Pescadores Islands, Chinese recognition of the independence of Korea, most favored nation status in trade with China, and a large indemnity. Japan's surprising victory alarmed Russia which had designs on the Liaodong Peninsula. France and Germany joined with Russia to compel Japan to give up its claim to the peninsula for an increased indemnity from China.

At the dawn of the twentieth century, Japan was the dominant power in Asia, and a rival of the United States as the dominant power in the Pacific Ocean. In 1902, the Anglo-Japanese Alliance was concluded. Japan was recognized as an equal by the world's greatest power of the day. It was the first non-European nation welcomed into the exclusive club of modern, civilized nations. Japan demonstrated its worthiness to be so honored when it defeated Russia in the Russo-Japanese War of 1904–1905. Russia, the nation that in 1812 defeated the great Napoleon, suffered a crushing defeat by a non-European nation. The implications of that fact were not lost on the colonial people around the world who were just beginning to feel the energy of nationalism.

Southeast Asia

At the beginning of the nineteenth century, Spain, Portugal, and the Netherlands still held territories in Southeast Asia, remnants of their empires created during the sixteenth and seventeenth centuries. Portugal held onto Timor, southeast of Bali. Spain still controlled the Philippine Islands and continued to do so until ceded to the United States following the Spanish-American War in 1898. The Dutch possessed the Indonesian archipelago. All of these were a part of what is known as Maritime Southeast Asia.

In 1819, the British founded Singapore ("Lion City") on a small island at the tip of the Malay Peninsula. By 1860, the population had increased from roughly 1000 to 80 000. It became a royal crown colony in 1858. Malacca, located on the southeast coast of the Malay Peninsula, was ceded to Britain by the Dutch in the Anglo-Dutch Treaty of 1824.

Great Britain extended control over portions of Burma (Myanmar) during the First Anglo-Burmese War (1824–1826) and the Second Anglo-Burmese War (1852–1853). The annexation of Burma was completed in January 1886, following the Third Anglo-Burmese War (1885). Burma was initially administered as a province of British India. The British advance in Burma was in response to French advances in Indochina.

French involvement in Indochina began with the arrival of French Jesuit missionaries in the early seventeenth century. During the eighteenth century, European interest in Indochina was largely restricted to trade. The need to protect French missionaries who were being threatened with expulsion served as an excuse for direct interference in the nineteenth century.

French gunships captured the ports of Tourane (Da Nang) in 1858 and Saigon in 1859. In 1862, Vietnam ceded three ports and all of Cochinchina (southern Vietnam) to France. In the following year, the king of Cambodia asked France to establish a protectorate over his kingdom. The French secured control of northern Vietnam as a result of the Sino-French War (1884–1885). In 1887, the provinces of Annam, Tonkin, Cochinchina, and Cambodia were joined together to form French Indochina. Laos was added in 1893.

The spread of France's colonial rule in Southeast Asia alarmed the British, who as noted above, were advancing eastward from India. There was the possibility that a colonial confrontation in Southeast Asia over the Kingdom of Siam could lead to war between the two European great powers. Neither was willing to allow the other to have Siam (Thailand).

Siam's King Mongkut (Rama IV, 1804–1868) and his son and successor King Chulalongkorn (Rama V, 1853–1910) were able to preserve Siam's independence through a twin policy of modernization and clever diplomacy that took advantage of Britain's and France's desire to preserve Siam as a buffer between them. Mongkut promoted Western education. In 1862, he employed Anna Harriette Emma Leonowens (1831–1915) to provide his 39 wives and 82 children with a Western education that was both secular and scientific. By recognizing the need to change, rather than cling hopelessly to the past, Siam and Japan were able to avoid the fate of most of the non-Western world during the Age of Western Imperialism.

American Empire

Americans do not normally think of the United States as being, or ever having been, an empire. Many are surprised to learn that the United States was one of the West's colonial powers at the end of the nineteenth century. Even more surprising is the assertion that the United States was from its beginning an imperialistic nation.

The causes of the colonial conflict (1775–1783) that led to Great Britain losing 13 of its colonies along the Atlantic coast and the founding of the United States of America were many and varied. One cause was the Royal Proclamation of 1763, aimed at halting the expansion of the European settlements beyond the Appalachian Mountains. Such restraint was unacceptable to wealthy colonial leaders who would shortly become the "Founding Fathers." Many, including George Washington (1732–1799), were land speculators with large holdings in, for example, the Ohio Valley.

As the new American nation pushed beyond the mountains, the Native Americans were pushed aside. If Western legal concepts unknown to the Native American tribes did not suffice for trading land for beads or other goods, then they were simply pushed out of the way. The case of the Cherokees provides a vivid example.

The Cherokees were one of the "Five Civilized Tribes," that were called such because they had adopted many of the Western ways. They developed a written language and published a newspaper, even drafted a constitution modeled after that of the United States. But, as "King Cotton" took over the Southern economy, and gold was discovered in Georgia in 1828, the White settlers demanded Cherokee lands. The Cherokees resisted. They took their case to the United States Supreme Court, where they won. Unfortunately for them, Andrew Jackson (1767–1845), a wealthy planter from Tennessee, was elected president in 1828.

As early as 1794, Jackson was a partner in a land speculation business that sold lands belonging by treaty to the Cherokee and Chickasaw tribes. As president, he chose to ignore the Supreme Court's ruling. He pushed the Indian Removal Act through Congress in 1830, authorizing the forced removal of the Cherokees from their ancestral lands to the territory that later became the state of Oklahoma. The removal of all of the Southeastern tribes between 1831 and 1838 is but one of the dark pages in the history of America's expansion across the continent.

Between 1803 and 1867, the United States created a continental empire by purchase, annexation, and conquest. The Louisiana Territory was purchased from France in 1803. It included approximately 828 000 square miles (2 144 510 km^2), out of which 15 new states were later formed. General Andrew Jackson's seizure of portions of Spanish West Florida led to negotiations that resulted in Spain ceding East and West Florida to the United States in 1818.

The territory of Texas declared its independence from Mexico on March 2, 1836. Cotton production was expanding into Texas, as Southern planters sought out fresh lands. Cotton production required, or so the Southern planters assumed, slave labor. Since slavery was prohibited by Mexico, it became an important issue leading to the declaration of independence and request that Texas be admitted to the United States as a slave state.

Annexing Texas became a part of the controversy over the spread of slavery to the western territories. The proponents of annexation prevailed. On December 29, 1845, President James K. Polk (1795–1849) signed the legislation admitting Texas to the United States as the twenty-eighth state. The Oregon Treaty signed in June 1846, settled the disputed border between the Oregon Territory and British Columbia by establishing the forty-ninth parallel as the border.

The border between Texas and Mexico was disputed. Mexico broke off relations with the United States following the latter's annexation of Texas. President Polk offered to settle the disputed border and purchase New Mexico and California for $30 million dollars. When Mexico refused to consider the offer, Polk sent American troops into the disputed territory and prepared to ask Congress for a declaration of war.

The Mexican-American War lasted from April 1846 to February 1848. The military phase ended in September 1847, with American forces occupying Mexico City. According to the Treaty of Guadalupe Hidalgo (1848), Mexico ceded 500 000 sq. miles (1 294 994.06 km^2) of its territory to the United States for $15 million. The states of New Mexico, Utah, Nevada, Arizona, California, Texas, and the western portion of Colorado were eventually carved out of the new acquisition.

Many Americans, then and since, considered the war an act of aggression on the part of the United States. The House of Representatives voted in January 1847, to censure Polk for starting a war with Mexico that was unnecessary and unconstitutional. Ulysses S. Grant (1822–1885), who served in the war and later served two terms as president (1869–1877), said that the Mexican-American War was "one of the most unjust ever waged by a stronger against a weaker nation" (Rickard 2006).

The United States made the transition from a continental to a maritime empire as a result of the Spanish-American War (1898) and the annexation of Hawaii in the same year. The Spanish-American War, like the war with Mexico, was a contest between David and Goliath, in which Goliath defeated David both times.

The war that lasted less than four months (April 21–August 13), began with American intervention in the Cuban revolt against Spain and effectively ended on July 17, with the Spanish surrender at Santiago, Cuba. The Treaty of Paris (1898) ceded Guam and Puerto Rico to the United States and gave sovereignty over the Philippines to the United States in exchange for $20 million. The Philippine Republic, founded in January 1899, fought a four-year guerilla war against the American occupation. Mark Twain (1835–1910), the beloved creator of Tom Sawyer and Huck Finn, said that America's conquest of the Philippines "debauched America's honor and blackened her face before the world" (Goldensohn 2006, p. 146).

Figure 13.4 The USS Maine exploded and sunk in Havana Harbor, Cuba, on February 15, 1898, resulting in a public outcry that contributed to the United States declaring war with Spain on April 21, 1898. *Source:* via pingnews.

There was interest in annexing Cuba, but Cuba was a large island occupied by people who were non-European, Roman Catholic, and spoke Spanish. The thought of trying to absorb such a large population with a very foreign culture nixed any chances of Cuba becoming a part of the United States.

Hawaii was a sovereign state, strategically located in the Pacific Ocean. Great Britain, France, and the United States all had treaties with the island kingdom. By 1875, American sugar planters dominated the Hawaiian economy. Missionaries viewed Hawaii as a stepping stone to the Christianization of the Philippines and China. As the European nations began dividing up the world and building large navies that required coaling stations around the world, the United States became alarmed at the possibility that Britain might seek control of Hawaii.

In 1893, Queen Liliuokalani (1838–1917) attempted to promulgate a new constitution that would strengthen the monarchy. A group of Americans deposed the Queen and proclaimed a republic with Sanford B. Dole (1844–1926) as president. The leaders of the coup were encouraged by President Benjamin Harrison (1833–1901), who sent marines to surround the royal palace. The new government of the Republic of Hawaii sent a delegation to Washington, D. C. requesting annexation. The Hawaiian Islands were formally annexed to the United States in July 1898.

Within the Western Hemisphere, the United States asserted a kind of informal sovereignty. With the Roosevelt Corollary (1904) to the Monroe Doctrine (1823), the United States asserted the right to intervene at will in the matters of any Latin American state. When Columbia refused an offer of $10 million for America's right to build a canal through Panama, the United States encouraged the Panamanians to revolt and declare independence from Columbia. Panama then became a virtual protectorate of the United States, to whom it "leased" the Canal Zone. In the following year, President Theodore Roosevelt (1858–1919) was instrumental in persuading his admirer, the German Kaiser, to agree to an international conference at Algeciras, to relieve tensions over the Moroccan crisis. In 1907, Roosevelt sent America's "Great White Fleet" of 16 battleships around the world, just to show the flag.

References

Bickers, R.A. and Tiedemann, R.G. (2008). *The Boxers, China, and the World*. Lanham, Md: Rowman & Littlefield.

Boulos (2010). Brown Man's Burden' of 1899 Was Prescient. Mondoweiss. https://mondoweiss.net/2010/07/brown-mans-burden-of-1899-was-prescient (accessed 21 October 2019).

Goldensohn, L. (2006). *American War Poetry: An Anthology*. New York: Columbia University Press.

Hochschild, A. (1998). *King Leopold's Ghost: A Story of Greed, Terror, and Heroism in Colonial Africa*. New York: Houghton Mifflin.

Kipling, R. (1899). The White Man's Burden. McClure's Magazine. http://historymuse.net/readings/KiplingWHITEMANSBURDEN1899.htm (accessed 21 October 2019).

Kissinger, H. (2011). *On China*. New York: Penguin Books.

Lai-Henderson, S. (2015). *Mark Twain in China*. Stanford, CA: Stanford University Press.

Macaulay, T.B. (1835). Minute on Education (1835) by Thomas Babington Macaulay. http://www.columbia.edu/itc/mealac/pritchett/00generallinks/macaulay/txt_minute_education_1835.html (accessed 21 October 2019).

Rickard, J. (2006). The Memoirs of General Ulysses S. Grant, Chapter 3. http://www.historyofwar.org/sources/acw/grant/chapter01.html (accessed 21 October 2019).

Part V

The Crisis of Western Civilization: An Overview

On July 28, 1914, a teenage terrorist shot the heir to the throne of the Austro-Hungarian empire in the town of Sarajevo in the Balkans. That single event altered the direction of world history and resulted in the twentieth century becoming the bloodiest century in history. The conflagration that resulted will ever be known as the Great War. The hundred-year peace that preceded it ended in a European civil war, the outcome of which was decided by the intervention of the United States of America. Tragically, America's entry guaranteed that a second Great War, bloodier than the first, would follow.

The horror of modern industrialized war caused many to question the basic assumptions of the Enlightenment. Faith in the innate goodness and rationality of human beings, along with belief in progress and optimism about the future were all mortally wounded by the war experience. The economic and social disruption of the interwar years culminating in the Great Depression, together with the seeming inability or unwillingness of governments to mitigate the suffering caused by the Great Depression, led many to question whether liberal democratic governments and *laissez faire* economics were outdated.

Many, particularly in Germany and the Soviet Union, turned to a new political ideology referred to as totalitarianism. The totalitarian state, whether of the right (Nazi Germany) or the left (Soviet Union), demanded that its citizens become "born again," true believers. They thrived by maintaining a perpetual "we against them" tension that eventually led to the outbreak of the second Great War, commonly known as World War II.

Oddly, war created two rather confusing alliance systems. Totalitarian Germany with its racist worldview allied with Imperial Japan, a militaristic non-European nation bent on dominating the Pacific. The so-called Axis Powers engaged in a life or death struggle with the Allies, who formed a Grand Alliance that included the totalitarian Soviet Union and the democratic United States, United Kingdom, and France. World War II, in some respects, surpassed World War I in its horrors and crimes against humanity. The attempted genocide of Europe's Jewish population, carpet bombing of cities in which tens of thousands of civilians were incinerated, and the dropping of atomic bombs on two Japanese cities, raised humanity's crimes against humanity to new heights.

Western Civilization: A Brief History, First Edition. Paul R. Waibel.
© 2020 John Wiley & Sons, Inc. Published 2020 by John Wiley & Sons, Inc.

14

The Great War: 1914–1918

Chronology

1879	Dual Alliance Between Germany and Austria-Hungary
1882	Triple Alliance Between Germany, Austria-Hungary, and Italy
1887	Reinsurance Treaty Between Germany and Russia
1914	Assassination of Archduke Franz Ferdinand
1914	First Battle of the Marne ("Miracle of the Marne")
1914	Battles of Tannenberg Forest and Masurian Lakes
1914	First "Bombs" Dropped on England by Zeppelins
1915	Sinking of the *Lusitania* by German a U-Boat
1915	First Major Use of Poison Gas in Second Battle of Ypres
1915–1916	Gallipoli Campaign
1916	Battle of Verdun, Great War Becomes War of Attrition
1916	Battle of the Somme, Bloodiest Battle of the Great War
1916	Sykes-Picot Agreement Between Great Britain and France
1917	Germany Resumes Unrestricted U-Boat Warfare
1917	Russian Revolution
1917	Balfour Declaration
1918	Treaty of Brest-Litovsk Between Germany and Russia
1918	Wilson's Fourteen Points
1918	War Ends at 11:00 a.m., November 11 ("All Quiet on the Western Front")

One of the most traumatic events in the history of Western Civilization occurred between 1914 and 1918. It was called "The Great War," in part because though it was mostly a European war, it was fought around the world. With the outbreak of a second global war in 1939, people began referring to the Great War as World War I and the new conflict as World War II. Indeed, some historians suggest that the Great War was only the first round of a truly great war that began in 1914 and did not end until 1945, with a ceasefire between 1918 and 1939.

Western Civilization: A Brief History, First Edition. Paul R. Waibel.
© 2020 John Wiley & Sons, Inc. Published 2020 by John Wiley & Sons, Inc.

Prelude to the Great War

The balance of power among the five European great powers – Great Britain, France, Prussia, Austria, and Russia – reestablished by the Vienna Congress in 1815 was upset by the unification of Germany in 1871. In place of balance of power as the mechanism for maintaining peace in Europe, a system of defensive alliances emerged after 1871, largely the work of Otto von Bismarck.

Bismarck concluded an alliance with Austria-Hungary in 1879 that lasted until 1918. The Dual Alliance assured each partner of the other's aid if attacked by Russia. In 1882, Germany, Austria-Hungary, and Italy formed the Triple Alliance, which committed the three members to act together in the event of an attack by France on either Germany or Italy, or an attack by Russia on Austria-Hungary. To reassure Russia that Germany was not a threat, Bismarck negotiated the Reinsurance Treaty with Russia in 1887, which provided for one partner assuming benevolent neutrality, if the other was attacked by a third power.

Bismarck's alliances effectively isolated France, which Bismarck considered the major threat to peace on the continent, especially since Great Britain was abstaining from entering into any formal alliances. Since Bismarck's foreign policy aimed at securing Germany's influence on the continent and did not threaten Britain's dominant position on the world stage, peace among the great powers appeared secure. Bismarck's retirement in 1890, followed by a fundamental change in German foreign policy, caused the alliance system to unravel.

Kaiser Wilhelm II (1859–1941) announced a "new course" in German foreign policy aimed at elevating Germany to world-power status. Such a change was a direct challenge to Great Britain's position in the world, since it meant that Germany must construct a navy that could rival the British navy for control of the seas. The growing belief that Germany was a threat to Britain, together with an increasing feeling of diplomatic isolation resulting from Britain's aggressive role in the South African Boer War (1899–1902), led Britain to abandon its "splendid isolation" and begin seeking allies of its own.

The German Kaiser's saber-rattling foreign policy caused Great Britain, France, and Russia to set aside their historic and colonial disputes in order to confront Germany's growing strength. Wilhelm II's decision in 1890 not to renew the Reinsurance Treaty with Russia increased fear of what might be Germany's intentions in both Russia and France. Though democratic France and autocratic Russia were unlikely allies, they entered into a formal alliance in December 1894. Britain concluded the Anglo-Japanese Alliance in 1902, followed in 1904 and 1907 by two informal "understandings," or "ententes," that resolved outstanding imperial disputes with France and Russia, respectively.

By 1907, Europe was divided into two hostile camps: the Triple Alliance composed of Germany, Austria-Hungary, and Italy, and what became known as the Triple Entente consisting of Great Britain, France, and Russia. The Triple Entente was not a formal alliance, but more of a "gentlemen's agreement" to coordinate their individual efforts at confronting the perceived threat from Germany.

It became evident at the Algeciras Conference in January 1906, that Wilhelm II's "new course" and desire for Germany to have "a place in the sun" caused alarm in Europe. The conference was called by President Theodore Roosevelt (1858–1919) at the urging of the

Kaiser to resolve a dispute between France and the Sultan of Morocco, arising from France's bid to establish a protectorate over Morocco. Wilhelm II hoped to drive a wedge between France and Britain and make a public demonstration of Germany's bid for recognition as a world power. In the end Britain, Russia, and the United States, joined by Italy, Germany's ally in the Triple Alliance, supported France. Only Austria-Hungary supported Germany. The outcome of the conference demonstrated that the alliance system designed by Bismarck to isolate France had come unraveled. Rather than demonstrating Germany's world-power status, Germany's isolation and vulnerability was exposed. It was the last time the European great powers would meet together in congress before the outbreak of the Great War.

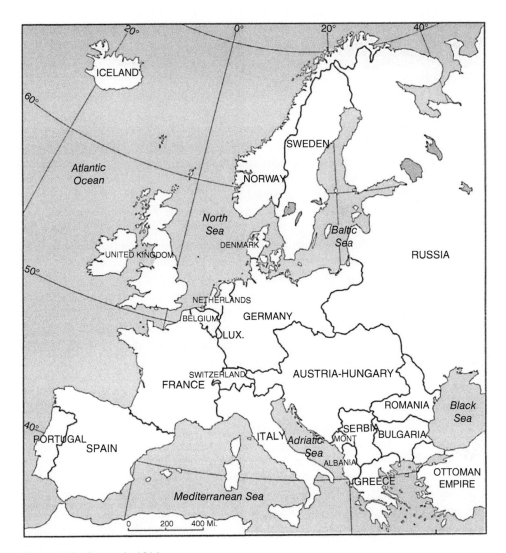

Figure 14.1 Europe in 1914.

Explosion in the Balkans

The unification of Italy and Germany left Europe with rigid borders except in the Balkans, where the decline of Turkish power and influence offered opportunities for inflamed nationalism and conflict between Austria-Hungary and Russia. Austria-Hungary's decision to annex the two provinces of Bosnia and Herzegovina in 1908 threatened the peace of Europe. Serbia saw it as a hostile act, since the Serbs hoped to create a Great Serbia in the Balkans that would include Bosnia with its large Serbian population. The fact that Austria-Hungary was allied with Germany and Russia supported its Slavic kinsmen in Serbia meant the so-called First Balkan Crisis threatened to ignite the whole of Europe.

Bismarck predicted decades earlier that a general European war would one day breakout over a minor incident in the Balkans, the whole of which, he had contended, was not worth "the healthy bones of a single Pomeranian musketeer" (Craig 1978, p. 110). The First Balkan Crisis was not the event Bismarck feared. The trigger for the Great War occurred on June 28, 1914, when the heir to the Austrian throne Archduke Franz Ferdinand (1863–1914) and his wife Sophie Chotek (1868–1914) were assassinated by a 19-year-old Serbian nationalist named Gavrilo Princip (1894–1918).

The European world was shocked by the assassination. Everyone expected Austria to take some punitive action against Serbia. If it had acted promptly, the rest of the world would no doubt have accepted the *fait accompli*. But the Austrians needed assurance from Germany that it would honor its commitment under the Dual Alliance to aid Austria-Hungary in the event that Russia intervened on Serbia's behalf. The delay in obtaining Germany's support allowed time for Russia to conclude that Russian prestige could not allow Serbia's destruction.

It was a well-known fact that Austria was no longer the great power that it was in 1815, or even in 1849. It was a multicultural land empire held together by soldiers, bureaucrats, parades, and an aging emperor who served as a living symbol of past glory. It was being torn apart by the spirit of nationalism that created the German Empire and strengthened both France and Great Britain. If Austria did not punish Serbia, how could it continue to be regarded as a great power? If Germany allowed its only sure ally to suffer further loss of prestige, would not Germany's future security be threatened? On July 5, the Kaiser assured Austria of Germany's support for whatever action it chose to take regarding Serbia. Russia's position hardened, and it warned the Austrians that it would honor its commitment to defend Serbia.

Russia's warning was ignored in Vienna. Instead, the Austrians presented Serbia with an ultimatum on July 23. Serbia accepted all but one or two of the demands that it felt would infringe on its sovereignty. Serbia's response was an effort to avoid conflict with Austria. Rejecting Serbia's offer, Austria mobilized its army and declared war on July 28. Russia responded by ordering partial mobilization on July 29 and full mobilization on July 30. Germany was left with a choice between activating the Schlieffen Plan or humiliation in the eyes of the world, something the Kaiser could not accept.

The Schlieffen Plan was the German plan for war. It assumed that any war in Europe would be one in which Germany would be compelled to fight a two-front war with France and Russia. Since the plan called for the Germans to eliminate France first, then quickly turn back to the east, each day that the Russians spent mobilizing before the Germans launched their drive to the west further jeopardized the success of the plan. The pace of events became a matter of railroad timetables, since the Schlieffen Plan called for troop trains to pass through towns within minutes of each other on their way to the front. It would be a quick war in which, as in the wars of German unification, rapid mobilization and deployment of armies would determine the outcome.

On August 3, Germany declared war on France and invaded neutral Belgium. Great Britain entered the war on August 4 to aid France and to honor its commitment to defend Belgium's neutrality. Of all of the European great powers, only Italy remained, for the time being, out of the conflict. What was meant to be a little war between Austria-Hungary and Serbia quickly became a general European war, and with the entry of Great Britain, it became a world war.

1914

There was no real reason for the outbreak of war in 1914. Numerous volumes have been written by historians trying to explain what caused the war or who, if anyone, was to blame. The popular explanation that Germany was somehow solely to blame is the product of wartime Allied propaganda and postwar attempts to explain a failed peace while burdening Germany with full responsibility for the rise of totalitarianism in Russia and Germany. When all the arguments and counterarguments have been considered, however, the comment of British prime minister, David Lloyd George (1863–1945), that the European great powers simply slithered over the brink into a war no one wanted remains the best explanation. The outbreak of the Great War resulted from a failure of diplomacy.

Kaiser Wilhelm II and his cousin Tsar Nicholas II (1868–1918) tried at the last moment to avert war. In an exchange of communications between the two, Nicholas pleaded with Wilhelm to restrain Austria, for he was being "overwhelmed by pressure" and would soon "be forced to take extreme measures" leading to war. Any of the three – Wilhelm II, Nicholas II, and Franz Joseph (1830–1916)– could have prevented the war by halting mobilization. But they did not. The fate of Europe, and the world, was in the hands of the generals, and they were captive to plans for mobilization and war, which they felt unable to tinker with, even in the minutest detail.

Germany's Schlieffen Plan was a daring gamble that looked good on paper, but did not allow for certain unforeseen exigencies, that together with a number of miscalculations, prevented its successful execution. Belgium's refusal on August 3 to allow German forces to pass through Belgium to France was followed by Germany's invasion of Belgium and Britain's declaration of war with Germany on August 4. Belgium's decision to fight slowed down the German advance. Surprisingly, the Russians were able to throw an army into East Prussia on August 17. General Helmuth von Moltke (1848–1916) detached two corps from his vital right wing, upon which the success of the Schlieffen Plan depended, and sent them east to meet the Russian threat. It was a fatal error.

On August 30, Moltke made another disastrous decision. He departed from the original plan and turned his right flank south while still east of Paris. Recognizing that something had gone wrong with the German advance, the French commander-in-chief, Joseph Joffre (1852–1931), launched a counterattack against the German left flank along the Marne

River. The battle that ensued, remembered as the "Miracle of the Marne," saved France from almost certain defeat by halting the German advance. The Schlieffen Plan had failed. General von Moltke resigned in disgrace.

The First Battle of the Marne was followed by the so-called "race to the sea," as the opposing armies tried to outflank each other as they steadily moved north to the English Channel. By December 25, the soldiers, who went into battle with expectations of being home for Christmas, stood opposite each other in a line of trenches that stretched from the English Channel in the north to Switzerland in the south. Over the next four years of conflict, the line of trenches remained virtually unchanged, despite the expenditure of millions of casualties in futile attempts to break through the lines and turn the stalemate into a war of motion.

While the French were blunting the German advance in the west, the German army under command of Field Marshal Paul von Hindenburg (1847–1934) and General Erich Ludendorff (1865–1937), was turning back the Russian advance in the East. The Battles of Tannenberg Forest (August 30) and Masurian Lakes (September 15) were crushing defeats for the Russians. Hindenburg and Ludendorff emerged as victorious heroes, while General Aleksandr Samsonov (1859–1914), the Russian commander at the Battle of Tannenberg, attempted to redeem his honor by committing suicide.

War in the Trenches

The generals assured their reluctant monarchs that the conflict would be a brief and glorious little war, but the war the diplomats failed to prevent was not the kind of war the generals were trained to fight. The generals were schooled in military strategies little different from those used during the Napoleonic wars one hundred years earlier. However, a century of remarkable technological "progress" – one that included the development of railroads, telegraphs and telephones, airplanes, submarines, machine guns, tanks, poison gas, flame throwers, and a great many other wonders of modern civilization – shortly transformed what was to be a glorious little war into a "troglodyte world" of trench warfare that would later strain the imaginations of artists, writers, and poets, as they tried to depict it for those who had not experienced the horror of it firsthand.

The Great War is often referred to as the first industrial war. The new reality was that unless there is a decisive victory at the beginning, an industrial war becomes a war of attrition, in which victory goes to the side best able to make use of its economic and manpower resources. The nation with the healthiest economy achieves victory by simply outlasting the enemy. The American Civil War (1861–1865), the Boer War (1899–1902), the Russo-Japanese War (1904–1905), and even the little wars in the colonies foreshadowed what industrialized warfare would mean. The effectiveness of rapid-firing machine guns at, for example, the Battle of Omdurman in the Sudan (1898), demonstrated the obsolescence of massed cavalry or infantry charges in modern warfare. But these lessons were lost on the generals who planned the battles of the Great War. They were not in the textbooks studied at Europe's prestigious military academies.

Confronted by machine guns, the soldiers literally dug in. "[W]hen all is said and done," commented Siegfried Sassoon (1886–1967), an English infantry officer and poet, "the war was mainly a matter of holes and ditches" (Richards 1982, p. 28). The line of trenches that existed by Christmas 1914, from the English Channel to Switzerland was not simply a matter of two ditches facing each other. Both sides tended to follow a three-trench system, though at times there could be more. There were certain characteristics common on both sides, but the German trenches tended to be deeper, drier, and more elaborate than either the British or French.

The frontline trenches were usually about eight feet (2.4 m) deep and four to six feet (1.3–1.8 m) wide with a parapet of earth or sandbags rising another two or three feet (0.6 or 0.9 m) high on the enemy side. Several hundred yards behind the frontline came the first support trench, followed after another 100 yards (91.4 m) by a third support, or reserve trench. First-aid stations and kitchens were included in the support trenches. There were also bunkers that served as command posts, storage for food and weapons, and communication centers. In addition to the parallel trenches, there were various communication trenches that ran between them through which ammunition, reinforcements, and food were brought up to the front. Approximately 100 ft. (30.5 m) out from the frontline trench were forward posts for observation, listening, grenade throwing, and machine-gun placements, connected by shallow ditches called "saps."

The space between the front lines of the opposing armies was called "no man's land," an area that averaged about 250 yards (230 m) deep. It was covered in craters created by artillery shells, row upon row of barbed wire, unexploded ordinance, and bodies and body parts in various stages of decomposition, the remains of failed assaults on the enemy's frontline.

Contrary to what is depicted in motion pictures and television dramas, war, any war, is mostly long periods of boredom broken by short periods of intense action. Life in the trenches of World War I was particularly horrific. There was nowhere to find relief from the extremes of weather. In the winter, wine could freeze, and rations turn to cubes of ice. When it rained, the soldiers stood for days at a time in stagnant water filled with sewage and decaying bodies.

A variety of vermin and pests were constant companions. Flies, fleas, and mosquitoes were a nuisance compared to the rats and lice. Rats, large and healthy looking, were attracted by the rotting bodies off which they fed. "Rat hunting" became a kind of trench sport, fought with spades, clubs, or whatever was handy. Lice were even more detested than the rats. Washing one's clothes or taking a bath was a rare luxury and of little defense against the lice that laid their eggs in the soldiers' clothing and multiplied with astonishing speed. A gas attack brought only temporary relief. Like the enemy across no man's land, the rats and lice always returned.

The generals, who conducted the war from positions well away from the front that any of them seldom, if ever, visited, did not know how to fight a war that became a stalemate. They hoped to break the stalemate on the Western Front and return to a war of motion, a war they could understand. The generals on both sides followed the same strategy. First, they bombarded the enemy trenches with an artillery barrage that lasted several days, in hopes of destroying the rows of barbed wire and to "soften up" the enemy. Then, when the artillery went silent, the infantrymen in the trenches were ordered to "go over the top" into a storm of machine gun fire that cut most of them down before they ever reached the enemy's frontline trenches. Almost invariably, the offensive failed, and the survivors fell back to their own trenches to await the usual counterattack. And so, it continued, again and again, without significantly altering the line of trenches, despite the tens, even hundreds, of thousands of casualties.

The war on the Western Front was, as one historian put it, "a war of the battering ram rather than the stiletto" (Palmer and Colton 1965, p. 673). The horse cavalry in brightly colored uniforms and armed with lances and sabers proved of little value charging into the face of machine-gun fire. After the Battle of the Marne and the stalemate of trench warfare on the Western Front, the war was fought mostly by the basic foot soldier, or infantryman. Airplanes played a minor role, mostly for reconnaissance until the last months of the war. Then the duels between fighter pilots added a bit of drama and romantic legend for the postwar period, but had little, if any, impact on the outcome of the war.

The experience of trench warfare was enough to change those who experienced it forever. Charles Delvert (1879–1940), a French veteran of the Battle of Verdun recorded the death of a colleague in his diary:

> The death of Jégoud was atrocious. He was on the first steps of the dugout when a shell (probably an Austrian 130) burst. His face was burned; one splinter entered his skull behind the ear; another slit open his stomach, broke his spine, and in the bloody mess one saw his spinal cord gliding about. His right leg was completely crushed above the knee. The most hideous part of it all was that he continued to live for four or five minutes. (Eksteins 1989, pp. 152–153)

Continuous exposure to such sights resulted in a numbness to the surrounding horror that helped the individual soldier to survive. Fritz Kreisler (1875–1962), an Austrian infantryman who survived the war to become a master violinist and composer, described it:

> A certain fierceness arises in you, an absolute indifference to anything the world holds except your duty of fighting. You are eating a crust of bread, and a man is shot in the trench next to you. You look calmly at him for a moment, and then go on eating your bread. Why not? There is nothing to be done. In the end you talk of your own death with as little excitement as you would of a luncheon engagement. (Eksteins 1989, p. 154)

Many of those who lost the ability to feel human emotion, to feel pity or fear, would be forever there in the trenches, never able to return to the life they knew before the war. They remained estranged from civilian life. Life in the trenches had to be experienced to be understood. Those who did not experience it could never really understand the veteran whose nights were filled with nightmares and whose days were filled with fear. If the civilians back home could somehow see it, wrote Wilfred Owen (1893–1918), one of England's greatest poets, who died one week before the Armistice, then

> My friend, you would not tell with such high zest,
> To children ardent for some desperate glory,
> The old Lie: Dulce et decorum est
> Pro patria mori.
> (Walter 2006, pp. 141–142)

("It is sweet and becoming to die for one's country," a quotation from the Roman poet Horace.)

Modern Weapons of War

Several new, modern weapons appeared during the Great War. The first ship sunk by a self-propelled torpedo fired from a submarine occurred on September 5, 1914, when the German U-boat *SM U-21* sunk the British light cruiser *HMS Pathfinder*. Germany declared the waters around Britain to be a war zone in which merchant ships would be sunk without warning. Unrestricted submarine warfare was suspended in September 1915, following protests and a warning from the United States after the sinking of the ocean liner, *Lusitania*, on May 7 off the southern coast of Ireland. Germany's renewal of unrestricted submarine attacks in January 1917 provided the justification for Woodrow Wilson's request for a declaration of war in April.

The first Zeppelins, cigar-shaped dirigible airships filled with flammable hydrogen gas, appeared over England in December 1914. At first, infantry shells dropped from the Zeppelins served as "bombs." Approximately 500 people were killed by 51 Zeppelin bombing raids during the war. Hence, they served as a psychological weapon, not as a weapon of mass destruction.

As with the Zeppelins, airplanes were initially used for reconnaissance. Quickly, however, pilots began dropping grenades and other objects on the enemy below and firing at enemy planes with pistols. The first plane equipped with a machine gun was French, flown by Louis Quenault (1892–1958) on October 5, 1914. During 1915, fighter planes were equipped with machine guns that fired bullets between the rotating propeller blades. Soon, fighter pilots were engaging in "dog fights" above the battlefields. A pilot with five "kills" was honored with the title "ace." Each country had its list of fighter aces, or knights of the air. The most famous ace of the Great War was the German, Manfred von Richthofen (1892–1918), the "Red Baron," who downed 80 enemy planes before being shot down and killed in April 1918.

Both the Allied and Central Powers engaged in strategic and revenge bombing during the war. At first, the pilots dropped the "bombs" by hand, using only their eyes to aim them. All sorts of aircraft were used. The first actual bomber airplane was the French Voisin III, a pusher (propeller in the back) biplane. In the autumn of 1916, the Germans developed the Gotha G.V. bomber, a biplane powered by two engines, with a wingspan over 77 ft. (23 m), and capable of carrying more than 1000 pounds (454 kg) of bombs. During May and June 1917, Gotha bombers made bombing raids on the English coastal town of Folkestone and London. Material damage was minimal, but the psychological impact was tremendous.

The first major gas attack was at the Second Battle of Ypres (April 22 May 24, 1915), when the Germans took advantage of favorable winds and released canisters of chlorine gas. There were three types of gas used by all the combatants during the war, chlorine, phosgene, and mustard. Phosgene was the gas of choice for the Allies. It was six times as deadly as chlorine. The victim did not know that he had received a fatal dose until a day or two after exposure, when his lungs began to fill with fluid, slowly suffocating him. An estimated 85% of deaths from gas during the war were due to phosgene gas. All of the combatants used chemical weapons, despite the fact that their use was classified as a war crime by international agreements in 1899 and 1907. Captain Harry S. Truman (1884–1972), who later became president of the United States, commanded an artillery unit that fired gas shells against the Germans in the last year of the war.

The armored tank developed out of the need to find a way to break the stalemate on the Western Front. Tanks, the generals hoped, would do what infantry charges and gas attacks failed to do. They could create a breach in the line of trenches through which the attack would advance, thus turning the stalemate into a war of motion. The first tanks were essentially a large armored box mounted on a tractor equipped with the recently invented caterpillar tracks.

The British were the first to deploy tanks on September 16, 1916, during the Battle of the Somme. They had only limited impact, though they did play a significant role in the final Allied offensives at the end of the war.

Apart from the machine gun, the most effective weapon of the Great War was not invented or developed as a result of the war. It was invented in the United States in 1874 as an aid to agriculture. It was barbed wire, used as a defensive weapon. Combined with the machine gun, barbed wire was a deadly obstacle for any infantry or cavalry charge. Trenches, machine guns, and barbed wire are the enduring nightmarish images of the Great War.

1915

The failure of the Schlieffen Plan led some among the civilian government in Berlin to conclude that the war was lost, and Germany should seek an armistice and a negotiated end to the war. As supreme warlord, the Kaiser could have followed their advice, but the generals, encouraged by victories on the Eastern Front, persuaded him that the war could be won. Wilhelm II basically abdicated leadership to his generals, Hindenburg and Ludendorff in particular.

On the Eastern Front in February 1915, the Russians suffered heavy losses in the Second Battle of Masurian Lakes. They were able to halt the German advance, but at the cost of between 56 000 and 92 000 casualties compared to 7500 for the Germans. The Austro-Hungarian advances during 1915 were unmitigated failures. An Austro-German offensive in April drove the Russians back into Poland. Warsaw fell to the Germans in August. The Russian casualties were so great that Tsar Nicholas II chose to take personal command of his armies in September, a decision that contributed to the Russian Revolution in 1917.

The Allies, acting on advice from Winston Churchill, First Lord of the Admiralty, committed a major blunder when they launched a poorly planned, poorly executed, and disastrous campaign aimed at opening the Dardanelles Straits and capturing Constantinople. Turkey joined the Central Powers in 1914, thus preventing the Western Allies from supplying the Russians. An Allied force of Australian, New Zealander, and French troops began landing on the shores of Sula Bay in present-day Turkey on August 8, 1915. They never got off the beaches. The Turks, who occupied the high ground rained shells down on the invaders, who suffered like ducks in a pound. Those who managed to survive were evacuated by mid-January 1916. Allied and Turkish losses amounted to roughly 250 000 each. It was a victory for the Turks. Winston Churchill resigned as First Lord of the Admiralty.

The Turks were of little help to the Germans, but the Austrians were not only of little help, but a burden as well. The Allies, too, found Italy's entry into the war on their side in May 1915 to be more of a burden than a resource. Bismarck once commented that the

Katholische Feldmesse und Abendmahlspendung.

vor der Schlacht in Russland, hinter Korkowo.

Zensiert
Paul Hoffmann & Co.
Berlin-Schöneberg.

N.V.E.
1226

Figure 14.2 A Roman Catholic priest celebrates Mass for German soldiers on the Eastern Front during the Great War. *Source:* From The New York Public Library.

Italians had a big appetite but not the teeth to match. Just as the Germans had to divert forces from the Western front to prevent an Austrian defeat on the Eastern front, so too did the Allies have to divert vital resources to the shore up Italians.

Sausage Machine: 1916

The image of trench warfare as a sausage machine, "because it was fed with live men, churned out corpses, and remained firmly screwed in place" (Davenport 2015), was an apt description of the major battles on the Western Front during 1916. Both sides attempted to end the stalemate by massing huge quantities of men and material along a small sector of the front, and then smashing through the enemy's line like a gigantic battering ram. Two battles in particular stand out as examples, the Battle of Verdun (February 22 to December 21) and the Battle of the Somme (July 1 to November 18).

The Germans opened the Battle of Verdun with the intent of bleeding the French to death by keeping the battle going. They reasoned that they could kill five French soldiers for every two German soldiers killed by the French. Verdun was of no strategic value to either side, but the German commander, General Erich von Falkenhayn (1861–1922) knew that the French would defend it at all costs. And they did. "They shall not pass," declared General Henri-Philippe Pétain (1856–1951), who defended Verdun. The Germans used

Die bei den Kämpfen
vor Verdun
gefangenen Franzosen werden mit
der Bahn weitertransportiert.

1417.
Zensiert
Paul Hoffmann & Co.
Berlin-Schöneberg.

Figure 14.3 French soldiers on their way to the Battle of Verdun. *Source:* From The New York Public Library.

flamethrowers and Storm Troops for the first time, and rained down two million artillery shells on Verdun and its surrounding forts. When the longest battle of the war finally ended, more than 250 000 had died and another million plus were wounded. The casualties were roughly the same for both sides.

If the Battle of Verdun was the longest battle of the war, the Battle of the Somme was the bloodiest. The British began the battle with a seven-day-and-night bombardment of the German trenches using 1500 artillery pieces along a 23-mile front. They fired four million rounds on the first day alone. The Allied commander, Sir Douglas Haig (1861–1925), believed that the artillery bombardment would break-up the rows of barbed wire and destroy or bury the German trenches. With the battle effectively won when the artillery ceased firing, the infantry, and possibly even cavalry, would move in to "mop up" whatever resistance remained. Once again, the strategy failed.

The German machine gunners went underground and waited. Once the Allied artillery stopped firing, they came out of their bunkers, set up their machine guns, and waited for the Allied infantry attack that followed. The British and French infantrymen were ordered to attack in formation carrying 66 pounds of equipment each. The slaughter that ensued challenges the imagination. It was the highest casualty rate in modern warfare, with the British suffering 60 000 casualties, including 40% of their officer corps, on the first day. A total of more than one and a quarter million men were sacrificed in the battle, and when it was over, the lines remained unchanged.

The only major naval battle of the war took place on May 31 and June 1, 1916, off the coast of Denmark's Jutland Peninsula. Germany's decision to build a high seas fleet was one of the major long-term causes of the war. Except for the Battle of Jutland, it remained in port, ostensibly to protect the German coastline. The battle between the German High Seas Fleet and the British Grand Navy was indecisive. British losses in ships and men was greater than the German losses, but the German High Seas Fleet returned to port and did not venture out to sea again during the war.

Romania entered the war on the side of the Allies in August, having been promised territorial gains at the expense of Austria-Hungary. Franz Joseph, who came to the Hapsburg throne in December 1848, died on November 21, 1916 after a 68-year reign. His successor, Karl I (1887–1922), sought without success to end the war. In Britain, David Lloyd George replaced David Asquith (1852–1928) as prime minister. Perhaps of greater significance for the future was the election of Woodrow Wilson as president of the United States.

Home Front

None of the nations that fought in the Great War were prepared for a long war. As noted earlier, a modern war between industrialized countries becomes a war of attrition, a "total war," in which victory goes to the side best able to organize its resources. Factories had to be retooled to produce the needed armament and other products needed to prosecute the war. That, in turn, meant that the factories had to be supplied with the raw materials and workers that they needed to meet the demand. There had to be peace between labor and management, so that strikes did not occur. The role of women in the war effort on the home front required rethinking the role of women in general. All such issues, and many more, required governments to expand their role in regulating the economic life of their countries.

Because Germany was blockaded and, therefore, denied access to vital raw materials, it was the first to mobilize its resources and, also, the most successful. The Auxiliary Service Law of 1916 placed all males between the ages of 17 and 60 at the disposal of the war effort. Germany's prewar leadership in the natural sciences proved beneficial when it became necessary to develop substitute and, in some cases, synthetically produced products.

Germany's ally, Austria-Hungary, found it difficult to bring organization to such a multinational empire. In addition to the competition between the two halves of the Dual Monarchy for limited supplies of food and other resources, there was the ever-present problem of diverse languages, varying legalities and customs governing the relationship between the various parts of the empire and the government in Vienna or Budapest, and the general backwardness of a medieval-like dynastic empire. The multinational nature of the Hapsburg empire made it easy for allied propaganda to undermine the war effort, especially after President Wilson issued his Fourteen Points.

Russia was the only one of the belligerents that never organized its home front. Any effort to coordinate the home front so as to bring together resources and solve the problems of supply and distribution that plagued Russia was viewed by Nicholas II and his government as an effort to introduce reform and revolutionary change, thereby undermining the autocracy. Crops rotted in the fields while citizens in the cities went hungry, simply because there was no person or agency to figure a means whereby scarce railroad stock could be used to transport soldiers and armaments to the front and food to the cities. Soldiers went into battle without rifles, because no one allocated raw materials and manpower to the factories. The suffering on the Russian home front due to such ineptness was a major cause of the Russian Revolution in 1917.

Britain and France both benefitted from the fact that they could draw upon their empires for material and manpower resources. Both enjoyed access to the enormous resources from the United States. Despite loudly proclaiming its neutrality, the United States favored the Allies from the beginning of the war. As Allied war debts in the United States increased, so too did America's interest in an Allied victory.

A Ministry of Munitions was created in Britain in July 1915 to allocate resources and men and monitor the level of profits from the manufacture of arms. Control of the munitions industry meant increased government regulation of the entire economy. The French government had extensive authority to commandeer resources in time of war, a tradition going back to the French Revolution. Everywhere, the increased role of government in the regulation of the economy was one of the most important legacies of the Great War.

Once the United States entered the war on the side of the Allies, the American government began a massive mobilization of both the economy and its citizens. A military force of almost five million men was raised through both a military draft and volunteer enlistments. The War Industries Board was created and charged with aiding private industry to produce for the war effort by, for example, assuring peace between labor and management so as to maintain high levels of industrial output. President Wilson created the United States Food Administration to oversee agricultural production. Farmers were assured of a fair price for what they produced. Various programs were created to encourage citizens to conserve food and other resources for the war effort. Domestic food consumption was reduced by 15%, agricultural yield increased by 25%, and exports to the Allies was increased more than threefold.

The total war effort required the mobilization of civilians. All of the nations at war introduced conscription to assure adequate fighting forces, and also to ensure that skilled workers remained in the factories. Women found employment opportunities not available before, as they filled positions left vacant by men serving in the armed forces. Both organized labor and women benefitted after the war from their cooperation and contributions to the war effort. There was an increased acceptance of worker's rights in general and trade unions and collective bargaining in particular. Likewise, it became harder after the war to resist the demand for women's suffrage.

Propaganda aimed at shoring up support for the war at home appealed to patriotism while demonizing the enemy. Atrocity stories about the enemy, often false or exaggerated, helped to transform the war into a moral crusade against evil and for justice. Opposition to the war on moral or other grounds was viewed as treasonous. Legislation such as the Defense of the Realm Act (1914) in Britain and the Espionage and Sedition Acts (1917 and 1918) in the United States empowered governments to suppress public dissent and impose censorship on the press, while at the same time, openly and "legally" violating the citizens's civil liberties.

In France, newspaper editors were drafted for publishing negative reports on the war or, in at least one case, executed for treason. In the United States, any criticism of the military, government, or even the American flag, became a federal offense, punishable by fines, imprisonment, or even death. Fear and hysteria increased in all of the warring nations as the war continued, producing a reaction that often called into question the very ideals they were fighting and dying to guarantee.

War around the World

Not all of the battles of the Great War were fought in Europe. Britain, France, Germany, and the United States possessed territories overseas and major naval forces. Russia stretched from eastern Europe to the Pacific Ocean. The Ottoman Empire had at least nominal control over much of the Middle East. The nature of modern industrial war meant that vital natural resources from outside Europe were even more important. Oil, in particular, became a vital strategic resource, thus making the fate of the Ottoman Empire a major concern.

The war with the Ottoman Empire was largely a British affair. A key part of British strategy was to incite an Arab revolt against the Turks. Colonel T. E. Lawrence (1888–1935), a British army intelligence officer serving in Cairo, Egypt in 1914, was instrumental in organizing and leading an Arab revolt against the Ottoman Turks. British General Edmund Allenby (1861–1936) captured Jerusalem in December 1917, and Damascus in October 1918.

British strategy in the Middle East created instability that remains in the twenty-first century. The Arab revolt was purchased with a promise to Sharif Hussein bin Ali of Mecca (1853–1949) of support for the establishment of an independent Arab state after the war. Shariff Hussein understood that to mean all of the Arab lands under Turkish rule, including Palestine.

At the same time, the British sought support from the Jewish people by promising to secure in Palestine as a national home for the Jews. The promise to the Jewish people was made by British Foreign Minister Arthur James Balfour (1848–1930), and is known as the Balfour Declaration. Both promises to the Arab and Jewish people were just that, promises. The British did not intend to honor either commitment. On May 19, 1916, the British and French concluded what is called the Sykes-Picot Agreement, in which they agreed to divide between them the Arab lands of the Ottoman Empire. The truth was that the European leaders did not envision a postwar world outside Europe significantly different from that before 1914. As they conspired to increase their overseas empires, they did not foresee that they were arousing nationalist feelings among the colonial people that would later destroy their empires.

Both Africa and Asia played bit parts in the war drama. When the war started, Japan declared war on Germany on August 21, 1914. As an ally of Britain since 1902, Japan was able to seize German possessions in China and some islands in the Pacific Ocean. New Zealand took control of German Samoa, while Australia took German New Guinea following a brief skirmish. The German colonies in Africa were quickly seized by Britain and France with one exception, German East Africa.

German East Africa was defended by a small mixed force of German and African (Askari) soldiers under the command of Colonel (later General) Paul Emil von Lettow-Vorbeck

(1870–1964). Lettow-Vorbeck's small army conducted a guerilla war against the British from November 1914 until he surrendered undefeated in November 1918, two weeks after the end of the war in Europe.

Year of Decision: 1917

At the beginning of 1917, both the Allies and the Central Powers were exhausted, but neither was willing to concede defeat or agree to a negotiated peace. The military leaders on both sides felt that it was still possible to snatch victory from defeat. Thus, both rebuffed overtures from President Wilson to arbitrate as President Roosevelt had done in the Russo-Japanese War. Just two weeks after Wilson announced his Fourteen Points (January 8, 1918) as a basis for peace negotiations, Germany and Austria-Hungary declined a joint American-British peace proposal.

From the beginning, it was almost certain that the United States would eventually enter the war and do so on the side of the Allies. There were many historical ties between the United States and the Allies that encouraged sympathy for the Allied cause among Americans. Despite the American Revolution, many Americans still looked upon England as the homeland. It was France, through its support of the American cause, that made American independence possible. And it was France that gave the Statue of Liberty to the American people, forever symbolizing the love of liberty shared by the two nations. Most important was the role played by President Woodrow Wilson.

Wilson was a very complex person, but like the German Kaiser and the Russian Tsar, he was a deeply flawed man, woefully unequal to the challenges he faced in foreign affairs, especially when it came to the war in Europe. Wilson had very little knowledge, and no real understanding, of European history or the challenges presented by the war. He suffered from personality flaws that had deep roots in lifelong physical illnesses and psychological traumas. He was a supreme egotist, who saw himself as the one person called by God to usher in a new age of world peace and justice. His vision of himself and his mission was, writes historian G. J. Meyer, "an expression of his egotism, his vision of himself as *the* indispensable man, *the* one voice able to speak for the freedom-loving people not only of the United States but of the world" (Meyer 2016, p. 9).

Wilson used Germany's renewal of unrestricted submarine warfare on January 31, 1917 as justification for America's entering the war on the side of the Allies as an "associated power," not an ally. He insisted from the beginning that the United States was merely defending the right of a neutral power to trade with either side in the conflict without interference. But the United States never behaved as a neutral power. After the sinking of the *Lusitania* in 1915, Secretary of State William Jennings Bryan (1860–1925) advised Wilson that the United States should pursue a policy of true neutrality, rather than, as was the case, favoring the Allies. Wilson ignored Bryan's advice. Bryan resigned, becoming the first person of such rank in American history to resign his position on moral grounds.

The United States was the chief financier for the Allies. As the war progressed, the Allies became increasingly dependent upon the United States for both food and war material. The necessary supplies were paid for partly through loans to the Allies from American banks. The Wilson administration encouraged such loans, while discouraging loans to Germany

(Spykman 1929, p. 156). By April 1917, the Allies were nearing the end of their financial resources. To ensure that American investors would not lose their investments due to a German victory, it was necessary for the United States to enter the war, and, as Wilson put it in his message to Congress on April 2, grant the Allies "the most liberal credits, in order that the resources of the United States might so far as possible be added to theirs" (Spykman 1929).

The argument for America's entry on the side of the Allies was made all the more plausible by three events that caused a shift in American public opinion. First was the German decision on January 31 to renew unrestricted submarine warfare, followed by the sinking of the American merchant ship *Housatonic* on February 3 by the German submarine *U-53*. The *Housatonic* was carrying supplies to Britain, and although the captain of *U-53*, before sinking it, allowed all of its crew off into lifeboats and towed them to safety, Americans were outraged by the violation of their nation's "neutrality."

Second was the so-called Zimmermann telegram. British naval intelligence intercepted a telegram from German foreign minister, Arthur Zimmermann (1864–1940), to the German envoy in Mexico, suggesting a possible alliance between Germany and Mexico. The telegram was sent on January 19. President Wilson learned of its content on February 26. On the following day, he proposed arming American ships and authorized the State Department to make the telegram public. The text of the telegram appeared on the front pages of newspapers all across the country on March 1. The resulting impact on American public opinion was predictable.

The third event was the outbreak of revolution in Russia during March 1917.[1] The Russian Revolution occurred in two phases; one could say that there were really two revolutions. The first occurred in March. It toppled the Tsarist autocracy and resulted, temporarily, in a constitutional Provisional Government. The Provisional Government was formed by former deputies of the Duma, a representative assembly suspended by the Tsar in September 1915, when he went to the front to take personal command of his armies. The fact that the members of the Duma were elected, though by a very restricted franchise, became the Provisional Government's claim to legitimacy.

The Provisional Government was overthrown in November, which marked the beginning of the second phase. It was led by the Bolsheviks, a radical faction within the Petrograd Soviet. The Petrograd Soviet was made up of delegates who were elected by individual soviets, or local governmental councils, of workers, soldiers, or sailors. They claimed to be the legitimate government on the basis of having been elected by the people. From the beginning, the Petrograd Soviet issued decrees of its own and countermanded decrees of the Provisional Government.

The Provisional Government failed for a variety of reasons, three in particular. First, it came to power because of the Tsar's failure to organize the home front. Increasing suffering on the part of the Russian people, together with continuous failure at the front, undermined historic support for the Tsar as God's ordained ruler of Russia. The Provisional Government, likewise, failed to take immediate and concrete measures to end the chaos.

---

1 The Julian calendar was 13 days behind the Gregorian calendar in use in the West. Hence the two-parts of the Russian Revolution are sometimes referred to as the "February" and "October" revolutions.

A second cause of the Provisional Government's failure was ideological in nature. The Provisional Government was a coalition of liberals committed to defending civil liberties, who felt that they did not have the authority to make any fundamental changes in Russian society until an elected Constituent Assembly met and drafted a constitution that defined the government's authority. Until such time, the Provisional Government saw itself as just that, "provisional," the transitory caretaker of national sovereignty. It simply failed to understand that the first responsibility of any government is to govern. Rather than address the demands of the masses, the Provisional Government committed a third, and fatal blunder, when it decided to continue the war, and even launched a new offensive in July. Opposition to continuing the war was widespread and very vocal.

It was Vladimir Ilyich Lenin (1870–1924), who recognized that extracting Russia from the war was necessary for a second revolution led by the Bolsheviks. Lenin was living in exile in Switzerland, when the March revolution occurred. Aware of his opposition to the war, the German military leaders facilitated Lenin's return to Russia, together with 31 other prominent Bolsheviks. Upon his arrival in Petrograd on April 16, Lenin published his "April Thesis," calling for immediate peace, a transfer of government authority to the Soviets, and a nationalization of land. The All-Russian Conference of Soviets of Workers' and Soldiers' Deputies adopted Lenin's program. Support for the Bolsheviks grew, while support for the Provisional Government declined.

The planned Russian offensive began on July 1. The Germans launched a counterattack on July 19, resulting in the rapid disintegration of the Russian army as an effective fighting force. Russian soldiers began deserting in large numbers. Lenin correctly observed that, "The army voted for peace with its feet."

Chaos ensued in Russia. Anarchy was the order of the day. The absence of any meaningful authority structure left the masses demanding order and change without anywhere to direct their demands. The opportunity to take charge lay open to anyone who could control the energy of the masses. Lenin seized the opportunity. He called for the immediate seizure of power, a second revolution, at a secret meeting of the Executive Committee of the Bolshevik faction of the Petrograd Soviet.

Lenin's call for a Bolshevik coup was approved by the Central Committee. The coup took place on November 7 (October 25 of the old calendar), 1917. There was only minor resistance. The transition of government authority was accepted in the cities and at the front. At most, a "wait and see" attitude prevailed where confusion had reigned.

The Constituent Assembly, elected in November following the Bolshevik coup, convened on January 18, 1918. The Bolsheviks were outnumbered with only 168 delegates out of a total of 703. The day was spent in debates that did not favor the Bolsheviks. Only minutes before five o'clock in the afternoon, the lights in the hall went out and the delegates left. The following day, Lenin formally dissolved the Constituent Assembly. What many hoped would mark the end of autocracy and beginning of constitutional government ended with the dawn of a new form of authoritarian government, one that demanded more than just obedience. Marxism-Leninism demanded a "born again" true believer, hence the term "totalitarianism."

End of the War: 1918

Though both the Allies and Central Powers were exhausted at the beginning of 1918, Germany was in a position to win. The new Bolshevik government in Russia asked for an armistice on December 5, 1917. Germany's demands were extensive. The Treaty of Brest-Litovsk, signed on March 3, 1918, required Russia to abandon Poland, the Ukraine, the Baltic provinces, Finland, and Transcaucasia. Russia lost major portions of its industrial capacity and food-raising capabilities. It was a substantial, but necessary sacrifice. Civil War broke out between the Reds and the Whites in Russia following the dismissal of the Constituent Assembly. The Whites were supported by the Allies, the United States, and Japan. Only by ending the war with Germany could the new Bolshevik government win the civil war.

Victory on the Eastern Front allowed Germany to transfer troops from there to the Western Front, where the final outcome of the Great War would be decided. Prospects for a German victory were enhanced further by delivering a crushing defeat to the Italians at the Battle of Caporetto (October 24 – November 19, 1917). Also, it was still questionable if the immense resources of the United States, then available to the Allies, would arrive in time to save them from defeat.

Germany launched its last major offensive on March 21, taking the Allies by surprise. The war became once again a war of motion, as the German army advanced to within 75 miles (120.7 km) of Paris by March 23. They began to bombard Paris, using the so-called "Paris Gun" (a.k.a., the "Williams Gun"), the largest artillery piece of the Great War. Between May 27 and June 6, the Germans advanced to within 37 miles (59.5 km) of Paris. People were fleeing from Paris, and, as in 1914, the French government made preparations to leave the capital. Time, however, was running out for Germany.

France was saved from defeat by the appearance of 355 thousand British troops and the arrival of an American force of 2 million. Buttressed by nine divisions of fresh American soldiers, the Allies launched a counteroffensive. On August 8, the British army began the "Hundred Day Offensive," assisted by 450 tanks. The trench war was over. It was once again a war of motion. The German lines began to crack. Ludendorff called August 8, "the black day" of the German army. The Germans retreated to the Siegfried Line (a.k.a., the Hindenburg Line), a defensive line from Arras to Laffaux in northern France.

Facing imminent military defeat, and fearful of a "revolution from below" as had occurred in Russia, Ludendorff and Hindenburg informed the Kaiser on September 29, that the war was lost, and Germany must seek an immediate armistice. Wilhelm II appointed his cousin, the liberal Prince Max von Baden (1867–1929), chancellor. The Prince asked Wilson for an armistice as a preliminary to a peace conference to negotiate a settlement on the basis of Wilson's Fourteen Points.

With Germany's allies already suing for peace, and with a mutiny among the sailors at Kiel, the Kaiser yielded to advice from Hindenburg and abdicated on November 9. At the request of the British royal family, he was granted exile in the Netherlands. Two days later, at 5 a.m., a German delegation signed the armistice. In accordance with the terms of the agreement, the fighting stopped at 11:00 a.m. on November 11, 1918. At long last, it was "all quiet on the Western Front."

References

Craig, G.A. (1978). *Germany, 1866–1945*. New York: Oxford University Press.

Davenport, M.J. (2015). *First over There: the Attack on Cantigny, Americas First Battle of World War I*. New York: Thomas Dunne Books, St. Martins Press.

Eksteins, M. (1989). *Rites of Spring: The Great War and the Birth of the Modern Age*. New York: Doubleday.

Meyer, G.J. (2016). *The World Remade: America in World War I*. New York: Bantam.

Palmer, R.R. and Colton, J. (1965). *A History of the Modern World*, 3e. New York: A.A. Knopf.

Richards, M.D. (1982). *Europe, 1900–1980 a Brief History*. St. Louis, MO: Forum Press.

Spykman, N.J. (1929). The United States and the Allied Debts. Max-Planck-Institut Für Ausländisches öffentliches Recht Und Völkerrecht. http://www.zaoerv.de/01_1929/1_1929_1_a_155_184.pdf (accessed 21 October 2019).

Walter, G. (ed.) (2006). *The Penguin Book of First World War Poetry*. London: Penguin Books.

15

Peace and Disillusionment

Chronology

1907	Picasso's *Les Demoiselles d'Avignon*
1915	*The Birth of a Nation* Premiers, First Blockbuster Film
1917	Marcel Duchamp's *Fountain*
1917	Woodrow Wilson's "Peace Without Victory" Speech
1918–1919	Worldwide Flu Pandemic
1919	Paris Peace Conference
1919	Treaty of Versailles Signed
1919	John Maynard Keynes' *The Economic Consequences of the Peace*
1919	League of Nations Charter Signed
1919	United States Senate Voted Against the Versailles Treaty
1920	KDKA in Pittsburgh, Pennsylvania is the First Licensed Radio Station
1920	Otto Dix's *Match-seller*
1922	James Joyce's *Ulysses*
1922	T.S. Eliot's *The Waste Land*
1923	Käthe Kollwitz's *Germany's Children are starving!*
1925	F. Scott's Fitzgerald's *The Great Gatsby*
1925	*Revue nègre* With Josephine Baker Introduces Jazz to Europe
1928	Bertolt Brecht's *The Threepenny Opera*
1928	D.H. Lawrence's *Lady Chatterley's Lover*
1931	Salvador Dali's *The Persistence of Memory*
1935	Christopher Isherwood's *The Last of Mr. Norris*
1939	Christopher Isherwood's *Goodbye to Berlin*

After the guns were silenced on November 11, 1918, the task of constructing a peace settlement began. The last such meeting of the Great Powers following an extended period of war was in 1815. The diplomats who met in Vienna in 1815 represented monarchies. They represented, and answered to, their sovereigns. They were free to make decisions on the basis of what would result in a just and lasting peace. They did not have to consider a public opinion shaped by years of state-sponsored propaganda. They did not have to return

Western Civilization: A Brief History, First Edition. Paul R. Waibel.
© 2020 John Wiley & Sons, Inc. Published 2020 by John Wiley & Sons, Inc.

home to win elections. Hence, the defeated and the victors met together to achieve a common goal: peace.

That was not the case in 1919. The peacemakers of 1919 represented constitutional states. They had to answer to a public who had suffered four long years of industrialized warfare, who had been subjected to a constant bombardment of propaganda aimed at demonizing the enemy, not only their governments, but their citizens as well. Citizens of the victorious nations expected that the evil enemy should suffer for, as they were taught to believe, causing the most destructive war in Western history.

The victorious European Allies were exhausted by the war. They were victorious only because a new, non-European great power, intervened on their behalf, thus assuring defeat of the Central Powers. The United States of America emerged from the Great War as the only country untouched, even strengthened, by the war. It was understandable, that having effectively determined the outcome of the war, the United States should play a pivotal role in shaping the peace settlement.

Unfortunately, President Woodrow Wilson, himself, chose to go to Paris rather than leaving negotiations to the diplomats. Wilson's role at the peace conference proved to be an obstacle to constructing a just peace. Just as the entrance of the United States into the war assured the defeat of the Central Powers, Wilson's influence at the peace conference contributed to its failure.

Paris Peace Conference: 1919

The victors gathered at Louis XIV's grand palace of Versailles just outside Paris on November 18, 1919 to draft a peace settlement that would mark the end of the Great War and assure peace for the future. A spirit of idealism was present, that is, among those who were victorious. Germany and its allies were not included. This was not to be a negotiated peace, such as previous attempts – Westphalia (1648), Utrecht (1713), and Vienna (1815) – to guarantee future peace after major wars. This was to be a victors's peace, a settlement based on two fallacious assumptions. First was the belief that Germany alone was to blame for the war. Second was the premise that future peace in Europe and the world required the destruction of Germany as a great power.

Germany requested, and agreed to, an armistice in November 1918, on the basis of Wilson's 14 Points. The armistice would halt the fighting, so that a peace conference, similar to that which followed the Napoleonic Wars, could meet and restore the balance of power. But such was not the intent of the victors. The terms of the armistice were such that Germany was rendered unable to resume fighting, if it did not accept the terms of the peace settlement. Germany was required to withdraw from all occupied territory on both the Western and Eastern Fronts in Europe and withdraw its forces on the Western Front to a specified distance east of the Rhine River. It was to disarm, meaning surrender all military vehicles, railroad stock, submarines, and naval vessels. Perhaps most indicative of the future nature of the peace settlement drafted by the victors was the continuation of the blockade of Germany until the treaty was completed and signed.

None of the Central Powers (Germany, Austria-Hungary, Turkey, or Bulgaria) were included. Neither was Russia, one of the original Allies. Russia was in the midst of a civil war between the Reds, as the forces of the new Bolshevik government were called, and the Whites, who claimed to be fighting for restoration of the constituent assembly but were perceived by the people to be fighting for restoration of the Tsarist autocracy. Which side would emerge victorious in the civil war and become the legitimate government of a new Russia remained to be seen. Until then, the Allies and the United States were committed to not recognizing the Bolshevik government. Indeed, they intervened on the side of the Whites.

As seen earlier in Chapter 10, the diplomats at the Vienna Congress were guided in their deliberations by the three principles of balance of power, legitimacy, and compensation. The only guiding principle at the Paris Peace Conference was the desire to present a united front to the defeated powers. There was no agreement among the peacemakers on what the post-peace conference world should look like. In fact, what each of the peacemakers desired was often at odds with what their colleagues wanted. Every decision, therefore, had to be a political compromise between idealism and realism, between what one knew was necessary for a lasting peace and what one's countrymen, conditioned by four years of wartime propaganda, expected.

The peace conference became a contest between new-world idealism represented by Woodrow Wilson and old-world realism represented by Georges Clemenceau. David Lloyd George found himself attempting to mediate between the two adversaries, or as he put it, do the best he could "considering I was seated between Jesus Christ and Napoleon" (Pettinger 2013). Vittorio Orlando (1860–1952), the fourth member of the "Big Four," as they were called, played a very minor role. His primary objective was to secure, for Italy, those territories promised by Britain and France in the 1915 Treaty of London. When Clemenceau and Lloyd George joined Wilson in denying what Orlando felt were Italy's just claims, he left Paris and did not return until May. "When … I knew they would not give us what we were entitled to," Orlando later said, "…I writhed on the floor. I knocked my head against the wall. I cried. I wanted to die" (ITALY: Last of the Big Four 1952). Such theatrics prompted Clemenceau to dub Orlando "The Weeper" (Ibid. 1952).

Georges Clemenceau, called "The Tiger" for his efforts to impose as harsh a treaty as possible on Germany, was a seasoned statesman. He supported the Paris Commune in 1871, and as a Radical Republican deputy in the National Assembly at Bordeaux, he vowed to avenge the humiliation of France by Prussia in the Franco-Prussian War. He twice witnessed Germany's invasion of France, and was, therefore, convinced in his own mind that France's future security could only be guaranteed if Germany was rendered unable to ever again disturb the peace of Europe.

David Lloyd George was a leader of Britain's Liberal Party who served as Chancellor of the Exchequer from 1908 to 1915. A pacifist in 1914, he quickly became a leader of Britain's war effort following the German invasion of Belgium. He was appointed Minister of Munitions in 1915 in charge of organizing the British economy to support a long war. In December 1916, Lloyd George became Prime Minister of a coalition government, a post he continued to hold until October 1922. At the peace conference, he was a pragmatist, focused on defending and expanding the interest of the British Empire.

Woodrow Wilson arrived at the conference, "as a latter-day Savior from the New World," notes historian A.J.P. Taylor, "convinced of his own intellectual superiority and righteousness" (Taylor [1966b], *From Sarajevo to Potsdam*, pp. 62, 45). Armed with his 14

Points, he was Don Quixote mounted on Rocinante, his noble steed, ready to battle the tainted leaders of the Old World and set the world aright. The Europeans who had no personal knowledge of the American president, cheered him, but those who met him, or had firsthand knowledge of his personality, had a different opinion. George V (1865–1936) told a friend after meeting Wilson: "I could not bear him" (Winter 1996, p. 340). In the eyes of the European leaders with whom Wilson had to negotiate, he appeared totally disconnected from the real world of 1919. Lloyd George later recalled:

> I really think that at first the idealistic President regarded himself as a missionary whose function it was to rescue the poor European heathen from their age-long worship of false and fiery gods. He was apt to address us in that vein, beginning with a few simple and elementary truths about right being more important than might, and justice being more eternal than force. (*Ibid.* 1996, p. 339)

It was not only the other members of the Big Four who found Wilson difficult to bear. At one point in the negotiations, the South African and Australian delegates refused Wilson's request that they give up the German colonies, which they had seized during the war. Wilson said to William Morris Hughes (1862–1952), Australia's Prime Minister: "Is Australia prepared to defy the appeal of the whole civilized world?" After adjusting his hearing aid, Hughes replied with a smile: "That's about the size of it, President Wilson" (Taylor [1966a], *A History of the First World War*, p. 169).

Back home, Wilson's support was waning. He became the Democratic candidate for President in 1912, only after 46 ballots and with the support of William Jennings Bryan, the "Peerless Leader" of the progressive forces in the Democratic Party. He was nominated because a majority of tired delegates agreed that he was the least unobjectionable of the options presented to them. He was elected only because the popular hero of the Spanish-American War and former President, Theodore Roosevelt, bolted the Republican Party and ran as a third-party candidate. Wilson was re-elected in 1916, because he promised to keep America out of the war in Europe.

Woodrow Wilson was born in Virginia, the son of a prominent Presbyterian minister and theologian who was wholly committed to the Confederate cause during the Civil War. The elder Wilson instilled in his son, not only an admiration for the antebellum South, but a belief in the Calvinist doctrines of divine providence and predestination. Evidence of the hold that Southern culture held over Wilson throughout his life can be seen in his comment after viewing with members of his cabinet D.W. Griffith's film, "Birth of a Nation." "It's like writing history with lightning," he supposedly said. "And my only regret is that it is all terribly true" (The Unfortunate Effects 2017). The film version of Thomas Dixon Jr.'s novel, *The Clansman* (1905), is a fantasy tale of the founding of the Ku Klux Klan and its role in "redeeming" the South from the burden of Reconstruction.

Wilson was a man of contradictions, much like that other famous Virginian, Thomas Jefferson, who wrote the Declaration of Independence which includes the famous line: "We hold these truths to be self-evident: that all men are created equal; that they are endowed by their Creator with certain unalienable rights; that among these are life, liberty, and the pursuit of happiness." But Jefferson was also a slave owner, who bought and sold human beings as property and fathered children by one of his slaves.

Figure 15.1 President Woodrow Wilson in Paris attending the peace conference in 1919.
Source: Library of Congress Prints and Photographs Division.

As a nineteenth-century liberal, Wilson believed in the innate goodness and perfectibility of human beings. His 14 Points were not simply high-sounding words on paper. He believed that well-meaning leaders could meet around the conference table and construct a just peace, if they were guided by the abstract principles proclaimed by Jefferson in the Declaration of Independence and other of his writings. At the same time, like Jefferson, he never really desired a fundamental change in the political or social structure of society. He could not bring himself to make the concessions necessary to see his principles become reality. In the end, his idealism was an illusion that deceived even him.

In his epic, *The Oxford History of the American People* (1965), Samuel Eliot Morison records a conversation between Wilson and Clemenceau regarding Wilson's belief that the creation of a League of Nations would prevent future wars. Clemenceau told Wilson that future wars could only be prevented if all could agree to, and include in the League charter, three basic principles, racial equality, freedom of immigration, and free trade. Wilson responded that he could not agree to, or accept, any of the three. To include racial equality would result in the Southern and Western senators rejecting the treaty. Congress was determined to ban Orientals from immigrating to the United States. And Congress would never agree to free trade between the United States and Europe, Asia, or Africa. "Very well, then;" Clemenceau replied, "the only way to maintain peace is to remain strong ourselves and keep our past and potential enemies weak. No conceivable League of Nations can do that" (Morison 1965, p. 877). Wilson repeatedly compromised on his 14 Points in an effort to win support for his beloved League of Nations. Whatever flaws in the treaty with Germany that he was forced to accept, he felt could later be corrected through the League of Nations.

The Treaty of Versailles with Germany was presented to the German delegation on May 7 and signed on June 28, five years to the date from the assassination of the Archduke in Sarajevo. The ceremony took place in the Hall of Mirrors, where on January 18, 1871, the German Empire was proclaimed. Individual treaties were signed between September 1919 and August 1920 with the other former members of the Central Powers. The Versailles Treaty required Germany to surrender all of its overseas colonies, and 13% of Germany, itself, which contained between 6.5 and 7 million people. The port city of Danzig (Gdansk) with a mostly German population became a Free City. A strip of territory linking the newly created state of Poland with the port city of Danzig was given to Poland, thus cutting off East Prussia from the rest of Germany. Other territorial adjustments included surrender of Alsace-Lorraine to France, French control of the industrial area of the Saar for 15 years, and minor portions of territory given to Belgium, Denmark, and Poland. Some were subject to the outcome of future plebiscites. The area west of the Rhine River, and a strip of territory 50 km (31 miles) deep along the east bank of the Rhine, were to be "demilitarized." Allied troops were to occupy the west bank for 15 years.

The military terms of the treaty were harsh. Germany was allowed an army limited to 100 000 volunteers (no conscription), no paramilitary groups, no air force, a small navy without submarines, and specified limits on certain weapons and other military equipment. Also, the General Staff was to be dissolved, and the army limited to only 4000 officers. The two articles of the treaty considered most unjust by the German people were the requirement that Germany accept full responsibility for the war and pay the total cost of the war. The former, Article 231, provided the legal basis for the reparations demanded, the total amount of which was to be decided later.

The Paris Peace Settlement in general, and particularly the Treaty of Versailles with Germany, was correctly characterized as a "Carthaginian Peace" by John Maynard Keynes, a member of the British delegation and one of the most influential economists of the twentieth century. His book, *The Economic Consequences of the Peace*, published in December 1919, proved to be one of the most devastating indictments of the Versailles Treaty. Keynes resigned his post with the British delegation in protest. In his letter of resignation to David Lloyd George he predicted that the treaty would lead to "the devastation of Europe."

> If we aim at the impoverishment of Central Europe, vengeance, I dare say, will not limp. Nothing can then delay for very long the forces of Reaction and the despairing

convulsions of Revolution, before which the horrors of the later German war will fade into nothing, and which will destroy, whoever is victor, the civilisation and the progress of our generation. (Keynes 1919)

Perhaps no one provided a better epitaph for the Versailles Treaty than Woodrow Wilson, himself, nearly 18 months earlier in his "Peace Without Victory" speech, before a joint session of Congress on January 22, 1917.

> Victory would mean peace forced upon the loser, a victor's terms imposed upon the vanquished. It would be accepted in humiliation, under duress, at an intolerable sacrifice, and would leave a sting, a resentment, a bitter memory upon which terms of peace would rest, not permanently, but only as upon quicksand. Only a peace between equals can last. (First World War 2008)

The greatest tragedy of Woodrow Wilson's career was that by leading the United States into the war and thereby ensuring an Allied victory, he made "a peace without victory" impossible to achieve (Kazin 2014). Unlike the Vienna Peace of 1815, that was hammered out by both the victors and the defeated determined to draft a just peace that would last, the Paris Peace of 1919 was a dictated peace that merely provided a 20-year ceasefire. The French poet Romain Roland (1866–1944) wrote in his diary on June 23, 1919: "Sad peace! Laughable interlude between the massacres of peoples" (Richards and Waibel 2014, p. 89).

League of Nations

The League of Nations Covenant was included in all five of the treaties that made up the Paris Peace Settlement. There was a General Assembly in which each member had one vote. The Council was made up of the wartime Allies (Britain, France, Italy, and Japan), minus Russia. An additional four (later nine) members were elected by the General Assembly to serve three-year terms on the Council. The Permanent Secretariat, headed by the Secretary General, who was appointed by the Council with approval of the General Assembly, was in charge of the day-to-day business of the League.

The League did not have any executive or legislative powers, since it was meant to be an open forum where arbitration of international disputes could take place. A Permanent Court of International Justice was established at The Hague in the Netherlands. The headquarters of the League and the meeting place of the General Assembly was located in Geneva, Switzerland.

With the benefit of historical hindsight, it is easy to argue that the League never had any realistic chance of succeeding. No one really wanted such a "parliament of man." The European powers saw it mainly as a means of assuring the continued involvement of the United States in postwar Europe. The postwar world was very different from what it was in 1914. The financial center of the world had shifted from Europe to the United States. The Pax Britannica ended with the Great War, but no one was willing to acknowledge its demise. The new reality in 1919 demanded that the United States assume the new responsibilities being thrust upon it. Instead of doing so, the United States chose to retreat into isolationism.

The League was a futile attempt to replace the balance of power among the great powers as a guarantee of peace, with an international association of nation states unwilling to surrender an iota of their sovereignty to such an assembly. Furthermore, how could the League serve its purpose of arbitrating international disputes, or guarantee peace through collective security, if four of the world's six great powers (Germany, Russia, Japan, and the United States) were not members? Perhaps most important, was the failure of the United States to join the League.

There were a variety of reasons why the United States did not join the League. Some had to do with American public opinion, and some had to do with Wilson's unwillingness to compromise. Wilson failed to make the treaty with Germany and the League a bipartisan political issue, thereby assuring opposition from the Republicans who controlled both houses of Congress during Wilson's last two years in office. Concern that joining the League might compromise the nation's sovereignty, and the increasing desire of the American public to get "back to normalcy," made it wise to separate the League from the Versailles Treaty. That would enable the Senate to vote on them separately. Wilson firmly rejected any such suggestion. In his mind, the two were inseparable.

The growing force of nativism in America, evident earlier in the question over Cuba's fate following the Spanish-American War, was yet another factor in the dispute over joining the League of Nations. Missouri Senator James A. Reed (1861–1944), a member of Wilson's party, expressed concern that the United States might find itself subject to instruction from non-European nations. "This colored league of nations," he said would initially consist of 15 white nations and 17 of "black, brown, yellow and red races, low in civilization and steeped in barbarism" (Winter 1996, p. 351). Senator Lawrence Y. Sherman (1858–1939) of Illinois, a Republican, expressed alarm that the proposed League would include 17 Catholic nations but only 11 that were Protestant. Would the United States find itself under papal influence (Ibid. 1996)?

Attempts at persuading Wilson to compromise were rejected. Republican Senator Frank B. Brandegee of Connecticut met with the president in an attempt to persuade him to change his position. He failed. After leaving Wilson, Brandegee said that he felt "as if I had been wandering with Alice in Wonderland and had tea with the Mad Hatter" (Ibid. 1996). Wilson tried to bypass the Senate and muster public opinion in support of the treaty and the League. While on a speaking tour across the country that covered 8000 miles (12 875 km) by train in just 22 days, he suffered a transient ischemic attack, or mini-stroke. After cutting short the tour and returning to Washington, D.C., he suffered a stroke on the morning of Oct. 2, 1919 that left him paralyzed on his left side. On November 19, the Senate voted down the Versailles Treaty. A separate treaty with Germany was signed in 1921.

The United States never joined the League of Nations. Neither did it enter into a defensive alliance with Great Britain and France, a promise Wilson made to Clemenceau in order to secure French support for the League and a more lenient treatment of Germany. By not signing the Versailles Treaty and not joining the League, the United States turned its back on Europe, with fatal consequences for the future.

Disillusionment

The cost of the Great War is impossible to calculate with any certainty. The economic impact was far reaching, but how much was a direct result of the war? The war on the Western Front was fought in the industrial area of northeastern France, but the overall material destruction wrought by the war was not as great as believed at the time. Though the war destroyed much, it also called into existence new industrial resources. Prewar production levels were surpassed by 1925, which soon resulted in overproduction that contributed to the onset of the Great Depression.

Perhaps the most important economic impact of the war and its aftermath was how it undermined the economic basis of the middle class in the Western nations. Since the Enlightenment, the middle class was always the driving force and backbone of political and economic liberalism. Indeed, the nineteenth century was the "golden age" of both classical liberalism and the middle class. The stability of Western society depended upon the stability of the middle class, and that in turn depended upon its members' ability to accumulate wealth and pass it on to the next generation.

The economic repercussions of the war seriously weakened the middle class by undermining its financial basis through taxes, inflation, and expropriation of wealth. There were few taxes before the war, but the war exposed the latent power of taxation to produce vast sums of money. Taxes that during wartime were meant to be only temporary, became an increasing burden during the years following peace. Inflation eroded the value of savings and investments. Interest income from an investment that would have allowed an individual to live comfortably in retirement before the war was inadequate after the war, even though it produced a higher annual income.

Erosion of their economic security caused the middle class to begin questioning the value of its labor and its contributions to civilization. Before the war, they believed that their work ethic and their frugality, which together enabled them to accumulate wealth, was a force for progress and peace. After the war, they were told that their pursuit of wealth and their exploitation of the working class was a cause of war. They began to question the validity of economic and political liberalism. Perhaps parliamentary democracy was too weak and unable to deal with the economic and political upheavals of the postwar period. Perhaps strong leadership was needed, or in any case, one more sympathetic to business. Such questions were dangerous, given the fact that it is the middle class, not the working class as the Marxists would have one to believe, that is historically the revolutionary class.

The insecurity and self-doubt that plagued the middle class, however, was due to much more than the new economic upheaval. The middle class understood everything in moral terms, and the moral basis of their traditional worldview was being eroded by the ongoing secularization of Western thought. The emerging, postmodern understanding of reality called into question the religious basis of middle-class morality. The nuclear family, the center of the middle-class lifestyle, was also changing at a rapid pace after the war.

The war hastened the emancipation of women by opening up new avenues of education and employment, as well as loosening traditional moral codes. Women were increasingly seen dressed in more revealing and comfortable clothing with their hair "bobbed." The sight of women smoking and drinking in public was shocking to some. The growth of a mass culture meant that individuals sought fulfillment outside of the home. Vaudeville and the cabaret replaced the piano in the parlor. Women's liberation and new opportunities for education and employment contributed to the weakening of family ties. To some extent, the sense of liberation that permeated the air acted as a kind of buffer between the individual and the constant reminder of the war.

The public was made aware of the horrors of industrialized warfare through the memoirs, poetry, and fiction of those who survived. Radio dramas and the new cinema enabled those who remained at home to vicariously experience the horror of war in the trenches. How could one continue to believe that humans were by nature reasonable beings, when one encountered daily on the streets the shattered bodies of wounded veterans or read about the nightmares that haunted them both day and night? The sheer numbers of the casualties seemed beyond comprehension.

Though statistics vary with respect to the number of casualties, it is generally agreed that the Allies suffered approximately 5.7 million[1] military deaths, 3.7 million civilian deaths, and 12.8 million wounded out of a total population of 806 million. Of those, only just over 100 000 were American military deaths. The Central Powers suffered 4 million military deaths, 3.1 million civilian deaths, and 8.4 million wounded from a total population of 143 million. The total number killed in the war was approximately 9.7 million military personnel and 6.8 million civilians. Those wounded in combat numbered approximately 21.2 million. Altogether, there was a grand total of 37.8 million casualties as a result of the assassination of the Archduke Ferdinand on June 28, 1914. Some scholars feel that the 664 000–1.2 million of people killed in the massacre of Armenian Christians in the Ottoman Empire during the spring and autumn of 1915 should be included in the total casualties caused by the war.

To add to the trauma, the deadliest flu pandemic in history spread around the world between the spring of 1918 and the summer of 1919. Of the roughly 500 million people infected worldwide, between 20 and 50 million died. The hardest hit were young adults between 18 and 29 years old. The elderly were largely bypassed by the deadly strain of Spanish flu (Mystery of 1918 2014). The brutality of the Russian Civil War triggered a famine along the Volga River in 1921 and 1922. Estimates of the number of deaths caused by the famine range anywhere from two to ten million. Death seemed to stalk the land everywhere but in America.

Culture

"As a man thinketh, so is he" is a saying based on the biblical proverb, "For as he thinketh in his heart, so is he" (Prov. 23:7 KJV). When we consider the culture of any period in the context of the dominant philosophical assumptions of that same period, the truth of that popular saying becomes clear. The individual artist's worldview is evident in his or her

---

1 All figures are rounded out to the nearest one-hundred thousand. The figures cited here are from Robert Schuman European Center House of Europe Scy-Chazelles (http://www.centre-robert-schuman.org/userfiles/files/REPERES%20%E2%80%93%20module%201-1-1%20-%20explanatory%20notes%20%E2%80%93%20World%20War%20I%20casualties%20%E2%80%93%20EN.pdf).

creative work. The creative arts "provide a direct and powerful, if incomplete, expression of the spirit of an age" (Cunningham and Reich 2006, p. 487). The same is true for a society or a historical period. That is why we can use terminology like abstract, baroque, impressionism, dada, romanticism, etc. to describe the styles of artistic expression and periods in cultural history.

In the period from 1900 to 1930, the shift from reason to unreason, or irrationalism (See Chapter 12), gave birth to a lifestyle and corresponding cultural expression that is referred to as "modernism." Modernism rejected all artistic models of expression and all accepted esthetic standards in favor of the free expression of the artist's own reality. Modernist artists and writers believed that reality differed for every individual, according to how the individual experienced and interpreted it. Previously, artists and writers were guided by the belief that their creativity should reflect the understanding that the universe consisted of a uniformity of cause and effect natural laws that could be understood and expressed mathematically. Modernists believed that reality was a matter of perspective that changed from individual to individual. Reality lay deep in the individual's unconscious mind, Freud's mysterious realm of irrational drives and suppressed desires that express themselves in dreams. It was this inner reality that modernist artists and writers tried to represent in their creative works. The Russian painter Wassily Kandinsky (1866–1944) asked those who viewed his art to "look at the picture as a graphic representation of a *mood* and not as a representation of *objects*" (Arthur 1919, p. 126).

Art

The transition to modernism in art began with the Impressionists, a group of artists who rebelled against the realist artists who attempted to portray their subject matter with photographic-like realism. They staged an art show in Paris in the spring of 1874. Louis Leroy (1812–1885), a French art critic, published a review of the show entitled "The Exhibition of the Impressionists." The artists were thereafter known as the Impressionists, and their style, impressionism, though they did not adopt the term themselves until their third art show in 1877.

The Impressionists tried to depict the combination of light and color as perceived by the artist's eye. The result was a painting that portrays the artist's impression of an object as seen through the interplay of light on it. It is a subjective, not an objective, response to the real world. The question becomes: What is "real," the object as it is, or the object as seen by the artist? Claude Monet's *Red Boats at Argenteuil*, painted the year after the first impressionist show, is one of the best examples of impressionism. Claude Monet (1840–1926), Pierre Auguste Renoir (1841–1919), Camille Pissarro (1830–1903), Alfred Sisley (1839–1899), and Edgar Degas (1834–1917) were among the best known of the Impressionists.

Postimpressionism is a term used to describe a group of artists who reacted to the impressionist style by emphasizing geometric forms. They continued to use bright colors and thick brush strokes, as did their predecessors. As with the Impressionists, their approach is subjective, but with emphasis on the artist's mental reflections upon the sensory images coming into the mind as light waves. Reality is in the mind of the artist. The

Postimpressionists had very different styles, but Paul Cézanne's *Mont Sainte-Victoire* (1904–1906) is a good example of a landscape reduced to geometric patterns on a flat plane. Cézanne (1839–1906) was the most outstanding of the Postimpressionists that included Vincent Van Gogh (1835–1890), Paul Gauguin (1848–1903), Georges Seurat (1859–1891), and Henri de Toulouse-Lautrec (1864–1901), among others.

The fauvists, like the Postimpressionists, used vivid colors and bold brushstrokes and had little in common except their rejection of all traditional values. Henri Matisse (1869–1954), André Derain (1880–1954), and Maurice de Vlaminck (1876–1958) are among the best-known fauvists. Fauvism got its name, like impressionism, from a review of their first art show in 1905. In his critique, Louis Vauxcelles (1870–1943) referred to the exhibiting artists as "the wild beasts" ("*les fauves*"). Fauvism was a short-lived movement, lasting only between 1905 and 1908, and was limited to France.

Fauvism influenced expressionism, a style in which the subjective experience was even more pronounced. Expressionist paintings "became *immensely expressive psychological profiles*, rather than realistic, objective depictions" (Whitaker 2015). The Norwegian painter Edvard Munch (1863–1944) is variously referred to as a forerunner of expressionism or its best example. *The Scream* (1893), multiple versions of which were painted by Munch between 1893 and 1910, depicts, in a very powerful way, the sense of loneliness and alienation that troubled the sensitive soul living in a reality that no longer made sense.

Expressionism originated in Dresden, Germany with a group known as "The Bridge" ("*Die Brücke*"), founded in 1905, and a second group known as "The Blue Rider" ("*Der Blaue Reiter*") founded in Munich in 1911. Ernst Ludwig Kirchner (1880–1938), whose painting *Street, Berlin* (1913) is representative of the artworks produced by members of The Bridge, was the main author of the *Programme*, a kind of manifesto of the group's goals handed out at their first exhibition in 1906. The Bridge derived its name from a line in Fredrich Nietzsche's *Thus Spoke Zarathustra* (1883–1885): "What is great in man is that he is a bridge and not an end" (Nietzsche 1954). Nietzsche's philosophy was a major influence on their art. The group disbanded after the outbreak of war in 1914.

The Blue Rider group got its name from a painting by Wassily Kandinsky, one of the group's founders and its chief representative. The most important of the group's members, in addition to Kandinsky, were Franz Marc (1880–1916), Paul Klee (1879–1940), and Auguste Macke (1887–1914). For them, art was a means of escaping or transcending the material world through a spiritual experience. Like The Bridge, The Blue Rider came to an end in 1914. Macke and Marc both died in the war, while Kandinsky was forced to return to Russia.

The artistic movement known as cubism began with Pablo Picasso (1881–1973) and Georges Braque (1882–1963). The name comes, once again, from a comment by the critic Louis Vauxcelles, who after viewing some paintings by Braque at an exhibition in Paris in 1908, described them as "reducing everything to 'geometric outlines, to cubes'" (Cubism – Art Term 2019). Picasso's painting *Les Demoiselles d'Avignon* (1907) marked the beginning of cubism in art. The title, which translates as *The Young Ladies of Avignon*, was provided by Andre Salmon (1881–1969) who first exhibited it. Salmon felt that Picasso's title, *Le Bordel d'Avignon* (*The Brothel of Avignon*) would provoke indignation from viewers.

Picasso combines geometric patterns with primitivism symbolized by the African masks worn by two of the figures in *Les Demoiselles d'Avignon*. The result is a chaotic menagerie of shapes and colors, a fragmented image of a fragmented worldview. Picasso's *Les Demoiselles d'Avignon* (1907), and *Daniel-Henry Kahnweiler* (1910), *Three Musicians* (1921), and George Braque's *Violin and Palette* (1909–1910) evidence the abandonment of all the principles of composition, perspective, shading, and color that governed art since the Renaissance. Just as the art of the Renaissance reflected a world that made sense, cubism reflected a world that seemed increasingly meaningless.

The Great War seemed to confirm what the intellectuals of the late nineteenth century claimed, that is, that human beings are not rational beings, but in fact irrational. The individual as a human being died in the trenches on the Western Front. What was left was "nothing but a machine, a very complex machine, an absurd machine" (Rookmaaker 1971, p. 129). Both Dada and surrealism reflected the new world of absurdity and meaninglessness.

The artistic movement known as Dada began in Zurich, Switzerland during the war and spread to the major centers of avant-garde art in Berlin, Paris, and New York, before giving way to surrealism. "Dada," wrote the Dutch art historian H.R. Rookmaaker, "was a nihilistic creed of disintegration, showing the meaninglessness of all western thought, art, morals, traditions. It destroyed them by tackling them in an ironic way, with black humor, by showing them in their absurdity, by making them absurd" (1971, p. 130). Simply stated, Dada was "anti-art art."

As a movement, surrealism viewed the individual as being lost, or imprisoned, in an absurd reality, unable to gain true freedom or true humanity. It rejected a rational reality and looked, instead, to the unconscious psyche and dreams. André Breton (1896–1966), considered by some to be the founder of surrealism, defined it in his *Surrealist Manifesto* (1924) as "Dictation of thought in the absence of all control exercised by reason, outside of all esthetic and moral preoccupation" (Surrealism – Art Term 2018).

Marcel Duchamp (1887–1968) and Salvador Dali (1904–1989) serve as exemplary examples of both Dada and surrealism. Two of Duchamp's works that are often cited as examples of Dada are *Fountain* (1917) and *L.H.O.O.Q.* (1919). *Fountain* is one of Duchamp's "ready-mades" for which he was well known. He merely took a urinal, mounted it upside down on a wall and signed it "R. Mutt 1917." *L.H.O.O.Q.* is a copy of Leonardo da Vinci's *Mona Lisa* on which Duchamp has drawn a mustache and goatee.

Salvador Dali's *The Persistence of Memory* (1931) is considered the best example of a surrealist painting. He cultivated a public persona that was as surrealist as his art. "The difference between me and the surrealists," Dali once said, "is that I am a surrealist" (Klingsohr-Leroy 2004, p. 44). André Breton, the leader of Surrealism, expelled Dali from the movement in part for his commercialism. The influence of Freudianism and the quest for reality in the unconscious mind and in dreams was evident in Dali's art.

Modern art during the period between the two world wars abandoned any attempt to depict the objective world. Like Einstein's physics, there is no longer any fixed reality. A work of art created reality as defined in the mind of the artist. No longer was there an objective standard by which to judge good from bad art. Both Dadaism and surrealism were anarchic, even nihilistic, responses to the insanity of war and the decadence of postwar society and politics, but without any hint of an answer.

It was a broken world after the Great War. No one could escape the new reality. Those who returned from the war mutilated both physically and mentally could be seen on the streets of the cities and villages, silent testimonies to a nightmare from which no one was allowed to awaken. A child saw a wounded soldier on a train. His face was horribly disfigured, and he was missing a leg. The child asked his mother, "What's wrong with that man?" The wounded warrior replied: "Have a good look, little one, and don't ever forget that this is war, this and nothing else" (Winter 1996, p. 368).

Skilled artists like Otto Dix (1891–1969), George Grosz (1893–1959), Max Beckmann (1884–1950), Käthe Kollwitz (1867–1945), and others employed a fragmented technique to create visual images of the broken world that the prewar *La Belle Époque* had become. Dix's *Match-seller* (1920) shows a blind, quadruple amputee sitting on a sidewalk selling matches, while people walk by avoiding him and a small dog urinates on the stump of his left leg. Käthe Kollwitz's two chalk lithograph posters, *Germany's Children are starving!* (1923) and *Bread* (1924), are powerful images of the suffering resulting from defeat in the war.

Literature

The modernist message of a subjective reality that passed through the artist's brush unto the canvas also passed through the poet's or novelist's pen unto the page. Modernism was informed by three developments. First was the passing of the great empires that dominated world affairs for centuries, and the appearance in their place of a host of new nations with uncertain futures. Second was Einstein's theories which begged the question of whether anything could be known for certain. But most important was Sigmund Freud's discovery of the unconscious, which opened up a dark labyrinth that inspired wonder as well as fear. All of these created a sense of discontinuity with the past and uncertainty about the future that was reflected in the creative works of the artists, poets, novelists, composers, and those who manufactured what became known as "popular culture."

Freudian themes are common in what later became known as the literature of the interwar years, as opposed to what is commonly called popular fiction. Oedipal complexes, illicit sex, and sexual liberation (especially of women), are common themes. Sexual desire, as an unconscious motivational force, is a frequent motif in the novels and short stories by D.H. Lawrence (1885–1930), James Joyce (1882–1941), Marcel Proust (1871–1922), Virginia Woolf (1882–1941), Franz Kafka (1883–1924), Thomas Mann (1875–1955), and William Faulkner (1897–1962). It was not necessary for a writer to be personally acquainted with Freud's work in order to have been influenced by him. The American author Sherwood Anderson (1876–1941) was allegedly surprised to find himself listed among those influenced by Freud, when he claimed to have never heard of him.

Because of the graphic sexual content of D.H. Lawrence's *Lady Chatterley's Lover*, it had to be published privately in Italy in 1928 and in France and Australia in 1929. A heavily censored edition was first published in the United States in 1928 and in Britain in 1932. An uncensored edition was not published in Britain until 1960, following a sensational obscenity trial. James Joyce's *Ulysses* likewise endured censorship and court battles. Because of the controversy caused by its serialization in *The Little Review*, an American literary magazine that published a variety of modernist literature and art, *Ulysses* was first published as a book in Paris in 1922 by Sylvia Beach (1887–1962).

Sylvia Beach's Parisian bookstore Shakespeare and Company became an aviary for modernist artists and writers. Gertrude Stein (1874–1946) hosted a salon in Paris that, like

Beach's Shakespeare and Company, was a gathering place for modernists. Stein is credited with originating the term "Lost Generation" to refer to a group of American writers who settled in Paris. The best known of them were Ernest Hemingway (1899–1961), F. Scott Fitzgerald (1896–1940), John Dos Passos (1896–1970), Ezra Pound (1885–1972), and T.S. Eliot (1888–1965).

Though the term "Lost Generation" is often used in reference to a particular group of expatriate American writers and poets, it has a more general application as well. It refers to a whole generation that came of age during the Great War. They found themselves in a world where the old values they were raised with no longer applied. It was only a small portion of that generation, however, who wrestled with the implications of finding a mooring in a new morally neutral universe occupied by human beings who were considered to be irrational animals.

Popular Culture

The masses of ordinary people did not gaze at Picasso's *Les Demoiselles d'Avignon*, read T.S. Eliot's poem titled *The Waste Land* (1922), or listen to a composition by Arnold Schoenberg (1871–1951) and see a fragmented artistic medium used to convey a fragmented worldview. The emerging postmodern worldview reached them slowly through the popular culture created and marketed by the mass media. Increasingly, more people were literate and possessed more disposable income. They purchased weekly and monthly magazines that included short stories and serialized novels. Radio broadcasts became available worldwide during the 1920s, giving ordinary people easy access to popular drama and music. Silent feature-length motion pictures, already available after 1906, became "talkies" in 1927.

Magazines were either "glossies" or "pulp" depending on the quality of paper used or their content. Popular fiction, sometimes referred to as "pulp fiction," was available at prices the common man or woman could afford. Albatross Books in Hamburg, Germany, began publishing paperback books in what became the standard size of 181×111 mm (7×4.3 in.) in 1932. The first Penguin paperback appeared in 1935, and the first Pocket Books paperback in 1939.

The first radio broadcast for entertainment took place on Christmas Eve 1906 from Brant Rock, Massachusetts, but it was not until 1920 that advertisement-supported commercial radio was born. Radio station KDKA in Pittsburgh, Pennsylvania was the first licensed station. Within two years, there were more than 500 licensed commercial radio stations in the United states. The first commercial radio network known as the National Broadcasting Company (NBC) was founded in 1926, followed in the next year by the Columbia Broadcasting System (CBS).

Hans Henricus Schotanus à Steringa Idzerd (1885–1944), a Dutch engineer, began regular radio broadcasts from The Hague on November 6, 1919. Because he published the program beforehand in the newspaper, it is considered the beginning of commercial radio broadcasts. Radio Paris began broadcasting in 1922, the same year that the British Broadcasting Company (BBC) was formed. The first German radio station went on the air in 1923. The European governments recognized the potential power of radio broadcasts early and took steps to assure that the medium was government regulated.

State-regulated broadcasts tended, not surprisingly, to provide music and drama programs that the guardians of good taste thought the public should hear, rather than the emerging popular music and drama. In December 1929, the centrally located Grand Duchy of Luxembourg granted a commercial broadcasting license to Luxembourg Broadcasting Company (a.k.a., Radio Luxembourg). Radio Luxembourg began English-language broadcasts of popular programs that were supported by revenue from British advertisers. Leonard Frank Plugge (1889–1981), a British businessman and Conservative politician, founded International Broadcasting Company (IBC) in 1931. The IBC provided a commercial alternative to the BBC by purchasing airtime on continental radio stations and collaborating with Radio Luxembourg. By the end of the decade, regular radio broadcasts were heard around the world.

Motion pictures made their appearance at the end of the nineteenth century. The first movie theater opened in Pittsburgh, Pennsylvania in 1905. Its name, Nickelodeon, was a combination of the Greek word for theater and "nickel," the cost of admission.[2] The first feature-length film, *The Story of the Kelly Gang*, appeared in 1906. The first blockbuster film was the 3-hour long, 12-reel *The Clansman* (later titled *The Birth of a Nation*) that premiered in 1915.

The center of the early motion picture industry was in Berlin, not Hollywood. It was in Germany, prior to the Nazis coming to power in 1933, that film became a serious artform. German expressionist films like *The Cabinet of Dr. Caligari* (1920), *The Golem: How He Came into the World* (1920), *Nosferatu* (1922), *Metropolis* (1927) and *M* (1931) are classics that profoundly influenced the history of motion pictures down to the present. *The Blue Angel* (1930), starring Marlene Dietrich (1901–1992), together with Bertolt Brecht's stage play, *The Threepenny Opera* (1928), epitomize the cultural life of Weimar, Germany.

Berlin, where "life was a cabaret," was the center of the avant-garde culture between the end of the Great War and the depth of the Great Depression, a period commonly referred to as the "Jazz Age." The term, attributed to F. Scott Fitzgerald, is appropriate, since the music genre known as jazz is perhaps the most enduring innovation in popular culture of the period.

Jazz was born in New Orleans, Louisiana at the turn of the twentieth century among African-American street musicians who had no formal musical education or training. From there, it spread to Chicago, Illinois, and then to Harlem in New York City. During the prohibition era in America (1920–1933), the Cotton Club in Harlem was the creative center of the new music, as it made the transition to the mainstream of popular music. Duke Ellington (1899–1974), Fats Waller (1904–1943), Ethel Waters (1896–1977), Bessie Smith (1894–1937), and many other pioneers of jazz music performed at the Cotton Club and helped make Harlem a center of American culture.

Jazz music and jazz culture crossed the Atlantic Ocean to Europe in the aftermath of the Great War. As in America, a major part of the attraction of the jazz culture was that it helped people deal with the suffering and pain caused by the war, and in America, by prohibition. In Germany, it helped distract one's attention from the suffering caused by military defeat and the injustices of the peace settlement. Also, embracing the radically

---

2 A nickel (5 cents) in 1905 would have the same purchasing power of $1.43 or £1.11 in 2018.

new culture was a way of rejecting the old order that many felt was a cause of the war. The appearance of black colonial and American troops in Europe during the war, created a certain fascination with black culture, and specifically African-American culture, of which jazz was seen as an integral part.

The "passion for black culture and a 'primitivised' existence" associated with jazz was referred to as "negrophilia," from the French *négrophilie* meaning "love of the negro." It was considered "modern and fashionable" among the avant-garde "to collect African art, to listen to black music and to dance with black people," notes art historian Petrine Archer-Straw (Archer-Straw 2000). The popularity of black performers was due, in part, to a skewed belief that they exemplified a "primitive African energy filtered through American modernism" (Black Philadelphia 2013).

Success of the *Revue nègre* (*Revue Negro*), a lavishly staged all-black musical starring Louis Douglas (1889–1939) and Josephine Baker (1906–1975) that opened in Paris in October 1925 played a key role in the introduction of jazz to Europe. No American performer did more to introduce jazz to Europeans than Josephine Baker. Often dubbed the "Black Pearl," the "Bronze Venus," or the "Creole Goddess," Ms. Baker mesmerized audiences in Paris and Berlin with her voice and especially her sexy modern dance routines. "Negroes dance with their senses," wrote a German critic, "while Europeans can dance only with their minds" (2013).

Many defenders of traditional culture condemned modernist culture, and jazz music in particular, as decadent, mass-produced entertainment reduced to the lowest common denominator in order to attract the widest possible audience. It was accused, much as rock "n" roll music of the fifties would later be, of undermining morality and threatening the psychological and physical health of those exposed to it.

Social Impact

Industrialized warfare required the mobilization of all layers of society. Military conscription, recruitment of women as laborers to replace men who went to war, and rationing of food and other essentials on the home front weakened class distinctions while making the burdens of the war more equitable. Many experienced a sense of self-respect and participation in the affairs of their country that they had not previously known. They were not willing to return to the prewar status quo when peace returned. Postwar governments found it difficult to deny women the right to vote or workers the right to organize. The United States and most European countries granted women's suffrage shortly after the return of peace.[3]

Homosexuals served alongside heterosexuals at home and at the front during the war. They, like women and workers, were no longer content after the war to be denied recognition as full members of society. Before the war, what would later be called the "gay-rights movement" focused on using scientific arguments to support their claim that homosexuality was normal. After the war, the movement shifted to demanding recognition of their rights as citizens, including repeal of sodomy laws and opening up of government employment and military service to known homosexuals.

---

3 France and Italy did not grant women the right to vote until the end of World War II. Women in Switzerland had to wait until 1971.

During the 1920s, there was a lively and largely unimpeded homosexual subculture in Paris, Berlin, and to a lesser extent in London. Men and women from around the world journeyed to Paris, and especially Berlin, to experience the newly liberated sexual norms. Thomas Mann, who visited Paris in 1926, expressed surprise at finding "the whores on the streets of Paris were predominantly male" (Woods 2016). The streets of Paris evidenced to him the internationalization of homosexuality. Art historians Vincent Bouvet and Gerard Durozoi concluded from their study of the cultural life of Paris during the interwar years, that "homosexuality and bisexuality were treated with relative tolerance in moneyed, cultural and artistic circles, and almost came to be regarded as a badge of modernity during the 1920s" (2016).

Berlin was the true capital of the homosexual subculture in Europe. Nowhere else during the 1920s did the homosexual subculture flourish as it did in Berlin. The English writer Christopher Isherwood (1904–1986) was one of many gay men and lesbian women who went to Berlin because of its reputation. One of Isherwood's relatives who lived in Berlin, told him that "you couldn't find anything more nauseating than what goes on there [in Berlin], quite openly, every day.... These people don't even realize how low they have sunk. Evil doesn't know itself there.... You could never imagine such things." "And then and there," Isherwood later said, "I made a decision ... that, no matter how, I would get to Berlin just as soon as ever I could" (Friedrich 1972, p. 304).

Isherwood followed his friend and sporadic partner, the English poet W.H. Auden (1907–1973), to Berlin in 1929. He remained in Berlin until May 1933, five months after Hitler came to power and began forcing homosexuals back into the shadows. Isherwood did, however, write two short semi-autobiographical novellas set in the Berlin he knew and loved, *The Last of Mr. Norris* (1935) and *Goodbye to Berlin* (1939). They were published together in 1945 as *The Berlin Stories*, which served as the inspiration for the Broadway play, *I Am a Camera* (1951) and the film by the same name in 1955. The highly successful Broadway musical *Cabaret* (1966) and its film version (1972) that won eight Academy Awards were also based on *The Berlin Stories*.

The twenties were a period of economic prosperity. They were called the "Roaring Twenties" in America, the "Golden Twenties" (*Goldene Zwanziger*) in Germany, and the "Crazy Years" (*années folles*) in France. It was a period of excess, new dances like the Charleston and black bottom, speakeasies and gangsters, motion pictures and radio, jazz music, professional sports, barn-storming pilots and transcontinental and intercontinental flights, and much, much more. Like one of Mr. Gatsby's parties, it seemed as though the fun would never end. No one could see, or wanted to see, that soon the music would stop, for just around the corner was the Great Depression.

References

Archer-Straw, P. (2000). Negrophilia: A Double-edged Infatuation. The Guardian. https://www. theguardian.com/books/2000/sep/23/features.weekend (accessed 21 October 2019).

Arthur, J.E. (1919). *Cubists and Post-Impressionism*. Chicago, IL: A.C. McClurg & Company.

Black Philadelphia Abroad: Louis Douglas (2013). The Philadelphia Dance History Journal. https://philadancehistoryjournal.wordpress.com/2013/02/ (accessed 15 November 2019).

Cunningham, L. and Reich, J.J. (2006). *Culture & Values: a Survey of the Humanities*. Boston, MA: Wadsworth Cengage Learning.

Friedrich, O. (1972). *Before the Deluge: A Portrait of Berlin in the 1920's*. New York: Harper & Row.

Hartsock, P.I. (2017). The Unfortunate Effects of 'The Birth of a Nation'. The Washington Post. https://www.washingtonpost.com/opinions/the-unfortunate-effects-of-the-birth-of-a-nation/2017/07/21/b6fc5920-6c1e-11e7-abbc-a53480672286_story.html?utm_term=.24cb0c2e7cd2 (accessed 21 October 2019).

Kazin, M. (2014). If the U.S. Had Not Entered World War I, Would There Have Been a World War II? The New Republic. https://newrepublic.com/article/118435/world-war-i-debate-should-us-have-entered (accessed 21 October 2019).

Keynes, J.M. (1919). Economic Consequences of the Peace, chapter 7. University of Texas. http://la.utexas.edu/users/hcleaver/368/368KeynesECP7remedies.html (accessed 7 November 2019).

Klingsohr-Leroy, C. (2004). *Surrealism*. Berlin: Taschen.

Morison, S.E. (1965). *The Oxford History of the American People*. New York: Oxford University Press.

National Geographic (2014). Mystery of 1918 Flu That Killed 50 Million Solved? https://news.nationalgeographic.com/news/2014/04/140428-1918-flu-avian-swine-science-health-science (accessed 21 October 2019).

Nietzsche, F. (1954). Thus Spoke Zarathustra. Translated by Walter Kaufmann. http://www2.hawaii.edu/~freeman/courses/phil394/Thus%20Spoke%20Zarathustra.pdf (accessed 11 November 2019).

Pettinger, T. (2013). Biography David Lloyd George. Biography Online. www.biographyonline.net (accessed 15 October 2019).

Richards, M.D. and Waibel, P.R. (2014). *Twentieth-Century Europe: A Brief History, 1900 to the Present*, 3e. Malden (MA): Wiley Blackwell.

Rookmaaker, H.R. (1971). *Modern Art and the Death of a Culture*. London: Inter-Varsity Press.

Tate (2019) Surrealism. http://www.tate.org.uk/art/art-terms/s/surrealism (accessed 21 October 2019).

Tate (2019). Cubism. www.tate.org.uk/art/art-terms/c/cubism (accessed 21 October 2019).

Taylor, A.J.P. (1966a). *A History of the First World War*. New York: Berkley Publishing Corp.

Taylor, A.J.P. (1966b). *From Sarajevo to Potsdam*. New York: Harcourt, Brace, Jovanovich.

The Guardian (2008). First World War: Extract from Woodrow Wilson's Speech to the American Senate on January 22 1917. https://www.theguardian.com/world/2008/nov/14/woodrow-wilson-senate-address-1917 (accessed 21 October 2019).

Time (1952). ITALY: Last of the Big Four. http://content.time.com/time/magazine/article/0,9171,817533,00.html (accessed 21 October 2019).

Whitaker, G. (2015). Art Movements. Symbolism, Fauvism, Expressionism. Visual & Decorative Arts Blog. http://blog.flametreepublishing.com/art-of-fine-gifts/art-movements-symbolism-fauvism-expressionism (accessed 21 October 2019).

Winter, J.M. (1996). *The Great War and the Shaping of the 20th Century*. New York: Penguin Studio.

Woods, G. (2016). Influence of Gay Culture on Modern Life. The Independent. http://www.independent.co.uk/arts-entertainment/books/features/gregory-woods-the-influence-of-homosexuality-on-western-culture-a6980451.html (accessed 21 October 2019).

16

A Failed Peace: 1919–1939

Chronology

1917–1922	Russian Civil War Between Reds and Whites
1918	Friedrich Ebert (SPD) Becomes Chancellor of Germany
1918	Karl Liebknecht (USPD) Proclaims Socialist Republic
1918	Philipp Scheidemann (SPD) Proclaims German Republic
1919–1920	"Red Scare" in United States
1919	Weimar Constitution Drafted for German Republic
1921–1922	Severe Famine in Russia
1922	Benito Mussolini Appointed Prime Minister of Italy
1923	Munich Beer Hall Putsch by Adolf Hitler
1923	Great Inflation in Germany
1923–1925	French Occupation of Ruhr
1924	Lenin Dies
1924	USA Immigration Act of 1924 Establishes Quotas
1926	General Strike in England
1928	Leon Trotsky Ousted, Stalin Becomes Leader of the Soviet Union
1929	Lateran Accords, or Lateran Treaties, Between Italy and the Vatican
1929	New York Stock Exchange Crashes, Great Depression Begins
1925–1927	Adolf Hitler's *Mein Kampf*
1930	Presidential Dictatorship Begins in Germany
1936	John Maynard Keynes' *The General Theory of Employment, Interest, and Money*
1933	Adolf Hitler Appointed Chancellor by President Paul von Hindenburg
1933	Reichstag Passes Enabling Act Marking the End of the Weimar Republic

Though the world that emerged from the Great War appeared in some ways to be a continuation of the world of 1914, there were many signs that there would be no return to the status quo ante bellum. Of the five prewar great powers, only two, the United Kingdom and France, remained. The historic dynasties that comprised the empires of Germany, Russia, and Austria-Hungary, together with a host of lesser princely houses in Europe, were gone. Germany was now a republic. Russia was embroiled in a civil war out of which

Western Civilization: A Brief History, First Edition. Paul R. Waibel.
© 2020 John Wiley & Sons, Inc. Published 2020 by John Wiley & Sons, Inc.

would emerge what was to be, at least on paper, a union of socialist republics. Austria-Hungary fragmented into Austria, Hungary, Czechoslovakia, Poland, and Yugoslavia.

Both the British and French empires expanded through acquisition of the former German colonies and the Middle Eastern territories of the former Ottoman Empire. This expansion of European imperialism in the world obscured the fact that both the United Kingdom and France suffered irreversible economic damage that weakened their positions within the new international power structure. Europe was no longer the center of the world. The industrial and financial leadership of the world's economy shifted overseas to the United States, the only power that benefitted from its participation in the Great War.

A destructive civil war in Europe in which non-European, colonial soldiers played a role in the defeat and subsequent occupation of Germany undermined the prestige of European rule in the world and the myth of European racial superiority. Wilson's Fourteen Points called for the right of "self-determination" for the different nationalities within the former Austro-Hungarian Empire and self-government for the "non-Turks in the old Turkish Empire," but did not include the colonial subjects of either the European or American empires. Lenin's vision of the new world order did, however, call for an end to imperialism throughout the world, and even pledged support for all people groups in the world seeking "national freedom."

The African-American intellectual and civil rights leader, W.E.B. Du Bois (1868–1963) saw clearly how the participation of non-European soldiers in the European civil war could further the cause of freedom and equality for both the colonial peoples and people of color in Europe and America. In an article published in 1918, Du Bois wrote:

> This war is an end and also a beginning. Never again will darker people of the world occupy just the place they had before. Out of this place will arise, soon or late, an independent China, a self-governing India, an Egypt with representative institutions, an Africa for the Africans, and not merely for business exploitation. Out of this war will rise, too, an American Negro with the right to vote and the right to work and the right to live without insult. (Emerson and Kilson 1965)

Japan's victory over imperial Russia in 1905 and the events of the Great War in Europe and around the world forever shattered the myth of European superiority. National liberation movements became a growing threat to Western imperialism.

The new reality in the international power structure after 1919 included two rivalries that shaped the twentieth century. One was the struggle for control of the Pacific Ocean between the United States of America and the Empire of Japan. The second was the competition between Woodrow Wilson's and Lenin's visions of a new world order. The former drew the United States in December 1941 into the second phase of the Great War, or World War II, as it is commonly called. The latter evolved into the Cold War between the United States and the Soviet Union that dominated the world between 1945 and 1991.

Recovery and Prosperity

While the leaders of the victorious nations and the newly created nation-states tried to recover from the war and establish a future void of national conflicts, most people shared a common desire to return to normalcy. Normalcy meant restoration of life as it was lived before the Great War. A return to normalcy was, however, not possible. The hope of doing so only prevented reasonable efforts to adjust to the new reality.

Great Britain

Great Britain's entry into the war on the continent on August 4, 1914 in response to Germany's violation of Belgium's neutrality proved to be a fateful decision for the future of the British Empire. Though Britain was one of the victors in 1918, the future demonstrated that all of the war's European participants were among the losers. For Britain's subjects, the end of the war in 1918 was followed by a brief period of economic boom as production shifted to meeting the pent-up demand for consumer goods. By March 1921, however, unemployment reached over two million. Chronic unemployment persisted through the 1920's and 1930's, never less than one million and at times more than two million. Many became dependent on government relief, or "dole," which led to widespread demoralization among the once proud working class. Some historians conclude that the Great Depression that was to strike Europe in the early 1930s actually began in Britain in 1920.

The cause of Britain's economic woes were related to the damage done to its dominant position in world trade. The demands of total war meant that British industry concentrated on producing for the war. Industrial development in the United States, Japan, and members of the British Dominions was stimulated by increasing demand previously met by Britain. Lost customers did not necessarily return to Britain at the war's end. Hence, its foreign markets shrank.

British industries found themselves unable to compete with their postwar competitors. Their industrial plants were out of date compared to the new industrial plants in the United States and elsewhere. Also, Britain did not participate in the newer industries like chemicals to the same extent as, for example, Germany and the United States. British industry was still concentrated on its traditional base of coal, iron, steel, textiles, and shipbuilding. It was in those labor-intensive industries that it lost the competitive edge. Recovery was further hampered by the decision to return to the gold standard in 1925. Interest rates rose, limiting the supply of money for investment in economic development. As the value of the British pound increased, British exports became too expensive compared to those of its competitors. By the mid-1920s, exports were only 75% of their prewar volume (Crafts 2014). As exports dropped, unemployment rose and strikes increased, culminating in the General Strike of May 3–12, 1926.

Other factors that hindered economic recovery included Britain's loss of status as the world's banker. Whereas it was a creditor nation before the war, it was a debtor nation after the war. The national debt that stood at 0.25 times the GDP[1] in 1913, was 1.3 times the GDP by 1920. The financial center of the world economy shifted to New York, as the United States became the world's leading industrial power.

Chronic unemployment and perpetual dependence on the public dole after making such supreme sacrifices during the war years led to widespread pessimism and lack of hope for a better future. The Labour Party favored policies aimed at establishing a welfare state and

---

1 GDP refers to "Gross Domestic Product," the total value of all goods and services produced in a year.

nationalization of heavy industry. The Labour Party was the party of the working class, but included members of the middle class who broke with the fading Liberal Party. The Liberals favored free trade, while the Conservative Party, the party of the propertied classes, favored protection. Of the three political parties, the Conservatives best represented the mood of the country during the interwar years.

At first, it is difficult to understand the persistent appeal of conservatism during the period, not only in Britain, but throughout Europe and the United States. No doubt a part of the answer can be found in the widespread fear that the Russian Revolution of 1917 might have unleashed a communist revolution that, like the flu pandemic of 1918–1919, might spread throughout the world. Even while fighting for its survival in a civil war, the Bolshevik government was promoting revolution in Europe, Asia, and the United States. The fear of Bolshevism that stalked the Western world during the 1920's is hard to comprehend in today's post-Cold War world.

The sheer cost in human lives was another factor. Out of a total population of 45.4 million, the United Kingdom of Great Britain and Ireland suffered over 885 000 military and 109 000 civilian deaths.[2] An additional 1.1 million British Imperial forces were killed (Nadège Mougel). Even more significant was the number of deaths among the young men of the ruling class, those who graduated from the elite "public" (i.e. private) schools, that reached as high as 20%. The generation who in the normal course of events would have become the leaders after the war lay dead in the trenches along the Western Front or returned a "lost generation," psychologically exhausted, cynical, and aimless. They found civilian life dull and frivolous compared to life in the trenches. They shunned politics, leaving direction of the future to the generation who caused the Great War.

The first postwar general election, the first in which all men over twenty-one and women over thirty could vote, was held in December 1918. The result was a coalition government led by David Lloyd George, leader of the Liberal Party and Prime Minister since December 1916. The election was largely a referendum on Lloyd George's leadership. The Liberal Party's coalition partner, the Conservative Party led by Andrew Bonar Law (1858–1923), won the lion's share of the votes cast. Lloyd George's personal popularity, together with his campaign slogan that called for making the United Kingdom "a country fit for heroes to live in," no doubt deserved credit for the coalition's victory at the polls.

Bonar Law led the Conservatives to victory in the general election held in November 1922. Significantly, the Labour Party emerged as "His Majesty's Loyal Opposition," while the divided Liberal Party continued its decline. The Conservative government was able to address the perpetual problem of Ireland. Protestant Northern Ireland and Roman Catholic southern Ireland were separated, and each given its own parliament in 1920. Southern Ireland became effectively independent in 1921, when it was granted dominion status as the Irish Free State, or Erie. Northern Ireland's parliament voted not to join the Irish Free State in 1922. It chose instead to retain Home Rule as a member of the United Kingdom. The Irish Free State changed its official name to Ireland, or Erie, in 1937 and became fully independent in 1949.

---

2 The figures cited here are from Robert Schuman European Center House of Europe Scy-Chazelles (http://www.centre-robert-schuman.org/userfiles/files/REPERES%20%E2%80%93%20module%201-1-1%20-%20explanatory%20notes%20%E2%80%93%20World%20War%20I%20casualties%20%E2%80%93%20EN.pdf) and rounded off to the nearest one-hundred thousand.

Women's rights made limited progress during the 1920's. Constance Georgine Markievicz (1868–1927) became the first woman elected to Parliament in December 1918. She was elected to represent the Irish constituency of Dublin St Patrick's but did not take her seat in the House of Commons. Nancy Witcher Langhorne Astor, Viscountess Astor (1879–1964) was the first woman who took her seat in Parliament. She served as a Conservative Member of Parliament (MP) from November 1919 to July 1945.

Lady Astor represented the combative spirit of the women's suffrage movement in the early twentieth century. A woman MP was too much for some of the more tradition-bound male MPs. In one encounter with Winston Churchill, the former First Lord of the Admiralty and future Prime Minister, Churchill is reported to have said: "When you took your seat I felt as if a woman had come into my bathroom and I had only a sponge with which to defend myself." She replied, "You're not handsome enough to have such fears" (McCleland 2015). It was the Conservative government of Stanley Baldwin (1867–1947) that granted the vote to women in 1928 on the same terms as men.

There were two brief Labour governments during the 1920's, both led by James Ramsay MacDonald (1866–1937). The first lasted only from January to November 1924. It lacked a majority in Parliament and ruled with support from the Liberal Party. Its only significant achievement was recognition of the USSR, or Union of Soviet Socialist Republics, as the new Russia was officially known beginning in 1924. Recognition of the Soviet Union was not a popular move with the British people.

The Conservative Party returned to power in November 1924, once again with Stanley Baldwin as Prime Minister. Baldwin acted quickly to break off relations with Russia. It was his economic policies, though, that proved unpopular with the working classes. He restored the gold standard in 1925, then refused to negotiate with the unions during the General Strike in 1926. After the collapse of the strike, Baldwin procured passage of the anti-union Trade Disputes Act in July 1927.

Ramsey MacDonald returned to office as Prime Minister of the second Labour government in June 1929. The new Labour government did nothing more radical than restore relations with the Soviet Union and appoint Margaret Bondfield (1873–1953) as Minister of Labour, the first woman in British history to be appointed a cabinet minister. MacDonald's timid leadership in line with policies set by the Conservatives, won the Labour Party respect among middle-class voters, but cost the party support among the working class, especially as the Great Depression began to impact Britain.

MacDonald resigned from office in August 1931, but continued as Prime Minister of a National Government at the request of King George V (1865–1936). Despite the suffering among the working classes, the conservative mood of the time became evident in the General Election in October 1931. The parties of the National Government won 67% of the votes and 554 seats out of 615. Of those, the Conservative Party held 470 and the Labour Party only 52.

Ramsey MacDonald retired in June 1935 due to failing health. He was succeeded by Stanley Baldwin as head of the National Government. Baldwin's last stint in office was unexciting, except for his successful handling of Edward VIII's abdication in December 1936. Baldwin resigned on May 28, 1937, just sixteen days after the coronation of George VI (1895–1952). His last act in office was to raise the salary of MPs from £400 a year to £600. The Leader of the Opposition was granted a salary for the first time, as well. Harold

Nicholson said of Baldwin's departure, "No man has ever left in such a blaze of affection" (Nicolson 1966, p. 301).

Arthur Neville Chamberlain (1869–1940) served as Prime Minister from Baldwin's resignation until May 1940. His term in office is forever associated with his failed foreign policy of appeasement. MacDonald, Baldwin, and Chamberlain all failed to muster enough nerve to confront the British public with the increasing danger presented by Germany's rearmament and aggressive foreign policy. They feared that doing so would have been disastrous at the polls. The risk of unleashing a second Great War was too much to ask of the public. It was easier to ignore the threat, hoping against hope that it would simply disappear.

France

France suffered proportionately most from the war. Out of a total population of 39.6 million, it sustained 4.3 million deaths, 1.8 million of them in the military. Another 4.3 million returned from the war wounded (Mougel 2011). The war on the Western Front was fought primarily on French soil, leaving behind extensive property damage. Whole villages, towns, factories, mines, railroad lines, and large swaths of farmland were destroyed. Most of France's coal and iron mines were flooded and many wells in or near the former combat zones were poisoned.

France financed the war by resorting mostly to loans, rather than taxes. The postwar governments borrowed heavily to rebuild the war-ravaged areas. The result was inflation, a rising national debt, and an unbalanced budget. For financial relief, the French, more than the British, looked to reparations from Germany. French policy toward Germany was largely determined by a combination of economic and national security concerns. It was a policy doomed from the start with serious consequences for both France and Europe. So long as the struggling German Republic was burdened with the harsh Versailles Treaty, it could neither recover from the war nor pay the reparations demanded.

Interwar France remained a greatly divided country. Neither conservative nor left-wing governments were able to bring unity to the nation that was soon to face the chief economic and international crises of the century. Politics remained confused and unstable, with governments of the left and right alternating in power. A wave of nationalism and patriotism, and a fear of Bolshevism, brought a coalition of right-wing parties to power in January 1920.

The National Bloc (*Bloc national*), as the right-wing bloc was called, won the national elections on the slogan, "Germany will pay!" They felt that the Versailles Treaty was too lenient with Germany. They wanted not only the return of Alsace-Lorraine granted by the treaty, but the annexation of the Ruhr industrial area of Germany. They pursued financing recovery and securing France's future security through strict enforcement of the treaty.

A financial crisis, together with a belief that Germany was intentionally failing to send shipments of coal to France as part of reparations, led the government of President Raymond Poincaré (1860–1934) to send French troops into the Ruhr in January 1923 against the advice of the British, who saw the French action as imperialism. The occupation proved fatal for the National Bloc as the French franc lost value and pressure from financial interests in London and on Wall Street mounted. The National Bloc lost the general election in May 1924 and disbanded shortly afterwards.

A coalition of four left-wing political groups, known as the Left Bloc (*Cartel de Gauches*) formed a government in May 1924 under Edouard Herriot (1872–1957) and governed until July 1926. They held a majority of seats in the Chamber of Deputies, but did not win a majority of the popular vote. The Left Bloc recognized the Soviet Union in 1924 and ended the Ruhr occupation in the summer of 1925. It failed to solve the major economic issues of inflation, rising debt, and the unbalanced budget. After Herriot's fall from power in April 1925, there were six short-lived ministries during the next fifteen months.

Raymond Poincaré returned to power in July 1926 as the leader of a National Union ministry that governed until July 1929. He took drastic measures to restore financial stability. France returned to the gold standard, a disguised repudiation of the national debt that was contracted in terms of the prewar franc. The devaluation of the franc caused suffering among the middle class, as many saw the value of their savings and investments undermined.

Poincaré's reforms did restore a measure of prosperity and stability that France had not enjoyed since before the war. France was better prepared for the coming depression than most European countries. Nevertheless, when it did arrive, France suffered as much as everyone else. But nowhere was the impact of the Great Depression greater than in Germany.

Weimar Germany

November 9, 1918 was a fateful day in the history of not only Germany and Europe, but for the world itself. On October 4, Prince Max von Baden, who was appointed Chancellor on the day before, requested an armistice on the basis of Wilson's Fourteen Points. Wilson was willing to negotiate only with a democratic government. After being encouraged to do so by Field Marshal Paul von Hindenburg, Wilhelm II abdicated under protest on November 9 as both German Emperor and King of Prussia. Max von Baden resigned later the same day, passing government authority on to Friedrich Ebert (1871–1925) with the comment: "Herr Ebert, I commit the German Empire to your keeping" (Friedrich 1972, p. 26).

Ebert was leader of the Social Democratic Party (SPD), a former saddle maker, bartender, journalist, and party bureaucrat. He did not wish to see the monarchy end and even urged von Baden to remain on as regent, or "administrator," until the Kaiser's son or grandson could replace him. The British favored preserving the monarchy, but Wilson's vision of the future did not include a Germany ruled by a monarch. Germany needed a liberal democracy, or so Wilson believed, as a part of his new world order.

The confused negotiations that preceded von Baden's announcement of Wilhelm II's abdication, an announcement he made on his own authority and without approval from the Kaiser, was part of an effort to preempt a revolution from below by engineering a revolution from above. Von Baden previously asked Ebert, would he support "the struggle against the social revolution?" Ebert's answer represented the wishes of all but the extreme left-wing radicals. "I do not want it – in fact," he said, "I hate it like sin" (Friedrich 1972, p. 20). All involved knew the success of a revolution from above depended upon cooperation between the civilian authority and the German army, still loyal to Hindenburg.

In a telephone conversation on November 10 with Wilhelm Gröner (1867–1939), Deputy Chief of the General Staff under Hindenburg, Ebert agreed to work with the old officer corps in suppressing the social revolution that both feared and "hated like sin." Historians remain divided over the significance of the so-called Ebert-Gröner Pact. Some feel that Ebert ensured that the new German republic was stillborn. Ebert understood, however, that without the army's support, the republic would not survive. Assured of the government's survival, Ebert proclaimed by decree, reforms that reassured the basically conservative population that Germany would not succumb to a Bolshevik revolution, even though a return to the golden years of the Wilhelmian era likely would not happen.

One Berliner, who many years later, reflected on those early days of November 1918, observed: "The really important thing during any crisis is whether the streetcars are running. If the streetcars keep running, then life is bearable" (Friedrich 1972, pp. 27–28). Ebert's government was able to ensure that the Berlin streetcars continued operating, as well as the telephones and all essential utilities.

The threat of a communist revolution was real. Karl Liebknecht (1871–1919), leader of the Independent Social Democratic Party (USPD), proclaimed Germany a socialist republic from the main balcony of the Royal Palace in Berlin. When he heard that Liebknecht was about to proclaim what amounted to a Bolshevik revolution, Philipp Scheidemann (1865–1939), deputy leader of the SPD, proclaimed the German Republic from a window of the Reichstag building. Scheidemann did not have time to consult Ebert, who was trying to establish a regency. Scheidemann later said that when Ebert learned of what he had done, "He banged his fist on the table and yelled at me. ... 'You have no right to proclaim the Republic'" (Friedrich 1972, p. 24). Instead of a smooth transition to some sort of constitutional monarchy, Germany became a republic, by accident.

Elections to a National Assembly were held in January 1919. Because a communist revolution, the so-called "Spartacist Uprising" led by Karl Liebknecht and Rosa Luxemburg (1871–1919), was underway in Berlin, the delegates met in the town of Weimar. There, they proceeded to elect Ebert as the first President of what became known as the Weimar Republic and drafted a democratic constitution.

Two provisions of the Weimar Constitution proved fatal for the Republic. Article 48 allowed the president to rule by decree in the event of a national emergency. The second was the provision that the Reichstag was to be elected according to a system of proportional representation. That provision made it virtually impossible for any one party to win an absolute majority in any national election. All of the governments of the Weimar Republic were by necessity coalition governments. The survival of the republic became dependent on the ability of three ideologically incompatible parties, the so-called Weimar parties – SPD, Catholic Center Party (Z, or *Zentrum*), and German Democratic Party (DDP) – to cooperate in coalitions to keep the republic afloat. They were able to do so by merely papering over the political and economic issues that divided them. There were 20 separate coalition governments during the republic's 14-year lifespan. It was government by crisis management.

The Weimar Republic was threatened from both the left and the right. In addition to the Spartacist Uprising in Berlin, a Bavarian Soviet Republic had a brief existence between April 6 and May 3, 1919. It was more of a comic opera than a serious attempt at establishing a nation state. There were other communist uprisings in Leipzig (1919), the Ruhr (1920), Saxony (1923), and Hamburg (1923). All were brutally suppressed by Freikorps units.

The Freikorps were paramilitary organizations made up largely of former combat soldiers. Since the Versailles Treaty denied Germany a military force capable of defending the republic, it turned to the Freikorps, even though the Freikorps did not accept the legitimacy of the Weimar Republic. The republic's dependence upon them in effect provided a license for the right-wing, anti-republican forces to prevent the threat of a revolution from below.

There were two attempted right-wing coups during the 1920s. The first was an attempted putsch in March 1920 by a group of Freikorps known as the Ehrhardt Brigade. The leader was Wolfgang Kapp (1858–1922), supported by Erich Ludendorff. When the army was called on to suppress the putsch, it refused to fire upon the Freikorps, whom they considered to be comrades in arms. The putsch collapsed after only four days due to a general strike called by the trade unions. All of the leaders of the putsch were able to leave the country with the aid of sympathetic officials, thus avoiding prosecution.

The second right-wing coup attempt occurred in Munich on November 8–9, 1923, and was led by Adolf Hitler (1889–1945), a minor nationalist agitator and leader of a regional political party named the National Socialist German Workers Party (NSADP), or more commonly the Nazi Party. Hitler disrupted a meeting of Bavarian nationalists in the Bürgerbräukeller, a large beer hall in Munich, on the evening of November 8 by jumping onto a chair, firing two shots into the ceiling, and announcing that he was forming a national government.

On the following day Hitler, joined by Erich Ludendorff, Hindenburg's partner in leadership of the German war effort during the Great War, led a group of followers in a march down Ludwigstrasse. They were confronted by Bavarian police who fired upon the marchers. Hitler and Ludendorff were subsequently arrested and tried for treason. Ludendorff was acquitted. Hitler was found guilty and sentenced to five years in prison. He was released after serving only nine months.

The greatest threat to the Weimar Republic's survival during the 1920s came not from the political right or left, but from the hyperinflation of 1923, caused in part by the Ruhr occupation. In July 1914, before the outbreak of the war, one U.S. dollar was worth 4.2 German marks. In January 1919, after the war was over, the same dollar was worth 8.9 marks. At the start of the Ruhr occupation in January 1923, inflation had reduced the value of the mark to 17 972 marks per dollar. On November 15, a single U.S. dollar was worth 4.2 trillion marks. The mark was worthless.

1914	$1 = 4.20 marks
1919 (July)	$1 = 14.00 marks
1921 (January)	$1 = 64.90 marks
1922 (January)	$1 = 191.80 marks
1922 (July)	$1 = 493.20 marks
1923 (January)	$1 = 17,972.00 marks
1923 (September)	$1 = 100 million marks
1923 (October)	$1 = 1 trillion marks
1923 (November)	$1 = 4.2 trillion marks

Figure 16.1 The Great Inflation of 1923 in Germany.

Factory workers were paid twice a day, at noon and the end of the workday. Earnings were handed out in bushels of paper currency. What a worker was paid at noon was virtually worthless by the end of the day. A former university student told of how he ordered a cup of coffee listed on the menu for 5000 marks. By the time he finished the first cup and ordered a second, the price had risen to 14000 marks.

A new government was formed led by Gustav Stressemann (1878–1929), a leading figure in the German People's Party (DVP), as chancellor. A new mark, the Rentenmark, was introduced. The old inflated currency could be traded in at the rate of one trillion old marks for one new Rentenmark. The value of the mark soon stabilized at the prewar value of 4.2 to the U.S. dollar.[3] A committee chaired by American banker Charles G. Dawes (1865–1951) came up with the Dawes Plan that enabled Germany to resume regular reparations payments. The plan included ending the Ruhr occupation and a loan of 800 million gold marks, mostly provided by Wall Street banks.

The issuance of the new currency enabled the government to pay off the national debt, but as when Britain and France returned to the gold standard, it hurt the middle class. The impact on the German middle class was devastating. They were wiped out financially, since the government ruled that a mark was a mark. Those who had access to solid currencies during the hyperinflation were able to pay off debts and purchase properties with the inflated marks.

The psychological impact on the middle class was even greater than the financial impact. They lost their sense of self-worth, and with it, their values, their faith in democracy, and for many, their faith in free-enterprise economics. In their search for an explanation of what was happening to them, they abandoned the center parties and turned to the rightist parties. The Weimar parties that previously worked together to keep the republic afloat began to lose support at the polls.

American bankers loaned approximately three billion gold marks to Germany by 1925. A portion went into economic development. Some was passed on to the French and British in the form of reparations payments. The French and British, in turn, were able to make payments on their wartime debts to the American banks which, in turn, made more loans to Germany. Money was put in circulation, leading to a measure of tranquility and prosperity not known since before the Great War. The last half of the 1920s were called the "roaring twenties" in America and Britain, the "crazy years" in France, and the "golden twenties" in Germany.

United States

Like their European counterparts, most Americans wanted to return to life as it was before America's entry into the war in Europe. Most Americans, being descendants of European emigrants, thought of the home of their ancestors as the "old country." Wilson's global idealism had little appeal for the average American citizen. The United States of America was still on the march to fulfill its "manifest destiny," to occupy the North American continent from the Atlantic to the Pacific oceans. The Indian Wars west of the Mississippi would not "officially" end until 1924.

---

3 There was a total of 1.2 sextillion (1 200 000 000 000 000 000 000) inflated, paper marks in circulation in July 1924.

Many Americans believed that their involvement in the Great War was a mistake. Now that the war was over "over there," as the lyrics of George M. Cohan's popular wartime tune put it, it was time for the boys to return home to the business at hand, that is, to the building of a great American republic uninterested and uninvolved with the world beyond its borders. It was a feeling that found expression in the 1920 Republican presidential candidate Warren G. Harding's plea: "America's present need is not heroics, but healing; not nostrums, but normalcy; not revolution, but restoration; not agitation, but adjustment; not surgery, but serenity; not the dramatic, but the dispassionate; not experiment, but equipoise; not submergence in internationality, but sustainment in triumphant nationality...." (Warren G. Harding 2019).

Harding (1865–1923) won all of the states except the traditionally Democratic South, and even made inroads there by winning Tennessee. His landslide victory with 60% of the popular vote and 404 electoral votes was a clear repudiation of Wilson's foreign policy. Harding died in office in August 1923 and was succeeded by Vice President Calvin Coolidge (1872–1933).

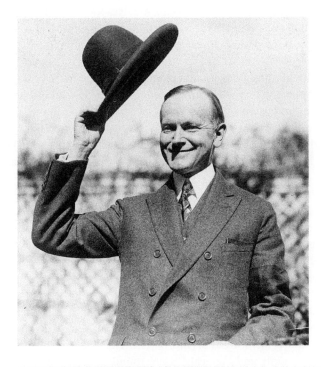

October 22nd 1924   32764

LC-F8-32764-slight

Figure 16.2 President Calvin Coolidge was a living embodiment of the optimism characterized in America during the "Roaring Twenties" before the Great Depression struck. *Source:* National Photo Company Collection.

Coolidge was the ideal leader for America experiencing the greatest era of prosperity in its history. He embodied the principles of nineteenth-century economic liberalism. The proper role of the president, as understood and practiced by Coolidge, was to step aside and allow the natural laws of laissez-faire to work their magic for the greater good of all. "After all," Coolidge told a meeting of the American Society of Newspaper Editors in January 1925, "the chief business of the American people is business. They are profoundly concerned with producing, buying, selling, investing, and prospering in the world. I am strongly of the opinion that the great majority of people will always find these are moving impulses of our life" (Sobel 1988).

Everyone, except small farmers, especially in the rural South, seemed to be enjoying the prosperity. The average worker who earned $750 per year in 1919 was earning $1236 in 1929. In his State of the Union address to Congress in January 1929, Coolidge pointed with pride to America's successes: "No Congress ever assembled has met with a more pleasing prospect than that which appears at the present time. In the domestic field there is tranquility and contentment ... and the highest record years of prosperity" (Galbraith 2009, p. 1). In his acceptance speech for the Republican nomination for the presidency in August 1929, Herbert Hoover (1874–1964) echoed Coolidge: "We in America today are nearer to the final triumph over poverty than ever before in the history of any land.... We shall soon, with the help of God, be in sight of the day when poverty will be banished from this nation" (Strout 1982).

America was not immune to the paranoia that was sweeping across Europe in the postwar years. Fear of things foreign, especially immigrants from predominantly Roman Catholic and non-English speaking parts of Europe, or areas of the globe occupied by non-Europeans, was a part of the warp and woof of American society since its founding. This often-ignored aspect of American history found fertile soil for its expression at various times in the nation's history. One such period was during the decades following the end of the Great War.

Socialist and Marxist theories never found widespread acceptance among the multinational and religiously diverse working class in America. Still, the fear that such ideas might catch on were widespread during the Gilded Age and throughout most of the twentieth century. The success of the Bolshevik Revolution in Russia in 1917, and the frequent communist uprisings in central and eastern Europe after the war, heightened fears in America of anything that might remotely be identified as "socialism," "Bolshevism," or "communism."

What historians call the "Red Scare" swept through America in 1919–1920 causing panic and violence. The flames were fueled by "Red hunters" who saw imaginary agents of Bolshevism everywhere. Chief among them was U.S. Attorney General A. Mitchell Palmer (1872–1936). Thousands of immigrants and "radicals" were rounded up in what were called "Palmer raids," the largest of which took place in January 1920. Six thousand alleged radicals were arrested in thirty-three cities across America. Many were arrested and held without warrants or being formally charged, denied contact with lawyers or relatives, and in some cases, coerced into signing confessions. Six hundred were eventually deported.

The Red Scare became mixed with a revival of nativism. Congress passed legislation in May 1921 that limited immigration from any given country to 3% of foreign-born residents of that nationality residing in the United States according to the 1910 census. Restrictions

Figure 16.3 Attorney General A. Mitchell Palmer presided over the "Red Scare" that swept America in 1919–1920. *Source:* National Photo Company Collection.

on immigration increased under the Immigration Act of 1924, which changed the percentage to 2% of a given nationality residing in the United States in 1890. It also limited immigration to a total of 150 000, down from 805 228 in 1920, and totally excluded the Japanese. Chinese immigration was effectively halted by the Chinese Exclusion Act of 1882, renewed in 1892 and 1902 by the Geary Act. Chinese residents could be deported but not granted citizenship. The Supreme Court ruled in 1923 that Asian Indians, though "Caucasians" and "of the same race as white Americans," were not eligible for citizenship, "because U.S. law allowed only free whites to become naturalized citizens," and "the average man knows perfectly well that there are unmistakable and profound differences" (Not All Caucasians are White 2019).

The Ku Klux Klan, newly revived in 1915, reached its peak in membership in 1923. Though primarily remembered as an anti-black, racist organization in the South, the KKK was more anti-Roman Catholic and anti-Jewish elsewhere. Jews were commonly discriminated against in education, in access to employment, and socially. Many in America during the 1920s associated Jews with Bolshevism. Anti-Semitic views were widely disseminated by such popular figures as the industrialist Henry Ford (1863–1947), the popular radio preacher Father Charles Edward Coughlin (1891–1979), and the aviator-pioneer, Charles Lindbergh (1902–1974).

Henry Ford purchased *The Dearborn Independent* newspaper in 1918 and used it to disseminate his belief that America was the victim of a vast Jewish conspiracy. He outlined his theory in a series of 91 articles that were later published in four volumes titled *The International Jew: The World's Foremost Problem* (1920). He also published *The Protocols of the Meetings of the Learned Elders of Zion*, an anti-Semitic book first published in Russia in 1903, claiming to be the minutes of a meeting of Jewish leaders who planned the domination of the world by the Jews. The *Protocols* were later serialized by Father Coughlin in his periodical *Social Justice* during 1938. Charles Lindbergh was a frequent visitor to the Ford home in Dearborn, and shared Ford's views regarding the negative influence of Jews in America. But Lindbergh was more than just an anti-Semite; he was a convinced eugenicist.

Anti-Semitism, nativist inspired anti-immigration mania, the pseudo-scientific theories of the eugenicists, and anti-Roman Catholicism were all a part of a witch's brew that was pervasive in America between the two world wars. During the presidential election of 1928, when the Republican Herbert Hoover, "the Great Humanitarian," ran against Al Smith, "the Happy Warrior," a campaign leaflet that circulated in upstate New York warned of what would happen, if Al Smith, the Roman Catholic Governor of New York and anti-prohibitionist was elected:

> When Catholics rule the United States
> And the Jew grows a Christian nose on his face
> When Pope Pius is head of the Ku Klux Klan
> In the land of Uncle Sam
> Then Al Smith will be our president
> And the country not worth a damn.
>
> (Cummins 2008)

This aspect of the American spirit during the 1920s and 1930s is largely forgotten today, perhaps because of what the same prejudices led to in Germany during the 1940's.

Soviet Russia

Russia was torn by civil war between 1917 and 1922, during which the new Bolshevik government struggled to survive opposition from within and intervention by its former allies and the United States. The Communist Party[4] led by Vladimir Lenin implemented a policy known a "War Communism." Some historians consider War Communism a series of emergency measures necessitated by the Russian Civil War. Others have concluded that it was a coordinated effort to undermine the economic basis for any opposition to the state, including those who clung to the idealistic slogans of the 1917 Revolution. All private property, including personal property, was nationalized. All banking became a state monopoly, and at one point, there was an attempt to replace money with an official barter system. Industry was nationalized, strikes forbidden, and compulsory labor introduced in 1918. By the end of the year, all land was nationalized as well.

---

4 The Bolsheviks became the Communist Party in 1918. The Russian Soviet Federated Socialist Republic (RSFSR) became the Union of Soviet Socialist Republics (USSR) in 1924, when a new constitution was drafted to replace that of 1918.

War Communism was an economic disaster. Industrial and agricultural production reached new lows. People fled the cities to the countryside, while the hardships of War Communism caused Russia's population to drop by 16 million, not including deaths from war or emigration. Serious resistance broke out during 1921 that led to the introduction of Lenin's New Economic Policy (NEP). Peasants were allowed to sell their surplus grain and produce on the open market, and some private enterprise and retail trade was allowed. What Lenin called the "commanding heights" of the economy – banking, large industry, transport, utilities, and foreign trade – remained state controlled.

Within a few years, the economy saw substantial recovery, but not soon enough to prevent a severe famine in 1921–1922 that caused an estimated five million deaths. Lenin's death in January 1924, after a series of three strokes, unleashed a power struggle within the Communist Party between Lenin's chosen successor, Leon Trotsky (Lev Davidovich Bronstein, 1879–1940) and Joseph Stalin (Iosif Vissarionovich Dzhugashvili, 1878–1953). By 1928, Trotsky was ousted and exiled first to Kazakhstan then to Turkey and eventually assassinated, in August 1940, at his residence in Mexico City.

Stalin launched the first of three Five-Year Plans in 1928 aimed at establishing the Soviet Union as a modern industrial nation capable of defending itself from the perceived threat of annihilation by hostile capitalist powers. The first two, 1928–1932 and 1933–1937, emphasized heavy industry and collectivization of agriculture with little benefit for the masses. Real wages for the workers remained at or near subsistence level. Millions were subjected to forced labor. In one sense, the Five-Year Plans succeeded. By 1940, the Soviet Union was the world's third industrial nation behind the United States and Germany.

The collectivization of agriculture served two purposes, to provide the necessary food supply for industrialization and to destroy the independence of the peasants. Collective farms were industrialized agriculture in which farms, like factories, were expected to meet production quotas assigned by central planners. When expected results did not materialize, government officials confiscated what grain was produced, leaving millions to starve. Failure to meet production quotas led to claims that the kulaks, a class of formerly prosperous farmers, were sabotaging the efforts at collectivizing the farms. Stalin declared the kulaks "enemies of the people" and set in motion policies aimed at "liquidating the Kulaks as a class" (Stalin's Forced Famine 2000). Resistance was met with severe repression, including an engineered famine that resulted in millions of deaths.

There is no agreement on how many died as a result of the collectivization and famine, or how many vanished into the system of forced labor camps known as the "Gulag." As many as 25000 per day may have died of starvation in the Ukraine at the height of the famine in the spring of 1933. Mikhail Gorbachev (b. 1931), who served as the last leader of the Soviet Union from 1985 to its demise in 1991, experienced the famine as a child in Stavropol Krai: "In that terrible year [in 1933] nearly half the population of my native village, Privolnoye, starved to death, including two sisters and one brother of my father" (Gorbachev and Collis 2006, p. 10). The State Duma of the Russian Federation in 2008 passed a resolution, "In memory of the victims of the famine of the 1930s on the territory of the USSR," that estimated total deaths at approximately seven million (Statement of State Duma 2008).

A third Five-Year Plan was launched in 1938 but was suspended when the German invasion of the Soviet Union began in 1941. The Five-Year Plans laid the basis for a modern industrial economy, while at the same time, the basis for the Stalinist totalitarian state.

Italy

Like the other European powers, Italy suffered from the economic aftershocks of the Great War. Also, the propertied classes feared that the economic hardships suffered by the working class would lead to a Bolshevik revolution. Unlike in Britain, Germany, and France, there was no willingness on the part of the various political parties to form working coalitions to deal with the problems the nation faced. Added to the economic woes was the fact that Italy's performance in the war was not very impressive, and so, the rewards promised to Italy for joining the Allies were not honored at the Paris Peace Conference. There was a great deal of resentment felt by the people just waiting for a charismatic political leader to focus it on "the enemies" within and without, and by doing so, become the leader of a new Italy.

In 1921, Benito Mussolini (1883–1945), a former schoolteacher, member of the prewar Socialist Party and editor of its newspaper, and a wounded war veteran, founded the National Fascist Party. The party's symbol was the fasces, a bundle of rods tied around with an axe with the blade exposed. The fasces was borrowed from the Roman Republic, where it served as a symbol of supreme authority or imperium.

Italian Fascism did not have a coherent ideology like Marxism-Leninism or National Socialism (Nazism). It was fundamentally a mass movement that emphasized action cloaked in more than a little romanticism. The Fascists appealed to the wounded national-ist pride of the people, presented themselves as a bulwark against communism and defender of the workers against exploitation by the capitalists. Italian Fascism was a curi-ous blend of two opposite ideologies, nationalism and socialism. What intellectual content there was came from a blend of ideas drawn from Friedrich Nietzsche, Georges Sorel, Henri Bergson, and other pre-1914 theorists. Mussolini was an admirer of Plato's *Republic*, which he often read, and from which he may have obtained his vision of a future Italy shaped and ruled by Fascism. Asked once to describe the future state he was creating in Italy, Mussolini coined the term "totalitarianism." It must be noted, however, that Mussolini's Italy was never a totalitarian state.

In October 1922, King Victor Emmanuel III (1869–1947) called upon Mussolini to form a government, believing that he could establish a stable government and govern responsibly. The Fascist Party emerged from the 1924 elections as the largest party with two-thirds of the seats in the Chamber of Deputies. Following the murder in 1924 of Giacomo Matteotti (1885–1924), a socialist deputy and strong critic of the Fascists, most of the non-Fascist representatives left the Chamber of Deputies in what was called the Aventine Secession.

During the immediate years following Matteotti's murder, Mussolini transformed Italy into a one-party state ruled by Il Duce, (The Leader), Mussolini's title as leader of the Fascist Party. Press censorship was imposed, and opposition parties were banned. Mussolini was granted authority to rule by decree in January 1926. Independent labor unions were disbanded, strikes outlawed, and arbitration of labor disputes that usually favored management were enforced. Schools were brought under state control and militarized youth movements introduced. Municipal and provincial elections were ended in 1926, and after 1928, only candidates approved by the Fascist Grand Council could be elected to office. As in Stalin's Soviet Union, Italian citizens had no real choice but to approve the Fascist Party's candidates.

Mussolini's Fascist state was a right-wing movement that staged impressive military parades and maintained an atmosphere of warlike delirium. The more romantic, like Mussolini himself, dreamed of a new Roman Empire. In reality, the Fascists never solved the economic problems that existed since the end of the Great War. Bankruptcies increased, the infrastructure remained largely unchanged, real wages did not rise, and the standard of living for most Italians did not improve.

Mussolini's single impressive achievement was his resolution of the conflict between the Italian state and the Roman Catholic Church going back to the unification of Italy with Rome as its capital. The Lateran Accords, or Lateran Treaties, were agreed to by the Kingdom of Italy and the Vatican in 1929. They established the Vatican City, all 109 acres (44.1 ha.) of it, as a sovereign state and formalized relations between the Roman Catholic Church and Italy. The pope agreed to remain neutral in international affairs. Also, Italy would be a confessional state, that is, Roman Catholicism would remain the state religion.

The Great Depression

The Roaring Twenties came to a sudden end on Tuesday, October 29, 1929, when the New York Stock Exchange crashed. The total losses in the value of stocks traded that day was greater than twice the value of all currency in circulation in the United States. Soon America and the developed world was experiencing what is referred to as "the Great Depression". The Great Depression had a profound impact on the economic and psychological health of people in America and Europe. Many from both the middle and working classes began to question if the natural laws of society and economics as explained by John Locke and Adam Smith (constitutional government and free enterprise economics), were obsolete. Perhaps the aftermath of the Great War and the Great Depression demanded new theories, new ideologies accompanied by action.

American Connection

The Great Depression was triggered by the New York Stock Market crash, but there were signs well before October 1929, and contrary to the outward gaiety of the 1920's, that there were serious unresolved problems in the economies of the United States and Europe emanating from the war. The agricultural sector of both economies never recovered during the 1920s. World trade was disrupted as producers and markets shifted, at times switching roles. The breakup of the Hapsburg Empire in Southeastern Europe created a number of competing national economies. As the Depression deepened, everywhere the tendency was to try and protect home industries by erecting high tariff walls. National leaders everywhere failed, or refused to recognize, that each nation's economy was but one part of an intricate world economy and, therefore, economic problems had to be addressed with that understanding.

The hidden weakness in the economic prosperity of the Roaring Twenties was the American economy. Prosperity in Europe was dependent on American finances, while American prosperity itself was financed by credit. Speculation in stocks, not the production and consumption of goods and services, was the force driving the boom. Fortunes were made on paper, mounds of stocks purchased on "margin" (credit), with the stocks themselves serving as collateral. While anyone could theoretically become a millionaire overnight by "playing the stock market," wages for workers remained mostly stagnant. Poor farmers and laborers could not afford to buy the goods they produced. Overproduction combined with underconsumption was a disastrous formula.

Economic depression spread rapidly after the crash on Wall Street. Banks failed. Factories closed. Layoffs increased exponentially. Between October 1929 and March 1933, the value of stocks fell from $87 billion to $19 billion. The gross national product (GDP) decreased by roughly one-third during the same period. By 1933, one-quarter of the American labor force was unemployed, and those who found work often worked for as little as 10 cents an hour, or less. According to some reports, department stores in New York City could require applicants for employment as elevator operators to have a college degree.

Many in America blamed the depression on President Herbert Hoover. He organized relief for Belgium during the Great War and relief for the starving in Soviet Russia during the famine of the 1920s. Why, many wondered, did he not do something to relieve the suffering at home caused by the depression? People began to refer to empty pockets as "Hoover flags," newspapers as "Hoover blankets," and shanty towns built on the edge of cities by the unemployed as "Hoovervilles" (Boardman 1989, p. 125).

Figure 16.4 A crowd gathers outside the New York Stock Exchange on news of the crash of 1929. *Source:* Library of Congress.

The depression spread from America to Europe. Even before the stock market crash, American investors slowed investments in Europe and began withdrawing funds from European banks. There were greater and quicker gains to be made by speculating in stocks. The pace quickened once the depression began. The international flow of money, stimulated by the Dawes Plan and American loans to Germany, halted, and when it did, the prosperity ended, giving way to depression. By 1931, Europe was feeling the full effects of what was becoming a worldwide depression.

The Soviet Union was largely outside the world economy during the Great Depression. It operated a command economy that insulated it from the international finance and market demand forces that were at the heart of the Great Depression. In fact, the Soviet economy grew rapidly, as the Soviet Union experienced an industrial revolution of its own, while the Western nations tried to find a way out of the depression.

Both the United States and the European nations tried to respond to the depression as if it were a national problem. Each clung tenaciously to the classic liberal economic theory associated with Adam Smith and his followers. Basic to their analysis was the belief that a loss of confidence in the monetary system and a failure to remain competitive in international markets was causing the depression. The solution was to tighten the belt, that is, balance the budget, reduce costs of production, and maintain the value of the currency. The hard times of the depression would weed out weak and inefficient sectors of the economy. Governments must not interfere in some ill-advised effort to shore up inefficient enterprises or mitigate the suffering of the masses by attempting to maintain wages or unemployment benefits through deficit financing. Such efforts would only result in a greater economic disaster in the future. Stay the course was the watchword of the day, and the economy would, in time, right itself.

An alternative approach was offered by the English economist John Maynard Keynes, a leading advocate of the new consumer-based economic theory. Keynes published his ideas in *The General Theory of Employment, Interest, and Money* (1936), one of the most influential books of the twentieth century. Keynes questioned the assumption that people, at least their governments, were helpless before the rigid economic laws of the classical economists. He rejected the notion that free enterprise necessarily meant governments must not attempt to manipulate the economy, or that deflationary policies were the only acceptable response to depression.

Keynes believed that governments could, and should, intervene with inflationary policies that would increase production and employment. Among the policies he advocated were public works programs to put the unemployed back to work, lowering interest rates, and printing more currency. More money would be available for investment and to pay for the stimulus package. Rather than remaining passive, governments possessed the capacity to create and maintain prosperity.

Keynes's critics accused him of advocating socialism. In fact, just the opposite was true. Keynesian economics, as his theories put into practice came to be called, proved to be the means by which free enterprise (capitalism or laissez-faire) was saved. Two leaders who came to power in early 1933, Franklin D. Roosevelt (1882–1945) and Adolf Hitler, ended the Great Depression in their respective countries by applying Keynes's activist economic policies. Roosevelt's New Deal programs, together with the massive defense spending during World War II ended the Great Depression in America. Likewise, the massive spending for rearmament ended the economic slump in Germany.

Hitler's Rise to Power

Adolf Hitler was released from prison in December 1924, after serving only nine months of his five-year sentence. While in prison, he began dictating much of *Mein Kampf* (*My Struggle*)[5] to his deputy, Rudolph Hess (1894–1987). *Mein Kampf* is an often-confusing narrative of Hitler's life, political philosophy, vision of Germany's revival, and racial theories, especially his virulent anti-Semitism. The first volume appeared in July 1925, and sold 9473 copies, just shy of the total 10 000 first printing. The second volume followed in 1927. It was not until after Hitler became Chancellor in 1933, that *Mein Kampf* became a best seller.

Very few people read *Mein Kampf* at first, and even fewer took it seriously. One who did was Johannes Stanjek (1873–1930), a Roman Catholic theologian and editor of the journal *Defense Papers* (*Abwehr-Blätter*). Using the penname Raphael Ahren, Stanjek wrote a four-page review of *Mein Kampf* for the October 20, 1925 issue. His review shows how even a learned scholar found it difficult to believe that a nation as well educated as Germany could succumb to such ideas. "One puts Hitler's book aside with a feeling of satisfaction," Stanjek concludes. "As long as the völkisch movement cannot find better leaders, much water will flow down the stream before they will be victorious in the land of poets and thinkers" (Ahren 2016).

Between March 1925 and March 1927, Hitler was banned from making public speeches. Once the ban was lifted, he was able to take advantage of his gift as a spellbinding speaker during the May 1928 parliamentary election. Some consider Hitler one of the two greatest orators of the twentieth century, Winston Churchill being the other. Forty-one political parties competed in the May 1928 parliamentary election. The governing coalition parties retained power with 58.5% of the popular vote, whereas the Nazi Party received only 2.6% of the popular vote (Deutschland Wahl Zum 4 1928).

The Great Depression began to impact Germany in 1930, with tragic results for the Weimar Republic's last truly parliamentary government led by Hermann Müller (1876–1931), a Social Democrat. As unemployment rose, and funds available for unemployment insurance evaporated, Müller proposed reducing benefits and increasing insurance rates in order to balance the budget. When Müller's own party refused to go along, his government collapsed. Hindenburg called upon Heinrich Brüning (1885–1970) from the Roman Catholic Center Party to lead a new government.

When the Reichstag rejected Brüning's proposed austerity budget, President Hindenburg called for new parliamentary elections. The elections held on September 14, 1930 marked the end of parliamentary government and the beginning of a presidential dictatorship. The Nazi Party increased its share of the popular vote from 2.6% in 1928 to 18.25% in 1930 (Deutschland Wahl Zum 5 1930). It became the second largest party behind the Social Democrats. All subsequent governments lacked a majority in the Reichstag and governed by presidential decree as allowed by Article 48 of the Weimar Constitution.

Germans went to the polls twice during 1932, in attempts to create a coalition that could command a majority in the Reichstag. Success was denied in both. The Nazi Party's percentage increased to 37.27%, thus making it the largest party in the Reichstag. The Weimar coalition parties that won 58.5% of the popular vote in 1928, won only 38.26% in

---

5 Hitler wrote a second book in 1928. It was first published in English in 1962 as *Hitler's Secret Book* and again in 2003 with a more accurate translation as *Hitler's Second Book*.

July 1932 (Deutschland: Wahl Zum 6 1932). Desperate to restore parliamentary government, Hindenburg offered the chancellorship to Adolf Hitler on January 30, 1933.

In his memoirs published after his death, Heinrich Brüning discussed last minute efforts by himself and others, including Kurt von Schleicher (1882–1934), Gregor Strasser (1892–1934), and some leading Social Democrats, to prevent one-party rule under Hitler. Schleicher served as chancellor from December 3, 1932 until January 28, 1933. Strasser was a prominent leader of the left-wing of the Nazi Party in northern Germany. According to Brüning, the conspirators tried to create a coalition government dedicated to restoration of the monarchy. The effort failed due to Hindenburg's loyalty to Wilhelm II and unwillingness to accept another member of his family as monarch. Though very interesting, most scholars do not consider Brüning's recollection of the events as creditable (Patch, Jr. 1998).

Erich Ludendorff, onetime supporter of Adolf Hitler, sent a telegram to Hindenburg warning him of the danger that Hitler's appointment represented for the future of Germany: "I prophesy that this man will plunge our Reich into the abyss and will inflict immeasurable woe on our nation. Future generations will curse you in your grave" (Kinzer 1993).

Hitler was able to persuade Hindenburg to issue the Decree of the Reich President for the Protection of People and State on February 27, 1933. The occasion was the burning of the Reichstag building, which Hitler argued was intended to be a signal for a communist revolution. The measure was meant to silence opposition from the SPD and the Communist Party (KPD). Despite efforts to silence the left-wing parties, the Nazis failed to win a majority in the March 5 parliamentary elections. The German National People's Party joined forces with the Nazis to form a majority in the Reichstag, but still not enough to change the constitution.

The end of the Weimar Republic came on March 23, when the Reichstag passed the Enabling Act (Law to Remedy the Distress of People and Reich), giving Hitler plenary power to pass laws without the participation of the Reichstag. Prior to the vote in the Reichstag, leaders of the Communist Party were arrested, and the party banned. Twenty-six of the Social Democrat delegates were in hiding, fearful for their lives. Only ninety-four risked attending and voting against the Enabling Act. In order to achieve the necessary votes to pass the Act, Hitler promised the Roman Catholic Center Party that in exchange for its support, he would respect the rights of the Catholic Church in Germany and improve relations between Germany and the Vatican. The Enabling Act passed by a vote of 444 to 94.

The Weimar Republic passed into history as the Nazis rose in the Reichstag, gave the Hitler salute, and sang the party's anthem the "Horst Wessel Song." Just three days earlier, Heinrich Himmler (1900–1945), head of the SS, opened the first concentration camp near the picturesque town of Dachau, a short distance northwest of Munich. The Enabling Act, that was to last for only four years, was renewed repeatedly until the end of World War II.

References

Ahren, R. (2016). Why Jews Didn't Blink an Eye When 'Mein Kampf' First Came Out. The Times of Israel. https://www.timesofisrael.com/why-jews-couldnt-care-less-about-mein-kampf-when-it-first-came-out (accessed 21 October 2019).

Boardman, B. (1989). *Flappers, Bootleggers, "Typhoid Mary," & the Bomb: An Anecdotal History of the United States from 1923–1945*. New York: Perennial Library.

Crafts, N. (2014). Walking Wounded: The British Economy in the Aftermath of World War I. VOX, CEPR's Policy Portal. https://voxeu.org/article/walking-wounded-british-economy-aftermath-world-war-i (accessed 21 October 2019).

Cummins, J. (2008). Dirty Campaigning in the Roaring Twenties: Herbert Hoover vs. Al Smith. Mental Floss. http://mentalfloss.com/article/19897/dirty-campaigning-roaring-twenties-herbert-hoover-vs-al-smith (accessed 21 October 2019).

Deutschland: Wahl Zum 4 (1928). Reichstag. http://www.gonschior.de/weimar/Deutschland/RT4.html (accessed 21 October 2019).

Deutschland: Wahl Zum 5 (1930). Reichstag. http://www.gonschior.de/weimar/Deutschland/RT5.html (accessed 21 October 2019).

Deutschland: Wahl Zum 6 (1932). Reichstag. http://www.gonschior.de/weimar/Deutschland/RT6.html (accessed 21 October 2019).

Emerson, R. and Kilson, M. (1965). The American dilemma in a changing world: the rise of Africa and the negro American. *Daedalus* 94 (4): 1055–1084.

Friedrich, O. (1972). *Before the Deluge: A Portrait of Berlin in the 1920's*. New York: Harper & Row.

Galbraith, J.K. (2009). *The Great Crash 1929*. Boston: Houghton Mifflin Harcourt.

Gorbachev, M.S. and Collis, J. (2006). *Manifesto for the Earth: Action Now for Peace, Global Justice and a Sustainable Future*. Forest Row, East Sussex: Clairview.

History Matters (n.d.). Not All Caucasians Are White: The Supreme Court Rejects Citizenship for Asian Indians. The U.S. Survey Course on the Web. http://historymatters.gmu.edu/d/5076 (accessed 21 October 2019).

Kinzer, S. (1993). Hitler's Rise Recalled With Sorrow. The New York Times. https://www.nytimes.com/1993/01/31/world/hitler-s-rise-recalled-with-sorrow.html (accessed 21 October 2019).

McCleland, D. (2015). Churchill vs Lady Astor: The Age of Classic Insults and Witticisms. The Casual Observer. http://thecasualobserver.co.za/churchill-lady-astor-classic-insults-and-witticisms (accessed 21 October 2019).

Mougel, N. (2011). World War I Casualties. Reperes. http://www.centre-robert-schuman.org/userfiles/files/REPERES%20%E2%80%93%20module%201-1-1%20-%20explanatory%20notes%20%E2%80%93%20World%20War%20I%20casualties%20%E2%80%93%20EN.pdf (accessed 21 October 2019).

Nicolson, H. (1966). *Diaries and Letters. 1930–1939*. London: Collins.

Patch, W.L. Jr. (1998). Heinrich Brüning's recollections of monarchism: the birth of a red herring. *The Journal of Modern History* 70 (2): 340–370.

Sobel, R. (1988). Essays, Papers & Addresses. Calvin Coolidge Presidential Foundation ICal. https://www.coolidgefoundation.org/resources/essays-papers-addresses-35 (accessed 21 October 2019).

Strout, R. (1982). 'Poor Hoover.' The Christian Science Monitor. https://www.csmonitor.com/1982/0326/032631.html (accessed 8 November 2019).

The History Place (2000). Stalin's Forced Famine 1932–1933, 7,000,000 Deaths. http://www.historyplace.com/worldhistory/genocide/stalin.htm (accessed 21 October 2019).

The White House (2006). Warren G. Harding. https://www.whitehouse.gov/about-the-white-house/presidents/warren-g-harding (Accessed 21 October 2019).

Wikisource (2008). Statement of the State Duma of the Russian Federation. In Memory of the Victims of the Famine of the 1930s on the Territory of the USSR. https://ru.wikisource.org/wiki/Заглавная_страница (accessed 21 October 2019).

17

A Second Great War

Chronology

1921–1922	Washington Naval Conference
1931	Japanese Invade Manchuria
1933	Reich Concordat Between Germany and the Vatican
1933	German Rearmament Begins
1935	Italy Invades Ethiopia
1938	Union (Anschluss) of Germany and Austria
1938	Munich Conference Surrenders Sudetenland to Germany
1939	Nazi-Soviet Nonaggression Pact
1939	World War II Begins with German Invasion of Poland
1939–1940	Winter War Between Finland and Soviet Union
1940	Fall of France, Free French and Vichy France Governments Formed
1940	Battle of Britain
1941	German Invasion of Soviet Union
1941	Japanese Attack on Pearl Harbor, Home of USA Pacific Fleet
1941	USA Declares War on Japan, Germany Declares War on USA
1942	Wannsee Conference Plans Genocide of Jews in Europe
1942	Battle of Midway, Tide Turns in War with Japan
1942–1943	Battle of Stalingrad, Tide Turns in Favor of Allies
1943	Allied Invasion of Sicily and Italy; Mussolini Deposed; Italy Surrenders
1943	German Forces Defeated in North Africa
1945	Hitler Commits Suicide, Germany Surrenders
1945	USA Drops Atomic Bombs on Hiroshima and Nagasaki, Japan Surrenders

What French poet Romain Rolland called a "Sad Peace! Laughable interlude between the massacres of peoples!" came to an end on September 1, 1939. An estimated one million German soldiers, in mechanized divisions and supported by overwhelming air power, crossed the German-Polish frontier, quickly overpowering and crushing the unprepared and poorly led Polish forces. The Free City of Danzig was occupied and declared reunited with Germany. Both Britain and France issued ultimatums to Germany demanding that

Western Civilization: A Brief History, First Edition. Paul R. Waibel.
© 2020 John Wiley & Sons, Inc. Published 2020 by John Wiley & Sons, Inc.

German forces withdraw from Poland. In England, blackout conditions were ordered for the duration of the war, and the evacuation of children from the large cities to safety in the countryside began. Across Europe, and even in distant areas of the globe, nations began declaring their neutrality, including Germany's ally Italy.

Both Britain and France declared war on Germany on September 3. Immediate military action against Germany, however, was limited to the Royal Air Force (RAF) dropping 5.4 million propaganda leaflets over northern Germany. Logistically speaking, Britain could not go to the rescue of Poland. Only France could have launched an attack on Germany, but France's military planning for another war with Germany was based on defense, not offense.

The fact that both Britain and France possessed overseas empires that spanned the globe meant that this new war in Eastern Europe, like that which began in 1914, became a worldwide war in a matter of days. An article appeared on September 12 in the *New York Times* in which the war in Europe was referred to as the "Second World War," (*New York Times* September 10, 1939) and Washington and Jefferson College in Washington, Pennsylvania announced a new history course on "the second world war" (*New York Times* September 12, 1939). Henceforth, the Great War would be known as the First World War, or World War I, and the war that began on September 1, 1939 would be known as the Second World War, or World War II.

In one sense, designating September 1, 1939 as the beginning of World War II is arbitrary. Historians like to have start and end dates for major historical events, and so, the German invasion of Poland and the final Japanese surrender on September 2, 1945 are the traditional dates for World War II. But the actual beginning of the war differed for the various participants. In the European theater, the beginning date could be given as July 1936, when Germany and Italy sent volunteers to Spain and provided combat air support for General Francisco Franco's (1892–1975) nationalist forces in the Spanish Civil War (1936–1939). The Italian invasion of Ethiopia in October 1935 could also be designated as the beginning of World War II. The Japanese invasion of Manchuria in September 1931 is a logical choice for the beginning of the war in the Asian theater.

World War II, unlike World War I, was actually two wars, one fought in Europe and the other fought in Asia and the Pacific. There was really no coordination of the two wars by either side. In January 1941, Britain and the United States agreed that if the United States entered the war against Germany and Japan, priority would be given to the defeat of Germany.

Road to War in Europe

It is commonly believed that a war in Europe was inevitable once Hitler came to power. His plans to avenge the wrongs imposed upon Germany by the Versailles Treaty, and to unite all Germans in one great German Reich that would last a thousand years, are clearly stated in *Mein Kampf*. During the first two years of his rule, Hitler did not make any aggressive moves in foreign affairs. He was well aware that Germany was in no position to alarm Britain and France. Before challenging the Western Allies, Hitler first had to construct a totalitarian system of government in Germany, while at the same time, ending the depression and covertly rearming.

Totalitarianism

The goal of a traditional dictatorship is essentially conservative. So long as the individual paid taxes, obeyed the laws, served in the military when called upon to do so, recognized the traditional class structure of society, and gave at least passive support to the regime, the individual enjoyed a considerable degree of personal freedom. Such governments were widespread in Europe by the latter 1930s. Spain, Portugal, the East European "successor states" (Poland, Hungary, and Yugoslavia) were all dictatorships of one form or another. Even Mussolini's Fascist Italy was, in reality, only a rightwing dictatorship.

National Socialist Germany and Marxist-Leninist Soviet Russia were something new and quite different from the traditional dictatorships or even the extreme autocracy that existed in Tsarist Russia. The new style authoritarian dictatorships are commonly referred to as "totalitarian." They were the very antithesis of liberalism. They are best understood as a kind of religious revival movement that harnessed the energy of the masses in an idolatrous worship of the state, the party, or the leader. Individualism disappeared as the individual became a born again, true believer, a faceless object at the disposal of the state.

The totalitarian rulers (Lenin, Stalin, Hitler) promised a classless state, a new order in which the banker would sit down at the table with the worker and the farmer. All classes would be united as one people, making whatever sacrifices were demanded to secure the future of a "thousand-year Reich" (Germany) or a classless society free from exploitation (Soviet Union). Slogans like the Nazis' *"Ein Volk, Ein Reich, Ein Führer"* ("one people, one nation, one leader") became the mantras that held the masses mesmerized.

Hitler spent the first two years after being appointed Chancellor in bringing every aspect of life in Germany under the control of the Nazi Party. The process by which it was achieved was called the *Gleichschaltung*, or coordination of society. The goal was to create a *Volksgemeinschaft*, a national or racial community in which traditional social classes would be replaced by a mass of "folk (i.e., racial) comrades." It entailed a new relationship between the individual and the state. Hitler's Minister of Propaganda and Public Enlightenment, Joseph Goebbels (1897–1945), characterized it in 1933: "If liberalism took as its starting point the individual and placed the individual man in the center of all things, we have replaced the individual by the nation and the individual man by the community" (Pipes 1981).

Germany was transformed for the first time into a centralized national state. All independent institutions, such as labor unions, teachers's associations, and youth organizations were abolished or merely integrated into Nazi-led organizations. All aspects of media production were brought under the Reich Chamber of Culture headed by Goebbels. The upper house of the federal legislature, the *Reichsrat*, that represented the state governments was abolished, together with all state legislatures.

Creation of the *Volksgemeinschaft* required that the churches should also become subservient. In order to neutralize the Catholic Church as a center of organized opposition, Hitler followed the example of Mussolini and negotiated a treaty with the Vatican. The Reich Concordat between Germany and the papacy was signed on July 20, 1933. According to the terms of the concordat, the Catholic Center Party was disbanded, and the Catholic clergy were to refrain from all political activity. In the future, any member of the Roman Catholic Church in Germany, whether clergy or layperson, who opposed the Nazi state and its policies (e.g., the Holocaust) had to do so as individuals, not as Roman Catholics. Many among the clergy and laity did so at great personal cost, but most capitulated.

An attempt to unite all the Protestant churches into one Reich National Church under Ludwig Müller (1883–1945) had limited success. A small group of Evangelical Christians including Karl Barth (1886–1968), Dietrich Bonhoeffer (1909–1945), and Martin Niemöller (1892–1984) formed the Confessing Church in opposition to the Reich Church. They issued the Barmen declaration in 1934, stating that the Christian's allegiance to Jesus Christ took precedence over one's loyalty to the state, or any other earthly authority. Barth emigrated to Switzerland in 1935. Niemöller was arrested in July 1937 and placed in "protective custody" in Sachsenhausen and Dachau concentration camps until 1945. Dietrich Bonhoeffer became active in the resistance. Implicated in the attempt to assassinate Hitler on July 20, 1944, Bonhoeffer was among the many arrested when the plot failed. He was executed on April 8, 1945, just two weeks before the camp was liberated.

Hitler and the Appeasers: 1933–1939

Adolf Hitler became Chancellor on January 30, 1933. On February 2–3, he met with his top generals and admirals and instructed them to begin rearmament. He also informed them of his intent to conquer territory in Eastern Europe. The following October, Hitler withdrew Germany from the Geneva Disarmament Conference and the League of Nations. One year later, in October 1934, he announced an increase in the size of the army to 300 000, expansion of the Navy, and the creation of an air force (*Luftwaffe*). All were violations of the Versailles Treaty.

Figure 17.1 Europe between the World Wars.

At the same time, Hitler gave assurances that his intentions were peaceful. In May 1934, Germany signed a 10-year non-aggression pact with Poland. One year later, in May 1935, he stated that he would not interfere in Austria or seek to unite Austria with Germany. During the following month, Germany and Britain signed the Anglo-German Naval Treaty, setting limits to the size of Germany's navy. By signing the treaty with Germany, Britain in effect legitimatized Hitler's violations of the Versailles Treaty.

In February 1936, Hitler felt the time was right to remilitarize the Rhineland. Such a move was a direct threat to France's future security, but France did nothing when, on March 7, German soldiers began occupying the Rhineland. The soldiers had orders to withdraw at any sign of resistance from France. But the French government had decided not to resist the German action without the support of Britain, and the British Cabinet had already decided in January 1935, that the Rhineland was not of vital interest to Britain. To encourage inaction from the British and French, Hitler offered to sign non-aggression pacts with all the countries bordering Germany.

Next on Hitler's agenda was Austria, the last remnant of the prewar Austro-Hungarian Empire. Engelbert Dollfuss (1892–1934), Chancellor of Austria with dictatorial power since 1933, banned the Austrian Nazi Party, which led to an attempted *coup d'état* in July 1934. Dollfuss was assassinated by Austrian Nazis. Believing that Hitler was somehow behind the attempted coup, Mussolini mobilized the Italian army along Italy's border with Austria and warned Hitler not to attempt to annex Austria. Earlier in 1934, when Hitler announced that Germany would rearm, Mussolini joined with France and Britain in what was called the Stresa Front to oppose Hitler. It was the last time that the three World War I Allies acted in one accord.

What brought the Stresa Front to an end was Italy's invasion of Ethiopia in October 1935. The League of Nations condemned Italy but took no effective action. Its weak-willed response merely offended Mussolini and propelled him into the waiting arms of Hitler. The resulting coalition referred to by Mussolini as the Rome-Berlin Axis (1936) and formalized by the Pact of Steel (1939), proved disastrous for both Germany and Italy.

In August 1936, Hitler ordered that the German economy and military should be readied for war in four years. Hermann Göring (1893–1946), head of the *Luftwaffe*, was put in charge of a Four-Year Plan to make Germany economically self-sufficient. Hitler met with his generals on November 5. He explained that Germany needed living space (*Lebensraum*) in the east, and that war would come no later than 1943–1945. In the meantime, Austria and Czechoslovakia must be destroyed.

In 1925, when Germany agreed to the Locarno Treaties in which Germany accepted as permanent the postwar border with France and Belgium as defined in the Versailles Treaty, Germany made it clear that future adjustments would need to be made regarding Germany's eastern borders. British Prime Minister Neville Chamberlain (1869–1940) sent Foreign Secretary Lord Halifax (1881–1959) to Berlin in November 1937 to meet with Hitler and discuss Germany's need to address certain border and minority disputes in the east. In his meeting with Hitler, Lord Halifax informed Hitler that Britain would accept peaceful change.

Chamberlain and Halifax were advocates of a foreign policy that became known as appeasement. Appeasement grew out of a desire to never again experience the horrors of 1914–1918, and guilt feelings regarding the harsh treatment of Germany in the Versailles

Treaty. It assumed that if Germany were treated like any other nation, the German people would regain their pride and reject the extreme policies voiced by Hitler. The mistake was to assume that Hitler was a traditional German statesman, that he could be reasoned with. But Hitler was not a traditional German statesman. His dreams, or megalomania, were not subject to reason. If the policy of appeasement had been pursued during the Weimar Republic, it would likely have succeeded. Applied to Hitler, however, it merely put off the inevitable.

Kurt von Schuschnigg (1897–1977), who had succeeded Engelbert Dollfuss as Chancellor of Austria, met with Hitler at Hitler's retreat in the Alps on the border with Austria. Hitler's demands amounted to Austria becoming a protectorate of the German Reich. When Schuschnigg attempted to hold a plebiscite on Austrian independence, he was forced to resign and was replaced by Arthur Seyss-Inquart (1892–1946), an Austrian Nazi politician. Seyss-Inquart invited the German army to enter Austria. On March 13, 1938 the union of Austria with Germany (*Anschluss*) was proclaimed, thus fulfilling a commitment Hitler made in *Mein Kampf*.

Hitler began immediately to make demands on Czechoslovakia, while urging his generals to prepare for war. Czechoslovakia was the only nation in Eastern Europe that had a democratic government and a healthy industrial economy. In an area and era when national minorities were oppressed, Czechoslovakia treated those within its borders fairly. Its security was guaranteed by treaties with both France and the Soviet Union. Once again, as with Austria, Hitler was prepared to confront France and Britain with an international crisis that would force them to choose between the likelihood of war with Germany or sacrifice a nation that many, certainly those in Britain, knew little of and cared even less.

The excuse for German demands on Czechoslovakia was the fate of Germans living in the Sudetenland, a region inside Czechoslovakia along its border with Germany. The pro-Nazi Sudeten German Party led by Konrad Henlein (1898–1945) demanded autonomy for the Sudeten Germans and, on September 12, 1938 called for annexation with Germany.

Theodor Kordt (1893–1962), German Ambassador to Britain and member of the German resistance, met with Lord Halifax at 10 Downing Street in London. He urged Britain to take a firm stand against Hitler's demands. If Britain did so, Kordt gave assurances that certain German generals would act against the Nazis. Also, Stalin promised to come to Czechoslovakia's aid, if Britain and France remained firm and war broke out. Chamberlain's government resisted all such calls for a courageous response to Hitler. The appeasers were committed to peace at any price.

On September 29, Neville Chamberlain, Eduard Daladier (1884–1970), Mussolini, and Hitler met in Munich to decide the fate of Czechoslovakia. Neither Czechoslovakia nor the Soviet Union was invited. Hitler was again victorious over the Western democracies and those in Germany who wished to take advantage of a foreign policy failure to remove Hitler from power. Czechoslovakia was faced with the choice of surrendering the Sudentenland or fighting alone. Chamberlain returned to London, where he waved a sheet of paper in the air signed by Hitler that guaranteed "peace in our time." The *Manchester Guardian* published an editorial christening the Munich Conference "The Funeral of British Honour."

On March 15, 1939, German army units occupied Bohemia and Moravia, whose independence Hitler guaranteed in the Munich agreement. Hitler demanded the surrender of all that was left of Czechoslovakia. The Czechoslovakian government capitulated. German troops entered the capital, Prague, as Hitler announced that "Czechoslovakia has ceased to exist" (Nazis Take Czechoslovakia 2001).

Two significant developments followed from the destruction of Czechoslovakia. The first was the fact that even Chamberlain had to acknowledge that the seizure of Bohemia and Moravia, and the designation of Slovakia as a protectorate of Germany, were clearly acts of aggression. For the first time, Hitler had annexed territory without a German population. Emboldened by his success at Munich, Hitler made demands on the Free City of Danzig and the Polish Corridor. Chamberlain reacted by writing, in his own hand, a commitment to defend Poland's sovereignty. Both Britain and France pledged military support if Poland was attacked by Germany.

The second significant fallout from the Munich Conference was a shift in the Soviet Union's foreign policy. Stalin had consistently urged the Western democracies to abandon appeasement and take a stand against Hitler's aggressive moves, but he was ignored. In addition to the general fear of the spread of communism, there was a reluctance on the part of Poland and the other East-European states to risk inviting Soviet military forces to enter their territories. After all, they had profited from the collapse of Tsarist Russia.

Stalin had his own understanding of what motivated the policy of appeasement. He became convinced that the Western democracies were attempting to direct Hitler's aggression against the Soviet Union. Thus, he decided to turn the tables on them by appeasing Hitler. The result was the Nazi-Soviet Nonaggression Pact signed on August 23, 1939. In a secret protocol, they agreed to the division of Eastern Europe after the fall of Poland.

German forces began the invasion of Poland on September 1, 1939. Both Britain and France declared war on Germany two days later. Stalin waited cautiously before invading Poland from the east on September 17, no doubt in part waiting to see if the British and French would repeat their performance at the Munich Conference. When their only action was to drop propaganda leaflets on Germany, Stalin apparently decided it was time to proceed with the terms of the secret protocol to the recently signed Nazi-Soviet Nonaggression Pact.

Blitzkrieg

The military tactic pioneered by the Wehrmacht and used from the invasion of Poland until the victories ended, was called *Blitzkrieg* (lightning war). It consisted of a combination of mechanized spearheads of troops that moved in quickly and surrounded the enemy's strongpoints, rather than frontal assaults against defended positions. The advancing troops were supported by motorized artillery, tanks in massed groups, with tactical support from fighters and dive-bombers. Its combination of surprise and overwhelming force usually resulted in a rapid and decisive victory.

The period between the fall of Poland and Hitler's offensive in 1940 is referred to as the "Phony War" (*Sitzkrieg*). It is called such because though Britain, France, and Germany were officially at war, no real military operations took place during that period. Hitler made offers of peace that were rebuffed.

Though Stalin had a nonaggression pact with Germany and participated in the dismembering of Poland and partition of Eastern Europe, he apparently anticipated war with Germany in the future. In late September and October, Stalin took steps to strengthen the defenses of Leningrad, the former St. Petersburg, including a request that Finland grant the Soviet Union military bases in exchange for territory. When the Finns rejected the offer, war broke out on November 30, 1939.

The so-called "Winter War" lasted from November 1939 to March 1940. The Finns put up a heroic defense, but eventually succumbed to the overwhelming resources available to the Russians. Finland ceded to the Soviet Union the territorial concessions sought by Stalin, as well as additional territory that increased the security of Leningrad. Stalin did not seek to annex Finland. After his victory over Finland, he proceeded to incorporate the Baltic states of Estonia, Latvia, and Lithuania, as well as Bessarabia and Northern Bukovina from Romania into the Soviet Union. In hindsight, it appears that Stalin was creating a buffer zone between the Soviet Union and Germany, something he would later do again at the end of World War II.

The Phony War ended in April 1940, when Hitler launched his western offensive. He informed his generals in September 1939, that he intended to attack France through Belgium and Holland in early November and thus isolate Britain. On October 9, he indicated that the offensive would preempt an occupation of Belgium and Holland by the Western Allies, while also protecting the Ruhr and securing northern France as a base for an offensive against Britain.

The offensive was postponed until April 9, when it began with an invasion of both Denmark and Norway. Denmark surrendered within hours. The Norwegians, supported by British forces, fought on until June 10, when the government and royal family went into exile in Britain. One outcome of the Norwegian campaign was the resignation of Neville Chamberlain, and his replacement as Prime Minister by Winston Churchill. The Norwegian resistance of 62 days proved to be the longest of any country attacked by Germany except the Soviet Union.

The German offensive against France began on May 10 with a *Blitzkrieg* assault on the Netherlands. The center of Rotterdam was flattened by German bombers with a loss of 40 000 civilians. It was a foreshadowing of the senseless brutality of this second Great War that would, in many ways, surpass that of the first. The Dutch surrendered on May 14. It was a prelude to one of the most stunning military events of the twentieth century, the fall of France.

The battle for France lasted only 46 days, from May 10 to June 25. Much has been written in an attempt to explain not just the defeat of France, that many at the time would not have considered possible, but the speed with which it happened. France was prepared to refight the war of 1914–1918. It emphasized defense against a German invasion, rather than an offensive against Germany that, if undertaken during Germany's invasion of Poland, might have changed the outcome of the war. Resources were wasted on the construction of the Maginot Line, a line of fortresses along the western border of France from Switzerland to Belgium, meant to stop a German invasion. For various reasons, the Maginot Line did not extend all the way to the English Channel. If anything, its construction weakened France by encouraging a false sense of security and a defensive mentality that surrendered the advantage to the invading Germans.

France was deeply divided between left and right, a legacy of the French Revolutions of 1789 and 1848, and the Paris Commune in 1871. Many on the right were more fearful of a communist revolution than defeat by the Germans. Both the political and military leadership proved incompetent. Much of the French aircraft never got off the ground, leaving a lingering mystery as to why. In brief, a widespread sense of defeatism, a military leadership that had no understanding of the mechanized warfare that propelled the *Blitzkrieg*, and the fact that the French were simply outgeneraled meant that the battle for France was a mismatch.

The German panzers (tanks) cut through the dense forests and rough terrain of the Ardennes in southeastern Belgium. By May 20, they had reached the English Channel, cutting the French and British forces in two and forcing some 338 000 of them to flee to the beaches at Dunkirk to await evacuation to England by an armada of small boats and ships. Prime Minister Paul Reynaud (1878–1966) resigned on June 16, unable to muster enough support from the government and military leaders to continue fighting. Marshal Henri Pétain, the hero of the Battle of Verdun in World War I, formed a new government and immediately asked for an armistice with Germany. The armistice was signed on June 22 in the Forest de Compiègne, in the very same railcar that was used for Germany's surrender to France in 1918.

Northern France, including Paris, was occupied by German forces. The remainder of France, with its capital at Vichy, and the French empire abroad, was under the authority of Pétain's government. General Charles de Gaulle (1890–1970) flew to London, where he formed a French government in Exile. Because de Gaulle's government of Free France was recognized by the Allies during the war, Pétain's government, though legitimate according to the constitution of the French Third Republic, was considered illegitimate and a puppet of Germany. After the war, Pétain was tried for treason and sentenced to prison. De Gaulle once commented that Pétain's life was "successively banal, then glorious, then deplorable, but never mediocre" (Fenby 2010, p. 296).

On June 10, when the defeat of France was certain, Italy declared war on Britain and France and began to invade France. The Italians advanced a few kilometers during the so-called Battle of the Alps (10–25 June) before stalling. It was a less than glorious performance that became characteristic of the Italian military during the war.

After the fall of France, Hitler's next move was an attack on Britain, code-named Operation Sea Lion. The battle began with a German air raid on July 10, 1940 and continued until October 31, when Hitler halted the air raids in order to begin preparations for his offensive against the Soviet Union. The objective was to gain control of the air over the English Channel and Southern England in order to allow an invasion of Britain. The outcome of the battle hung in the balance between August 13 and September 7, during which the *Luftwaffe* concentrated on attacking the airfields and communications centers in Southeast England. On September 7, the Germans committed a fatal error, when they shifted to bombing London, thus giving the RAF time to recover. By the fall, Hermann Göring's (1893–1946) boast that the *Luftwaffe* would bomb the British into surrender proved overoptimistic. Without command of the air, an invasion of Britain in the face of British sea power was simply not possible.

There were a number of reasons for the British victory, other than their courage. The *Luftwaffe* was designed for tactical support of the *Blitzkrieg*, not extended, long distance bombing. Its bombers were slow and lacked adequate fighter support. The German fighter planes were limited in range and inferior to the RAF's Hurricanes and Spitfires. "The few" to whom the British owed so much, according to Churchill, included pilots from all over the British Commonwealth, occupied Europe, and even the neutral United States. The top ace of the Battle of Britain was Josef Frantisek (1914–1940), a Czech pilot who shot down 17, possibly 18, German aircraft in September 1940. Perhaps the greatest advantage the British enjoyed was radar, which gave them a crucial few minutes warning, enabling the RAF to meet the German aircraft over the English Channel. Its important role in the victory was summed up by Wing Commander Max Aitken (1879–1964): "Radar really won the Battle of Britain .... We wasted no petrol, no energy, no time" (Roberts 2008).

Hitler had certain long-range objectives from which he never deviated. One was to obtain "living space" for the German people in Eastern Europe. The belief that the Germans were destined to expand German culture, language, and settlements in Northern and Eastern Europe, lands occupied by people of Slavic ethnicity, went back to the High Middle Ages. One might think of it as being similar to the concept of Manifest Destiny in American history. With Hitler, however, it meant the destruction of those people, especially Jews and Slavs, Hitler considered subhumans (*Untermenschen*). He believed that because Germany lacked adequate space for population growth, the best of the German race was forced to emigrate in the past. Hence, conquest of Eastern Europe, including war with the Soviet Union, was an integral part of his future plans. Also, it had the added benefit of destroying what Hitler called "Jewish Bolshevism."

On December 18, 1940 Hitler issued orders for the German military forces to prepare for a rapid campaign to crush Soviet Russia in the coming spring. "Operation Barbarossa," as the campaign was code-named, was aimed at gaining the rich agricultural Ukraine, the oil rich Caucasus, and creation of a barrier against Asiatic Russia from the Volga River in the south to Archangel in the north. Stalin had been warned of Hitler's intended invasion many times by his own and foreign intelligence sources. Hitler's directive of December 18 was sent to Stalin by the Soviet Attaché in Berlin. A German Communist working in Japan actually provided the date of the invasion, but Stalin chose to ignore all warnings.

The Russian military was caught off guard when the German invasion began on June 22, 1941. Hitler intended for it to begin on May 15, but was delayed for a month because the Germans had to rescue the Italians. Mussolini launched a surprise invasion of Greece on October 28, 1940. It was a disaster. By mid-November, the Italian invasion was stopped and retreated before a Greek counter offensive. Fearful of what British intervention on the side of Greece meant as a threat to Germany's rear during the invasion of Russia, Hitler ordered the German forces to advance into Greece. The Greek and British forces were soon defeated, and Greece surrendered to the Germans on April 20.

Three million soldiers, mostly German, but including Finns, Rumanians, Hungarians, and Italians, invaded Russia along a 2000-mile (3219 km) front. Caught by surprise and suffering heavy losses, the Russian forces retreated ever deeper into the vast Russian interior, scorching the earth as they went. Hitler insisted upon mounting three simultaneous offensives, one to the north against Leningrad, one to the south into the Ukraine, and one in the center aimed at Moscow. As the German forces went deeper into Russia, their supply lines became overextended. By late autumn, they were besieging Leningrad, had captured most of the Ukraine, entered the Crimea, and were within 19 miles (30 km) of Moscow. Then, disaster struck caused in part by the delayed launch of the invasion.

First came the torrential rains that turned the unpaved roads into mud, and then the early arrival of the cruel Russian winter. Temperatures around Moscow dropped to −22 °F (−30 °C). The German army, not equipped for winter weather, began freezing to death in front of Moscow. Fires had to be kept burning under the tanks to keep the oil from freezing. The tires on the trucks froze. Soldiers suffered congelation of the anus when they squatted to relieve themselves. German women back home were urged to donate their winter coats for the soldiers on the Eastern Front.

On December 5, the Russians launched a counteroffensive. Like Napoleon's army in 1812, the German army began the long and bloody retreat westward that would end with the Russian capture of Berlin in May 1945. Hitler made an immense blunder, when he invaded Russia without ending the war with Britain. He made an even greater blunder when he declared war on the United States on December 11, 1941, just four days after the Japanese attacked the American Pacific fleet at Pearl Harbor, and three days after the United States declared war on Japan.

Road to War in the Pacific

The war in the Pacific was largely a contest between the United States and Japan for control of the Pacific. It originated in the latter part of the nineteenth century, when Japanese and American imperial aspirations came into conflict. The Meiji Restoration in Japan (1868–1912) created a modern, westernized Japan with imperial ambitions, demonstrated by its defeat of China in the Sino-Japanese War (1894–1895), their participation in the suppression of the Boxer Rebellion (1899–1901), and its victory over Russia in the Russo-Japanese War (1904–1905).

Steam-powered ships encouraged American commercial interests in the Pacific, especially for a share of the lucrative Chinese trade. The United States signed a treaty of friendship with Hawaii in 1849. It was meant to create a bond between the two that would prevent Hawaii from becoming a colony of Britain or France. Hawaii was desirable as a base for American whaling ships and a new source of cane sugar. And of course, there was always the argument that Hawaii was a fertile mission field for Protestant Christians.

In January 1893, a group of American sugar planters carried out a coup that deposed Queen Lili'uokalani (1838–1917) and established the Republic of Hawaii with the goal of seeking annexation to the United States. A treaty of annexation was signed but failed to gain the necessary two-thirds majority in the Senate. When the Spanish-American War broke out in April 1898, Hawaii assumed strategic importance. On July 4, 1898, Congress passed a joint resolution (Newlands Resolution) to annex the independent Republic of Hawaii. Opposition to such a blatant act of imperialism and fear that the United States was joining the ranks of nations with colonial empires remained strong. Some feared that annexing Hawaii as a territory might lead in the future to the admission of a state with a non-white majority. Fear that Japan would acquire Hawaii, American acquisition of the Philippine Islands and Guam from Spain in 1898, and increased access to the growing trade with China, led to the formal creation of Hawaii as a territory (Hawaiian Organic Act of 1900), with its own elected government and a territorial governor answerable to the President.

The Japanese victory in the Sino-Japanese War increased fears that China would face the same fate as Africa. When American commercial interests in China grew following annexation of the Philippines, the United States put forth the Open-Door Policy aimed at guaranteeing open access to Chinese markets for all nations. Britain turned the policing of the Pacific Ocean over to Japan after concluding the Anglo-Japanese Alliance (1902). With Japan as the dominant naval power in the Pacific, American policy makers saw Japan as a serious threat to American interests. In response, the American military adopted "War Plan Orange" (1911), a plan for a possible war with Japan that remained valid until 1939.

Relations were further strained when Japan, as one of the Allies, quickly seized the German territory of Kiaochow in China at opening of World War I. Then, in January 1915, Japan presented China with an ultimatum backed by threat of war if refused. Known as the 21 Demands, China was required to cease leasing territory to foreign powers and, in effect, become a protectorate of Japan. Suspicious of Japan's intentions and their implications for American interests, the United States joined with Britain to check Japan's move.

Japan was present as one of the Allies at the Paris Peace Conference (1919), but not on a par with the "Big Four." When Woodrow Wilson blocked inclusion of a declaration of racial equality in the League of Nations Charter, the Japanese saw it as an expression of American anti-Japanese racism. The San Francisco School Board began segregating Asian students in public schools in 1906. The 1913 California Alien Land Law banned Japanese from purchasing land. The Immigration Act of 1924, meant to preserve the racial homogeneity of the United States, banned Japanese immigration. Chinese were already barred by the Chinese Exclusion Act of 1882, made permanent in 1902.

The United States felt that Japan's acquisition of the former German colonies in the Pacific (German Caroline, Marianna, Marshall, and Palau islands) threatened American supply lines. In response, the United States sponsored the Washington Naval Conference (November 12, 1921–February 6, 1923). Britain was prevailed upon to cancel the Anglo-Japanese Alliance of 1902 and, in its place, substitute an agreement to limit the size of the navies of United States, Great Britain, Japan, France, and Italy. The agreement set a ratio of 5:5:3:1.75:1.75 for capital ships, meaning that for every three capital ships that the Japanese had, the British and the United States were permitted to have five and France and Italy were permitted to have 1.75. Understandably, Japan took it as an afront to Japanese pride and an attempt to limit legitimate Japanese imperial interests. The agreement remained in effect until 1936.

Despite mutual distrust, relations between the United States and Japan remained cordial during the 1920s. Both had prosperous economies. Forty percent of Japan's industrial product went to the United States, its number one trading partner. Both suffered setbacks with the onset of the Great Depression, but the situation in Japan was made all the worse by a 25% increase in tariff on Japanese goods imported into the United States. One half of Japan's rural population suffered extreme poverty as rice prices fell below cost and silk prices collapsed.

Instead of a Franklin Roosevelt appearing with a New Deal, in Japan the real power in government passed into the hands of the military leaders. They saw the answer to Japan's problems in an aggressive foreign policy aimed at obtaining economic control of China and Southeast Asia. Also included was expulsion of the Western presence and creation of

Japanese hegemony in Asia. Not surprisingly, the new leadership's aggressive foreign policy goals brought Japan into conflict with both the Soviet Union and the United States.

After the Japanese invasion of Manchuria in 1931 and the creation of Manchukuo as a puppet state of Japan, border disputes occurred along the border between Manchukuo and the Soviet Union. Most of the skirmishes were minor, but at least one escalated into a major conflict, the Battles of Khalkhin Gol, between May 11 and September 16, 1939. Soviet forces won a decisive victory over the Japanese forces. The two nations signed the Soviet-Japanese Neutrality Pact on April 13, 1941, in which the two pledged to remain neutral in the event that either was attacked by a third party. The pact proved beneficial to both Japan and the Soviet Union during World War II.

The course of events in Europe, especially the fall of the Netherlands and France, and Britain's struggle for survival in the Battle of Britain, was too great a temptation for Japan's expansionist ambitions in East and Southeast Asia. Japan signed the Tripartite Pact with Germany and Italy in September 1940 but refused to attack the Soviet Union when Germany launched Operation Barbarossa in June 1941. Only the United States remained as a serious check on Japanese ambitions.

President Roosevelt was limited in what he could do to help the Allies in Europe or check Japanese aggression in Asia. A Gallup poll conducted in March 1937 showed that 94% of Americans wanted the United States to stay out of all foreign wars. Taken again in March 1939, the percentage rose to 99%. "America First" rallies were held in major cities with Charles Lindbergh as a popular speaker. Lindbergh spiced his speeches with a generous sprinkle of anti-Semitism. Despite the public's reluctance to prepare for possible war, Roosevelt did manage to funnel some aid to Britain through passage of the Lend-Lease Act in March 1941. When Japanese forces occupied northern French Indochina in September 1940, Roosevelt imposed an embargo on the export of aviation fuel, scrap iron, and steel to Japan. Oil was added to the embargo in June 1941.

The oil embargo left Japan with only two choices, either yield to American demands and give up the goal of creating a so-called Greater East Asia Co-Prosperity Sphere under Japanese leadership, or seize the oil resources in the Dutch East Indies. In order to achieve the latter, they had to first disable the British and American fleets in the Pacific. That led to the decision to attack the American Pacific Fleet based at Pearl Harbor in Hawaii. The objective was not to invade Hawaii, much less any idea of following up the attack on Pearl Harbor with an invasion of the Western United States. The goal was to neutralize the ability of the United States to respond to Japan's plans for at least six months. By then, those who favored war with America believed that Japan's position in Southeast Asia and the Western Pacific would be strong enough that the United States and Britain would accept the *fait accompli*.

Japan launched a surprise air attack on the American naval base at Pearl Harbor early on Sunday morning, December 7, 1941. The impact was devastating, but not fatal. A total of 21 ships were either lost or damaged. Of the 402 aircraft stationed in Hawaii, 188 were destroyed and 159 damaged. However, the submarine base, naval repair yards, the oil depots, and the Old Administration Building, in which the Navy's signals monitoring and cryptographic unit (Fleet Radio Unit Pacific) was housed, were undamaged. Most important was the fact that the three aircraft carriers assigned to the Pacific fleet were out to sea, and therefore spared. Japan launched simultaneous attacks on the Philippines, Guam, Midway, Hong Kong, Malaya, and Singapore.

Both the United States and Britain declared war on Japan on December 8. In a move that seems to defy all logic, Hitler decided to declare war on the United States on December 9. The formal announcement was made in a speech to the Reichstag on December 11. Mussolini, following Hitler's lead, declared war on the United States. Not surprisingly, the United States responded with declarations of war on both Germany and Italy on the same day.

Turning of the Tide

Years later, reflecting on the situation during the first half of 1942, General George C. Marshall commented: "Few realized how close to complete domination of the world were Germany and Japan and how thin the thread of Allied survival had been stretched" (Gruhl 2017). It was not the actions of the United States that got the Allies through those dark hours. "It is certain," he wrote, "that the refusal of the British and Russian peoples to accept what appeared to be inevitable defeat was the great factor in the salvage of our civilization" (Payne 2016).

By the summer of 1942, the Japanese occupied or controlled Manchuria and portions of mainland China, Hong Kong, French Indochina, Malaysia, Philippines, Singapore, Dutch East Indies, Burma, Portuguese Timor, Guam, Wake Island, Papua, and New Guinea, Kiribati, and two of the Aleutian Islands (Attu and Kiska). German forces had advanced to the Caucasus Mountains in the Soviet Union and were approaching the Nile River in North Africa. German U-boats were sinking Allied ships at an alarming rate during what the Germans called the "Second happy time" in the Battle of the Atlantic. The U-boats were active in American waters from January to July 1942.

There is no doubt that once the United States joined the war against the Axis, and once mobilization and conversion of industries to war production was completed in early 1943, the defeat of the Axis powers was only a matter of time. There was no way, really, that the Axis could successfully attack the United States, protected as it was by two oceans. Invasion of North America by either Germany or Japan was never a possibility, not even in the wildest imaginations. As with World War I, the entry of the United States decided the outcome of World War II.

The tide turned against the Axis in the late summer and early fall of 1942. The Italian Tenth Army began to invade Egypt on September 30, 1940. British and Commonwealth forces began a counteroffensive on December 9. Thinking of tanks as ships on a sea of sand, the British General Archibald Wavell (1883–1950) used the advantage of mobility to defeat the Italians, who took up positions in fortified camps. After repeated defeats, the Italian Tenth Army surrendered on February 7, 1941. More than 13 000 prisoners were taken along with more than 400 hundred tanks and more than 800 guns.

Hitler sent General Erwin Rommel (1891–1944) to North Africa to rescue the Italians. Rommel, later known as the "Desert Fox," pushed the British back across Libya and into Egypt. An Anglo-American force landed in Algeria and Morocco in November 1942 and moved across North Africa. Rommel's Africa Korps held unto North Africa, even as it became pinched between two Allied armies. Hitler ordered Rommel back to Germany in

March 1943. The end came on May 13, 1943, when the German forces surrendered. North Africa was liberated.

Allied forces landed in Sicily during the night of July 9–10, 1943. The liberation of Sicily was complete on August 17. Support among the Italian people for continuing the war evaporated quickly after Allied aircraft bombed Rome on July 19. King Victor Emmanuel III (1869–1947) dismissed Mussolini as Prime Minister on July 26. British, American, and Canadian forces began invading Italy on September 9. General Pietro Badoglio (1871–1956) formed a new government and began seeking an armistice. The unconditional surrender of Italy was announced on September 8, 1943.

The turning point of the war in Europe, and some would say, for the whole of World War II, was the Battle of Stalingrad, July 17, 1942–February 2, 1943. Hitler ordered the German Sixth Army under command of General Friedrich W.E. Paulus (1890–1957) to take the city. When the army became trapped in the city, Hitler would not allow a strategic retreat. The Russians were determined to defend the city named in honor of Stalin. The fighting was intense, waged block by block, house by house, and even room by room. On February 2, 1943, what was left of the Sixth Army, about one-third of the original number, surrendered. Of the roughly 90 000 who surrendered, about one-half died on the march to the Siberian prison camps. Only about 6000 ever returned to Germany.

The fact that the war had become a war of attrition like World War I was clear in the Battle of Kursk (July 5–16, 1943), the largest tank battle in military history. The Russians had the advantage in numbers. They fielded 1 900 000 troops, 5000 tanks, and 3500 aircraft. Opposing their forces were 780 000 German troops, 3000 tanks, and 2000 aircraft (Carson 2018). The Soviet forces suffered much larger losses, but their losses could be replaced. The Germans could not replace their losses. The Russian steamroller could be slowed down, but not stopped.

On June 6, 1944, almost three years to the date since the German invasion of the Soviet Union began, American, British, and Canadian forces landed on the beaches of Normandy in Northern France. Within a month, one million men were advancing eastward toward Germany. Paris was liberated on August 25, and by mid-September, the Allies crossed the German frontier. In a desperate attempt to halt the Allied advance, the Germans launched their last major offensive on December 16 through the Ardennes. Their objective was to split the Allied armies, deny the Allies use of the Belgium port of Antwerp, and possibly negotiate an end to the war on the Western Front. The German offensive stalled on Christmas Eve. The Allies launched a major offensive all along the Western Front in February.

The Russians began a major offensive on the Eastern Front on January 12, 1945. They liberated Warsaw two weeks later. Advancing as much as 37 miles (60 km) per day, they began the siege of Berlin on April 16. Roosevelt died on April 12. Mussolini was captured by Italian partisans and hung on April 28. Hitler committed suicide two days later in his underground bunker beneath the Reich Chancellery in Berlin, shortly after marrying his mistress Eva Braun (1912–1945). Admiral Karl Dönitz (1891–1980) succeeded Hitler as the last leader of the Third Reich. Acting in accordance with instructions from Dönitz and representing the German High Command, General Alfred Jodl (1890–1946) signed the unconditional surrender of all German forces on May 7, 1945.

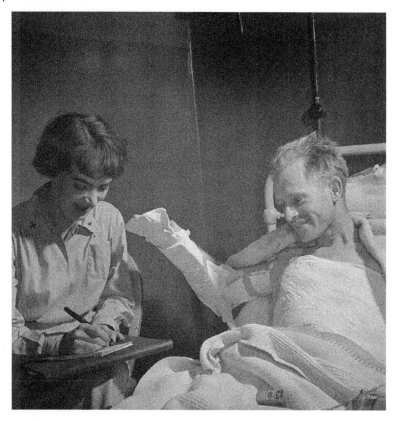

Figure 17.2 A Red Cross worker in England assists a wounded American soldier write a letter back home, 1944. *Source:* Library of Congress Prints and Photographs Division.

The war was over in Europe, but there was still a war in the Pacific to be won. The turning point in the Pacific was the Battle of Midway, June 4–7, 1942. The decisive weapon in the Pacific theater was the aircraft carrier. It was the Japanese failure to sink the American aircraft carriers during the attack on Pearl Harbor that eventually cost them the war. The Japanese hoped to finish what they started at Peral Harbor by luring the American aircraft carriers into a trap. If successful, the United States would suffer another humiliating defeat that would eliminate it as a strategic power in the Pacific. Demoralized, the United States would accept Japanese control of the Pacific and bow out of the war.

The Japanese put the bulk of their fleet, including seven aircraft carriers, into the battle. The Americans were aware of the Japanese plans, having broken the Japanese naval code. The American fleet, with three heavy carriers and additional land-based aircraft from Midway and Hawaii, was waiting. The battle began on June 4, when American dive bombers and torpedo planes attacked the Japanese armada. An interesting feature of the battle is that it was fought entirely by aircraft. The big ships with their big guns never saw each other and remained out of range of their guns. Three of Japan's four heavy aircraft carriers and one heavy cruiser were sunk. Unlike the Americans, the Japanese could not replace either the ships or the skilled personnel. As in the European theater, the war had become a war of attrition that favored the Allies.

Figure 17.3 The remains of Hiroshima, Japan after the United States dropped the first atomic bomb on August 9, 1945. *Source:* Library of Congress Prints and Photographs Division.

American forces landed on Guadalcanal on August 7, 1942. From there, it was essentially a matter of island hopping, as the Americans moved northwestwardly through the Pacific toward the Japanese home islands. After the war ended in Europe, many felt it might be necessary to invade Japan. Potential losses were estimated at as many as one million. The Soviet Union declared war on Japan on August 8, 1945 and began invading Manchuria. Perhaps, in part to shut the Russians out of postwar Japan, as well as to avoid the horrendous losses caused by an invasion of Japan, the United States dropped the first atomic bomb on Hiroshima on August 9, followed three days later, by a second dropped on Nagasaki. The Japanese decided to surrender unconditionally on August 14. The formal surrender ceremony took place on September 2, on board the *U.S.S. Missouri*. World War II, the second Great War in the first half of the twentieth century, was over.

Banality of Evil

World War II surpassed its predecessor in its images of the depths to which humans can descend in their cruelty to their fellow human beings. Before the war ended, as images of the Nazi death camps became known, the victors decided to hold the leaders of the Axis powers, and those personally responsible for what were deemed to be war crimes and crimes against humanity, accountable for their actions. It was a noble attempt to say that some things are simply wrong by any reasonable standard.

The war crimes trials and tribunals were also a means of diverting attention away from war crimes committed by the Allies. The fire-bombing of German and Japanese cities, and the dropping of atomic bombs on Hiroshima and Nagasaki that killed hundreds of thousands of civilians were obvious war crimes. British and American bombers dropped 650 000 incendiary and high-explosive bombs on Dresden, whose normal population was 630 000, creating a firestorm that reached temperatures of 800–1000°C (1472–1832 °F). Between 35 000 and 135 000 people died in Dresden and 90 000–146 000 in Hiroshima.

Not all of those tried were government officials. Some leading German industrialists, including Alfried Krupp von Bohlen und Halbach (1907–1967), Friedrich Flick (1883–1972), and directors of the chemical firm IG Farben, were tried for war crimes and crimes against humanity. But no mention was made of American corporations that profited from their participation in the Holocaust. Among them were IBM, ITT Inc., Chase National Bank, and the two automakers, Ford Motor and General Motors ("List of Companies Involved in the Holocaust" 2018; Rich 1998). Recent research has exposed how "neutral" Switzerland laundered hundreds of millions of dollars of gold and other treasures looted from Jews and other victims of the Nazi terror ("The Sinister Face of 'Neutrality'" 2018). If we learn anything from the history of civilizations, it is that both good and evil lie in the hearts of all humankind. That the horrors of the Holocaust occurred in Germany and not France, Britain, or even the United States is more an accident of history than any particular characteristic of German history.

Racism and Anti-Semitism – they are not the same thing – were at the very core of Adolf Hitler's twisted worldview, as well as, those educated individuals who tried to carry out, with typical German efficiency, his will to rid Europe of all its Jews and those classified as subhumans.

Holocaust

Hitler was appointed chancellor of Germany on January 30, 1933. By mid-March, the first concentration camp, located at the medieval town of Dachau, was established. It was intended for political prisoners, but later evolved into a death camp. Just a week later, a boycott of Jewish businesses was organized. The Law for the Restoration of the Professional Civil Service was passed on April 7, barring Jews and political opponents of the Nazi regime from holding civil service positions. Another measure required that all non-Aryan lawyers be disbarred by the end of September. Both measures initially allowed exemptions for Jews who served in the military during World War I.

The National Socialist German Students' Association organized ceremonial burnings of "un-German" books at universities throughout Germany on May 10. It was not only books by Jews, but also other noted German and foreign authors, including, for example, works by Bertolt Brecht, Thomas Mann, Erich Maria Remarque, Stefan Zweig, Jack London, Ernest Hemingway, and Helen Keller. During the following summer, the universities were "cleansed" of Jewish influence by expelling Jewish professors.

In September 1935, the Reichstag passed the Reich Citizenship Law and the Law for the Protection of German Blood and German Honor, commonly referred to as the Nuremberg Laws. Jews were stripped of their citizenship, prohibited from marrying or having sexual relations with non-Jews, hiring German maids under the age of 45, or flying the German flag. The laws defined a Jew as anyone with three Jewish grandparents, anyone married to a Jew, or anyone with a Jewish parent. The status of being racially Jewish was passed by parents to their children and grandchildren. Those individuals who did not fit the definition of being racially German or Jewish were classified as "mixed-race" (*Mischlinge*). Their constitutional rights were steadily reduced over time. The Nuremberg Laws served as the legal basis for the Holocaust. Hitler was very careful to make sure that every aspect of the persecution of the Jews was done "legally."

The persecution intensified during 1938. Jews were required to register all property in April, and in November, they were required to transfer all retail businesses to Aryans. In August, Jews who had names that were not recognized as Jewish by the authorities, were required to add "Israel" or "Sarah" as their middle name. In October, Jewish passports were marked with a large red letter "J" to prevent them from fleeing to Switzerland. An outburst of violence against Jews all across Germany occurred on the night of November 9 known as "the night of broken glass" (*Kristallnacht*). Hundreds of synagogues were burned, and windows of Jewish shops broken. Approximately 20 000 Jews were rounded up and sent to concentration camps. The Jews were required, as a community, to pay a fine of one billion marks for the damage done during that night. Jewish children were expelled from public schools on November 15.

Less than 1% of the German population (502 799, or 0.75%) in 1933 was Jewish by religion according to the June 16, 1933 census.[1] A census taken on May 17, 1939, in which Jews were classified as "racial Jews" as defined by the Nuremberg Laws, showed there were 233 539 within the 1933 borders, and 330 539, when those living in Austria and the Sudetenland were included. At the end of the war, there were only 19 000 remaining (Blau 1950).

The German occupation of Eastern Europe and the invasion of the Soviet Union brought large numbers of Jews under German control. Between 1939 and 1942, Jews throughout German-occupied Europe were required to wear a yellow star of David, except in Denmark. During 1940, the Polish Jews were forced into ghettos. The Warsaw Ghetto had approximately 500 000 inhabitants in 1.3 square miles (3.4 km^2). Construction on Auschwitz concentration camp began in May 1940. Eventually, Auschwitz was a large complex with 50 sub-camps. Some camps were extermination centers, while others included factories that used inmates as slave laborers, for example, Krupp, Siemens-Schuckert, IG Farben, and Ford Motor. Fifty-one companies made use of slave labor at Auschwitz, according to the Holocaust Education Trust (HET). Altogether five hundred firms had ties to Auschwitz (Borger 1999). Though Jews constituted by far the majority of those imprisoned at Auschwitz, Roma, Soviet Prisoners of War, and individuals from 20 different nationalities suffered and died there. The first gassing at Auschwitz occurred on September 3, 1941, when 600 Russian prisoners of war were killed using Zyklon B gas. Historians estimate that at least 1.1 million people died at Auschwitz before the gassing was halted on November 2, 1944.

---

1 Approximately 505 000 out of a total population of 67 million. There were only 37 000 Jews living in Germany in 1950 (German Jewish Population in 1933).
"German Jewish Population in 1933." United States Holocaust Memorial Museum. Accessed October 24, 2018. https://encyclopedia.ushmm.org/content/en/article/germany-jewish-population-in-1933 (Accessed October 29, 2018).

Some of the most brutal and indiscriminate slaughter of Jews occurred as the German armies moved eastward. Local Anti-Semites, ordinary people, saw in the German invasion, an opportunity to massacre the Jews who had been living among them for centuries. Lithuania, Hungary, and Croatia provided particularly graphic examples.

As the German armies invaded Latvia, Lithuania, Poland, Belarus, Russia, Ukraine, Moldova, and Romania, they were followed by *Einsatzgruppen* (special commando units) entrusted with the task of rounding up and executing Jews, Roma, members of the intelligentsia, political commissars, and generally anyone they wished to see as a threat to the "new order." There were ten death squads of battalion size, composed mostly of SS and police personnel, together with locals recruited for "service as clerks, grave diggers, wagon drivers, and cooks to provide support for the mass killing actions" ("Einsatzgruppen" n.d.). The victims were lined up along the edge of trenches and shot. Over a period of just two days, 33 771 Jews were killed at Babi Yar in the Ukrainian capital of Kiev.

In a speech before the Reichstag on January 30, 1939, seven months before the invasion of Poland, Hitler said that another world war would result in the "destruction of the Jewish race in Europe" ("Hitler's Threat" n.d.). The mass shootings and other means of killing proved psychologically trying for the soldiers involved, costly, inefficient, and lacking order. Thus, on January 20, 1942, 15 high-ranking Nazi officials met at a villa in Wannsee, a suburb of Berlin, instructed by Hermann Göring (1893–1946) "to make all the necessary preparations ... for the Final Solution of the Jewish problem in the German sphere of influence in Europe" (Wannsee Conference 2018). Chairman of the conference, Reinhard Heydrich (1904–1942), informed the attendees that 11 million Jews would be included in the program.

The Wannsee Conference lasted only about 90 minutes. Its role in the Holocaust was not to initiate the extermination program. That was already well underway. It was, one might say, to smooth out the details of responsibility for the collection, transport, killing, and disposal of the millions of human beings under the control of the SS. It was very much like a meeting of a corporation's department heads during which the marketing of a product was discussed. Who was in charge of which aspects of the manufacturing and distribution? How could cost be kept down? "Time is money; money is time." "Everything is business." Questions about humanity never entered the picture.

The whole program of the Final Solution was continued until the very end of the war. As the Soviet armies pushed deeper into Poland and the death camps were slowly liberated, surviving inmates were taken on death marches to camps inside Germany, so that as many Jews as possible could be killed before time ran out on the Thousand-year Reich.

No Room

Much of the persecution of Jews before 1941 was aimed at encouraging them to emigrate, to leave Germany. But no one wanted to accept Jewish refugees. On May 13, 1939, the luxury liner *MS St. Louis* departed Hamburg, Germany for Cuba with 900 Jews onboard. They reached their destination on June 4 but were refused permission to disembark in Cuba. President Roosevelt was at first open to allowing them to enter the United States, but strong opposition from Secretary of State Cordell Hull (1871–1955) and Southern Democrats, whose support Roosevelt needed for the upcoming 1940 presidential election, kept him from doing so. Faced with no alternative, the MS *St. Louis* returned to Europe, where most of its passengers later perished in the Holocaust.

A bill to allow Jewish children to enter the United States, despite the official immigration quotas, was offered by two members of Congress, one Republican and one Democrat. The bill ignited a public debate, but never came up for a vote in Congress. Anti-Semitism in the United States rose during the 1930s and 1940s. One public poll taken in 1944, showed that one-quarter of Americans considered Jews to be a "menace." Breckinridge Long (1881–1958) served as an Assistant Secretary in the U.S. State Department between 1939 and 1944, were he supervised the Visa Division. Under his direction, numerous barriers were erected to impede Jews and others fleeing Nazi persecution from obtaining visas. In a memorandum of June 26, 1940, Long advised on how a strict anti-immigration policy might best be implemented:

> We can delay and effectively stop for a temporary period of indefinite length the number of immigrants into the United States. We could do this by simply advising our consuls, to put every obstacle in the way and to require additional evidence and to resort to various administrative devices which would postpone and postpone and postpone the granting of the visas. (Breckinridge Long's Memorandum 1940)

Individuals fleeing the Holocaust were met with a series of hurdles to overcome that delayed their receiving a visa to enter the United States until the issue resolved itself, that is, they disappeared in the SS's parallel universe.

When the war ended in 1945, Europe was a vast wasteland of rubble among which a sea of people moved about like ants on an ant hill. Survivors from the death camps, slave laborers returning home, and countless displaced persons were on the move. If it were possible for one to go back in time to Europe in the fall of 1945, one would surely wonder if recovery were possible. Likewise, witnessing the joyous meeting of American and Soviet soldiers at Torgau on the Elbe River, our time traveler would not expect that within five years the two wartime allies would be leaders of opposing alliances that threatened the very existence of civilization on planet earth.

References

Blau, B. (1950). The Jewish population of Germany 1939–1945. *Jewish Social Studies* 12 (2): 161–172. http://www.jstor.org/stable/4464869 (accessed October 29, 2018).

Borger, J. (1999). Nazi Documents Reveal That Ford Had Links to Auschwitz. The Guardian. https://www.theguardian.com/world/1999/aug/20/julianborger1 (accessed 21 October 2019).

Carson, J. (2018). The Battle of Kursk in Numbers. HistoryHit. https://www.historyhit.com/the-battle-of-kursk-in-numbers (accessed 21 October 2019).

Fenby, J. (2010). *The General: Charles de Gaulle and the France He Saved*. New York: Skyhorse Publishing.

Gruhl, W. (2017). *Imperial Japan's World War Two: 1931–1945*. New York: Routledge.

Hitler's Threat (n.d.). Hitler Threatens the Jews. http://stevenlehrer.com/Hitler_threat.htm (accessed 21 October 2019).

New York Times (1939a). September 10, 1939. Volume 88, Number 29814.

New York Times (1939b). September 12, 1939, Volume 88, Number 29816.

Payne, R. (2016). *The Marshall Story: A Biography of General George C. Marshall*. Pickle Partners Publishing.

PBS (2018). The Sinister Face of 'Neutrality'. https://www.pbs.org/wgbh/pages/frontline/shows/nazis/readings/sinister.html (accessed 21 October 2019).

PBS (2019). Breckinridge Long (1881–1958). http://www.pbs.org/wgbh/americanexperience/features/holocaust-long (accessed 21 October 2019).

Pipes, R. (1981). *Modern Europe*. Homewood: Dorsey Press.

Rich, F. (1998). What's Good for General Motors. The New York Times. https://www.nytimes.com/1998/12/02/opinion/journal-what-s-good-for-general-motors.html (accessed 21 October 2019).

Roberts, A. (2008). Britain at War: The Battle of Britain. The Telegraph. www.telegraph.co.uk/history/britain-at-war/3195155/Britain-at-War-The-Battle-of-Britain.html (accessed 21 October 2019).

The History Place (2001). Nazis Take Czechoslovakia. http://www.historyplace.com/worldwar2/triumph/tr-czech.htm (accessed 21 October 2019).

The World Holocaust Remembrance Center (n.d.). The Wannsee Conference. https://www.yadvashem.org/holocaust/about/final-solution-beginning/wannsee-conference.html?gclid=CjwKCAjw9sreBRBAEiwARroYm2ocmmXyCfr8YIwFtLtQHURfcxQryUvI9fdqZ9NmUJjgFFmlVPa5eRoC7koQAvD_BwE (accessed 21 October 2019).

United States Holocaust Memorial Museum (n.d.). Einsatzgruppen. https://encyclopedia.ushmm.org/content/en/article/einsatzgruppen (accessed 21 October 2019).

United States Holocaust Memorial Museum (n.d.). Germany: Jewish Population in 1933. https://encyclopedia.ushmm.org/content/en/article/germany-jewish-population-in-1933 (accessed 21 October 2019).

Wikipedia (2018). List of Companies Involved in the Holocaust https://en.wikipedia.org/wiki/List_of_companies_involved_in_the_Holocaust (accessed 21 October 2019).

Part VI

The End of Europe: An Overview

The Allied coalition during World War II was never more than a coalition of necessity, or at best, of convenience. Not one or two of the so-called "Big Three" (United Kingdom, United States, and Soviet Union) was capable of defeating Germany alone. The Western Allies and the Soviet Union were ideologically incompatible. Once the war was over in Europe, the coalition began to break apart, despite efforts to hold it together long enough to end the war with Japan and establish the United Nations Organization.

Both the Western democracies and the Soviet Union had reasons enough to be fearful of the other's intentions. The fact that the United States possessed the atomic bomb, and had already demonstrated its willingness to use it, increased the Soviet Union's distrust of the Western democracies going back to their intervention in the Russian Civil War (1917–1922). At the same time, Stalin's efforts to create a network of satellite states in Eastern Europe as a kind of first line of defense against any future attack from a revived Germany or, as many in the Soviet Union believed, an attack from the Western capitalists, provided sufficient reason for the Western democracies to fear the spread of Soviet influence.

By the end of the 1940s, two alliance systems faced each other in a Cold War that could, at any moment, burst into a nuclear holocaust engulfing the entire world. From the late 1940s until the end of the 1980s, a bipolar world existed in which the United States-led alliance confronted the Soviet-led alliance. The competition between the two took the form of proxy wars fought by client states in various parts of the world, for example in Korea, China, Vietnam, and the Middle East. Other less obvious civil disorders around the globe were encouraged and fueled by the two superpowers.

The collapse of the Soviet Union between 1989 and 1991 ended the Cold War, but in many ways created a more dangerous multipolar world. The new age of religious-based ideological struggles replaced the more predictable and stable Cold War superpower confrontation. The revolution in technology opened up previously isolated areas of the globe, forcing "modernity" with its diverse worldviews and moral values onto hitherto closed societies, as for example, the Muslim world. The West may no longer be the epicenter of world power, but there can be no denying that Western culture has conquered, and continues to shape, the world in the twenty-first century.

Western Civilization: A Brief History, First Edition. Paul R. Waibel.
© 2020 John Wiley & Sons, Inc. Published 2020 by John Wiley & Sons, Inc.

18

Cold War and Recovery: 1945–1962

Chronology

1945	Yalta Conference
1945	Potsdam Conference
1945	Ho Chi Minh Proclaims Democratic State of Vietnam
1946	George F. Kennan's Long Telegram
1946	Winston Churchill's Iron Curtain Speech
1947	Truman Doctrine
1947	European Recovery Act (Marshall Plan)
1948–1949	Berlin Airlift
1949	North Atlantic Treaty Organization (NATO)
1949	Federal Republic of Germany and German Democratic Republic Founded
1949	People's Republic of China Proclaimed at End of Chinese Civil War
1949	Soviet Union Explodes First Atomic Bomb
1950–1953	Korean War
1954	Southeast Treaty Organization (SEATO)
1954	French Defeated at Battle of Dien Bien Phu in Vietnam
1954	Geneva Accords
1955	Central Treaty Organization (CENTO)
1956	Hungarian Revolt
1957	Soviet Union Launch First Artificial Earth Satellite, Sputnik I
1957	Rome Treaty Creates European Economic Community
1959	Fidel Castro Comes to Power in Cuba
1961	Berlin Wall Erected and Berlin Crisis
1962	Cuban Missile Crisis

When the war ended in Europe in the summer of 1945, Europe was in ruins. Certain decisions regarding postwar Europe were made at the Yalta and Potsdam conferences. It was evident, at both conferences, that the wartime alliance was an alliance made necessary by the fact that neither the Western Allies nor the Soviet Union alone was able to defeat Germany. The core, incompatible ideological differences between the two political and economic systems were set aside during the war to secure victory over Nazism. The American

Western Civilization: A Brief History, First Edition. Paul R. Waibel.
© 2020 John Wiley & Sons, Inc. Published 2020 by John Wiley & Sons, Inc.

public, for example, was fed a diet of propaganda that portrayed the people of the Soviet Union as freedom-loving people not unlike themselves.

Once victory over the common enemy was achieved, the tensions reemerged, and the world began to polarize into two competing camps representing the two different visions of the future, originally represented by Woodrow Wilson and Vladimir Lenin. The gradual emergence of what was soon called a "Cold War" stimulated the recovery of war-ravaged Europe and Japan, while at the same time, hastened the demise of the colonial empires, setting the stage for the new, underdeveloped nations of the so-called "Third World" to become the site of "proxy wars" between the two superpowers and their allies.

Origins of the Cold War

It is possible to trace the roots of the Cold War back to the Russian Revolution of 1917 and American military intervention on the side of the Whites in the Russian Civil War that followed. During the interwar period, the United States saw communism as a world threat directed from Moscow. Communist agents were sent out from Moscow to various parts of the world to promote the worldwide revolution prophesied by Karl Marx. The "Red Scare" in post-World War I America was one reason why the United States was the last of the Great Powers to recognize the Soviet Union (1933).

For most Americans, World War II was a war against anti-democratic, authoritarian rule. They went to war to liberate the conquered peoples of Europe and Asia. Naturally, they expected to see democratic governments established following victory over the enemies of freedom. America's allies, Britain and France, were critically wounded by the war. They were destined to lose their overseas empires, much of their wealth and international prestige, and become submissive allies of the United States in the Cold War. In contrast, the United States emerged from the war as the world's leading industrial nation, having gained much at comparatively little cost from its participation in the war.

The United States suffered a combined total of 418 500 military and civilian deaths caused by its participation in the war. The United Kingdom's total was 450 700. The Soviet Union, in contrast, suffered between 8 800 000 and 10 700 000 military deaths. When the civilian deaths caused by the war are included, the total rises to somewhere between 24 and 27 million, or roughly 90 times the number of American deaths from the war (Gaddis 2005, p. 9; "Research Starters: Worldwide Deaths in World War II" n.d.). When one adds to that, the fact that much of European Russia was devastated, compared to none of the United States and rather little of Britain, it is not difficult to understand why Stalin's aims for postwar Europe were so very different from those of Franklin Roosevelt or Winston Churchill.

There was always tension between Stalin and his British and American allies. Stalin felt that they had ulterior motives behind their delays in invading France and thus giving the Soviet forces some relief on the Eastern Front. When the three leaders met at Yalta in the Crimea during early February 1945, the defeat of Germany was eminent. Roosevelt was primarily interested in winning the war with Japan, once the war with Germany ended. With that goal uppermost in his mind, Roosevelt wanted to secure Stalin's commitment to enter the war against Japan after Germany's defeat. Hence, he did not wish to clash with Stalin over Stalin's demands regarding postwar Eastern Europe. Also, Roosevelt tended to see Stalin as the heroic leader of the Russian people, one with whom he was able to work for the benefit of the liberated peoples of Europe. And there was the matter of the United Nations Organization, in which Roosevelt wanted the Soviet Union to participate.

Winston Churchill had a more realistic understanding of Stalin, but he was at a clear disadvantage. His primary goal during the war was for the United Kingdom to survive. In order to achieve that goal, he recognized the need to relinquish leadership of the Anglo-American coalition to Roosevelt. Churchill understood that once Germany was removed as a check on Soviet expansion, the Soviet Union would dominate Europe. His efforts to deal with Stalin in an old-fashioned way by dividing Europe into spheres of influence was thwarted by Roosevelt. Clearly, Britain was no longer the world's superpower that it had been at the dawn of the century. The sun was beginning to set on the British Empire.

Stalin was focused on ensuring that the postwar settlement guaranteed the future security of the Soviet Union. Never again should the Soviet Union fear a German invasion. As when he dueled with Trotsky over the future of the Russian Revolution, Stalin put the Soviet Union before the interests of communists elsewhere. Beyond security for the Soviet Union, Stalin believed it possible for the Soviet Union to secure the future domination of Europe that Hitler failed to achieve for Germany.

Figure 18.1 The Big Three leaders met at the Yalta Conference in February 1945 to discuss the status of postwar Europe and the continuing war with Japan. *Source:* Library of Congress Prints and Photographs Division.

Tension rose as conflicting goals and personalities clashed at the Yalta Conference. There was a general agreement that Germany would be divided into occupation zones, but only until a peace conference met, as in 1919, to determine the ultimate fate of Germany and Europe. It was also agreed that, with respect to those countries liberated, free democratic elections would be held to determine their form of government. The future of Poland became a point of conflict. Britain and France went to war with Germany over Poland. Churchill and Roosevelt wanted to see a democratic Poland.

Stalin believed that the enormous sacrifices made by the Russian people entitled the Soviet Union to retain the portion of Poland gained as a result of the non-aggression pact with Germany (1939), as well as portions of Finland and Romania, the Baltic states of Latvia, Lithuania, and Estonia, and territorial concessions from Iran and Turkey. Stalin further hoped to obtain control of the Turkish Straits and naval bases in the Mediterranean Sea. As for Germany, though it was to remain united, the Soviet Union should receive the lion's share of reparations. Stalin apparently believed that postwar Germany would embrace Marxism.

Roosevelt succeeded in getting Stalin to agree to declare war on Japan three months after the defeat of Germany. In exchange, the Soviet Union would receive back territories lost to Japan in the Russo-Japanese War (1904–1905) and additional territory in East Asia, together with the "special rights" once enjoyed by Russia in Manchuria. To secure Stalin's support for the United Nations Organization, the Soviet Union was granted three votes in the General Assembly, one for itself and one each for the Ukraine and Belorussia. As for Poland, the Soviet Union was to retain the territory seized in 1939, and Poland was to be compensated with territory taken from Germany. Stalin also agreed that "free and unfettered" elections would be held in Poland.

Once the Cold War was underway, some critics suggested that Roosevelt effectively surrendered Eastern Europe to the Soviet Union. No doubt Roosevelt trusted Stalin more than he should have, and distrusted Churchill, who he regarded as an old-fashioned British imperialist. It is more correct to say, as historian Richard Pipes (1923–2018) pointed out, that the appeasement of Stalin resulted from an "overwhelming desire for peace, ignorance of history, and inability to understand the totalitarian mind...." (Pipes 1981, p. 286). Roosevelt's confidant and close advisor, Harry Hopkins (1890–1946), later spoke of their shared feeling that the Yalta Conference was a success:

> We really believed in our hearts that this was the dawn of a new day we had all been praying for and talking about for so many years. ... The Russians had proved that they could be reasonable and farseeing and there wasn't any doubt in the minds of the President or any of us that we could live with them peacefully as far into the future as any of us could imagine. (Pipes 1981, pp. 286–287)

Hopkins's comment seems very similar to that of Neville Chamberlain's after his return to London following the Munich Conference in 1938.

When the three Allied leaders met again from July 17 to August 2, 1945 at Potsdam, a suburb of Berlin, the war in Europe was over. The goal of the Potsdam Conference was to clarify the agreements made at Yalta, that is, divide Germany and Austria into occupation zones, as well as Berlin and Vienna, administer occupied Germany until the anticipated peace conference, define the borders of Poland, assign reparations from Germany, clarify the Soviet Union's role in Eastern Europe, and bring to a close the war with Japan.

There was a new set of realities at Potsdam, however, that played an important role in what was decided. First, Roosevelt died on April 12, and was succeeded by Vice President Harry Truman (1884–1972). Unfortunately, vice presidential candidates in American politics are chosen to strengthen the party's presidential campaign ticket, that is, to win an election. Little, if any, thought is given to the possibility that the vice president might assume the presidency in the event of the president's death while in office. Hence, when Truman arrived in Potsdam, he was largely in the dark as to what his predecessor agreed to at Yalta. For example, Truman was not fully informed about the Manhattan Project that produced the atomic bomb until April 24, 12 days after Roosevelt's death and his becoming President. Stalin, who had spies embedded in the Manhattan Project, knew more about the atomic bomb than Truman.

Winston Churchill was present until July 5, when the Labour Party dealt Churchill's Conservative Party a crushing defeat in the general election. Churchill was replaced at Potsdam by Clement Attlee (1883–1967), the new Labour Prime Minister. Because the United Kingdom has a parliamentary system, the loyal opposition party keeps a "shadow" government ready to assume office at any moment. Therefore, Attlee was better informed than Truman, but he was no Churchill. The Labour Party won the election committed to building a welfare state, an implicit turn away from an emphasis on foreign policy.

Stalin was the man clearly in command at Potsdam. He was the only one who had participated in the planning and prosecution of the Allied war effort to defeat Nazi Germany. He was the only one who knew, or could define, what had been decided at Yalta. Germany's fate became the major issue at Potsdam.

It was assumed that Germany would remain united, but the unspoken reality recognized by all concerned, was that a united Germany would serve either as a bulwark against the spread of Communism, or as the means by which the Soviet Union might dominate postwar Europe. As the Cold War began to emerge, it became ever more apparent that if Germany remained united, it would have to lean toward one or the other emerging Cold War alliances, and whichever side it chose, would dominate Europe.

The other unspoken reality that influenced the negotiations at Potsdam and played a major role in bringing about the Cold War, was America's possession of the atomic bomb. Stalin did not react as expected when Truman told him that the United States had developed "a new weapon of unusual destructive force." If Truman meant to use the A-bomb to somehow influence Stalin to make concessions regarding postwar Germany and Eastern Europe, he failed. When, from Stalin's perspective, the atomic bombs were dropped on Hiroshima and Nagasaki, two "peaceful and densely-populated Japanese cities," "[w]ithout any military need whatsoever" (Dannen 2015, "Truman Tells Stalin, July 24, 1945"), Stalin assumed that the United States meant to use its monopoly on the atomic bomb to blackmail the Soviet Union.

1946

During 1946, it became apparent that there would be no peace conference. In a speech on February 9, Stalin said that future wars were inevitable due to capitalism and Western imperialism. George F. Kennan (1904–2005), a career diplomat stationed in Moscow, sent a cablegram, since known as the "Long Telegram," to Washington, D.C., in which he argued that American foreign policy toward the Soviet Union should confront Soviet expansion with creditable opposition, or confrontation. Kennan's analysis in the Long Telegram, together with an article he wrote for *Foreign Affairs* in July 1947 ("X" [George F. Kennan] 1947, pp. 566–582), shaped American policy toward the Soviet Union. The "policy of containment" gave its name to the first phase of the Cold War, known as the period of containment, from the Truman Doctrine to Khrushchev's coming to power in the Soviet Union.

Stalin consolidated Soviet control of Eastern Europe during the first years after the war. He pursued a policy characterized as "salami tactics," whereby coalition governments were formed in which the two key ministries of defense and security were assigned to the Communists. Then, step by step, the coalition parties were removed until the country in question had a one-party communist regime subservient to Moscow.

In accordance with agreements reached at Yalta, industrial plants in the western zones of Germany were dismantled and shipped to the Soviet Union, but the Soviet Union failed to ship agricultural products from its occupation zone to the western zones as agreed. The British and Americans stopped the Soviet Union from taking reparations from their zones in 1946. President Truman had already halted Lend Lease aid to the Soviet Union in May 1945. In January 1947, the British and American zones were united administratively into what became known as Bizonia. The French zone did not join to form Trizonia until April 1949. Just six weeks later, the three western zones became the Federal Republic of Germany, or West Germany.

On March 5, 1946, Winston Churchill, who was then leader of the Opposition in Parliament, went to Westminster College in Fulton, Missouri, where he delivered his famous Iron Curtain Speech. In it, he observed that Europe had been divided into two camps by what he called an "Iron Curtain:"

> From Stettin in the Baltic to Trieste in the Adriatic an "iron curtain" has descended across the continent. Behind that line lie all the capitals of the ancient states of Central and Eastern Europe. Warsaw, Berlin, Prague, Vienna, Budapest, Belgrade, Bucharest and Sofia; all these famous cities and the populations around them lie in what I must call the Soviet sphere, and all are subject, in one form or another, not only to Soviet influence but to a very high and in some cases increasing measure of control from Moscow. ("Churchill's Iron Curtain Speech" 2019)

Churchill's speech is considered by Russian historians to mark the beginning of the Cold War, but picking a specific date is arbitrary. Forty-six years later on May 7, 1992, Mikhail Gorbachev, the last president of the Soviet Union, gave a speech at Westminster College, in which he noted that the Iron Curtain had come down, "a victory for common sense, reason, democracy, and common human values" (Clines 1992).

Containment

Two developments during 1947 showed that a Cold War was a reality. First was President Truman's response to Britain's announcement in February that it would end its support for the governments of Greece and Turkey, who were resisting Soviet supported communist insurgencies. It was no longer possible for Britain to serve as the world's policeman. It was time for the United States, the strongest nation in the world at the time, to step up to the plate and assume the burden of defending the free world. On March 12, 1947, Truman spoke before a joint session of Congress. He asked Congress to provide $400 million (roughly $4.7 trillion [£3.5 trillion] in 2019) in aid to Greece and Turkey that would include sending civilian and military personnel and equipment. One sentence in particular has been understood to announce what became known as the Truman Doctrine: "I believe that it must be the policy of the United States to support free peoples who are resisting attempted subjugation by armed minorities or by outside pressures" (Eidenmuller 2017).

Figure 18.2 Europe during the Cold War.

The Truman Doctrine pledged American military support to contain the spread of communism within its then existing borders. But what good was there in threatening military intervention, if the people of Western Europe freely voted for Communists in free elections? The French Communist Party (PCF) won 28.26% of the popular vote in the November 1946 legislative election in France, making it the largest political party. The Italian Communist Party (PCI) emerged from the June 1946 general election in Italy as the third largest political party. It appeared that the people of Western Europe, living among the ruins of the war, were leaning left, that is, voting for political parties that believed in government intervention to alleviate the people's suffering. The only effective way to combat the spread of communism was to remove the economic and social problems that nurtured it. Only people who feel there is no hope for the future turn to communism.

The remedy came in the form of the European Recovery Act, better known as the Marshall Plan, announced by Secretary of State George C. Marshall (1880–1959) in a commencement address at Harvard University on June 5, 1947. The Marshall Plan offered $12 billion (roughly $140 trillion [£ 109.6 trillion] in 2019) in economic aid to rebuild the European economies. It was offered to all the European countries, including the Soviet Union. Stalin's initial response was positive, but he soon saw it as a plot to undermine the form of socialism being constructed in the Soviet Union and its East-European satellite states. Thus, the Soviet Union refused to participate and blocked its satellites from doing so. When Czechoslovakia indicated its interest in participating, the communists carried out a coup in February 1948 that resulted in a new government subservient to Moscow.

On June 21, 1948, the three Western zones in Germany introduced a new currency, the Deutsche Mark. Perhaps more than any other policy change, the introduction of the new currency in the western zones made the separation of Germany into West and East Germany a reality for the foreseeable future. Stalin responded on June 24 by closing all road, rail, and canal access to the western sectors of Berlin. Stalin apparently hoped that if the Western Allies were unable to supply their sectors, they would be forced to abandon Berlin. It is unlikely that Stalin intended, or would have allowed, armed conflict to erupt over Berlin. Neither were the Western Allies willing to go to war. It is likely that Stalin's aim all along was to apply pressure in order to extract concessions.

The Western Allies faced a dilemma. They could not abandon Berlin, nor could they force the blockade. The answer was found in what became known as the Berlin Airlift. Between June 26, 1948 and May 12, 1949, American and British airplanes supplied Berliners in the blockaded sectors of Berlin with 2.3 million tons (1 043 262.5 kg) of supplies, including food, coal, and even Christmas candy for the children. The Allies imposed an embargo on specific exports from the Eastern satellite states, and the United States sent strategic bombers to Britain. The blockade ended on May 12, 1949 and, supplies once again moved freely along road and railways. The airlift, itself, did not officially end until September 30, when sufficient surplus of necessary supplies was stored up.

By the time of the Berlin Blockade, the United States army stood at only half-a-million men, with only 98 000 stationed in West Germany, of which, only 31 000 were combat soldiers. Also, there was only one reserve division in the United States ready for deployment, if needed. In contrast, Soviet military forces in East Germany surrounding Berlin numbered 1.5 million. The United States was relying on its nuclear monopoly in the event of war. However, only 50 atomic bombs were available to the military at the time of the Berlin

Blockade, and none of the bombers deployed to Europe before April 1949 were capable of delivering an atomic bomb (Dawson and Rosecrance 1966).

On April 4, 1949, ten European nations joined with the United States and Canada in signing the North Atlantic Treaty that established the North Atlantic Treaty Organization, or NATO, a military alliance. The signatories pledged to respond collectively to any attack on any member of the alliance by an outside party. NATO extended the American nuclear umbrella to include Western Europe. It set up a military fence to prevent any westward expansion of the Soviet Union's control in Europe. The Soviet Union organized the Warsaw Pact, a defensive alliance between the Soviet Union and its seven satellite states in Central and Eastern Europe in May 1955 as a counterweight to NATO.

The military fence around the Soviet Union was expanded when the United States created SEATO (Southeast Asia Treaty Organization) in September 1954 and CENTO (Central Treaty Organization) in February 1955. The former was an attempt to create a military alliance that would block further communist expansion in Southeast Asia. The latter was an alliance of the United Kingdom, Iran, Iraq, Pakistan, and Turkey. American support for Israel effectively prevented the United States from becoming a formal member of CENTO. Neither SEATO nor CENTO proved successful. Of the three, only NATO continues in the post-Cold War era.

Cold War in Asia

Two events in 1949 that sent shockwaves through the American consciousness and ignited a new Red Scare were the Soviet Union's successful testing of an atomic bomb in August and the Communist victory in the Chinese civil war. America's loss of its nuclear monopoly meant that a future war between the United States and the Soviet Union would likely include the use of atomic bombs. The American public's sense of security was severely shaken. It was widely believed that someone had given the secret of the atomic bomb to the Soviets. A number of American citizens were arrested and charged with spying for the Soviet Union. Some received prison sentences of various lengths. Julius Rosenberg (1918–1953) and his wife, Ethel (1915–1953), were convicted of conspiracy to commit espionage and sentenced to death.

China

The proclamation of the People's Republic of China on October 1, 1949 came as a shock to Americans who knew very little about China other than the fact that it was an ally during World War II. The Qing dynasty that ruled China since 1644 ended in 1912, with the forced abdication of the six-year-old Xuantong Emperor Puyi (1906–1967). A republic was proclaimed, but there really was not any true central government from 1912 until 1949. China dissolved into a medieval-like patchwork quilt of competing warlords who ruled their territories at will, while at times, giving only token allegiance to a central government. Between 1927 and 1949, Chiang Kai-shek (1887–1975), one of the many warlords, claimed central authority. Under Chiang Kai-shek's rule, the so-called Republic of China existed as an authoritarian one-party military dictatorship.

In April 1927, Chiang Kai-shek declared martial law in Shanghai and sent a secret order to all areas under his control to purge the Kuomintang (Nationalist Party of China) of all Communists. Bai Chongxi (1893–1966), a former warlord and, in April 1927, Chief of Staff of the National Revolutionary Army and garrison commander in Shanghai, carried out the purge in what has become known as the Shanghai massacre of 1927. General Bai, who Western reporters nicknamed "The Hewer of Communist Heads," arrested thousands and executed hundreds of workers, mostly members of Communist labor unions, and students.

A civil war between the nationalist Kuomintang forces and the Communists led by Mao Zedong (1893–1976) broke out following the 1927 purge. The civil war continued intermittently until the final victory of the Communists in 1949. Despite extensive material aid from the United States, Chiang Kai-shek's nationalist army was handily defeated by Mao Zedong's People's Liberation Army. As in the Russian Civil War, where the Bolsheviks won the hearts and minds of the people, the Chinese Communists did likewise. In December 1949, Chiang Kai-shek and roughly two million nationalist soldiers retreated to the island of Taiwan (Formosa).

Taiwan belonged to Japan from 1895 until Japan's defeat in World War II. China did not have legal title to Taiwan in 1949. According to the agreements reached at the Cairo Conference in November 1943, attended by Roosevelt, Churchill, Stalin, and Chiang Kai-shek, and the Potsdam Conference in July–August 1945, sovereignty over Taiwan was to be transferred to China after the peace treaty with Japan was signed. But the peace treaty was not signed until 1952. Chiang Kai-shek's authority over Taiwan rested on General Douglas MacArthur allowing Chiang Kai-shek to accept the surrender of Japanese forces on the island. That act by MacArthur appeared to give Chiang Kai-shek de facto control of Taiwan.

Taiwanese resentment of China's occupation led to a revolt in February 1947. The Nationalist suppression of the revolt and "pacification" of the island resulted in the death of an estimated 10 000 Taiwanese, including many leaders and those with advanced education. The "White Terror," as it is often called, was halted after American diplomatic intervention (Cheng 1988). The Chinese Nationalists imposed martial law in Taiwan that lasted from May 19, 1949 to July 15, 1987.

The United States did not intend to defend Chiang Kai-shek's government in exile on Taiwan from an invasion by Mao's forces. What saved the miniature Republic of China on Taiwan was the invasion of South Korea by North Korea on June 25, 1950. Korea was under Japanese rule from 1910 to 1945. At the end of World War II, Soviet forces occupied northern Korea and American forces occupied southern Korea. As with Germany, efforts to keep Korea united fell victim to the emerging Cold War. Elections were held in southern Korea in 1948, which resulted in the founding of the United States' supported Republic of Korea. In response, the Democratic People's Republic of Korea was founded with Soviet sponsorship in northern Korea. Neither were republics except in name. Marxism-Leninism prevailed in the north, while an authoritarian dictatorship was the rule in the south.

Having secured Stalin's approval for an invasion of South Korea aimed at uniting the country under the communist regime in the north, North Korean forces began the invasion early on Sunday morning, June 25, 1950. The South Korean forces were inferior in number, equipment, and leadership. Though there were a large number of American forces stationed in Japan, there were only 200–300 American soldiers stationed in South Korea.

The southern capital of Seoul fell on June 28. Syngman Rhee (1875–1965), president of South Korea, ordered the massacre of suspected political opponents in the south. Estimates of those who died in the so-called Bodo League massacre vary between 100 000 and 200 000 (McDonald 2008). The fact that the massacre took place was not made public until after the end of the dictatorship in 1990.

On the day before the fall of Seoul, the United Nations Security Council passed a resolution authorizing member states to aid South Korea. The Soviet Union was boycotting the meeting, and therefore, was not present to veto the resolution. By September 12, South Korean and UN forces controlled only a small 5000-square-mile (12 950 sq. km) piece of territory around the southeastern port of Pusan. Between September 15 and 19, American forces carried out a daring amphibious landing at Inchon, a port on the western coast, 150 miles (241.4 km) behind the North Korean lines.

The mostly American UN forces pushed the North Koreans back into North Korea, but as they drew near the Yalu River that serves as a border between North Korea and China, "volunteer" Chinese soldiers in massive numbers crossed the border and confronted the UN forces. Fighting continued in a back-and-forth manner until a ceasefire was negotiated and signed on July 27, 1953. A demilitarized zone was established separating North and South Korea along the 38th parallel, roughly the same border that existed before the war. As of 2019, there has been no peace treaty ending the Korean War.

Vietnam

Communism seemed to gain ground in Southeast Asia when France acknowledged defeat in their attempt to hold onto Vietnam. It was agreed at the Potsdam Conference (1954) that France's prewar colonies in Southeast Asia would be returned to France. Though the United States did not favor the return of French colonial rule, the emerging Cold War in Europe and the United States's need for French support in building a Western alliance to oppose Soviet expansion left the United States with little choice but to support the return of French rule in Vietnam.

During World War II, contacts between the United States's Office of Strategic Services (OSS), predecessor of Central Intelligence agency (CIA), and the nationalist Vietnam Independence League (Viet Minh), led to an informal agreement that, in return for the Viet Minh's harassment of the Japanese and rescue of downed American pilots, the United States would support an independent Vietnam. Ho Chi Minh (1890–1969), founder of both the Viet Minh (1941) and the Indochinese Communist Party (1930) was an admirer of both Marxism and American democracy. But, above all else, he was a nationalist committed to the liberation of Vietnam from French colonial rule.

On September 2, 1945, the very same day as the surrender of the Japanese onboard the USS *Missouri*, Ho Chi Minh proclaimed the Democratic State of Vietnam with Hanoi as its capital. Ho's admiration for the United States was evident in his proclamation speech:

> All men are created equal; they are endowed by their Creator with certain unalienable Rights; among these are Life, Liberty, and the pursuit of Happiness. This immortal statement was made in the Declaration of Independence of the United

States of America in 1776. In a broader sense, this means: All the peoples on the earth are equal from birth, all the peoples have a right to live, to be happy and free. The Declaration of The French Revolution made in 1791 on the Rights of Man and the Citizen also states: "All men are born free and with equal rights, and must always remain free and have equal rights". Those are undeniable truths ("Ho Chi Minh, Declaration of Independence of the Democratic Republic of Viet–Nam" n.d.).

Unfortunately, Ho Chi Minh's appeal for recognition from the United States was ignored.

Hoi Chi Minh spent four months during 1946 in France in a failed attempt to get French recognition of an independent and unified Vietnam. While Ho Chi Minh was in France, the French established a government in the south under Bao Dai (Nguyen Vinh Thuy, 1913–1997), the last emperor of Vietnam. War broke out in December 1946 between the Democratic State of Vietnam in the north and the Republic of Chochinchina in the south. Alarmed by Mao Zedong's victory in China in 1949, and the outbreak of the Korean War in 1950, the United States began providing military hardware and advisors to the French in what was later called the First Vietnam War (1946–1954). American pilots flew missions in support of the French. In 2005, it was revealed that two American CIA pilots out of 24, were killed in action during the Battle of Dien Bien Phu (Mar 13, 1954–May 7, 1954), the decisive battle of the war.

Following their decisive defeat at the Battle of Dien Bien Phu, the French began a complete withdrawal from Vietnam. The Geneva Conference on Indochina met between May 8 and July 21, 1954 with the mission of bringing peace to Southeast Asia. The conference was attended by representatives from the United States, Britain, China, the Soviet Union, France, both North and South Vietnam, Cambodia, and Laos. The Geneva Accords that were agreed to at the conference included the division of Vietnam into two zones, one in the north and one in the south, with the dividing line approximating the seventeenth parallel. The division was to be temporary, until a general election was held throughout Vietnam in July 1956 for a unified Vietnam.

Though the United States and the government of South Vietnam participated in drafting the Geneva Accords, neither actually signed them. Assuming a free election in all of Vietnam on unification would result in a victory for North Vietnam, South Vietnam, supported by the United States, chose not to hold the election in 1956. In December 1957, both the Soviet Union and the Peoples Republic of China agreed to a proposal to recognize North and South Vietnam, with both being admitted to the United Nations. The North Vietnamese rejected the proposal, since it would undercut their primary goal of unification. The Viet Minh began a guerrilla war in the South in October. Ho Chi Minh declared a People's War in March 1959 for the unification of Vietnam.

The United States backed the government in South Vietnam as they formerly backed the French. Two American advisors were killed by Viet Minh guerrillas in July 1959, marking the beginning of the Second Vietnam War. Though South Vietnam was a "republic" in name it was, in fact, a military dictatorship under President Ngo Dinh Diem (1901–1963), a devout Roman Catholic Christian in a Buddhist country. As Diem's government grew increasingly corrupt, it lost the support of the people.

As the United States became more deeply involved in Vietnam, the "domino theory" was used to argue that the defense of South Vietnam was of great strategic importance in

America's defense of freedom around the world. According to the "domino theory" that emerged during the early 1950s, if South Vietnam fell to communism, then all Southeast Asia would be lost like a row of dominos when the first one is toppled. After returning from a visit to South Vietnam to assess the military situation in October 1961, General Maxwell Taylor (1901–1987) recommended to President John F. Kennedy (1917–1963) that he send 8000 combat soldiers to Vietnam. General Taylor concluded, "if Vietnam goes, it will be exceedingly difficult if not impossible to hold Southeast Asia" (Gibbons 1995, p. 7). Secretary of Defense, Robert McNamara (1916–2009) and the Joint Chiefs of Staff suggested sending 200 000 as a show of strength. The president did neither. Instead, he increased the number of military advisors to more than 16 000.

By December 1961, American military advisors were assisting in combat missions, Viet Cong guerrillas controlled much of the South Vietnamese countryside, and the American taxpayers were spending $1million ($8 430 638 [£6 363 446] in 2019) per day to support the increasingly ineffective South Vietnamese Army. Fearful that the war might be lost unless Diem was replaced, President Kennedy approved a military coup in November 1963, that resulted in Diem's death and the first of a succession of generals who came to power through coups, and who attempted, unsuccessfully, to lead South Vietnam.

Europe

Joseph Stalin died on March 5, 1953. After a brief period of collective leadership, Nikita Khrushchev (1894–1971) emerged as the leader of the Soviet Union. Khrushchev denounced Stalin's legacy in a speech before the Twentieth Party Congress of the Communist Party of the Soviet Union in February 1956. He accused Stalin of a number of crimes, including having created a cult of personality around himself and creating "conditions of insecurity, fear, and even desperation" (Hunt 2015, p. 153). Under Khrushchev's leadership, a number of political and cultural reforms were instituted that allowed a greater degree of freedom in both the Soviet Union and its satellites.

When the iron fist of Stalin was removed, it appeared that Khrushchev would allow the satellite states more freedom in finding their own way to the socialist future, but they soon found that there were limits to what they might achieve. Confusion and frustration resulted in revolts in East Berlin in 1953, and in Poland and Hungary during 1956.

The uprising in East Berlin began as an unauthorized strike that was soon suppressed by Soviet tanks. The Polish revolt also began with a strike and demonstrations in Poznań. Polish nationalism played a role as the demonstrations spread to various cities across Poland. The nationalists, communists who wanted an independent Poland, were able to remove the Stalinists from the Central Committee of the Polish Communist Party (KPP) and elect, as its First Chairman, a popular Communist who had been jailed by Stalin for his advocacy of Polish nationalism. A visit by government officials from Moscow restored order by threatening Soviet military intervention.

A full-fledged revolution broke out in Hungary in late October, when the Hungarian army joined the revolution. A new government was formed under the Communist Imre Nagy (1896–1958), who announced an end to one-party rule and that Hungary was leaving the Warsaw Pact. Nagy appealed for recognition from the United States and the

United Kingdom, as well as other nations of the free world, but none was given. Fear of igniting a war between the United States and the Soviet Union outweighed any desire to aid the Hungarians.

Soviet military forces entered Hungary on November 4. Within six days, the revolution was over. and a Moscow-obedient regime put back in power. Nagy and the generals who participated in the revolt were eventually shot. Many others were imprisoned. An estimated 200 000 Hungarians took advantage of the disorder to leave Hungary.

More shocking to American leaders than the Soviet suppression of the Hungarian revolt was the Soviet Union's successful launch of the first artificial earth satellite on October 4, 1957. Sputnik I, as it was named, orbited the earth about every 98 minutes, giving off a pulsating radio signal that could be picked up by amateur radio operators, and was called the "deep beep-beep" by the Associated Press. It was even possible to see the satellite with the naked eye in the early morning or late evening when conditions were just right.

What was most significant about Sputnik I was the fact that if the Soviets had a rocket that could place a satellite in orbit, it had the capability to develop ballistic missiles that could deliver nuclear bombs to the United States. No longer was the United States protected by two oceans. What Americans had done to Hiroshima and Nagasaki could conceivably be done to American cities. America's program to launch a satellite was put on a fast track, resulting in the first successful launch of a satellite on January 31, 1958. In the meantime, the Soviet Union launched Sputnik II, carrying the first living creature into space, the space dog "Laika." The race to space was suddenly a part of the Cold War arms race.

To the Brink of Nuclear War

Just as the United States was being drawn deeper into the struggle between North and South Vietnam over unification, the stage was being set for two of the most dangerous Cold War crises, the Berlin Crisis of 1961 and the Cuban Missile Crisis in 1962. In both, but most certainly the latter, the world teetered on the brink of nuclear war.

The founding of the Federal Republic of Germany, or West Germany, and the German Democratic Republic, or East Germany, in 1949 was an admission that all hope for a peace conference and a united Germany were abandoned, at least for any foreseeable future. Both claimed to be the true successor of the German Third Reich and the only representative of the German people. Both claimed Berlin as its capital, though West Germany established a provisional capital in the university town of Bonn on the Rhine River. Neither Germany recognized the other until 1972. The Western sectors of Berlin were regarded by West Germany as an unofficial de facto federal state (*Bundesland*), though the Federal Republic did not have title to them. The whole of Berlin remained under the authority of the Allied Control Council. Indeed, the New Occupation Statute (1949) reserved the right for the four Allies to intervene in Germany, West and East, if deemed necessary. Full sovereignty was not restored to Germany until The Treaty on the Final Settlement with Respect to Germany was signed in 1990.

Divided Berlin with its island of democracy and capitalism surrounded by the drab reality of a Marxist-Leninist totalitarian state was, throughout the Cold War, a constant reminder of the human tragedy of the failed peace and the danger that an accidental spark could ignite a nuclear holocaust. It almost happened on October 27–28, 1961, when Soviet and American tanks, armed, and with orders to fire if fired upon, faced each other at Checkpoint Charlie with only 164–329 ft (100–200 m) between them. The incident was in the making for some time.

Prior to August 13, 1961, an East German citizen could exit the German Democratic Republic through Berlin. One needed only to board a streetcar or subway car to one of the Western sectors and, from there, go to West Germany. Prior to 1961, an estimated 4.5 million East Germans, approximately 20 % of East Germany's population, used the Berlin route to freedom in West Germany. Since many were highly educated, professional people needed in East Germany to build the highly touted Democratic Republic, their loss represented a serious "brain drain" that had to be stopped.

The solution was found in the erection of a wall that circled the Western zones of Berlin, cutting them off from the surrounding Democratic Republic. What became known as the Berlin Wall went up so fast, beginning on August 13, that family members were caught on one side or the other. The wall was more than just a wall. It was actually a series of obstacles, fences, and open spaces, as well as the wall itself, that stretched 96 miles (155 km) around West Berlin. The construction of the wall was a violation of the Allied agreement regarding occupied Berlin that led to the American and Soviet tank standoff at Checkpoint Charlie on October 27–28. The danger that it represented was real, but neither the Soviet Union nor the United States was willing to let it ignite a war between them.

Once in place, only military force could have removed the wall, and that was never an option. The United States and its allies resigned themselves to its existence. President Kennedy later said of the outcome of the crisis: "It's not a very nice solution, but a wall is a hell of a lot better than a war" (Gaddis, p. 115). Premier Khrushchev said that the wall was a "hateful thing," but "[T]he East German economy would have collapsed if we hadn't done something soon against the mass flight.... So, the Wall was the only remaining option" (Gaddis, p. 115). Berlin remained a hot spot for the remainder of the Cold War. Khrushchev once commented that Berlin "is the testicle of the West.... When I want the West to scream, I squeeze on Berlin" (Berlin from Wall to Ball 2005).

A war, potentially a nuclear war, was very unlikely to occur over Berlin in 1961, but it was a very real possibility over the Soviet Union's decision to base missiles armed with nuclear warheads in Cuba during the fall of 1962. The American-backed dictator of Cuba, Fulgencio Batista (1901–1973), was overthrown in 1959 in a revolution led by Fidel Castro (1926–2016). When Castro, a self-proclaimed Marxist, began to nationalize American-owned properties, the United States ended diplomatic relations with Cuba and imposed a trade embargo. Many Cubans, especially middle-and upper-class citizens who had much to lose, both in terms of property and personal freedom, began seeking refuge in the United States.

In April 1961, a band of approximately 1400 Cuban exiles, trained and equipped by the United States Central Intelligence Agency (CIA), attempted to overthrow Castro's regime. They were landed by the CIA on the beaches near the Bay of Pigs. The venture was a disaster. The promised air support was withdrawn at the last moment, leaving the exiles at the mercy of Castro's forces. More than 100 died in the fighting, while the remainder were taken prisoner.

Fearful of an American invasion of Cuba, and suffering from the trade embargo, Cuba became increasingly dependent on the Soviet Union, both economically and militarily.

On October 15, 1962, an American U-2 spy plane took pictures of Soviet medium-range missiles in Cuba. There followed 13 days, during which the United States and the Soviet Union danced on the edge of nuclear war. Two days later, additional photos showed long-range missiles present capable of flying 2200 miles (3541 km). It was later revealed that short-range missiles, armed with nuclear warheads that could be used to repel an American invasion, were dispatched to Cuba. Most alarming was the fact that in the event of an invasion, local commanders were authorized to use them (Gaddis, p. 77).

In a speech to the nation on October 22, President Kennedy informed the American people of the missiles, and added that he ordered a naval quarantine around Cuba to intercept Soviet ships that might be carrying nuclear warheads for the missiles. He also warned the Soviet Union of the consequences should any missiles be launched from Cuba: "It shall be the policy of this nation to regard any nuclear missile launched from Cuba against any nation in the Western Hemisphere as an attack by the Soviet Union on the United States, requiring a full retaliatory response upon the Soviet Union" (President John F. Kennedy n.d.).

It remains to be known, and may never be known, all that took place during the tense meetings between President Kennedy and his advisors during those 13 days. Neither will we ever know who blinked first, Kennedy or Khrushchev. The only sane outcome was one where both could claim to have saved the world from war. Khrushchev withdrew the missiles from Cuba and Kennedy pledged that the United States would not attempt or support a future invasion of Cuba. Also, Kennedy agreed to the withdrawal of missiles in Turkey targeted on the Soviet Union. Looking back at the crisis, Ted Sorensen (1928–2010), the man who wrote Kennedy's history making speech, aptly expressed the unspoken relief of people throughout the world, when he said: "It was a giant gamble on our part. ... [But] we succeeded ... [and] the world stepped back from the very brink of destruction and has never come that close again" (Stern 2008).

The Cuban Missile Crisis marked the end of the Cold War period known as coexistence, that began with Khrushchev's ascension to leadership of the Soviet Union, and the beginning of the period known as détente. The world came so close to a nuclear holocaust that both the Soviet Union and the United States took steps to try and assure that such a crisis would never occur again.

Postwar Recovery

To look back at photos of the piles of rubble that dominated the landscape of Western Europe when the war ended in the spring of 1945 is to wonder how it ever recovered, not to mention experienced unprecedented prosperity in the 1950s and 1960s. The same may be said of postwar Japan or South Korea after the Korean War. Certainly, a major reason for the speed of recovery was the Cold War. To offset the attractiveness of communism, the United States extended extensive economic aid for rebuilding their economies, and by extension, the quality of life for all their citizens. Also, the presence of large numbers of American military personnel did much to boost economic recovery. The fact that Japan served as the base for American forces during the Korean War was a major factor in Japan's recovery.

The wartime damage in Europe was not as great as first thought. The war's destruction of industries and cities actually contributed to recovery and subsequent prosperity. Destroyed or damaged plants were modernized or replaced by more efficient and competitive plants. That was an advantage enjoyed by West Germany when compared to Britain. There was a great demand for just about everything, especially housing and food. The one thing that was in short supply was investment capital.

The Marshall Plan provided the necessary capital to jumpstart the economies of Western Europe. Once the recovery was underway, expansion was financed by earnings from exports. By 1950, production levels were nearly a third greater than before the war. Full employment was the norm during the 1950s and 1960s, necessitating the introduction of foreign "guest workers."

The Marshall Plan aided recovery in two other important ways. First, receiving Marshall funds carried with it the requirement that the recipients cooperate in the recovery. The result was formation of the Organization for European Economic Cooperation (OEEC) in 1948, to foster trade among its members. Its success led to creation of the European Coal and Steel Community (ECSC) in 1951 and the European Atomic Energy Community (EUROATOM) in 1957. The former eliminated tariffs and other trade barriers between the member nations. The latter promoted research and development of nuclear energy.

A major milestone in the development of European unity came with the Rome Treaty in 1957 that established the European Economic Community (EEC), better known as the Common Market. The EEC provided a common market and a common trade policy for trade with non-members. Trade among its members quadrupled in the decade from 1958 to 1968. Not to be overlooked as an incentive for European economic integration was the belief that anything that integrated West Germany into Europe would lessen the fear, especially among the French, of a healthy Germany.

The need for speedy recovery of war-ravaged Western Europe caused a leftward swing in postwar elections. Parties that were not ideologically opposed to government playing a key role in the economy were preferable to those that were committed to the old "hands off" approach. Also, the old conservative parties that dominated the interwar years were perceived as those whose policies were responsible for the war. As noted above, the communist parties did well in the French legislative election in 1946 and in the Italian general election in 1947. Communist parties in the Benelux countries (Belgium, Netherlands, and Luxemburg) showed strength in the general elections held in 1945 and 1946.

The early postwar success of the Communists was short lived, however, due in part to their being "guided" by Moscow. The Soviet Union saw the communist parties outside the Soviet bloc as serving the interests of the Soviet Union. They were expected to follow policy decided in Moscow. Images of Stalinist suppression in the satellite states, together with the ongoing economic recovery in the West, meant that communism became less attractive to Western Europeans.

The socialist parties, like the Communists, did well initially, but then suffered a decline. They were hampered by their early association with the communist parties. The fact that they had their origin in late nineteenth-century revisionism that split Marxism into orthodox and revisionist Marxism, meant that their party programs still included the standard Marxist concepts of class struggle, international solidarity of the working class, and the inevitability of the classless society. The party program of the German Social Democratic

Party (SPD), for example, was still the Heidelberg Program of 1925. So long as the SPD avowed Marxism, it was unacceptable to Christians in general and Roman Catholics in particular.

In order to gain acceptance among the voters, the Social Democratic parties had to purge their party programs of Marxism. The SPD adopted the new Bad Godesberg Program in 1959. Gone was the traditional Marxist philosophy and rhetoric. In its place, was a democratic socialism based on human dignity, that is, individual freedom growing out of mutual respect for right and justice (Waibel 1983, pp. 91–95). Their goal was creation of a welfare state, gas and water socialism, not the classless utopia of the Communists.

As the Social Democratic parties changed their image to more accurately represent what they really stood for, they were able to become mass parties that cut across all confessional, social, and economic divisions. With the change came success at the polls. For example, in the parliamentary elections in 1966, the SPD was able to join in a grand coalition government with the Christian Democratic Union/Christian Social Union (CDU/CSU). In 1969, the SPD was able to head a government for the first time since 1928 in coalition with the liberal Free Democratic Party (FDP).

Rise of Christian Democracy

Such was the attraction of the leftist parties, especially the Social Democratic parties, that those who feared the spread of communism tried to unite those who favored a minimal role of government involvement in the economy and a shared anxiety over the increasing secularization of society and culture. Christian Democracy, with its origins in nineteenth-century Roman Catholic social teachings and Neo-Calvinism, offered a right-center alternative to left-center Social Democracy. Both Christian Democracy and Social Democracy favor a simple formula for, or approach to, the state's role in the economy, as well as social and cultural issues: "As much freedom as possible; as much control as necessary." Both believe in a free market economy. Both want to see the prosperity that comes from a free economy shared by all members of society.

So long as Social Democracy remained linked with atheistic Communism (Marxism), both Protestant and Roman Catholic Christians were hesitant to vote Social Democratic, even though they shared the Social Democrats's desire to create a postwar society with a greater degree of economic and social justice. At the same time, they understood that if Protestants revived their prewar conservative parties, and the Roman Catholics revived their confessional parties, the working-class based Social Democrats would likely win the elections. What was needed was a new kind of political party modeled after those in the United States, a party based upon common shared values, able to appeal to all socio-economic classes, Christians of both Protestant and Roman Catholic confessions, and those without any religious identity. That was the strength of the Christian Democratic parties that were successful in both Italy and Germany, but especially in Germany.

The occupation authorities in West Germany were fearful of what a Social Democratic victory might mean in the new Federal Republic founded in 1949. Hence, they encouraged and aided the emergence of the Christian Democratic Union, known as the Christian Social Union in Bavaria. The Roman Catholic bishops agreed not to support a revival of the prewar Catholic Center Party. Instead, they favored the founding of a non-confessional party based upon shared Christian values. The result was the founding of the CDU/CSU that governed West Germany in coalition with the FDP from 1949 to 1966, except between 1957 and 1961.

Konrad Adenauer (1876–1967), who served as Chancellor from 1949 to 1963, worked to integrate West Germany with the American-led alliance in the Cold War, even to the extent of rearming Germany and integrating West Germany into NATO. Also, under Adenauer's leadership, West Germany experienced an economic recovery that Germans refer to as the *Wirtschaftswunder* (economic miracle).

The extraordinary economic recovery was largely the work of Adenauer's Federal Minister for Economic Affairs (1949–1963) and Vice Chancellor (1957–1963), Ludwig Erhard (1897–1977). Erhard's "social market" approach emphasized a free market economy, while accepting government regulations that "protects its citizens against illness and unemployment through a network of social insurance schemes" (70 Years of Social Market Economy 2018). Supporting free enterprise produced prosperity and not only enriched the stockholders, but also supported high wages and a comprehensive welfare system that assured peace between labor and management. In Britain, labor disputes discouraged investments in, and modernization of industries, that, in turn, resulted in unemployment. In Germany, cooperation between government, management, and labor produced unprecedented prosperity and the need to import guest workers.

Building the Welfare State

A characteristic of recovery in Europe was the emergence of the welfare state, the realization of gas and water socialism. State-sponsored social welfare legislation was not something new. Germany provided the precedent with Bismarck's social legislation between 1883 and 1889 that provided workers with health, accident, old age, and disability insurance. After Bismarck's retirement from office, the Reichstag continued and expanded Bismarck's legislation by passing the Worker's Protection Act of 1891 and the Children's Protection Act of 1903.

Britain's Parliament began passing welfare legislation in the early twentieth century. Beginning with the Education Act of 1902, the Conservative-led government passed the Unemployed Workmen Act and Employment of Children Act in 1905. Under the Liberal-led government, a whole host of social legislation was passed. Subsidized meals for school children was introduced in 1906 and expanded in 1914. The Labour Exchanges Act (1909) established labor exchanges to aid the unemployed in finding work. The National Insurance Acts (1911) made health insurance, sick pay for up to 26 weeks, and unemployment insurance for up to 15 weeks available to workers, all of which, was financed by contributions from workers, employers, and the government. Pensions for retired workers over 70 was provided for those who qualified.

The motivation behind the earlier social legislation was to win the support of the working class that was gaining the right to vote and organizing political parties to represent their interests, as for example the Labour Party in Britain and the Social Democratic Party in Germany. The motivation behind the modern, post-World War II welfare states was different. They arose from the conviction that the state should play a role in establishing a basic standard of living below which none of its citizens could fall. That meant making education available to all, providing medical services for all, enabling the elderly to live out their lives with dignity, and eliminating poverty and homelessness. All the welfare states had the same goals and similar programs. They differed mainly in how they were financed.

One development that contributed to the creation of welfare states was what might be called the retreat from empire. Unlike the aftermath of World War I, when the Allies took advantage of their victory over Germany and Turkey to expand their empires, after World War II, there was little resistance to granting independence to their colonies. The colonial powers were exhausted, both materially and psychologically in 1945. Their citizens were no longer willing to forswear a minimal standard of living in order to take pride in the fact that they ruled large native populations in distant colonies. They were no longer willing to devote funds to the maintenance of colonies, when those funds could be used to improve the standard of living for all back home. The victory of Britain's Labour Party in the May 1945 parliamentary elections gave evidence that the pledge to build a welfare state at home was more attractive to the voters than the history of the British Empire as personified in the person of Sir Winston Churchill.

The appearance of the modern welfare state is but one example of the economic prosperity that came to characterize the 1950s and 1960s in the industrialized nations of the free world. Class distinctions blurred as a meritocracy based on education and experience began to displace the importance of one's ancestry or school tie. Peace between labor and management in a market economy produced higher wages, increased benefits, and provided a shorter workweek for workers. Prosperity gave birth to the postwar consumer society. Such things as automobiles, refrigerators, washing machines, and televisions became increasingly more common. Working-class and middle-class families shared a similar diet, enjoyed similar recreational activities, watched the same television programs, and fell in love and married across vanishing class lines.

Postwar America

As was true after World War I, the United States was the only nation to benefit from its participation in World War II. Americans were confident of their new role as leader of the free world. Affluence became characteristic of American life during the two decades after the war's end. The nation's GDP (Gross Domestic Profit, or value of all goods and services produced) "jumped from about $200 thousand-million in 1940 to $300 thousand-million in 1950 to more than $500 thousand-million in 1960" (The Postwar Economy: 1945–1960).

It was spending for the war that ended the Great Depression in America. Once the war production ended, the American economy began transitioning to a consumer economy to keep the prosperity going. There were four times as many automobiles produced in 1955 as were produced in 1946. Whereas fewer than 17 000 homes had a television set in 1946, in 1960, 250 000 were being sold every month. Seventy-five percent of American homes had at least one television set in 1960, and the average family spent four to five hours in front of their televisions (The Postwar Economy: 1945–1960). The picture of a postwar suburb with individual homes that looked as if made from the same mold, and with a television antenna mounted on each roof, became the symbol of American prosperity.

During the first decade after the war, the prosperity and optimism about the future was mostly characteristic of the white majority of the nation's citizens. But by the mid-fifties, African Americans were beginning to demand greater access to the American dream. Within ten years, women and other minority groups, including what would later become known as the LGBTQ community, were likewise demanding their piece of the dream.

There was evidence of the darker side of human nature in the anti-Communist paranoia that mimicked the Red Scare of the 1920s. Joseph McCarthy (1908–1957), the junior senator from Wisconsin, played the role of the Red Scare's A. Mitchell Palmer. McCarthy fueled the paranoia with his sensational campaign to uncover what he alleged were known "members of the Communist Party and who nevertheless are still working and shaping policy in the State Department" (Peurifoy 1950). McCarthy and the House Committee on Un-American Activities, founded in 1947, hunted for alleged, hidden communist operatives in Hollywood and other areas of the entertainment industry, in public schools, colleges, and universities. It seemed that no area of public or private life was safe from those who were committed to infiltrating every aspect of American life with the intent to destroy freedom.

When the decade of the 1960s opened, few people in Europe or the United States could have known that within the next 30 years the Soviet Union would disappear without a war and the Chinese dragon would awaken and threaten to challenge the United States for leadership in a new post-modern, post-Western world.

References

American History (2012). The Postwas Economy: 1945–1960. http://www.let.rug.nl/usa/outlines/history-1994/postwar-america/the-postwar-economy-1945-1960.php (accessed 21 October 2019).

Cheng, P.P.C. (1988). Taiwan under Chiang Kai-shek's Era: 1946-1976. *Asian Profile* 16 (4 (August)): 301.

Clines, F.X. (1992). At Site of 'Iron Curtain' Speech, Gorbachev Buries the Cold War. *New York Times* (7 March).

Dannen, G. (2015). Truman Tells Stalin, July 24, 1945. http://www.dannen.com/decision/potsdam.html (accessed 21 October 2019).

Dawson, R. and Rosecrance, R. (1966). Theory and reality in the Anglo-American Alliance. *World Politics* 19 (1): 21–51. https://doi.org/10.2307/2009841 (accessed 29 November 2018).

Deutschland.de (2018). 70 Years of Social Market Economy. https://www.deutschland.de/en/topic/business/social-market-economy-in-germany-growth-and-prosperity (accessed 21 October 2019).

Eidenmuller, M.E. (2017). Harry S. Truman: The Truman Doctrine. American Rhetoric. https://www.americanrhetoric.com/speeches/harrystrumantrumandoctrine.html (accessed 21 October 2019).

Gaddis, J.L. (2005). *The Cold War: A New History*. London: Penguin Books.

Gibbons, W.C. (1995). *The U. S. Government and the Vietnam War: Executive and Legislative Roles and Relationships*. Princeton, NJ: Princeton University Press.

Hunt, M.H. (2015). *The World Transformed: 1945 to the Present*. New York: Oxford University Press.

Kennan, G.F. ["X"]. (1947). The sources of soviet conduct. *Foreign Affairs* 25 (4): 566–582.

Liberty, Equality, Fraternity (n.d.). Ho Chi Minh, Declaration of Independence of the Democratic Republic of Viet–Nam. http://chnm.gmu.edu/revolution/d/583 (accessed 9 November 2019).

McDonald, H. (2008). South Korea owns up to brutal past. *The Sydney Morning Herald* (November 15).

Peurifoy, J.E. (1950). The Deputy Under Secretary of State for Administration (Peurifoy) to Senator Joseph R. McCarthy. https://history.state.gov/historicaldocuments/frus1952-54v01p2/d174 (accessed 21 October 2019).

Pipes, R. (1981). *Modern Europe*. Homewood: Dorsey Press.

Stern, S.M. (2008). Ted Sorensen's Fallible Memory of the Cuban Missile Crisis. History News Network. https://historynewsnetwork.org/article/51487#_edn2 (accessed 21 October 2019).

The History Place (n.d.) President John F. Kennedy on the Cuban Missile Crisis. http://www.historyplace.com/speeches/jfk-cuban.htm (accessed 21 October 2019).

The National WWII Museum (n.d.). Research Starters: Worldwide Deaths in World War II. https://www.nationalww2museum.org/students-teachers/student-resources/research-starters/research-starters-worldwide-deaths-world-war (accessed 21 October 2019).

The Telegraph (2005). Berlin from Wall to ball. www.telegraph.co.uk/travel/destinations/europe/germany/berlin/734189/Berlin-from-Wall-to-ball.html (accessed 21 October 2019).

Waibel, P.R. (1983). *Politics of Accommodation: German Social Democracy and the Catholic Church, 1945–1959*. Frankfurt am Main: Peter Lang.

Westminster College (2019). Churchill's Iron Curtain Speech. https://www.westminster-mo.edu/explore/history-traditions/IronCurtainSpeech.html (accessed 21 October 2019).

19

Cold War: 1962–1991

Chronology

1946–1954	First Vietnam War
1959	USA "Project Horizon: Proposal to Establish a Lunar Outpost"
1962	Cuban Missile Crisis
1963	President John F. Kennedy Assassinated
1964	China Explodes First Atomic Bomb
1964	Tonkin Gulf Resolution (Vietnam War) Passed by Congress
1965	US Marines Arrive in Vietnam; Battle of la Drang Valley
1967	Six Day War in Middle East
1967	China Explodes First Hydrogen Bomb
1968	Tet Offensive; Siege of Marine Base at Khe Sanh
1968	Paris Riots; Riots at Democratic Convention in Chicago
1968	Prague Spring; Brezhnev Doctrine
1971	Last USA Combat Troops Leave Vietnam
1973	Yom Kippur War in Middle East; OPEC Oil Embargo
1975	North Vietnamese Victory in Vietnam War
1979	USA Recognizes People's Republic of China and Taiwan as Part of It
1979	Pope John Paul II's Pilgrimage to Poland
1989	Berlin Wall Comes Down
1990	Reunification of Germany
1991	USSR Officially Dissolved After 74 Years; End of Cold War

President John F. Kennedy and Premier Nikita Khrushchev faced each other in Berlin and Cuba like two gunslingers in a movie of the old American West. In both incidents, but especially in the latter, their standoff to see who would blink first brought the world to the brink of nuclear annihilation. Both leaders took measures afterward to provide whatever assurance possible that such a dangerous confrontation would not occur again. For example, a telephone "hot line" was established on June 20, 1963 to provide direct communications between the leaders of the world's two super powers. At a time in modern history when a perceived threat of nuclear attack required a decision on a counterstrike

Western Civilization: A Brief History, First Edition. Paul R. Waibel.
© 2020 John Wiley & Sons, Inc. Published 2020 by John Wiley & Sons, Inc.

within minutes, direct and immediate communication between the two leaders whose hands were on the nuclear buttons was critically important. Coexistence was replaced by détente, the effort to identify and resolve, or lessen, points of conflict.

Within two years of the Cuban Missile Crisis, both Kennedy and Khrushchev were gone from the world scene. President Kennedy was assassinated in Dallas, Texas on November 22, 1963, and Khrushchev was forced from office on October 14, 1964. Not until 1989–1990, when George H. W. Bush was president of the United States and Mikhail Gorbachev (b. 1931) was president of the Soviet Union, did two leaders work together with greater benefit for humankind.

The period from the Cuban Missile Crisis to the breakup of the Soviet Union was an era of revolutionary change. Few periods in history have seen as much change. Whether one considers international relations or intellectual, cultural, and social life, the difference between the world at the beginning of the 1960's and the world after 1990, was as between night and day.

The Space Race

The space race was a part of the Cold War during the period of détente. Behind the glamor of exploring the heavens and competing to be the first nation to place a human being on the moon, there was always the prospect of the military advantage to be gained. As noted earlier, the United States's effort to respond to the Soviet Union's launch of the Sputnik I satellite by launching its own satellite into space aboard the Navy's Vanguard rocket was less than impressive. The Vanguard was launched from Cape Canaveral, Florida on December 6, 1957. It rose some four feet off the launching pad before falling down and bursting into a huge ball of fire. The satellite it was carrying broke loose from the rocket and "was later allegedly found near a dumpster not far from the now-scorched launch pad, it's radio transmitter still faithfully beeping away" (Pyle 2017). The press variously referred to the effort as "Flopnik" and "Kaputnik," as well as other unflattering terms.

After the failure of the Navy's Vanguard rocket, President Eisenhower turned to Werner von Braun (1912–1977), one of the German rocket scientists who developed Germany's V-2 rockets during World War II. Eighty-four days after von Braun took charge, on February 1, 1958, America's first satellite, Explorer 1, was placed in orbit.

Project Horizon was launched in March to study the feasibility of establishing a lunar base for both scientific and military purposes. According to the opening statement of Project Horizon's Report, "Proposal to Establish a Lunar Outpost," dated March 20, 1959 and declassified in 2014:

> There is a requirement for a manned military outpost on the moon. The lunar outpost is required to develop and protect potential United States interests on the moon; to devclop [*sic*] techniques in moon-based survcillance [*sic*] of the earth and space, in conmunications [*sic*] relay, and in operations on the surface of the moon; to serve as a base €or [*sic*] exploration of the nioon [*sic*], for further exploration into space and for military operations on the moon if required; and to support scientific investigations on the moon. (United States Army 1959)

The report also noted, that "Materials on the moon itself may prove to be valuable and commercially exploitable" (United States Army 1959). As with the early explorers and later imperialists, motives were a mixture of adventure, discovery, national prestige and power, and commercial advantage.

There were no international treaties regarding territorial claims in outer space in 1959, and so, it was assumed that whoever established a base on the moon, or conceivably any planet, could claim it just as the European nations did the new lands they discovered during the fifteenth century and later. "To be second to the Soviet Union in establishing an outpost on the moon," the report warned, "would be disastrous to our nation's prestige and, in turn, to our democratic philosophy. Though it is contrary to United States policy, the Soviet Union, in establishing the first permanent base, may claim the moon or critical areas thereof for its own" (United States Army 1959). The Project Horizon's Report included a timeline for establishing orbiting space stations and the construction of a lunar base by 1965. It included maps of the moon marking possible landing sites, drawings of buildings, living quarters, and even a "Typical Lunar Suit."

The Soviet Union led in the space race through the mid-1960s with the first earth-orbiting satellite (1957), first dogs in orbit (1958), first monkeys sent into space (1959), first man to orbit earth (1961), first woman to orbit earth (1963), and first man to leave a spacecraft and float in space (1965). The United States began to challenge the Soviet Union's list of "firsts" in 1966 with the first linkup in space followed by the greatest-attention grabbing event to date, the first manned landing on the moon in 1969, the same year that the Soviet Union achieved the first docking of two manned spacecraft, and the first transfer of a crew from one spacecraft to another, accomplished by a spacewalk. In 1986, the Soviet Union began construction of the first modular space station (Mir), completed in 1996 and operated until 2001. In 1998, after the collapse of the Soviet Union and end of the Cold War, the United States and the Russian Confederation began cooperating in the International Space Station (ISS) venture.

Globalizing the Cold War

As the European overseas empires vanished during the 1950s and 1960s, Europe itself, the hub around which the world wheel revolved at the dawn of the twentieth century, became the potential prize in the Cold War competition between the United States and the Soviet Union. By the end of 1949, the competition for Europe was a stalemate, and the contest shifted to the new nations that emerged from the former colonies. The two superpowers competed for influence by supplying needed economic and/or military aid. An example of this was the competition between the United States and the Soviet Union to fund construction of the Aswan High Dam on the Nile River. Supposedly, funding for the dam would earn Egypt's support for the benefactor. The competition for influence with the new postcolonial nations could, and did at times, take the form of "proxy wars" fought by client states, since direct military conflict between the two superpowers was, by mutual and informal agreement, simply unthinkable.

The new nations were not mere puppets. In fact, for those blessed with gifted leaders, the puppet was able, at times, to become the puppet master, or to use another metaphor, the tail wagging the dog. Some chose to follow a path of "non-alignment," which provided them with the freedom to lean to one side or the other to receive the greatest benefit. Others allied with one or the other of the superpowers, thus positioning themselves vis-à-vis their sponsor to extort concessions that otherwise might not have been forthcoming. Knowing that their sponsor "needed" them, they could convincingly suggest that without the desired support, their government might fall, with the prospect that the sponsor might lose a vital ally in the Cold War. It was a reality that both the United States and the Soviet Union found limited their ability to act freely in their diplomacy toward each other.

There are a number of examples on both sides of the Cold War of how minor powers were able to use the threat of possible collapse to, in effect, blackmail their superpower sponsor. Minor powers such as North or South Vietnam, North or South Korea, East or West Germany, the People's Republic of China or Chiang Kai-shek's nationalist government on Taiwan, and Israel could not credibly threaten to switch sides in the Cold War, but what they could do, as noted by Cold War historian John Lewis Gaddis, "was encourage fears that their regimes might fall if their respective superpower sponsors did not support them. The 'dominos,' found it useful, from time to time, to *advertise* a propensity to topple" (Gaddis 2005, p. 129).

The superpowers found themselves in a position where they were coerced into supporting an ally's policies, even when those policies caused unnecessary and undesirable conflicts between themselves. The two Germanies serve as an example. West German Chancellor Konrad Adenauer repeatedly called for reunification of Germany, which he knew was necessary for continued victories in the West German elections. His counterpart in East Germany, Walter Ulbricht (1893–1973), though not dependent upon free elections, continued to insist that there was but one Germany, and the German Democratic Republic was it. Their sponsors, the United States and the Soviet Union respectively, could only put forward scenarios for German reunification that they knew were unacceptable to all parties concerned. In truth, neither Adenauer or Ulbricht nor the United States or the Soviet Union desired a reunified Germany.

The two best examples of the "tail wagging the dog" were France for the United States and China for the Soviet Union. As noted earlier, the need for France's support in Europe during the immediate postwar era required the United States to support the return of French colonial rule in Vietnam. Americans were drawn into what was a French colonial war to suppress Vietnamese nationalism, a foreign policy stance opposed by Washington. After France's defeat and exit from Vietnam, the United States continued to find France a thorn in the flesh.

After Charles de Gaulle returned to power as the leader of the French Fifth Republic in 1958, he took every opportunity to assert France's claim to great power status at the expense of the United States's claim to sole leadership of the free world in the existing bipolar international system of the Cold War. De Gaulle's independence frustrated Washington. President Eisenhower accused de Gaulle of having a "Messiah complex," that is, being a "cross between Napoleon and Joan of Arc" (Gaddis 2005, p. 139). De Gaulle not only wanted to assert France's claim to great power status, but also establish Europe as a third center of power, thus ending the bipolarity that characterized the Cold War. To that end, he withdrew France from NATO, insisted on France developing its own nuclear arsenal, criticized America's role in Vietnam, recognized the People's Republic of China in 1964, and championed a united Europe. President Johnson lamented the fact that the United States had no control over de Gaulle and his foreign policy. Both Johnson and de Gaulle knew that the United States could never refuse to defend France, no matter how offensive de Gaulle's foreign policy might be.

The United States experienced a similar relationship with the authoritarian ruler of South Korea, Syngman Rhee (1875-1965). President Eisenhower found it necessary to bring an end to the Korean War in July 1953 before it could escalate into war with the People's Republic of China which, in turn, may well have escalated into a nuclear war with the Soviet Union. America's allies in Europe were quick to point out that such a war might be won by the United States, but it would likely be fought in Europe. Pressure from America's allies in Europe contributed to President Truman's firing of the flamboyant but unruly General Douglas MacArthur in April 1951.

Rhee, who had little respect for democracy, was able to secure a bilateral security treaty with the United States that kept American forces stationed in South Korea indefinitely to defend South Korea's independence, and with it, Syngman Rhee's regime. In effect, the United States found itself defending an authoritarian regime while publicly claiming to be defending freedom and democracy. Rhee could always claim that if his government was to fall, the consequences for America's leadership would be significant. He knew the United States needed him as much as he needed the protection of the United States. President Eisenhower admitted that America had little choice. The United States could threaten to withdraw from South Korea, "but the truth of the matter was, of course," said Eisenhower, "that we couldn't actually leave" (Gaddis 2005, p. 130).

Throughout the Cold War, the United States found itself with limited freedom of action, in particular cases, due to the leverage an unruly ally was able to assert. Chiang Kai-shek maneuvered the United States into defending, not only his government on the island of Taiwan, but also the rocky Channel Islands of Quemoy and Matsu. Chiang Kai-shek claimed that the two islands were needed to stage a future invasion of mainland China, something only a defeated former warlord who thought of himself as the leader of China could think possible. Quemoy and Matsu played a similar role in Asia to that of Berlin in Europe. Just as Khrushchev likened Berlin to the West's testicles that he could squeeze whenever he wished, Mao Zedong likened the Channel Islands to a noose around America's neck that he could loosen or tighten at will (Gaddis 2005, p. 130).

It was not only the United States that found itself doing the bidding of its minor allies. The Soviet Union experienced similar frustrations with the German Democratic Republic and the People's Republic of China. The Soviet Union had to save the East German regime in 1953. After that, Walter Ulbricht was able to use the threat of regime collapse to extract economic aid from the Soviets, and in 1961, compel Khrushchev to approve construction of the Berlin Wall.

The Soviet Union's most difficult ally was the People's Republic of China and its charismatic leader, Mao Zedong. Russia and China shared a long history of mutual enmity. The Russians blamed their backwardness in comparison to the West on the Mongolian conquest of Russia in the mid-thirteenth century and its subjugation to the Golden Horde which lasted until the last quarter of the fifteenth century. Russian participation in the imperialist exploitation of a weak China, that lasted from the mid-nineteenth century to the Chinese Communist victory in 1949, only deepened the mistrust.

Contrary to what many in the West thought during the Cold War, just because Mao Zedong looked to Karl Marx for theoretical inspiration, did not mean that Communism in China and Communism in the Soviet Union were the same thing, or that either was what Karl Marx envisioned. Both Lenin and Mao "revised" Marxism to produce their own brand of socialism that made possible a revolution in two countries where revolution was not possible, according to Marx. Marx argued that the working-class revolution required the existence of an industrial economy and a liberal government controlled by the propertied classes. Both Marxism-Leninism and Maoism leapfrogged over the period where the industrial working class was pitted against the capitalists who owned and controlled the means of production. Both revised Marxism to fit their needs.

With Mao's victory in 1949, it was logical that China would be allied with the Soviet Union. Mao Zedong was an admirer of Stalin. At first, the relationship between the two nations was good. Stalin saw himself and the Soviet Union as the senior partner, the legitimate leader of the communist movement worldwide. Mao was willing to accept assistance from the Soviet Union and guidance from Stalin, though he did not always follow lock step. The relationship changed with Stalin's death and Khrushchev's leadership.

Khrushchev's de-Stalinization, his advocacy of coexistence, and his cooperation in efforts to achieve détente in the Cold War caused stress and eventually alienation between the two leaders, resulting in what is commonly referred to as the Sino-Soviet split. Mao was not willing to concede leadership of the communist movement to Khrushchev, whom he viewed as an overcautious, perhaps even weak, leader.

In August 1958, China began an artillery bombardment of the Channel Islands of Matsu and Quemoy without consulting Khrushchev. The Nationalist Chinese forces responded in kind, while appealing for aid from the United States. President Eisenhower authorized strengthening of American forces in the area. Mao's reckless independence alarmed Khrushchev, who feared the Taiwan Strait Crisis risked escalating into a war that could involve the two superpowers. Mao hurled insults at Khrushchev's efforts to work with President Kennedy in bringing to fruition the Limited Nuclear Test Ban Treaty, signed by the United States, the Soviet Union, and the United Kingdom on August 5, 1963, just one day before the eighteenth anniversary of America's dropping the atomic bomb on Hiroshima.

On October 20, 1962, while the Soviet Union and the United States were in the midst of the Cuban Missile Crisis, China attacked India over their disputed Himalayan border. Requests from India's Prime Minister Jawaharlal Nehru (1889–1964) for military aid from the United States were rejected by President Kennedy. Once the Cuban Missile Crisis was over, Khrushchev decided to support India. Mao interpreted Khrushchev's position as support for India's attempts to subvert China's claim to Tibet. By the end of 1962, the Sino-Soviet split was a reality.

Fighting along the border between the Soviet Union and China broke out in March 1969. The Central Intelligence Agency's (CIA) *President's Daily Brief* for August 14, 1969, referring to a clash between Soviet and Chinese forces on the previous day, noted that though "[n]either side wishes the inflamed border situation to get out of hand. ... This latest flare-up can only increase the explosive potential of the border situation" (United States Central Intelligence Agency 1969). What might appear, at first, as a minor border incident in Central Asia was a concern for the United States, particularly since the People's Republic of China was a nuclear power since 1964.

China exploded its first atomic bomb in October 1964, and its first hydrogen bomb on June 14, 1967. Given the unpredictable nature of China's leadership, a nuclear China, especially one that felt increasing threatened by both the Soviet Union and the United States, was a matter of serious concern for the two superpowers. Both President Kennedy and President Johnson considered a joint American-Soviet preemptive strike against China's nuclear program, but the Soviet Union was not interested.

During mid-October 1969, in the midst of the Soviet-Chinese border dispute, the Soviet Union made plans "to wipe out the Chinese threat" (The Telegraph 2010) with a nuclear attack on China and asked the United States to remain neutral. In a reversal of its position five years earlier, the United States responded with a warning that a Soviet nuclear attack on China would be met with an American nuclear attack on the Soviet Union. Henry Kissinger (b. 1923), President Nixon's National Security Advisor at the time, commented later on the incident: "It was a major event in American foreign policy, when a President declared that we had a strategic interest in the survival of a major Communist country, long an enemy, and with which we had no contact" (Kissinger 1979, pp. 182–183).

The Sino-Soviet split opened the door for a major change in the international scene. Henry Kissinger visited the People's Republic during 1971 for secret talks with China's Premier Zhou Enlai (1898–1976) that paved the way for President Nixon's historic week-long visit to China in February 1972. It was a week that Nixon correctly characterized as "the week that changed the world" ("Assignment: China" 2012). Once the door was open, relations between the United States and the Peoples' Republic of China continued to improve, until finally, in January 1979, the United States agreed that there was only one China, and Taiwan was a part of that one China. Already in November 1971, the People's Republic of China took its seat on the United Nations Security Council as the representative of China.

Vietnam War

The rapprochement between the United States and China was all the more significant since it occurred during the Vietnam War, one of several proxy wars between the superpowers during the Cold War. The American approved coup that overthrew South Vietnam's President Ngo Dinh Diem was followed by a succession of 12 military coups between 1963 and 1965. Instability became the chief characteristic of South Vietnam's government. Vice President Lyndon B. Johnson (1908–1973), who was sworn in as President following President Kennedy's assassination on November 22, 1963, inherited the Vietnam War along with the office of President.

An incident in the Gulf of Tonkin off the coast of North Vietnam in August 1964 led eventually to over 500 000 American military personnel being deployed to Vietnam. The *USS Maddox*, a naval destroyer patrolling in international waters, was thought to have been attacked by North Vietnamese patrol boats. Long after the war ended, historians concluded that no attack actually took place. Nevertheless, convinced that there was an attack, President Johnson ordered airstrikes against targets inside North Vietnam, after first notifying the Soviet Union by way of the "hot line" that the United States was not widening the war in Vietnam. Within days, Congress passed the Tonkin Gulf Resolution authorizing

Figure 19.1 Secretary of Defense Robert McNamara discussing the Vietnam War in a press conference in April 1965. *Source:* Library of Congress Prints and Photographs Division.

the President "to take all necessary measures to repel any armed attack against the forces of the United States and to prevent further aggression" (National Archives 1964).

Direct American involvement increased with the arrival of 3500 combat-ready marines on March 8, 1965. The move was necessitated by the awareness that South Vietnam was losing the war. By July, it was obvious that Americans were divided on their nation's deepening involvement. President Johnson was getting conflicting advice on how to proceed. George W. Ball (1909–1994), Undersecretary of State advised against a buildup: "The Viet Cong – while supported and guided from the North – is largely an indigenous movement" and "although we have emphasized its Cold War aspects, the conflict in South Vietnam is essentially a civil war within that country" (Gilbert 2002, p. 167).

General William Westmoreland (1914–2005), commander of American forces in South Vietnam, told Defense Secretary McNamara that with an additional 57 battalions and additional helicopter companies and support units, he could defeat the Viet Cong by the end of 1967. General Wallace Martin Greene, Jr. (1907–2003), Commandant of the Marine Corps, advised President Johnson that it would take 500 000 soldiers five years to win the war. Johnson, himself, had doubts about the willingness of the American public to support a sudden massive increase in America's involvement in the war.

The four-day Battle of la Drang Valley, fought in mid-November 1965, proved to be one of the most significant battles of the war. American and North Vietnamese armies faced each other for the first time. Nearly 237 American soldiers were killed, compared to 1037 North Vietnamese. General Westmoreland believed that American forces could win a war of attrition. Marine Corps General Victor Krulak (1913–2008) disagreed. Such a strategy, he concluded, was "wasteful of American lives, promising a protracted strength-sapping battle with small likelihood of a successful outcome" (Cutler 2016, p. 69). McNamara, on the other hand, predicted that 1000 Americans per month would die in a war that the United States had only "even odds" of winning. In October 1966, McNamara observed that despite the enemy's heavy loses, "there is no sign of an impending break in enemy morale and it appears that he can more than replace his losses by infiltration from North Vietnam and recruitment in South Vietnam" (United States Department of State 1966). Outcome of the Battle of la Drang Valley convinced North Vietnam's President Ho Chi Minh (1890–1969) that the war would be won using the same tactics that defeated the French.

The year 1968 proved to be the turning point in the war. On the morning of January 31, the North Vietnamese launched coordinated attacks on 100 cities and American military outposts throughout South Vietnam. It was the lunar new year known as Tet, the "Feast of the First Morning of the First Day." Viet Cong guerillas occupied the United States Embassy in Saigon for six hours, a humiliating scene viewed on the nightly news back home in America.

A part of the offensive was the siege of the American Marine base at Khe Sanh near the border with Laos by North Vietnamese and Viet Cong forces. The siege, which began on January 21, and lasted for 77 days between January 21 and July 9, was meant to divert American attention and forces away from targets of the Tet offensive. General Westmoreland and other American leaders mistakenly thought that Khe Sanh was the main objective of the offensive, perhaps an attempt by the North Vietnamese to repeat their victory over the French at the Battle of Dien Bien Phu in 1954.

American casualties escalated during the Tet offensive. February 11–17 proved to be the bloodiest week for American forces, with a total of 543 killed and 2547 wounded. With the war being fought every night on American television news, the nation's mood began to turn decisively against the war. On February 27, Walter Cronkite (1916–2009), America's most trusted network news anchor, returned from a visit to Saigon and reported his conviction that, "It seems now more certain than ever that the bloody experience of Vietnam is to end in a stalemate" (Walsh 2018).

Clark Clifford (1906–1998), Chairman of the President's Intelligence Advisory Board, assembled a group of 12 elder statesmen and military leaders at the State Department in Washington, DC on March 25 and 26 to assess the situation in Vietnam and advise the president. After a sober assessment, eight of the 12 concluded that a military victory was unlikely and advised that the United States withdraw from Vietnam.

With his approval ratings plummeting, public support for the war eroding, news of a massacre of 300 Vietnamese civilians in My Lai hamlet by American soldiers made public, advisors urging withdrawal from Vietnam, and the likelihood of a battle with Robert F. Kennedy for the Democratic Party's nomination for president, Johnson announced in a television speech on March 31, 1968 his decision not to run for reelection. His presidency was destroyed by the war he inherited from his predecessor, a war he could neither win nor exit. A president who hoped to do for his country with his War on Poverty programs what Franklin Roosevelt did with his New Deal, became as much a tragedy of the war as the many American servicemen who died in combat.

America seemed to be coming apart in 1968 amidst a cloud of teargas, as the antiwar movement tried to nominate a candidate for the presidency who would bring peace to

Figure 19.2 Not all fighting in the Vietnam War involved jungle patrols and bombing. Mobile artillery fire, pictured here, was used to support combat units. *Source:* Photo courtesy of Wllliam Penn, Jr.., private collection.

Vietnam and the streets and campuses of America. Not only did Americans watch the war fought each night on the evening news, they also watched American citizens being attacked by police dogs, beaten by police armed with truncheons, and dispersed with high-power water hoses for demanding the same rights for all Americans, that the nation's armed forces were fighting and dying to defend in Vietnam. Robert F. Kennedy (1925–1968), brother of the slain president and hope of the antiwar movement for President Johnson's successor, was gunned down on June 5, 1968, following his victory in the California Democratic Primary. Just two months earlier, Rev. Martin Luther King, Jr. (1929–1968), the foremost leader of the civil rights movement, was gunned down in Memphis, Tennessee, where he went to support a strike by African-American sanitation workers.

Angry, frightened, and horrified, the American people elected Richard M. Nixon (1913–1994), the Republican Party candidate, as the 37th president of the United States. In his first Inaugural Address on January 20, 1969, Nixon pledged to seek "peace with honor" in Vietnam. Peace talks opened in Paris five days later between representatives of the United States, South Vietnam, North Vietnam, and the Viet Cong. The war continued, even expanded, as President Nixon authorized bombing North Vietnamese supply sanctuaries inside Cambodia. Later, in April 1970, American and South Vietnamese soldiers crossed into Cambodia in an attempt to weaken the North Vietnamese forces as the United States began to drawdown its forces from Vietnam. Nixon's aim was "Vietnamization" of the war, meaning that the fighting should become the responsibility of the South Vietnamese Army. By the end of 1970, American troop levels were reduced to 280 000.

Morale and discipline became problems among America's forces during 1969. Drugs were easily obtained. It was estimated that nearly 50% experimented with marijuana, opium, or heroin during 1969. Casualties from drug abuse began to outnumber those from combat. More than 200 incidents of officers being killed by soldiers under their command using fragmentation grenades, called "fragging," occurred during the year. Racial unrest among the soldiers increased, perhaps caused by news of the Civil Rights struggle back home. By the fall of 1971, there were reports of American ground troops refusing to go on patrols.

The last Marine combat units left Vietnam on April 30, 1971. The last combat troops were withdrawn in August 1972. The year 1973 opened with hopes of peace. President Nixon announced that negotiations in Paris had produced an agreement that would provide a "stable peace in Vietnam and contribute to the preservation of lasting peace in Indochina and Southeast Asia" (Nixon 1973). The Paris Peace Accords were signed on January 27. They were really a face-saving means by which the United States was able to end its participation in the Vietnam War with, as Nixon put it, "honor."

During a meeting with South Vietnam's President Nguyen Van Thieu (1923–2001) in April 1973, Nixon pledged that American forces would return to Vietnam, if North Vietnam violated the terms of the peace agreement. The pledge proved to be worthless. Faced with the prospect of impeachment, Nixon resigned the presidency on August 4, 1974. He was succeeded by Vice President Gerald Ford (1913–2006), who became Vice President in November 1973, following the resignation of Vice President Spiro Agnew (1918–1996).

Confident that the United States would not return to Vietnam, North Vietnam launched their final offensive against the South on March 10, 1975. On April 23, as North Vietnamese troops surrounded Saigon, President Ford announced that the war in Vietnam was "a war that is finished as far as America is concerned" (United Press International 1975). The last Americans, ten marines, were lifted off the roof of the United States Embassy on the morning of April 30. Within hours, the North Vietnamese flag flew above the presidential palace. The war was over. Vietnam was united and independent.

Between August 5, 1964 and May 7, 1975, more than 2.5 million American military personnel served in Vietnam. Of that number, 58 148 died. The youngest was 16, and the oldest was 62. Sixty-one percent of those killed were under 21 years old; 11 465 were under 20. The average age of those who died was 23.1 years. Eighty-six percent were Caucasians, 12.5% were African Americans, and 1.2% were from other races. During the course of the war, the United States dropped seven million tons of bombs on Vietnam, Laos, and Cambodia, "more than twice the amount of bombs dropped on Europe and Asia in World War II" ("1957–1975: The Vietnam War" 2006).

Turbulent 1960s

By the early 1960s, Western Europe had recovered from the devastation left by World War II. The bombed-out city centers were rebuilt with modern department stores and office buildings. New factories with the latest technology replaced those destroyed by Allied bombing campaigns. An American professor enjoying a sabbatical in West Germany in 1975, pointed to candy wrappers lying on the neatly trimmed grass of a park and remarked that it was evidence of what the Germans called their "economic miracle." Supposedly, seats in the Bundestag had to be replaced with larger ones since newer members were healthier, evidenced by their greater girth. The transition to consumerism was a sign of prosperity in Europe as well as the United States.

Some of the more sensitive members of the immediate postwar generation, known as "baby boomers" in America, began to question the benefits of such material prosperity. They began to feel that the prosperity burdened society with only two impoverished values: personal peace and affluence.

> *Personal peace means just to be let alone, not to be troubled by the troubles of other people, whether across the world or across the city–to live one's life with minimal possibilities of being personally disturbed.... Affluence means an overwhelming and ever-increasing prosperity–a life made up of things, things, and more things–a success judged by an ever-higher level of material abundance.* ([emphasis in original] Schaeffer 1976)

The feeling was that the individual was little more than a series of punches on an IBM computer card, or just another widget in a consumer economy whose value was determined by its utility and could be tossed aside like any other outdated, out of fashion, or worn out item. Revolt against consumerism was not the only motivation for the youth protests of the 1960s.

Some saw in the idealistic side of Marxism the possibility of a new society based upon cooperation rather than competition, a society that saw the wealth generated by the modern economy used to create a more just society for all. For them, the whole social, economic, and political structure of the postwar West was designed to do only one thing, "to perpetuate political and economic power in the hands of ruling cliques while keeping the masses both ignorant of the true situation through manipulation of the media and satisfied through the production of inexpensive consumer goods" (Richards and Waibel 2014, p. 277). They also claimed that perpetuation of the Western lifestyle depended upon economic imperialism and support of authoritarian, pro-Western regimes abroad.

Most of those who participated in the demonstrations that attracted the attention of the media were merely "present," that is, there because it was the "in thing" to do for students in the 1960s and early 1970s. They did not know the meaning of the slogans they chanted or the jargon they tried to work into conversations. There was a minority, however, who had specific and achievable goals. In the United States's civil rights struggle, for example, the charismatic leadership of Martin Luther King, Jr. touched the conscience of white, middle-class students, who then linked arms with their African-American peers to force open the doors to equal opportunities for all in education, employment, and housing. For others, it was the struggle to awaken the conscience of Americans to the war in Vietnam, a war that was wasting the lives of America's best-educated generation.

The United States was a nation founded upon Judeo-Christian and Enlightenment principles that were embodied in a written Constitution. The task was to awaken the masses of citizens to the need of bringing society into line with those principles. It was different elsewhere. Europe, despite being the birthplace of constitutional government and the natural rights ideas of the Enlightenment, was still a world dominated by a rigid class system where birth and/or wealth determined whether or not one was able to obtain the education necessary for success. It was possible, though unusual, for a very bright or talented individual (male, of course) to be co-opted into the existing system, but the system itself worked to perpetuate the elites.

In Europe, as in America, there were also those who identified themselves as part of a worldwide revolution to bring true Marxism to fruition, or claimed to be anarchists, though what that meant, no one really knew. But those in Europe who aimed at reforming the highly selective and elitist educational systems achieved the most success. New universities were opened that provided more opportunities for admission. As of 2019, except for living expenses, higher education is essentially free for those admitted to a university in many European Union countries.

In the United States, the most positive impact of the turbulent 1960s was in the Civil Rights movement. Legal segregation was ended, and legislation passed to open access to housing and employment without regard to race. Little was achieved for women's rights, and any forward movement in lesbian, gay, bisexual, transgender, and queer (LGBTQ) rights remained for the future. The anti-war movement did not end the Vietnam War. Indeed, many believe that it may well have prolonged it.

Paris: 1968

The student revolt peaked in the Paris riots of May 1968. Dissatisfaction with de Gaulle's conservative government was growing for some time, but it was a seemingly minor incident that triggered the May riots. Police entered the Sorbonne, the best-known part of the University of Paris, on May 3 and arrested a group of students who were demonstrating against the war in Vietnam. The police action was a violation of the cherished tradition of academic freedom. Demonstrations and confrontations followed between the students and police throughout the Latin Quarter of Paris.

During the following days of May, tens of thousands of students, teachers, and others who supported them, clashed with riot police. Barricades, as many as 60, went up across the narrow streets of the Latin Quarter. Police fired teargas at the demonstrators, who responded with Molotov cocktails and cries of "Long Live the Paris Commune!" The students were joined by striking workers, as the major trade unions called for a general strike on May 13. By the last week of May, roughly 10 million workers across France were on strike and clashes between demonstrators and police broke out in Strasbourg, Bordeaux, Nantes, and Lyon. It appeared that de Gaulle might resign, leaving France to descend into revolution and an uncertain future. By the beginning of June, the tide was turning in favor of de Gaulle and his government.

Many, especially among the working class, really wanted only moderate reforms. They began to fear that the violence and the possibility that some of the more radical demands, if realized, might endanger the prosperity France enjoyed. The radicals did not understand the aspirations of either the workers or the middle class. They labeled the "establishment" the enemy, without knowing who was included in the establishment. They chanted Marxist and anarchist slogans, without any real understanding of economics in the real world.

De Gaulle moved decisively on May 30. He dissolved the National Assembly, and scheduled elections for June 23. On the following day, Prime Minister Georges Pompidou (1911–1974) announced a reshuffling of the government. The streets were soon filled with pro-de Gaulle supporters. An estimated 800 000 marched down the Champs-Élysées waving the tricolor national flag. The workers returned to work, and the French Communist Party, that on May 29 called for a "people's government," endorsed the June 23 elections. When held, the elections showed clearly that the people of France rejected the radicals, giving de Gaulle's party, the Union for the Defense of the Republic (UDR), 354 seats in the National Assembly compared to only 57 for the socialists and 34 for the Communists ("1968 French Legislative Election" 1968).

By the end of June, the Paris Spring was over. What was accomplished? The utopian demands and visions of the radical students lived on in the romanticized histories and documentaries of 1968, side by side with romanticized accounts of the Democratic National Convention in Chicago and the Woodstock Music Festival, both of which occurred during August. It was the workers who gained the most. The trade unions were strengthened and the workers' rights increased along with their wages. As late as September, busses with riot police could be seen parked on side streets near the Sorbonne. The Fifth Republic remained largely unchanged.

The Prague Spring: 1968

The post-Khrushchev Soviet Union of Leonid Brezhnev (1906–1982) was very unlike the classless society promised by Karl Marx and those who brought down Tsarist Russia in 1917. It was a society in which certain groups enjoyed a privileged position. In addition to those who held special status from the beginning of the Soviet Union (military and party leaders, high-level bureaucrats, and KGB members), there was a "new" class of technocrats, scientists, performance and visual artists, world-class athletes, and certain literary and intellectual figures who received higher incomes and had access to a range of special privileges. These included access to special stores that offered fashionable, even imported, goods that were not available to the average citizen, as well as special clinics, and doctors who made house calls. An automobile, or use of an official car, as well as use of a cottage (*dacha*) for weekend outings or vacations were additional benefits for those who were "more equal" than the ordinary workers.

The simple truth was that a command economy and totalitarian political system could not generate a society that provided material comfort or a sense of individual worth and fulfillment. Still, there were those who felt that socialism could work. In the satellite states of Eastern Europe, and later in the Soviet Union itself, attempts were made to replace the image of Orwell's Big Brother with "socialism with a human face." They wanted to find their own way to the socialist future without being forced to adhere to Moscow's leadership. The so-called "Prague Spring" of 1968 was the most outstanding example.

Alexander Dubček (1921–1992), a Slovakian politician who studied Communist management, economics, and ideology in Moscow where Mikhail Gorbachev was a classmate, became First Secretary of the Czechoslovak Communist Party in January 1968. Dubček believed that if the Soviet Union was assured of Czechoslovakia's loyalty, it would be allowed to pursue its own path. An Action Program was published by the Communist

Party of Czechoslovakia (KSČ) on April 5. It called for freedom of speech and expression, freedom of association, and freedom of movement. The last included travel to the West. Economic reforms included legalization of workers' strikes, withdrawal of Soviet economic advisors, and more freedom for industries in seeking new markets, in short, a decentralization of the economy. In foreign relations, new relationships with the Western nations would be maintained while continuing to cooperate with the Soviet Union and the members of the Eastern Bloc.

The reforms in Czechoslovakia caused alarm among the communist leaders of the Eastern Bloc countries. Freedom of choice, in any area, must eventually lead to a questioning of the Communist Party's monopoly of power. Open relations with the Western countries would likely lead to a weakening and possible end to the alliance with the Soviet Union. The intervention in Hungary in 1956 made clear, or should have made clear, that the Soviet Union demanded that the Communist Party retain absolute control in each of the satellite states, and that they remain securely allied with the Soviet Union.

Fearful that the reforms in Czechoslovakia might spread like a virus to their own countries, the leadership of East Germany, Poland, and of course the Soviet Union, decided to take action. During the night of August 20–21, Warsaw Pact forces from the Soviet Union, Poland, Hungary, and Bulgaria occupied Czechoslovakia, while Czech troops remained confined to their barracks. East German forces were not included for fear of reviving memories of the German invasion of 1938. Dubček was replaced by Gustáv Husák (1913–1991), who had spent six years in prison following a Stalinist purge in 1950. Dubček was allowed to continue living in the comfort of his villa in Bratislava, but was demoted to the Forestry Service. Brezhnev justified the intervention in September 1968 by claiming that the Soviet Union had the right and obligation to intervene in any socialist country, with military force if necessary, where the government's decisions or actions "should damage either socialism in their country or the fundamental interests of other socialist countries, and the whole working class movement, which is working for socialism" (The Brezhnev Doctrine 1997).

Criticism of the so-called Brezhnev Doctrine came loudest from Communist parties abroad and the People's Republic of China. If Communist parties in Italy or France, for example, came to power, would the Soviet Union feel justified to intervene if the Communists were to lose power? Could the Brezhnev Doctrine be a justification for a Soviet attack on China?

The use of the Brezhnev Doctrine to justify the Soviet Union's intervention in Czechoslovakia was not so different, however, from the United States using the Monroe Doctrine to justify intervention in the Dominican Republic in 1965. Just as the Soviets saw Czechoslovakia's threatened opening to the West as a danger to socialism in the Eastern Bloc countries, the United States intervened in the Dominican Republic to prevent what it feared might become a second Cuban Revolution.

Economic Slump

On October 6, 1973, Yom Kippur, the Day of Atonement and holiest day of the year in Judaism, Syria and Egypt launched a coordinated attack on Israel. Taken by surprise, the Israelis suffered setbacks during the first three days, but once they began a counterattack against both invading armies, Israel's enemies were in retreat. The Soviet Union and the United States backed their respective allies transforming the Arab–Israeli War into a proxy war between the two superpowers. As an Israeli victory became certain with the possibility of territorial losses by both Syria and Egypt, the Soviet Union threatened to intervene militarily unless the United States joined with them in imposing a ceasefire. In an urgent message from Leonid Brezhnev to President Nixon on the evening of October 24–25, Brezhnev warned, "I will say it straight that if you find it impossible to act jointly with us in this matter, we should be faced with the necessity urgently to consider taking appropriate steps unilaterally. We cannot allow arbitrariness on the part of Israel" (Brezhnev 1973).

The Yom Kippur War ended on October 28. Humiliated again as in the Six Day War in June 1967, the Arab members of OPEC (Organization of the Petroleum Exporting Countries) persuaded the other members to impose an oil embargo on the United States and its allies who supported Israel during the war. Soon the embargo caused a 400% increase in oil prices worldwide. Understandably, such a sudden increase in energy costs impacted every area of the economy, especially in the United States and Western Europe. Because the oil embargo coincided with an economic slump during the mid- and late-1970s, it was almost universally blamed for the slump.

Western Europe was already experiencing a slowing down of economic growth accompanied by rising inflation before the oil crisis. The Western European economies were facing structural problems that would have brought on the slump, even if there had not been an oil crisis. One was the fact that the postwar reconstruction that fueled the boom of the 1950s and 1960s was over. The housing shortage was gone, for the most part, and the new housing units were filled with such former luxuries as refrigerators and televisions. Many were enjoying a honeymoon with the automobile. Consumption was slowing down, even before the increased energy costs caused a sudden increase in the price of consumer goods.

Another cause was the fact that the welfare programs, common in Europe, were becoming a strain on national economies as growth slowed down. Most Europeans after World War II believed that all citizens should be guaranteed a basic standard of living that included food, shelter, education, healthcare, care for the elderly, and insurance against unexpected calamities such as unemployment, work-related injuries, and sickness. The basic goal of the welfare state was much the same everywhere in Europe. What differed was how the welfare programs were financed, that is, who paid for them. For example, in the United Kingdom and the Scandinavian countries the costs were paid by taxpayers, funneled through the state. Employers covered two-thirds of the costs in France and Italy, while employers and employees paid 80% of the bill in West Germany.

The welfare programs might not have become a financial burden except for the fact that by the late-1970s, and certainly during the 1980s, they included a number of "extras" that went well beyond guaranteeing a basic standard of living for everyone. Well-kept parks, theaters for the performing arts, libraries, and subsidies for writers and filmmakers were among the extras funded under the welfare systems. To make matters worse, many of those who grew up under the welfare systems tended to view their benefits as entitlements, rather than privileges bestowed by a benevolent society. Critics accused the welfare systems of creating a generation of citizens who lacked initiative and a sense of self-reliance. Increased juvenile delinquency, drug use, and promiscuous sex were charges made against the welfare systems by their persistent critics. Strangely, the same criticisms were heard in the United States which, apart from the Social Security System, a leftover from Franklin Roosevelt's New Deal legislation, could not be considered a welfare state.

Recovery

It was a new style of conservative leadership during the 1980s that brought an end to the economic downturn. The exemplar of the new conservatism was the United Kingdom's Margaret Thatcher (1925–2013), who served as prime minister from 1979 to 1990. The "Iron Lady," as she was sometimes called, implemented an economic policy based on three principles. The first was privatizing nationalized industries and national utilities. Second was to reduce the power of the trade unions which would encourage industries to modernize and thereby become more competitive. Third was reducing inflation, which stood at more than 20% during the late 1970s. Her monetarist policies (control inflation by controlling the money supply) reduced the rate of inflation to 3.7% by 1983 (Richards and Waibel 2014, p. 299).

Mrs. Thatcher's economic policies, at times referred to as Thatcherism, emphasized free markets and downsizing government "to the bare essentials: defense of the realm and the currency" ("What Is Thatcherism?" 2013). They were adopted to one degree or another by François Mitterrand (1916–1996) in France, Helmut Kohl (1930–2017) in West Germany, and Ronald Reagan (1911–2004) in the United States. There were both winners and losers in the recovery. There was a small class of individuals who did extraordinarily well, a large group who were somewhat better off, or at least held their own, and a group who were worse off and had little hope of improving their lives.

Revolution of 1989 and End of the Russian Revolution of 1917

If any single event during the second half of the twentieth century could rival that of Neil Armstrong's setting foot on the surface of the moon on July 20, 1969, it occurred 20 years later on the evening of November 9, 1989, when the Berlin Wall was peacefully breached. Shortly after 7 p.m., Guenter Schabowski (1929–2015), member of the East German legislature (*Volkskammer*) and Communist Party official, announced that East German citizens, "effective immediately, without delay," could travel freely to West Germany. Within hours, East Berliners were crossing to West Berlin. Guards, who until then were instructed to shoot anyone attempting to cross into West Berlin, began helping their fellow citizens through the Brandenburg Gate and other crossing points. The pictures of Berliners atop the wall dancing, drinking champagne, and otherwise celebrating will forever remain the symbol of communism's failure.

Within two years, the Soviet Empire collapsed with barely a whimper. Only in Romania did the regime choose to resist the transition to democracy with military force. Everyone was taken by surprise. No one expected to see a reunited Germany, much less the end of the Soviet Union and with it the Cold War. Historians, political scientists, journalists, and many others have written numerous books in an attempt to explain the Revolution of 1989.

Perhaps Marxism-Leninism simply died of old age, so to speak. The world was undergoing a technological and information revolution during the last quarter of the twentieth century. How could a totalitarian system in which the possession of a typewriter might be interpreted as subversive, survive when information about any part of the world was almost instantly available? How could a command economy survive in a world economy that was increasingly based on consumerism? Capitalism thrives in a consumer economy, while Marxism contradicts the natural laws of economics and human nature. It is at least questionable if a society that denies freedom of thought and choice can survive in a high-tech world.

There were key players in the drama that unfolded between November 9, 1989 and December 26, 1991, the day on which the Supreme Soviet met and officially dissolved the Soviet Union that was created on December 30, 1922. United States presidents Ronald Reagan and George H.W. Bush, Soviet president Mikhail Gorbachev, British prime minister Margaret Thatcher, West German chancellor Helmut Kohl, and Pope John Paul II played leading roles, while many others played supporting roles. But great events in history are not solely the work of great men and women. That vast amorphous mass of human beings who go about their daily lives must not be left out. The Revolution of 1989 was, above all, a revolution of the human spirit.

It is an often-overlooked truism that no government, however authoritarian or totalitarian, can survive without at least the passive support of a majority of its subjects. When the time comes, as it inevitably does, that the majority says "enough is enough" and refuses to continue being submissive, then the government changes.[1] The Czechoslovakian playwright and future president of Czechoslovakia, Václav Havel (1936–2011), illustrates that aspect of human nature upon which any authoritarian system depends for its survival in his parable of the greengrocer:

> The manager of a fruit-and-vegetable shop places in his window, among the onions and carrots, the slogan: "Workers of the world, unite!" Why does he do it? What is he trying to communicate to the world? Is he genuinely enthusiastic about the idea of unity among the workers of the world? Is his enthusiasm so great that he feels an irrepressible impulse to acquaint the public with his ideals? Has he really given more than a moments [*sic.*] thought to how such a unification might occur and what it would mean?
>
> I think it can safely be assumed that the overwhelming majority of shopkeepers never think about the slogans they put in their windows, nor do they use them to express their real opinions. That poster was delivered to our greengrocer from the enterprise headquarters along with the onions and carrots. He put them all into the window simply because it has been done that way for years, because everyone does it, and because that is the way it has to be. If he were to refuse, there could be trouble. He could be reproached for not having the proper decoration in his window; someone might even accuse him of disloyalty. He does it because these things must be done if one is to get along in life. It is one of the thousands of details that guarantee him a relatively tranquil life "in harmony with society", as they say. (Havel 1979)

---

1 The exception is Nazi Germany. The majority of Germans remained loyal to Hitler's regime until the very end.

The greengrocer in Havel's parable wants simply to live his life in peace. He wants simply to "get along." He is no different than his counterpart in a democratic, free-enterprise country in the West. The greengrocer in the West wants personal peace and affluence. The greengrocer unfortunate enough to find himself in a communist country only wants personal peace and a tranquil life.

During the Fall of 1989, the mass of ordinary citizens in the Soviet Union and its satellite states simply had enough of life under communism. They sensed an opportunity for change and seized on it. But what happened to create that opportunity? It is in searching for the answer to that question, that one can see how certain individuals made choices that together created a new world order.

The Soviet Union was a world power in decline during the 1980s. It was one of two world powers, each with an empire, each with the military might to destroy world civilization. But there were signs of a downward trend in the indices of national well-being. Infant mortality rates were on the rise. Life expectancy, particularly for men, was declining. Alcoholism and suicide rates were also increasing. And, as if in need of proving its world-power status, the Soviet Union embarked on risky foreign policy initiatives in, for example, Afghanistan and the Horn of Africa.

Leonid Brezhnev died in 1982 after 18 years at the helm. He was succeeded first by Yuri Andropov (1914–1984), a career politician who served in a number of posts, most recently as Chairman of the KGB from 1967 until 1982. It was Andropov who persuaded Nikita Khrushchev to use military force to suppress the Hungarian uprising in 1956, and who played a key role in suppressing the Prague Spring in 1968. His tenure was brief, only 15 months. After Andropov's death in 1984, Konstantin Chernenko (1911–1985) served as leader of the Soviet Union for 13 months. Andropov and Chernenko were the last of the old guard.

Chernenko's successor, Mikhail Gorbachev, was a new kind of Soviet leader. At only 50, he was one of a new generation of leaders who grew up after the Russian Revolution. With Gorbachev's arrival, socialism with a human face that inspired the Prague Spring in 1968 was reborn, but this time in the Soviet Union itself. Gorbachev understood that the Soviet Union could not continue as a totalitarian state. He chose to alter the trajectory of Soviet history by introducing two new principles, glasnost and perestroika.

Glasnost meant openness and transparency, an end to censorship and freedom of expression. The past could be investigated and the truth freely told. No longer would mistakes and failures be covered up. No attempt was made in April 1986 to coverup the nuclear accident at Chernobyl, or minimize the extent of it. Perestroika meant transparency, openness, new thinking, freeing the economic sector from the bureaucratic obstructionism that is inherent in a command economy, and even allowing some private enterprise. Such reforms, however, led to questioning the primacy of the Communist Party.

Gorbachev's mistake was to think that he could save socialism by introducing social democracy. His understanding of Marxism was more akin to Eduard Bernstein's revisionism. Glasnost succeeded, but perestroika failed. After the collapse of the Soviet Union, Gorbachev explained why. "The Achilles heel of socialism was the inability to link the socialist goal with the provision of incentives for efficient labor and the encouragement of initiative on the part of individuals. It became clear, in practice, that a market provides such incentives best of all" (Gorbachev and Mlynář 2002, p. 160).

Elections were held in March 1989 for a new Congress of People's Deputies. Prior to the elections, Gorbachev removed the constitutional requirement that the only legal political organization was the Communist Party. Many of the senior party leaders who ran for election were defeated. In the spirit of glasnost, the convening of the Congress in May was televised. The Supreme Soviet elected by the Congress of Deputies proceeded to enact new legislation on freedom of religion and press. "[I]t was already clear to everybody," Gorbachev recalled in his memoirs, "that the days of the Party dictatorship were over" (Gaddis 2005, p. 242).

The Eastern Bloc countries found in the Soviet Union under Gorbachev something new. It was not the Western countries that served as a model for change, but the Soviet Union, that under Gorbachev's leadership proved that Marxism had in itself the potential for reform. During the 1980s, the Eastern Bloc countries had, as their goal, to realize the socialism with a human face that the Prague Spring promised possible. It was even more so, after Gorbachev announced in July 1989 that each of the East European states should take its own path to socialism.

Already in June, semi-free elections were held in Poland that resulted in Solidarity, an independent labor union and political opposition party, winning all but one of the seats in the Polish parliament that it was allowed to contend. It was the first election since the Communist Party renounced its monopoly on power in April, and the closest thing to a free election in Poland since 1928. The first non-communist government in Eastern Europe since creation of the Iron Curtain was installed on August 24, 1989.

Reform came to Hungary as well. Prime Minister Miklós Németh (b. 1948) removed funds from the government's budget for 1989 for maintenance of the barbed wire fence along the border with Austria. The dismantling of the Hungary's portion of the Iron Curtain began in June, providing an easy exit route for East Germans. Since it was a violation of treaty agreements between East Germany and the other Warsaw Pact countries, the East Germans protested to Moscow, but to no avail.

In Czechoslovakia, the end of communist rule came by way of the Velvet Revolution between November 17 and December 29, 1989. It was called "velvet," because it was a peaceful transition. On January 1, 1993, Czechoslovakia split peacefully into two nations, Slovakia and the Czech Republic, an event commonly referred to as the "Velvet Divorce." The People's Republic of Hungary became the Republic of Hungary on October 23, 1989. Bulgaria did likewise on November 15, 1990.

Wherever Gorbachev went during 1989, he was met with enthusiastic crowds. What journalists began calling "Gorbymania" seemed to be everywhere. When Gorbachev visited Bonn, West Germany's provisional capital, he was greeted in the town's center by thousands of West Germans chanting "Gorby! Gorby! Gorby!" who "wildly waved red hammer-and-sickle flags" (Parks 1989). Everywhere, there were banners and placards with slogans like "Gorbachev--the Evangelist of Peace," "Keep It Up, Gorbachev," and "Bring Us Peace" (Parks 1989).

When Gorbachev arrived in East Berlin in October 1989 for the celebration of the 40th anniversary of the founding of the German Democratic Republic, he was greeted by crowds of East Berliners shouting, "Gorby, help us! Gorby, stay here!" Gorbachev stood on the reviewing stand along with Erich Honecker (1912–1994), Walter Ulbricht's successor and the man who oversaw construction of the Berlin Wall in 1961. The soldiers and military hardware paraded past them while the crowd chanted "Gorby! Gorby!" Gorbachev later recalled that, "[Jaruzelski], the Polish leader, came up to us and said, 'Do you understand German?' I said, 'I do, a little bit.' 'Can you hear?' I said, 'I can.' He said, 'This is the end.' And that was the end: The regime was doomed" (Gaddis 2005, pp. 244–245). Honecker, said Gorbachev, "did not really perceive any more what was actually going on." Gorbachev tried to warn Honecker, as he had other leaders in the Soviet bloc, that only those who refused to change need fear the future. But trying to get Honecker to face reality was, said Gorbachev, "like throwing peas against the wall" (Gaddis 2005, p. 245).

Gorbachev's counterparts in the West found themselves reacting to the Soviet leader's initiatives and the will of the people. Margaret Thatcher was the first to correctly judge Gorbachev as one who she and the other leaders in the Western democracies could work with to end the fear of a third world war. It was Thatcher who persuaded Ronald Reagan to tone down his Cold War rhetoric and work with Gorbachev, something that Reagan's successor, George H.W. Bush would continue with greater skill and success.

Just one month and two days after celebrating the 40th anniversary of the German Democratic Republic, the Berlin Wall was opened. West German chancellor Helmut Kohl saw an opportunity to unite the two Germanies and seized on it. Reunification of Germany was something that could only happen with the approval of the four wartime Allies. On August 31, 1990, the two Germanies signed the Unification Treaty. The Treaty on the Final Settlement with Respect to Germany, commonly referred to as "Two Plus Four Treaty", between the two Germanies and the four World War II Allies was signed in Moscow on September 12, 1990, and went into force on March 15, 1991. The newly unified Federal Republic of Germany was henceforth a sovereign nation.

The Soviet Union, itself, was coming unglued during 1989. In May, the Baltic states of Latvia, Lithuania, and Estonia declared themselves sovereign. The central government in Moscow responded with harsh rhetoric, but nothing more. Lithuania and Estonia declared independence in March 1990, followed by Latvia in May. One by one the individual republics that made up the USSR began declaring their sovereignty.

The old guard of the Communist Party hardliners, together with high-ranking officers in the armed forces, and leaders in the military-industrial complex became increasingly alarmed by what they saw as a descent into anarchy. In August 1991, they acted. Their goal was to save the Soviet Union as it existed before Gorbachev's reforms. They attempted to achieve their goal through a coup that began on August 19. For reasons unknown, the coup leaders did not arrest Boris Yeltsin (1931–2007), who was elected president of the Russian Soviet Federative Socialist Republic (RSFSR) in July.

Yeltsin called upon the people of Russia to go out into the streets to show their opposition to the coup. Gorbachev was released from his dacha in the Crimea, where he was being held by the coup's leaders. It was clear on August 21 that the coup had failed, but the coup's attempt, and Boris Yeltsin's role in its failure, marked the end of the Soviet Union. On August 24, Gorbachev resigned as General Secretary of the Communist Party of the Soviet Union (CPSU). The USSR rapidly began coming undone, as various of the Soviet Republics declared their independence.

On Christmas Day 1991, Gorbachev resigned as president of the Soviet Union. On the following day, the Supreme Soviet approved the ending of the 74-year-old USSR. Russia became the recognized successor state of the Soviet Union. Russia assumed the former

Soviet Union's seat on the Security Council of the United Nations. By 1996, the former Soviet republics transferred the nuclear weapons in their possession to Russia.

A complex combination of forces wove together to bring about the fall of communism and the end of the Cold War. Pope John Paul II's pilgrimage to his Polish homeland in June 1979 exposed to everyone how decades of Soviet rule, persecution of the churches, and ideological indoctrination failed to win the hearts and minds of the people. Poland was a country in which more than 90% of the people were Roman Catholics, despite the fervent efforts of the Communists to replace Christianity, and all religion, with atheism. John Paul II reminded the Poles that, as Christians, they testify to the truth that in God there is an absolute by which all human activity, including political activity, can and must be judged. Despite all the efforts of the state machinery to downplay the Pope's visit, millions turned out to greet him. Slightly less than 300 000 assembled in Warsaw's Victory Square on June 29, 1979 to hear John Paul II celebrate mass.

What remains a perplexing question is why, when he clearly saw that the Soviet Union would not survive, Gorbachev did not unleash the dogs of war. Why did he not choose for the Soviet Union to go down, if it must, in an Armageddon-like battle? Just as President Kennedy did during the Cuban Missile Crisis, Mikhail Gorbachev chose peace over war and life over death.

References

BBC News (2013). What is Thatcherism? https://www.bbc.com/news/uk-politics-22079683 (accessed 21 October 2019).

Brezhnev, L. (1973). Letter From Soviet General Secretary Brezhnev to President Nixon. U.S. Department of State. https://history.state.gov/historicaldocuments/frus1969-76v15/d146 (accessed 21 October 2019).

Cutler, T. (2016). *The U.S. Naval Institute on Vietnam: A Retrospective*. Annapolis, MD: Naval Institute Press.

Fordham University (1997). Modern History Sourcebook: The Brezhnev Doctrine, 1968. https://sourcebooks.fordham.edu/mod/1968brezhnev.asp (accessed 21 October 2019).

Gaddis, J.L. (2005). *The Cold War: A New History*. London: Penguin Books.

Gilbert, M.J. (ed.) (2002). *Why the North Won the Vietnam War*. New York: Palgrave.

Gorbachev, M. and Mlynář, Z. (2002). *Conversations with Gorbachev: On Perestroika, the Prague Spring, and the Crossroads of Socialism* (trans. G. Schriver). New York: Columbia University Press.

Havel, V. (1979). The power of the powerless. *International Journal of Politics* https://www.nonviolent-conflict.org/resource/the-power-of-the-powerless (accessed January 3, 2019).

Kissinger, H.A. (1979). *White House Years*. Boston: Little, Brown.

Libcom.org (2006). 1957–1975: The Vietman War. https://libcom.org/history/1957-1975-the-vietnam-war (accessed 21 October 2019).

National Archives and Records Administration (1964). Joint Resolution for the Maintenance of Peace and Security in Southeast Asia. https://catalog.archives.gov/id/2803448 (accessed 21 October 2019).

Nixon, R.M. (1973). Address to the Nation Announcing Conclusion of an Agreement on Ending the War and Restoring Peace in Vietnam - January 23, 1973. Richard Nixon Foundation. https://www.nixonfoundation.org/2017/08/address-nation-announcing-conclusion-agreement-ending-war-restoring-peace-vietnam-january-23-1973 (accessed 21 October 2019).

Parks, M. (1989). 'Gorbymania' Captures Bonn--It's a Challenge to the West, Aide Says. Los Angeles Times. http://articles.latimes.com/1989-06-14/news/mn-2050_1_soviet-leader-gorbachev-challenge-mikhail-s-gorbachev (accessed 21 October 2019).

Pyle, R. (2017). *Amazing Stories of the Space Age*. Amherst, NY: Prometheus Books.

Richards, M.D. and Waibel, P.R. (2014). *Twentieth Century Europe: A Brief History, 1900 to the Present*, 3e. Hoboken: John Wiley & Sons.

Schaeffer, F.A. (1976). *How Should We Then Live? The Rise and Decline of Western Thought and Culture*. Old Tappan, NJ: Fleming H. Revell Co.

The Telegraph (2010). USSR Planned Nuclear Attack on China in 1969. www.telegraph.co.uk/news/worldnews/asia/china/7720461/USSR-planned-nuclear-attack-on-China-in-1969.html (accessed 21 October 2019).

United Press International (1975). Text: President Ford's Speech. *The New York Times*. https://archive.nytimes.com/www.nytimes.com/library/world/asia/042475vietnam-ford-speech.html (accessed 15 November 2019).

United States Army (1959). *Project Horizon*. Vol. I: Summary and Supporting Considerations. https://history.army.mil/faq/horizon/Horizon_V1.pdf (accessed 21 October 2019).

United States Central Intelligence Agency (1969). The President's Daily Brief. https://www.cia.gov/library/readingroom/docs/DOC_0005976932.pdf (accessed 21 October 2019).

United States Department of State (1966). 268. Memorandum From Secretary of Defense McNamara to President Johnson. https://history.state.gov/historicaldocuments/frus1964-68v04/d268 (accessed 21 October 2019).

US-China Institute (2012). Assignment: China – The Week That Changed The World. https://china.usc.edu/assignment-china-week-changed-world (accessed 21 October 2019).

Walsh, K.T. (2018). 50 Years Ago, Walter Cronkite Changed a Nation. U.S. News & World Report. https://www.usnews.com/news/ken-walshs-washington/articles/2018-02-27/50-years-ago-walter-cronkite-changed-a-nation (accessed 21 October 2019).

Wikipedia (1968). 1968 French Legislative Election. https://en.wikipedia.org/wiki/1968_French_legislative_election (accessed 21 October 2019).

20

A New World Order

Chronology

1979–1989	Soviet Troops Intervene in Afghanistan Until 1989
1980	Marshal Tito Dies
1988	Gorbachev Addresses United Nations on New World Order
1990 and 1991	George H.W. Bush on New World Order
1990–2003	Mapping of the Human Genome Project
1991	Croatia and Slovenia Declare Independence
1992	Bosnia Declares Independence; Siege of Sarajevo Begins
1996	Taliban Establishes the Islamic Emirate of Afghanistan
1997	Cassini–Huygens Probe Launched
1998	USA Congress Passes Iraq Liberation Act of 1998
2000	International Space Station Gets First Crew
2001	Dennis Tito Becomes First Tourist in Space
2001	Terrorist Attack on USA ("9/11"); Afghan War Begins
2003	Iraq War Begins
2003	China Launches Its First Manned Space Flight
2004	NASA's Opportunity Rover lands on Mars
2004	Facebook Founded by Mark Zuckerberg
2011	"Arab Spring" in Tunisia, Oman, Yemen, Egypt, Syria, Morocco, and Libya
2012	Voyager 1 (Launched 1977) Exits Our Solar System into Interstellar Space
2017	Donald Trump Elected President of USA
2019	Horizons Spacecraft Passes Ultima Thule, Four Billion Miles from Earth
2019	China Makes First Soft Landing on Far Side of Moon
2019	First Photo of a Black Hole

The world was transformed by the events of 1989–1991. The end of the Cold War, together with the technological revolution under way, the awakening of the masses of humanity across the globe, and the loss of a balance of power among the world's great powers ushered in a "new world order" that in the third decade of the twenty-first century was still taking shape. The sudden collapse of the "old world order" that took form after World War II, sometimes referred to as the "Yalta world," caught most of the world leaders off guard

Western Civilization: A Brief History, First Edition. Paul R. Waibel.
© 2020 John Wiley & Sons, Inc. Published 2020 by John Wiley & Sons, Inc.

and without a plan for the future. Instead of new foreign policies based on a recognition of the emerging new reality, they tried to apply the old, unimaginative foreign policies of the Cold War era.

Perhaps the most important trend shaping the new reality was the fact that the traditional nation state was no longer the sole focus of international relations. Conflicts between different worldviews, ultimately grounded in religious-based understandings of what is real, or to use the title of one of Paul Gauguin's paintings, "Whence Come We? What are We? Whither Do We Go?" overshadowed the conflicts between nation states in the early twenty-first century.

The conflict between two worldviews, Islam and Western Civilization, serves as an obvious example of what is frequently called the "Clash of Civilizations."[1] The revolution in information technology meant that cultures once isolated, or primarily limited to a part of the globe, were exposed to diverse cultural influences. The results were wars and international terrorism.

The end of a bipolar world, together with ongoing war, increased the gap between the affluent, developed nations and the underdeveloped nations stuck in poverty with little hope of change. The suffering and sense of hopelessness regarding the future fueled a mass migration of people fleeing poverty, war, and crime to seek refuge in the developed nations of Europe and North America.

Visions of a New World Order

Mikhail Gorbachev, who at the time was still leader of the Soviet Union, understood how the world was changing and took the initiative of proposing a plan for a new world order. In an address to the United Nations General Assembly on December 7, 1988, he outlined his vision of a new world order based upon recognition of the diversity of the world community. Tolerance of that diversity by all the members of the world community was crucial for cooperation between them. Through tolerance and cooperation humanity could find "a way to the supremacy of the common human idea over the countless multiplicity of centrifugal forces, to preserving the vitality of a civilization which is possibly the only one in the universe" (Gorbachev 1988).

It is worth reading a lengthy quote from Gorbachev's address to accurately understand what he proposed:

> "The history of the past centuries and millennia has been a history of almost ubiquitous wars, and sometimes desperate battles, leading to mutual destruction. They occurred in the clash of social and political interests and national hostility, be it from ideological or religious incompatibility. All that was the case, and even now many still claim that this past – which has not been overcome – is an immutable pattern. However, parallel with the process of wars, hostility, and alienation of

---

1 The phrase is attributed to Samuel P. Huntington's article, "The clash of civilizations?" *Foreign Affairs* (Summer 1993). Some prefer to think of a clash of cultures as clashing worldviews. I am of the opinion that culture reflects worldview, which is in the final analysis rooted in religion.

peoples and countries, another process, just as objectively conditioned, was in motion and gaining force: The process of the emergence of a mutually connected and integral world.

'Further world progress is now possible only through the search for a consensus of all mankind, in movement toward a new world order. We have arrived at a frontier at which controlled spontaneity leads to a dead end. The world community must learn to shape and direct the process in such a way as to preserve civilization, to make it safe for all and more pleasant for normal life. It is a question of cooperation that could be more accurately called 'co-creation' and 'co-development.' The formula of development 'at another's expense' is becoming outdated. In light of present realities, genuine progress by infringing upon the rights and liberties of man and peoples, or at the expense of nature, is impossible.'

The very tackling of global problems requires a new "volume" and "quality" of cooperation by states and sociopolitical currents regardless of ideological and other differences." (Gorbachev 1988)

At first Gorbachev's vision of a new world order appears too idealistic, too visionary, and too radically different from the basic assumptions upon which much of the West's history since the Commercial Revolution of Late Middle Ages, and certainly since the appearance of classical liberalism during the Enlightenment. Indeed, it is! It is the vision of the ancient and medieval Church, that the human community must be based upon cooperation, not competition. It is also the underlying assumption of socialism. One may debate what brand of socialism Gorbachev aligns with, but he should not be accused of being a follower of Adam Smith's *laissez faire* or John Locke's social contract. In a sense, Gorbachev was suggesting that the twin principles of glasnost and perestroika, that were reforming the Soviet Union, might be used to reform the world community.

Gorbachev's idealistic vision enhanced his popularity in Europe. Since there was as yet no competing vision of a new world order offered by United States's President George H.W. Bush, Gorbachev held the moral high ground. Would the world look to the Soviet leader and the Soviet Union to lead the way to a future where the threats of nuclear war and military alliances were banished, and replaced by a community of nations under the rule of law?

President George H.W. Bush outlined what was understood by many at the time as an alternative vision of a new world order in two speeches before joint sessions of Congress in 1990 and 1991. The first was on September 11, 1990, in which Bush addressed the role of the United States as leader of a coalition of 20 nations taking military action to liberate the Persian Gulf state of Kuwait, invaded and occupied by Iraq in August. The second was his 1991 State of the Union Address on January 29.

There were similarities in the two visions. Bush foresaw "a new world order, where diverse nations are drawn together in common cause to achieve the universal aspirations of mankind: peace and security, freedom, and the rule of law" (Bush 1991). But what Gorbachev foresaw as a world community of "diverse people," Bush saw as "diverse nations," an important distinction. For Bush, the end of the Cold War was a victory "for all humanity," because it was a victory for freedom and liberty as represented by the United States. "For two centuries," said Bush, "America has served the world as an inspiring

Figure 20.1 Karl Marx, Joseph Stalin, and Vladimir Lenin look down from Communist Paradise on the funeral of Communism led by Mikhail Gorbachev. *Source:* Library of Congress.

example of freedom and democracy. For generations, America has led the struggle to preserve and extend the blessings of liberty. And today, in a rapidly changing world, American leadership is indispensable" (Bush 1991).

Bush's new world order would be one in which the world's nations looked to "America [as] the beacon of freedom in a searching world" (Bush 1991). The new world order would be a unipolar world led by the United States in which the Soviet Union would play a supporting role. The "hopes of humanity turn to us," said Bush, because "only the United States of America has had both the moral standing, and the means to back it up. We are the only nation on this earth that could assemble the forces of peace" (Bush 1991).

Neither vision was realized. Gorbachev's new world order fell victim to the internal power struggle within the Soviet Union. The result was the end of the Soviet Union, and with it, Gorbachev's leadership. The Soviet Union's demise also doomed Bush's new world order. The balance of power between the United States and the Soviet Union ended. It was replaced by a unipolar world in which the United States was clearly the one superpower.

What Bush saw as an opportunity for a new world order under American leadership proved a miscalculation. The diplomats who gathered in Vienna at the end of the Napoleonic Wars (1814–1815) understood from past history that an absence of a balance of power among the great powers results in war. By restoring the balance of power, they assured peace in Europe for the next hundred years, except for the wars of German unification.

When the balance of power disappeared at the end of the nineteenth century, World War I resulted. The diplomats who gathered at the Paris Peace Conference in 1919 ignored the example set at the Vienna Congress, resulting 20 years later in the outbreak of World War II. The emergence of the Cold War effectively restored a balance of power. The end of the Cold War ushered in a new period of international instability characterized by international terrorism and war, resulting from the absence of a balance of power and the Clash of Civilizations.

War in the Balkans

The breakup of Yugoslavia and the resulting civil war during the 1990s presaged what was to become normal. The postwar Socialist Federal Republic of Yugoslavia was a forced union of at least 26 ethnic groups, both Slavic and non-Slavic, plus the non-European Roma, or Gypsies. Adding to that diversity was the presence of three major religions – Roman Catholic, Orthodox, and Muslim. The conflict between Christians and Muslims was a byproduct of the almost four centuries during which the Ottoman Turks ruled the Balkans. The conflict between the two major Slavic peoples, Serbs and Croats, reflected both the history and the religious and cultural differences of the two.

The Serbs were united by their Orthodox Christian religion. Also, unlike Croatia that was a part of the Austro-Hungarian Empire until the end of World War I, the Serbs won their independence from the Turks during the nineteenth century. The Kingdom of Serbia was recognized by the Great Powers at the Berlin Congress in 1878. Although both Croats and Serbs share a similar language, Serbian is written in Cyrillic and Croatian in Latin script. Historically, the Serbs looked eastward to Russia, while the Croats looked to Central Europe and Germany.

In 1918, the Croats, Slovenians, and Serbs united as the Kingdom of the Serbs, Croats, and Slovenes under a Serbian king. Yugoslavia, as it was officially known after 1921, was occupied by Germany during World War II. Unlike the rest of Eastern Europe, Yugoslavia was not liberated by the Russians, but by Communist guerillas led by Marshal Tito (Josip Broz, 1892–1980). Tito's guerillas defeated both the German occupation and those guerillas fighting to restore the prewar monarchy.

During its postwar period as the Socialist Federal Republic of Yugoslavia, Marshal Tito was able to keep the lid on the ethnic and religious conflicts by force of his personality and authoritarian rule. After his death in May 1980, the economy began to collapse leading to widespread unemployment and the rise of ethnic nationalism. Slobodan Milosevic (1941–2006), President of Serbia, and Franjo Tudjman (1922–1999), President of Croatia, fanned

Figure 20.2 Europe today.

the flames of ethnic conflict. Croatia and Slovenia declared independence in June 1991. Serbia used the Yugoslavian army against the rebellious states, thus igniting a civil war.

Bosnia declared its independence in May 1992. Previously, Bosnia was one area within Yugoslavia where Serbs, Croats, and Muslims lived together peacefully. The Winter Olympics were held in the capital city, Sarajevo, in 1984. Between April 5, 1992 and February 29, 1999, Serbian forces besieged Sarajevo. The Serbs began a campaign of "ethnic cleansing," a euphemism for genocide as was "final solution" a euphemism for genocide of the Jews in Nazi Germany. Finally, NATO intervened with airstrikes against the Serbs during August and September, 1995. A peace settlement was negotiated in Dayton, Ohio (USA) during November 1995, and signed in Paris on December 14.

Terrorism and War

The Clash of Civilizations is discernable in the fact that war and terrorism have become almost inseparable. We speak of war when nation-states are the actors, and terrorism when ideologies are the actors. The Prussian general and military theorist Carl von Clausewitz (1780–1835) is remembered for having said, "War is the continuation of politics by other means." Today, at least since the 1990s, one might say that terrorism is war by other means.

Afghanistan

A Marxist government came to power in Afghanistan in April 1978. The newly created Democratic Republic of Afghanistan signed a treaty of friendship with the Soviet Union in December. As resistance to the atheistic government grew among the Muslim population, the Soviet Union began giving massive military aid to the government. Soviet troops were sent into Afghanistan in December 1979.

The various guerilla groups called Mujahideen,[2] both moderate and fundamentalist Muslims, received finances and arms from the United States, Pakistan, and Saudi Arabia. The United States began supplying the Mujahideen with Stinger missiles in 1986, that enabled the guerillas to shoot down Soviet helicopter gunships. China's People's Liberation Army trained Mujahideen fighters in camps in Pakistan and China. The war in Afghanistan was just another proxy war during the Cold War period. Peace accords were signed in 1988 between Afghanistan, the Soviet Union, the United States, and Pakistan. The last Soviet soldiers left Afghanistan in February 1989. The Mujahideen continued the war until the Communist government in Kabul was defeated.

American interest in Afghanistan waned after the Soviet departure. The future of the war-torn nation was left to the United States's allies Saudi Arabia and Pakistan. Pakistan took advantage of the breakdown of law and order and lack of a strong central government to establish relations with the numerous warlords and the Taliban, a Sunni Islamic fundamentalist political movement. In September 1996, the Taliban established the Islamic Emirate of Afghanistan that ruled 90% of the country until December 2001.

Afghanistan, and to a lesser extent Pakistan, provided a safe environment where radical Muslims could recruit, educate, and train jihadists to continue the jihad, or holy war, through terrorist attacks. Among them was a militant Sunni Islamist multi-national group called al-Qaeda, founded during the struggle to liberate Afghanistan. Al-Qaeda was led by Osama bin Laden (1957–2011), a member of the wealthy Saudi Arabian bin Laden family.

Al-Qaeda trained terrorists began attacking Americans abroad in 1992, using suicide bombers. In February 1993 a car bomb exploded in an underground garage beneath the World Trade Center in New York City. Al-Qaeda was credited also with the successful terrorist attacks on the landmark Twin Towers in New York City on September 11, 2001. The terrorists hijacked four commercial airliners. Two were flown into the Twin Towers. A third was crashed into the Pentagon building, headquarters of the United States Department of Defense, located in Arlington County, Virginia. A fourth was meant to crash into the White House in Washington, D. C., but crashed into a field in Pennsylvania as the passengers struggled with the terrorists for control of the plane.

When the government of Afghanistan refused to surrender Osama bin Laden and other al-Qaeda leaders, the United States, supported by the United Kingdom, Canada, and Australia, invaded Afghanistan on October 7, 2001. The stated aim of the invasion was to destroy al-Qaeda in Afghanistan and remove the Taliban from power. The Afghan capital, Kabul, fell in November. An interim government led by Hamid Karzai (b. 1957) was installed. The Taliban retreated to the mountains from which it continued fighting the American-led coalition forces and the new Afghan government. Osama bin Laden escaped

---

2 The term is used in reference to Islamic fighters fighting non-Muslims inside Muslim countries.

capture by fleeing to safety inside Pakistan. He was killed on May 1, 2011 during an American military raid on his compound near Islamabad, Pakistan.

Iraq

The United States Congress passed, and President Bill Clinton (b. 1946) signed, the Iraq Liberation Act of 1998, making it the policy of the United States "to support efforts to remove the regime headed by Saddam Hussein from power in Iraq..." (Gilman 1998). George W. Bush (b. 1946) was elected president in 2001 on a platform that included full implementation of the Iraq Liberation Act. Supposedly, Iraq possessed weapons of mass destruction (WMDs) and, according to Vice President Dick Cheney (b. 1941), was the "geographic base of the terrorists who had us under assault now for many years, but most especially on 9/11" (Milbank 2004).

The Iraq War, sometimes called the Second Iraq War, began on March 20, 2003. The initial American-led invasion force was made up of roughly 177 000, mostly American and British soldiers, together with 2000 Australian and 197 Polish soldiers. After Iraqi forces were defeated, the Coalition Provisional Authority governed Iraq until the Iraqi Transitional Government took over following elections during December 2005. The first permanent government led by Nouri al-Maliki (b. 1950) assumed power in May 2006.

After Saddam Hussein's defeat, American and British combat troops remained in Iraq fighting an insurgency. On December 15, 2011, the United States declared the Iraq War over.

Figure 20.3 US Army soldiers patrolling the streets of Old Baqubah, Iraq in 2007. *Source:* DOD/USAF/Stacy L. Pearsall.

The last American troops left Iraq on December 18. Things soon spiraled out of control in Iraq, as sectarian war broke out between Shite and Sunni factions. In 2014, the Iraqi army collapsed under an attack from Islamic State (IS), also called Islamic State in Iraq and the Levant (ISIL) and Islamic State in Syria (ISIS).

Islamic State originated among those who fought the Soviet invaders in Afghanistan. They believe in the use of violence and terrorism in their war against all things non-Muslim. They are at war against the modern world. Western Civilization is targeted as the creator and chief vehicle of modern culture. Followers of Islamic State make an absolute commitment to jihad (holy war), "whose number-one target had to be America, perceived as the greatest enemy of the faith" (Kepel 2006, p. 220).

Arab Spring

The invasion of Iraq resulted in the destabilization of the whole Middle East, indeed the whole Islamic world. During the 2010s, the Middle East was once again, as in ancient history, a battleground. What was called the "Arab Spring" in 2011 expanded the chaos across North Africa.

The Arab Spring was a mixture of popular pro-democracy uprisings that began in Tunisia in December 2010 and soon spread to Oman, Yemen, Egypt, Syria, Morocco, and Libya. The government of Muammar Gadhafi (1942–2011) in Libya was overthrown in October. Post-Gadhafi Libya is ruled by "innumerable armed factions loyal to their home cities, political or religious ideology, or foreign backers" (Mandhai 2017). Civil war broke out in Syria in July 2011, that remained active in 2019.

Iran, Turkey, and to a lesser extent Egypt, competed for status as the region's dominant power. The United States found itself competing with Russia for influence in the region, as was the case during the Cold War. Because Islam refuses to accept the existence of Israel, and Israel remains the only dependable ally of the United States in the Middle East, the United States could not avoid continued involvement. As of January 2019, the United States was actively engaged in combating terrorism in 80 countries on 6 continents. During the 17 years following President George W. Bush's declaration of a global war on terrorism, the United States military alone spent $1.9 trillion fighting terrorism, and the U. S. State Department an additional $127 billion (Savell 2019).

World Migration

Throughout human history there have been periods of mass migrations of people groups brought about by climate change, overpopulation, war, and a host of other causes. The earliest migrations resulted in the populating of our world, as well as the creation of its distinctive racial and ethnic diversity. The numerous migrations during the historical period resulted in the mixing of cultures, either negatively, or more often, positively. What, for example, would American country and Western music be like, if it were not for the Moorish migration into the Iberian Peninsula (Spain and Portugal) that is often credited with introducing the guitar?

During the first quarter of the twenty-first century, both Europe and North America have been impacted by migrants and refugees fleeing war, terrorism, lawlessness, famine, and even cases of ethnic cleansing. Some are refugees seeking temporary asylum and wish to return to their home countries in the future. Many are emigrants in search of a better life in the developed nations of the European Union and North America. They come as individuals, or as families, even children unaccompanied by their parents or other family members.

Their journey to Europe, whether overland or by boat is perilous. Women risk being raped. Children risk being kidnapped and possibly sold into slavery. Those attempting to cross the Mediterranean Sea, sometimes in small, flimsy, overcrowded rubber boats, are at the greatest risk. As of September 2018, as many as 20% of migrants who left Libya either drowned at sea or disappeared. Those rescued, or intercepted by the Libyan coast guard, and returned to Libya were sometimes sold to smugglers, who in turn sold them on the slave market, or ransomed them to family members. If the ransom was not paid, they were often tortured or simply killed. The fact that the migrants take such risks says a lot about the conditions they are attempting to flee.

Migrants going to the United States from South and Central America, often entering illegally, did not face the same degree of danger as those crossing from Africa or the Middle East to Europe. They were mostly people, individuals and families, seeking a better life. They were leaving behind poverty in hope of finding employment, however humble, in the United States. More recent migrants were often fleeing Central American countries where lawlessness and gangs were the daily reality. Many were seeking asylum hoping to remain and eventually become American citizens.

The large numbers of immigrants going to Europe and the United States have aroused fears among the host countries. In Europe, where birthrates have been low, workers, especially skilled workers, are welcomed. But large numbers of immigrants from wholly different historical, ethnic, and cultural backgrounds are hard to assimilate, especially in such large numbers. Many of those seeking entrance to European countries are Muslim, thus presenting a clash of cultures. That is not as true with those from Central America seeking admission to the United States. Although they are predominately Roman Catholic and Hispanic, and often speak only Spanish when they arrive, they are a part of Western culture. Tragically, many Americans have been slow to accept Spanish as a second language or accept the fact that the Hispanic population is rapidly increasing.

Fear of the immigrants has caused a nativist, or populist reaction, in the host countries. Political parties and individual politicians have found exploiting that reaction a road to success, especially those right of center. Some European countries have tried to restrict emigration, or even close their borders to immigrants from non-Western countries. Others have tried to force assimilation by, for example, banning the traditional headscarves worn by many Muslim women. Serious questions have arisen regarding religious freedom and the extent to which people should defend their culture from the threat represented by foreign cultures.

The noted French author, Jean Raspail (b. 1925), published a novel in 1973 with the title *Le Camp des Saints*, translated into English as *The Camp of the Saints*, that became controversial during the migration crisis. *The Camp of Saints* is an apocalyptic novel with a simple plot. Given little attention when first published, except for a few prominent French literary figures, *The Camp of the Saints* became a best seller again in 2011, and has continued to be popular despite being accused by some of being a racist novel.

The plot is simple. An armada of nearly a million starving and disease-ridden Indians aboard old freighters and other vessels are on their way from India to Europe. They seek food and a better life in the West, but have no desire to assimilate. Thus, they represent a threat to the very existence of Western Civilization, meaning civilization itself. Should the armada be stopped, or should Europe welcome the needy refugees? It is easy to see the attraction Raspail's novel holds for many since the appearance of the migrant crisis. It is a mistake, however, to dismiss it as being somehow "racist," just as it is a mistake to accuse the fear of mass migration among Europeans and Americans as racist. As one reviewer put it, "But the central issue of the novel is not race but culture and political principles" (Owens 2016). To what lengths can a Western nation go to defend its culture against multiculturalism without violating the very principles upon which Western Civilization is founded?

Donald Trump (b. 1946), elected president of the United States in 2017, pledged to construct a wall along the southern border with Mexico. Illegal immigration, President Trump claimed, had become a national crisis in 2019. The issue of the "border wall" in particular, and immigration in general, sharply polarized the American public along political party lines. The image of poor, uneducated, illegal immigrants, allegedly including terrorists and criminals of all kinds, proved to be a powerful political issue for both Republican and Democratic parties. Working-class Americans, who suffer from the decline of the United States as an industrial nation, feel their livelihood threatened by the immigrants, whether legal or illegal. Middle-class Americans, many of whom are university educated, living in and near large metropolitan areas, feel less threatened. The immigrants they encounter are more like them, that is, well-educated, upwardly mobile, white-collar, and vocationally trained for the modern service economy of modern America.

Studies done by nonpartisan researchers and government offices indicate that immigrants have a positive, rather than negative, impact on the American economy. They increase the nation's productivity, while contributing to state and federal coffers. According to one study, it is "estimated that foreign-born workers contributed roughly \$2 trillion [€1.75 trillion] to the US economy in 2016" (Edwards 2019, p. 40). The largest group of immigrants to the United States (41%) come from Asia, not Latin America. Also, 45% have college degrees, whereas only 35% of non-Hispanic white Americans do. New York Times columnist and author, Thomas L. Friedman (b. 1953), noted in 2005 that nearly 25% of America's scientists and engineers are immigrants, and 51% of doctorates in engineering awarded by American educational institutions go to foreigners (Zakaria 2005).

Despite widespread bipartisan support for comprehensive immigration reform, all efforts to address the issue as of 1919 have stalled in Congress. So long as keeping the "crisis" alive benefits both major political parties, there is very little hope for any change.

The Search for Meaning in a Multicultural World[3]

Many of those who survived the trauma of World War I lived on to experience the Great Depression and World War II. Twenty-five million Americans were unemployed during the Great Depression without any real relief available from local, state, or federal governments.

---

3 For a more thorough discussion see my chapter, "Searching for Meaning in a Multicultural World," in Richards and Waibel (2014).

The Great War, the Great Inflation of 1923 in Germany, the spread of the Great Depression to Europe less than 10 years later, scenes of the Russian famine during the early 1920s, ongoing civil war in China followed by the Japanese invasion, and World War II, the Holocaust, and the war crimes and crimes against humanity committed by both the Axis and Allied powers, proved to be more than the human psyche could bear. It seemed no longer possible to have faith in reason, believe in the innate goodness of human beings, or the inherent value of the individual. All fell victim to reality, as did belief in universal truths and values, or principles upon which to construct a humane world. The frightening prospect of a thermonuclear holocaust was visited upon the world, not by Germany or Japan, but by the United States, the most perfect historical embodiment of the Enlightenment tradition.

The challenge that confronted the post-World War II intellectuals was how to make sense out of a universe in which there was no longer any God or absolute truth that might provide unity or meaning. At first, they turned to the philosophy of existentialism, which taught that the individual could find, or create, meaning for his or her existence. Existentialism assumed that human beings live in a universe that is silent and indifferent to their existence. Therefore, the individual must validate and give meaning to his or her existence by choosing to act. Faced with a choice, the individual must choose, but which option is chosen does not matter. There is no right or wrong choice. The individual must struggle against the absurdity of the universe, knowing the struggle is in vain. Echoing Nietzsche, Jean-Paul Sartre (1905–1980), one of the best-known postwar existentialists, wrote in 1947:

> Not only is man what he conceives himself to be but he is also only what he wills himself to be .... *Man is nothing else but what he makes of himself* [emphasis added]. ...existentialism's first move is to make every man aware of what he is and to make the full responsibility of his existence rest on him. (Sartre 1947)

Existentialism gave way to structuralism during the 1960s.

Structuralism assumes that there is a universal structure, a kind of hidden harmony or universal code that exists independent of humans but determines their behavior. There are thought processes in the human mind that are unconscious but determine consciousness. Because those thought processes are universal, the same in every human being everywhere, there is an alleged unity to humanity that supersedes all cultural, racial, and class distinctions. The individual as master of his or her own fate becomes a mere plaything of hidden mechanistic forces.

The French anthropologist and ethnologist, Claude Lévi-Strauss (1908–2009), is credited with being the founder of structuralism. The structuralists, however, were unable to uncover, or identify, the hidden structures that supposedly control the human mind and all that humans do. By the late 1970s, it was yielding the field to deconstruction.

Deconstructionists argued that there is no hidden structure to be discovered. In literary criticism, for example, the deconstructionist is free to interpret a literary piece anyway he or she wishes. There is no relationship between the author's intent and the words on the page. The decoder is interested in what the author left out, what Jacques Lacan (1901–1981) called the "holes in the discourse." The obvious problem with deconstructionism is that there are as many valid interpretations as there are decoders, since every deconstruction can itself be deconstructed.

If deconstructionism is used in an attempt to understand civilization and Western Civilization in particular, one soon discovers that there are "no 'great books,' no treasure trove of wisdom from the past that defines, inspires, or provides a standard for modern civilization" (Richards and Waibel, p. 323). Historical facts disappear, as the deconstructionist looks for the meaning of what lies hidden behind the facts. In place of history as a record of past events, a story is created to provide the desired meaning. Myth becomes history. Houston Stewart Chamberlain's *The Foundations of the Nineteenth Century* (1911) and Marin Bernal's *Black Athena* (1987–2006) are examples of how myth can become history.

It is easy to understand the acceptance of deconstruction among some intellectuals as cultural pluralism, multiculturalism, and diversity increased since the mid-1960s. Historians from different cultural backgrounds will naturally interpret history differently. The history of nineteenth-century Europe, or the United States, written by a middle-class European or Euro American will differ from the same written by a historian whose ancestry is African, Asian, or Middle Eastern. As diversity increases, can one justify requiring students in Europe or the United States to study the history of Western Civilization? For those whose cultural and ethnic heritage is non-Western, the history of Western Civilization "is only the story of deeds done by 'dead white males' told by their descendants who seek authority through perpetuating their memory" (Richards and Waibel, p. 323).

Postmodernism is the term often used to describe the attempt to answer those ever-troublesome questions of meaning and purpose. The term originated in the latter nineteenth century to refer to what was later called postimpressionist art. During the last quarter of the twentieth century it was used to refer to whatever was considered avant-garde in the arts. Postmodern art is an eclectic style, a kind of collage in which bits and pieces of diverse styles are put together without any unifying theme. It is a fragmented style that reflects a fragmented worldview.

Postmodernity, or postmodernism, refers to the third division of Western intellectual history, with the first being premodernity (the medieval synthesis), and the second being modernity (the Enlightenment tradition). Because it rejects all of the fundamental assumptions of the Enlightenment, it represents the Enlightenment tradition in disarray. To better understand postmodernity, it helps to contrast it with premodernity and modernity.

Premodernity (see Chapters 6 and 7) understood that reality was an orderly universe created by God and able to be understood by human beings created by God in his image. There was meaning and purpose for both the individual and for history. Those who were entrusted with interpreting God's revelation in Scripture and nature, the theologians and philosophers, were the wisemen, or experts to whom one could turn for help with understanding. Modernity taught that the universe existed as a uniformity of cause and effect natural laws. It was an orderly universe created by God who was seen as the great architect, but unlike with premodernity, God was not actively involved with his creation (see Chapter 9). There was still meaning and purpose for both the individual and history. The scientists, those who discovered and interpreted the natural laws, were the experts.

Postmodernity begins with the assumption that reality is a random chance universe without meaning. History is meaningless. The individual's life is meaningless. Neither God the creator as revealed in Scripture, nor God the great architect of Enlightenment Deism exists. Reality is only what anyone says it is at any given moment. Any attempt to create a metanarrative (e.g. the Bible) to explain reality is futile, a fallacious expression by a particular subculture at a particular point in time. Referring back to the tripartite division of Western intellectual history mentioned above, premodernity can be understood as the house that God built, modernity as the house that man built, and postmodernity as the house that never got built.

Culture

As noted in earlier chapters, when discussing the cultural expression of the different periods of Western Civilization's history, there is a connection between worldview and creativity. The creative art produced by an individual reflects the individual's worldview, or one might say, the inner life of the mind. The same thing is true in the collective, whether in reference to a particular group of people, or a particular period of history. As the understanding of reality changed, for example from premodernity to modernity, so did artistic styles. A painting of the Madonna from the High Middle Ages is different from one done during the nineteenth century.

The creative arts of the post-World War II period reflect the growing sense of alienation and despair and the fragmentation that came with the disappearance of any absolute reference point or metanarrative that could make sense out of, to borrow from the title of an old English ballad, a world turned upside down. The United States played a prominent role in the rise of postmodernism, thanks to the many creative artists who came to America fleeing the totalitarian regimes in Germany and the Soviet Union.

"Abstract expressionism," also called the "New York School," was dominant during the first decade or so after the war. One characteristic of the abstract expressionists was their individualism. An accurate description of abstract expressionism would require a study of each artist. Their art is recognizable by its lack of recognizable content and emphasis on gesture and/or color. Jackson Pollock (1912–1956), who was perhaps the best known of the school, might create a painting by throwing paint from the tip of a brush at a canvas, or walking around on a canvas while dripping paint from a brush.

During the mid-1950s, the artistic movement known as "Pop Art" appeared. Unlike the abstractionists, they wanted to paint the real postwar world obsessed with commercialism and mass culture. They condemned the twin values of personal peace and affluence of the 1960s and 1970s. Andy Warhol (1930–2008), known as "The Prince of Pop," painted pictures of Campbell's soup cans, a Brillo soap box, Elvis Presley, and much more. "Pop artists," said Warhol, "did images that anybody walking down Broadway could recognize in a split second – comics, picnic tables, men's trousers, celebrities, shower curtains, refrigerators, Coke bottles – all the great modern things that the Abstract Expressionists tried hard not to notice" (Danto 2010).

Minimalism followed Pop Art during the 1970s. It is characterized by the absence of any emotional content or personal meaning. Ellsworth Kelly (1923–2015) serves as a good example. His painting *Red, Orange, White, Green, Blue* (1968) is a succession of colored stripes on canvas. The *Vietnam Veterans' Memorial* (1982) is representative of minimalist sculpture.

During the last two decades of the twentieth century, artistic expression went in various directions. Some artists explored the limits of abstraction, while others tried reproducing objects with photographic precision. It was difficult at times to tell if the artist was in fact an artist or a mischievous Leprechaun tricking the art-loving public for a golden coin, or maybe two. Since postmodern art is the king of "premeditated chaos," it is transient and dependent upon the viewer interacting with it. Understandably, it has to become ever more spectacular in order not to lose the public's attention and go out of style.

Christo Javacheff (b. 1935) simply wrapped an object, any object, big or small, a technique called *Empaquetage*. Together with his wife, Jeanne-Claude Denat de Guillebon (1935–2009) they wrapped the Reichstag building in Berlin and the Pont-Neuf bridge in Paris. They always insisted that their art had no deep meaning. Asked what was the purpose of their art, Jeanne-Claude replied: "It's for nothing. It's only a work of art. Nothing more" (Vogel 2005).

Post-World War I Dadaism inspired what in the 1990s became known as "performance art." Artist Janine Antoni (b. 1962) "mopped the floor of the gallery with her hair soaked in Loving Care hair dye" for a work she titled *Loving Care* (1993). Performance art became increasingly more sensational, shocking, and even pornographic. Religious and patriotic symbols and objects were sometimes used in ways considered intentionally offensive or blasphemous.

Europe, the home of Western Civilization, at the beginning of the twenty-first century is no longer the center of the world, as it was at the dawn of the twentieth century. The West (Europe and America) has disappeared into a global village that resembles more a crazy quilt or a Jackson Pollack painting. Multiculturalism has done away with a commonly accepted history that can serve as a basis for an aesthetic standard. There is no longer any way to define what constitutes art, much less whether something is good or bad art. Is graffiti sprayed on a wall or a railroad car, or images drawn on the wall of a public restroom art?

The search for meaning in what appeared to be a meaningless universe was reflected in the literature, drama, cinema, and music. Some of the writers who embraced Marxism early in their lives, later became disillusioned. They later wrote powerful indictments of totalitarianism. Ignazio Silone (1900–1978), Arthur Koestler (1905–1983), George Orwell (1903–1950), and Aleksandr Solzhenitsyn (1918–2008) were prolific writers who produced both fiction and non-fiction indictments of what Koestler called in the title of one of his non-fiction books, *The God That Failed* (1949).

The existentialist message of the individual desperately searching for meaning in a universe without any, filtered down to the masses in the novels of Albert Camus, John-Paul Sartre, and Simone de Beauvoir (1908–1986). But the novel was not the only medium. What is called the Theater of the Absurd was a popular medium for existentialism during the 1950s and 1960s. Eugene Ionesco (1912–1994), Harold Pinter (1930–2008), and Samuel Beckett (1906–1989) are the best-known playwrights of that genre. Beckett's *Waiting for Godot* (1952) portrays two tramps waiting for the coming of a mysterious person named Godot, who never appears. Perhaps he is only someone the two tramps believe in, but does not really exist. Nevertheless, their belief in him and his eventual appearance gives them a reason to go on living.

The cinema as art is ideally suited to communicating philosophical ideas. That is particularly true of the European cinema which is less driven by the demands of mass-marketed entertainment. Films by Alain Resnais (1922–2014), Michelangelo Antonioni (1912–2007), Federico Fellini (1920–1993), and Ingmar Bergman (1918–2007) have as their theme the search for meaning in an alienated world. The leading characters in Bergman's films "wonder whether they are in this world for a reason. They feel themselves alienated from others, meaningless entities walking around on the earth for a few years and then vanishing into endless night" (Janaro and Altshuler 2003).

John Cage (1912–1992) composed music by chance to fit a universe of random chance. Inspired by Marcel Duchamp's (1887–1992) "ready-mades," Cage composed music by chance. His best-known work titled *4'33"* is performed by a pianist sitting motionless at the piano for 4 minutes and 33 seconds. The "music" is the "ready-made sounds," or random noises coming from the surrounding environment.

Popular Culture

American popular culture has dominated throughout much of the world since the late 1940s. The United States transitioned from an industrial economy to a consumer economy. While much of the world was struggling to recover from the devastation caused by the war, the American economy grew by 37% during the 1950s. By the end of the decade, the purchasing power of the median family had increased by 30%. Americans who grew up during the Great Depression and endured the rationing of basic goods during World War II were ready to spend, and spend they did. Although Americans represented only 6% of the world's population, they were consuming one-third of the world's goods and services.

Whereas earlier generations were "careful to save and reuse," postwar Americans became consumers buying and throwing away. The spending for war was what really ended the Great Depression. Once the war ended, the switch from production to consumption enabled the nation's economy to expand rather than contract. Advertisers created demand for products and services people did not know they needed, and made them feel guilty if they did not throw away last year's styles for the latest fashion. In 1956, Robert Sarnoff (1918–1997), president of the National Broadcasting Company (NBC), attributed America's high standard of living to the fact that "advertising has created an American frame of mind that makes people want more things, better things, and newer things" (Miller 1977, p. 118).

To the people still suffering from the war, American prosperity reinforced the image of the United States as the land of opportunity, glamor, youth, and all that was the newest, latest, and avant-garde. American movies, music, and television programs, together with the presence of American armed forces stationed abroad after 1945, assured that the American lifestyle would enrich, or corrupt, the postwar world.

The collapse of the Soviet Union in 1991 was heralded as a victory for capitalism over communism. The United States as the flagship of capitalism reaped the benefits of that victory. By the dawn of the twenty-first century symbols of America's cultural dominance could be seen everywhere. By the end of the 2010s, the signs of American franchises could be seen everywhere in the world. More people recognize McDonald's "golden arches," or Kentucky Fried Chicken's "Colonel Saunders," than the historical symbols of their own country.

2000–2019

The world events arising from the end of the Cold War were important, but there were other developments that inspired hope for the future. There were signs that despite all of the apparent chaos in the world, progress was being made in recognizing and defending human rights.

Women made significant progress in having their right to equality with men recognized. Beginning in 2006, the "Me Too" movement encouraged women to no longer suffer in silence sexual abuse from men in positions of power. In many culturally underdeveloped, mostly non-Western countries, women still suffer legalized discrimination and outright abuse at the hands of men who cling to primitive, often religious based, notions of a woman's place in society. In the more modern areas of the world, especially those influenced by the West, even men are showing justifiable outrage at honor killings, attacks, torture, beatings, and the reprehensible practice of female genital mutilation that remain legal, or at a minimum tolerated, in unenlightened areas of the globe.[4]

Advances were made in recognizing the human rights of members of the LGBTQ community. As of January 2019, same-sex marriage (sometimes called marriage equality) was legal in 28 countries and recognized in four more. All but five were located in Europe or the Western Hemisphere. In contrast, the Sultan of Brunei, Hassanal Bolkiah (b. 1946), announced in April 2019, that homosexuality in Brunei would be punished by stoning to death. The announcement marked "the grand finale of a five-year roll out" (Callaghan 2019) of Islamic sharia law. To many, it seemed as though Brunei was competing with Saudi Arabia for recognition as the wealthiest and least civilized nation in the twenty-first century world.

The spread of terrorism and the mass migration of people throughout the world are important trends that are changing our world in ways that cannot be fully comprehended. But as important as they are, they must take a backseat to what is no doubt the most important development so far in the twenty-first century, globalization.

Worldwide Internet

One educational website defines globalization as "a term used to describe increasing social, economic, and political interaction and interrelation across political and cultural boundaries" (Explain 2015). There are three forms of globalization: political, social, and economic. Globalization's greatest impact has been felt in two areas, sharing of ideas and information, and the interconnectedness of the world's economies. Driving both is the revolution in internet technology.

The appearance of virtual communities through the internet's social networking created the potential of transforming the world's diverse population into a single virtual community.

---

4 United States federal law (the Female Genital Mutilation of Act 1996) prohibits genital mutilation of females under 18. Twenty-eight states prohibit the practice as of January 2019. Perhaps an example to which cultural diversity has undermined civilized values in Western nations is the ruling by a federal judge in Michigan that the Female Genital Mutilation of Act 1996 violated the Constitution (Domonoske 2018).

The first social network site, Six Degrees, appeared in 1997. The real breakthrough came in 2006, when Facebook and Twitter became available worldwide.

Facebook, the world's most popular social network, was founded in 2004 by Mark Zuckerberg (b. 1984), a sophomore at Harvard University. By the third quarter of 2012, Facebook had more than one billion active members. That number rose to 2.27 billion in the third quarter of 2018. Twitter, with its 280 characters limit on messages, appeared in March 2006. The first message, or "Tweet," was sent at 9:50 p.m. (PST) on March 26, and read, "just setting up my twttr." As of November 24, 2018, there were 500 million Tweets sent each day by 326 million active Twitter Users, 261 million of which are outside the United States.

The growth of the worldwide internet has produced statistics that challenge comprehension. As of January 2019, there were 1.5 billion websites worldwide, compared to only one in 1991. More than 380 new websites are created every minute. There were roughly 3.58 billion users of the internet as of November 2018, roughly 51% of the earth's population. China accounts for just over 25 percent, or three-times the population of the United States. In 2018, it was estimated that by 2019 "the global traffic on the Internet will reach 2 zettabytes or 2 billion-billion bytes for the year" (How Many 2019).

Probing the Limits of Space

Major steps were taken in the exploration of outer space during the first two decades of the twenty-first century. The first crew of three, one American and two Russians, occupied the International Space Station between October 2000 and March 2001. Dennis Tito (b. 1940) became the first tourist in space in April–May 2001, after paying a reported $20 million to join to Russian cosmonauts on a trip to the International Space Station. China launched its first manned space flight in October 2003, becoming the third nation to do so.

Opportunity Rover, launched by the United States's National Aeronautics and Space Administration (NASA) landed on Mars on January 24, 2004. Among the information sent back by Opportunity Rover was evidence that water once existed on Mars. Cassini–Huygens Probe launched in 1997 began orbiting Saturn in July 2004. In December, the Huygens module separated from Cassini and landed on Saturn's largest moon, Titan.

Medieval and Renaissance map makers would often draw images of sea monsters to indicate their ignorance of what lay beyond the known limits, or in the vast oceans between known land masses. The mystery of what lies beyond what is known geographically and otherwise has inspired humans since they first gazed up at the night sky with curiosity, or wondered what lay beyond the horizon. It is why science fiction will always be a popular genre of fiction and motion pictures. Perhaps the greatest mystery, apart from the human mind, is what lies beyond our solar system, beyond the Milky Way Galaxy, in which our solar system is but a grain of sand, if even that. There are hundreds of billions of stars like our sun in the Milky Way Galaxy, and there are billions of galaxies in the universe.

The door to the infinity of the universe was jarred open just a small crack by images sent back to earth from the Hubble Space Telescope launched on April 24, 1990. Using data collected between 2003 and 2004, an image called the Hubble Ultra Deep Field of a small area of space in the constellation Fornax, containing an estimated 10 000 galaxies, was created and published. Launched in 1977, Voyager 1 exited our solar system into interstellar space in August 2012. After nine years and a journey of 4.6 billion miles (7.4 billion km), NASA's New Horizons Spacecraft passed within 7750 miles (12 400 km) of Pluto in July 2015. On January 1, 2019, it flew past Ultima Thule, a space object four billion miles from earth. Two days later, China succeeded in making the first soft landing on the far side of the moon, the side of the moon that is never seen from Earth. It was first photographed in 1959 by a Soviet satellite.

At a news conference in early April 2019, Shep Doeleman, an astrophysicist at the Harvard-Smithsonian Center for Astrophysics in Cambridge, Massachusetts and director of the Event Horizon Telescope Project made public the first ever picture of a "black hole," previously thought to be unseeable. A black hole is "a region of space having a gravitational field so intense that no matter or radiation can escape." The existence of black holes was predicted by Einstein's theory of relativity.

The black hole, whose image has been captured, is located about 55 million light-years from earth at the center of the galaxy Messier 87 (M87), which is located in the constellation Virgo. Its mass is estimated to be 6.5 billion times that of our Sun. "M87 is a monster even by supermassive black hole standards," observed Sera Markoff, a theoretical astrophysicist at the University of Amsterdam (Grossman and Conover 2019).

Human Genome Project

Equally as impressive as humankind's journey into outer space is progress made in understanding the biological complexity of a human being. An international research project began during 1990 with the goal of "to determine the sequence of the human genome ['A genome is an organism's complete set of DNA, including all of its genes.'] and identify the genes that it contains" ("What was the Human Genome Project" 2019). The project was completed in 2003 and the results published.

The knowledge gained opened up the possibility of identifying and treating hereditary diseases, but at the same time it raised numerous complicated ethical issues. Images of "babies on order," or maybe creating a race of humans bred for mindless labor, or with whatever physical or mental characteristics are considered desirable at the time, occupied the popular mind. For some, the use of genetic testing to discover possible genetic issues of an unborn baby raises questions about the sanctity of life. Some see the possibility of knowing whether or not one possesses a genetic code that makes one likely to develop a particular disease later in life as a blessing.

The seriousness of the ethical issues raised by such knowledge were dramatically made known in November 2018, when a researcher at the Southern University of Science and Technology in Shenzhen, China, announced he had removed a gene from the embryos of two twin girls born in November 2018. The researcher's experiment was done in violation of Chinese law and immediately condemned worldwide. Once again, increased knowledge of the natural laws of the universe proved both a blessing and a curse. Human beings are by nature neither good nor evil, but capable of both, and destined to do both.

Western Civilization and the World

The knowledge that we live in a cause and effect natural law universe, and our understanding of human nature, were discovered during the history of Western Civilization. They originated with the ancient Hebrews and made possible both the Scientific Revolution and later the Industrial Revolution. Contact with the other civilizations of the world spread that knowledge. Today, that core knowledge enables further discoveries by curious individuals around the world. Only those societies that deny or reject that fundamental core of useful knowledge remain trapped in the dark ages without the comforts resulting from scientific discovery and with no appreciation for individual human rights.

Reflecting on the horrors of World War II – the ashes of the death camps, Dresden, and Hiroshima – English historian A.J.P. Taylor noted that there are two faces to Western Civilization. One is represented by centuries of willful injustices perpetrated on its own people and the various people groups of the non-Western world victimized by economic and political imperialism, the exploitation of the weak by the strong and powerful, and the sacrifice of innocent lives in numerous wars. The other is represented by the banishment of superstition and the rise of modern science and the fundamental assumption of civilized life, that every human being, male and female, of whatever mental capacity or physical condition, is of equal value and entitled to life, freedom, and justice. "Civilization," concluded Taylor, is "held together by the civilized behavior of ordinary people" (Taylor 1966, p. 62).

The twentieth century is often referred to as "the American Century" with some justification. But there are many signs that the United States is no longer the sun around which the rest of the world's countries revolve. Likewise, Western Civilization is no longer, to paraphrase Protagoras, "the measure of all things." That said, it remains true that all the world's diverse people groups live in a world largely shaped by the history of Western Civilization.

References

Bush, G.H. (1991). George Herbert Walker Bush's Third State of the Union Address. https://en.wikisource.org/wiki/George_Herbert_Walker_Bush's_Third_State_of_the_Union_Address (accessed 21 October 2019).

Callaghan, G. (2019). So Wrong to See Brunei's Anti-gay Laws as an Exception to the Rule. The Sydney Morning Herald. www.smh.com.au/world/asia/so-wrong-to-see-brunei-s-anti-gay-laws-as-an-exception-to-the-rule-20190413-p51dw6.html (accessed 21 October 2019).

Danto, A.C. (2010). *Andy Warhol*. New Haven, CT: Yale University Press.

Domonoske, C. (2018). Judge Says Federal Law Against Female Genital Mutilation Violates U.S. Constitution. NPRhttps://www.npr.org/2018/11/21/669945997/judge-says-federal-law-against-female-genital-mutilation-violates-u-s-constituti (accessed 21 October 2019).

Edwards, H.S. (2019). Dividing Lines, The Human Face of Global Migration. *Time* (February 4/February 11).

eNotes (2015). Explain the concept of globalization and its advantages and disadvantages for social, political, and economic development. https://www.enotes.com/homework-help/explain-concept-golobization-its-advantages-567033 (accessed 21 October 2019).

Gilman, B.A. (1998). H.R.4655 - 105th Congress (1997–1998): Iraq Liberation Act of 1998. Congress.gov. https://www.congress.gov/bill/105th-congress/house-bill/4655 (accessed 21 October 2019).

Gorbachev, M. (1988). Address by Mikhail Gorbachev at the UN General Assembly Session (Excerpts). History and Public Policy Program Digital Archive, CWIHP Archive. https://digitalarchive.wilsoncenter.org/document/116224 (accessed 21 October 2019).

Grossman, L. and Conover, E. (2019). The First Picture of a Black Hole Opens a New Era of Astrophysics. Science News. https://www.sciencenews.org/article/black-hole-first-picture-event-horizon-telescope (accessed 21 October 2019).

Janaro, R. and Altshuler, T (2003). *The Art of Being Human*. New York: Pearson.

Kepel, G. (2006). *Jihad: The Trail of Political Islam*. London: I.B. Tauris.

Mandhai, S. (2017). Libya Six Years On: No Regrets over Gaddafi's Demise. GCC News | Al Jazeera. https://www.aljazeera.com/news/2017/10/years-regrets-libya-gaddafi-demise-171019073901622.html (accessed 21 October 2019).

Milbank, D. (2004). Bush Defends Assertions of Iraq-Al Qaeda Relationship. The Washington Post. http://www.washingtonpost.com/wp-dyn/articles/A50679-2004Jun17.html (accessed 21 October 2019).

Mill for Business (2019). How Many Websites Are There Around the World? https://www.millforbusiness.com/how-many-websites-are-there (accessed 21 October 2019).

Miller, D.T. (1977). *The Fifties: The Way We Really Were*, 118. Garden City, NY: Doubledayp.

Owens, M.T. (2016). Camp of the Saints, 2014 Style? National Review. https://www.nationalreview.com/2014/06/camp-saints-2014-style-mackubin-thomas-owens (accessed 21 October 2019).

Richards, M.D. and Waibel, P.R. (2014). *Twentieth Century Europe: A Brief History, 1900 to the Present*, 3e. Wiley-Blackwell: Malden, MA.

Sartre, J.-P. (1947). *Existentialism*. New York: Philosophical Library (Quoted in Marvin Perry (1992). An Intellectual History of Modern Europe. Boston: Wordsworth Publishing, p. 449).

Savell, S. (2019). This Map Shows Where in the World the U.S. Military Is Combatting Terrorism. https://www.smithsonianmag.com/history/map-shows-places-world-where-us-military-operates-180970997 (accessed 21 October 2019).

Taylor, A.J.P. (1966). *From Sarajevo to Potsdam*. London: Thames & Hudson.

U.S. National Library of Medicine (2019). What was the Human Genome Project and why has it been important? https://ghr.nlm.nih.gov/primer/hgp/description (accessed 21 October 2019).

Vogel, C. (2005). Art Project Pilgrims Prepare to Install 'The Gates'. The New York Times. https://www.nytimes.com/2005/02/05/arts/design/art-project-pilgrims-prepare-to-install-the-gates.html (accessed 21 October 2019).

Zakaria, F. (2005). Book Review: 'The World Is Flat': The Wealth of Yet More Nations. The New York Times. https://www.nytimes.com/2005/05/01/books/review/book-review-the-world-is-flat-the-wealth-of-yet-more-nations.html (accessed 21 October 2019).

Index

Western Civilization: A Brief History, First Edition. Paul R. Waibel.
© 2020 John Wiley & Sons, Inc. Published 2020 by John Wiley & Sons, Inc.